History of Universities

VOLUME VII
1988

History of Universities

VOLUME VII
1988

Oxford University Press
1988

History of Universities is published annually as a single volume.

Editor:
Laurence Brockliss (Magdalen College, Oxford).

Assistant Editor:
Mark Curthoys (Nuffield College, Oxford).

Bibliography Editor:
John Fletcher (University of Aston in Birmingham).

Editorial Board:
P. Denley (Westfield College, London)
W. Frijhoff (Erasmus Universiteit, Rotterdam)
N. Hammerstein (University of Frankfurt)
D. Julia (Centre de recherches historiques, EHESS, Paris)
J. K. McConica (St Michael's College, Toronto University)
N. G. Siraisi (Hunter College, New York)

Papers for publication in History of Universities as well as books for review should be sent to the editor, Dr. L. W. B. Brockliss, Magdalen College, Oxford, OX1 4AU, United Kingdom.

A leaflet 'Notes to OUP Authors' is available on request from the editor.

Details of subscription rates and terms are available from Oxford Journals Subscription Department, Walton Street, Oxford, OX2 6DP, United Kindom.

British Library Cataloguing in Publication Data
History of Universities.—Vol. 7-
1. Universities. History. Serials
378' .009
ISBN 0-19-822742-6

Library of Congress Cataloging in Publication Data
Cataloging Card No. 82-642421

Typeset by Computerised Typesetting Services
Printed in Great Britain by
Biddles Ltd, Guildford and King's Lynn.

Contents

Articles

Research in Progress

Conference Reports

Book Reviews

Russia's 'University Question': Origins to Great Reforms 1802–1863

James T. Flynn

The foundation of the Russian universities early in the reign of Alexander I was one of a series of reforms which attempted to use western models to help Russia meet its needs by matching the West in Progress. This is the origin of the 'University Question', the dilemma of having the free western university serve the Russian autocracy. One could have either the free western university or the Russian autocracy, not both, for the two were fundamentally opposed. The history of the university question in Russia is, therefor, the story of the failure of the western-model university to realize its potential because the autocracy repeatedly cracked down, severely restricting the autonomy, the *Lehr-und Lernfreiheit,* necessary for the western university's success. First outlined in Pirogov's famous 1863 essay, 'The University Question', this interpretation of the consequence of Alexander's university reform remains the standard one.[1]

It hardly needs saying that much evidence supports that interpretation. In 1819, for example, Minister of Education Golitsyn became convinced that commitment to academic freedom and the autonomy of the university showed that the faculty of St Petersburg University was infected by a 'spirit of self-love' which inescapably led to the horrors of revolution. He fired several professors, accepted gladly the resignation in protest of many more, and pressed for the dismissal of nearly half the students. It would not be difficult to multiply such examples of repression in the history of the Russian university. Nonetheless, the point of this paper is to argue that to make repression the main theme overstresses one aspect while missing something important. Study of the universities in their first, formative, stage shows that both Ministry of Education and the universities tried, often with considerable success, to ward off the dilemma. Accommodating the western-model university to the Russian political and social environment presented many difficult problems, among them the sort of repression carried out by Golitsyn and other loyal servitors of the tsarist state. Nonetheless, there were other equally loyal servitors who worked at the university reform by developing a series of compromises which kept the essentials of the original liberal reform. They achieved a good deal of success by accepting neither horn of the dilemma, complete autonomy for the university or its opposite, complete subservience to the state.

The successful development of compromise solutions to many problems encountered in the effort to introduce the western-model university into Russia shows that in some ways Russia could borrow successfully from the West, and in other ways it could not.[2] Discriminating between these ways is worth attention because Russia's relationship with the West is in some important respects what Russian history is about. Peter the Great indeed began modern Russian history when he opened his 'window to the West'. It might be argued that this was the true origin of Russia's university question, for Peter tried to keep that window suitably narrow, to profit from borrowing technology while minimising the threat to autocracy in much western political and social practice. Peter, and most subsequent Russian rulers, knew that Russia had somehow to respond to the West's example, either by borrowing or by rejecting institutions and practices. So, indeed, did the *intelligentsia*, who came to oppose the state because they disagreed with the choices that state made in borrowing and rejecting western models. Thus, Russia was the first major society whose leaders realized, in some way to some degree, that it was 'backward' compared with the West and, further, that to preserve its own values, or perhaps even political independence, it had to borrow from the West some things it needed to make 'Progress', i.e. acquire what it needed to compete with the West. The 'University Question', the consequences of borrowing the western university to help Russia make progress, is only one aspect of that larger question of Russia's relationship to the West. It is, however, an important one, not least because the university became a battleground on which struggled partisans of quite different conceptions of Russia's relationship to the West and therefore of quite different answers to the most important 'question' in Russian history: 'What is to be done?'

In the spring of 1801, when his father's assassination suddenly elevated him to the throne, Alexander I considered many answers to that question. At his initiative, there were serious discussions of reform in most areas of public life, from the role of the Senate to the size and character of the army, from serfdom to the role of the church. In sum, the reign of Alexander I began as a time of reform. Education, while it was not at the top of the reformers' list, was an obvious as well as important candidate for the reformers' attention. The Secret Committee, the group of trusted advisors Alexander gathered about him, met for several months before getting around to the subject of education. There had been much discussion of educational reform in the eighteenth century, and many models for reform developed, not least of which were the reformed system of the Polish National Education Commission and the Felbiger system imported to Russia from Prussia and the Habsburg Empire. There was, then, ample material to be drawn upon by would-be assistants such as LaHarpe and Karazin as well as members of the committee such as Czartoryski and Novosil'tsev, all of whom provided Alexander and the committee with detailed recommendations. Moreover, the staff of the School Commission founded by Catherine the Great included men like Theodor Iankovich, able professional educators well schooled in the question and well motivated as well to accomplish worthwhile development in the schools. Not surprisingly, therefore, the discussions went quickly as well as smoothly.[3]

It soon was agreed, in 1802, to found a Ministry of Education whose governing body, called the Main School Administration, would direct all education throughtout the empire through six universities, which were founded between 1802 and 1804. The senior official for each university, the 'curator', served the Main School Administration. Though there were a number of sources for various aspects of the reform, the universities were modelled mainly after the example of Göttingen, in large part because Göttingen scholars had served at Moscow University (founded in 1755, redesigned in 1804), which had sent many of its graduates to study at Göttingen. Among the Moscow men with experience, and long-lasting scholarly connections, with Göttingen was M. N. Murav'ev, former tutor to the tsar who joined the educational reformers as Moscow curator. Murav'ev chaired the ministry subcommittee which worked on drafting legislation, the statutes, for the new universities as well as a new statute for Moscow. He was convinced not only that Russian universities should strive to emulate Göttingen's excellence in scholarship but also that Göttingen's academic freedom was 'necessary' both to develop learning in Russia and also to 'raise public morals'.[4] All agreed on the goals to be sought by developing Göttingen-like institutions, the preparation of well trained and highly motivated candidates for the state services and also learned teachers to bring enlightenment to the whole nation.

The means to achieve these three interlocking and overlapping goals, development of excellent universities, provision of well prepared civil servants, and well trained teachers, included four of particular importance. First was the autonomy of the university. Not only was the organization and curriculum of the Protestant German university adopted, but also the notion that the university was a self-governing corporation whose service to society was the unconditioned pursuit of learning. That was an ideal more often rejected than achieved in the West, particularly in eighteenth century absolutist states. Nonetheless the reformers about Alexander I took it seriously. They required each university to elect its rector from among, and by, its own professors and that the council made up of all senior faculty members decide all questions regarding academic matters as well as all questions of student, and for that matter faculty, discipline. The faculties were charged also with the financial management of each institution. Various parts of these responsibilities were assigned to faculty committees, to be elected by the faculty council. The statutes which founded the universities also gave very detailed regulations to be followed in many matters. For example, the courses to be given and the degree requirements were listed in the statute, not left for the decision of the faculties. Such detailed regulations naturally limited in practice the scope of faculty action. Nonetheless, it seemed obvious as well as important to the reformers that self-governing autonomy was a necessary aspect of a modern university.

A second means adopted to achieve the goals of the Alexandrine reform was the universities' control of the public schools, organized in a ladder system right down to the village school. Each university was to provide teacher training in a special faculty, the Pedagogical Institute, to staff the gymnasia, which in turn were to provide similar service for the lower schools. Every village in the vast

Russian empire, said the statute founding the system, 'should have' a school. The graduates of the village school were entitled to enter the district [uezd] middle school, whose graduates were prepared for the gymnasium, which prepared for the university. The universities were to provide not only teacher training for the secondary level, but administration and supervision at all levels. A faculty-elected committee was to provide on site visitations on a regular basis, to guide and encourage the lower schools on their way.

A third important element was absence of class restrictions for admission. Each village school was to be open to all, including the children of private serfs, who by success in study became eligible to move up the social as well as the academic ladder and so to move out of their original class. This provision may have seemed necessary if the government were to have a latent pool large enough to recruit its future servicemen, but this all-class provision was seldom stated that way. It was usually put in moral terms, as required because it was right that those who 'contributed through learning to the welfare of the nation' earned promotion out of the 'obligated' classes and into the nobility.[5]

Finally, the curriculum adopted for the system was an important means in the pursuit of the reformers' goals. The question was whether the goal of bringing enlightenment to the whole nation meant stressing the studies which go by the name of the liberal arts, including mathematics, physics, languages, and other subjects whose practical utility was more obvious than that of, say, Latin or ancient history.[6] The question was whether the new system was to provide learning or training, preparation for careers which might well bring with them upward social mobility, or training for the improved performance of jobs traditionally associated with one or another of Russia's classes. With a remarkable minimum of qualification, the planners opted for learning as the best training, and thus for a liberal arts curriculum, right down to the village school, confident that it was best for both training and learning. This decision was acerbically attacked by well known liberals, such as Pnin and Martynov, as well as by conservatives and reactionaries, on the grounds that it attempted the impossible and thus was doomed to failure.[7]

The clarity and apparent coherence of these goals and methods agreed upon the 1802–4 was in some measure deceptive, for the reformers had not provided clear answers, indeed had not even considered, some important questions about the task ahead. The reformers made no effort to sort out their goals by considering priorities. Should one or another of these goals and methods impinge on another, no consideration had been given to deciding which was more important. The university statutes were quite specific on budgets, including the number of professors (twenty-eight for each university) and their salaries as well as the number of state-supported positions for students in each faculty. But the reformers had not made at all specific what might be required for the universities to achieve success. It was not considered, for example, how many students the universities should attempt to enroll, or how long it might take for the new teacher training programs to begin producing graduates in numbers adequate to make enough of a difference to the school system to count the reform a success. Thus, though the reformers were obviously serious about meeting some of Russia's most important needs and in a general way represented the concept of the enlightened absolutist, using state power to make reforms for the common good, their plans in some important respects remained vague, high hopes of generous spirit rather than carefully conceived blueprints.

In practice, in the decade 1804–14, each of the univerisities was left alone for the most part, to achieve the reformers' general goals as best each could. The views and abilities of the individual curators as well as the local circumstances, therefore, became the most important factors in the development of each university, contributing to great diversity among the universities' despite their common origin in a reform planned by a central organ of an absolutist state. The first task for each university was the gathering of a faculty to meet the requirements of the new statutes. The second was to recruit a student body both able and willing to provide suitable candidates for the public services and teachers for the lower schools. After a decade's work, the first task had been accomplished in three universities, failed in two others and not attempted in the sixth. Building the student bodies proved even more difficult and was clearly achieved in only one of the six. Some among the reformers thought this record indicated the failure of the reform. Even those reluctant to accept so harsh a judgement could not argue that the reform needed no significant revision, for after a decade of work even the most successful of the universities could not plausibly claim that it had met the goals of the reform launched in 1802–4.

The university for the Baltic provinces, Dorpat, was among the more successful. The first rector, Georg Parrot, was a distinguished scholar, as well as well known agitator for good causes. Parrot and his faculty colleagues had no difficulty in recruiting, by 1805, the full complement of professors. All came from German Protestant universities. Many were distinguished scholars, all were at least professionally competent. They had no difficulty making a success of university self-government through the faculty council and committees. Moreover, almost to a man they were in religious ideology self-confessed 'rationalists'. Since the university theology faculty was also to function as the Lutheran seminary for the empire, there was some discomfort in church circles at having its clergy trained by a faculty of secular-minded rationalists, but the discomfort proved minor. In 1809, the Lutheran Church in the Baltic provinces decided to require its own examinations for graduates from the Dorpat theology faculty, but the examinations tested the clerical candidates' knowledge of the local languages, not their doctrinal orthodoxy.[8]

Similarly, it might be expected that the local traditional elites, the oligarchies of serf-owning nobles and of merchants who ran the Baltic provinces, would not find congenial the work of a university faculty of 'rationalists' who governed themselves in a little 'academic republic' and who taught, to cite but one example, economics which stressed the practical and moral superiority of free labour. Initially, indeed, the foundation of the university was a bitter struggle over just those issues. The faculty choice for rector, Parrot, was among the most insistent on the universities' right to admit all academically qualified students regardless of class origin and was well known among the local nobility for holding liberal views on most questions of the day. As soon as the tsar spoke, however, and adopted Parrot's position, inviting him to St Petersburg to take part in the work of planning the new system, the quarrel ended. Nobles served on the university finance committee, chaired by Parrot, and made financial contributions, if on a modest scale.

They did not, however, hasten to enroll their sons in the university. Success in developing the faculty was not matched by the growth of a student body. In some years students were outnumbered by the professors. Enrolled students numbered a few more than two hundred and fifty in 1812. Few completed the course. Indeed, more than half stayed less than one year. Thus, it proved impossible to offer the planned three year cycle of courses for the first degree, the *kandidat*, for too often there were no students for the courses. The Pedagogical Institute, the teacher training faculty which had funds to support all its students on state stipends, was the most under-enrolled. Many, perhaps most, of its students tried, usually successfully, to transfer to another faculty, thus avoiding the institute graduate's obligation to serve six years in teaching in public schools. Naturally, there were few candidates for work towards higher degrees. Students were very visible in Dorpat, however, despite their numbers, for they promoted an almost constant round of fights, assaults on townspeople as well as each other, and general trouble making. At one point, the curator advised the faculty council that professors should not have windows on the street sides of their homes since there was no way to prevent students from repeatedly breaking them. At the end of the university's first decade, not surprisingly, it was not obvious to many observers that the university reform at Dorpat had proven worth its costs. The university was well run. Its faculty of able scholars taught their disciplines well and contributed to learning through their research and writing. Their work, however, had little impact on either the public services or public schools of the provinces.

At the other end of the scale, as well as opposite side of the empire, the university at Kazan clearly was a failure. Many professors had been recruited from German universities, but few stayed long in Kazan. At no time did the faculty number more than half that required by the statutes, while the student body never exceeded fifty. University autonomy, i.e. faculty self government, was not attempted, for the curator simply appointed a 'director', while not permitting election of a rector or the convening of a council until late in the decade. Most of the new professors appointed bitterly complained at this policy, but there seemed little they could do about it, except leave. Moreover, the few professors who stayed very long found themselves victims of local xenophobia, not the welcome bearers of the fruits of progress they had assumed. They found themselves overworked too, for many had to teach in more than one subject area, while also teaching the preparatory courses in the gymnasium. Some compensated for that by collecting double salaries, yet none doubted that their responsibilities were more than they could manage. Providing supervision of the lower schools of Kazan's district, the fifteen eastern-most provinces of the empire, proved an extraordinarily burdensome additional task.

Moscow acquired an excellent faculty of Germans recruited from Göttingen and Russians educated there. One of the Germans proudly reported to Göttingen that 'every day' Moscow came closer of Göttingen's standard.[9] By the end of the decade well prepared Russians outnumbered Germans. The language of instruction was Russian, in all but a few cases. The university stirred a good deal of local pride, stimulating gifts to the library and to funds for student aid. Moreover, the student body really was drawn from many classes. Nobles and clergy made up the largest groups, but neither was ever the majority. Nonetheless, enrollment remained discouragingly low, reaching a peak of 215 on the eve of the university's destruction in the fires which destroyed much of the city in 1812. Rowdy student behaviour prompted the Moscow faculty in 1808 to draw up a new, much tightened, discipline regulation, which required that students attend classes as well as go to church on Sundays. The reformers had planned a faculty of theology for Moscow, and St Petersburg, Kazan, and Kharkov as well, but in fact theology faculties were founded only at Dorpat and Vilna. Nonetheless, during the first decade when the faculty councils of all the new foundations, except Vilna, found it necessary to issue new regulations which demanded better behaviour of students, the new rules required not only that students attend class, and study as well, but also that they attend church.

Vilna was the exception in this matter, and in nearly all others too. Vilna soon filled its staff with able scholars who received their higher education in western universities, in France as often as not. The medical faculty was made up in large measure by Germans educated in German universities but all others were filled by Poles, despite Curator Czartoryski's complaint that the Vilna faculty's continued preference for even 'mediocre' Poles over 'eminent' foreigners was not likely to advance the 'progress of learning'.[10] Vilna soon had more than five hundred students, nearly half of whom stayed long enough to complete the degree of 'diploma'. This degree was not provided for in the statutes, but by the end of the first decade it was the usual practice at Vilna and Moscow, and not unknown at the others, to award a diploma to those who had completed two or more years of the three year *kandidat* programme in part because so few were able to complete the courses, thesis, and thesis defence required for the *kandidat*. The development of the diploma for those who accomplished a good deal, if not a *kandidat*, was itself a worthwhile adjustment to reality which helped Vilna, and to a lesser degree the other universities, to begin providing better prepared men for the public services. Vilna's student body was almost entirely noble, however, and its graduates seldom entered the teaching profession. Thus, even Vilna, the most successful of the new universities in most respects, had an influence in its district which remained a good deal less than revolutionary.

Kharkov was not so badly off as Kazan, in great part because its curator, S. O. Potocki, energetically pursued his task in recruiting faculty, insisted on the election of rector and council according to the statutes, and even found a way to borrow students from the church's local college, when too few students enrolled to make feasible the opening of the university in 1805. Nonetheless, Kharkov's difficulties remained acute. The faculty council was the scene of struggles between the Germans and the Russians so bitter that the functioning of the university often was nearly impossible. The student body, whch grew to 150 by 1812, was often the subject of the faculty quarrels, for the Germans were more than disappointed at what they found the abysmally low quality of the students, while the Russians (who often in actuality were Slavs from the Hapsburg Empire educated in one or another Austrian university) found the Germans' complaints irrelevant to the work at hand, preparing Russians for service to the Russian state.

St Petersburg University saw almost none of Kharkov's problems. Curator Novosil'tsev did not want a university on the Göttingen model. Therefore he stalled, postponing the foundation of the university. At the same time, however, he quickly developed a teacher's college, described as the pedagogical faculty of a 'future' university. There was no effort to develop a Göttingen-like institution. Novosil'tsev recruited a staff of Russians, usually from the Orthodox clergy, educated in church schools and having experience both in teaching and in service in one or another government ministry. There was no elected rector, but an appointed director who used monthly faculty meetings not to discuss policy with his faculty, let alone encourage their independent research, but to inform the staff of the administration's directives for their work with a student body of 350, recruited almost entirely from the clergy. Un-Göttingen-like though it was, St Petersburg was the only institution of the six declared founded in 1804 which soon began producing well trained teachers for the district's lower schools, if on a decidedly class-bound and narrowly vocational basis.[11]

The universities' record was so mixed that it was not surprising that some among the reformers expressed disappointment and called for reconsideration of the educational reform. The basic problems to be solved were two. Three of the six universities still needed to be organized according to the reform statutes, by recruiting the faculties and developing effective university self-government. Also, with the exception of Vilna, an exception all but irrelevant for Russia, the local societies the universities were founded to serve seldom perceived the universities as opportunities for progress but often as unwelcome intrusions to be ignored if not resisted. Thus, all but Vilna had yet to develop student bodies capable of making progress at the reform's goals. It was not obvious that religion was helped or hindered by the universities, or explained the public's indifference and hostility to them. Nonetheless, the introduction of pietistical religion was offered as the likely solution to the universities' problems.

The university faculties were not hostile to religion, or so aggressively secularistic that they provoked or frightened defenders of traditional Russian values into vigorous response, if not indeed reaction. There were many provoked and frightened defenders of Russian values, especially religious, who would have gladly taken up the cause of reaction, but they held in equal contempt the liberal 'enlightened rationalists' who advised Alexander I in the early years of his reign and the conservative 'pietists' of the Bible Society who replaced them after 1812.[12] They were frightened not so much by what had happened in Russian universities, about which they knew rather little, but by the progress of revolution in France and all its works, particularly as its effects multiplied in central and eastern Europe. They were the sort who the curator of St Petersburg University, S. S. Uvarov, in 1813 complained 'lump together the French army and French books'. Tsar Alexander was not among them, however, disappointed and perhaps even frightened though he was by the results of applying western 'rationalism' to Russia. He turned not to traditionalists, such as Shishkov, but to the Bible Society, to work out better answers to the university questions.

Bible Society reformers were reformers, not reactionaries intent on repealing, or somehow undoing, the original reform. Nonetheless, the Bible Society reform did much harm in the universities, both because some Society men entrusted with responsibility for the universities were not well informed about them and because others were not serious about Bible Society goals but merely used their Bible Society connections for self-advancement. It was no secret, of course, that the universities had serious problems. Serious Bible Society men proposed to meet those problems by providing the motivation of deeply felt religious conviction to inspire people to mutually supportive effort for the common good. In the decade 1804–14, university autonomy had proven difficult to manage, for the faculty councils were clearly overburdened with more work than a relatively small group of men could handle. Equally important, some councils saw nearly continuous wrangling, which in varying degrees in various places, saw faculties divided into opposing sides, foreigners against Russians, or liberals against conservatives, 'enlightenmentists' against those favouring career-training, and many permutations of all three. Repeatedly, factions of faculty councils asked the ministry to intervene, to abrogate one decision or another, or even to appoint the rector, since the elections of rectors were often the occasion for particularly sharp fighting in council. Bible Society reformers found such conflict and lack of cooperation evidence that the universities lacked the moral commitment to cooperation in a great common enterprise of providing enlightenment for the whole nation and training competent, well motivated officials for the manifold areas of state activity, all for the common good. Bible Society men made few efforts to change the organization of the university, or the ladder system in the lower schools, or end the all-class admission policy. Aside from adding courses in religion to the offerings of the universities, the Bible Society reform made little effort to alter the curriculum, proposed no new balance between liberal arts and career training, and in particular made no more attempt to cater to the needs and tastes of local societies than had the original reform.

In institutions where the Bible Society provided able and honest leaders (Lieven at Dorpat and Obelenskii at Moscow were the outstanding examples), the Bible Society reform worked well, promoting growth and steady progress at achieving the original reform's goals. In places where the Bible Society reformer was a hypocritical careerist (Magnitskii at Kazan) or a mean-spirited blockhead (Runich at St Petersburg), the Bible Society reform wreaked great harm. Both Magnitskii and Runich harrassed and bullied faculty members, clearly in violation of the statutory authority. For that reason, some members of St Petersburg's faculty defied Runich, refused to leave, and continued teaching at the university long after Runich's departure. Such goings on naturally promoted much confusion which undercut the effectiveness of the university's work and, not incidentally, drove students away. Much of what Bible Society officials contributed, indeed, was not only confused but silly. For example, when some students at Kharkov caused an uproar, by throwing apples at an actor on stage in the local theatre, Golitsyn, the Bible Society minister, brought the case to the Council of Ministers. He unsuccessfully sought authority for criminal trials to deal with students whose exhibition of un-Christian and dangerous 'self-love', he found a serious threat to the well being of the empire. It was July 1826, after Golitsyn had already resigned, before the Bible Society ministry got around to such questions as the university's right to elect its rector. In July 1826, the ministry granted Novosil'tsev's request to appoint the rector at Vilna, rejected Runich's request for authorization to appoint the rector for St Petersburg, and denounced a plan to amend the statutes to permit the ministry to appoint rectors as 'contrary to the proper organization of a university'.[13]

The occasional attack of silliness was not the reason that Bible Society men gave mutually contradictory answers to the question of elected rectors. The Bible Society reform made little significant change in this or other key elements of the original reform because most Bible Society reformers aimed at changing the hearts of the men in the system, not the design of the system. In the short run, it was obvious that Magnitskii and Runich made nonsense of university autonomy in practice, and severely hurt their universities, by arbitrary abuse of their authority as curators. But when the impulse behind the Bible Society effort spent itself and disappeared in the early 1820s, it had achieved little of long term significance.

When the most famous of the Bible Society curators, Magnitskii, was dismissed from his curatorship for stealing university funds, it was clear that the Bible Society era had passed. Alexander I and Golitsyn regretfully agreed that the Ministry of Education should begin a search for another answer to the university question. Alexander chose Admiral Shishkov to succeed Golitsyn as minister, an appointment which seemed to signify rejection of the facile optimism associated with the 'rationalist' version of enlightenment and rejection of the equally facile pietism of the Bible Society as solutions to the universities' problems. Though Shishkov's appointment signified what had been tried and found wanting, it did not indicate what path was to be taken.

In the end the path that was taken reaffirmed much of the original reform of 1802–4. The search for new guidelines for the universities took ten years to settle on new statutes which kept the essentials of the original reform, the development of Göttingen-like institutions to meet Russia's needs for civil servants and teachers. The work undertaken in the late 1820s, which culminated in the university statute of 1835, made one important and permanent change in the system. The universities' direction of the lower schools was abandoned. In other respects, however, the reforms seen to enactment early in the ministry of S. S. Uvarov were successful in maintaining the original reform goals and methods. This was a remarkable turn of events, for the Minister of Education who presided over the transition from the Bible Society days into the reign of Nicholas I called for significant changes. Chosen minister by Alexander I because he promised to make no hasty changes, Admiral Shishkov nonetheless recommended (1) the abolition of the elected rectorship for the universities and, (2) abolition of the ladder system by reorganizing the lower schools on the basis of social class, providing terminal and clearly vocational education for the lower classes well short of gymnasium level, which (3) would end effectively all-class university admissions, and finally (4) Shishkov made many proposals for revamping the curriculum, to make it 'truly Russian' by making the education of Russian servicemen-in-training more practical. Since Nicholas I shared these views, it was extraordinary that the new legislation when it came in 1828 and 1835 retained the elected rectorship for the universities, indeed all the autonomy the university faculties could be persuaded to keep, as well as all-class admissions, and a unitary curriculum which stressed the liberal arts.[14]

Uvarov, who came to dominate the proceedings long before his appointment as assistant minister in 1833, found many willing allies, including most university faculties. Nearly all filed repeated complaints with the ministry that the multiple responsibilities imposed by the statute of 1804 was an impossible burden, for the professors had not the hours in the day actually to provide full time administration, manage the finances, serve as 'inspectors' (i.e. the police and disciplinary officials) for the students, and also run the public school system, while also managing to serve as full time teachers and, not incidentally, scholars devoted to the development of higher learning.

The reform committees worked very slowly through masses of

materials submitted by the faculties and many others. The ideologically motivated pronouncements of Shishkov and many others, though striking and clear in general, remained general. The proposals from the faculties and the academic professionals who served in the ministry (for example, the mathematician N. I. Fuss) provided detailed, practical reforms in adoptable form. The professors and the academic professionals remained committed to the goals and means of the original reform. The changes they introduced were modifications designed to promote achievement of the original reform goals.

Thus, in the 1835 university statute, as the faculties had urged repeatedly, nearly all administraative functions, most notably the onerous obligations of student discipline, were turned over to officials appointed for those tasks. These officials were subordinates of the curator, who continued to be the appointed member of the ministry responsible for all schools in the district of his university, thus in effect serving as assistant minister of education for his district. The university rector, however, remained elected. He chaired a five man committee for administration, which included two non-elected members (variations were possible) which could be joined by the curator, if and when he chose, and reported to the faculty council. The council retained responsibility for all academic matters, with one very significant change. The management of the lower schools was removed to the curator's office. While the curator was empowered to ask his university for help, in the main, the university faculties had been granted their wish, for the burden of attempting to provide enlightenment for the whole nation by having the university run a ladder school system right down into the villages had proven impossibly difficult for the universities to manage.

This was a confession of failure. The lower schools were beyond the ability of the universities to assist. Ending the vain expenditure of university time and effort on those schools doubtless was of benefit to the universities. At any rate the university faculties had received what they wanted. Nonetheless, that left the lower schools to the management of others who had no more resources, perhaps fewer, than the universities. Uvarov often praised this arrangement as a wonderful success but he must have known that it was surrender of an important part of the original reform.[15] In January 1834 his ministry journal published an article on the educational system of

Prussia which reported that the smallest of the eight Prussian districts, Posen, i.e. Prussia's share of partitioned Poland, enrolled more than 96,000 pupils in schools below university level. Moscow, the largest of the six Russian districts, enrolled not quite 11,000. Uvarov did not make explicit comparisons but it was clear that in the wealth, culture, and social development necessary to generate wide interest in formal schooling there was a great disparity between Russia and her nearest western neighbour, even in its share of partitioned Poland. The disparity, Uvarov seemed to realize, was far too great to be overcome by anything within the power of the Ministry of Education.[16]

Uvarov gave up on no other significant element of the original Alexandrine reform. To be sure, in dealing with Nicholas I, Uvarov often was less than candid. It was characteristic of his work that the reform statutes of 1828 and 1835 contained no statements of goals, beyond vague references to 'completing' the reforms of 1802–4, and left unsaid a good deal, though many supporters and foes of the reforms had offered clear statements of goals. The clarity of Shishkov's opposition was matched by Professor Balugianskii's support. The first elected rector of St Petersburg University, Balugianskii proposed a statute which included a very detailed description of the process by which students from lower classes qualified for advancement up the educational ladder. He also wanted a complete description of the courses to be given (not just a list of courses to be taught as the professors saw fit) and detailed rules for student behaviour.[17] The 1835 statute as enacted contained none of these features. The statutes retained the elected rectorship, but said nothing about social classes. Most members of the ministry and university faculties remained committed to the original reform as the best answer possible for Russia's situation. They joined Uvarov in omitting publication of detailed statements which could stir the hopes or fears of the less prudent. The changes in the system which were made, saving that of ending university responsibility for the lower schools, were not the extreme solutions put forward by those who opposed the system, such as Shishkov, or by those who ardently favoured it, such as Balugianskii. Instead, Uvarov proved a moderate pragmatist, as well as an able administrator, who was convinced of the long range effectiveness of the original reform of 1802–4 and worked to make it succeed.[18]

The reform legislation was made significant in practice by the progress made by each of the universities. Uvarov, in spring 1834, reported to the tsar that Kharkov University 'lags far behind the other universities'.[19] His judgement was correct, but it proved more important that the Kharkov University which compared poorly with the other universities in 1834 was markedly stronger than it was a decade earlier and was indeed nearly ready to emerge as the sort of institution envisioned, if not quite planned, by the reformers of 1803–4. As late as 1827 more than half the 'chairs' at Kharkov remained vacant, while the curator complained that it was nearly impossible to persuade faculty members to participate in the university council's work, or to engage in scholarly research and writing. Not a decade later, when the student body had risen to more than four hundred, it was finally possible to undertake the sequence of courses provided for by the statutes. Meanwhile, while the addition of a splendid new library and chapel provided welcome opportunities for ceremonial rejoicing, the almost complete renewal of the faculty between 1835 and 1840 made Kharkov academically up to its assigned tasks. Many of the older faculty members were persuaded to accept early retirements, on full pension, while Uvarov took the lead in developing new faculty. Typical of the new additions was A. O. Valitskii, who had completed the *kandidat* at Vilna, the 'Professors' Institute' programme at Dorpat, and two years at Berlin. Valitskii was a well trained professional academic when in 1835 he began a long productive career in teaching and writing.

The Professors' Institute at Dorpat where Valitskii received a good part of his education, was important to the success of all the universities, though it was in existence long enough to graduate only two classes. At Parrot's suggestion, in 1827 Uvarov secured the tsar's assent to a programme which recruited talented graduates of the Russian universities to undertake studies at Dorpat University, where they would get first class instruction as well as enough experience with the German language to be able to pursue graduate work at Berlin, though a few returned to St Petersburg to finish their doctorates. In either case, the development of nearly three dozen well trained professional academics committed to making careers in the Russian universities went far to completing their foundation. The Dorpat trained men were too few to make up the majority on any faculty, but their work and the influence of their example had profound effects, particularly at Kharkov and Kazan, but also at St

Petersburg and Moscow. It may be worth noting too that these young Russians went to the Berlin University, founded in 1811 by the Prussian reformer Humboldt. Berlin yielded nothing to the model of Göttingen in academic excellence, the development of higher learning, or indeed in devotion of *Lehr-und Lernfreiheit*. But the Berlin professor, less ambiguously than the model provided by his Göttingen predecessor a quarter century earlier, was a civil servant who worked to achieve goals on which he and the state agreed in conscience as well as practice. This gradual shift in understanding of which western model was more appropriate for Russian needs was not clearly articulated by Parrot or Uvarov in the planning and administration of the Professors' Institute programme. Nonetheless, the change was made. The next generation of Russian professors had in mind the model of Berlin rather than Göttingen.[20]

By the late 1830s, none of the universities had fewer than four hundred students while Moscow enrolled nearly nine hundred. Moreover, while large numbers of the students continued to be recruits from poor gentry, clergy, and others driven into state service more by econonmic need than aspiration for learning, increasingly large percentages of the students came from noble families well situated enough to have choices. This development was particulary important at Kharkov and St Petersburg, the two most seriously affected in their first decades by the hostility or indifference of nobility whose sons the universities needed to train for careers in service. For reasons having nothing to do with education, and decisions in which no member of the Ministry of Education, including Uvarov, had any part, Vilna University was replaced by the St Vladimir University at Kiev. For political reasons, the new university at Kiev had difficulty building a professorial staff.[21] No other university had problems in that area.

The successful establishment of the Alexandrine universities marked not only the erection of a dilemma hard, perhaps impossible, for Russia to solve. There was, to be sure, a dilemma, for university autonomy, and the preservation of the *Lehr-und Lernfreiheit* necessary to make it meaningful, were not easily reconciled with the legacy of Peter the Great, the great modernizer himself. Nonetheless, in 1835, six universities were securely operating, developing native faculties whose academic competence none could doubt, training slowly increasing—but ever increasing—numbers of students for careers in public services where none could doubt their usefulness to society as well as state.

None could doubt also that the faculty members of Russian universities were civil servants in the service of an autocratic state, with significant limits on *Lehr-und Lernfreiheit* obvious to all. Pirogov, who became the best known of the graduates from the Dorpat Professors' Institute programme, in his famous essay 'The Univesity Question' in 1863 lamented that. 'A scholar striving for independence is a very common phenomenon, but a *chinovnik* [civil servant/bureaucrat] with that goal is inconceivable.' Pirogov concluded that 'In the contemporary centralized state, university autonomy is only that which makes the university as little bureaucratic as possible . . .'.[22] Uvarov and a good many others had come to a similar view, with little of Pirogov's sense of regret. Moreover, they had achieved enough in developing the Russian universities by the mid-1830s to suggest that although dilemmas are uncomfortable, they need not prove fatal to some of the most laudable goals of any university system.

Tsar Nicholas I, and many others, wanted something else. They wanted a system designed to defend and preserve autocratic Russia, whose values could be undermined in the not-very-long run by the practice and example of university autonomy, by social mobility through education, and the independence of mind and aspiration which seemed to some the intent, as well as result, of pursuit of the higher learning. Not unreasonably for him, Nicholas I wanted that undermining stopped. Made especially agitated and fearful by the 1848 upheavals in the West, Nicholas launched his own reform, for he realized by then that he could not count on the Uvarovs to do it. Uvarov's dismissal, in fall 1849, was followed by many orders, including commands to abolish the election of university rectors, to impose severe limits on university admissions, and to alter sharply the curriculum.

Nicholas I meant clearly to answer the university question by blocking the university's ability to promote change. He wanted the universities to serve the common good by supporting the autocratic Russia he had inherited from Peter the Great and his successors. This proved difficult, perhaps impossible, even in the short run. It was difficult even to find new rectors, unless the government was willing to pass over the men obviously best qualified for the posts. Thus, the rectors appointed were the same men previously elected. Pletnev at St Petersburg and Perevoshchikov at Moscow were the best known examples, but the appointment of the same man previously elected rector took place in all the universities, for those

men had not only the confidence of their colleagues but demonstrated ability and patriotism to recommend them. Similarly, practical necessity, the obvious need for medical doctors and teachers,
soon required so many exceptions to the limits on enrollments that
they soon lost much of their meaning. It was difficult even to block
admissions for able members of the low classes, for the Table of
Ranks, the mechanism of advancement, was part of the autocratic
system, a treasured legacy of the great Peter himself. Little wonder,
then, that in 1850 Uvarov's successor, the devoted conservative
P. A. Shirinskii-Shikhmatov, reported that 'as before, the doors of
the universities remain open to all classes'.[23] Though Nicholas I had
a clear answer for the university question, his answer was not
capable of meeting Russia's needs for very long. The collapse of
Nicholaivan Russia in the debacle of the Crimean War was, thus,
the occasion, not the reason, to re-examine the university question.

The regime imposed by Nicholas I on the universities had significance, for its contrast with Uvarov's solutions to the dilemma of the
university question helped mark the range of possibilities. The
autocratic state had founded a system which included university
autonomy in order to promote its own efficiency. But the successful
universities produced not only well trained, up-to-date professionals to staff the state services but also men of independent judgement
who developed their own notions of the path ahead, a development
unwelcome to those who cherished autocracy. The obvious cure for
that was to suppress autonomy, providing tight management both
to focus efficiently scarce resources and to promote social and
political stability. But the suppression of autonomy minimized, if
not crushed, important elements needed to make successful
reform, as the dead unproductiveness of the universities after
Uvarov's fall in 1849, or Kazan and St Petersburg in the days of
Magnitskii and Runich, well testified. Faced with this dilemma,
Nicholas I chose one of the obvious alternatives, suppress autonomy. Given a chance, a Pirogov or Balugianskii would choose the
other alternative. Uvarov chose neither, but tried to ward off the
dilemma by keeping as much autonomy as he could manage while
also minimizing the likelihood of precipitous change. He hoped that
given adequate time to succeed, the reform which included university autonomy, social mobility through education, a fundamentally
liberal arts orientation, and with it the development of institutions
devoted to the higher learning ('temples of learning' as he and his

successors usually phrased it) would promote the sort of change which would permit Russia to advance to another, more progressive, stage of history without paying too high a price in instability and violence.[24]

Thus, until and unless new developments fundamentally changed the situation, the choices were few as well as clear: the one made by Nicholas I, its opposite as in proposals such as Balugianskii's, or an Uvarov-like middle ground. The choice made by Nicholas I was blundered into also by Putiatin, Minister of Education in 1861. That solution, events would show, could succeed only if vigorously pushed by a government willing and able to adopt, and single-minded enough to persevere in, measures sufficiently draconian to force its choice on the universities. Successive governments of Tsarist Russia were perhaps unable and certainly unwilling to do either with the consistency necessary to succeed.

The appointment of four ministers of education in six years (1855–61) indicated not only that the government of Alexander II, though committed to the Great Reforms, had difficulty making up its mind on the university question. It pointed also to the sudden appearance of a new factor, 'corporatism' among newly enlarged student bodies, which complicated and distorted the already difficult questions. The government which laboured from 1855 to 1863 to produce the reform statute for the universities did not handle well this new problem. Rather, it was bungled, with consequences whose intractability and extent multiplied to the end of the life of Imperial Russia. Yet, the turmoil, and even the terror felt in some circles, of the mass demonstrations by St Petersburg's suddenly mass student body in the 1860s did not block development of the reform statute of 1863, which provided for university autonomy, including the elected rector, and maintained the all-class admissions policy and the unified, basically liberal arts curriculum. This solution was reached because it seemed to those who had to choose the best solution to Russia's needs, as it had to those who had to choose in 1804 and 1835.

A. S. Norov was Nicholas I's last Minister of Education, selected because he had the warm recommendation of his predecessor, Shirinskii-Shikhmatov, with whom he shared deep piety and devotion to the Orthodox faith. Norov chaired one of the many committees appointed by Nicholas I to study the problems of the bureaucracy. Norov's 1852 report concluded that the chief problem was over-centralization, i.e. Nicholas I's solution to the problem, and recommended that the government trust more the judgement of the men who staffed the services and encourage decision making at levels closer to the local peoples to be served. Nothing came of this recommendation, for it was not the answer Nicholas I wanted, but it helps to explain Norov's admiration for educational liberals such as Granovskii and Pirogov. Norov's appointment as minister in 1854 pleased the university faculties, though one of his first recommendations, urging cancellation of the limits on university enrollments imposed by Nicholas, was ignored by the tsar.[25]

Nikitenko, who worked closely with Norov on a reform of the censorship law, thought that Norov's proposals in education were unlikely to succeed because they were 'completely utopian'.[26] In fact they were no more than a return to Uvarov's policies. The struggle to enact them was serous and bitter, and the outcome hardly foregone, as the pessimism of Nikitenko suggested. The reforming tsar, Alexander II, often opposed the reformers and on some matters seemed unable to grasp the issues. Norov reiterated the view held by Uvarov, and many others, that liberal arts, specifically to include classical languages, were the best fundamental education for future servicemen. Alexander II wrote on Norov's margin, 'I do not share this conviction!'[27] Norov's successor, E. P. Kovalevskii, guided through the bureaucratic machinery Norov's proposals, which expressed his own views as well, against particularly sharp opposition from Count S. G. Stroganov in the State Council and from the Minister of Interior, P. A. Valuev. Successful at last, Kovalevskii in 1861, over seventy years of age, requested retirement. The tsar granted the request, then offered Kovalevskii's post to his chief opponents, Stroganov ad Valuev, without apparent realization of the difficulty in asking them to carry out a programme which they opposed. Both declined the tsar's request but Admiral Putiatin, to whom the tsar turned next, did not. Putiatin's appointment as Minister of Education showed that military officers raised under Nicholas I could yet be counted on to accept the tsar's assignments no matter how inappropriate. Putiatin's appointment also demonstrated that the tsar did not notice the mismatch between candidate and office until too late, when Putiatin's well intentioned blunders pushed the university faculties into open refusal to obey ministry orders and drove masses of students into the streets in what soon became violent protests.[28]

In essentials the issues were not complicated. In 1856 Norov proposed, in effect, a return to Uvarov's programme. By 1860, the worst of the restrictions imposed by Nicholas I had been revoked. It remained to provide the means to achieve the university goals, both in finances and in new personnel, and to rework the curriculum. Though many agreed that a fundamentally liberal arts education was best, developments in world scholarship, to whose standards Russian academics had long since come to aspire, and the sudden influx of new students (St Petersburg University, for example, had fewer than four hundred students in 1855, nearly twelve hundred in 1861) called for much up-dating and expansion in order to provide that liberal education. Unlike the issues, the path to enactment was excessively complicated. Norov proposed in 1856 education 'based in Orthodoxy' and marked by a 'return to the classics' while 'not slighting' technical education, but 'restoring harmony' to the curriculum.[29] Norov also declared necessary a massive increase in funding and the recruiting of new faculty in much greater numbers than previously possible, in part by sending abroad for graduate education promising young candidates, much the same programme Uvarov initiated some two decades earlier.

Norov appointed a committee to work up the proposal, whose draft was submitted for the consideration of the St Petersburg faculty in 1858. Meanwhile, as Nikitenko noted, reform was 'in the air', and the curator of the university invited the quickly growing student body to take some responsibility for itself. The *skhodki* which responded, a mass meeting of students modelled vaguely after the general meeting of the peasant commune, expressed the views of the students, often through delegations chosen to make presentations to the authorities. The *skhodki* provided a means of informing students of developments, and of getting their support for communially run book-exchanges, housing and feeding arrangements, and even cultural and intellectual affairs. Once under way, the *skhodki* were difficult to suppress, for in short order the 'corporatism' they embodied seemed to many but a normal extension of the self-governing autonomy of a self-governing university.

To many outside the universities, however, the *skhodki* seemed threats to good order, especially since the growing numbers of students in the capital overwhelmed the capacity of the university to deal with them. In spring and fall 1857, moreover, came news of violent incidents between students and police or soldiers in Kazan, Kiev, and Moscow. Since Norov could not convince the tsar that he could meet this problem of student disorder, the tsar replaced him with E. P. Kovalevskii, the curator of Moscow University. Kovalevskii was a successful mining engineer, and administrator of mining enterprises, and senior member of the Senate staff in 1858 when Alexander II named him curator of Moscow University. At Moscow he cooperated with the faculty in quickly dismantling the Nicholaivan regime and worked to further the reforms put forward by Norov. But no more than Norov could Kovalevskii quickly solve the student problem. His 1859 decision that students off-campus were out of university control, and thus subject to the ordinary police, only recognized the obvious, not answered the needs of the students or the government.[30]

The tsar added another complication in 1860 by appointing a special committee, chaired by Count Stroganov, to reconsider the proposals but forward by Norov and Kovalevskii. Stroganov used this committee to attack the proposals. Kovalevskii in the end succeeded in overcoming that opposition and by spring 1861 had the support of the State council for his concept of the legislation needed. In May 1861 he agreed to set of intermediate steps and in June retired. The 'May Rules' agreed to by Kovalevskii and Stroganov provided for stress on classical languages and rigorous examinations for admissions to universities, required students to attend classes, forbade students from applauding or jeering professors, exempted only the very poor from payment of tuition, called for the election of rectors 'in exact conformity with the state of 1835', and forbade *skhodki* unless they had the prior permission of university authorities. The obvious intent of these rules was to get under control not only the suddenly rising admissions but also control over the students themselves. Some of the rules testified to the impact of another problem by providing for the expulsion of Polish students who took part in any disorder and by requiring Russian as the language of instruction in all courses at Kiev University. Most important was rule number 15: 'All the measures indicated above are to be carried out gradually and in so far as they prove possible'. The newly appointed Minister of Education, Admiral Putiatin, decided to implement them all at once.[31]

The faculty council of St Petersburg University declared it 'impractical or impossible to fulfill' the May Rules, as ordered by

Putiatin, and refused to try. The students, many suddenly finding themselves in effect dismissed since they could not pay full tuition, turned *skhodki* quickly in mass demonstrations of protest. The disorders quickly escalated, until the university was closed in December, Putiatin dismissed, a new committee on university reform appointed, and the curators of all the universities asked to assemble to discuss the crisis.[32] The new Minister of Education, A. V. Golovnin, was among the reforming bureaucrats who gathered around Grand Duke Constantine in the last years of the reign of Nicholas I, serving as Constantine's personal secretary as well. He first entered the Ministry of Education as a staff member in 1859. Von Bradke, appointed chairman of the new committee on the reform statute, had assisted Uvarov in pulling together the 1835 statute. In 1862, he was nearly on his death bed. He won much admiration for the courage he showed, as well as his commitment to reform, working to the limits of his strength to advance the draft statute through yet more committees, the last a new Stroganov committee. Golovnin and Von Bradke had a difficult task in the mileau of fear created by rebellion in Poland, the terrorist threats of Velikoruss, and the series of mysterious fires which horrified much of St Petersburg in 1862. Not surprisingly in that climate of opinion, the student demonstrators lost all support from the public. Indeed, the faculty of St Petersburg University soon was joined by the other faculties in cooperating with the government to eliminate all signs of student self-government, especially the *skhodki*.[33]

The 'General Statute for Imperial Russian Universities', issued in June 1863, was in most important respects a faithful return to the statute of 1835. Golovnin sent to the State Council with the final draft a cover letter which pointed that out, detailing the continuity between the reform of 1804, 1835, and 1863 and arguing that in order to make good the goals of that continuing reform, it was necessary to increase markedly the financial commitment to the universities and to increase the supply of well prepared faculty members. The statute aimed to do that: faculty salaries more than doubled, the number of faculty authorized increased by nearly seventy per cent, funds for libraries and laboratories increased four-fold. The budget of St Petersburg University increased nearly four-fold, that of the other universities doubled, and a new programme sent abroad for advanced study eighty-four candidates for faculty positions. Striking as all this was, it was more important that the statute reaffirmed the autonomy of the 1804 and 1835 statutes, the all-class admissions, and the basically liberal arts curriculum. As Golovnin put put it, in answer to critics who protested that the reformers paid too much attention to the views of foreign scholars, 'All universities in the Christian world have much the same organization and exist for much the same goals . . .'.[34] Thus, the organization and goals adapted from the example of Göttingen more than a half century before, and refined in 1835, remained the best solution to Russia's needs.

The university faculties had little difficulty agreeing that such indeed was the best solution. There were some, such as Count Stroganov, who continued to think that all-class admissions were a serious mistake. But there were others who thought it wrong to restrict admissions at all. Kovalevskii was among them. In May 1859 he argued that 'the temple of learning should be open to all, in the same way as the temple of worship . . .' Neither man's proposal, to restrict university admissions on the basis of class or to adopt completely open admissions, survived the process to enactment, for they seemed to many, including the State Council as well as the university faculties, impractical extremes. A similar result befell Pirigov's recommendation to abolish all required courses. In his essay on the 'University Question', Pirogov expressed an oft repeated regret: the 'early organization of universities was closer to the ideal than ours . . . . Both teachers and students were united in pursuit of learning, they were *commilitones*. With the development of the modern state, with the spread of education to the masses, it was not possible to keep this original pure ideal. The governments, churches, society, all have their demands. The unconditioned pursuit of pure learning could not stand against the conditions of life. And thus we see that for a long time now universities have not been institutions of pure learning, but of governments, churches, academic-societies, and national institutions'.[35] Pirogov was right. The 'pure ideal' could not stand, for it was an unacceptably extreme as its opposite, the attempt to limit the universities to professional or vocational training for servicemen. I. D. Delianov, curator of St. Petersburg University, replied that 'though recognizing that there is much justice in Mr Pirogov's ideas', nonetheless, there is the need to educate the 'teachers, judges, investigators', and others who are 'indispensable for the purposes of the government'.[36]

In sum, the 1863 statute, Russia's 'Great Reform' for the universities, was a return to Uvarov's refusal to choose complete autonomy or its suppression. Its adoption, and the arguments both for and against it, indicate the remarkable consistency of the debate and the answers proposed. Serious and searching as the debate was, the answers proposed to the university question never indicated serious reconsideration of the assumptions and terms of the original 1804 reform. In 1814 and 1834, to be sure, senior officials, Kochubei of the State Council and Count V. V. Levashev, governor-general of Kiev, suggested replacing some, if not all, universities with a different type of institution, the *lycée*, which they argued was better suited to meet Russia's needs.[37] A few such institutions were opened, and some became important. But they did not indicate serious consideration to replacing the universities with another kind of institution, for that suggestion was brushed aside with little discussion. The terms of the debate had been set in the early years and were not seriously questioned thereafter.

The universities were to contribute to Russia graduates to staff the public services who had been educated in the liberal arts, as opposed to prepared for their jobs in professional, if not quite vocational, schools. It seemed to matter little from the point of view of the system whether the curriculum was rooted in the secular, perhaps better 'rationalist', Enlightenment favoured by the reformers of 1802–4, the pietism of the Bible Society generation, the classicism cherished by Uvarov, or the romantic generation's remarkable combination of reverence for science with focus on the special, if not rationally definable, something which made Russia unique. The universities were to remain as faithful as possible to their western models, because, as Golovnin had put it, 'all universities in the Christian world have much the same organization and exist for much the same goals . . .' with only the modifications required pragmatically to keep the essentials of the system in place. The Great Reform's answer to the university question, then, marked the fruition of a consistent pursuit of laudable goals, if also a narrow reading of both the possibilities and needs of Russia. While there was in all this a bit of obstinacy perhaps, it is worth noting also that there was a large measure of idealism, tempered with pragmatism, in the consistency with which Russia's educational bureaucracy returned to the essentials of the programmes launched in 1802–4 as the best answer for Russia's 'University Question'.[38]

College of the Holy Cross
Worcester
Massachusetts, 01610
U.S.A.

REFERENCES

1. The dilemma of the university question had many ramifications in the increasingly complex relationships among the university, the state, and society for the whole nineteenth century. For an excellent introduction see Klaus Meyer, 'L'histoire de la question universitaire au XIXe siècle', *Cahiers du Monde Russe et Soviétique*, XIX (1978), 301–3 and the same author's 'Die Entstehung der 'Universitätsfrage in Russland. Zum Verhältnis von Universität, Staat und Gesellschaft zu Begin des Neunzehnten Jahrhunderts', *Forschungen zur Osteuropäischen Geschichte*, Bd 25 (1978), 229–38. For Pirogov's essay, 'Universitetskii vopros', see N. I. Pirogov, *Izbrannye pedagogicheskie sochineniia*, ed. V. Z. Smirnov, (Moscow, 1952), 324–93.
2. For description and analysis of the many factors at work in this successful development, see James T. Flynn, *The University Reform of Tsar Alexander I: 1801–1835* (Catholic University of America Press, forthcoming).
3. It has been asserted now and again that the Alexandrine educational reform was a copy of one or another model or project. See, e.g., A. G. Sliusarskii, *V. N. Karazin: ego nauchnaia i obshchestvennaia deiatel'nost'* (Kharkov, 1955), 15–16 and Nicholas Hans, *History of Russian Educational Policy 1701–1917* (London, 1931), 37–41 for arguments that a single 'enlightened' advisor, Karazin, was chiefly responsible for drawing up the reform plans or that the system was basically copied from the Polish 18th century reform. The evidence does not support such assertions.
4. S. V. Rozhdestvenskii, *Istoricheskii obzor deiatel'nosti Ministerstva Narodnago Prosveshcheniia* (St Petersburg, 1902), 39. Rozhdestvenskii's discussion of the planning of the university reform in the early stages of Alexander I's reign (*ibid*, 39–57) is based on a thorough knowledge of the ministry files. Moscow's new statute was completed in May 1803 (Tsentral'nyi gosudarstvennyi istoricheskii arkhiv, Leningrad, fond 733, opis' 28, delo 23, listy 1–11 [hereafter TsGIAL]) but was not promulgated until November 1804 (*Sbornik postanovlenii po Ministerstva Narodnago Prosveshcheniia* (15 vols.; St Petersburg, 1866–1901), I, 295–331. The only source for the Secret

Committee's discussion is the notes kept by Stroganov, printed in Nikolai Milkhailovich, *Graf Pavel Aleksandrovich Stroganov* (3 vols.; St Petersburg, 1903), II. For the committee's cool reception of the plan recommended by LaHarpe, who made much of French examples, see *Ibid.*, II, 144–8. On the appeal of Göttingen's example to another absolutist state seeking educational reform, see Grete Klingenstein, 'Despotismus und Wissenschaft: Zur Kritik norddeutscher Aufklärer an der österreichischen Universität 1750–1790', *Formen der europäischen Aufklärung,* Friedrich Engel-Janosi, others (eds.), in *Wiener Beiträge zur Geschichte der Neuzeit,* Bd 3 (1976), 127–57.

5. *Sbornik postanovlenii,* I, 759 (Ukaz of 10 November 1811). Rozhdestvenskii is still the best guide to this issue. See particularly his 'Iz istorii idei narodnogo prosveshcheniia v Aleksandrovskiuiu epokhu', *Sbornik statei po Russkoi istorii posviashchennykh S. F. Platonovu* (Petrograd, 1922), 382–96.

6. Russian reformers, from the time of Peter the Great, had no more success than others in spelling out precisely what made liberal education liberal. One of Peters's most important foundations was the Moscow School, designed to train military personnel for technical specialties. The entire curriculum was the *Arifmetika* of Leontii Magnitskii, a practical manual of mathematics, arranged in catechetical format for memorization by students. The course ignored all theoretical and abstract questions, providing instead training in problem solving. Yet, Magnitskii's introduction to his work described it as a contribution to 'liberal arts' helping students to develop their minds, the faculties which distinguish humankind from the rest of creation. Max J. Okenfuss, 'Technical Training in Russia under Peter the Great', *History of Education Quarterly,* 13 (1973), 329–332. A particularly insightful discussion of what Russians made of the nature of the liberal arts is in the same author's 'The Jesuit Origins of Petrine Education', in J. Garrard (ed.), *The Eighteenth Century in Russia* (Oxford, 1973), 106–130. James C. McClelland, *Autocrats and Academics: Education, Culture, and Society in Tsarist Russia* (Chicago, 1979) surveys the question for the whole life of Tsarist Russia, concluding that both state and academia in Russia tended to overstress 'liberal' education, defined as development of 'abstract intellectual skills', at the expense of practical technical training.

7. S. V. Rozhdestvenskii, 'Universitetskii vopros v tsarstvovanie imp. Ekaterina IIoi i sistema narodnago prosveshcheniia po Ustavam 1804 goda', *Vestnik Evropy,* 1904 (No. 8), 440–4 is an insightful discussion of the question and in particular of the objections raised by Pnin and Martynov, i.e. that Russia needed improved vocational training, not more people receiving general education. It was striking that even those who reacted negatively to the new system seldom argued that the means to the reform goals were not adequate. For example, the *uezd*

school programme called for a two year course that included instruction in religion (to include both doctrine and history), a study of the text on the obligations of citizenship introduced into the schools by Catherine the Great, grammar, writing, world and Russian geography and history, arithmetic and geometry, physics and biology (natural history), drawing, and a course on 'fundamentals' of technology. This curriculum was to be taught by a staff composed of two teachers, each to spend twenty-eight hours per week in the classroom. No critic argued that the workload required by such a curriculum would likely prove beyond the capacities of the available teachers.

8. E. V. Petukhov, *Imperatorskii Iurevskii, byvshii Derptskii, Universitet 1802–1865* (Iurev, 1902), 297. Petukhov's work is richly documented and detailed. On Parrot see Friedrich Bienemann, *Der Dorpater Professor Georg Friedrich Parrot und Kaiser Alexander I* (Reval, 1902). Parrot's role in the first decade of the university's existence is described in detail also in E. E. Martinson, *Istoria osnovaniia tartuskogo (b. Derptskogo-iurevskogo) universiteta* (Leningrad, 1954).

9. Markus Wischnitzer, *Die Universität Göttingen und die Entwicklung der Liberalen Ideen in Russland in ersten Viertel des 19 Jahrhunderts* (Berlin, 1907), 34. The literature on Moscow University is extensive but does not match in quality that for the other universities. The most usefully detailed study for the period before 1825 is M. N. Tikhomirov (ed.), *Istoriia Moskovskogo Universiteta* (2 vols.; Moscow, 1955).

10. Daniel Beauvois, *Lumières et Société en l'Europe de l'Est: l'Université de Vilna et les écoles polonaises de l'Empire Russe (1803–1832)* (2 vols.; Paris, 1977), I, 61. Beauvois' study is the best work on all aspects of the university's development and is thoroughly in command of the sources both published and archival. Józef Bieliński, *Uniwersytet Wilenski, 1579–1831,* (2 vols.; Cracow, 1899–1900), remains useful, especially for the contributions of individual faculty members.

11. St Petersburg received its university status in 1819, but was almost at once turned over to the curatorship of D. P. Runich , whose administration made impossible any efforts to develop the university. By the mid-1830s, however, St Petersburg had recovered from the Runich years and soon proved one of the academically strongest of the Russian universities. The most detailed treatment remains V. V. Grigorev, *Imperatorskii S. Peterburgskii universitet v techenie pervych piatidesiati let ego sushchestvovaniia* (St Petersburg, 1870). For Kharkov and Kazan see two richly detailed works published on the hundredth anniversary of their foundations, D. I. Bagalei, *Opyt istorii Khar'kovskago Universiteta* (2 vols.; Kharkov, 1893–1904); B. N. Bulich, *Iz pervykh let Kazanskago Universiteta, 1805–1819* (2 vols.; St Petersburg, 1904).

12. For a discussion of two of the most important such defenders of Russian values, see my articles on Admiral A. S. Shishkov and A. S. Sturdza in *Modern Encyclopedia for Russian and Soviet History*, 35

(1983) and 38 (1984). For Uvarov's dealings with them, and with the worst of the Bible Society men, see my article, 'S. S. Uvarov's "Liberal" Years', *Jahrbücher für Geschichte Osteuropas*, Bd 20 (1972), 481–91.

13. Runich's request is in TsGIAL, fond 733, opis 20, delo 219, listy 158, 182, 260–4; Novosil'tsev's in *Sbornik postanovlenii*, II, 31–3. Novosil'tsev's choice was well known for his public protests against Magnitskii's obscurantist attacks on academic freedom. Beauvois, *L'Universite de Vilna*, I, 70–2. The proposal to amend the statues and the ministry's rejection are printed in Bagalei, *Opyt istorii*, II, 145–64. Two scholars have produced important studies of the Bible Society which regrettably remain unpublished. Judith Cohen Zacek, 'The Russian Bible Society 1812–1826' (Ph.D., Columbia, 1964) is the best treatment of its subject in any language. Zacek concludes (p. 187) that Golitsyn all but ignored issues of organization, administration, and curriculum, concentrating on attempts to 'infuse education with a new spirit'. W. W. Sawatsky, 'Prince Alexander N. Golitsyn (1773–1844): Tsarist Minister of Piety' (Ph.D., Minnesota, 1976) is a treasure trove of materials, including (pp. 252–290) a well-informed discussion of the ideas on education of Bible Society leaders.

14. The Committee on the organization of schools, appointed by Nicholas I in May 1826, was the main agency in the reform, replacing the 'temporary committee on statutes' appointed by Shishkov in January 1825. Rozhdestvenskii, *Istoricheskii obzor*, 176–219; Steven H. Allister, 'The Reform of Higher Education in Russia during the Reign of Nicholas I, 1825–1855' (Ph.D., Princeton, 1974), 20–107; and Constantin Galskoy, 'The Ministry of Education under Nicholas I: 1826–1836' (Ph.D., Stanford, 1977), 166–193 provide excellent guides, all showing thorough knowledge of the committee files and journal, which are in TsGIAL, f.737.

15. Cynthia H. Whittaker, *The Origins of Modern Russian Education: An Intellectual Biography of Count Sergei Uvarov 1786–1855* (DeKalb, 1984), 128–51 makes obsolete all previous discussions of Uvarov's work with the schools below university level.

16. Uvarov in 1843 reported to Nicholas I the great success of the schools in reaching enrolments of more than 100,000 pupils, an increase of nearly 40% over the levels of 1833. Accurate statistics were difficult develop, and so remain difficult to find, but the rough magnitudes in Uvarov's reports seem beyond reasonable doubt. *Desiatiletie Ministerstva narodnago prosveshcheniia 1833–1843* (St Petersburg, 1863), 103–5. A computational, or typographical, error in the table (*ibid.*, 104) results in a total enrolment figure for 1842 twice the actual number. The error is so obvious that it must be merely a slip, not an effort to exaggerate. Uvarov did not point out, to be sure, that France had more than three million pupils in such schools, or that even Ireland, whose

population was not one tenth of Russia's, had five times more pupils in such schools. Mary Daly, 'The Development of the National School System, 1831–40', in A. Cosgrove and D. McCartney (eds.), *Studies in Irish History presented to R. Dudley Edwards* (Dublin, 1979), 156.

17. Balugianskii's proposed statute included strict rules against 'making noise in class or library' and provided that students 'who make noise during church services may be arrested'. TsGIAL, f.1260 , op.1, d. 341, listy 35–6. He also recommended that the universities retain management of the lower schools, though he granted in a covering letter (*ibid.*, 43–4) that there were advantages in assigning the lower schools to the curators' authority. The statute of 1828 in *Sbornik postanovlenii*, II, 200–57; of 1835 in *ibid.*, 969–95. Rozhdestvenskii, *Istoricheskii obzor,* 195 pointed out that the statutes continued the essentials of the 1802–4 legislation, a point missed by many scholars since, for it is easy to take the pronouncements of Shishkov, calling for reversal of the earlier reform on most essential points, as policy though in fact his recommendations were not acted upon. For examples see P. Miliukov, *Ocherki po istorii russkoi kultury*, II (St Petersburg, 1905), 344–6; Patrick L. Alston, *Education and the State in Tsarist Russia* (Stanford, 1969), 32–5. For examples of Uvarov's usual craft, if not deviousness, in dealing with Tsar Nicholas I, see my article, 'Tuition and Social Class in the Russian Universities: S. S. Uvarov and "Reaction" in the Russia of Nicholas I', *Slavic Review*, 35 (1976), 233–248.

18. This is the message of Uvarov's 1818 address *Rech prezidenta imperatorskoi Akademii Nauk, popechitelia SPB uchebnogo okruga v torzhestvennom sobranii Glavnogo pedagogicheskogo instituta 22 marta 1818 goda* (St Petersburg, 1818). Cynthia Whittaker has published an abridged translation of this speech in *Slavic and European Education Review*, 1978 (1), 32–8. Whittaker's article, 'The Ideology of Sergei Uvarov: An Interpretive Essay', *The Russian Review*, 37 (1978), 158–76 well presents the case that Uvarov remained loyal throughout his life to the ideals expressed in his 1818 speech.

19. Bagalei, *Opyt istorii*, II, 244.

20. For discussions of the Professors' Institute, see Rozhdestvenskii, *Istoricheskii obzor,* 186–7; Petukhov, *Derptskii universitet,* 486–9. Parrot's plan and Uvarov's draft legislation are in *Sbornik postanovlenii*, II, 95–101, 108–111. On Valitskii's career, see M. G. Khalanskii, D. I. Bagalei, (eds.) *Istoriko-filologicheskii fakultet khar'kovskago universiteta za pervyia 100 let ego sushchestvovania 1805–1905* (Kharkov, 1905), 175–83.

21. For a discussion of the issues involved in foundation of the Kiev university, see my article 'Uvarov and the "Western Provinces": A Study of Russia's Polish Problem', *Slavonic and East European Review*, 64 (1986), 212–36.

22. Pirogov, 'Universitetskii vopros', *Izbrannye sochineniia*, 397. The

development of Pirogov's views is most cogently studied in W. L. Mathes, 'N. I. Pirogov and the Reform of University Government, 1856–1866', *Slavic Review*, 31 (1972), 29–51 and 'N. I. Pirogov and the University Queston in the Era of the Great Reforms: Reconsiderations' (unpublished paper, Convention, American Association for the Advancement of Slavic Studies, New Orleans, LA, 21 November 1986).

23. *Sbornik postanovlenii*, II, sec. 2, 1137–38 (26 January 1850).
24. For a sensitive discussion of Uvarov's point here, see Whittaker, *Uvarov*, 87–94.
25. Norov is the subject of an admirably detailed study, Peter R. Weisensel, 'Avram Sergeevich Norov: Nineteenth Century Russian Traveler, Bureaucrat, and Educator' (Ph.D., Minnesota, 1973). Norov was not among the circles of liberal bureaucrats which formed about Grand Duke Constantine and Grand Duchess Elena Pavlovna in the late years of the reign of Nicholas I and which played an important role in the development of the Great Reforms. Nonetheless, he shared many of their views. Compare his 1852 report on the state services (Weisensel, 204–6) with the views of N. A. Miliutin and others discussed in W. Bruce Lincoln, 'The Genesis of an "Enlightened" Bureaucracy in Russia 1825–1856', *Jahrbücher für Geschichte Osteuropas*, Bd 20 (1972), 321–30.
26. A. V. Nikitenko, *Zapiski i dnevnik* (2 vols.; St Petersburg, 1905), I, 517 (diary entry for 8 May 1858).
27. Weisensel, 'Norov', 238.
28. Putiatin's career has not been much studied, but it seems safe to say that he was not simply the blockhead often pictured (e.g. Alston, *Education and the State*, 47–51). He had a respectable navy career, including successful completion of difficult negotiations with Japan during the Crimean War (the source of Herzen's jibe at 'our Japanese minister') and was serving in the embassy in London when the tsar called him to take on the Ministry of Education. Nothing in his background or training suggested fitness for that post. A sympathetic discussion of Putiatin's career is in *Russkii biograficheskii slovar'*, vol. 15 (St Petersburg, 1910), 162–4.
29. Norov's proposal is in *Sbornik postanovlenii*, III, 75–84 (5 March 1856). Of the many brief accounts of the path to enactment of the 1863 statute, the best in English is Alston, *Education and the State*, 44–57, which provides a perceptive reading of the memoir literature. The best informed Soviet account is R. G. Eimontova, 'Universitetskaia reforma 1863 g.', *Istoricheskie zapiski*, 70 (1961), 163–96. The classic Russian liberal interpretation is I. N. Borozdin, 'Universitety v Rossii v epokhu 60-kh godov', *Istoriia Rossii v XIX veke* (9 vols., Granat, St Petersburg, n.d., 1910?), IV, 185–212. Mastery of the sources makes Rozhdestvenskii, *Istoricheskii obzor*, much the superior account. See especially *Ibid.*, 352–66 on Norov and *Ibid.*, 413–30 on Golovnin.

However, Rozhdestvenskii (*Ibid.,* 356) found that 'The university question in the early years of Alexander II's reign . . . was whether to return the universities to the normal order of the 1835 statute'. Regarding the 1835 statute as 'normal', Rozhdestvenskii gave short shrift to those who opposed it, thus missing the seriousness of Stroganov, Valuev and others who worked to defeat the reformers' proposals.

30. The sudden increase in student numbers was part of a dramatic surge in public spiritedness in Russia in the wake of the humiliating defeat of repressive Nicholaivan Russia in the Crimean War. The young Russians who made up the 'generation of the sixties' came to the universities not only in greater numbers but with a much greater sense of mission, an optimistic faith that their generation would place learning at the service of society. The emergence of this phenomenon and its manifold consequences are well presented in two superior works which, regrettably, remain unpublished; Thomas J. Hegarty, 'Student Movements in Russian Universities 1855–1861' (Ph.D., Harvard, 1965) and William L. Mathes, 'The Struggle for University Autonomy in the Russian Empire During the First Decade of the Reign of Alexander II' (Ph.D., Columbia, 1966). On Kovalevskii, see also *Russkii biograficheskii slovar'*, 9 (1903), 22–4 and N. Rodzevich, 'Otstavka E. P. Kovalevkago', *Istoricheskii vestnik* (January, 1905), 98–129, whose close reading of the archival documents provides a useful corrective to the usual memoir-based accounts.

31. The May Rules are printed in *Sbornik postanovlenii*, III, 732–35 and in translation as an appendix in Hegarty, 'Student Movements', 383–84. In addition to the Stroganov committee, two other special study groups worked on aspects of the issue. The curator of St Peterburg University, I. D. Delianov, in 1860 asked a faculty committee, chaired by Professor K. D. Kavelin, to study ways to meet the student problem, while another ministry committee appointed by Kovalevskii involved Pirogov, and others, in reviews of the projected reform. This work occasioned Pirogov's famous essay, 'The University Question'. The essay was completed in 1862 but not published until after the enactment of the new statute.

32. Mathes, 'Struggle', 108–17, well presents Putiatin's efforts and the responses he provoked at St Petersburg University. For a richly detailed description, see Hegarty, 'Student Movements', 67–142. Valuev, the Minister of Interior, took credit for the government's response to the crisis engendered by Putiatin's action in forcing the May Rules, arguing that neither the Ministry of Education nor the State Council were capable of producing solutions. *Dnevnik P. A. Valueva: Ministra vnutrennykh del,* ed. P. A. Zaionchkovskii (2 vols., Moscow, 1961), I, 130–131.

33. Important though he was to the university reform, Golovnin is better known for his contribution to the reform of censorship. See Charles A.

Ruud, *Fighting Words: Imperial Censorship and the Russian Press 1804–1906* (Toronto, 1983), 118–45; W. Bruce Lincoln, *In The Vanguard of Reform: Russia's Enlightened Bureaucrats 1825–1861* (DeKalb, 1982), 72–95, 143–6.

34. Rozhdestvenskii, *Istoricheskii obzor*, 413. The text of the statute is in *Sbornik postanovlenii*, III, 1040–75, together with Golovnin's cover-letter (*ibid.*, 1075–90). A translation is in Mathes, 'Struggle', 503–55 (appendix C). The universities did not reassume responsibility for the lower schools, but they were again assigned responsibility for student discipline, a feature of the 1804 statutes which the faculties had cheerfully relinquished to the curators in 1835. The faculty councils were not enthusiastic about regaining responsibility for management of student discipline, but the staff appointed for the task had not proven successful at keeping order and something had to be done. See Mathes, 'Struggle', 207–9.

35. Pirogov, *Izbrannye sochineniia*, 380.

36. Mathes, 'Struggle', 159. For the debate on curriculum, see *Ibid.*, 157–61; Rozhdestvenskii, *Istoricheskii obzor,* 353–5. On the social class and admissions question, *Ibid.,* 361–6 (Kovalevskii quoted, 362); Mathes, 'Struggle', 107–8; Hegarty, 'Student Movements', 59–60.

37. Rozhdestvenskii, *Istoricheskii obzor*, 75–6; Vitaliia Shulgin, *Istoriia Universiteta Sv. Vladimira* (St Petersburg, 1860), 37–8.

38. 'Obstinate' is the term used by Meyer, 'L'histoire de la question universitaire', *Cahiers du Monde Russe et Soviétique* (1978), 301. An aspect of the university question which grew in importance throughout the life of Tsarist Russia was the emergence of the intelligentsia. This development has received more attention than all others in the history of education in Russia and in fact has become a subject of study itself, quite distinct from the history of the schools. A recent work, Maria Wawrykowa, *Für eure und unsere Freiheit: Studentenschaft und junge Intelligenz in Ost- und Mitteleuropa in der ersten Hälfte des 19. Jahrhunderts* (Stuttgart, 1985), well summarizes the extensive literature, finding the rise of a similar 'intelligentsia' in Russia, Poland, and Germany, and concluding that the main element in all was the Romantic 'sons'' rejection of the 'fathers'' faith in enlightened rationalism as the guide to reform. N. V. Riasanovsky, *A Parting of Ways: Government and the Educated Public in Russia 1801–1855* (Oxford, 1976), 148–245 provides a richly nuanced discussion of the ideas developed by intelligentsia leaders. Daniel R. Brower, *Training the Nihilists: Education and Radicalism in Tsarist Russia* (Ithaca, 1975) establishes the social origins and make-up of the radical intelligentsia.

American Higher Education in the Age of the College

Jurgen Herbst

The Historiographical Issue

No period in the history of American higher education stands more in need of reappraisal and reinterpretation than the 'age of the college'. Until quite recently historians have treated the decades between the Revolution and 'the emergence of the American university' in the years after the Civil War with faint distaste and little appreciation for what they found in it.[1] They saw it as a time of declining standards and dissipation of energies dominated by large numbers of weak and small institutions, many of which came and went without leaving any permanent trace.[2] The 'old-time college' with its uniform curriculum was the period's typical institution. It smelled of the mustiness of old-fashioned frock coats and brought up images of roll-top desks, their cubbyholes stuffed with yellowing papers in much the same fashion that the 'faculties' of students' minds were to be crammed with the facts and qualities the old-time college professor so faithfully dispensed and promoted.[3]

A newer literature has now appeared that dissents rather strikingly from this traditional interpretation. The old-time college no longer is the only educational institution worth noting in this period. Quite to the contrary, an appreciation of diversity now permits us to recognize a whole series of specialized schools that devoted themselves to some form of post-common school education.[4] To use just one example: in the years before 1855 Illinois reported the existence of female high schools and teacher seminaries, literary and theological institutions, female academies, liberal institutes for the establishment and support of education, and seminaries of learning for the advancement of religion, science, and 'the cause of education generally'. The state had at least one seminary for the promotion of 'English and German literature', one commercial and mathematical institute to teach 'double-entry bookkeeping and the laws of trade, of commercial calculations and the higher mathematics', as well as manual labour colleges, schools, seminaries, and universities. Then there were medical and literary colleges and universities as well as agricultural and female colleges and universities.[5] To be sure, the differences of what was being taught in these institutions were not always pronounced. They depended, after all, on the students' state of prior education or the lack of it. But they were nonetheless novel and remarkable when contrasted with collegiate education during the colonial period.

It is therefore useful to try to take the measure of the changes that have occurred in the historiography of this period and to investigate a few themes that have now emerged as significant starting points for a re-interpretation of American higher education in the ante-bellum years.[6] After a brief characterization of the traditional view, I want to consider the colleges as they reflected the 'politeia', their society's political orientation and commitment, and to highlight their commitment to tradition within diversity by pointing to the role of the ubiquitous 'college course'. At the same time I want to show that this emphasis on tradition did not rule out a careful and measured response to demands for innovation which took the form of partial and parallel courses and schools.

I should like to argue, too, that what has been called the 'great retrogression' needs to be balanced with a consideration of the progressive social role the colleges performed in ante-bellum America.[7] Academic decline and economic and social stimulus may be seen as two sides of the same coin, each requiring the other to enable higher education to survive and perform its traditional function in a frontier society. Finally, I want to end with a brief sketch of the diversity of institutions that came to characterize American higher education in the ante-bellum period. The search for ways to teach practical and applied science, to train teachers for the common schools, and to open collegiate doors for men and women of middle and working class origins introduced novel institutions into ante-bellum higher education.

The Traditional View and its Problems

The 'age of the college' was endorsed, if not to say sanctified, as a fixed notion in our historiography by Richard Hofstadter and

Walter Metzger in their influential study on the history of academic freedom. They divided their work into an 'age of the college' and an 'age of the university'.[8] The latter was said to have begun somewhere around 1876. In that year the Johns Hopkins University opened its doors in Baltimore, Reconstruction ended in the American South, and at about that time the nation was said to have entered the age of organized or corporate capitalism. With the importation of the German university model for graduate education and the emergence of the research university a new era had begun in the history of American higher education.

The distinction between the 'age of the college' and the 'age of the university' raised all sorts of difficulties. Not only did universities with several faculties, colleges, or schools exist in the United States during the 'age of the college', but colleges as one-faculty institutions continued and continue to thrive in the 'age of the university'. Taken from a curricular rather than an institutional point of view, the distinction was equally problematical. Medical, theological, and legal instruction—i.e. university subjects—were offered already in eighteenth century colleges, and the liberal arts course has never disappeared from American higher education.[9]

But this was not all. The typological distinction was imbued also with a qualitative dimension. The 'age of the university' was the modern age in which was born the academic world we know today and in which we feel at home. By contrast, the 'age of the college' was filled with local institutions out-of-touch with national or state issues, stuck in the past, and, particularly as concerned their curricula, unresponsive to their critics. When compared to the institutions that preceded and that followed them, the colleges of the ante-bellum period came to be portrayed as academic backwaters.

Problematic, too, was the contrast between the fall from grace that Richard Hofstadter attributed to the ante-bellum colleges and the tremendous economic and demographic 'take-off' that many scholars noted for the new nation during the first half of the nineteenth century.[10] Willard Hurst chose the felicitous phrase of 'the release of energy' to characterize the expansion in territory, spirit, and political experience that now buoyed the young democracy.[11] Along with all other institutions colleges, too, proliferated. But Hofstadter wrote of 'the great retrogression' to deplore the disregard for academic standards in the multiplying collegiate institutions and to express regret over the loss of, nay the deliberate disregard for, the presumed academic rigour inherited from the colonial colleges and the European past.

American higher education was criticized not only for the 'great retrogression', but also for the presumed unwillingness or inability of the colleges during the ante-bellum era to respond to the demands of the American people for instruction in practical scientific tasks. Here, too, the colonial and the post-bellum period were made to shine by contrast. In the colonial colleges professorships of mathematics and natural philosophy had usually been established soon after the initial appointment of a professor of divinity. In New York and Philadelphia professorships of medicine had been the first professional faculty appointments outside the colleges proper.[12] The rise of the modern university to scientific eminence obviously needs no additional comment.

By contrast, the colleges of the ante-bellum period were said to have paid mere lip-service to science. 'The scientists remained second-rate citizens in the academic world and their influence was negligible', wrote George P. Schmidt.[13] Frederick Rudolph followed the same line when he declared that in the colleges all the curricular experiments with the teaching of science 'were adopted as props for the classical course'.[14] And the classical course, it was asserted by implication if not explicitly, was dominated by the teaching of Latin and Greek.

Colleges in an Age of Revolution

This disparaging view of American higher education in the ante-bellum period clouds and misrepresents more than it illuminates our understanding. It portrays the colleges as being out-of-touch with their society when it can be argued that just the opposite was the case. In the decades between 1780 and 1860 the institutions and views of collegiate, Latin-based education underwent far-reaching changes that in their legal, organizational, and curricular aspects reflected the deep-seated transformation of the society in which they existed and which they served. Not only do we during the early years of this period have to face the obvious issue of the American Revolution as a war for national independence, but joined to it was the gradually accelerating struggle for republican forms of government and democratic patterns of social relations. With the victory of Andrew Jackson in 1828 the common people would compete for the spoils of politics on equal terms with the sons of the country's established and wealthy families. Should we not assume that changes of such magnitude in the political and social configurations of a people would have made their impact on collegiate institutions as well?

The events educational historians describe do not exist in a vacuum. In the colonial period as throughout western history higher education had been part of the political and ecclesiastical establishment of empire, province, or nation. As present and future leaders of their society, professors and students in the colonial colleges had closely followed and participated in the momentous events that were to bring independence for a new nation. Faculty members educated their students for public service. Patriotic professors, tutors, and students debated and promoted the propagation of republican principles.[15] None was more engaged in this effort inside and outside his college than Princeton's president John Witherspoon who in 1776 became a member of the Continental Congress. At Yale, Princeton, Harvard, and Brown students took the initiative in founding literary societies which soon became centres for political debate and agitation.

Once independence had been won the colleges, willy-nilly, became drawn into the political battles of the new nation. What financial, foreign, and social policies were appropriate for the new republic? The first presidents of the new nation from Washington to Monroe had themselves belonged to the revolutionary generation and saw to it that republican ways would replace the monarchical traditions of the past. By 1828 the victory of Andrew Jackson signalled the ascendency of democracy over aristocracy and feudalism. Faculty members and students in the established colleges continued debating these national issues in familiar ways. If anything, as Robson has pointed out, they increased the fervour of their partisanship.[16]

For students the professorial and tutorial sermons of a new republicanism and democracy often translated themselves into protests against the collegiate traditions of *in loco parentis*.[17] Students demanded that colleges be seen as civil rather than domestic societies and their rights as citizens be recognized and protected against faculty encroachment. Thus Professor Pearson of Harvard could remind his colleagues in 1789 that if students were taught 'that they are entitled to all the civil rights of freemen . . . it is no wonder that they rebel against the constitution of College which, at present, is not founded on such principles'.[18]

Newly founded colleges in the hinterland and on the frontier were far more likely than their Eastern sister institutions to depend on local support and to respond to local issues. Their students came from rural areas and relatively poor families; they were older on the average and often worked and attended college part-time or inter-mittently. They were also less likely than their younger classmates to board or room together and to feel themselves as members of a college class.[19] In many cases the institutions themselves were sup-ported by religious groups or were part of a promotional effort to encourage development and attract desirable settlers with fam-ilies.[20] For these new colleges national issues seemed further removed than for their sister institutions in the older areas along the coast. Missionary concerns for the self-imposed mandate of 'taming a wilderness' and bringing civilization and religion to 'the ends of the world' crowded out a secular, republican political culture that had been cherished in the East.[21]

This new collegiate culture was intimately related to the 'release of energy' on the frontier, a release that created a veritable patch-work of local centres across the country with few unifying strands. Diversity and localism marked the new America and the colleges it established beyond the Appalachians.[22] Here Americans looked outward, not backward to the metropolises of the East. Their republicanism translated itself into a democratic localism that saw no need and felt no love for central direction. Local associations of citizens, frequently held together by bonds of a common religion, acted as godfathers for the new colleges. Tocqueville observed it well in 1831: 'In democratic countries the science of association is the mother of science; the progress of all the rest depends upon the progress it has made.'[23] The new colleges sprang up as evidences of democracy in higher education, just as the colonial colleges had served as the academic incubators of republicanism.

Tradition within Diversity: The College Course

Despite these differences between East and West, between republican tradition and democratic innovation, the colleges were held together by a common commitment to educating the country's future professional, religious, political, and scientific leaders. In Eastern as well as Western colleges the same questions were raised: how to educate for leadership in a democracy? How to harmonize the urgent need for an educated intelligence that was to seek above all the welfare of the commonwealth with the proud boasts of a rough-hewn democracy that believed in the natural ability of everyone to seek their own best interests?

The complexity and confusion of the answers are mirrored in the pages of James Fenimore Cooper's *The American Democrat*. Writing in 1838 Cooper asked the colleges to graduate students who were to be gentlemen of public or private station, who belonged to a class that was 'the natural repository of the manners, tastes, tone, and to a certain extent, of the principles of a country'. With a paternalism incongruous to his professed preference for democracy Cooper exhorted these gentlemen to be stewards of the liberties of their fellow citizens and to assert at all times the principles of democratic government. In turn, Cooper and like-minded Americans felt, the great masses of Americans ought to respect the college-educated gentlemen for the contributions they made to civilization. 'Where many such are found, the arts are more advanced, and men learn to see that there are tastes more desirable than those of the mere animal . . . He who would honor learning, and taste, and sentiment, and refinement of every sort, ought to respect its possessors, and, in all things but those which affect rights, defer to their superior advantages'.[24]

This, to be sure, was a tall order that was bound to remain unfilled. But the colleges, by and large, accepted it and sought to make it their educational mission. The key to its attempted realization lay in their loyalty to the traditional college course as the required uniform curriculum for candidates for the bachelor of arts degree. That course became the mainstay of a college education in the ante-bellum years. The colleges refuted all accusations that in their adherence to it they were inflexible and impractical and unresponsive to the demands of an expanding country for instruction in modern subjects. To the contrary, they argued that only by preserving the traditional curriculum could they perform their function of educating the country's future leaders.

The manifesto of the ante-bellum college was the 1827 report of the Yale Faculty on their curriculum. President Jeremiah Day, the author of the report's first part, made it clear that colleges were concerned with basic intellectual skills and acquirements in literature and science. When young men were exposed to these they would gain the 'foundation of a superior education,' not a complete edifice. The 'discipline and the furniture of the mind' were the aims, not the myriad details of every conceivable subject. The college would select with care its curriculum, but every part of it had to qualify for a particular mission. Thus mathematics would train the faculty of demonstrative reasoning, the physical sciences would instill respect for facts and give practice in inductive reasoning. Classical literature would develop taste and logic would teach its students how to think, as rhetoric would accomplish the same for the art of speaking. The educated graduate would combine solid learning with skills of eloquence; he would have something to say, and he would know how to say it well. He was the college-bred gentleman whom James Fenimore Cooper would hold up ten years later as the ideal American democrat.

The task of the college was the education of character. But that could be achieved only by a balanced approach that would stress the languages as much as the sciences. Concern for 'a proper symmetry and balance of character' in the students made it improper and unlikely that a college would neglect the modern scientific subjects. The Yale faculty pointed out that chemistry, mineralogy, geology, and political economy had been introduced in recent years. Their study required effort no less 'vigorous and steady and systematic' as the study of all other collegiate subjects. A collegiate education, after all, was an education of mind and character to prepare students for the future proper execution of professional tasks.

Thus the Yale faculty and thereafter the faculties of America's colleges throughout the land rejected the accusations of the impracticality of their studies and of their unwillingness to respond to demands for fundamental curricular changes. What they insisted upon was that college studies had to remain general and theoretical or, as they would put it, preparatory to professional study. They embodied the principles of science which were 'the common foundation of all high intellectual attainments,' which in turn were needed among merchants, manufacturers, and farmers as much as among statesmen and politicians. In a democracy—and here Cooper would later echo the report—the college course was to be open to all who contributed in their different ways to the welfare of the nation.[25]

Tradition and Innovation

As much as they upheld tradition, the colleges had not been averse to innovation. Yale had made that point in 1777 when its then president-elect Ezra Stiles had submitted to the college corporation proposals for strengthening the traditional role of the college in educating Connecticut's civic and political leaders. Stiles had urged the creation of professorships in belles lettres, oratory, civil history, and law. The new chairs were to be endowed in the college where they could serve the general education of the students 'in that knowledge which may qualify them to become useful members of society as select men, justices of the peace, members of the legislature, judges of courts, and delegates in Congress'. Legal instruction in government, Stiles emphasized, was general education. It was '*civil history* of the best kind. It is not a dull and unanimated narrative of events—it is tracing great events, great political phenomena to their operative and efficient causes—it is the *true spirit of history*'.[26]

The same endorsement of general and theoretical education applied to the so-called partial and parallel courses that several colleges had introduced into their curriculum. Responding to demands from the outside, partial courses allowed non-degree candidates to enroll for part of the regular college programme, and parallel courses substituted more scientific instruction for one of the classical languages in the regular course. In every case, however, the approach remained preparatory and avoided professional instruction.

The colleges acted with great caution. Afraid that increased or novel offerings would detract from the value of the regular college course leading to the bachelor's degree, Princeton in 1796 and Union College in 1802 permitted only non-degree students to attend lectures in the parallel course. Between 1825 and 1828 more such reforms were discussed and adopted at Harvard, Amherst, the University of Vermont, Columbia, Williams, Union, and Dartmouth.[27] By 1828 only President Nott of Union was adventurous enough to award the BA degree to graduates of the regular as well as of the parallel course.[28]

It cannot be said, then, that the colleges had shut their doors, eyes, and ears to the demands of innovation. They had indeed endorsed curricular experiments. They knew that only thus could they keep open the gates to social mobility for many of their students as they had done in the past with remarkable success. Between 1748 and 1768 half of Princeton's students had been sons of farmers of middling to poor economic status, and three-quarters of them later became clergymen, lawyers, or physicians.[29] And what had been true for Princeton had also been true with only minor variations for the other colleges of the colonial period.

This need for colleges to offer a solid and respected basis for a professional career and to respond to changing times and conditions was even more in evidence after 1800 in the new foundations in the hinterland and on the frontier. Because these institutions were marked by diversity and localism and because their students lacked family connections, apprenticeship arrangements, or access to some proprietary professional school that growing up in an established society might have supplied, the regular college course that led to the bachelor of arts degree was even more a necessity for them than for their Eastern brethren. It was the road to opportunity in a democratic society, the most promising pathway to a professional career.

If the Western colleges were to fulfill their function as gateways to professional opportunity, they had to insist on the regular college course to establish their academic respectability and forge a bond of unity among their students. The education societies of churches and denominations that served as college founders in the West could wholeheartedly endorse its literary and scientific contents. As Douglas Sloan has reminded us, in the ante-bellum years the dispute of science with religion lay yet in the future. Charles G. Finney, the great revivalist at Oberlin College, admonished his students to study works on medicine and natural science 'for all these declare the wonderful works of God'.[30] The course thus became the staple fare of the new students in the colleges of the West.

As in the older colleges in the East, the study of the natural sciences was at times introduced in a partial or parallel course. Many of the western colleges also responded to the urgent call for teachers in private academies and public high schools and introduced teacher training. Eventually they allowed women to enroll as well.[31] Part-time school teaching in conjunction with 'normal instruction' then provided welcome opportunity for the many older students from relatively poor families to help defray their college expenses. But whether full or part-time student, male or female, those who had completed the regular college course had earned the bachelor degree and were full-fledged college graduates.

The philosophy of the Yale Report, then, did not rule out responsiveness to new conditions. In fact, it could be argued that it was the combination of upholding academic standards symbolized by the regular college course and being responsive to new developments that allowed the colleges, old as well as new, to play the role the people wanted and the nation needed. In its fusion of tradition and responsiveness, in its ability to accept the new without discarding the old, lay the strength of the ante-bellum college.

The Other Side of the Coin: The Great Retrogression

If we thus have stressed the strength of the ante-bellum college in its reliance on the traditional college course and its willingness to respond carefully to the needs and demands of their students, what are we to make of Professor Hofstadter's 'great retrogression', that undermining of academic standards and that dispersal of both financial and intellectual resources in the many new and diverse collegiate institutions in the West? I suggest that we see it as the flip side of the 'take-off' and 'the release of energy', and that we acknowledge it as the inevitable consequence of the local initiatives and the associationist nature that characterized so many of the new foundations. As individuals and associations played ever larger roles when they attempted to meet the demand for ministers, physicians, and lawyers in the expanding country, their efforts could not but lead to dispersion of efforts and a weakening of traditional standards.

The need for trained professionals was huge and urgent, and financial and institutional resources were wanting. Individual ministers would respond by opening Latin schools or academies in their localities to prepare boys and young men for college. In many cases they also offered non-classical instruction for girls and young women. Whenever they thought it feasible, clergymen and laymen would band together and draw on their community's resources to establish a college in their midst. Local initiative and personal commitment rather than organizational policy provided the initiative for these educational boot-strap operations.[32]

Where personal and community resources were insufficient, help was sought from the voluntary societies that had been formed to aid educational efforts in the West. The American Education Society, founded in 1815 as the American Society for the Education of Pious

Youth for the Gospel Ministry, sought funds to lend money to students and to supply churches with ministers.[33] Thirty years later the Society for the Promotion of Collegiate and Theological Education at the West would assist the colleges directly rather than funding their students.[34] Americans found that it was easier to summon help from their neighbours and friends and from like-minded associates in their churches and interdenominational societies than to call upon the governments of states and nation. The response would come more quickly and directly.

Keeping in mind, then, that the newer colleges sprang up in newly settled country through largely local initiatives and depended for their survival and continuing support on the college societies, it is easier to understand that in many cases the regular college course leading to the bachelor of arts degree was a hope and a goal rather than a presence to be taken for granted. Colleges stood in want of both qualified instructors and prepared students. While professors and tutors, the great majority of them ministers or students of divinity, had in almost every case themselves been trained in the classics, their liabilities had less to do with the kind of education they had received than with its quality and depth.

But the case was different with students. Here the lack of college preparatory training was the real reason for 'the great retrogression'. Colleges in the hinterland and on the frontier could not rely on Latin-trained freshmen. Thus they had to supply that training in their preparatory departments which also functioned as academies to train teachers for the common schools. For many years such colleges failed to graduate students with degrees. They reported larger enrollments in their preparatory than in their college classes. As one of their professors once remarked: 'We call our institutions colleges on the same principle upon which we call Christians saints; not for what they are but for what we expect they will be'.[35] Thus the charters of the ante-bellum colleges can best be seen as promissory notes than as certificates of character. Or, to mix metaphors, foundations had to be laid first that later generations might build their colleges and universities.

The lack of preparatory institutions in the new country also contributed to the blurring of the line between what we today define as secondary and higher education. The 'release of energy' gave small room to public ventures. The New England tradition of municipal Latin grammar schools faded out in the West, and Latin education became for all intents and purposes a field for private initiatives and enterprise. The law distinguished the colleges that were authorized by legislatures to grant degrees from institutions or individuals who were not. The latter therefore offered their Latin lessons in parsonages, churches, academies, and other schools of various designations and descriptions. By virtue of their charters the colleges could offer a Latin education on every level. If their students were inadequately prepared, they were admitted to the preparatory course or school; if they passed muster on admission, they enrolled in the college proper. Still, the phrase college or collegiate education encompassed the whole field of Latin instruction whether in preparatory school or class, academy, or college.

In the long view of history the local character of ante-bellum colleges and their founders and initial supporters not only distinguished them from the colleges of the colonial era, but also led most decisively to a legal re-definition of American higher education. The colonial colleges had all been provincial rather than local institutions. Harvard College had been the college of the Massachusetts Bay Colony, Princeton had functioned as the College of New Jersey, and the College of William and Mary had been the college for Virginia. With the single exception of Queen's College in New Jersey, the remaining colonial colleges, too, had each played a similar public role and enjoyed a collegiate monopoly in its province. Together with established or dominant church and with provincial assembly and governor, the colleges had represented public authority—a reminder of the old medieval arrangement of *sacerdotium, regnum, and studium* as the three public powers of the realm.[36]

This, however, could no longer be said of the colleges and churches in the ante-bellum years. The Dartmouth College Case decision of the United States Supreme Court in 1819 had recognized that colleges could be local or community institutions. No longer was it to be taken for granted that a college was a public institution. Its legal status was to depend on its charter of incorporation. The charter would reveal whether a state or other public agency had founded, i.e. funded the college, or whether a private person or group had supplied the first funds. The founder's public or private character would determine the legal status of the college. If the institution were a private foundation, the charter would protect it against interference by public authority without the consent of the college governors.[37]

The Dartmouth decision had ushered in a new era in the legal history of American higher education. By encouraging the private sponsorship of colleges as a means of promoting settlement and economic development, the Supreme Court aided the break with the exclusively public character of European and colonial Latin education. The nature of the new country, the 'release of energy' above all, invited this new departure and ushered in an era in which public and private institutions of higher education would develop side by side.[38] For the ante-bellum period in particular, it is the proliferation of the colleges as private institutions and the 'great retrogression' that accompanied it that catches the attention and the imagination. It is here and then that diversity became the hall-mark of American higher education.[39]

The Diversity of Ante-Bellum Education

Legally diversity manifested itself in ante-bellum American higher education in the side-by-side existence and appearance of public and non-public colleges. This was the legacy of the Dartmouth decision. From a curricular point of view, the repeated calls for opportunities for the children of 'farmers and mechanics' to receive training in practical and applied scientific fields as well as for teaching in the common schools found only a reluctant hearing in the colleges. But they did result in the creation of various academy and high school level institutions and public as well as private normal schools. This added to 'the great retrogession' and kept fluid the distinction between secondary and higher education.

At the outset of the national period the tradition of the colleges as public institutions continued. The old colonial colleges now emerged as bastions of republicanism. The College of Philadelphia reappeared as the University of Pennsylvania, the Yale Corporation added state officials to its members, and the new state constitution of Massachusetts devoted an entire section to 'the University at Cambridge'. The trustees of Dartmouth College found themselves before the bar of the United States Supreme Court because the New Hampshire legislature had taken it as axiomatic that a provincial college was a public institution and that the legislators had the power to amend its charter.

New public colleges were founded in the young republic. State universities were chartered in Georgia in 1785, in North Carolina in 1789, in Vermont in 1791, and in South Carolina in 1801. Though founded by Presbyterians, Transylvania University in Kentucky as well as Blount College and Cumberland College in Tennessee functioned for years as public institutions.[40] Other state universities followed in Ohio in 1804, in Maryland in 1812, in Michigan in 1817, and in Virginia in 1819. Still more were opened in Alabama, Delaware, Indiana, and Missouri during the thirties, and in Iowa, Wisconsin, and Mississippi during the forties.

Yet Americans, by and large, were relunctant to support their public institutions. Given the similar nature of literary and scientific instruction in the regular college course in public as well as private colleges, few legislatures were ready to vote occasional or regular appropriations for their state universities. A college was a college, most legislators thought, and why should some schools be funded by the public when others were not? The predicament of public institutions was made worse because unlike the denominational and the local booster colleges they could not call for aid on member congregations and communities. In Tennessee President Phillip Lindsley would complain that as he and his University of Nashville belonged to no sect or party, they had no one to stand by and befriend them.[41] In North Carolina the friends of the university had tried in 1793 to persuade others to help: 'Episcopalians, Presbyterians, Methodists, Baptists, Universalists, and Society of Friends, peaceful Quakers, give!' But few of them did. Far too many thought the university to be a secular institution rife with infidelity and harbouring atheism.[42]

Life for public institutions remained precarious until long after the Civil War. Newspaper editorials and popular lecturers accused the public universities of ignoring the demands for a higher education responsive to the needs and interests of farmers and mechanics. In Wisconsin in 1850 the *Southport Telegraph* took the 'stall-fed denizens of Madison' to task for their preference to have the state university train doctors, lawyers, and ministers. 'If the friends of this literary hierarchy wish to find favor for it in the eyes of those who will be compelled to support it', the paper editorialized, 'let them make it an institution that shall be useful to the masses . . . and establish those departments which shall be open for the farmer and mechanic . . .'[43]

The key to the ineffectiveness of the early state universities lay in their failure to forge a bridge between the traditional liberal and professional education and the rising demand for practical studies in the sciences applied to agriculture and mechanics. As the regular college course was everywhere meant to remain scientific in a general and theoretical sense, the attempts to introduce new subjects such as chemistry into the curriculum usually stopped short of practical applications. At the time of its enactment, not even the Morrill Act with its injunction that in each state at least one university teach 'such branches of learning as are related to agriculture and the mechanic arts . . .' brought the desired change.[44]

Agriculture and, to some extent, engineering as well as other applied sciences remained the step-children of American collegiate education during the ante-bellum years. If we are to believe the complaints of President Francis Wayland of Brown, farmers and mechanics in particular desired such instruction for their sons. Wayland stated repeatedly that a college 'must carefully survey the wants of the various classes of the community in its vicinity' and then adapt its courses 'not for the benefit of one class, but for the benefit of all classes'. If Brown University were to offer instruction in agriculture, applied chemistry, and science, Wayland wrote, it would attract 'the agriculturist, the manufacturer, the mechanic, or the merchant . . .'[45]

Crusading for federal aid for a 'a university for the industrial classes', Jonathan Baldwin Turner predicted in Illinois that 'if every farmer's and mechanic's son . . . could now visit such an institution but for a single day in the year, it would do him more good in arousing and directing the dormant energies of mind, than all the cost incurred, and'—getting in his sally at the colleges with their regular course—'far more good than many a six months of professed study of things he will never need and never want to know'.[46]

But it wasn't the colleges or the universities that sought to meet this demand. Academies and high schools, the so-called 'people's colleges', offered agricultural and mechanical studies for students from farming and working class families. The first institution of this kind to become widely and favourably known was a public institution chartered by the Congress in 1802. This was the United States Military Academy at West Point, the country's first genuine scientific school. Engineering, drawing, and French were among the subjects studied.[47] Seventeen years later Captain Alden Partridge opened his Literary, Scientific and Military Academy at Norwich, Vermont, and offered instruction in engineering and linguistic, agricultural, and military studies. Students could take as much or as little time as they wished to finish the certificate course.[48]

A businessman followed where the soldiers had trod. Stephen Van Rensselaer endowed the Polytechnic Institute named after him at Troy, New York, in 1824 to afford 'an opportunity to the farmer, the mechanic, the clergyman, the lawyer, the physician, the merchant, and in short to the man of business or leisure, of any calling whatever, to become practically scientific'.[49] Rensselaer's message was clear: while the colleges would prepare young men for professional careers with the bachelor of arts course, the people's colleges were going to offer practical scientific instruction for vocational and professional purposes for as long and to whatever degree as all those who wanted it desired.

By 1815 proprietary medical schools had entered the list of institutions offering practical instruction without requiring a regular college course. In many ways their establishment paralleled the founding of the many local colleges across the country. Both types of schools suffered from the lack of well prepared students. The medical schools offered their doctoral course without requiring the completion of a prior bachelor of arts or medicine degree. As one historian put it, these proprietary medical colleges 'competed to provide the fastest, cheapest, and easiest education. The college that could make good on its claims to do all three could plan on having its benches filled to overflowing'.[50] Compared to the medical schools of the colonial period, the ante-bellum schools were retrograde indeed.

Gradually, the established colleges began to experiment with new and different ways to expand their scientific instruction. At Yale professorships in agricultural chemistry and in practical chemistry were established in 1846 'for the purpose of giving instruction to graduates and others not members of the undergraduate classes'. Thus began the School of Applied Chemistry and in 1854, after the addition two years earlier of a School of Engineering, the Yale Scientific School.[51] These foundations permitted the additions of new subjects for different students without either overloading or distorting the literary and scientific curriculum of the regular undergraduate course. Similar developments occurred at Harvard with the opening of the Lawrence Scientific School in 1847 and at Dartmouth with the Chandler School of Science.

A new step was taken with the opening in 1857 of one of the earliest public scientific schools. The Agricultural College of the State of Michigan in East Lansing began as a separate institution to train farmers and offer a bachelor's degree. From the start it offered a four-year curriculum of the liberal arts and sciences. Its students, so they, their parents, faculty members, and friends in the state's agricultural society argued, did not need practical instruction in agriculture. That was something they knew firsthand. What they needed was an understanding of scientific principles underlying agriculture so that they might be able to improve their farming practice, crops, and herds, and increase their marketing abilities. The college curriculum therefore stressed traditional college subjects and such practical fields as engineering, surveying, technology, and household economy.[52]

The college faced difficulties on two different fronts. Opposition arose in the legislature and the governing board. In order to hold down expenses, the members of these two bodies pushed for the elimination of the liberal arts curriculum as inappropriate to an agricultural school.[53] The college and its friends, however, successfully resisted and defeated these moves. More perplexing and frustrating because pointing to the heart of the agriculturalists' dilemma was the absence of a true agricultural science and of specialized teaching materials and techniques. For agricultural education on a college or university level to succeed, these had first to be developed.

Thus the real pioneering work of the college took place during the 1850s and 1860s in its laboratories and on its experimental fields where the means and methods for agricultural instruction had first to be created. The pay-off would come much later when by 1885 forty per cent of the graduates had been trained for and had gone into farming, a far higher percentage than achieved by the state universities. Building on the foundations laid in the 1860s the college then demonstrated how instruction in practical applications could be successfully joined to a rigorous collegiate curriculum in the liberal arts and sciences and a base of experimental research.[54]

As these concerns for scientific, agricultural, and medical education led to the founding of the new scientific schools, a similar felt need for professionally trained teachers led to other new initiatives. The new colleges in the West had provided a ready supply of male teachers for the secondary schools. Private academies, public normal schools, and female seminaries had sprung up to prepare teachers for the common schools. As by the 1840s elementary school teaching had become an occupation dominated by young women of college age, a small but growing number of these women teachers had been prepared in normal schools, female seminaries, and colleges. Here, too, as with the scientific schools, sustained growth would set in after the War. The ante-bellum years were years of incubation and hesitant beginnings.[55]

Far from being an age of retardation, retrogression, and stultifying monotony, the 'age of the college' contained in vibrant tension the demands of tradition and innovation. Its educational institutions reflected and served rather directly the varied components of its population in settled urban centres and on the raw agrarian frontier. Colleges took seriously their task of civilizing and humanizing a young and growing population, and scientists and scholars began to glimpse and to experiment with the task of mastering new skills and techniques of applied scientific, agricultural, and mechanical education. The call for teacher education could not be overheard. New institutions set off on their shake-down cruise, and if many of them failed their trials and tests, many others overcame their shortcomings and made permanent contributions.

Above all the ante-bellum years opened the colleges to men and women who until then had never dreamed of entering academic life. The sons and daughters of middle-class and poor families in city and country sought out colleges and normal schools, scientific academies and female seminaries to create for themselves a new place and role in life. Aided by their elders through voluntary education societies they availed themselves of private and of public generosity. They demonstrated their need and their determination to be educated. Together with the founders and supporters of all these colleges, schools, institutes, seminars, and academies in all their variety, haphazardness, and precarious abandon, they translated their faith in a democratic society into educational reality.

University of Wisconsin—Madison
455 North Park Street
Madison
Wisconsin 53706, U.S.A.

REFERENCES

1. The reference is to Laurence R. Veysey, *The Emergence of the American University* (Chicago, 1965).
2. The classic expression of this view is Donald G. Tewksbury, *The Founding of American Colleges and Universities* (New York, 1932 and 1965); see also the critique, Natalie A. Naylor, 'The Ante-Bellum College Movement: A Reappraisal of Tewksbury's Founding of American Colleges and Universities', *History of Education Quarterly*, XIII (Fall 1973), 261–274.
3. George P. Schmidt, *The Liberal Arts College: A Chapter in American Cultural History* (New Brunswick, 1957). Schmidt uses the phrase 'old-time college' and also published *The Old Time College President* (New York, 1930).
4. For a comprehensive statement of the newer view see Colin B. Burke, *American Collegiate Populations: A Test of the Traditional View* (New York, 1982). If Burke seems less willing than I am to credit the ante-bellum period with the diversification of academic institutions, it is because he compares that period with the decades after the Civil War when institutional diversification increased even more rapidly, whereas I compare the ante-bellum years with the colonial period and stress the diversification that had been unknown in the eighteenth century. On other aspects of contrasting the ante-bellum with the post-bellum period see David Potts, 'Students and the Social History of American Higher Education', *History of Education Quarterly*, XV (Fall 1975), 322.
5. I have taken the various names from the Illinois State Statutes of the period. See my 'Diversification in American Higher Education', in Konrad H. Jarausch (ed.), *The Transformation of Higher Learning 1860–1930* (Chicago, 1983), 196–206.
6. Such appraisals have been carried out before; see Douglas Sloan, 'Harmony, Chaos, and Consensus: The American College Curriculum', *Teachers College Record*. LXXIII (1971), 221–251; David Potts, 'American Colleges in the Nineteenth Century: From Localism to Denominationalism', *History of Education Quarterly*, XI (Winter 1971), 363–380; my own, 'American College History: Re-Examination Underway', *History of Education Quarterly*, XIV (Summer 1974), 259–266; and James McLachlan, 'The American College in the Nineteenth Century: Toward a Reappraisal', *Teachers College Record*, LXXX (December 1978), 287–306.
7. 'The great retrogession' is the title of a section in Richard Hofstadter's chapter on 'The Old-Time College' in his and Walter P. Metzger's, *The Development of Academic Freedom in the United States* (New York, 1955).

8. Hofstadter and Metzger, *The Development of Academic Freedom*. Their distinction was first severely criticized by James Axtell in his sparkling essay on 'The Death of the Liberal Arts College', *History of Education Quarterly*, XI (Winter 1971), 339–352.

9. For the latter point see George E. Peterson, *The New England College in the Age of the University* (Amherst, 1964).

10. I refer to the 'take-off' as set forth in W. W. Rostow, *The Stages of Economic Growth* (New York, 1963).

11. See Willard Hurst, *Law and the Conditions of Freedom in the Nineteenth-Century United States* (Madison, 1956), 3–32.

12. Jurgen Herbst, *From Crisis to Crisis: American College Government, 1636–1819* (Cambridge, MA, 1982), 94, 160.

13. Schmidt, *The Liberal Arts College*, 51.

14. Frederick Rudolph, *Curriculum: A History of the Undergraduate Course of Study since 1636* (San Francisco, 1977), p. 115. See also the trenchant critique of Rudolph's approach in David B. Potts, 'Curriculum and Enrollments: Some Thoughts on Assessing the Popularity of Antebellum Colleges', *History of Higher Education Annual*, I (1981), 88–109.

15. See David W. Robson, *Educating Republicans: The College in the Era of the American Revolution, 1750–1800* (Westport, CT, 1985), 29.

16. Robson, *Educating Republicans*, 177.

17. See Steven J. Novak, *The Rights of Youth: American Colleges and Student Revolt, 1798–1815* (Cambridge, MA, 1977).

18. Quoted in James McLachlan, 'The *Choice of Hercules*: American Student Societies in the Early 19th Century'. In Lawrence Stone (ed.), *The University in Society* (2 vols.; Princeton, 1974), ii. 463–464.

19. See David F. Allmendinger, Jr., *Paupers and Scholars: The Transformation of Student Life in Nineteenth Century New England* (New York, 1975), 8–27.

20. See Daniel J. Boorstin, who in his *The Americans: The National Experience* (New York, 1965), 152–161, introduced the concept of the 'booster college'.

21. On the role of colleges on the frontier see the chapter on 'The Small Colleges' in Peter C. Mode, *The Frontier Spirit in American Christianity* (New York, 1923).

22. See David B. Potts, '"College Enthusiasm!" As Public Response, 1800–1860', *Harvard Educational Review*, XLVII (February 1977), 31.

23. Alexis de Tocqueville, *Democracy in America*, ed. Phillips Bradley (2 vols.; New York, 1956), ii. 118.

24. James Fenimore Cooper, *The American Democrat* (New York, 1956), 89, 90.

25. Quotations are from the 'Original Papers in Relation to a Course of Liberal Education', *The American Journal of Science and Arts*, XV (January, 1829), 297–351.

26. Ezra Stiles, *Plan of a University: A Proposal Addressed to the Corporation of Yale College, 3 December 1777* (New Haven, 1953).
27. Stanley M. Guralnick, *Science and the Ante-Bellum American College* (Philadelphia, 1975), 24–41.
28. Codman Hislop, *Eliphalet Nott* (Middletown, CT, 1971), 226–227.
29. McLachlan, 'The American College in the Nineteenth Century', 294.
30. Quoted in Sloan, 'Harmony, Chaos, and Consensus', 236.
31. See James Findlay, '"Western" Colleges, 1830–1870: Educational Institutions in Transition', *History of Higher Education Annual*, II (1982), 37.
32. See Potts, 'American Colleges in the Nineteenth Century', 367, and Timothy L. Smith, 'Uncommon Schools: Christian Colleges and Social Idealism in Midwestern America, 1820–1950', *Lectures 1976–1977: The History of Education in the Middle West* (Indianapolis, 1978), 20.
33. Natalie A. Naylor, '"Holding High the Standard": The Influence of the American Education Society in Ante-Bellum America,' *History of Education Quarterly*, XXIV (Winter 1984), 479–497.
34. James Findlay, 'The SPCTEW and Western Colleges: Religion and Higher Education in Mid-Nineteenth Century America', *History of Education Quarterly*, XVII (Spring 1977), 31–62, and 'Agency, Denominations and the Western Colleges, 1830–1860: Some Connections between Evangelicalism and American Higher Education', *Church History*, L (1981), 64–80.
35. President Merriman of Ripon College, as quoted by J. P. Gulliver, 'Commencement at a Frontier College', in *College Days*, Ripon College, Ripon, Wisconsin, I (September 1868), 107.
36. Herbst, *From Crisis to Crisis*, 2.
37. For the nuances of terminology—whether local, private, or community—see my debate with John Whitehead in Whitehead and Herbst. 'How to Think About the Dartmouth College Case', *History of Education Quarterly*, XXVI (Fall 1986), 333–349.
38. Herbst, *From Crisis to Crisis*, 241–243.
39. See my 'Diversification in American Higher Education', in Jarausch (ed.), *The Transformation of Higher Learning 1860–1930*, 196–206.
40. See Merle Borrowman, 'The False Dawn of the State University', *History of Education Quarterly*, I (June 1961), 6–22.
41. From Lindsley's 1848 Commencement Address, quoted in Richard Hofstadter and Wilson Smith (edd.), *American Higher Education: A Documentary History* (Chicago, 1961), i. 378–379.
42. Quoted in Kemp P. Battle, *History of the University of North Carolina* (Raleigh, NC, 1907), i. 17.
43. *Southport Telegraph*, February 15, 1850.
44. Indiana and Wisconsin are cases in point. The legislature scorned Indiana University and gave the land grant funds to newly founded Purdue University, a private institution at Lafayette. In Wisconsin the

land-grant state university was to develop the 'Wisconsin Idea' of faculty involvement in agriculture, business, and government in answer to the institution's critics. See Merle Curti and Vernon Carstensen, *The University of Wisconsin: A History, 1848–1925* (Madison, WI, 1949), ii. 109–110. For the Morrill Act see Edward Danforth Eddy, Jr., *Colleges for Our Land and Time: The Land-Grant Idea in American Education* (New York, 1956).

45. From Francis Wayland, 'Report to the Corporation of Brown University (1850)', in Theodore Rawson Crane (ed.), *The Colleges and the Public, 1787–1862* (New York, 1963), 136–141, *passim.*

46. Jonathan Baldwin Turner, 'A State University for the Industrial Classes (1850)', in Richard A. Hatch (ed.), *Some Founding Papers of the University of Illinois* (Urbana; 1967), 41.

47. Sidney Forman, *West Point: A History of the United States Military Academy* (New York, 1950), 51–60; Stephen E. Ambrose, *Duty, Honor, Country: A History of West Point* (Baltimore, 1966), 87–90.

48. William Arba Ellis, (ed.), *Norwich University 1819–1911: Her History, Her Graduates, Her Roll of Honor,* vol. I *General History 1819–1911* (Montpelier, VT, 1911), 12–13.

49. Palmer C. Ricketts, *History of the Rensselaer Polytechnic Institute, 1824–1894* (New York, 1895), 55.

50. Martin Kaufman, *American Medical Education: The Formative Years, 1765–1910* (Westport, CT, 1976), 42.

51. Brooks Mather Kelley, *Yale: A History* (New Haven and London, 1974), 181–183. In 1861 the Yale Scientific School was renamed the Sheffield Scientific School.

52. Madison Kuhn, *Michigan State: The First Hundred Years, 1855–1955* (East Lansing, 1955), 62–64.

53. Willis F. Dunbar, *The Michigan Record in Higher Education* (Detroit, 1963), 85, 86, and Kuhn, *Michigan State,* 26, 27.

54. Kuhn, *Michigan State,* 118, 119.

55. Maris A. Vinovskis and Richard M. Bernard. 'The Female School Teacher in Ante-Bellum Massachusetts', *Journal of Social History,* X (Spring 1977), 322–345. See also the use of the same data by Carl F. Kaestle and Maris A. Vinovskis, *Education and Social Change in Nineteenth Century Massachusetts* (Cambridge, England, 1980).

The Oxford Idea of a Liberal Education 1800–1860: The Invention of Tradition and The Manufacture of Practice

Peter Slee

Introduction

In 1800, Oxford University, in keeping with its status as a private corporation, was autonomous. It directed its own affairs. It had control over its curriculum and the standards required for admission to its degrees. It had, within the more stringent confines of the law, full control over the admission of its students. Colleges made their own appointments to academic posts, on conditions they either defined or freely consented to. Freedom of development, though it may require the repeal of some ancient statutes was, as yet, unhindered and unhampered by any external agency. Oxford University was in full control of its own affairs, and while there were always a good many ideas about what Oxford University *ought* to be doing in a changing world, only those held in consensus by its governing body were effective in influencing what it actually *did*. This general consensus within the university of its overall purposes—'the academic ethos'[2]—acted as a mechanism for filtering and evaluating ideas about what were, or were not appropriate forms of educational activity. It defined the broad limits within which the practical business of education could feasibly be conducted, and it therefore exercised direct bearing on the range of provision made formally accessible to students. Any meaningful discussion about extending the type, level, or quality of provision was either conducted within the matrix of the academic ethos, or else began by proposing a modification of it. What then were the major constituents of the Oxford academic ethos? In 1800 they were threefold.

First, Oxford was an ecclesiastical institution tied seemingly inextricably to the Church of England. It aimed in this capacity at inculcating sound religion. Most College fellows were obliged to take holy orders shortly after their election. Every undergraduate was required under oath to subscribe to the 39 Articles before matriculating. Attendance at College Chapel was compulsory. Divinity was a part of every undergraduate's studies. Almost one third of all Oxford students were the sons of clergymen and almost two thirds of all Oxford graduates went into the Church. But as discrimination against dissenters subsided in the early and middle years of the nineteenth century, and as the activities of the Oxford Movement attracted public notice and parliamentary disapproval, Oxford was forced gradually to reconsider and slowly to relinquish its exclusive ties with the Anglican faith. Oxford admitted dissenters to degrees in 1854, and then to fellowships from 1871 when compulsory chapel was abandoned. By 1881 less than a third of all Oxford dons were in holy orders, and only about 30 per cent of their students made a career in the Church.[3]

Second, Oxford was a politically conservative and socially exclusive institution. It could hardly have been otherwise. Four years residence at an Oxford College was a costly business. In the early years of the nineteenth century even the thriftiest, most temperate young man, well schooled enough to dispense with the services of a private tutor, would expect to run up bills of £150 a year. And when a 'middling' middle-class family might hope to command an annual income of around £300 it is clear that few but the wealthiest fathers could begin to consider an Oxford education for theirs sons.[4] Oxford was a closed society. As a socio-political institution it formed a finishing school for gentry, aristocracy and clergy. As Mr Larkyns the Rector said to Verdant Green Senior, where else but the University would the young Verdant 'be able to meet with so great a number of those of his own class, with whom he will have to mix in the after-changes of life, and for whose feelings and tone a college-course will give him the proper key-note?' The communal collegiate lifestyle and the core curriculum of classics, mathematics, and Divinity formed a lasting and exclusive class bond. The experience sealed the stamp of a gentleman and created a series of social norms to which the scholarship boy from a poorer background must emulate to achieve a measure of social mobility. But, from the early years of the nineteenth century, with the emergence of new, commercial, industrial and professional groupings who sought social status and political power commensurate with their wealth, sharp consensus as to what constituted a proper social tone broke down. By the middle 1880s Edward Freeman claimed to be unable to recognise the university of his youth.[5]

Third, Oxford was an educational institution. And it is with Oxford as an educational institution that this paper is concerned. To break down the functions of the university in such a clear cut fashion is of course to make sharp distinctions where they were in practice blurred. Oxford continued throughout the nineteenth century to retain a distinctive Anglican and socially aristocratic tone. But what is important to note is that after 1864 when the principle of freedom of choice in final degree subjects was established, the curriculum became progressively less a mechanism of social, political or religious confirmation and more a positive educational element in its own right. Indeed by 1900 Oxford was once again regarded as a leading international university.

This paper addresses three questions that arise if the model of educational change within educational institutions, which was set out above, is accepted. First, what were the main features of the Oxford educational ethos in the early years of the nineteenth century and how are these features to be explained? Second, to what extent, in what ways and for what reasons did Oxford modify or redefine its assessment of its proper relationship with the intellectual world in mid-century: in short, how and why did the educational element in the academic ethos change? And third, how closely was the practical business of teaching and study constrained by the dictates of the academic ethos? To what extent were official ideas about the university's function reflected in academic practice? These three questions will now be examined in turn.

Part One: The creation of an academic educational ethos 1800–1830

Oxford has never been without its critics. But rarely can they have seemed quite so shrill as they did towards the close of the eighteenth century. The extent to which teaching, learning and acceptable moral standards fell into abeyance in Georgian times is a nice question. The pessimistic but longstanding interpretation of many contemporares—notably Napleton, Knox, Gillray and Gibbon[6]—portraying torpor, indolence, vice and a chronic dearth of learning has been subject to modification. Knox and his fellow critics directed their fiercest invective at the formal requirements the university demanded of the student who read for a degree. There is no doubt that administration of the examination system was lax and open to abuse. But recent research shows equally clearly that there were always some able, learned and well-read men in whom curiosity and conscience took over in the absence of formal compulsion to study, and a good deal more who *were* compelled to work by their colleges.[7] Quite simply, the system, such as it was, was uneven. Some colleges were more effective than others in fostering scholarship and sound moral and political principles. The Public Examination Statute of 1800 was drawn up in response to these problems.[8] The subjects of study, the choice of texts, the style of teaching all remained substantially unrevised. The reforms of 1800 were a positive restatement of traditional values. They aimed simply to regulate and to standardize; to enact a basic minimum level of attainment for all undergraduates reading for a degree.

These reforms, and those that followed in 1807, attracted interest and criticism. The introduction of Responsions in 1808 prompted the *Edinburgh Review* to question publicly the scope and purpose of an English university education. The *Review* did not dispute that classics, Divinity, and mathematics were valuable instruments of education. But that they should be the *only* subjects of formal study was scandalous. Oxford was openly maintaining an outdated, outmoded curriculum that was little more than a minor adaption of the Laudian code. The university seemed torn between the idea of educating gentlemen for social reasons, and that of providing a rigorous academic training. The very purpose of an English university education was vague. It lacked clear definition. The *Edinburgh Review* provided one.

Influenced by the teaching of Dugald Stewart the *Review* called on Oxford to prepare its alumni more actively for the pressures and problems of the nineteenth century. In a rapidly changing world it was vital that the citizen understood the social, economic and political forces at work around him. To the *Reviewers* knowledge was power and the key to constructive social action. A man must be equipped with a stock of cultural information possession of which would enable him directly to influence his surroundings. The means to this end lay not in the study of dead languages or outmoded mathematics but in a curriculum restructured to encompass the developing technologies of an expanding, diversifying society— political economy, modern languages, natural science, commerce, law, and modern history.[9]

Cogent, persuasive, direct and to the point, the arguments put by the *Review* left the onus on Oxford to justify its position. This it did. The early nineteenth-century ethos of university study as mental training was developed and articulated in direct response to the challenge laid down by the *Edinburgh Review*. The resultant con- cept of a 'liberal education' developed by Edward Copleston was in origin defensive, that is to say it was conceived as an ex post facto justification of the status quo developed and expressed as a counter to external criticism. Furthermore the theory of the value and function of higher education that emerged was holistic. It was more than a statement of specified ends. Expressly by defining the importance of the subjects to be studied and the right method of teaching them, it related the ends of higher education to the means by which they were to be achieved. The ends of higher education postulated by Edward Copleston were in deliberate and direct contrast to those stipulated by the *Review*, while the means of achieving them were precisely those embodied in the traditional Oxford curriculum. The theory of the value of a classical education offered an explanation of educational ends to which the university had already committed itself.

In upholding the traditional studies against the charge of dis- utility Copleston was aware that the scientific and informative element in the classics could no longer seriously be defended on the grounds that it offered the most up-to-date and practical scientific knowledge. He formed his defence accordingly.

In a world grown increasingly mechanistic, in the age of accumulative, acquisitive man, the purpose of the university was to counter the effects upon the individual of gross materialism. National efficiency had been increased markedly by the application of the principle of the division of labour. But at the cost of human dignity. Specialization narrowed the individual's vision until he became 'a subordinate part of some powerful machinery useful in its place, but insignificant and worthless out of it.' But society, and indeed, successful business, required more from the individual than simply the exercise of technical skills. Broad liberal sympathies and creative, flexible intelligence were at a premium in a society experiencing radical change and deep social division. Through the teaching of classics the university was aiming not to train its alumni directly for any specific profession but rather to develop an elevated tone and flexible habit of mind which would enable them to overcome the constricting tendencies of modern life and to carry out with zeal and efficiency 'all the offices, both private and public, of peace and war'. The function of the university was to provide, through the subjects best suited to the task, a unifying, binding, cultural education and an exercise in method. It was not the knowledge imparted through the study of classics and mathematics that was valuable but the skills, qualities and habit of mind developed by the nature of the subjects themselves.

But what exactly made classics and mathematics so valuable a medium in the training of minds? The answer was disarmingly simple. They were uncongenial, unpleasant and downright difficult. This was their strength. They were conducted in their own mode according to their own stringent rules of procedure. To make progress, basic skills appropriate to that mode—linguistic or notational—must be mastered. There was no shortcut. Greek grammar and mathematical theorems could be acquired only with effort and discipline. Furthermore, the syllabus, be it construing texts or solving mathematical problems, involved the constant and methodical application of these basic skills. By requiring the student to adopt skills appropriate to another—alien—mode of experience the curriculum required more effort on his part than could reasonably be elicited from any subject read in English alone. Such subjects, easily digested, simply conveyed information and could therefore readily be crammed for the purposes of examination. Furthermore the traditional studies lent themselves to the catechetical method of instruction practised at most Oxford colleges. *Active* personal contact between student and teacher was held to be a more efficient aid to learning and mental development than the *passive* receptivity elicited by lectures. Small groups could be arranged according to ability and there was constant contact and feedback between teacher and student. The greater familiarity between the two was expressed by the direct contact of mind with mind. The student's level of ability was raised by the greater intellect and gentle persuasion of his tutor.

Contrary, then, to the views commonly expressed, the idea of the university as an educational agency for developing minds and of classics and mathematics as disciplines and as the best means of achieving those ends did not precede, underlie or lead to the construction of the fixed curriculum or the system of administration and teaching, but was developed consciously under pressure in order to bolster them. But if the promotion of the academic ethos as 'mental training' does not explain how the traditional subjects attained their preeminence it does go some way to explaining why they maintained it. The idea of a 'liberal education' as mental rather than direct vocational training, and for that reason the proper end of a university education, became canonical. It formed what Edward Shils had described as a 'normative tradition'. The idea of the university—the 'academic ethos'—became synonymous with the idea of mental training. The curriculum was cultivated and defended within the matrix of this 'normative tradition' and formed its own series of 'substantive traditions'. In the early years of the nineteenth century the 'substantive traditions' of classics and mathematics, and of personal tuition rather than lectures, were complementary to the Oxford 'academic ethos' of a liberal education, but for no greater reason than that the ethos was created in order to protect them. Defenders of the university system inherited a powerful tradition which they had bequeathed themselves. What began with Copleston, as a defence of tradition, became, in effect, a traditional defence. It was a stratagem brought continually into play throughout the 1820's and '30's but never to greater effect than in 1848 when the universities were forced by fears of parliamentary intervention to consider expanding the curriculum.[10]

Part Two: Response to change: the academic ethos and the expanding curriculum 1830–1850

Though discussions of curricular change were prompted by fears of external interference, the practical measures of reform were postulated by small but active groups emergent within the tutorial body. They had little sympathy with those who wished to restructure the curriculum to meet an alternative set of academic, social or economic values. Most college teachers were happy to define their function as arbiters of intellect and inculcators of sound religion and, as their livelihood was invariably bound to the methods inherent in the teaching of classics and mathematics, to subscribe readily to their superiority in this respect. They aimed simply to make the system of teaching more efficient by removing from it certain iniquities which had become apparent in the 1830s as the unexpected side effects of efforts to strengthen the competitive ethos.

Fortified by a strong justification of the curriculum, the university had been content simply to refine the machinery of examination. To have only one test of knowledge and ability, and that at the end of a course, seemed inefficient. It was too great a temptation to idleness. It encouraged too many undergraduates to neglect serious study until the weeks immediately preceding finals, when the less industrious would seek out a private tutor with whom they would cram the rudiments required for examination. The university authorities adopted the view that more frequent examinations would serve admirably to encourage regular and consistent study. Responsions and termly College Collections soon became a sobering feature of university life. College lectures were developed as the master key to their successful negotiation. Consequently most students—particularly those deficient in schooling—found their time and industry occupied solely by the subjects of the official curriculum. This had two direct effects.

The first and most immediate was to empty the benches at professorial lectures. Chairs had been founded to encourage interest in developing studies which lay outside the formal curriculum. They played an important part in the intellectual life of the university. The vigour and eminence of many of the professors was considered by defenders of the traditional studies largely to offset criticism that the university did not recognize new and important areas of science and learning. At Oxford the student was in receipt of the best possible mental training and was also able to attend lectures in history, political economy, law, languages and natural sciences which would keep him up to date with the latest developments in these areas. But, with the arrival of compulsory college lectures, students simply did not have time for anything much outside the prescribed course of study. Even the most reputable professors were left without an audience.[11]

Opinion ran high. The university was now more vulnerable to the charge of narrowness. While the status of subjects like history and chemistry was growing nationally, a fixed and immovable examination system had removed all opportunity to profit from them. Furthermore, by removing the professors' audience the university was seeming to revert to the old vice of sinecure chairs. It was dispensing stipends while a considerable store of teaching capital lay dormant and untapped.

Second, compulsory college lectures and examinations increased contact between tutor and student and revealed clearly to the former that, while the fixed curriculum conferred undoubted educational benefits on some students, on most it exercised a largely negative effect. Tutors found the dividing line drawn between two distinct classes of student: those who read for honours, and those who did not.

Tutors had few worries about the 'reading men'. Honours courses were exacting and stimulating tests of ability. Competition was intense. Success required high levels of intelligence, accuracy, motivation and effort. The university was determined to keep it that way. But by rigorously maintaining high academic standards it unwittingly created an unbridgeable divide in the student body. Less than a third of all undergraduates read for Honours. Just over half of the rest followed the pass course, and tutors found them sunk in a mire of apathy.[12]

The problem was readily defined. Disqualified from the honours course for whatever reason—be it inadequate schooling, lack of natural talent or inclination—the pass man was forced to study the same subjects but at a lower and less interesting level. Jowett and Stanley, reforming tutors, described the Oxford pass degree as comprising 'a meagre knowledge of divinity, an indifferent acquaintance with three or four volumes of Latin and Greek, a piece of Latin, about two-thirds of Aldrich's *Logic*, or a few books of Euclid'; another as 'four years spent in preparing about fourteen books, only for examination . . . text books read, re-read, digested, worked, got up, until they became part and parcel of the mind'. 'Such', said Jowett, 'is the sum and accomplishment of school and college education'. Whatever the pleasures for Socrates under the English university system, the pig, it seemed, would remain perpetually unsatisfied.[13]

Tutors became convinced that the routine of low-level lectures in the traditional subjects could be of little benefit to the man who lacked either the talent or the inclination to pursue his studies enthusiastically. Nor were they convinced that all pass men were incorrigibly dull. 'This inanimate being who sits in your room with vacant stare', said Jowett and Stanley, 'is not really stupid . . . [but] ten thousand construing lectures in Herodotus will not elicit a ray of intelligence for him'. The problem was largely one of motivation. Undergraduates could not be induced to take any notice of a course which 'neither fully occupies their time, nor gives them any subjects of interest'. Yet it was clear, said Jowett, that 'the stupidest undergraduate in a Livy lecture, will brighten in conversation, if you speak to him of the Revolution in France'. The tutors maintained that a liberal education ought to encourage mental gymnastic. Any system of teaching which did not elicit mental effort could not claim to educate. Such was the pass degree. They called for a broader, student-centred system of study to be developed *within* the matrix of a traditional liberal education.[14]

The tutors became, in effect, a small but active body of 'conservative reformers' who, while preserving its main features, aimed to rectify what they considered to be serious shortcomings in the system of study and teaching. They initiated and directed the hand of internal reform, and did so by playing on very real fears of government interference in university affairs.

Criticism of almost all aspects of university life—financial, administrative, moral, religious and academic—had continued unabated since the early years of the century. But the controversies engendered by the Oxford Movement focused parliamentary attention on the university, and by the middle 1840s it was becoming clear that the university's unwillingness to consider any change in government or system of education was regarded less as a sign of strength than of reactionary weakness. Benjamin Jowett asked if it was

at all probable that we shall be allowed to remain as we are for twenty years longer, the one solitary, exclusive, unnational Corporation—. . . a place, the studies of which belong to the past, and unfortunately seem to have no power of incorporating new branches of knowledge?

Rumbles in parliament suggested not. It was assumed that parliamentary intervention would lead to far-reaching radical change. Something had to be done to prevent it. Jowett and Stanley claimed:

our only defence against attacks from without, is to build up from within, to enlarge our borders that we may increase the number of our friends. . . Neither Commission nor Committee of Enquiry need have any terror for us, if it could truly be said 'The University and the Colleges have the will and power to reform themselves'.

So much was agreed generally. But the problem still remained. What shape would the reforming legislation take?[15]

It would not be fundamental. Hebdomadal Board, Congregation, Convocation, all were united in 'admitting the superiority of classics and mathematics as the basis of a general education', and therefore as indisputably the best means to the true end of a university education. On that they stood their ground. Reform, such as it was, must be conducted within the matrix of the traditional academic ethos. Jowett pointed at the solution. The university could silence its external critics simply by remedying the practical problems that had become evident in the 1830s. The reforms would be a cosmetic exercise designed to change the face of university studies without disturbing its psyche. The practical legislation that ensued was ingenious. There were now to be four examination schools. Literae Humaniores was revamped. Mathematics was resurrected. To them were added two new schools comprising an amalgamation of different studies. The School of Natural Science contained Mechanical Philosophy, Chemistry and Physiology and the School of Law and Modern History involved the student in the study of Civil and International Law, Political Economy and Modern History. These 'new' subjects were those for the teaching of which the university already possessed some means—namely an endowed professor. It was hoped that these new studies would prove of some stimulation to those who had little interest in classics—namely those aiming for pass degrees ('passmen'). If the reforms were a success then the university would solve all its problems at one stroke. The introduction of six new subjects would silence external criticism that the university did not show adequate regard for new or useful knowledge, and would do it without incurring extra expense. The pass men would find something to interest them and the professors would recover some of their audience.

Nevertheless, there was the problem of ensuring that the traditional form of a liberal education was preserved. Consisting simply of information, and taught passively by means of lectures these new subjects did not require real mental effort and could not, therefore, be said to educate. They might be interesting, they might be useful, but they were not the suitable subjects of true academic study. The curricular hegemony of classics was retained by an ironic twist of legislation.

All candidates for a degree must read Literae Humaniores and one other of the three remaining examination schools. But their second school, be it Mathematics, Natural Science or the 'Fourth School' of Law and Modern History could only be taken after passing successfully Final Schools in Literae Humaniores and candidates could not present themselves for that until their fourth year of residence. All students had then further to extend their residence in order to read for a second, less prestigious school, which sought only to compound their financial burdens and proved a great incentive to rendering that study as brief as was possible. The new disciplines were hardly likely therefore to have far reaching influence. But they were not intended to do so. They were introduced simply to take the sting out of external criticism that the university did not teach new or useful knowledge, and to remedy internal rumblings within the existing system. But the format of the reforms was designed to limit their impact and to ensure that the new subjects played a very minor secondary role. The university justified its stand within the academic ethos of a general liberal education and maintained doggedly the substantive traditions of classics and mathematics.

Part Three: The academic ethos and the management of new subjects: a short case study

Two new sets of academic subjects had been created. But not without a fight. The problem lay with the 'Fourth School', the subjects which comprised it and the methods by which it was to be taught. It became the focus of two years' fierce debate.[16] The school's final form, promulgated by statute on April 23rd 1850, was shaped by the interplay of four converging forces: necessity, utility, convenience, and coherence.

Few in Oxford doubted the necessity of establishing new examination schools. They were the most vital ploy in a stratagem intended to disarm criticism and forestall external interference in university affairs. Most agreed that they should comprise 'useful' developing subjects, which, for the sake of convenience, were already represented in the university by existing Chairs. But which subjects were suitable? At Oxford great concern was voiced about the intellectual coherence of the new schools. In this respect mathematics and natural science caused little trouble. The problem lay entirely with the fourth, 'modern' school. Numerous combinations of subjects were proposed and then rejected because they appeared to be little more than odds and ends swept together 'for no better reason than that there was no room for them elsewhere'.[17]

Convocation was agreed that the new subjects had little educational value. They were not suitable media for developing the mind. Their intrinsic worth—such as it was—lay in the stimulating information they conveyed. Intellectual coherence was therefore sought in subject matter. The 'Fourth School' was to comprise modern history, law and political economy, all subjects with a common basis in the study of political phenomena, and all deemed useful to future citizens, legislators and landowners.

But one further problem remained. How would the subjects be organized? On what basis would teaching and study be grounded? At what level would standards be set? Henry Halford Vaughan, Regius Professor of Modern History, summed up the difficulties neatly. 'The whole Classical system', he said,

has been the development of years and years—Details have always been prescribed with more or less rigour by custom—legislation has had existing custom for its basis. But with regard to Modern History and jurisprudence there is no theory whatsoever in existence. The Statute is absolutely creative. There is at present no theory to develope—our first want will be order, unity and guidance.[18]

The legislators sought 'order, unity and guidance' in tradition. While the academic ethos firmly discounted it as a serious educative discipline the Oxford School of Law and Modern History was to rest squarely upon the substantive traditions of Literae Humaniores. Law and Modern History was to be taught and studied through the medium of set texts. This blunted a series of pertinent objections that had been levelled against the introduction of history into the Oxford curriculum.

First, some had claimed that it was impossible to study a subject so large as modern history, even if it was confined to Britain and Europe. But to commit students to a round of textual study served admirably to delimit a potentially endless field of detail. Oxford history was made manageable by confining it to what was contained between the covers of a dozen books.

The choice of books varied a little throughout the 1850s, but for the purposes of examination candidates exhibited little deviation around a standard mean of historical classics. The *Oxford University Calendar* for the year 1859 enters into exceptional detail over the constitution of the school and demonstrates clearly the emphasis on mastering books rather than periods.

The *Calendar* reads:

Candidates for the higher Classes in Modern History may be expected to offer for Examination:

Either   (First Period)

Necessary   (History of England to the Accession of Henry VIII Hallam, *Middle Ages*)

And any three more of the following works:

(1) Gibbon—Chapters equalling in extent 2 vols. . . ., especially c.38, 44, 45, 49, 50, 55, 56, 58, 59, 68, 69, 70.

(2) Guizot—History of Civilisation in France

(3) Sismondi—Histoire des Francais, from Hugh Capet (987) to the death of Louis XI (1483).

This may be divided into three periods, each of which may be taken in separately as one work:

(4)(1) To the death of Louis VIII.

   (2) To the death of John.

(5)(3) To the death of Louis XI.

   (6)   William of Malmesbury—Gesta Regum Anglorum B. III, IV, V, and Historia Novella.

(7)   Parts of Milman's Latin Christianity, e.g., the period from Gregory VIII. to Innocent III, or the rest of Volumes IV and V, or Vol. VI. Only one of these periods to count as a book.

The *Calendar* enters into similar detail for the second period, and also for the special subjects introduced in 1854 to encourage close study of 'some original authorities'. Again the phraseology is instructive. With regard to the special subjects:

(a) The time of Charlemagne—to be studied in Eginhard's Life and Annals, and Guizot's Civilisation in France.

(b) The period of the Norman Conquest . . . in the Saxon Chronicle and Florence of Worcester.[19]

Soon the choice of books became standardized. Candidates generally drew from a narrow selection, chosen for ease of prose or simply tutorial expertise. The calendar for 1864 specifies that:

The books in History commonly brought in by Candidates for Honours are these:

for the First Period: Lingard's History of England; Hallam's Middle Ages; Gibbon from ch.38; Milman's Latin Christianity, Gregory VIII—Innocent III, with Book XIV. Candidates for the highest Honours are expected also to bring in two of the three following original authors, Philip de Commines, Joinville, William of Malmesbury; studying them minutely. . .[20]

Second, the study of 'books' was an effective counter for those who believed that history could not be 'dispassionately considered'. Such views were represented eloquently by J. A. Froude.

The problem, said Froude, was that history had become a political weapon. It was fuel to political and religious dispute. History was manipulated to support any point of issue between warring factions. The Conquest, the Civil War, the Glorious Revolution— all important junctures in English history—were battlegrounds of controversy. 'What', Froude asked, 'is to become of the poor students . . . if their notions of history are to sway this way or that way, according to the majorities in the House of Commons?'

But whereas some maintained that such difficulties must surely disqualify history from all serious consideration as an academic subject, Froude disagreed. Students should know something of history, if only as a basis from which to evaluate the claims of political rhetoric. True, every professor, every tutor was potentially the purveyor of bias. As such they must be controlled. With this even E. A. Freeman agreed. The answer, said Froude, was set texts. If they could not completely 'prevent difference of opinion' they could 'limit, to some extent at least, the effect of such difference upon the teaching, and coerce the character of what is learnt into some kind of consistency'. By basing teaching on the diligent study of 'books' the university would create an 'authority which shall control professors, tutors, students all alike', and a body of information which none could, 'be at liberty to set aside, something concrete 'students shall definitely learn, the tutors definitely teach, and professors' lectures assume'. The study of texts would put an end to the 'idle' often pointed speculation to which modern studies seemed specially prone.[21]

It was a solution which the Oxford examiners readily adopted. History examination papers were arranged according to the geo-chronological scope of the texts. So in 1853 the classman who opted to study the first period, from the Conquest to the death of Henry VII, sat four papers. The first, 'Hume, Lingard, Hallam', covered English political history between 1066 and 1509; the second, 'Gibbon, Guizot, Hallam', covered the corresponding period of European history. The third was a 'General Paper' asking direct questions of set texts, while the fourth comprised essay questions demanding a broad knowledge of English history from the Conquest to the reign of Queen Victoria. This format was repeated for the second period.

The questions were deliberately factual. They avoid any hint of controversy by calling for simple statements of fact. They fall into two distinct categories. The first ask direct questions of a particular text:

By what proofs does Lingard justify the claims of Edward I to be Lord Superior of Scotland? Give analogous cases of Feudal Supremacy over a Kingdom.

The second demand explicit factual recall:

What institutions as to the administration of Justice were established by Henry II, or existed in his time?

Give a sketch of the social and political history of Ireland in the 12th century. What was the immediate cause of Henry II's invasion?

Both species of question are related. Evidence required for the second would be drawn directly from the texts themselves. So it was that in 1853 the general paper set for candidates examined on the second period draws on knowledge of Robertson's *Charles V* and Ranke's *Popes*. Nine questions are listed. The last two test knowledge of chronology and geography, but answers to the previous seven questions can be drawn directly from the texts themselves. So question (1):

What were, according to Ranke, the distinct characteristics of Papl policy (1) in its relation with the German Emperors, (2) in the 14th century, (3) in the latter part of the 15th? Mention some important event characteristics of their policy in each of these periods

can be tackled by reading Ranke's *Popes*, volume I (translated by Sara Austin, second edition, London, 1841) from p. 22 to p. 42. Question (3) on the same paper comprises a series of quotations drawn from pp. 290–3 of the same volume. The other questions may be answered accordingly.[22]

The questions demand precise answers. One private tutor warned his students that:

it may be safely asserted that a First Class is seldom, if ever, gained nowadays without accounting for a very decided majority of the whole number of questions. A great deal of pains expended on only half the Paper will be considered as evidence of ignorance concerning the rest.[23]

The examiners wanted facts, nothing more. The greater number of questions answered correctly, the higher the mark. There was no room for 'opinion'. The tutor advised his students that, as their goal was to complete every question, they should not waste time by reading the paper through but should begin writing immediately. They should write quickly and avoid thinking too deeply about the questions.

If students were left with any doubt as to the value of this advice the answer sheets would soon have resolved them. To consult the examination papers tackled by Oxford undergraduates throughout the 1850s is instructive. On pale blue paper of quarto size, the questions were printed with a two-inch space between. It was there that answers to questions like:

Shew what was, at the time of Charles I, the social position and importance, and also the prevailing temper of the Country gentlemen, more especially in their relations to the Nobility. Trace their progress from the time of Henry VII to that of Charles I

were to be entered. Direct factual answers from unimpeachable authorities certainly reduced the likelihood of bias intruding between tutor and student. They banished any temptation to indulge in unscholarly flights of fancy and imagination. And, further, they made it plain that precision was a virtue actively to be encouraged. The Oxford history student learned early that prolixity was by no means an acceptable by-product of the recently discovered faculty of English composition.[24]

Finally, the study of texts helped overcome one pressing practical problem. Oxford colleges were reluctant to appoint specialist teachers in the new subject. It was expensive and the subjects were hardly prestigious. But it was made clear from the outset that, for law and modern history at least, such appointments would hardly be necessary. The Regius Professor explained that:

The tutors have given instruction in the history of the Old Testament and in Ancient History, and therefore . . . they can do so in regard to Modern History. In all there are textbooks on which the tutors can catechise and comment.[25]

Colleges could do one of two things. They could direct their own

tutors to teach the subjects of the new School, or they could turn
their students out to private tutors who, given the precarious hand-
to-mouth nature of their existence, would doubtless adapt readily
to meet the new circumstances.

Most adopted the latter course—some even agreeing to defray
part of the expense incurred by students who gained a good Class.
Only four colleges offered direct instruction in history, and all
initially on a part-time basis.[26] Exeter, for instance, organized a
system of team teaching. The Sub-rector and two assistants covered
the course together. And they did it without incurring extra
expense. The college had appointed them as teachers of the traditional studies and insisted they deliver their full complement of
classical lectures. The tripartite division of labour proved unnecessary, and in the following year the system was streamlined. Full
responsibility for history teaching devolved on Charles Boase. But
he was not allowed off so lightly. The college caused him to deliver
annual lectures on Divinity and classical subjects for some ten years
more.[27]

Vaughan's prediction was wholly accurate. Tutors—collegiate or
private—experienced little difficulty in adapting to the demands of
teaching for the new School. And for one simple reason—it was
designed so as to ensure that they did not have to change their
teaching technique. The cart was put very firmly in front of the
horse. The books were different, but the approach was the same.
Montagu Burrows described it neatly in a manual called *Pass and
Class*. His shrewd little book is a pragmatic statement of official
rhetoric, a guide to success within a rigid system. It is a statement of
fact, without polemic purpose and devoid of reforming intent.

'Thoroughness', said Burrows, was the key to success at Oxford,
and 'a thorough knowledge of books' was 'only to be got in one way,
viz. by laborious exercise of thought', which we may translate
loosely as memory. But every student could ease his burden by
being organized. The best method of getting up a book was as
simple and straightforward as it was universal. 'Suppose we are
reading Thucydides', explained Burrows:

A blank book may be provided for this alone, or, if large enough, may take
in the whole Greek History course, which will be better still. As soon as the
text of each of the author's eight books has been mastered, a short but
careful abstract of the contents should be made upon every alternate page
of the note-book, leaving room for the dates at the side. The opposite page

should contain, in one column, a second and shorter abstract of the first,— the most prominent facts of all, with the most important dates; the rest of the page should be left for remarks.

This method, coupled with a high degree of motivation, was the chief requisite for success. It was followed by most tutors—as Boase's lecture books bear testimony—and drilled into all students. With technique at a premium, Burrows saw no reason to increase the size of one's college bill by extending residence to read for the optional school. 'The preparation for both of them,' he declared, 'is of a sort which can be steadily and effectually made while the chief attention is given 'to the more important subject.' Indeed, Burrows maintained that, far from being a chore, study for the fourth school made for 'an agreeable recreation' and was much to be preferred to other less worthy pursuits, like cricket.[28]

In practice, regardless of whether they spent their leisure hours studying or in athletic pursuits, most undergraduates did extend residence to prepare for the examination, if only for a month. Most spent longer, and as Mandell Creighton discovered, to do well was no mean feat of memory. He took a Second. The cramming defeated him.[29]

Having first mastered the technique of gutting a book, the second task facing the student was to choose his texts. As a private tutor Burrows found that the pressing need with most men was their 'wish to know what is practically the best list to present to the Examiners, and also what it is best to begin with'. The rationale underlying Burrows' selection shows very clearly that the capital letter of the law, as expressed by the statute, did not correspond greatly with the lower-case of practice. While the statute declared that the student must be conversant with 'the facts of Modern History to 1789', Burrows gently assured his pupils that once they had chosen their optional period the facts pertaining to the other need be known 'only incidentally and in a very subordinate degree'.

How, then, did the student go about choosing his special period? In strict accordance with the ultimate aim of passing the examination at the highest level and with the minimum of effort, the determining factor was prior knowledge. But, all things being equal, Burrows advised the earlier course, for 'scarcely one Classman in ten takes up the other'. This was no exaggeration. A perusal of the Oxford examination papers reveals that no papers were set on the second period in 1863 or in 1865, reflecting the fact that students had not notified the proctors of their intention to 'bring up' works pertaining to the early modern era. Burrows gave two other reasons for the choice. Firstly, that without the early period the second was almost unintelligible, and that 'the spirit of historical study acquired in pursuing the earlier course will scarcely fail to lead a man on to complete the later'. This theoretical justification rings hollow in the face of the second, more pragmatic, reason, that the modern period was 'harder to tackle'. The issues involved were more complex; they required more detailed reading. As a result, few college tutors lectured on it.

Hallam and Lingard were compulsory reading for the first period. Burrows then recommended that Gibbon be read from chapter 38, taking up the chapters which the calendar discarded; which would count as two books. Guizot would complete the fifth. This, he noted, was not an entirely satisfactory selection, but it offered the most comprehensive route through the course.

The special subject should be 'got up like the rest, from particular books, only as their range is much more limited, a more minute acquaintance with detail is required'. All involved a similar work load, but Burrows suggested a choice from three—Eginhard, Commines and Sismondi. He noted that, with his simple, plain Latin, Eginhard was perhaps the easiest and safest option. He noted with seeming regret that few candidates took the opportunity to 'get up' Adam Smith. But he accepted the fact philosophically. It was after all a difficult book.[30]

How did the books themselves relate to the examination structure? English history was 'the basis of the whole course'. Those who wished to master it required an accurate acquaintance with the dates of English kings, the major events of their reigns, the leading constitutional features and the basic geography of the British Isles. Knowledge was essentially of political events and centred firmly on the constitution and the sources of royal power. Burrows advocated that when reading his texts the student should divide 'English history into general facts, special constitutional facts, and special ecclesiastical facts', arranging the information by carving it up into periods. Burrows based his advice upon careful study of the examinations. Thus the English history paper (first period) for 1863 asked:

What English sovereigns during the Middle Ages died mysteriously? Sift the evidence, and balance the probabilities as to the fate of each

and:

Compare the position of Cnut with that of William the Conqueror.[31]

In this respect the paper was little different from that set ten years earlier. By 1859, however, there were questions requiring more discursive treatment, and it was in recognition of this that Burrows advocated a measure of caution to students reading any one of the set texts. In so doing he expressed an unconscious but increasing awareness of the anomalous situation in which the student reading modern history was placed.

Gibbon, he stressed, must be read through completely. The dictates of the examination required it. There was a growing feeling among examiners that Gibbon's ecclesiastical history was neglected by students, who chose to draw their facts from other works. As a result the examiners would be sure to emphasize this aspect of Gibbon in the examination. There was the anomaly. Burrows was aware that under the light of recent research Gibbon's treatment of ecclesiastical history was defective. But the dictates of the Schools meant that it had to be 'got up' regardless. All he could suggest was that students read as a corrective Robertson's *History of the Christian Church* and Hooker on heresies, fifth book, chapters 51–4; Finlay on the Byzantines, Hallam on the Mahometan movement, and Freeman on the Saracens. Lingard was more contentious still, but, bar Hume, his was the only substantial 'authority' which dealt thoroughly with English history in medieval times. Lingard's 'Romanism' apart, Burrows was only too aware of the problems his work uncovered. 'The great progress of recent research into this part of our history', had rendered many details inaccurate. The obvious answer was, as Burrows noted, to consult the original documents. But this, he feared, was, 'out of the question for most who are preparing for examination in the Second Final School'.[32]

Here was the rub. Though the study of texts provided a sound basis upon which to rest the School of Modern History, the progress of scholarship had begun to render it inappropriate. As a supporter of the system Burrows had touched briefly on its weaknesses. Were the substantive traditions of Greats really appropriate to Modern

History? In the years after 1859 it became increasingly clear that they were not. The teaching of history—the manner and the matter of it—did not square with the history that was being written, and being read, by well-educated men. A number of options were open. Nothing need be changed. But then Oxford would be open to criticism that its standards of scholarship were poor. History could be dropped from the curriculum on the grounds that it could not be adapted to the Oxford idea of education. But that, surely, would be a reactionary and dangerous step. The last option was that history could be placed on a new, more radical footing. But it would then require more teaching time, more teachers, and, most obviously, elevation to degree status. But how would this be squared with the Oxford academic ethos? In his Inaugural Lecture as Chichele Professor Modern History delivered in 1862, Montagu Burrows provided the answer. History, he said, was in truth, 'very different from a mere acquaintance with a multitude of facts.' Teaching history properly would,

form habits of systematically organising those facts; of dealing with them accurately, of weighing evidence, of attending to both sides of a question, of patient suspension of judgement where sufficient data are not present. . .

If forming 'the judicial mind for the purpose of dealing in the best manner with all the problems of practical life is the principal object of all education', said Burrows, then history could be adapted as successfully to this end as classics.[33] Burrows was stressing that rather than being the result of a particular type of subject matter, mental training was the function of methodical study of a systematic and organized discipline. Organization and method were the crucial factors underlying any viable academic discipline. He was arguing that, far from being simply a mass of facts and dates, history had its own special methods and procedures, and they were thorough and vigorous enough to fulfil the stringent criteria of a liberal education.

Burrows' ideas about the potential educational value of history were shared by teachers of mathematics and natural science. They lent support to a memorial sent to the Hebdomadal Council in 1862. Signed by 83 members of Congregation, it complained that the classman's time was broken into by pass examinations in other subsidiary subjects. The constraints of the Oxford system mean that this second examination was too slight to be of any value, yet the classman had still to prepare for some six months in order to pass it and take his degree. This was clearly a substantial drain on financial resources, and it induced many students to read for both Schools simultaneously, causing severe strain, and in many cases poor results. If the situation was irritating to the serious student of Literae Humaniores, how much more so to the man interested in one of the newer disciplines? He had first to wade through twelve terms of classical study before being allowed to take-up the subject of his choosing. The Memorial suggested that if Oxford was seriously to sponsor a full range of subjects they should all be placed on a similar footing and given equal opportunity to develop.[34]

The memorialists won their case. The Examination Statute of 1864 ensured that some vestige of tradition remained. Students had still to read for Moderations before progressing to the Final School of their choice. But a new principle in education had been established. The traditional academic ethos, defined by Copleston, remained undisturbed. The university's supreme function was still to train minds. But now a distinction was drawn between the *means* and the *ends* inherent in this view of higher education. While the ends of education were to remain the same, the means to those ends were to be multiplied and broadened. No longer would the substantive traditions developed within the matrix of mental training emphasize a rigid curriculum compulsory on all. The onus now lay with each student to develop his own talents through a number of optional subjects. The criteria for the developing disciplines was the application of strict method and organisation to raw subject matter. The *manner* of teaching was still more important than the information conveyed and was the crucial distinction between a 'subject' and a new phase of curricular and pedagogic development. For the historians the process of manufacturing an academic discipline was begun again.

Conclusion

The theory and practice of higher education in mid nineteenth century Oxford meshed very closely. But only because the theory was developed openly to support and bolster a traditional, well-established administrative framework. Oxford did indeed take steps to silence external criticisms that its curriculum was outdated. But the reforms of 1848–50 were not far-reaching. Oxford refused to consider suggestions that it should broaden its academic ethos. The new legislation was intended to strengthen rather than to restructure existing practice and ideals. When the curriculum was genuinely extended between 1864 and 1872 it was the idea of the university as the guardian of scholarship and arbiter of mental training rather than—as has been suggested elsewhere—a training school for civil servants that prompted the change.[35] The ends of higher education inherent in the Coplestonian ethos remained undisturbed. It was not until the late 1870s and the Campaign for the Endowment of Research that the ethos had substantially to be broadened to accommodate radical new perceptions of the university's role.[36]

Department of History
University of Durham
43/46 North Bailey
Durham DH1 3EX

REFERENCES

1. This paper draws on Chapters 1–4 of my comparative history, *Learning and a Liberal Education: The Study of Modern History in the Universities of Oxford, Cambridge and Manchester 1800–1914* (Manchester, 1986). I wish to thank Mark Curthoys for his helpful criticism of this piece. Needless to say, the shortcomings and failings of this work are entirely my own.
2. Edward Shils, *Tradition* (London, 1981), 182.
3. Figures taken from; Michael Sanderson (ed.), *The Universities in the Nineteenth Century* (London, 1975), 9; Arthur Engel, *From Clergyman to Don: The Rise of the Academic Profession in Nineteenth-Century Oxford* (Oxford, 1983), 286; and from unpublished material compiled by the History of Oxford University Project.
4. James Heywood, *The Recommendations of the Oxford University Commissioners* (London, 1853), 204. Patricia Branca, *Silent Sisterhood: Middle Class Women in the Victorian Home* (Pittsburgh, 1975), 40–45; F. Musgrove, 'Middle Class Education and Employment in the Nineteenth Century', *Economic History Review*, XII (1959–60), 99–111; H. Perkin, 'Middle Class Education and Employment in the Nineteenth Century: A critical note', *Economic History Review* (XIV), 1961–62, 122–30.
5. Cuthbert Bede (pseud), *The Adventures of Mr Verdant Green, An Oxford Undergraduate* (1853, new ed. Oxford, 1982), 11. E. A. Freeman, 'Oxford After Forty Years', *Contemporary Review*, 51 (1887), 609–623, 814–30. Freeman matriculated in 1841.

6. W. R. Ward, *Victorian Oxford* (London, 1965), 6–20.

7. V. H. H. Green, 'Reformers and Reform in the University' in L. S. Sutherland and L. G. Mitchell (edd.), *The History of the University of Oxford, Vol. V: The Eighteenth Century* (Oxford, 1986), 607–639.

8. Mark Curthoys, 'The Early Years of the Oxford Examination System, 1800–1830' (unpublished conference paper).

9. 'Traite de Mechanique celeste par P. S. La Place' *Edinburgh Review* XXII, Vol. XI, (1808), 249–84; 'The Oxford edition of Strabo', *ER* XXVII, Vol. XIV, 1809, 429–41; 'Essays on professional education by R. L. Edgeworth', *ER* XXIX, Vol. XV, (1809), 40–53.

10. Edward Copleston, *A Reply to the Calumnies of the Edinburgh Review against Oxford Containing an account of the Studies pursued in that University* (2nd ed. Oxford, 1810), 108–112. For alternative views see: Sheldon Rothblatt, *Tradition and Change in English Liberal Education: An Essay in History and Culture* (London, 1975), 75–173; R. G. McPherson, *Theory of Higher Education in Nineteenth Century England* (Athens, 1959), 15–29; M. M. Garland, *Cambridge Before Darwin: The Ideal of a Liberal Education, 1800–1860* (Cambridge, 1980), 28–47.

11. E. G. W. Bill, *University Reform in Nineteenth Century Oxford: A study of Henry Halford Vaughan 1811–1885* (Oxford, 1973), 12–23; Charles Daubeny, *Brief Remarks on the Correlation of the Natural Sciences* (Oxford, 1848), 23; Bodleian Library, O.U.A. WpB/11/3/fol. 6.

12. *Report of Her Majesty's Commissioners appointed to inquire into the State, Discipline, Studies and Revenues of the University and Colleges of Oxford* (London, 1852), Evidence of Travers Twiss 293–4; (B. Jowett and A. P. Stanley) *Suggestions for an Improvement of the Examination Statute* (Oxford, 1848), 10.

13. (Jowett and Stanley), pp. 10–11; M. L. Clarke, *Classical Education in Britain 1500–1900* (Cambridge, 1959), 12.

14. (Jowett and Stanley), 12.

15. (Jowett and Stanley), 7–8.

16. Peter Slee, *History as a Discipline in the Universities of Oxford and Cambridge* (Cambridge PhD thesis, 1983), 35–46.

17. Bodleian Library, GA Oxon C65(37.38), GA Oxon b.26; E. G. W. Bill, *University Reform*, 80.

18. Bodleian Library, Ms.Eng.Lett. d440 fols. 28–29, H. H. Vaughan to F. Jeune, Jan 1850.

19. *Oxford University Calendar* 1859, 147–148.

20. *Calendar* 1864, 124.

21. J. A. Froude, 'Suggestions on the best means of teaching English history' in *Oxford Essays* (Oxford, 1855), 47–50, 62–63; E. A. Freeman and F. H. Dickinson, *Suggestions with regard to certain proposed alterations in the University and Colleges of Oxford* (Oxford, 1854), 157.

22. W. Robertson, *History of the Reign of Charles V* (London, 1857); L. Von Ranke, *History of the Popes*, transl. Sara Austin (London, 1841);

Q. 4 from Robertson, 5–6, 71, 161–78, Q. 5 from Robertson, 385, and Ranke, Vol. 1, Book 3, Q. 6 from Ranke, Vol. 1, 135–47, Q. 7 from Ranke, 570–74.

23. M. Burrows, *Pass and Class* (Oxford, 1860), 169.

24. *Oxford University Examination Papers* 1854, 'Hallam and Clarendon' Q. 5.

25. E. G. W. Bill, *University Reform*, 256.

26. New College Oxford, Archives, Motions set before the Stated General Meeting 1860–66, min 14 Nov. 1860; *Report of Her Majesty's Commissioners*, 216–17. The four Colleges were Balliol, Corpus Christi, Exeter, and Oriel.

27. Exeter College Oxford Archives, C. IV. 8. College Lectures 1855–77.

28. M. Burrows, *Pass and Class*, 69, 43–44, 177, 40–41. Boase's Lecture Books are the property of Exeter College, Archive Ref. JI-1-21, JII-1-6.

29. Estimates vary wildly. Burrows in, *Is Educational Reform required in Oxford, and What?* (Oxford, 1859), 24, claimed that by cramming *hard* a student could sit and pass through the School with credit with only six weeks preparation. I find this estimate wildly optimistic. Burrows, I would guess, was being less than objective in his assessment. He himself spent some four months preparing for his First—see *Autobiography of Montagu Burrows*, ed. J. M. Burrows (London, 1908), 204. For Creighton see, *Life and Letters of Mandell Creighton*, ed. L. Creighton (London, 1904), vol. 1, 41–42. After a short spell as tutor in history at Merton between 1867–75 Creighton took up the rural living of Embleton in Northumberland, returning to academic life in 1884 as Dixie Professor of Ecclesiastical History at Cambridge.

30. Burrows, *Pass and Class*, pp. 205–211; *Special Report from the Select Committee on the Oxford and Cambridge University Education Bill 31 July 1867*, 80, para. 1448.

31. Burrows, *Pass and Class*, 208–218; *Oxford University Examination Papers, School of Law and Modern History 1863*.

33. M. Burrows, *Inaugural Lecture delivered October 30th 1862* (privately printed and circulated), 16.

34. Bodleian Library, WPY/28/1 Hebdomadal Council Reports 1855–65; C. W. Sandford (and 82 others), *The Oxford Examination Statute. [Repeating the Memorial on which the measure was founded. . .]* (Oxford, 1863).

35. For dissenting views see, S. Rothblatt, *The Revolution of the Dons: Cambridge and Society in Victorian England* (London, 1968), 181–273, R. Soffer, 'Nation, Duty, Character and Confidence: History at Oxford, 1850–1914' *Historical Journal* 30.1 (1987), 77–104. For a more detailed criticism of Professor Soffer's views see Peter Slee, 'Professor Soffer's "History at Oxford"', *Historical Journal* 30.4 (1987), 933–942.

36. For discussion of these changes see: T. W. Heyck, *The Transformation*

of Intellectual Life in Victorian England (London, 1982), 155–190; Renate Simpson, *How the PhD came to Britain: A Century of Struggle for postgraduate education* (Guildford, 1983), 22–83; Peter Slee, *Learning and a Liberal Education,* 122–164.

Artibus Academicis Inserenda: Chemistry's Place in Eighteenth and Early Nineteenth Century Universities

Christoph Meinel

When, in 1731, Hieronymus David Gaubius succeeded his teacher Herman Boerhaave as professor of chemistry at Leyden, he took the opportunity to deliver an inaugural speech aimed at proving that chemistry had a right to be received among the academic disciplines, *chemiam artibus academicis jure esse inserendam*.[1] Given the fact that Gaubius occupied one of the most famous chairs for chemistry in Europe, such a claim for the subject might seem superfluous. Yet, Gaubius was not trying to enmesh his audience in a rhetorical *petitio principii*. From the way he pictured chemistry, it is clear that the academic status of the field was by no means universally agreed upon: instead of well-ordered bookshelves and literary elegance chemistry possessed only furnaces and vessels, and its adept did not sit leisurely at the writing-desk but blackened his hands, 'fumo, cineribus, fuligine obsitum'.[2] When Gaubius concluded his oration with the call 'the laboratory is waiting, the furnaces are burning, come and sweat there with me!',[3] he could confidently expect that few of his auditors would respond to his invitation.

With chemistry, a new type of scholarly pursuit had entered the traditional seats of learning. Its proper place was not the pulpit, but rather the laboratory, if admittedly the discipline was not yet devoted to experimental research, but rather to teaching by demonstration. Hence the professor of chemistry, who had to brush off soot and ash from his gown when he met with his colleagues, was an odd figure among scholars who oriented themselves towards the vanities of lower nobility and the local court.[4] Though Gaubius was one of the few to have an assistant for the rude and technical tasks, the very nature of laboratory work made it difficult for chemistry to be accepted as a legitimate academic pursuit.

Through much of its history, the position of chemistry within higher education and its demand for recognition have been questioned. Even in the second half of the nineteenth century, it was discussed whether a purely practical and empirical subject such as chemistry should not be banned from the universities or at least from the philosophical faculties. Position and status, the hierarchy of public offices and their reputation within and outside academia, rank and the value of specific disciplines and faculties, all of these were most important issues for the little world of learning, all the more since the world outside took an interest in such hierarchies. This quarrel was not about intellectual values alone. Office and power, competence and influence, salaries and career opportunities, in fact the most tangible values of institutionalized knowledge were involved. From this point of view, chemistry's claims for recognition and an academic position reveal the driving forces behind the mechanisms of continuity, change, and evolution of a scientific discipline.

Scientific disciplines are by no means socially and intellectually homogeneous, and this is especially true during their formative periods.[5] They comprise different groups and individuals, each of which has its own norms and traditions, and pursues its own programmes of research and its own strategies of institutionalization.[6] The various ways in which a discipline and its members respond to their social and institutional context result in a variety of styles and approaches. The Darwinian metaphor 'ecology of knowledge' has quite adequately been applied to the resulting process of competition and adaptation.[7] In this view, the formation of scientific disciplines results from a collective, competitive attempt to create social structures for intellectual activity and to stabilize them institutionally according to the demands and conditions of a changing environment. Success or failure depend to a great extent on the degree of correspondence between the disciplinary programme and the historical opportunities for its realization. The emergence and transformation of a scientific discipline imply intellectual, social, and economic processes at various levels with a constant interaction between them. The overall process of emergence and institutionalization of a discipline is, therefore, unlikely to be a linear succession of logical steps directed more or less towards the same ultimate aim.

Instead, a multilayered and multidirectional growth would be expected, each section of which may very well be aimed at a different destination.

During the eighteenth and early nineteenth centuries, the academic discipline of chemistry traversed various models of institutionalization, each of which can be identified by its underlying assumptions about chemistry's place and destination within the university and society. The purpose of this paper is to distinguish and reflect on those various models. The historical material on which the following analysis is based comes from more than 100 institutions of higher education, such as universities, Jesuit Colleges, Medical Schools for surgeon-physicians, Mining Academies, and technical schools.[8] Central European countries, and especially the German-speaking territories have provided most of the data. This is not only because of availability of sources and literature, but also because in these countries the universities have traditionally been the major centres for the transmission of academic knowledge. However, the demarcation criterion was neither national nor institutional, as opposed to the usual approach favoured by historians of science, but disciplinary, viz. whether or not the teaching of chemistry played any substantial role in that particular institution of higher education. Without understating the importance of national and institutional differences, from the point of view of disciplinary history, the similarities and correspondences are so remarkable and the simultaneousness of disciplinary developments so striking that they justify this approach. After all, through most of the period under discussion, the literature of academic chemistry was in Latin and part of a common European tradition, at least on the Continent.

For well known reasons the German universities have received considerable attention by historians of science and chemistry.[9] Often, however, this has been done from a somewhat distorted point of view by identifying 'the' German university with those features that characterized the major Prussian universities or Göttingen at the turn of the nineteenth century, but did not apply to other German universities such as Greifswald, Rinteln, Ingolstadt or Freiburg. From the scientific aspect, however, the institutional differences between the latter and, for instance, Halle were much greater than those between, say, Vienna and Utrecht, or Leyden and Jena. In addition, historians of science are usually biased in

favour of research-orientation as the decisive if not the only criterion for a true science. From this point of view, however, much of
the pre-nineteenth-century history of universities would be of little
interest.[10] Yet research is only one, and a rather recent, aspect in
the history of an academic discipline. By no means should it be used
as a demarcation criterion in disciplinary or institutional history.
Teaching was in fact the core of a professor's role and by no means
considered as second-rank or merely derivative.[11] By its very
nature, a scholarly discipline is formed and maintained by those
interactions which transmit a body of knowledge in a well-defined
and teachable form.[12] Thus the history of a scientific discipline and
the history of a particular science are clearly distinct.[13] Hence, for
the purpose of this paper only university-like teaching institutions
are considered, and their rivals such as the academies, scientific
societies and more practical teaching establishments, are ignored,
though, especially during the eighteenth century, the role of the
latter in promoting scientific knowledge became a constant challenge to the traditional seats of learning.

The initial institutional context for the development of an academic
chemistry was the seventeenth-century medical faculty. As a crucial
aspect of the reform of learning intended by the Paracelsians,
chemistry entered the universities throughout Europe.[14] Its rise was
as spectacular as it was universal. But soon the original, all-embrac-
ing cosmological goal of Paracelsianism gave way to more practical
and pharmaceutical ends. When, in 1609, Moritz of Hessen, the
learned prince-practitioner, created the first chair of medical chemistry (*chemiatria*) at any university, he imagined that chemistry
would be the noble keystone of an ideal system of arts and sciences.[15] Shortly afterwards, however, the chemists found themselves in a rather marginal position in the medical curriculum.
Faculty statutes of the time mention the subject as an auxiliary to
medicine. 'Medicina atque chimia tamquam domina et serva con-
junguntur',[16] said Zacharias Brendel, professor of chemistry at
Jena, in 1630. It was a servant, moreover, whose service was not yet
in great demand. Before the middle of the seventeenth century
some eight universities offered chemistry courses on a more or less
regular basis, but only Jena (from 1639) and the *Jardin du Roi* at
Paris (from 1648) created a special teaching position of *demonstrator*. During the second half of the century, more universities

included chemistry among the statutory duties of one of the professors of medicine: Utrecht and Leipzig in 1668, Leyden in 1669, Erfurt in 1673, Montpellier in 1675, Altdorf in 1677, Oxford and Stockholm in 1683, Strasbourg, Leuven, and Marburg in 1685, and Helmstedt in 1688. At other places the subject appeared in lecture catalogues from time to time, but did not belong to one professor's permanent duties.

The reception of chemistry into the medical faculty was a very decisive step in shaping the subject's content and academic position. It not only liberated chemistry from the suspicion of alchemical obscurity, but also removed it from the rigid framework of both neo-Aristotelian and physico-mechanical natural philosophy, which had proved equally sterile in terms of chemical theory and application. Concrete and well-defined tasks in the field of pharmacy not only supplied, at least in principle, a means of testing chemistry's practical performance; they also challenged the previous direction of its cognitive development. Consequently, this first wave of institutionalization almost entirely emancipated chemistry from the traditional interest of the Aristotelian and later on Cartesian philosophers in causation.[17] Chemistry was now taught by medical men to future physicians, and its main subject was how to prescribe and prepare chemical medicines.

The incorporation of chemistry into the medical faculty was, however, only partly advantageous for the future development of the discipline. As long as chemistry was merely an auxiliary to medicine and usually taught by a low-rank junior professor along with anatomy, botany, or pharmacy, its humble position within the hierarchy of the faculty was inevitably confirmed. As a mere ancillary subject, chemistry was deemed to be useful only insofar as it catered to the needs of its master, medicine. Moreover, an autonomous development was almost impossible, since in the traditional university system faculty chairs devoted to particular sub-disciplines did not exist. Usually the different professorships of a medical faculty were divided only roughly between the theoretical and practical branches of the science. In addition, there was often a distinction between the chairs in terms of rank, privileges, and salary, which reflected their social reputation within and outside academia. Each faculty had its peculiar pecking order and professors succeeded to higher chairs almost exclusively according to seniority.[18] Emancipative attempts of a discipline to obtain a higher rank would have most automatically provoked opposition from all other parties involved in this rearrangement.[19] Consequently, the professor of chemistry, who usually occupied the least respected and least rewarding chair in the faculty, would have taken the earliest opportunity to proceed to the next in order in the hope of becoming, eventually, *professor primarius*. In this latter position he was able to combine his teaching duties with a more profitable private practice or a position as court physician. This system of succession by seniority (*Aufrücken*), a heritage of the medieval university, continued well into the eighteenth century, although its deficiencies had been recognized much earlier. A junior professor who devoted too much effort to an auxiliary subject such as chemistry would have endangered his subsequent academic career. As a consequence, the teaching of chemistry was frequently neglected by those who were more ambitious. Chemistry became therefore a favourite field for extra-mural teachers, *doctores legentes* or *Fakultäts-Assessoren* who, in this manner, tried to make their way into an academic position.[20] As an evaluation of eighteenth-century academic careers in science proves, the teaching of chemistry was almost regularly a transitional stage, considered as a tedious and, due to the experiments, costly burden, that was reluctantly passed on to assistants or *amanuenses* who in turn used it merely as a stepping-stone to higher positions.

Under these circumstances, different models of justification and institutionalization were proposed in the early eighteenth century, aimed at liberating chemistry from its close ancillary association with medicine. By those who perceived a demand for chemistry and were trying to build their career on it, its humble position within the academic hierarchy was felt not only as personally insulting, but also as an impediment to greater intellectual autonomy and disciplinary differentiation. For that purpose, the subject needed a new identity, a new self-consciousness. Two competing lines of argumentation can be easily distinguished. The first one originated in the Leyden iatromechanical school of medicine. Its aim was to make chemistry the basis for a rational, empirically accessible physiology and pathology. The second type of argumentation, more indebted to the physical sciences in a Cartesian or Newtonian tradition, imagined chemistry to be a general science of matter, based upon corpuscles and acting forces.[21] In both cases a programmatic revaluation from an auxiliary subject to a basic science was intended. This shift of perspective was by no means restricted to the rhetorical stratagems of introductory chapters and inaugural speeches. Its proponents developed programmes of research and counselled new strategies of institutionalization. With reference to the two alternative guidelines for the disciplinary development of chemistry Johann Bartholomaeus Trommsdorff wrote in 1803:

Having earlier elevated chemistry to the status of a maid of medicine and secured its representation within the teaching faculty, the physicians' control over chemistry was now in decline; and while practising doctors had previously had to plead that their maid be tolerated, the university was now allowed to promote chemistry publicly and to praise it as the grandest science and mother of physics.[22]

Eighteenth-century universities did not regard themselves as institutions of research. They prepared for one of the traditional professions: theology, law, public administration, medicine, and higher education. They were notoriously concerned with their financial difficulties and poor student attendance.[23] Therefore only the first strategy of institutionalization had any real chance of success. The medical faculties alone, though usually the smallest of the four classical faculties, provided a possible base for more serious consideration of chemistry as an academic discipline. Even if still an auxiliary to medicine, chemistry, now that it regarded itself as fundamental to physiology and pathology was in a better position to enhance its status. As Immanuel Kant was to remark in *Der Streit der Fakultäten,* it makes a great difference whether the maid carries the torch ahead of her mistress, or the train of her gown behind her.[24]

It was still a long time, however, before separate chairs exclusively and permanently devoted to chemistry could be established. The most important prerequisite was the abandonment of the succession by seniority, which would have blocked any development towards greater specialization and differentiation. This was clearly recognized by many contemporaries. During the 1730s the universities of Würzburg (1734) and Königsberg (1737), the *Collegium Medico-Chirurgicum* in Berlin (1737), and the universities of Prague (1747) and Erfurt (1756) made early, if unsuccessful, attempts to abandon the seniority principle. In Vienna Gerard van Swieten, a pupil of Boerhaave in charge of the Austrian medical policy and university system, tried to establish specialized

Fachprofessuren for chemistry and botany throughout the Habsburg empire, and his measures were reinforced again during the reforms of Joseph II in 1786. In most cases, however, these attempts failed. This was not so much because of a stubborn tradition, but mainly because of economic difficulties resulting from the decreasing number of students, a typical feature of the latter part of the eighteenth century. Sometimes the universities had no other choice than to combine nominally independent professorships by endowing one professor with the duties and salary of a second, third, or even fourth chair. Boerhaave occupied four medical chairs in addition to his *professio chemiae*, although Leyden, at that time, was much better off than most other universities. In Helmstedt, with fewer than 200 students in the mid-eighteenth century, the combining of chairs proved the only way to provide a livelihood for the professors and to stop their continuous complaints.[25] Consequently, chairs devoted to particular fields of expertise (*Fachprofessuren*) were confined to the very few universities large enough to enable differentiation and specialization. Here chemistry was combined with botany and/or pharmacy, but no longer bound to purely medical topics such as anatomy. Neither did the holders of this new type of chair proceed to higher medical ranks during their subsequent career. Nor were these chairs given to other subjects once a position had become vacant. For the first time, it thus became possible, if still not easy, for practical chemists and especially for apothecaries to be nominated professors of chemistry. Perhaps the earliest example is Johann Conrad Barchusen who in, 1703, was appointed extraordinary professor of chemistry at Utrecht although he had no previous academic qualifications whatsoever and took little interest in the medical applications of the subject.[26] In this way, the medical faculty provided new career opportunities for those who wanted to specialize in chemistry, botany, or pharmacy, rather than necessarily abandoning these subjects in order to become physicians.

At the same time as chemistry gradually began to be differentiated as a specific discipline within the medical curriculum, other factors helped it break free of its dependency on medicine altogether. In the first place, in the course of the eighteenth century, interest in the discipline ceased to be primarily oriented towards the medical use of chemistry and was concentrated instead on its commercial applications and potential impact on the domestic economy. In 1750 the Swedish chemist Johan Gottschalk Wallerius coined the programmatic notion 'applied chemistry', *chemia applicata*, for this new understanding of chemistry's role.[27] By means of this new conception chemistry gained a wider utilitarian justification which fitted perfectly the general idea of science promoted in the enlightenment.[28] Within a few decades the notion and concept of 'applied chemistry' were adopted throughout Europe. It created an intellectual framework for an institutional development of the discipline in which non-medical applications were to become of crucial importance. Mineralogy, metallurgy, agriculture, the production of glass and ceramics, all began to be recognized as dependent on chemical knowledge. As a result, chemistry became a truly academic pursuit that did not have to justify its position. This development was encouraged by the fact that chemistry's value was far easier to prove in the commerical field than in physiology and pharmacology where its application was highly complex. The new areas of professional competence provided chemistry with a territory of its own, independent of the controversial systems of the various medical schools. According to Trommsdorff it was exactly this fact which enabled chemistry to formulate theoretical conceptions more adequate to its subject matter than had been possible when the discipline was controlled by merely medical questions.[29]

A second, complementary factor influencing the disciplinary development of academic chemistry was cameralism. This was a new discipline which emerged in the German-speaking universities during the last half of the eighteenth century in response to the educational requirements for the administration of the new territorial states.[30] For several decades the 'economic sciences',[31] as they were often called (i.e. mainly agriculture, commerce, and technology[32]), played a decisive role in recommending academic chemistry to state administrators and the general public alike. Five functions were especially important in this regard[33]: (i) the cameralists interpreted chemistry's role in society; (ii) they subsumed chemistry's scientific aims under the broader economic and administrative goals of the state; (iii) in this way they legitimated chemistry's claim to be independent and its demand for adequate support; (iv) they underlined the socio-economic importance of a chemically founded science of industrial production; and (v) they presented society with new perspectives in development and modernization which could be effected by means of university-based training in the applied sciences. Thus the association of cameralism and chemistry enabled a fundamental revaluation of the latter's academic status and public role.

The institutional consequences of this changed perspective and subsequent disciplinary reorientation were especially apparent at universities where the chemical chairs were not from the very beginning exclusively devoted to the training of future physicians. In that regard the Swedish model proved influential, since in Uppsala (1750), Lund (1758) and Åbo (1761) the universities had established their new chairs of chemistry not in the medical faculties, but in the philosophical faculties as part of the economics and administration curriculum. A second model was provided by the various schools of mining, some of which had been given full university status during the last third of the century. These institutions represent a remarkable, though little studied, departure from the traditional patterns of higher education. Primarily devoted to applied science and practical purposes they were, unlike the universities, part of the state's mining monopoly and under immediate administrative control of the mining authorities.[34] The most important of these schools were the mining academies (*Bergakademien*) in Freiberg/Saxony (university status from 1765), Schemnitz/Slovakia (1770), Berlin (1770), and the *École des Mines* in Paris (1783). Here a new kind of chemical professoriate began to emerge, which was neither intellectually, socially, nor institutionally tied to the medical tradition. Consequently the first professors of chemistry who had not initially gone through a medical education appear at these institutions.[35] Several German universities responded to this challenge by creating their own non-medical chairs for chemistry in connection with economics or technology. These chairs were especially common between 1775 and 1820. Sometimes they were incorporated into Cameralist Faculties especially established to receive new disciplines that did not easily fit into the traditional institutional schema. Chemical professorships of this 'economic' type were established in 1760 at the newly founded university of Bützow, at the *Cameral-Hohe Schule* at Lautern (1774–84), at the universities of Giessen (1777–85) and Mainz (1784–98), at the *Staatswirthschafts-Hohe Schule* of Heidelberg (1784–1813), and at the universities in Dillingen (1784–93), Bonn (1789–94), Marburg (1789–1844) and Vienna (1838–42). In some of these institutions the professor of chemistry belonged to the philosophical faculty and was also responsible for natural history, technology, or economics; in other cases he taught chemistry and pharmacy within the medical faculty, but was also a member of an inter-departmental institute for public economy or of an inter-faculty board of examinations. In other cases the professors of chemistry even belonged to two separate faculties (medical/philosophical or medical/cameralist) at the same time. In this way chemistry had conquered university territory, where it neither had to assert itself against the medical tradition nor to defend itself against charges of being merely a non-academic craft. The scientific and economic results chemistry was now able to promise provided the discipline with a more up-to-date strategy of institutionalization, and opened up new perspectives of professionalization that received public recognition and official support.

Taken together, there were basically four rival forms of institutionalization competing for the limited financial and personal resources the unviersities had to offer for chemical teaching during the second half of the eighteenth century: (i) the more traditional, ancillary chemistry course associated with a predominantly medical chair; (ii) more independent specialized professorships for chemistry and botany, or chemistry and pharmacy in the medical faculties; (iii) chemical positions connected to the teaching of metallurgy, technology, or cameralism outside the medical faculties; and (iv) the first attempts to establish truly independent chemical chairs, usually combined with pharmacy, within the philosophical faculties.

It might be worthwhile to have some quantitative idea of the respective momentum of each strategy of institutionalization. In this field, however, the quantitative methodology has its limitations. The numbers of institutions and individuals involved were small, so that local circumstances, the accidents of history and individual fate interfere with the establishment of secular trends without being eliminated statistically by large numbers. Social historians of science sometimes ignore the fact that 'normal' or 'typical': i.e. more or less standardized biographies began to develop only with the normalization of life expectancy during the nineteenth century. Another limitation of this kind of statistics is that only quantitative changes are recorded whereas the historian of science will usually find information about the quality of teaching and the academic standard of research more worthwhile. In this paper, the method of counting individuals and positions is only used to

Figure 1: Academic teaching positions for chemistry, 1660–1850, cumulative presentation

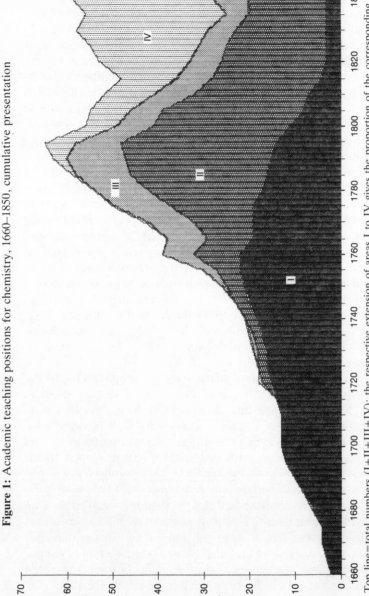

Top line=total numbers (I+II+III+IV); the respective extension of areas I to IV gives the proportion of the corresponding type of professoriate: I=ancillary connection to a predominantly medical chair, II=specialized professorship of chemistry (and botany/pharmacy) in a medical context, III=non-medical chemistry connected to mining or cameralist curricula, IV=chairs of chemistry in purely scientific, non-medical curricula.

indicate tendencies and general changes, and to give some hints as to developments in the cognitive content of the discipline. It is not meant to be an exact description of the processes under consideration, or to replace a more thorough historical analysis.

In preparing Figs 1 and 2, teaching positions in chemistry at universities and similar institutions of higher education before 1840 were evaluated. This was supplemented by a prosopographical study of the people who occupied these positions. Special attention was paid to career patterns and educational background. In order to eradicate short-term variations the institutional data were recorded as five-year averages. The resulting graph for this overall count (Fig. 1, top line) displays what one would expect: the usual, exponential growth in total numbers with a turning point near 1760, a slight fallback due to the Seven Years War, and a clear depression during the Napoleonic Wars when many of the small and moribund continental universities were abandoned and the entire university system of France and her newly conquered *départements* reorganized. The resulting numerical loss of academic positions was, however, to some extent balanced by the emergence of new institutions such as the *Écoles Centrales* and *Höhere Gewerbeschulen*. Three factors were responsible for the relatively slow recovery after 1815. Firstly, there is evidence that, beginning with the 1790s, chemistry was losing its prominent place as a fashionable 'Lieblingswissenschaft der Großen';[36] a decline of public interest definitely affected the institutional development of the discipline.[37] Secondly, saturation effects appear as soon as the great majority of institutions included in this sample had some kind of teaching position for chemistry, so that the much slower multiplication rate of institutions in the first half of the nineteenth century became a limiting factor for further growth. Finally, these statistics do not include purely pharmaceutical chairs after their institutional separation from chemistry in the early nineteenth century.

An even more interesting picture results if each form of institutionalization is considered on its own (Fig. 2). Graph I charts the number of chemical chairs where the discipline was merely a preparatory subject for medicine and tightly bound to the medical curriculum. Criterion for inclusion was that, in these cases, chemistry was always connected with teaching duties in a purely medical subject, and regularly given up if the respective professor, according to seniority, moved on to higher, purely medical disciplines.

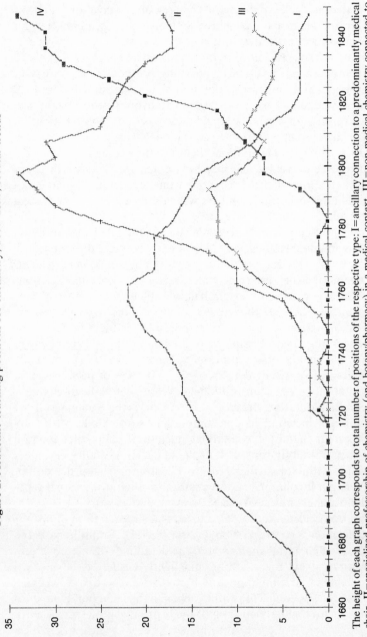

Figure 2: Academic teaching positions for chemistry, 1660–1850, secular trends

The height of each graph corresponds to total number of positions of the respective type: I = ancillary connection to a predominantly medical chair, II = specialized professorship of chemistry (and botany/pharmacy) in a medical context, III = non-medical chemistry connected to mining or cameralist curricula, IV = chairs of chemistry in purely scientific, non-medical curricula.

From the graph it is obvious that this form of institutionalization reached its zenith in the 1750s and declined considerably in importance immediately afterwards.

Instead, the tendency towards the creation of specialized chemical or botanical professorships within the medical faculties gained in momentum (Graph II). The teaching of chemistry still remained primarily addressed to medical students, but it was taken more seriously and enjoyed greater disciplinary autonomy. In research and publications, non-medical aspects became more important and the scientists who held the chairs continued to profess the subject for all of their academic career. Institutionally and socially, the two first lines (I and II) were, of course, interrelated. The process described by curves I and II can be seen, therefore, as primarily a rearrangement within the medical faculty in favour of a more independent chemical discipline, which became clearly differentiated within its traditional institutional context.

The development represented by Graph III, which depicts chemical teaching positions in connection with metallurgy, technology, economics, or cameralism, reflects a very different phenomenon. The association of chemistry with the applied side of these economic subjects proved a feasible way to liberate the discipline from its former domination by medicine and led to a new determination of its place within the academic system and within society as a whole. Consequently, a revaluation of chemistry's cognitive content was possible, in which the practical and commercial aspects received more attention. The type of student, the forms of institutional differentiation, and the professional orientation of the course differ remarkably from the traditional character of academic chemistry. Interestingly, a parallel move towards the practical and the useful can be observed in the chemical publications of university professors after the 1750s. However, the steep rise of this particular curve of institutionalization gave way to an equally sudden decline only a few decades later. There are various reasons underlying this phenomenon. Firstly, the utilitarian *leitmotiv* of enlightenment science, which had been so appealing at first glance, was short lived as the expected material results did not immediately arrive. In addition, Beckmann's programme of technology as an academic subject did not succeed. Finally, cameralism lost its traditional unity, divesting itself of its scientific and natural history aspects and eventually collapsing altogether during the first third of the nineteenth

century.[38] As a consequence, most universities lost their econom-
ically-oriented chemistry chairs. Only the limited number of mining
schools and polytechnics continued to offer teaching in applied and
technical chemistry at an academic level. Nevertheless, the importance of this short intermezzo must not been underestimated. When
in the 1790s the new antiphlogistic chemistry with its predominantly
non-medical approach made its way through the universities of
Europe, the conceptual and institutional framework for a chemical
discipline outside of the medical curriculum had already been
prepared.

At that time a fourth and last form of institutionalization was just
beginning: the establishment of chemical chairs within the philosophical faculty (Graph IV). While the preoccupation with the
useful and the needs of the state was exhausting itself, a new
concept of a university which would be dedicated to scholarship and
pure research was emerging at Göttingen and Halle within the first
seminars of history and philology.[39] The institutional place of this
new scholarly ideal was to be the philosophical faculty as opposed to
the professionally-oriented faculties of medicine, law, and theology. However, most of the early attempts to transfer teaching
positions in chemistry from the medical into the philosophical
faculty, such as at Ingolstadt (1773), Göttingen (1775), and Halle
(1788), failed sooner or later because of limited access to financial
resources available in tuition and examination fees.[40] Jena, then the
third largest university in the country, was the first German university to create, in 1789, a permanent chair for chemistry, combined
with pharmacy and technology in the philosophical faculty. Even
then, however, this was not in response to the new challenge posed
by the changed role of the faculty, for the foundation at Jena
belonged to the old technological and commercial tradition. In fact
the earliest foundations of independent chemical positions within
the philosophical faculty were almost entirely due to the declining
association between chemistry and cameralism. Hence an additional impetus was required to enable the transition of chemistry
from the medical to the philosophical faculty and to transform the
subject into the new type of research-oriented science that was to
prevail in the latter part of the nineteenth century.

In Dutch universities the new institutional setting was provided
by state intervention. In 1815 a royal decree on the organization of

higher education in the Northern Provinces divided the philosophical faculty into a faculty of mathematics and natural sciences which included chemistry, and a faculty of speculative philosophy and arts.[41] By this measure chemistry in the Netherlands was disconnected from medicine institutionally once and for all. In the beginning, however, most students were still future doctors, since there were few professional prospects in non-medical chemistry at the time. Nevertheless, the separation at least brought to an end the quarrel between chemistry and medicine about their respective rank in academia.

In Germany, on the other hand, the very idea of a separate science faculty would have been alien to the Humboldtian neo-humanist ideal of a university. The demand for a faculty of natural sciences was uttered for the first time during the revolutionary year of 1848, but it was not before 1863 that Tübingen succeeded in establishing the first science faculty. Even then the division was preceded by controversies between the representatives of medical and 'scientific' chemistry.[42] It is interesting, therefore, to note that it was pharmacy which played the crucial part in the final institutionalization of its sister-discipline, chemistry. During the last decades of the eighteenth century, the traditional way of training apothecaries, in the form of a craft-like apprenticeship, was criticized both by medical officials and within the profession. The access to academic education, however, was difficult since most pharmacists did not have the entrance requirements for a university matriculation. Therefore, leading representatives of the pharmaceutical profession, concerned with both the social and the scientific status of pharmacy, insisted on a reform of their own professional training. They wanted to make pharmacy more of an academic, science-based profession. A thorough training in chemistry, above all in chemical analysis, was seen as the best way to reach this goal. Following the model provided by Johann Christian Wiegleb, one of the leading figures in German chemistry in the 1780s, many private scientific boarding schools were established, designed to train not only future apothecaries, but also chemical manufacturers, food producers, and civil servants, in practical chemistry and the related natural sciences.[43] The most famous of these private institutions was Johann Bartholomäus Trommsdorff's *Chemisch-physikalische und pharmaceutische Pensionsanstalt für Jünglinge* which was opened in

Erfurt in 1795. It received official recognition as equivalent to a regular university training from 1823.[44]

These private pharmaceutical institutes played a decisive role in the subsequent development of university chemistry. In many cases their owners also held chairs in chemistry or pharmacy at the local university, and, over the years, these professors were able to incorporate their formerly private schools into the institutional and financial framework of the universities.[45] The philosophical faculty was the most obvious place for these teaching establishments, since it was the faculty where the journeymen-apothecaries could matriculate as full-time students without the usual requirement of having completed their studies at a *Gymnasium* first—a reflection of the philosophical faculty's ancient role as a preparatory school for the upper faculties. The small *Chemisch-pharmaceutisches Institut* established by Justus Liebig, then a 22 year old professor of chemistry at Giessen, together with Friedrich Christian Gregor Wernekinck, a mineralogist, Georg Gottlieb Schmitt, a physicist, and Hermann Umpfenbach, a mathematician, was a direct adoption of Trommsdorff's model—even though Liebig, in his later years, made every effort to make it appear as an immediate imitation of the chemical laboratory of the *Ecole Polytechnique* in Paris. It was run as an entirely private and quite profitable enterprise in the shadow of the official university. At the beginning, the university officials were, for obvious reasons, rather suspicious about this new kind of establishment. As one member of Senate stated, it was the university's duty to train professionals for the civil service; but it was not its trask to create pharmacists, soap-boilers, brewers, liquor distillers, dyers, vinegar workers, druggists and the like, for all of these were private entrepreneurs. Although the owners were allowed to continue their private teaching, the institute was not recognized as part of the university until 1835.[46]

After several countries had introduced a compulsory university training for apothecaries in imitation of Austria (1804), Bavaria (1808) and Prussia (1825), the former private institutes lost their importance or were transformed into regular university laboratories for chemistry and pharmacy. Many of them now belonged to the philosophical faculty which, at that time, would not otherwise have been able to sustain a purely chemical discipline, had not pharmacy provided a practical justification for the subject's support. From the point of view of the subsequent development of academic chemistry this may very well appear as a, to some extent, conscious strategy. Humboldtian professors of chemistry made use of the traditional function of the university as a training-ground for professionals needed by the state, in order to promote a new concept within academia of chemistry as a research-oriented, narrowly specialized scientific discipline.[47] Liebig, for one, until 1840, followed this strategy with unparalleled success, teaching pharmacy but making it perfectly clear that the training of apothecaries was not one of his primary concerns.[48] His conception of academic chemistry centred on pure chemistry and not on its application.[49] It was exactly this aspect of the Giessen school that constituted its international fame.[50] Liebig launched fierce attacks against the proponents of the old utilitarian lines, especially in Prussia and Austria, the two countries with the strongest cameralist tradition. His vision of chemistry was of a scientific discipline whose primary goal was to educate the mind.[51]

From the 1830s it was this neo-humanist, Humboldtian concept of university education which provided the conceptual framework for the promotion of an institutionally-independent chemical discipline. It is not yet entirely clear why the sciences, and especially why chemistry, the most applied of all, so reluctantly accepted the Humboldtian challenge. Nevertheless, its acceptance was crucial. Unlike pharmacy, training in which was publicly needed and even legally required, the independence of chemistry remained insecure and questioned as long as there was no real governmental or industrial demand for trained chemists. As a result, chemistry's utilitarian and applied aspects were given much less consideration in justificatory discourse, in order not to strengthen the hand of those who once again demanded that chemistry and similarly applied branches of science should be banned entirely from the universities and confined to polytechnics and professional schools.[52] Characteristically, the academic status of chemistry was now defended by comparing it not with the professional studies of theology, law, or medicine, but rather with philology and history.

The logical way of establishing chemistry's academic independence was to separate the discipline institutionally from pharmacy, since the latter had never denied its immediate ties to the needs of the profession. Most universities took this measure at sometime during the nineteenth century, beginning with Erlangen (1818), Jena (1820), Bonn (1821), Würzburg and Vienna (1836). When this occurred pharmacy often remained within the medical curriculum, whereas chemistry was transferred into the philosophical faculty. Figure 2 clearly shows how, between the 1810s and 1840s, the number of positions in medical chemistry (Graph II) decreased, if the decrease was not so dramatic as it appears from the graph since the separate pharmaceutical chairs have not been taken into account. Simultaneously, the number of chairs dedicated to chemistry as an independent science was increasing at the expense of the medical ones.

In this way the process of disciplinary differentiation and distinction of chemistry from neighbouring sciences had reached fruition. The former, mainly hierarchical stratification of these sciences had given way to a more functional division into academic disciplines with more narrowly specialized areas of competence and expertise, a typical feature of the modern understanding of the structure of knowledge.[53] Once this 'external' differentiation had been largely completed, processes of 'internal' differentiation and specialization became more dominant.

While the debates about the position and academic value of chemistry were losing their original vigour, a new quarrel between the different types of institution emerged. The rise of technical and commercial schools fighting for academic recognition polarized the entire system of higher education and also influenced the disciplinary development of chemistry at the respective institutional level. As a consequence the Humboldtian universities almost exclusively favoured pure, organic chemistry as the basis for the study of chemical theory, whereas applied, analytical, and inorganic chemistry were considered merely introductory or auxiliary subjects. This tendency was by no means confined to the German countries; it rather applied more or less wherever chemistry was institutionalized according to the guidelines laid down by Liebig's Giessen model.[54] It was defended by the somewhat contradictory claim that it was exactly its character as a pure and disinterested science which made university chemistry so eminently useful for the national economy. It is still a source of controversy among historians whether in the course of the nineteenth century there was a real polarization between academic chemistry and the requirements of industry.[55] What can be certainly said is that applied and technical chemistry, with a few exceptions such as the Leipzig chair of Otto Linné Erdmann, had to depart again from the universities and turn to the new polytechnics and *Gewerbeschulen*. Eventually, in the 1870s, there was no academic institution in all of Europe for the study of advanced inorganic chemistry except in Zurich and Paris.[56]

From the seventeenth century the academic discipline of chemistry, originally an ancillary subject of medicine, went through several stages of institutionalization which finally removed it from the medical context and turned it into an independent scientific discipline. The quasi-quantitative evaluation of this process supports the conclusion that several alternative strategies of institutionalization were competing with each other, leading to different forms of disciplinary differentiation. Accordingly, the overall process was not a straight development towards an already fixed end, but rather consisted of a succession of clearly distinct phases of differentiation, each of which had its specific underlying assumptions about what constituted the discipline and how it would best be institutionalized. It would not be illegitimate, therefore, to say that, during these two centuries, different types of chemistry were struggling for survival within the intellectual, cultural and social framework provided by the university system. Therefore, the common notion of a discipline's 'emergence' or 'development' is misleading, for it implies a, so to speak, pre-Darwinian idea of the subject as pre-existent from the very beginning and needing only to be freed from accidental disguises. This is equally true for the distinction commonly made between a discipline's prehistory, its emergence or genesis proper, and its subsequent development.[57] Historically it makes little sense to presuppose the present-day definition of a particular scientific discipline, and then to look for continuity rather than vicissitudes in its history. Disciplines are not metaphysical entities that retain their essence throughout their changing modes of existence. To assign them a 'hidden potentiality'[58] of development, antedating their real genesis or existence, would be historiographical scholasticism. It is our habit of looking back at these historical processes which creates the illusion of a coherent path of logical steps leading to the present. For a more adequate 'epigenetic' description we should rather study the ongoing tension between change and continuity. Subsequent adaptation and transformation processes affect both the institutional structure and the cognitive content of a scientific discipline. Its identity and definition, both internally and externally, are constantly being revised and continue to be open to future change.

For the purpose of this paper, we have had to focus on structural aspects and could touch on changes in the content of chemistry only briefly. But there is no doubt that both these aspects are closely related and affect each other, as they relate in turn to the wider transformation of cognitive, social, political, and economic structures within society. The universities, insofar as they play a key role in acculturation, are at the intersection of all these influences. Continuity and change in a society are necessarily reflected in the universities; but at the same time, the universities provide mechanisms to create continuity, as well as to enable intellectual and social change.

Universität Hamburg, Institut für Geschichte der Naturwissenschaften, Bundesstrasse 55, D-2000 Hamburg 13, West Germany

REFERENCES

1. Hieronymus David Gaubius, *Oratio inauguralis qua ostenditur chemiam artibus academicis jure esse inserendam* (Leyden, 1731 [this edn. quoted]; 2nd edn Leyden, 1786); reprinted with a French translation in *Opuscula selecta Neerlandicorum de arte medica*, Fasc. 1 (Amsterdam, 1907), 200–51.
2. Gaubius, *Oratio*, 7.
3. *Ibid.*, 48: 'patet rursum officina, ardebunt furni, accedite et mecum ad hoc desudate'.
4. Notger Hammerstein, 'Zur Geschichte der deutschen Universität im Zeitalter der Aufklärung', in Hellmuth Rössler and Günther Franz (eds.), *Universität und Gelehrtenstand, 1400–1800* (Deutsche Führungsschichten in der Neuzeit, 4; Limburg, 1970), 145–82, p. 156.
5. R. W. Home, 'Out of a Newtonian Straitjacket: Alternative Approaches to Eighteenth-Century Physical Science', in R. F. Brissenden and J. C. Eade (eds.), *Studies in the Eighteenth Century*, vol. IV (Canberra, 1979), 235–49.
6. Peter Weingart, 'Wissenschaftlicher Wandel als Institutionalisierungsstrategie', in Peter Weingart (ed.), *Wissenschaftssoziologie II: Determinanten wissenschaftlicher Entwicklung* (Fischer Athenäum Taschenbücher Sozialwissenschaften, 4008; Frankfurt, 1974), 11–35.
7. Charles E. Rosenberg, 'Toward an Ecology of Knowledge: On Discipline, Context and History', in Alexandra Oleson and John Voss (eds.), *The Organization of Knowledge in Modern America, 1860–1920* (Baltimore, 1979), 440–55.
8. This survey is based on data from 105 institutions, 48 of which were

German, 14 Habsburg, 9 French, 7 Russian, 6 British and Italian, and 5 Dutch, Swedish, or Swiss respectively. Among them university-like institutions (68) exceed the number of medical schools (10), schools of mines (7), and other, predominantly technical, establishments (20).

9. Karl Hufbauer, *The Formation of the German Chemical Community, 1720–1795* (Berkeley/Los Angeles/London, 1982).

10. The question to what extent a university should engage in research rather than in teaching was extensively discussed at the time; e.g. [Johann David Michaelis] *Raisonnement über die protestantischen Universitäten in Deutschland,* ii (Frankfurt/Leipzig, 1770), 123–42.

11. Cf. Brendan Dooley, 'Science Teaching as a Career at Padua in the Early Eighteenth Century: The Case of Giovanni Poleni', *History of Universities,* 4 (1984), 115–51.

12. This very aspect has been shown to be the point of departure for chemistry as a discipline; see Owen Hannaway, *The Chemists and the Word: The Didactic Origins of Chemistry* (Baltimore/London, 1975).

13. Cf. the often-quoted scholastic definition: 'quando discitur, disciplina vocatur, quando perfecta in habitu mentis est, ars nuncupatur', from Johannes Scotus, *Annotationes in Marcianum,* ed. C. E. Lutz (Cambridge, Mass., 1939), 60,3.

14. Allen G. Debus, 'Chemistry and the Universities in the Seventeenth Century', *Academiae Analecta: Mededelingen van de Koninklijke Academie voor Wetenschappen, Letteren en Schone Kunsten van België,* Klasse der Wetenschappen, 48/4, (1986), 13–33.

15. Bruce T. Moran, 'Privilege, Communication and Chemiatry: The Hermetic-Alchemical Circle of Moritz of Hessen-Kassel', *Ambix,* 32 (1985), 110–26.

16. Zacharias Brendel, *Chimia in artis formam redacta* [1630], ed. Werner Rolfinck (Jena, 1641), 7.

17. Charles B. Schmitt, *Aristotle and the Renaissance* (Martin Classical Lectures, 27; Cambridge, Mass./London, 1983).

18. Hans-Heinz Eulner, *Die Entwicklung der medizinischen Spezialfächer an den Universitäten des deutschen Sprachgebietes* (Studien zur Medizingeschichte des 19. Jahrhunderts, 4; Stuttgart, 1970), 7–8.

19. Virgilio Giormani, 'Le vicende della cattedra di chimica a Padova dal 1726 al 1749', in Paola Antoniotti and Luigi Cerruti (eds.), *Atti del I° Convegno di Storia della Chimica* (Turin, 1985), 99–106; *id.,* 'L'insegnamento della chimica all'Università di Padova dal 1749 al 1808', *Quaderni per la Storia dell'Università di Padova,* 17 (1984), 91–133, on pp. 92–3.

20. Günther Beer, 'Der Versuch Johann Christoph Cron's zur Errichtung eines ersten chemischen Laboratoriums an der Universität Göttingen im Jahre 1735', *Göttinger Jahrbuch,* 28 (1980), 97–108. Extra-mural lecturers were also frequent in Halle and especially at British universities; cf. F. W. Gibbs, 'Itinerant Lecturers in Natural Philosophy', *Ambix,* 8 (1960), 111–17; J. B. Morrell, 'Practical Chemistry in

the University of Edinburgh', 1799–1843', *Ambix*, 16 (1969), 66–80; and Christopher Lawrence's paper on the Edinburgh medical school in this present volume.

21. Christoph Meinel, '*De praestantia et utilitate Chemiae*: Selbstdarstellung einer jungen Disziplin im Spiegel ihres programmatischen Schrifttums', *Sudhoffs Archiv*, 65 (1981), 366–89.

22. J[ohann] B[artholomäus] Trommsdorf[f], *Versuch einer allgemeinen Geschichte der Chemie* (Erfurt, 1806), iii, 32–33; first published in *Trommsdorffs Taschenbuch für Aerzte, Chemiker und Pharmazeutiker auf das Jahr 1803* (Erfurt, 1803): 'Hatte man vorher die Chemie als Gehülfin der Arzneikunst erhoben und ihr Sitz und Stimme auf dem akademischen Katheder erstritten: so nahm jetzt das Präkonisiren der Aerzte zum Vortheil der Chemie ab; und seufzte vorher der laborirende Arzt um Duldung seiner Gehülfin: so durfte jetzt öffentlich die Akademie sich der Chemie befleißigen und sie die erhabenste Naturwissenschaft und die Mutter der Physik (*rerum naturalium praestantem sociam et maternam adjutricem*) nennen.'

23. E. Th. Nauk, 'Die Zahl der Medizinstudenten der deutschen Hochschulen im 14.–18. Jahrhundert', *Sudhoffs Archiv*, 38 (1954), 175–86; for student numbers in general see Franz Eulenburg, *Die Frequenz der deutschen Universitäten von ihrer Gründung bis zur Gegenwart* (Abhandlungen der phil.-hist. Klasse der Kgl. Sächsischen Gesellschaft der Wissenschaften, 24/2; Leipzig, 1904).

24. Immanuel Kant, *Der Streit der Fakultäten* [1798], in *Immanuel Kant Werke*, ed. Wilhelm Weischedel, ix (Darmstadt, 1975), 261–393, on p. 291.

25. Heinrich Nentwig, *Die Physik an der Universität Helmstedt* (Wolfenbüttel, 1891), 100.

26. Owen Hannaway, 'Johann Conrad Barchusen (1666–1723): Contemporary and Rival of Boerhaave', *Ambix*, 14 (1967), 96–111.

27. Christoph Meinel, 'Reine und Angewandte Chemie: Die Entstehung einer neuen Wissenschaftskonzeption in der Chemie der Aufklärung', *Berichte zur Wissenschaftsgeschichte*, 8 (1985), 25–45.

28. Karl Hufbauer, 'Chemistry's Enlightened Audience', *Studies on Voltaire and the Eighteenth Century*, 153 (1976), 1069–86.

29. Trommsdorff, *Versuch* iii, 27–8.

30. Focko Eulen, 'Die Technologie als ökonomische und technische Wissenschaft an deutschen Universitäten des 18. Jahrhunderts', *Technikgeschichte*, 36 (1969), 245–56; Wilhelm Stieda, *Die Nationalökonomie als Universitätswissenschaft* (Abhandlungen der Kgl. Sächsischen Gesellschaft der Wissenschaften, phil.-hist. Klasse, 25/2; Leipzig, 1906).

31. Early eighteenth-century 'economics' is a cross between agriculture, husbandry, and commercial administration.

32. According to its founder Johann Beckmann technology was conceived

of as the science of exploiting, processing and refining natural resources. See Ulrich Troitzsch, *Ansätze technologischen Denkens bei den Kameralisten des 17. und 18. Jahrhunderts* (Schriften zur Wirtschafts- und Sozialgeschichte, 5; Berlin, 1966), 154–61.

33. Rudof Stichweh, *Zur Entstehung des modernen Systems wissenschaftlicher Disziplinen: Physik in Deutschland 1740–1890* (Frankfurt, 1984), 57.

34. Wolfhard Weber, *Innovationen im frühindustriellen deutschen Bergbau und Hüttenwesen: Friedrich Anton von Heynitz* (Studien zur Naturwissenschaft, Technik und Wirtschaft im Neunzehnten Jahrhundert, 6; Göttingen, 1976), 1952–67.

35. E.g. Christian Ehregott Gellert, 1765 professor of chemistry and metallurgy at Freiberg's *Bergakademie*; Valentin Rose, 1770 professor of chemistry at Berlin's *Bergakademie*; Thaddäus Peithner, 1772 professor for chemistry and natural sciences at the mining academy in Schemnitz.

36. Johann Friedrich Gmelin, *Geschichte der Chemie* (Göttingen, 1797), i, 2.

37. The most prominent case is the one of the *Ecole Polytechnique*; see Janis Langins, 'The Decline of Chemistry at the *Ecole Polytechnique* (1794–1805)', *Ambix*, 28 (1981), 1–19.

38. The remaining parts of cameralism continued to be taught in the law faculties as a precursor of modern economics.

39. R. Steven Turner, 'The Bildungsbürgertum and the Learned Professions in Prussia, 1770–1830: The Origins of a Class', *Histoire Sociale—Social History*, 13 (1980), 105–80.

40. Christoph Meinel, 'Zur Sozialgeschichte des chemischen Hochschulfaches im 18. Jahrhundert', *Berichte zur Wissenschaftsgeschichte*, 10 (1987), 147–68.

41. H. A. M. Snelders, 'Chemistry at the Dutch Universities, 1669–1900', *Academiae Analecta: Mededelingen van de Koninklijke Academie voor Wetenschappen, Letteren en Schone Kunsten van België*, Klasse der Wetenschappen, 48/4, (1986), 59–75.

42. Armin Hermann and Armin Wankmüller, *Physik, Physiologische Chemie und Pharmazie an der Universität Tübingen*, ed. Wolf von Engelhardt (Contubernium, 21; Tübingen, 1980), 49–50.

43. Dieter Pohl, *Zur Geschichte der pharmazeutischen Privatinstitute in Deutschland von 1779 bis 1873*, Dr.rer.nat. thesis (Marburg, 1972); H. H. Egglmaier, 'Deutsche pharmazeutische Institute, 1848', *Mitteilungen der Österreichischen Gesellschaft für Geschichte der Naturwissenschaften*, 4 (1984), 119–28.

44. Pohl, *Geschichte* 38–69; Wolfgang Götz, *Zu Leben und Werk von Johann Bartholomäus Trommsdorff (1770–1837): Darstellung anhand bisher unveröffentlichten Archivmaterials* (Quellen und Studien zur Geschichte der Pharmzaie, 16; Würzburg, 1977), 35–9, 123–9.

45. Bernard Gustin, 'The Emergence of the German Chemical Profession, 1790–1867', Ph.D. thesis (Chicago, 1975); Erika Hickel, 'Der Apothekerberuf als Keimzelle naturwissenschaftlicher Berufe in Deutschland', *Medizinhistorisches Journal*, 13 (1978), 259–76.
46. G. Weihrich, 'Beiträge zur Geschichte des chemischen Unterrichtes an der Universität Giessen', *Jahres-Bericht des Großherzoglichen Realgymnasiums und der Realschule zu Giessen*, 634 (1891), 3–39, on pp. 18–19.
47. R. Steven Turner, 'The Growth of Professorial Research in Prussia, 1818 to 1848: Causes and Context', *Historical Studies in the Physical Sciences*, 3 (1971), 137–82; *id.*, 'University Reformers and Professorial Scholarship in Germany, 1760–1806', in L. Stone (ed.), *The University in Society* (Princeton, N.J., 1974), ii, 495–531; *id.*, 'The Prussian Professoriate and the Research Imperative 1790–1840', in H. N. Jahnke and M. Otte (eds.), *Epistemological and Social Problems of the Sciences in the Early Nineteenth Century* (Dordrecht, 1981), 109–21.
48. R. Steven Turner, 'Justus Liebig versus Prussian Chemistry: Reflections on early Institute-Building in Germany', *Historical Studies in the Physical Sciences*, 13 (1980), 129–62.
49. It should not be forgotten, however, that Liebig somewhat suddenly changed his mind in that regard, following the publication of his *Organic Chemistry in its Applications to Agriculture and Physiology* (London, 1840). The motives behind this reorientation are not yet entirely clear and need further investigation.
50. William H. Brock, 'Liebigiana: Old and New Perspectives', *History of Science*, 19 (1981), 201–18; Eric Gray Forbes, 'Liebig in Großbritannien', *Nachrichtenblatt der Deutschen Gesellschaft für Geschichte der Medizin, Naturwissenschaft und Technik*, 33 (1983), 115–33; Alois Kernbauer, 'Die Emanzipation der Chemie in Österreich um die Mitte des 19. Jahrhunderts: Von der Hilfswissenschaft zur freien Wissenschaftsdisziplin', *Mitteilungen der Österreichischen Gesellschaft für Geschichte der Naturwissenschaften*, 4 (1984), 11–44; *id.*, *Das Fach Chemie an der Philosophischen Fakultät der Universität Graz* (Publikationen aus dem Archiv der Universität Graz, 17; Graz, 1985).
51. Justus Liebig, 'Über das Studium der Naturwissenschaften und über den Zustand der Chemie in Preußen' [1840], in Justus von Liebig, *Reden und Abhandlungen* (Leipzig, 1874), 7–36.
52. Rudolph Fittig, *Das Wesen und die Ziele der chemischen Forschung und des chemischen Studiums* (Leipzig, 1870), 3.
53. Rudolf Stichweh, 'Differenzierung der Wissenschaft', *Zeitschrift für Soziologie*, 8 (1979), 82–101.
54. Robert Bud and Gerrylynn K. Roberts, *Science versus Practice: Chemistry in Victorian Britain* (Manchester, 1984).

55. Paul A. Zimmermann, 'Chemie, Politik, Fortschritt: Notizen zur Entwicklung eines Industriezweiges im Europa des 19. Jahrhunderts', *Technikgeschichte,* 41 (1974), 53–67; Bud/Roberts, *Science.*

56. Richard Lorenz, *Denkschrift über den Zustand der anorganischen Chemie in Preußen und Deutschland* ([Zürich], 1898), 36.

57. Martin Guntau and Hubert Laitko (eds.), *Der Ursprung der modernen Wissenschaften: Studien zur Entstehung wissenschaftlicher Disziplinen* (Berlin, 1987).

58. Martin Guntau and Hubert Laitko, 'Entstehung und Wesen wissenschaftlicher Disziplinen', in *eid., Ursprung,* 17–89, on p. 50.

The Limits of University: The Study of Language in some British Universities and Academies 1750–1800

Yusef Azad

The years from 1750 to 1800 in Britain are years in which to investigate 'the study of language', rather than linguistics or philology. These latter two disciplines, concerned with an autonomous examination of language using a 'scientific' and historically accurate method, are a more recent solution to the question of what to learn about language. The last decades of the eighteenth century offer an alternative perspective, in which language is subsumed within other disciplines and wider interests. This paper will examine the various opportunities in this period for the study of language in higher education, the intellectual contexts in which such study took place, and the reasons and purposes given for it. A comparison of such study in the universities with that taking place in the dissenting academies reveals in two separate ways 'the limits of university'. First, the universities are hampered by a narrow curriculum and restrictive traditions in educational practice. Oxford and Cambridge fail to tackle many intellectual issues of the time and are severely criticized by contemporaries for not preparing their students for the complexities of the modern world. Second, the academies too have a 'university', this being the universality of their education, the attempt to impart a system of 'extensive knowledge' in which all studies interconnect and are interdependent. This also results in limits to scope and insight as language is discussed in the terms of a broadly Lockean philosophy of mind.

I

The study of language in British higher education of the late eighteenth century is an eloquent register of the contemporary theories

of education and its relationship to society. The tutors of the
dissenting academies are keenly aware of the power of education,
both as a social and as a moral force. The academies were free from
the restrictive traditions and statutes which still held sway in the
universities, and they exploited this freedom to experiment in new
patterns of teaching and a much wider curriculum than anything
previously offered. The academies were originally established for
the training of nonconformist ministers but they were soon educating laymen as well, usually because of their refusal to subscribe to
the Thirty Nine Articles which effectively excluded them from
university education in England. There were also some Anglicans
who went to the academies because of the low academic and moral
standards at Oxford and Cambridge. From the writings of tutors at
the academies it is clear that there were two main classes of students, those destined for 'the learned professions', such as medicine, law or the ministry, and those who were to be merchants or
engaged in industry, the 'Civil and Active Life' of Joseph Priestley's
description. The balance between these two groups varied. Warrington Academy has been described as 'providing a comprehensive liberal education for the sons of wealthy dissenters', while its
successor academy at Manchester had a majority of future businessmen and so gave 'more general educational opportunties'.[1] Subjects
studied had to be justified as useful to both of these groups.

The town of Warrington earned for itself the title 'the Athens of
the North' and many dissenters saw the academies as universities in
their own right. Priestley in a letter to the students at 'New College'
in Hackney expresses the hope that the new academy will outshine
Oxford and Cambridge.[2] An understanding of academy education
is complicated by the fact that this concern to be a dissenters'
university is only one academy self-image. It is, for instance, more
true of Warrington and Hackney than it is of Manchester Academy.
Another description of the academy's course is as a 'scheme of
agreeable transition' from the grammar school to 'the higher
regions of professional science', bringing with it 'the advantages of
cultivated understanding and improved taste'.[3] There is a broad
agreement among tutors in viewing the academy education as transitional and preparatory. This preparation had two quite distinct
ends in view, professional academic specialization and the life of
business, yet for both it is claimed that 'the attainment of knowledge in general'[4] is an essential foundation. Priestley put forward

proposals for the education of future men of commerce in *An Essay on a Course of Liberal Education for Civil and Active Life* (1760). In line with the changes he had already effected at Warrington, he argues for a fuller range of subjects so that the merchant as well as the lawyer can receive an education adequate to his future needs:

It seems to be a defect in our present system of public education, that a proper course of studies is not provided for gentlemen who are designed to fill the principal stations of active life, distinct from those which are adapted to the learned professions.[5]

The education of the man of business was seen to be of special importance. Andrew Kippis, tutor at Hackney, declares:

Here they will not only furnish themselves with a perpetual refuge against the allurements of dissipation, folly, and vice, but be capacitated for appearing with credit, if they should arise to important magistracies, or become members of the legislature.[6]

This combination of moral and political reasoning in the justification of an academy education for merchants is common in the period. Warrington printed a letter advertising the usefulness of its course of study for prospective businessmen, saying that it would 'lead them to an early acquaintance with, and just concern for, the true principles of Religion and Liberty; of which great interests, they must in future life be the supporters'.[7] The acquisition of knowledge was seen as a necessary accompaniment to the acquisition of power. The middle-classes were also encouraged in the establishment of intellectual interests by ministers concerned at how people would use or misuse the leisure that came with wealth.

In Priestley's *Essay* we find a further reason for such education. Not only does it equip the merchant for politics, religion and the use of leisure, it is also necessary for the effectiveness of business. If the merchant is to be master of his business rather than merely a clerk, he must be able to think creatively and not just take orders. He must be aware of those possibilities and alternatives which make creativity available, and these can only be provided by the 'extensive knowledge' learned at the academy. The *Essay* demands that a scheme of education be established which deals with 'topics of sensible conversation'.[8] Focussing attention on the new political and economic world of the late eighteenth century, the *Essay* recommends subjects such as French and Geography which are of some practical use, but the emphasis is again upon an extensive plan of knowledge rather than a deep investigation of specifics. This stems from an observation of the inter-related complexities of modern life, the multifaceted responsibilities of the entrepreneur.

The range of subjects available at academies in this period astonished many. In addition to the traditional subjects of divinity, logic and 'the learned languages', there was the introduction of modern languages, history, geography, chemistry, to name but a few. This variety brought adverse comment. *The Monthly Repository* was to remark in 1810: 'The grand error in almost every dissenting academy has been the attempt to teach and to learn too much'.[9] Andrew Kippis, preaching on the opening of the new academy at Hackney, makes the same point: 'It may be reckoned among the frequent errors of the present age, that too much is taught at once, the consequence of which is that scarcely anything is well taught.'[10] Yet there were plenty of reasons given for such a wide-ranging sweep of disciplines. There was a contemporary stress upon the interconnection and interdependence of all knowledge. Thus Ralph Harrison denies that any science or branch of learning is 'frivolous and unimportant' because of 'the affinity and connection between the sciences.'[11] It is this system of knowledge which has to be communicated. Thomas Barnes, Harrison's colleague at Manchester, proves that to learn theology an understanding of history is required, and he continues:

But here again the field still opens upon us. For History, as well as Revelation, demands the knowledge of languages; and these again, of Customs and of Arts, of Chronology and Manners—the stream of science still branching out into more and wider channels.[12]

This system of knowledge, in which even very different sciences are connected, demands a corresponding system of education:

Education, upon such a scale as we have now imagined, demands the aid of numerous and distant sciences; none of which can be omitted without narrowing, in some degree, a system which, to be perfect, ought to be as various, as extensive, and as full as possible.[13]

Priestley, although writing of specific scientific disciplines at this point, shows very clearly why 'System' was held to be so important:

When subjects which have a connection are explained in a regular system, every article is placed where the most light is reflected upon it from the neighbouring subjects. The plainest things are discussed in the first place, and are made to serve as axioms, and as the foundation of those which are treated of afterwards. Without this regular method of studying the elements of any science, it seems impossible ever to gain a clear and comprehensive view of it.[14]

He later asks for 'a regular systematical instruction' in those areas of contemporary concern so far neglected in education. Just as in the system of a given science clarity can only be achieved through the regularity of a geometrical method, so in the system of knowledge as a whole, no discipline can be truly understood apart from the context of the others. Only after the system becomes familiar can the professional have the necessary knowledge from which to specialize and the merchant that understanding with which to make informed decisions in politics and business. Thus education becomes a liberating activity. Any attempt to examine the study of language in academies of this period must first come to terms with this model of what many of the academies were trying to achieve. They were not demanding detailed knowledge of each subject but 'the attainment of knowledge in general', 'that more general acquaintance, for which alone we plead'.[15] There was, of course, a gap between theory and practice. Many future businessmen, despite Priestley, must have questioned the value of what they were studying, and many did not complete the course. They did leave with 'a feeling for the latest religious and intellectual ideas',[16] encouraging involvement in that world of science, literary and philosophical societies which brought coherence to middle-class culture.

The universities were less motivated to see their teaching engage with the new society. It was left to radical and heterodox tutors such as John Jebb from Peterhouse College, Cambridge, to advocate an education for students which would 'fit them for the various scenes of social life'.[17] One subject, however, which did progress in the universities, albeit at a slower rate than in the academies, was history. We will discover how closely linked the study of history was with that of language at this time. In Edinburgh Adam Ferguson, Professor of Moral Philosophy 1764–1785, began studying mankind in terms of groupings and units, charting the progress of entire societies. Joseph Priestley introduced the study of modern history at Warrington in lectures which were later recommended to students at Cambridge by John Symonds, Professor of Modern History. Behind the increasing pressure for the study of history in higher education there was a concern for the political education of the traditionally and newly powerful. Only from history can society be understood as a dynamic rather than static institution, as an entity capable of realising change and accommodating alternatives.

The study of language in British universities and academies was limited in scope. A traditional discipline in which some thinking on language would occur was logic. In the latter half of the eighteenth century the 'new logic', following Locke, was predominant. A typical and highly influential textbook was Isaac Watts' *Logick: Or, The Right Use of Reason*.[18] A good part of the book is taken up with an account of Locke's theory of ideas as found in the *Essay concerning Human Understanding*. This included material on the nature of words as set out by Locke in *Book III*. Locke traced much of the argumentation and confusion in knowledge to confusion over the nature of words. He insisted that words name ideas and from this principle warned of the imperfection of words and against their abuse. In the logics of the period language is not explored beyond the definitions of the nature of words and their resulting capacities and deficiencies as found in Locke. But this account of language as a naming of the world of ideas rather than the world of things was to have a decisive influence on the study of language in the period. One Oxford Don, Edward Bentham, in his *Reflexions upon Logick*, compares logic with grammar, claiming that 'to know the nature of words in general and their several kinds'[19] is a necessary basis for clear thought. He later continues the link between words and ideas: '. . . such is the connexion between thinking and speaking, that Logick and philosophical Grammar must often coincide'.[20] He then admits that each language has its own 'peculiarities', but these are of little interest when compared with language's epistemological significance. Hans Aarsleff summarises the difference between the study of language in the late eighteenth century and the comparative philology of the nineteenth:

. . . it is universally agreed that the decisive turn in language study occurred when the philosophical, a priori method of the eighteenth century was abandoned in favour of the historical, a posteriori method of the nineteenth. The former began with mental categories and sought their exemplification in language, as in universal grammar, and based etymologies on conjectures about the origin of language. The latter sought only facts, evidence, demonstration; it divorced the study of language from the study of mind.[21]

It was in universal, or philosophical, grammar, rather than in logic, that most of the study of language took place.

Universal grammar was taught in the academies as part of 'polite literature' or 'the Belles-Lettres'. Barnes enthuses: 'These various subjects open so many views into Human Nature, as cannot fail of delighting the mind, and improving it, in its best principles and operations.'[22] Thus the universal grammar interconnects with various related disciplines to form a course in 'human nature', again, language being studied as an index to mind. The upsurge of interest in the Belles Lettres in the academies reveals the dissolution of the formerly strong sacred-secular divide in nonconformist thought. With the higher view of Man's spiritual standing and capacities that Unitarianism introduced, there came also a confidence in the value of Man's social and secular existence as progressive and providentially regulated. The Belles Lettres, as Barnes puts it, attempted to examine and thus further improve the 'best principles and operations' of the mind. There were problems in convincing students of the relevance of the study. Mr Seddon writes to Revd Eaton about Warrington's Tutor in Languages:

The greatest difficulty Mr Aikin meets with is to render his lectures upon Universal Grammar and oratory of general use. But this is a difficulty every Professor of the Belles Lettres circumstanced as he is must meet with, and we think he obviates it in the best manner possible.[23]

There was clearly a tension between the education of the merchant as a pragmatic equipment for business life and the more theoretical concerns of the tutors to impart a general literary refinement and understanding of human intellectual and social activity. At Warrington Academy students in their first year had to attend the lectures on Universal Grammar. The heterogeneity of the Belles Lettres emerges from the list of subjects Ralph Harrison was to lecture on at Manchester every session 'namely, The Theory of Language, particularly the English; Oratory; Criticism; Composition; History; and Geography'.[24] In a similar vein, Andrew Kippis had to teach 'Ancient Geography, Mythology, Roman Antiquities, Universal Grammar, Rhetoric and Criticism, Chronology, History, and the general Principles of Law and Government, and the English Constitution'.[25]

Although mainly taught in the academies, there were at least voices calling for the introduction of universal grammar into the universities. Vicesimus Knox implies the suitability of universal grammar for academic study when he writes 'on the learning necessary to be acquired previously to an entrance at the universities':

The elements of grammar should be perfectly understood; I mean not philosophical or universal grammar, but the grammars of the English, the Greek, and the Latin languages. Universal grammar is a fine science of itself; but at schools grammar is only taught as a preliminary step to learning in general.[26]

The respectability of universal grammar as an academic subject is further evinced by questions from the fellowship examinations at Trinity College, Cambridge in 1797. Eleven grammatical questions were asked, including: 1. Is language most probably a gift of the Creator, or an effect of human institution? 2. Whence arises the diversity of languages, and in what manner was it most likely effected?[27] From these questions it is clear that universal grammar had a strong historical dimension in its inclusion of the issue of the origin and early development of languages. William Scott, Professor of Ancient History at Oxford 1773–85, is said in his introductory lecture to have 'urged the impossibility of language itself being originally acquired by human effort, and thence inferred the necessity of recurring to the theory of miraculous interposition'.[28]

Universal grammar became the focal point for debates on the relationship between language and society, the rival claims for the divine and human origin of language, the nature and progress of primitive communities. It modelled a universality of human thought and experience, a universality based not upon extensive empirical observation but upon assumed philosophical principles and the inherited grammatical tradition. Many works on or related to universal grammar were not written by professional academics but interested individuals, such as James Harris, Lord Monboddo and Horne Tooke. Joseph Priestley also published some *Lectures on the Theory of Language and Universal Grammar* (1762) and a brief examination of these will give some understanding of the scope of the subject. The *Lectures* were popular in the academies, being used elsewhere by tutors, as was the custom. In the Introduction, Priestley claims that language is a 'measure of our intellectual powers'.[29] This results in a compulsion to explain all linguistic phenomena in terms of comprehensible operations of the mind.

Priestley's organization of the lectures begins by following in subject-matter that of an elementary grammar for school. He first discusses articulation and letters, then examines in general the division of words into classes before dealing with the individual parts of speech and syntax. But the content of the lectures is strikingly different from the chapters of a school grammar. There are no detailed rules for English grammar and usage based on elementary and authoritative definitions. Instead, in a quasi-comparative manner, rules of syntax and parts of speech are held to be of universal validity and their nature is discussed in much more depth. The principles for discussion are historical and psychological. Locke in his *Essay* found difficulty in explaining 'particles' as signs of ideas. Priestley, following Locke, explains conjunctions as contractions of phrases. 'And' is short for 'I', with the same truth, affirm'.[30] 'Wisely' replaces 'in a wise manner' since 'Adverbs are also contractions of other words, or rather clusters of words'.[31] But like Locke, he stumbles over prepositions, saying they represnt 'other affects or relations'[32] of ideas, though quite what these are he does not explain in detail. In the lectures there is an attempt to find the order and progress of human reason in the phenomenon of language.

Not only must Priestley relate each word to clear ideas in the mind, there is also the historical dimension. Priestley writes a conjectural history of the beginnings of language which acts as a justification for the division of words into classes. The classes are attached to different and successive operations of the mind, separated from each other by an undisclosed period of time. He thus charts the origin of concrete nouns, abstract nouns, adjectives and verbs before his pseudo-history breaks down and particles have to be explained in a purely theoretical way. Condillac is credited with causing the late eighteenth century's concern with etymology and the origin of language. For Condillac language and thought are interdependent; one cannot progress without the other. Thus the origin of language is also the origin of thought, and so crucial to an understanding of the distinctively human faculty of reason and reflection. A further reason for this procedure in the *Lectures* is Priestley's remark: 'Now the method of learning and using a language that is formed must be analogous to the method of its formation at first'.[33] To explore the nature of language via its (hypothesized) history is to learn and understand effectively because it produces a precise knowledge of the relationship between part of speech and act of mind.

Priestley's *Lectures* also afford a clear example of the frequently made link between universal grammar and the history of society. Given the universal grammar and single origin of all languages, their present diversity has also to be explained. Language, he claims, does not develop in a vacuum but according to the needs of usage. As people come across more and more of the world about them or are forced by circumstances 'to have recourse to the improvements of art',[34] the language changes to meet that new and particular situation. This imposes upon language a historical development identical to that of society. 'The progress of human life in general is from poverty to riches, and from riches to luxury, and ruin.'[35] Languages with great expressive capacity emerge from democracy, but with the decline of that liberty '. . . persons addicted to letters having no occasion for the ancient manly and free eloquence, fell, through an affectation of novelty, into a number of trifling and puerile refinements of style'.[36] Decline is described in terms of the withdrawal of language from external, socially committed reference. Language is thus examined by Priestley both as a product of universal human reflection and as a product of society. Language as the product of the human mind results in Priestley's conjectural history of the formation of the parts of speech. Language as the product of society results in his final lectures on such topics as the regular growth and corruption of languages, the complex structure of Latin and Greek, revolutions in languages, and the origins and uses of linguistic diversity. Though most of Priestley's history is speculative, his stress upon language as a social phenomenon is important. He makes eloquently explicit the place the study of language held for so many as a means of insight into the social and psychological life of Man.

In *The Rudiments of English Grammar* (1761) Priestley discusses articles in *Section II. Of Nouns* but writes in a note, 'In universal grammar they should be considered as belonging to the class of adjectives'.[37] This exemplifies a frequently encountered contrast between the universal grammar of the academy and the grammar of the classroom, the latter being subject to pragmatic and communicative constraints. It is, however, in *The Rudiments of English Grammar* that Priestley's most original comments on language are found. It is here that he questions the absolute value of word-class divisions and insists that English has only two tenses through his exclusive use of formal criteria. For school, Priestley had the task of clearly communicating rules. This freed him somewhat from that theoretical tradition which combined Locke with classical grammar. Instead, he could examine formal criteria freshly and come to independent conclusions. Despite its seemingly historical framework, universal grammar was speculative rather than investigative, more often a hindrance than a spur to genuine discovery.

The invention of history in the study of language should also be noted in two works both of which were extremely popular in this period. One is Horne Tooke's *Diversions of Purley* (1798 and 1805), and the other Hugh Blair's *Lectures on Rhetoric and Belles Lettres* (1780). Blair was Professor of the newly created chair of Rhetoric and Belles Lettres at Edinburgh from 1762 to 1784. In two of these lectures Blair summarises the commonplace themes of universal grammar, again in a historical framework. It was clearly felt that 'Rhetoric and Belles Lettres' had to include some instruction in universal grammar. Blair borrows thoughts from many writers, including Harris and Monboddo. Prior to the foundation of Blair's professorship, rhetoric was taught by John Stevenson, the Professor of Logic. This move of rhetoric from the domain of logic to that of polite literature is another evidence of the new interest in linguistic and literary studies and their connection with mind and culture. Horne Tooke constructed a largely imaginary etymology of English particles to prove after Locke that all words are names of sensible ideas. This accounted for those parts of speech which Locke found it so difficult to explain and which contemporary thinkers were describing as metaphysical operations of the mind. Tooke declared that he had discovered this truth by a priori reasoning, etymological evidence only coming much later and not being necessary to prove the argument. Again we find in the study of language the coincidence of conjectural history and the defence of traditional theories of the human mind and their relation to language. Tooke was not, of course, an orthodox disciple of Locke but his rewriting of Locke's philosophy was performed with a consistent application of Locke's central principle. Though Tooke's etymologies now appear absurd, at the time they were hailed as revelatory and certainly taken very seriously in the academic world. Dugald Stewart, substituting for Adam Ferguson, was lecturing at

Edinburgh on Tooke's *Letter to Mr Dunning* as early as 1778–1779, almost immediately after its publication.[38] It was, however, to be Dugald Stewart who in the early decades of the nineteenth century 'divorced philosophy from the study of language and thus helped prepare the ground for philology proper as an autonomous discipline'.[39]

In addition to universal grammar, the English language was studied and debated in the period. The demand for greater study of English was a familiar note in the eighteenth century. The academies began teaching in English rather than in Latin some decades before the universities, with Doddridge's Northampton Academy (1729–52) being the main influence. The tutors were often forced to write their own textbooks to supply the want of relevant material in English. English grammar was taught to younger students in the academies, though it was neglected in the universities. For the most part, as we shall see later, grammar was expected to be learned at school, but many of the academies considered it to be so important as to have lectures devoted to it. At Warrington in 1762 the Report reads, 'The English Grammar is taught to the younger students, and they are trained up in a regular course of English composition'.[40] At Manchester Ralph Harrison is advertised as lecturing on 'the Theory of Language, particularly the English'.[41] This was, perhaps, an attempt to smuggle in some teaching on English grammar aboard the respectable ship 'Theory of Language'. Especially popular among grammars used at academies are those of Robert Lowth and John Ash.[42]

Much study of the English language was concentrated on the growing interest in oratory and elocution. As early as 1712 Richard Steele had complained in *The Spectator* that the universities were 'dumb in the study of eloquence'. The academies, however, were concerned with oratory from early in the century because of the great importance attached to preaching in nonconformist churches. Isaac Watts and Phillip Doddridge both emphasized the importance of delivery, and Doddridge's *Lectures on Preaching* became a standard textbook throughout the century. The Warrington Report for July 10th 1760 promises that:

Constant Attention will be held to their pronouncing the English Language well, both in speaking and reading; this will be done particularly in the Lectures on Oratory and Grammar, in which the Tutor will frequently direct them to read before him; and all their exercises will be performed publicly before the whole Academy.[43]

In 1772 we read of Mr Enfield teaching 'Elocution and Composition'.[44] At both Daventry and Warrington lectures on oratory were heard and when Priestley was appointed Tutor in Languages at Warrington elocution exercises were begun at his suggestion. This widespread concern for English pronunciation and delivery might well have received added impetus from the publication of Thomas Sheridan's *British Education* (1756) which was 'A design to revive the long lost art of oratory, and to correct, ascertain, and fix the English language'.[45] Although many disagreed with Sheridan's suggestions as to what 'the long lost art of oratory' actually was, his connection between the improvement of oratory and improvement in the English language was widely held. Through the teaching of oratory, pronunciation would be standardized and knowledge effectively communicated. He emphasized that the spoken language had as great a need to be 'correct' as the written language. The British Constitution depended upon the Christian religion which would only be preserved if preaching clearly communicated truth to ordinary people. Behind these various lectures and courses in oratory there was a concern to see 'correctness' come to a spoken English which would then be of greater political and religious power in the world.

There were attempts to introduce oratory to the universities. Hely-Hutchinson, Provost of Trinity College, Dublin, encouraged composition and elocution with prizes and exams. In *Free Thoughts upon University Education; occasioned by the Present Debates at Cambridge* (London, 1751) the author writes:

It will be of use likewise [for the students] to desire their own thoughts upon a subject, and that, generally speaking, in their own language. By this means, the genius will be less cramped, and the justness or impropriety of their sentiments the easier discerned. Great pity it is, that the study of that language should be neglected, of which we shall constantly stand in need in our daily converse and concerns; in which causes at our Courts of Judicature are pleaded and determined, the true interests of our country inquired into, and thoroughly discussed in our two august assemblies . . .[46]

He mentions with approval recently considered plans at Pembroke-Hall for the appointment of four fellows to teach English composition, pronunciation and oratory. John Jebb attempted to get elocution included in the curriculum, to which an anonymous reply protested that this was unnecessary, since there already existed 'Latin and English declamations' which afforded 'opportunities of

shining in classical and historical knowledge, and the more requisite
qualifications of speaking and writing the English language.'[47] Vice-
simums Knox arguing for reform at Oxford suggests: 'That a public
school of elocution should be established; that the best speakers
should be appointed by the convocation to preside in it in rotation,
and for a liberal salary'.[48] Knox notes the nonconformist zeal in
oratory with regret, writing of the number of:

. . . sectaries, and persons irregularly educated, who spare no endeavours
to acquire that forcible and serious kind of delivery, which powerfully
affects the devout mind. The consequence is natural, though lamentable.
Tabernacles are crowded, and churches deserted.[49]

We can thus see greater emphasis being placed in these decades on
English as a living, spoken language. The English language was to
be studied as a necessary tool for effectiveness and influence in
society.

II

The study of particular foreign languages in this period also reveals
the predominance of pragmatic, social and philosophical concerns
rather than a linguistic interest. The teaching of a foreign language
invariably proclaims itself as the means towards some better end.
Greek and Latin were the prime educational diet of Oxford and
most of the academies. Cambridge, however, concentrated to a
significant extent on Mathematics and Science.[50] John Jebb argued
for change at Cambridge in *Remarks upon the Present Mode of
Education in the University of Cambridge to which is added a
Proposal for its Improvement* (Cambridge, 1773): '. . . surely the
study of mathematics, and of Nature's operations, should not intir-
ely engross the youthful mind. Enquiry into metaphysical, and
moral truth, is accompanied with numerous advantages'.[51] He
stresses the importance of 'the finished compositions of Greece and
Rome' but complains, 'Classical Merit is altogether disregarded'.[52]
Some of the academies, such as Northampton and Daventry, also
paid little regard to the classical languages, but for the most part
considerable skill was expected in these tongues. Greek was of
particular importance in ministerial training as the language of the
New Testament, but most commonly Greek and Latin were both
praised for the 'metaphysical, and moral truth' their literatures

contained. In higher education, the grammatical aspect of classical education was of little interest compared with the literary and the cultivation of the skills of translation and oration. Priestley complains in the *Essay* that there is a general neglect of classical grammar in the schools which means most boys are ill prepared for university.[53] Grammar was the particular province of the school. Warrington Academy felt the tension caused by the need to maintain its claims to a university standard of education but also the clear need of many of its students to be instructed in the basics of grammar. The Rector, Mr Seddon, writes to the Revd Dr Eaton about Mr Aikin, the Tutor in Languages. Aiken '. . . not only reads and comments upon the best Greek and Latin writers to the young gentlemen himself, but obliges them to read to him in both languages every day, condescending where necessary almost to the pains of a schoolmaster'.[54]

Though praiseworthy, this dedication was clearly meeting a very unsatisfactory situation. At the next meeting of the academy's committee Seddon notes:

There were two or three more recommended to the Society as intended for the Ministry; but upon examining them they appeared a little deficient in Grammar Learning, on which account their friends keep them to school, another year, and they remain upon the list till the next general meeting.[55]

In 1762 another possible student was rejected because he was 'rather too young and does not seem to have made sufficient progress in his Grammar Learning'.[56] The previous year the committee had stipulated that no young gentlemen were to be admitted to the Academy under the age of fourteen. There was evidently a worry that unless standards were rigorously maintained the Academy would turn into merely another school teaching the rules of grammar. Another solution was attempted. In the minutes for 26 June 1766 we read:

Agreed unanimously upon a full and mature consideration of the question, that the provision of a grammar school for the elements of the learned languages, in this Academy hath not, from the experience of the last two years, been attended with those advantages which were hoped from it: that for the future it be discontinued . . .[57]

It seems that this attempt to meet the need for elementary grammar teaching had not resulted in any significant improvement in the

learning of those studying there. Academies differed in the extent
to which they were prepared to offer the simple grammar instruction of a school, but certainly the more established and prestigious
academies attempted to maintain distinctions. The Greek and Latin
languages were taught, but at a higher level than mere rote learning. In the advertisement of 1788 for the new Hackney Academy we
are told that Hugh Worthington was to 'deliver lectures on the
Structure of the Greek Language'.[58] The main emphasis, however,
was on the leaving of the grammar of a language as assumed
knowledge and concentrating on greater things when studying at an
academy. A Report from Warrington speaks of the student fresh
from school who had studied 'the Languages, which are the great
Foundation for all future Improvement; in which tis supposed he
will now appear more as a Critick; and from the meer Study of
Words, go on to the Beauties and Art of Composition . . .'[59].
Thomas Barnes argues:

It is surely desirable, that he shall now rise, from Words to Things, from
Language to Sentiment. All that he has yet been doing, is only preparatory
to real knowledge. Language of itself, is but a scaffolding to science.[60]

Few quotations so reveal the confines of the study of language in the
late eighteenth century. Barnes places language outside the boundaries of 'real knowledge', relegating it to a necessary skill to be
learned at school. Language communicates knowledge but does not
contain it.

In Oxford the state of affairs was no better. Henry Fynes-Clinton
entered Christ Church in 1799 and was later to complain that he
'never received a single syllable of instruction concerning Greek
accents, or Greek metres, or the idiom of Greek sentences; in short
no information upon *any one point* of Grammar, or Syntax, or
Metre. These subjects were never named to me'.[61] Even allowing
for over-statement, M. L. Carke has described this education as 'a
scholarship which was content with an empirical knowledge of the
ancient languages' but which 'did not encourage a more profound
and critical study'.[62] There were college exercises in which students
continued to construe Greek and Latin texts, as they had done at
school, but there seems to have been little if any formal instruction
in the grammar of these languages. The intelligent student would
have to read and think for himself if he wanted to pursue grammatical questions for their own sake.

The lectures in the classics at the academies exemplify some of the educational ideas discussed at the beginning of this paper. Ralph Harrison was appointed 'Professor of the Greek and Latin Languages, and of Polite Literature' at Manchester Academy in 1786. We are told that Harrison when lecturing on the classics 'will illustrate his lectures with observations on the History, Mythology, Manners and Philosophy of the Ancients'.[63] The teaching of languages takes its place in a web of intellectual interest which centre upon national distinctives placed in a cultural, social and historical context. The foreign language becomes a window through which political truth can shine. By a nice irony, it was this same interest in national history and distinctiveness that was in the early nineteenth century to have such an influence upon the development of comparative philology. The same preoccupations are found in the study of oriental languages. William Jones spent most of his time studying at Oxford in the acquisition of oriental languages. One fruit of this work was his *Grammar of the Persian Language* (London, 1771). He admits in its preface that many will not have the time to learn Persian:

. . . but the civil and natural history of such mighty empires as India, Persia, Arabia, and Tartary cannot fail of delighting those who love to view the great picture of the universe, or to learn by what degrees the most obscure states have risen to glory, and the most flourishing kingdoms have sunk to decay: the philosopher will consider those works as highly valuable by which he may trace the human mind in all its appearances, from the rudest to the most cultivated state: and the man of taste will undoubtedly be pleased to unlock the stores of native genius, and to gather the flowers of unrestrained and luxuriant fancy.[64]

Shortly before the Grammar, Warren Hastings printed *A Proposal for Establishing a Professorship of the Persian Language in the University of Oxford:*

It is not unreasonable to suppose that the powers of the mind are distributed in equal perfection to the whole race of mankind, however, differently cultivated and variously applied: and even from that difference in their improvements, and from that variety in their pursuits, a powerful argument may be drawn of the advantages which might be derived to every branch of knowledge, from an acquaintance with the manners, customs, and practice of the most remote nations.[65]

Jones's account is the more fanciful and traditional. He sees mankind on a straight road from 'rudeness' to 'cultivation' with cultures at different stages along this route. The exotic languages reveal 'the human mind in all its appearances' and implicitly corroborate this hierarchical and European-centred vision of cultural advance. Hastings avoids such value-judgements and talks in terms of variation rather than hierarchy. Yet what is of particular interest to Hastings is not the difference which oriental languages reveal but rather the sameness in difference, the way a comparison of the cultures and languages of different nations will uncover analogies and similarites. These in turn will lead us to the origin of humanity. Both Jones and Hastings claim that it is through the learning of an oriental language that access can be gained to distant nations and thus human nature can be better understood, be it in terms of origin or destiny. Neither consider that such new knowledge will question or undermine their preconceived notions of human nature and its history.

Both also admit other reasons for the study of Persian, following the by now familiar pattern of mixing academic and pragmatic arguments. Jones writes that 'interest was the charm, which gave the languages of the East a real and solid importance'.[66] He is referring to the political and economic involvement of Britain in India, where Persian was the language of government. The learning of Persian received great impetus from this consideration. Hastings argues:

The Persian Tongue, whether considered as introductory to new discoveries in literature, or even as an object of national concern in its tendency to promote the interests which this country has lately acquired in the political, as well as the commercial affairs of Indostan; may be deemed of sufficient importance to justify an attempt to introduce the study of it into our Seminaries of Learning.[67]

Hastings goes on to argue how much more efficient it would be if people bound for India learned Persian well at Oxford rather than fumblingly when out there. The Professor of Persian would have an assistant who would have to be a native of Persia or India so as to know 'the true idiom, or the exact pronunciation'.[68] Use would be made of 'a large collection of manuscripts in the Persic language in the University of Oxford'.[69] Although both Dr Johnson and the Chancellor of the University approved of the project, the proposal was ignored into oblivion.

In the universities of this period such study of oriental languages as took place would be largely self-motivated. Dr Somerville writes of his Hebrew class at Edinburgh that, 'when I was a student of divinity Hebrew was little cultivated, or altogether omitted, by the greater number of the theological students'.[70] At Cambridge, as Christopher Wordsworth calmly puts it, 'The Hebrew Professors do not appear to have produced much'.[71] The Professors of Arabic at Oxford argued for the usefulness of the language on similar grounds of intellectual interest as those quoted earlier for Persian. Arabic was also of interest as an explicator of some of the problems in Hebrew. This comparative approach to semitic studies in Oxford aroused controversy and shows the strength of conservative and mystical ideas about language well into the eighteenth century. The followers of the theologian and philosopher John Hutchinson (1674–1737) proclaimed the corrupt artificiality of Arabic when compared with the purity of Hebrew. In 1754 B. Holloway published *The Primaevity and Preeminence of the Sacred Hebrew . . . vindicated from the repeated attempts of the Reverend Dr Hunt to level it with the Arabic, and other dialects.* The next year, the anonymous author of *Four Letters concerning the Study of the Hebrew Scriptures* insisted that Hebrew 'is uniform, as built upon one and the same principle, and becomes hereby explicative of itself'.[72] He was appalled, then, to learn from his fictitious correspondent 'that the knowledge of the Arabic is generally at Oxford thought absolutely necessary towards the explication of the Hebrew Scriptures'.[73] Following Hutchinson he proceeded to attack strongly such an opinion. The ripples of this controversy were still being felt many years later. In 1782 John James wanted to attend Hebrew lectures and:

. . . waited upon my tutor, whose opinions on many things of this nature are not the most liberal. He granted, however, his certificate, but not without marks of indifference, and some observations on the disrepute into which he said the study of the language had been brought by the extravagancies of some Hutchinsonian divines of this University.[74]

In the academies, however, the teaching of Hebrew flourished and there were a number of tutors exceptionally skilled in many of the oriental languages. Again, reason for this can be found in the dissenters' stress on doctrine being formulated from a careful and impartial examination of the text.

There was little formal teaching of modern languages in the universities and academies of this period. In Oxford and Cambridge

Professorships of Modern History had been established in 1724. The Professor was to be paid £400 per annum from which he had to pay two assistants to teach the modern languages. Also instituted at this time were the King's Scholarships, with which twenty young men both in Oxford and in Cambridge were to be taught modern history and modern languages free of charge. They were to be equipped in this way for the service of the state at home or abroad. There seems to have been no interest in French, German, Italian and Spanish as objects of purely linguistic study and research. Instead, they were useful assets for the politician and merchant involved in European affairs and for the gentleman with the refinement and leisure to read foreign literature. The Professor of History had only to give four lectures a year, his main task being the oversight of the modern language teachers. Modern languages was certainly the more important of the two disciplines and both Bishop Gibson in his plan for the professorship and Lord Townsend in writing to the universities stress this aspect of the new chair. Soon, however, patronage replaced excellence as the criterion in the choice of scholars and this resulted in their decline into sinecures and a consequent decline in the teaching of modern languages. There were attempts to revive the professorship and its duties but they met with little success. Interested students had to seek private tuition. John James, while an undergraduate at Queen's College, Oxford, writes to his father on 21 November 1778:

I begin with French the week after next. There is only one master. Chamberlain, very clever, and a native of France. He gives twelve lectures for one guinea, and I shall have the very serious advantage of conversing with him in French as long as I stay here.[75]

In fact, James was to discover that Chamberlain was not able to take on any more pupils and that, in any case, James did not have the time to include this advantageous but extra-curricular activity in his more regular course of study. While modern language teaching was clearly available in Oxford in the late eighteenth century, the fact that at this time there was only one French master, albeit busy, suggests it was not in very great demand.

The place of modern languages was a matter for debate at Cambridge. During the middle decades of the century the Professor of Modern History was Shallet Turner who did nothing in this capacity nor lived in Cambridge. In 1751, the author of *Free*

Thoughts upon University Education appeals for the Professor to reside and lecture in the University with his Assistants. Similar reasons for the teaching of modern languages are adduced as those noted above for the classical and oriental languages:

If our Young Nobility and Gentry were well versed in History and Chronology; if they were tolerable Masters of French and Italian, and had clear notions of the several forms of government, particularly that of our own country; if such a foundation were once laid, how easy would it be to raise a superstructure the most noble and magnificent.[76]

Languages are of interest as the communicators of historical and political phenomena. They enable us to travel and to read more widely, to come to terms with other nations and so advance in political sensitivity and wisdom. The writer believes that such a course of study will in its interest and usefulness engage the students' attention and reduce misbehaviour. The proposals had no effect, however, and it is clear that other voices seriously questioned the value of modern languages. In *Considerations on the Oaths* (1788) the author complains that in 1782 the Syndics of the Press had spent £500 on printing a facsimile of the Beza manuscript and some 'Italian Sonnets'.[77]

At Trinity College, Dublin, however, the Provost did establish a Professorship of French and German in 1775 and one of Italian and Spanish in 1776. These, he claims, '. . . will be a great saving to this country, will be the means of enabling young gentlemen of fortune to finish their education at home, and will send them abroad more capable of receiving improvement from their travels, when they are acquainted with the languages of the countries which they visit.'[78] The teaching of modern languages would also better equip those students who in later life would spend time as private tutors. These Professors were in fact little more than licensed crammers and modern languages did not become part of the curriculum until the 1870's. It does not seem that the appointment of these new professors had a great impact on the intellectual life of the college. F. M. Higman examines the records of the college library and comments, '. . . it must be said that the appointment of professors of modern languages does not appear to have stimulated any systematic book buying; rather the contrary'.[79] Dublin was also the scene of much hostility to the new proposals though it is difficult to distinguish genuine disapproval of the proposals from intense dislike of the Provost. A volume entitled *Pranceriana* appeared in 1775 which mercilessly satirized the Provost and his schemes and this was to be followed by further volumes. A typical note is struck in *Pranceriana Poetica* with some lines from *Harlequin Prancer*:

> Nor can Prancer be ever rewarded too much,
> For his skill in Italian, French, Spanish, and Dutch;
> As no other P[rovo]st before him was able
> To hold a Discourse with the Workmen of Babel;
> In all other tongues he cou'd chatter a Week,
> Provided they touch'd not on Latin and Greek.[80]

The verse insinuates that a concern for the modern languages can only emerge from a shameful ignorance of the classics. The fact that the Provost introduced with the languages, fencing and riding gave ammunition to the satirists in their claims that Trinity College, Dublin was turning from true learning to trivial pursuits.

The teaching of modern languages in the academies was not greatly superior to that of the universities. Most academies had no formal modern languages teaching. At Daventry (1752–89) French was an optional part of the instituted course but not, it seems, very popular. Elsewhere, modern languages were very often ignored altogether, though there is a greater emphasis upon them as the century draws to a close. Some of the reason for this must be the upsurge of interest in the Belles Lettres in the latter half of the century. An advertisement published in 1788 for the *New Academical Institution* in Hackney says: '. . . that the situation of the Institution affords opportunity of obtaining the best means of instruction in French and the other Modern Languages, Drawing, & c. at a separate expense'.[81] A very similar statement is made by the supporters of Manchester Academy in 1786—'able Masters in French, Italian, Music, Writing, Drawing and Merchant Accompts, are settled in the town'.[82] This does not mean that French and Drawing were considered on a par academically. Music, Drawing and the like are described as 'subordinate attainments'[83] when compared with the modern languages. Nevertheless, the languages are considered an extra refinement, entirely optional, for the teaching of which external tutors would have to be hired 'upon the usual terms'.

One reason why both Manchester and Hackney academies would emphasize the advantage of conveniently situated masters in modern languages was that they were both designed to fill the gap left by the closing of the Warrington Academy. Warrington was unique in places of higher education at this time in the importance placed upon the modern languages. French was a part of the regular course of instruction in all three years and Italian was also taught. Warrington examined its students with 'public academical exercises' which included a translation from Greek, Latin or French, and an oration or dissertation alternatively in English, Latin or French. An insight into the way in which French was taught is found in Seddon's letter to Eaton about Aikin:

In the French language he has two classes, one for those who have made some progress, and the other for such as are but just initiated, and both these classes are obliged to read and construe French every day.[84]

A few years later Warrington was employing a native German as tutor, John Reinhold Forster, and describing his appointment as one of the 'improvements'[85] to the Academy. In 1769, after Forster's resignation, Fantin La Tour, a Frenchman, was appointed tutor, with the proviso that he should only teach pupils of the academy. The minutes tersely note that Forster's teaching of private pupils 'was found inconvenient'.[86] Evidently Forster was still acting in part as the private 'master of foreign languages' in the town and the academy's concern to end this practice is a sign of their elevation of modern languages to an equal status with that of the other academic disciplines.

It seems in academies at large the teaching of French, Italian and German often left much to be desired, especially in pronunciation. H. McLachlan quotes one example—'At Kibworth the tutor required his pupils to read it "without regarding the pronunciation" which he did not know'.[87] This would suggest the inclusion of these languages merely to enable students to broaden their reading rather than speak the language. Such a context would explain the repeated emphases given by Warrington concerning the pronunciation of their tutors. Forster speaks 'fluently and with a proper accent'[88] and of Aikin the minutes record:

That with respect to French in particular, he not only writes but speaks and pronounces it well; having had the advantage of living many months in a French family, where that language was constantly used.[89]

It is clear that such competence was not be assumed.

There was a deliberately reforming concern in this unusual

emphasis at Warrington. In 1757 Seddon writes to Samuel Dyer to accept the post of Tutor in the Languages and polite literature '. . . to review that branch of learning, which has been so strangely neglected, and especially amongst the Dissenters . . .'.[90] French was part of 'polite literature' or 'Belles Lettres', a concept examined earlier. In Seddon's remarks to Dyer we can hear the regret of the liberal dissenters at the more 'narrow' evangelical concerns of their forefathers, a desire for the dissenting middle-classes to hold their own in polite society. Such an attitude was not confined to liberals; the evangelical John Newton in *A Plan of Academical Preparation for the Ministry* (1782) while denying any great intrinsic value to the Belles Lettres (in this being very much at odds with such men as Kippis, Barnes, Harrison, and Priestley), nevertheless admits the social argument: '. . . in such an age as ours, it is of some disadvantage to a man in public life, if he is quite a stranger to them. To a Tutor they are in a manner necessary'.[91] Joseph Priestley argues that the man in civil and active life 'should understand French very well'[92] but it is Vicesimus Knox, when arguing for the teaching of French in school, who in fact most clearly expresses the double motivation for the teaching of French at Warrington: 'I need not use argument in recommending the study of French and geography to the intended merchant. Their obvious utility is universally understood'.[93]

and then in the next section: 'The French language abounds with authors elegant, lively, learned, and classical. A scholar cannot, in this age, dispense with it.'[94]

These two quotations refer to the man of business who needs French for commerce and the gentleman, quite probably moving into a 'learned profession', who has to be at ease in polite society. The two categories are fluid. The merchant could transcend his origin and be educated to take a place in that society to which his wealth raises him. His commercial activities, if successful, produce leisure in which taste and intellect can be cultivated. Warrington realized how French suited so well the educational needs of both classes of students who attended the academy. Vicesimus Knox went on to argue that the teaching of modern languages should not be confined to school but extended to university, in particular Oxford:

. . . the professor of modern languages should employ one foreign assistant at least, in each language, to teach such pupils as should be recommended by the senior tutor in each college, the language of his country . . .[95]

In the Bodleian Library's copy of the *Letter* in which this proposal comes, the first word in the above quotation has been crossed out and 'A' deliberately penned into the margin. Perhaps nothing could so concisely express the confusion which had descended upon much of Oxford education in the late eighteenth century.

A final issue to be examined from the study of language 1750 to 1800 is the relationship between universal grammar and the grammars of particular languages. Joseph Priestley in *Lecture XIX* of his course on *the Theory of Language and Universal Grammar* discusses advantages that accrue from the diversity of languages in the world. One of them is that in the comparison of languages the nature and rationale of language is better understood. A universal language would have afforded no 'greater principles' by which to use that language with greater precision.[96] An anonymous annotator to this lecture, who studied at Hackney, summarises helpfully, '. . . unless we be acquainted with several languages, we cannot entirely comprehend universal grammar'.[97] This is the point being made in *Free Thoughts upon University Education* when the author writes of 'the knowledge of modern languages, without which there is no understanding our own to any degree of perfection'.[98] The comparison of languages produces those universal principles of grammar which are then reapplied to the individual languages, bringing to light 'superfluities' and 'defects', and thus revealing how the language can be improved. By contrast, in school, universal grammar is not proven from comparison but taught through the grammatical rules of one language. Robert Lowth comments:

Universal Grammar cannot be taught abstractedly: it must be done with reference to some language already known; in which the terms are to be explained, and the rules exemplified.[99]

He argues that English is the language through which universal grammar should be taught, as does the author of *An Essay upon Education* (1755): '. . . an English Grammar might be a proper Introduction to other Languages: For the general Principles of all are the same . . .'.[100] This latter work goes on to suggest that the grammars of other languages, instead of each being learned separately, should only be learned in those areas where they deviate from the norm set by English. Vicesimus Knox argues similarly but for him the base grammar is Latin rather than English. Whereas many disliked the teaching of Latin to the very young because of its difficulty, it was this same fact which convinced Knox that Latin should be taught from an early age since it is then that their minds are most receptive to the labour of rote learning.[101] These various attitudes show the great divide between how school and how university or academy education were conceived. The school begins where the academy finishes, teaching the grammar of just one language and so communicating those universal rules to be applied to other languages. It thus reverses the process of the academy, where various languages are compared to learn universal grammar which is then applied to a particular language. In the academy we have an education of discovery while in the school we are concerned with the efficient communication of conclusions. The contrast is, of course, more in the realm of theory than practice. The teaching of universal grammar in the academies was in fact very far from being comparative, inheriting instead the universal rules of previous generations.

This paper has only touched upon many issues that require a far more detailed examination; the study of language in the Scottish universities and universities on the continent; the influence of European thought upon British study and teaching methods; the relationship between the study pursued in universities and academies, and that done by private individuals.[102] Much more work can be done on the kinds of grammar taught and their dependence on theories of mind and of education. In attempting an overall perspective of the period's aims and motivations in the study of language, we have uncovered a complex structure of theoretical and practical concerns, of political, commercial and psychological interests. The theory of language was prized as revealing the universally human. The practice of language was coveted to further the binding of men together in economic and social organization. These aims stimulated some valuable thought upon the role of language in society but they also imposed limits on how language was viewed. Differences and irregularities were forgotten in the light of similarities and analogies. It was, however, the stress upon language as central to national and social life which in Europe paved the way for the more scientific, comparative and historical work of the next century.

Merton College
Oxford

REFERENCES

1. D. Wykes, *Sons and Subscribers: Lay Support and the College 1786–1840* in B. Smith (ed.), *Truth, Liberty, Religion* (Oxford, 1986) 62.
2. J. Rutt (ed.), *The Life and Correspondence of Joseph Priestley* 2 vols. (London, 1832) ii. 159.
3. T. Barnes, *A Dicourse delivered at the Commencement of Manchester Academy* (n.p, 1786) 20–21.
4. R. Harrison, *A Sermon preached at the Dissenting Chapel in Cross Street . . . On the Occasion of the Establishment of an Academy in that Town* (Warrington, 1786) 9.
5. J. Priestley, *An Essay on a Course of Liberal Education for Civil and Active Life* (Bath, 1778) 185.
6. A. Kippis, *A Sermon preached at the Old Jewry . . . on occasion of a New Academical Institution* (n.p, 1786) 17.
7. The letter can be found pasted into the first volume of the Warrington Academy's Minutes Books. The Minutes Books are in the library of Manchester College, Oxford.
8. Priestley, *Essay* 212.
9. *The Monthly Repository* Vol. V. (1819) 560.
10. Kippis, *Sermon* 19.
11. Harrison, *Sermon* 9.
12. Barnes, *Discourse* 14.
13. *Ibid.* 15.
14. Priestley, *Essay* 203.
15. Barnes, *Discourse* 16.
16. Wykes, *Sons and Subscribers* 53.
17. J. Jebb, *Remarks upon the Present Mode of Education in the University of Cambridge* (Cambridge, 1773) 1.
18. I. Watts, *Logick: Or The Right Use of Reason* (London, 1725). Watts' *Logick* was immensely popular in the eighteenth century. By 1768 it had reached a fourteenth edition.
19. E. Bentham, *Reflexions upon Logick* (Oxford, 1755) 16.
20. *Ibid.* 24.
21. H. Aarsleff, *The Study of Language in England 1780–1860* (Princeton, 1967) 127.

22. T. Barnes, *Proposals for Establishing in Manchester a Plan of Liberal Education for Young Men designed for Civil and Active Life* (Warrington, 1783) 3.
23. *Warrington Academy Minutes*. Vol I. 90.
24. *Manchester Academy Instituted February XXII, 1786. Appendix II.* (1786) 8.
25. *New Academical Institution London 24 June 1788.* 1.
26. V. Knox, *Liberal Education: or, A Practical Treatise on the Methods of Acquiring Useful and Polite Learning* 2 vols. (London, 1788) ii. 262.
27. C. Wordsworth, *Scholae Academicae: Studies at the English Universities in the Eighteenth Century* (Cambridge, 1877) 349.
28. An editorial note to J. Priestley, *A Course of Lectures on the Theory of Language and Universal Grammar* in J. Rutt (ed.) *Works of Joseph Priestley* (London, 1824) Vol. XXIII. 133.
29. Priestley, *Lectures* 125.
30. *Ibid.* 150.
31. *Ibid.* 150.
32. *Ibid.* 149.
33. *Ibid.* 185.
34. *Ibid.* 191.
35. *Ibid.* 193.
36. *Ibid.* 194.
37. J. Priestley, *The Rudiments of English Grammar* (London, 1761) 6 note g.
38. Aarsleff, *The Study of Language in England 1780–1860* 102.
   John Horne Tooke (1736–1812) gained fame in his day both as a radical, if eccentric, political agitator, and also as a writer on the nature of language. His thoughts on language were much more influential than his political opinions, yet for Tooke politics and language were very much interconnected. This is made clear in his *Letter to Mr Dunning* (1778), published while Tooke was in prison for a political offence. In this work, Tooke links the judge's unjust treatment of his case with widespread misconceptions as to the nature of language. Though it appeared eight years before the first volume of *The Diversions of Purley*, it contains the essential of Tooke's linguistic theory.
39. Aarsleff, 102.
40. *Report on the State of the Academy at Warrington 1762* 3.
41. *Manchester Academy Instituted. Appendix II* 8.
42. Robert Lowth (1710–1807), Bishop of London, was a celebrated critic of Hebrew poetry. With the publication of *A Short Introduction to English Grammar* (London, 1762) he also produced the eighteenth century's most popular and influential English Grammar. Its influence was extended through imitators such as Lindley Murray. By the end of the century, Lowth's *Grammar* alone had gone through at least

forty eight different editions. John Ash (1724–1779), minister at Pershore, first published his *Grammatical Institutes* in 1760, but in 1768 entitled it *The Easiest Introduction to Dr Lowth's English Grammar.*

43. *Report on the State of the Academy at Warrington 1760* 3.
44. *Report on the State of the Academy at Warrington 1772* 1.
45. T. Sheridan, *British Education: Or, The Source of the Disorders of Great Britain* (London, 1756) vi.
46. *Free Thoughts upon University Education* (London, 1751) 31.
47. *A Letter to the Author of the Proposal for the Establishment of Public Examination* (Cambridge, 1774) 9.
48. V. Knox, *A Letter to the Right Hon. Lord North* (Oxford, 1789) x.
49. Knox, *Liberal Education* i. 242.
50. Though the grammatical study of Greek and Latin was of little importance in Oxford, great emphasis was placed upon the study of their literatures, especially the Greek classics. Cambridge meanwhile consigned both language and literature to relative neglect in comparison to its interest in science and mathematics. This interest developed particularly in the second half of the eighteenth century. Admittedly Cambridge did nurture some of the most proficient Greek scholars in England just before and after 1800.
51. J. Jebb, *Remarks upon the Present Mode of Education in the University of Cambridge* (Cambridge, 1773) 8.
52. *Ibid.* 8.
53. Priestley, *Essay* 192.
54. *Warrington Academy Minutes* Vol. I. 90.
55. *Ibid.* 102.
56. *Ibid.* 118.
57. *Ibid.* 129.
58. *New Academical Institution* 2.
59. *Report on the State of the Academy at Warrington 1760* 3.
60. Barnes, *Proposals* 1.
61. C. Fynes-Clinton (ed.), *Literary remains of Henry Fynes-Clinton, Esq., M.A.* (1854) p. 22 quoted in M. Clarke, 'Classical Studies' from L. Sutherland and L. Mitchell (eds.) *The History of the University of Oxford Vol. V. The Eighteenth Century* (Oxford, 1986) 525.
62. Clarke, 'Classical Studies' 525.
63. *Manchester Academy Instituted. Appendix II* 8.
64. W. Jones, *Grammar of the Persian Language* (London, 1771) *Preface* xxiii-xxiv.
65. W. Hastings, *A Proposal for Establishing a Professorship of the Persian Language in the University of Oxford* (n.p, n.d) 5.
66. Jones, *Grammar of the Persian Language Preface* xi.
67. Hastings, *Proposal* 3.
68. *Ibid.* 13.

69. *Ibid.* 10.
70. A Grant, *The Story of the University of Edinburgh* (London, 1884) Vol. I. 335.
71. Wordsworth, *Scholae Academicae* 166.
72. *Four Letters Concerning the Study of the Hebrew Scriptures* (London, 1755) 39.
73. *Ibid.* 23.
74. M. Evans (ed.), *Letters of Richard Radcliffe and John James of Queen's College, Oxford 1755–83* (Oxford, 1888) p. 190. At Oxford in the eighteenth century parallels between Hebrew and other semitic languages were promoted in particular by Robert Lowth (1710–87). Lowth, however, popularized his ideas through the chair of poetry. There is no evidence that he ever taught Hebrew even privately. In the universities the interesting developments in Hebraic studies were definitely the work of interested 'outsiders', not the appointed professors in the language. On Lowth, see James L. Kugel, *The Idea of Biblical Parallelism and Its History* (Yale, 1981).
75. *Ibid.* 51–2.
76. *Free Thoughts upon University Education* (London, 1751) 15.
77. Wordsworth, *Scholae Academicae* 153.
78. J. Hely-Hutchinson, *An Account of some regulations made in Trinity College, Dublin, since the appointment of the present Provost* (Dublin, 1775) 4–5.
79. F. Higman, 'French texts in the Library of Trinity College, Dublin', *Hermathena 121* (1976), 100–108.
80. *Pranceriana Poetica* (Dublin, 1779) 5.
81. *New Academical Institution London 24 June 1788* 3.
82. *Manchester Academy Instituted. Appendix II* 2.
83. *Manchester Academical Institution, or, The New College, At Manchester* (n.p, 1800) 1.
84. *Warrington Academy Minutes* Vol. I. 90.
85. *Ibid.* 132.
86. *Ibid.* 141.
87. H. McLachlan, *Warrington Academy: Its History and Influence* (Manchester, 1943) 27.
88. *Report on the State of the Academy at Warrington 1767* 3.
89. *Warrington Academy Minutes* Vol. I. 68.
90. *Ibid.* 68.
91. J. Newton, *A Plan of Academical Preparation for the Ministry* (n.p., 1782) 10.
92. Priestley, *Essay* 206.
93. Knox, *Liberal Education* i. 181.
94. *Ibid.* 183.
95. Knox, *Letter to Lord North* xi.
96. Priestley, *Lectures* 247.

97. *Ibid.* 246.
98. *Free Thoughts upon University Education* 15.
99. R. Lowth, *A Short Introduction to English Grammar* (London, 1762) *Preface* xi.
100. S. Butler, *An Essay upon Education* (London, n.d) 76.
101. Knox, *Liberal Education* i. 166.
102. For a detailed study of the teaching of languages in France at this time, see L. Brockliss, *French Higher Education in the Seventeenth and Eighteenth Centuries: a cultural history* (Oxford, 1987) Ch. 3.

Lux veritatis, magistra vitae:
The Teaching of History at the University of Utrecht in the Eighteenth and the Early Nineteenth Centuries

Johanna Roelevink

In the Dutch Republic, halfway between the sea and the German border, not very far from Leyden and Amsterdam, the academic traveller encountered the small province of Utrecht and its capital of the same name. In medieval times Utrecht had been the centre of a large bishopric. After the Reformation a modest but thriving industry ensured the dignified and quiet character of the town. The former ecclesiastical and monastic properties, partly in private hands, party confiscated for the benefit of the city, still yielded a large income. In 1636 the town council decided to use these funds for the foundation of an Athenaeum Illustre, which was soon converted into a fully fledged university. After a rather hesitant start this institution acquired a reputation for sound teaching and scholarship, combined with Calvinist orthodoxy. Students flocked to Utrecht, not only from the other provinces of the Netherlands, but also from foreign parts, notably Germany, Hungary and Great Britain. In the eighteenth century the University of Utrecht had become, after Leyden, the second in importance of the five Dutch universities.[1]

From about 1760 the general decline in the number of students all over Europe and the virtual disappearance of the academic *per-egrinatio* made itself felt in Utrecht too.[2] In particular German students stayed away, preferring their own *Landesuniversität* or one of the new foundations like Göttingen.[3] In Utrecht things were made even worse by economic and political problems. The impoverished town experienced great difficulties in maintaining the standards of the university. In the 1780s the city became the centre of the revolt of the Patriots against the Prince of Orange, which was only ended when drastic action by the King of Prussia brought his brother in law back to power in 1787. The University after a short but serious upheaval occasioned by the revolt tried to return to its old routine, but the old glories of the first part of the century seemed to have gone for ever. The Batavian revolution in 1795 again threatened continuity, but, apart from the downfall of individual Orangist professors and a decrease in the number of students, it had only a very small effect on the institution itself or on its methods of teaching.

In 1811 Napoleon decided that the University of Utrecht should be an *École secondaire*, but his own downfall prevented the actual execution of this measure. King William I, in the beginning of his reign, immediately re-established Utrecht as one of three state universities in what was shortly to be the northern part of the United Kingdom of the Netherlands. At the same time a Royal Decree of August 1815 introduced a new law on higher education, replacing the 'old system'.[4]

Structurally the eighteenth century university of Utrecht belonged to the humanist, Protestant, continental type. There were three higher faculties of theology, law, and medicine plus a lower faculty of arts, originally meant to prepare all new students for their further studies. However, in the Dutch universities of the period there was no formal compulsion whatsoever to attend lectures in arts before entering one of the higher faculties. Consequently the position of the arts faculty within the university was even weaker than the scholarly status of the subjects warranted.[5]

In practice many students skipped those courses in arts which were not of immediate value to their main subject. As a result conventional combinations of courses developed according to the social and scholarly aims of the students. Owing to the general lack of external and internal rules governing arts education, the lower faculty had not only to compete with the impecunity or slackness of many students but also, as in many other European countries, with institutional rivals (Latin schools, boarding schools, *athenaea*) and private tutors. This affected the faculty's teaching in classical languages (of which history was a component) even more than its courses in philosophy and mathematics because it was not possible to take a university degree in these subjects. The title of master of arts had fallen into oblivion and the lower faculty, now often significantly called the philosophical faculty after the German fashion, only created doctors of philosophy.[6]

The new law of 1815 did not throw away the underlying and useful tradition that particular, if different, parts of the arts course were propaedeutic to studies in the three 'higher' faculties. On the contrary, these conventions were formalized. The new faculty of philosophy and letters, which together with a faculty of mathematics and physics replaced the old arts faculty, still had to provide propaedeutic courses, leading to the degree of *candidaat* for future students of law, theology and medicine. But at the same time the new faculty now became fully independent, on a par with the others, with the right to confer both a *candidaat's* and a doctor's degree. This meant the formal recognition that the study of the humanities could be an end in itself. Thus an independent scientific status of these subjects, history among them, was guaranteed. Through the new law both professors and students lost much of their freedom, though more in theory than in practice. There again the professor gained in professional security and the students benefited through the provision of broader, if still expensive, educational opportunities. All in all continuity is much more in evidence than change.[7]

It is only to be expected that during the eighteenth century lectures in the arts were less well attended than the professors liked them to be. Nevertheless the course of universal history (the subject of this present paper) did very well in comparison with the other humanities courses, certainly at Utrecht.[8] In the first place this success reflects and proves the growing interest in history during the eighteenth century. Secondly it is a tribute to the teachers. From 1815 the situation was, in this respect, entirely different. Most students simply had to take—or at least to pay for—the lessons in universal history as a part of the official propaedeutic curriculum. Without the degree of *candidaat* in the faculty of philosophy and languages, taken after an examination, nobody was allowed to enter the doctoral course of that faculty or to proceed to *candidaats* in theology or law. Not surprisingly in those days the propaedeutic lectures on general history were among the best attended of the whole university. It was even difficult to find an adequate lectureroom.[9]

What was the function of courses in history within the structure of university teaching before 1815? It is becoming more and more evident that any answer to this question must allow for considerable differences between the sixteenth and seventeenth centuries on the one hand and the eighteenth century on the other. Details are not clear, but it is certain that some subsidiary parts of the discipline such as geography lost ground. Others, especially the so called *antiquitates*, came to the fore while partly changing character. Here we are only concerned with the eighteenth century. To complicate matters many subjects which now come under the heading of history were then scattered over three different faculties and over many more courses.

The first feature that strikes the eye is the division between history and *antiquitates*, a time honoured segregation which had its roots in the ancient world and apparently affected the various scholarly and educational structures of European countries in different ways. In the course of the early-modern period *antiquitates* became a discipline with rather hazy chronological, linguistic, geographic and political connotations, in which the juridical element became gradually more important. At the same time professional scholars took over from well-meaning amateurs and critical methods were introduced.[10] This certainly blurred the lines between history and antiquities, but in the Dutch academic curriculum and hence in the mind of many students and scholars, the division was still sharp. This was due partly to the very strong humanist interest in classical civilisation still prevalent in the eighteenth century, partly to the influence of scholars like Gronovius and Graevius, and partly to the lasting effect of Roman law on Dutch lawyers which caused them to have a marked preference for Roman antiquities.[11]

Historia as an academic subject in eighteenth century Utrecht was concerned with the deeds and motives of individuals. According to the aims of the teacher the courses might take the form of general history, Church history, *historia literaria* or Dutch history. *Antiquitates*, taught as Jewish, Greek, Roman and Dutch antiquities respectively, dealt with patterns of public and private behaviour and with the social institutions resulting from these conventions. Without referring to the geography of the country the lectures described the institutional structure of religious life, institutions of state and law, the tactics and equipment of armies and the customs and rites which in daily life accompanied birth, marriage and death.[12]

Didactically history and *antiquitates* were considered to be complimentary. Christophorus Saxe, professor in Utrecht from 1753 till 1806, told his students that history teaches what has been done, where, by whom and when. Antiquities, on the other hand, show under which circumstances, for what reasons and by what cause something has happened. Both subjects, still according to Saxe, belong together like flesh and bones.[13] With slight oversimplification we may conclude that, in teaching, history dealt with the dynamic aspect of the past and *antiquitates* with the static aspect.[14]

This more or less rigid distinction between *historia* and *antiquitates* was encouraged rather than dissolved by the institutional vagaries of the university. All separate courses on either *historia* or *antiquitates* had their own well defined subject matter and their own didactic aim. According to these they were alloted to and jealously guarded by the several faculties: Church history by theologians, Dutch antiquities by the faculty of law. Universal history, Greek antiquities, Roman antiquities, Dutch history and *historia literaria* were taught in the arts faculty, but often taken by different professors. The latter had a stake in the lecture fees, paid to them directly for each separate course, so naturally the professors wanted to attract as many subscribers to their several lessons as possible.[15]

An enlightened teacher could not be but completely dissatisfied with this state of affairs. He wanted to analyse the past as a whole and to describe the development of mankind in all aspects. Consequently he tended to integrate the subject matter of history and *antiquitates* into one single history of mankind. In Utrecht this finally happened when professor Van Heusde took over as *professor historiarum, antiquitatum, eloquentiae necnon linguae Graecae* in 1803. The changes he made were confirmed by the law on higher education of 1815. By then the *antiquitates* were formally degraded to narrowly defined courses of special interest for certain students only. The contents dwindled to a bare minimum. Greek antiquities were confined to describing religion for the benefit of theologians, and Roman antiquities to dealing with public institutions for law students. At the same time not only these same themes but also the other subjects of the antiquities were swallowed up by the new enlightened course on the history of man.[16]

We will now concentrate on universal history as it was taught in Utrecht during the eighteenth and the early nineteenth centuries.

The universities of the Republic in general offer excellent opportunities to do so. Dutch students were in the habit of writing
notebooks, taking down verbally the text the professors dictated.[17]
Whereas in most other countries, notably in Germany, only textbooks are available and the *viva vox* has been lost in the mists of
time, it is possible in the case of the Dutch Republic to bring lecture
rooms to life and to assess the difference between the compendium
and the actual course. The university of Utrecht has been chosen
because it was fortunate enough to have several professors who
were historians or antiquarians of repute.

In the seventeenth century the university of Leyden had made an
outstanding contribution to classical scholarship. In the field of
history and antiquities Gronovius both father and son displayed a
profound knowledge of the ancient world, while Jacobus Perizonius
was one of the leading chronologists and historians of his time.[18] In
the eighteenth and the early nineteenth century the emphasis
shifted to Greek philology. Hemsterhuis, with his famous edition of
Lucian, was succeeded by men like David Ruhnkenius and Daniel
Wyttenbach who devoted their time to Greek literary and philosophical texts. In the nineteenth century philology reached new
heights with Bake and Cobet.[19]

Leyden's reputation for classical scholarship was still
unrivalled in eighteenth century northern Europe, where
Oxford's Bentley, some German predecessors of the *Altertumswissenschaft*, like Gesner and Heyne, and maybe a few scholars in France, were internationally the only serious competitors.[20]
In the Dutch Republic Utrecht held its own. Three Utrecht professors between them produced four widely acclaimed editions of
ancient historians. Arnoldus Drakenborch edited Livius, Carolus
Duker Thucydides, and Petrus Wesseling, who also contributed an
edition of late classical *itineraria*, Diodorus Siculus and
Herodotus.[21]

In the university teaching of medieval and modern history in the
eighteenth century, on the other hand, Germany had taken the lead
under the strong influence of the faculty of law. In England the
study of civil law was in decline and modern history does not seem
to have attracted much attention before it became a tripos in
Cambridge and Oxford in the 1850s.[22] There, as in the France of
Mabillon, La Curne de Sainte Palaye and Montesquieu, virtually all
the important work was done outside the universities.[23] But in the

modern university foundations of the Protestant part of the German Empire, the study of law and history thrived, spreading new branches of *Statistik, Staatengeschichte* and other *Kameralwissenschaften.*[24] In this respect, the Netherlands lagged behind Germany. *Jus publicum Romano-Germanicum* had been taught in Leyden and Utrecht in the seventeenth century, but only in the 1740s did Dutch public law become an academic subject.[25] Significantly, this happended first in Utrecht, always open to German influence, where in the arts faculty of the early eighteenth century Drakenborch and Wesseling had already done research into the medieval past.[26] It is not by chance that the best Dutch medievalist of the Republican era, Adriaan Kluit, who was to become *professor antiquitatum et historiae diplomaticae Foederati Belgii* at Leyden in 1779, was the product of an Utrecht education.[27]

Let us move from the background to the Utrecht professors themselves whose teaching is the focus of this paper. In 1735 Petrus Wesseling (1692–1764) was appointed professor of history, eloquence and Greek. Born in Westphalia, he had been educated at the universities of Franeker and Leyden, where he attended the lectures of the famous philologist and historian Jacobus Perizonius.[28] Wesseling, who had completed a study of theology, was a Greek scholar in the tradition of his friend Tiberius Hemsterhuis. But his interest was not mainly linguistic, as his editions of the *Vetera Romanorum Itineraria*, Diodorus Siculus and Herodotus testify. An authority on geography, antiquities and history he commanded a great knowledge of the ancient world. On top of this Wesseling was equally well acquainted with medieval and modern history and its sources. Therefore it is not suprising that in 1746 he was appointed professor of natural law and *Jus publicum Romano-Germanicum* as well.[29] However in line with the Dutch tradition he did not give up his professorship in the arts faculty. He even continued to devote all his spare time to classical research. Wesseling was certainly a polyhistorian, but also a good scholar and a gifted teacher.

His collegue Christophorus Saxe (1714–1806), *professor antiquitatum et humaniorum litterarum* from 1753 was of a totally different disposition. In his native Saxony he studied arts and theology at the University of Leipzig. After his arrival in the Netherlands as a private tutor his great learning in Roman antiquities and archaeology gained him a professorship at Utrecht. There he continued teaching till he was nearly ninety. Saxe was not only well versed in Latin and in Roman antiquities but also a bibliographer of repute. In fact he was a conservative representative of the type prevalent in the more old-fashioned German universities, never really at home in the much more critical Dutch climate. Again, his strong Lutheran persuasions, his abrupt political about-turn from an Orangist into a fervent Patriot, his lack of gifts as a teacher and above all his unpleasant character isolated him both from his students and his fellow professors.[30]

In 1803 Saxe was succeeded by a very young man, Philip Willem van Heusde (1778–1839'.[31] This Dutchman had studied humanities and law in Amsterdam and Leyden. Much later he admitted that, having distinguished himself in Greek philology under the guidance of Daniel Wyttenbach, he did not know much about history at the time of his appointment. But what he lacked in erudition he made up for through enthusiasm and hard work. His subsequent publications were mainly concerned with and inspired by Platonism, but they exuded an eclectic commonsense philosophy hard to define. Being neither a systematic philosopher nor, in his later years, a meticulous scholar, Van Heusde admired the Enlightenment in its moderate, Protestant, character. In history his guides were William Robertson from Scotland, and Friedrich Creuzer and Arnold H. L. Heeren from Germany. Van Heusde was an excellent teacher who strikes us as a very amiable if slightly dull man. His lectures made a great impact on the students, especially during his heyday in the early 1820s.[32] He was one of those who seem to epitomize the thought of their age and exert an enormous if diffuse influence on the next generation.

If Van Heusde adhered to the moderate enlightened principles of his day, Wesseling and Saxe had decidedly different affiliations, as did two other Utrecht professors of history about whose teaching we know next to nothing, Johann Friedrich Reitz, who taught from 1748 till 1778 and Rijklof Michaël van Goens who left the university after occupying his chair for ten years in 1776.[33] To understand where their loyalty lay and the consequences for both the methods and the actual content of history teaching, it is necessary to expand a little on historical scholarship at the Dutch universities in the eighteenth century. The main problem is, whether this scholarship is entitled to be labelled 'enlightened' and if not, whether it was just simply very old-fashioned and arid or whether it had its own characteristics as opposed to those of Renaissance humanism.

Because of the very moderation of the Dutch Enlightenment, it is difficult to trace isolated 'enlightened' points of view in university teaching. The touchstone should be whether the Enlightenment essentially permeated its structure, aims and methods. And to that, the answer must be in the negative. It is much more illuminating to label the eighteenth century Dutch professors of history 'critical polyhistorians' rather than use slightly pejorative descriptions like 'erudite' or 'antiquarian' or even 'baroque', terms coined with an eye to the writing not the academic teaching of history.[34]

Jacobus Perizonius and Tiberius Hemsterhuis may be termed renewers of the old polyhistorical tradition which stressed the unity of all knowledge and the necessity of universal erudition, based on the achievement of the ancients. Like their predecessors these two scholars were concerned on the one hand with the gathering of factual information and the arrangement of facts in a certain order. New facts were integrated into the system of sciences, if necessary by creating new subjects, but without changing the system itself. The overall aim was to bring to society at large the profit of factual and moral knowledge. Their encyclopaedical erudition went together with a strong urge to initiate an ethical revival in the Dutch universities along the lines of Christian precepts and classical concepts of virtue.[35] Politically conservative, socially members of the upper middle class, professors in this tradition fully accepted the world in which they lived.

Yet it is utterly misleading to call these polyhistorians old-fashioned. They did not act as an unreflective medium between the wisdom and knowledge of the past and the needs of their pupils. Historical pyrrhonism had made them painfully aware of the unreliability of many so called truths. But their reaction was by no means a convulsive, dogmatic one. They took to a quiet watchfulness, a careful revaluation of the sources of historical knowledge.[36] In Utrecht Wesseling, whose inaugural *Pro historiis Oratio* was entirely in the line of Perizonius, told his students without fuss or long dissertations on the authority of Holy Scripture, that the Bible was a very old, authentic and consequently dependable source. He conceded that faulty tradition had caused minor errors, but all in all Wesseling was very confident that this historical document was of the highest order.[37] The classics, valuable in themselves, were also welcomed as a second witness to Biblical facts.[38] In general all sources, Scriptural and other, old and modern, were considered to be equally important. Erudition as a compilation of facts established by careful assessment but not necessarily by common sense alone, became in itself an excellent instrument for discerning the truth with a critical, questioning mind.[39]

Critical polyhistorians willingly conformed to the existing, slightly modified but essentially humanist structure of university teaching. In actual research they went beyond the accepted boundaries of the historical discipline in quest of facts, but nevertheless they accepted that the resulting knowledge was normally divided into well defined compartments, each with their own scientific and didactic aims, contents and results. The polyhistorians also realized that these aims might be very limited and that the arts would always be dependent on other disciplines. As a result university teachers treated history as an important course, which was nevertheless subservient to theology and law. Wesseling and Saxe at Utrecht would, like Perizonius at Leyden before them, always explain why historical knowledge was absolutely indispensable to the theologian and the lawyer. And they acted upon these principles, both by providing interesting subject matter and by framing their course in an appropriately modest way.[40]

The contrast between the critical polyhistorian and the enlightened teacher of history is immediately clear to the observer. An *Aufklärer* could not possibly stick to the old ways. His aim was not to harmonize disparate facts or to offer a logically consistent causal explanation of the past, but to expound the inner system of reality as it existed in the actual world as well as in the mind.[41] This called for a very different treatment of history in the classroom. The professor did not condone the division of one well defined unity of knowledge, the science of the history of mankind, into several independent courses. He wanted to explain antiquities and all other historical subjects as aspects of the one truth about the past, using one and the same scientific method to reach the one ultimate aim, knowledge about man, his society, and his environment. In addition the enlightened teacher considered history to be an independent science and the historian capable of a full explanation of the past. Therefore general history as an academic subject devoured the other courses within the arts faculty and claimed a new, very central position in the university teaching system. Well before the law of 1815, Van Heusde like the Göttingen historians in Germany taught an all inclusive and all important course on *historia gentium*.[42]

The didactic and practical difference between polyhistorical and enlightened teaching of history may be illustrated with examples from the Utrecht courses of Wesseling and Saxe who taught universal history from 1735 to 1764 and from 1764 to 1803 respectively.[43] This private course, for which the students had to pay a fee, extended over one academic year, with four lectures a week. Wesseling and Saxe both depended on the aid of a textbook for their lessons. Contrary to most German professors, they did not write their own, but chose the *Epitome historiae universalis* compiled by the Italian Jesuit Horatius Tursellinus at the end of the sixteenth century.[44]

It is rather surprising that this particular textbook was used, because both Utrecht professors, of course, fiercely opposed Roman Catholic opinions. They also chided the author for all kinds of factual error.[45] This seemingly odd approach must have been as bewildering to the students as it was to the German traveller Beckmann who bluntly tackled Wesseling about it. The answer was predictably evasive. Everybody did so, Wesseling said, especially all former pupils of Perizonius.[46] Yet it is possible to find some sound reasons in favour of Tursellinus. For one, the strict chronological structure of the book appealed to the critical polyhistorian, as we will see shortly. Again the Jesuit wrote elegant Latin and offered a fairly concise text, divided into short handy paragraphs and with a minimum of periodization. The chronological system on which Tursellinus depended, was also a mark in its favour for it corresponded roughly to Scaliger's, the system adopted by most Dutch scholars. Jacobus Perizonius seems to have recognized there advantages and initiated the new career of this book which was by no means restricted to Leyden and Utrecht. From that time onwards the sheer weight of tradition added to the usefulness of the *Epitome*.

As mentioned before, Wesseling and Saxe dictated a commentary on this manual which the students took down verbally in their notebooks, entirely in the medieval tradition. So in fact there was a duality between the textbook and the teacher, not only on the level of facts but also on that of explanations and of religious and moral example. This was fully compatible with the aims and methods of polyhistorical teaching, but would have been completely unthinkable to the promotors of enlightened historiography.

According to classical definition history was not only *lux veritatis*, but also *magistra vitae*. These two attributes corresponded to the two didactic aims of polyhistoric teaching. So in the first place, history was to the student the light of truth, especially of factual truth and knowledge, not in a passive, but in an active way. The basic structure of general history was conceived as a 'continua rerum gestarum series' (a continuous series of human acts), a chain of contingent human reactions, defined by time and space and established according to the rigorous canons of scientific empiricism.[48] Time was the most important aspect in this series, because *ordo*, time, and the cause of a human reaction to something that had happened previously were so closely intertwined.

As a result every action was defined as something causing a chain of reactions which affected either a few or many people and lasted for a shorter or a longer time. All grades between the general and the specific were to be found on this particular scale, although the cause itself might be quite insignificant. As Saxe told his pupils: 'an event may proceed from a trivial beginning'.[49] With absence of activity, a long period of peace and rest, a polyhistorian could do nothing whatsoever but praise it and go on.

The beginning of the *series*, the creation of the world, had to be defined in the most rigorous way with the aid of chronology, a vitally important and much debated subject. Perizonius, to cite him once more, referred to a 'historia systematica seu chronologica' (a systematical or chronological history) and called chronology the soul of history. Without it, he stated, nobody would ever be able to gather the fruits of history, that is ethical and political observations.[50] The Utrecht professors agreed with him implicitly. They too treated the chain of divine and human actions as a result of conscious use of willpower, with its causes and effects, with its simulated and true reasons for human behaviour and with its tragic misunderstandings.

The view of history as a time-engendered series of human actions implied the exclusion of the conventional and the customary. The static or only slowly moving backdrop to the great human dramas of the past was and remained effectively banished to the lectures on antiquities. This severe amputation marred the vista of the human past as seen by the student who did not attend these lectures. Yet, despite its restrictions, history as a course was able to fulfil several important functions within the curriculum.

In the first place the description of the *rerum gestarum series* enabled the student to assess critically the new facts that came to his knowledge through reading authors and studying inscriptions or, indeed, any other relic of the past. Once pieced together, the chain of human actions as observed by the scholar became a means of weighing new evidence, in a quest for harmony and consistency. Because of this major concern the professor devoted much time to equipping his student with techniques for establishing the trust-worthiness of a given fact. He usually did so in short asides, some-times still called *quaestiones*.[51] Arguments of this kind linked the lectures with the other main method of teaching, the *disputatio*. But this was a steadily declining genre and the Dutch, unlike some German universities did not develop anything like an institu-tionalized seminar.[52] For this reason the lecture room became the proper and only place to sharpen the critical faculties of the pupils.

Secondly a course in history was a preparation for study in the higher faculties of theology and law. Many eighteenth century Dutch theologians were under the diffuse influence of *Foederaltheologie* and more specifically Coccejanism. This theol-ogy, with its sequence of covenants between God and man and its reliance on the fulfilment of prophesies in history, required fam-iliarity with historical events throughout all ages from the creation till the present.[53] The critical polyhistorians were willing and able to give the information required. Moreover Saxe stated that history was useful for theologians in other respects as well, notably Biblical exegesis and apologetic debates.[54] In consequence, he and Wesse-ling paid special attention to the history of the Jews, to the Hellenis-tic world and to the Christians within the Roman Empire. The apological potential of the subject was displayed in occasional remarks against heresies and in frequent denunciations of Roman Catholic theology and the superstitions which came in its wake.

History also was a preparation for the study of law. Strictly speaking Greek and Roman antiquities were intrinsically more interesting to students of law than ancient history, but nevertheless they needed a smattering of that as well. With medieval and modern history things were different because of the distribution of subjects concerning the past over the several faculties. Dutch antiquities, the immediate background of the existing laws, was taught in the law faculty itself along with other courses like statistics. But it was essential for law students to know the history of the states of Europe as well. Wesseling complied with this need by covering the history of modern times up to the eighteenth century, with emphasis on the Dutch Republic.[55] Saxe, who was not really very interested in modern history, at first only taught ancient and medieval history, but in 1778 he started a separate course on Dutch history for reasons of his own.[56] All in all it was Wesseling who catered best for the needs of the law students.

Universal history was not only meant to be a treasure of factual information, but also to be a *magistra vitae* to the students. To polyhistorians like Wesseling and Saxe general history served as a guide to religion and ethics. The task was performed by examples, both good and bad, which the professor pointed out from time to time. Wesseling told his students these examples served 'ad vitam human recte regundam et administrandam' (towards leading a well regulated life) and, in his later life, he said they were simply 'ad usum generis humani' (useful for man).[57]

The polyhistorian was fully aware of anachronism, yet saw it as relative. He tacitly assumed that there was a link between the human experience of the past and the present, since total anachronism would have reduced the value of examples to nothing. Nearly always these took the form of a description of an individual action and led to a general observation. Apparently there was no didactic planning behind these precepts. The moral observations were rather unsystematic and few and far between, while explicit theological interpretations of history were almost non-existent.[58] There certainly was no indoctrination which could become an unbearable chore to the student. In fact the examples stood fairly isolated from the *rerum gestarum series*, although Saxe still compared history to a play which drew applause or distaste from the spectator.[59]

In Utrecht the polyhistorical teaching of general history consisted of a balanced survey of the series of human actions from Adam to the present, with emphasis on rulers, Church leaders and scholars whose actions really mattered because they were a link in the chain of events. The structure of this survey with its co-ordinates of time and place, its well defined didactic purpose and its strict segregation from other courses covering the past, was rigid. On the other hand the series itself was flexible enough to absorb new facts, to shift the emphasis from one period to another or, conversely, to pay full attention to all periods indiscriminately, including the Hellenistic world, the later Roman Empire and the Dark Ages. But the real interest of the teachers focused on the critical assessment of facts. The professors frequently referred to sources and to literature for further reading. Their explanation of causal relations was entirely based on the immediate inducements for individual action. General observations and examples were attached to a discussion of the motives of the actors, which were either good, bad or tragically mistaken, the result of underestimating the real possibilities of a situation. As a body of religious and political thought, these observations were more or less consistent, but of course this unity bore no relation to the actual development of history.

The scholarly qualities of the professors had a decisive influence on the success of this sort of factual and moral teaching. It is not difficult to see that the success of Wesseling as a teacher and the unsatisfactory result of Saxe's exertions were not only due to differences in character. Though both did research in their own favourite subject, only Wesseling acquired the immense erudition necessary for the critical evaluation of information. Also he more successfully adapted his course on general history to changing circumstances than Saxe did. As a theologian of the Franeker school of Coccejanism Wesseling was also able to comply with the wishes of future students of theology. At the same time his good knowledge of the *Jus Publicum Romano-Germanicum* and Dutch antiquities enabled him to teach medieval and modern history to law students in a satisfactory way.

Saxe lacked this breadth altogether. He had actually fled Germany because of his love for classical scholarship, hoping to find inspiration in the glories of the Dutch scholars of the past. As a Lutheran he had no affinity with the Calvinist climate of *Foederaltheologie*. His attitude towards critical innovation was considered to be conservative even by his own teacher, the far from revolutionary Matthias Gesner, then professor in Leipzig and subsequently in Göttingen.[60] Only Saxe's interest in Roman archaeology, partly inspired by J. F. Christ, the learned German archaeologist, and by Winckelmann pointed towards the future.[61] Not surprisingly, unlike Wesseling, Saxe was never able to inspire his pupils or even to hold their attention for a long time.

In all respects the contrast between the polyhistorians and Saxe's successor Van Heusde was very sharp. Having skipped the lectures on universal history as a student, Van Heusde had to depend on books for his knowledge, and upon his appointment he instantly became an assiduous reader of the modern, enlightened historians. Van Heusde felt even freer to reject his academic inheritance because in Utrecht everybody was pleased with a new man in the arts faculty, no matter what he was actually going to do.[62] Van Heusde therefore simply set out to teach history in the enlightened sense, as an independent science of the development of mankind. Having no example within the Dutch Republic, Van Heusde struggled to supply an adequate course of his own, changing the structure of his lectures frequently. At least he found an inspiring example in the *Göttinger Schule*.

Enlightened university teaching was strikingly different from the polyhistoric courses of the past. In the first place its didactic aim was fundamentally new. Secondly, by changing not only the content but also the methods of teaching general history, it effected a breach in the old structure of the sciences and arts. Van Heusde's own enlightened interpretation of history can be mentioned only briefly here. He described it as the growth of mankind analogous to an individual's development.[63] In his opinion the nations of the east lived in infancy and boyhood, the Greeks and Romans in adolescence and early manhood, and the nations of Europe, after rebirth through Christianity, in adulthood. Van Heusde's view was only new within the Dutch context. He drew heavily on existing German, French, English and Scottish literature. Over the years he came to attribute more and more significance to the influence of Christianity, adapting and modifying his descriptions of the causes of human development. But the steady rational development of mankind remained the focus and the mainstay of his course till his death in 1839. Over the years, too, if the subject matter of the teaching was always enlightened, it gained Romantic overtones in his increasing interest in languages and in early medieval poetry.

Already in 1803 Van Heusde set out to clarify the difference between his own teaching and that of his polyhistoric predecessors. He told his students that he did not want to talk about *res gestae*, but about the intrinsic causes of the development of nations. History should not only chart their vicissitudes but also describe their civilisation, their *mores*, their culture, their arts and their science. Its ultimate aim would be *philosophia vera*, the science of man.[64]

It is obvious that Van Heusde firmly ignored the compartimental-ization of university teaching, although he did not strive to change the traditions and structures of university life as such. In his lectures on 'Historia gentium', as he pointedly called his course on universal history, he also treated subjects which traditionally belonged to Greek, Roman and even Dutch antiquities. Consequently he reduced his own courses on Greek and Roman antiquities to the bare essentials that theologians, lawyers and arts students would need for further study. These courses were not a complement, but an addition to the one on universal history. Dutch history was not treated separately by Van Heusde, because he considered all nations equally important as far as they made a real contribution to the development of mankind. In 1815 the new law on university education endorsed this state of affairs. History became a fully independent science within the faculty of philosophy and letters, whereas at the same time in terms of teaching it served as an instructive propaedeutical course for theologians, law students and students of the humanities.[65]

Van Heusde's propaedeutic course on 'Historia gentium' took two or even three years to complete. It comprised a systematic survey of all nations which had in any way contributed to the history of mankind; it was in fact a cultural pedigree of contemporary European civilisation. In the first decade of his professorship Van Heusde used Von Schloezer's ethnographic-synchronic method, combining the individual description of all important nations which had contributed to the present world with a shorter chronological enumeration of events within which the key contributions could be located.[66] But Van Heusde was not really satisfied with this, because his chief aim was not to help students memorize facts, but to make them understand the development of mankind as a whole. To him periodization was only a means towards imparting this insight. In his later lectures periodization was related not to dates but to unities of development and place. In his division of history mentioned above: the nations of the east first, then the Greeks and the Romans, and finally the European nations, he remained within the broad tradition of Montesquieu, Iselin, Herder and others. From 1819 Van Heusde gave a supplementary course in *historia humanitatis*, essentially a very abstract historical anthropology.[67]

To Van Heusde, the *lux veritatis* of history shone not from isolated facts but from the consistency and the complex interrela-tion of everything that had happened in the past during the constant

growth of mankind towards manhood. As a result Van Heusde did
not waste time on the critical assessment of sources and facts. He
took the rather facile stance that one had better stick to absolutely
trustworthy evidence, the *certissima quaeque*, excluding anything
that was subject to reasonable doubt.[68] Van Heusde had grown
tired of the meticulous methods of the critical polyhistorians. Like
enlightened writers of history he did not interrupt the flowing
discourse of his lectures to discuss critical problems.

Where the polyhistorians appealed to the relatively exceptional
sense, memory and moral sincerity of their pupils, all of which they
hoped to improve, Van Heusde addressed his students as men
endowed with common reason, a reason which would enable any of
them to grasp eventually the essence of historical development.
From his point of view the professor was only there to accelerate the
process. In fact, his course was meant to be a short cut to a
knowledge which the teacher had already attained and which his
audience would have acquired all by themselves if they had only
been given sufficient time to do so. Once the latent understanding in
the students' brains was awakened, they would be able to incorporate new knowledge within the existing structure.[69]

To Van Heusde, history as *magistra vitae* simply meant that the
student gained insight into the past of mankind and into his own
possibilities as a human being. Reality, even past reality was a
consistent unity of matters of fact, held together by causes and
effects of many kinds, human, social, climatic, personal and so on.
General observations not isolated examples were called for. Since
the pupil was able to draw his own moral conclusions, the professor
merely arranged the subject matter so as to give him the opportunity to do so.[70]

It is abundantly clear that Van Heusde could not make use of the
old textbooks on *historia universalis*. Neither was he able find a
suitable enlightened substitute because compendia of this kind
were always written in the vernacular whereas all Dutch university
teaching—with Van Heusde's full approval—was still in Latin. Yet
Van Heusde did not set out to write or translate a textbook, partly
because he just was not the right person to do so, partly because his
difficulties were more fundamental.[71] The old duality between compendium and commentator had to vanish, because there was only
one consistent and valid view of history, that of the professor.
Within the limitations of Dutch academic traditions and structures

this view had to be explained fully during the lectures, because there were no seminars in which to expand certain themes. So Van Heusde kept dictating the gist of his own course verbatim, while the ensuing disputations and *responsiecolleges*, where students were given the chance to put forward their own ideas, were reduced to polite conversation. On such occasions the students simply developed the view of the teacher and the debate ended with at the very least an acceptance of Van Heusde's general framework.[72] Certainly the outcome was never very surprising.

In comparison with the limited aims of polyhistoric teaching, Van Heusde in his lessons imposed his own views on his students. There was no real possibility of disagreeing with him, because he saw a direct relation between the causal consistency of the past and his own interpretation of history. Even the representation of facts depended entirely on this interpretation, for the lectures were uncluttered by irrelevant detail and sometimes quite disagreeable in their bland perspicuity.

In consequence, in his choice of illustrations Van Heusde tended to avoid the unpleasant, the cruel and the shocking.[73] In contrast to polyhistorical teaching Van Heusde knew no bad examples, no tragic occurrences or unsuccessful plans and actions, for he had no way of interpreting facts which did not suit his own convictions. One inconvenient fact would have required the modification of the overall interpretation, something which was scarcely conceivable. Van Heusde turned a blind eye, not only to Kant and his successors, but also to the German *Altertumswissenschaft*, to the rise of political history and to the new interest, inspired by Romanticism in the sources of medieval and modern history. Thus this vigorous reformer of the teaching of history at the University of Utrecht, the first enlightened professor of history at any Dutch university, ended his life as an *Aufklärer* who had outstayed his welcome. But his influence on many pupils was very strong. Nobody who wants to understand anything about Dutch intellectual life during this period can ignore him.

From what has been said, it is clear that in the eighteenth and the first half of the nineteenth century a well qualified teacher of history was continuously available at the university of Utrecht. A wide and interesting range of lectures on historical subjects was always provided.[74] This is in itself quite remarkable. The Roman Catholic universities of France, Belgium and Germany did not provide anything comparable at all. At Protestant universities in Britain and Germany, with the well known exceptions of Göttingen, Halle and, in Scotland Edinburgh, similar courses were not always part of the official curriculum either, and if they were, they might be ignored in practice or given by young or incompetent scholars waiting for something better.

The quality of the history teaching at Utrecht, moreover, stands up well under scrutiny, the course being neither too old-fashioned nor too avant-garde. In comparison with eighteenth-century professors at Leipzig, Oxford and Cambridge, Wesseling was well able to hold his own against the best historians in Europe. Till his death in 1764 he was also able to keep in touch with the development of *Statistik* and *Jus publicum* in Germany. Saxe, though an able scholar, definitely lost ground in comparison with enlightened teachers at Göttingen and Edinburgh. But he introduced the work of Winckelmann into the Netherlands and he belonged to a bibliographical tradition which in Germany lasted well into the nineteenth century.[75] On the other hand, Van Heusde did catch up with the moderate Protestant Enlightenment, but at the same time completely avoided the wilder flights of Romanticism and Kantianism. It is a pity that he was not interested in the political sciences which held the key to the future. Yet in his philosophical eclecticism and his sophisticated lectures Van Heusde, too, did not lose contact with his more eminent contemporaries.

In terms of the development of historical studies within the university world in the eighteenth and early-nineteenth centuries, therefore, Utrecht's performance was creditable. Though never in the front line, Utrecht fitted well into the Dutch scholarly climate with its specific classical flavour. On this basis the university provided an historical education which was excellent until the 1770s, old-fashioned but sound from then till about 1800, and certainly far above average in the first decades of the nineteenth century. Of course, if Utrecht's performance was judged against contemporary developments in historiography and literary studies outside the universities during this period, its contribution would seem rather thin. But such a comparison is invidious. In most countries university history teaching responded only slowly to new intellectual currents.

Bureau der Rijkscommissie voor
Vaderlandse Geschiedenis
Prins Willem-Alexanderhof 7
2595 BE 's-Gravenhage
The Netherlands

REFERENCES

1. On the university of Utrecht: *De Utrechtsche Universiteit 1636–1936,* vol. i, G. W. Kernkamp, *De Utrechtsche Academie 1636–1815* vol. ii, S. J. Fockema Andreae *et al. De Utrechtsche Universiteit 1815–1936* (Utrecht, 1936) and *Acta et decreta senatus, vroedschapsresolutiën en andere bescheiden betreffende de Utrechtsche Academie,* G. W. Kernkamp ed., 3 vols. (Utrecht, 1936–1940). On the position of the university in Dutch society W. Th. M. Frijhoff, *La Société néerlandaise et ses gradués, 1575–1814* (Amsterdam and Maarssen, 1981).
2. W. Frijhoff, 'Grandeur des nombres et misères des réalites: la courbe de Franz Eulenberg et le débat sur le nombre d'intellectuels en Allemagne, 1576–1815', D. Julia, J. Revel, R. Chartier (edd.) *Les Universités Européennes du XVIe au XVIIIe siècle. Histoire sociale des populations étudiantes,* vol. i. (Paris, 1986), 23–64.
3. H. Schneppen, *Niederländische Universitäten und Deutsches Geistesleben, von der Gründung der Universität Leiden bis ins späte 18. Jahrhundert* (Münster, 1960), 13 and *passim.*
4. General State Archives, The Hague, IIe Afdeling, Staatssecretarie 127, Koninklijk Besluit, 2 August 1815 no. 14. Printed in the *Nederlandsche Staatscourant,* no. 242 12 October 1815, and no. 243 13 October 1815. A French translation is to be found in V. Cousin, *De l' instruction publique en Hollande* (Paris, 1837), 336–586. A useful guide to nineteenth century institutional history of Dutch universities is M. Groen, *Het wetenschappelijk onderwijs in Nederland van 1815 tot 1980,* vol. i *Wetgeving. Civiel effect. Godgeleerdheid. Rechtsgeleerdheid. Indologie. Geneeskunde* (Eindhoven, 1987).
5. J. Roelevink, *Gedicteerd verleden. Het onderwijs in de algemene geschiedenis aan de universiteit te Utrecht, 1735–1839* (Amsterdam and Maarssen, 1986), 27–46. This doctoral thesis (English summary 331–337) discusses the themes of this article more fully. It will, I hope, be followed by a second volume analysing the social and scholarly network within which the professors operated, the professors' colleagues and pupils, the interaction between research and teaching, and the actual content of the lectures and their significance for the development of methods of research.

6. For the degrees Frijhoff, *Gradués,* 42, 43. On the philosophical faculty Roelevink, *Verleden,* 30, and Ch. E. McClelland, *State, Society, and University in Germany 1700–1914* (Cambridge, 1980), 65.

7. Roelevink, *Verleden,* 67–99.

8. J. Roelevink, 'Utrecht Student *testimonia* in the Second Half of the Eighteenth Century', *Lias* 13 (1986), 87–124 and Roelevink, *Verleden,* 38, 39.

9. Roelevink, *Verleden,* 74–88, 107 with the appropriate tables and graphs.

10. A. Momigliano, 'Ancient History and the Antiquarian', *Studies in Historiography* (London, 1966), 1–39; E. Cochrane, *Historians and Historiography in the Italian Renaissance* (Chicago and London, 1981), 423–444; D. Hay, *Annalists and Historians. Western Historiography from the VIIIth to the XVIIIth Century* (London, 1977), 133–185. On Dutch universities Roelevink, *Verleden,* 187–192, 233–238.

11. J. Gronovius (1645–1715) edited a *Thesaurus antiquitatum Graecarum* and J. Graevius (1632–1703) a *Thesaurus antiquitatum Romanarum* and a *Thesaurus antiquitatum et historiarum Italiae.* On Dutch jurists of the 'elegant school' B. H. Stolte jr., *Hendrik Brenkman (1681–1736) Jurist and Classicist. A Chapter from the History of Roman Law as Part of the Classical Tradition* (Groningen, 1981).

12. Roelevink, *Verleden,* 187–193. Apart from the well known and often re-edited book by Johannes Rosinus (Rossfield), many textbooks on Greek and Roman antiquities by J. Potter, B. Kennett, G. H. Nieupoort, P. Burmannus and L. Bos were edited, altered and used frequently in the eighteenth century.

13. University Library, Utrecht, MS 5 N 9, 'Antiquitatis Graecae Institutiones', (autograph, after 1758) 2; MS 8 D 27, 'Praelectiones ad L. Annaeum Florum', fly leaf (undated autograph); MS O F 1, 'Animadversiones in *Descriptionem brevem antiquitatum,* ut vulgo dicuntur, *Romanarum*' (autograph, probably 1753), fo. 5r; MS 5 N 8, 'Praelectiones de vario quaestionum literarum genere, disserendae exercitationibus accommodatae' (autograph, from 1755), fo. 7r.

14. Roelevink, *Verleden,* 187, 188.

15. Roelevink, *Verleden,* 177–211 (on the various subjects) and 101–117, 132–141 (on lectures and fees).

16. Roelevink, *Verleden,* 75, 192.

17. Roelevink, *Verleden,* 109–113. On the teaching of history at Dutch universities also: A. Th. van Deursen, *Leonard Offerhaus, professor historiarum Groninganus (1699–1779)* (Groningen, 1957); A. Th. van Deursen, *Jacobus de Rhoer 1722–1813. Een historicus op de drempel van een nieuwe tijd* (Groningen, 1970), 56–70; J. Roelevink, 'Historia en antiquitates. Het geschiedenisonderwijs aan het Athenaeum Illustre van Amsterdam in de achttiende eeuw tussen Polyhistorie en Verlichting', *Theoretische Geschiedenis* 10 (1983), 281–301; J.

Roelevink, 'Historia gentium. Ph. W. van Heusde and the Teaching of History at the University of Utrecht in the First Decade of the XIXth Century', *Lias* 13 (1986), 123–137.

18. Th. J. Meijer, *Kritiek als herwaardering. Het levenswerk van Jacob Perizonius (1651–1715)* (Leiden, 1971).

19. J. H. Gerretzen, *Schola Hemsterhusiana. De herleving der Grieksche studien aan de Nederlandse universiteiten in de achttiende eeuw van Perizonius tot en met Valckenaer* (Nijmegen and Utrecht, 1940); D. C. A. J. Schouten, *Het Grieks aan de Nederlandse universiteiten in de negentiende eeuw, bijzonder gedurende de periode 1815–1876* (Utrecht, 1964).

20. A survey in English: R. Pfeiffer, *History of Classical Scholarship from 1300 to 1850* (Oxford, 1976) 124–163.

21. A. Drakenborch, *T. Livii Historiarum ab urbe condita libri qui supersunt* (Amsterdam, 1738–1746); C. A. Duker, *Thucydides de bello Peloponnesiaco libri octo* (Amsterdam, 1731); P. Wesseling, *Diodori Siculi Bibliothecae historicae libri qui supersunt*, 2 vols. (Amsterdam, 1746); P. Wesseling and L. C. Valckenaer, *Herodoti Halicarnassei historiarum libri IX* (Utrecht, 1763); P. Wesseling, *Vetera Romanorum itineraria, sive Antonini Augusti itinerarium* (Amsterdam, 1735).

22. N. Hammerstein, *Jus und Historie. Ein Beitrag zur Geschichte des historischen Denkens an deutschen Universitäten im späten 17. und im 18. Jahrhundert* (Göttingen, 1972); *The History of the University of Oxford* vol. v, *The Eighteenth Century* L. S. Sutherland and L. G. Mitchell (edd.), 487; P. R. H. Slee, *Learning and a Liberal Education. The Study of Modern History in the Universities of Oxford, Cambridge and Manchester 1800–1914* (Manchester, 1986).

23. L. Gossman, *Medievalism and the Ideologies of the Enlightenment. The world and Work of La Curne de Sainte-Palaye* (Baltimore, 1968); L. W. B. Brockliss, *French Higher Education in the Seventeenth and Eighteenth centuries. A Cultural History* (Oxford, 1987), 151–163.

24. A recent publication in this field: H. E. Bödeker *et al.* (edd.), *Aufklärung und Geschichte. Studien zur deutschen Geschichtswissenschaft im 18 Jahrhundert*, (Göttingen, 1986).

25. A. Th. van Deursen, *Geschiedenis en toekomstverwachting. Het onderwijs in de statistiek aan de universiteiten in de achttiende eeuw* (Kampen, 1971); J. Roelevink, 'Bewezen met authenticque stukken. Juridisch-oudheidkundige drijfveren tot het uitgeven van teksten op het terrein van de vaderlandse geschiedenis in de achttiende eeuw' (in K. Kooijmans, (edd.). *Bron en publikatie. Voordrachten en opstellen over de ontsluiting van geschiedkundige bronnen, uitgegeven bij het 75-jarig bestaan van het Bureau der Rijkscommissie voor Vaderlandse Geschiedenis* (The Hague 1985), 78–99; C. J. H. Jansen, 'Over de 18e eeuwse docenten natuurrecht aan Nederlandse universiteiten en de door hen gebruikte leerboeken', *Tijdschrift voor Rechtsgeschiedenis:*

Revue d'histoire de droit: The Legal History Review 55 (1987), 103–115; C. J. H. Jansen, *Natuurrecht of Romeins recht. Een studie over leven en werk van F. A. van der Marck (1719–1800) in het licht van de opvattingen van zijn tijd* (Leiden, 1987).

26. Roelevink, 'Bewezen', 81, 82.
27. I. L. Leeb, *The Ideological Origins of the Batavian Revolution. History and Politics in the Dutch Republic 1747–1800* (The Hague, 1973); F. W. N. Hugenholtz, 'Adriaan Kluit en het onderwijs in de mediaevistiek' *Geschiedschrijving in Nederland. Studies over de historiografie van de nieuwe tijd*, vol. i (The Hague, 1981), 143–162.
28. I. C. G. Boot, *De vita et scriptis Petri Wesselingii* (Utrecht, 1874); Roelevink, *Verleden*, 154–159.
29. Roelevink, *Verleden*, 157.
30. Roelevink, *Verleden*, 160–170.
31. J. A. C. Rovers, *Memoria Heusdii* (Utrecht, 1841); A. J. Lakke, *Ph. W. van Heusde (1778–1839)* (Leiden, 1908); Roelevink, *Verleden*, 171–176.
32. Roelevink, *Verleden*, 82–85 and a list of the ninety-nine MSS lecture notes on various subjects traced so far, 346–354.
33. J. Wille, *De literator R. M. van Goens en zijn kring. Studiën over de achttiende eeuw* vol. i (Zutphen, 1937) and Roelevink, *Verleden*, 159, 164.
34. For instance E. Breisach, *Historiography, Ancient, Medieval and Modern* (Chicago and London, 1983), 193; D. Hay, *Annalists and Historians. Western Historiography*, chapters 7 and 8; S. Bertelli, *Ribelli, libertini e ortodossi nella storiografia barocca* (Florence, 1973). See also P. H. Reill, *The German Enlightenment and the Rise of Historicism* (Berkeley, 1975), 34, and G. Gusdorf, *Les Sciences et la conscience occidentale*, vol. vi, *L'Avènement des sciences humaines au siècle des Lumières* (Paris, 1973), 225. A. Grafton, 'Polyhistor into Philolog. Notes on the Transformation of German Classical Scholarship, 1780–1850', *History of Universities* 3 (1983), 159–192, obviously prefers the word polyhistor. See also Roelevink, 'Historia', 283, 284 and *Verleden*, 220–228.
35. Roelevink, *Verleden*, 293–298.
36. Meijer, *Perizonius*, 142–193; Roelevink; *Verleden*, 263–277.
37. P. Wesseling, *Pro historiis oratio* (Utrecht, 1735); Bodleian Library, Oxford, MS Hertford College E 22, P. Wesseling, 'Dictata in historiam universalem', 1758, fo. 14.
38. Burgsteinfurt Castle Archives, MS 19a, P. Wesseling, 27; Van Deursen, *De Rhoer*, 20–25.
39. Roelevink, *Verleden*, 270, 274.
40. Hammerstein, *Jus*, 144; Roelevink, *Verleden*, 177–178, 238–261.
41. P. Gay, *The Enlightenment: An Interpretation* 2 vols. (London, 1970), II, 388; Reill, *German Enlightenment*, 127–189.

42. University Library, Utrecht, MS 1645 (7 D 38), Ph. W. van Heusde, 'Dictata in historiam gentium', 1804–1805 and MS 1645 (7 D 39) with the same title.

43. So far forty two MSS with notes, taken during Wesseling's lectures, have been traced and twenty MSS concerning Saxe, mainly autographs (Roelevink, *Verleden*, 339–345).

44. The book was first edited in 1598 (E. C. Scherer, *Geschichte und Kirchengeschichte an den Deutschen Universitäten* (Freiburg im Breisgau, 1927), 115; J. H. J. van der Pot, *De periodisering der geschiedenis, een overzicht der theorieen* (The Hague, 1951) 152).

45. Roelevink, *Verleden*, 181, 182.

46. *Johann Beckmann's dagboek van zijne reis door Nederland in 1762*, G. W. Kernkamp, (ed.), *Bijdragen en mededeelingen van het Historisch Genootschap* 33 (1912), 417.

47. Meijer, *Perizonius*, 185, 186; D. Wyttenbach, *Vita Davidis Ruhnkenii* (Leiden, 1799), 95, 96; J. Engel, 'Die Deutschen Universitäten und die Geschichtswissenschaft', *Historische Zeitschrift* 189 (1959), 255, 256.

48. Roelevink, *Verleden*, 277–288.

49. University Library, Utrecht, MS 0 D 25, Saxe, 'Horatii Tursellini *Epitome Historiarum* interprete C. Saxio' (autograph, after 1764) fo. 131.

50. F. E. Manuel, *Isaac Newton Historian* (Cambridge, 1963), 38, ('The pivotal problem'); A. Seifert, *Cognitio historica. Die Geschichte als Namengeberin der frühneuzeitlichen Empiri* (Berlin, 1976), 138 ('Dispositionsprinzip of universal history'). For Perizonius see Bodleian Library, Oxford, MS D'Orville 226, 'Dictata in Tursellini Epitomen', fo. 1; MS D'Orville 228, 'Dictata in Tursellini Epitomen', fo. 1; and Meijer, *Perizonius*, 156–162.

51. Wesseling's earliest known lectures, delivered in Franeker in 1732, are interspersed with *quaestiones* (University Library, Leyden, MS Bibliotheca Publica Latina 523 I and II, 'Dictata in historiam universalem', taken down by L. C. Valckenaer). Comparison with Valckenaer's 'Adversaria juvenilia' (MS Bibliotheca Publica Latina 475) and a look at Saxe's *Quaestiones Literariae*, edited in Utrecht in 1767 suffice to see the close link between lecture and exercise.

52. Roelevink, *Verleden*, 117–132 about disputations and dissertations.

53. J. F. G. Goeters, *Theologische Realenzyklopedie* 11 (1983), 246 ff.; H. Faulenbach, *Weg und Ziel der Erkenntnis Christi. Eine Untersuchung zur Theologie des Johannes Coccejus* (1973) and more specifically G. Möller, 'Föderalismus und Geschichtsbetrachtung im XVII. und XVIII. Jahrhundert', *Zeitschrift fur Kirchengeschichte*, Dritte Folge I, 50 (1931), 393–400. A recent discussion of chiliasm in the seventeenth century Dutch Republic, E. G. E. van der Wall, *De mystieke chiliast Petrus Serrarius (1600–1669) en zijn wereld* (Leiden, 1987).

54. C. Saxe, *Oratio de veteris et medii aevi historia in academiis potissimum discenda docendaque* (Utrecht, 1776).

55. University Library, Utrecht, MS 0 F 18, P. Wesseling, 'In historiam Belgicam secundum continuatorem Tursellini dictata' (1758) and British Library, London, MS 11,529, P. Wesseling, 'Historia saeculi XVII' (after 1750).

56. Roelevink, *Verleden*, 193, 194.

57. University Library, Leyden, MS Bibliotheca Publica Latina 523, P. Wesseling, 'Dictata in historiam universalem', fo. 5; Bodleian Library, Oxford, MS Hertford College E 22, P. Wesseling, 'Dictata in historiam universalem', fo. 6.

58. Roelevink, *Verleden*, 193, 194.

59. University Library, Utrecht, MS 0 D 23, 'Horatii Tursellini *Epitome Historiarum* interprete C. Saxio' (autograph, in or after 1764), fo. 14.

60. Royal Library, The Hague, MS 74 D 9, J. M. Gesner to C. Saxe, 24 April 1746. For Gesner see U. Muhlack, 'Klassische Philologie zwischen Humanismus und Neuhumanismus', in R. Vierhaus, (ed.), *Wissenschaften im Zeitalter der Aufklärung*, (Göttingen, 1985), 108, 109.

61. In 1753 Saxe introduced a course on 'Archaeologia sive ars critica monumentorum veterum' (University Library, Utrecht, MS 5 N 20). For the Leipzig professor Johann Friedrich Christ: E. Dörffel, *Johann Friedrich Christ, sein Leben und seine Schriften. Ein Beitrag zur Gelehrtengeschichte des 18. Jahrhunderts* (Leipzig, 1878).

62. Roelevink, *Verleden*, 39, 174.

63. Apart from the numerous lecture notes see Ph. W. van Heusde, *De school van Polybius of geschiedkunde voor de negentiende eeuw* (Amsterdam, 1841).

64. Roelevink, 'Historia gentium', 127 ff.

65. Roelevink, *Verleden*, 74, 75.

66. A. L. von Schloezer, *Vorstellung seiner Universal-Historie* (Göttingen, 1772, 1773).

67. Roelevink, *Verleden*, 186, 349.

68. Roelevink, *Verleden*, 276, 277 and University Library, Utrecht, MS Var. 752, Ph. W. van Heusde, 'Dictata in historiam gentium' (1808–1809), fo. 1–4, edited Roelevink, 'Historia Gentium', 130–132.

69. Roelevink, *Verleden*, 312.

70. Roelevink, *Verleden*, 313, 314.

71. Roelevink, 'Historia Gentium', 287, 288.

72. Roelevink, *Verleden*, 116, 131, 132, 314.

73. Roelevink, *Verleden*, 314.

74. On Germany recently K. H. Jarausch, 'The Institutionalization of History in 18th-Century Germany', *Aufklärung und Geschichte*, 25–48, with a chart of lectures at Göttingen, based on the *series lectionum*.

75. S. von Lempicki, *Geschichte der deutschen Literaturwissenschaft bis zum Ende des 18. Jahrhunderts* (Göttingen, 1968).

Experimental Physics and the Natural Science Curriculum in Eighteenth Century Louvain

Geert Vanpaemel

During much of the eighteenth century, the scientific and cultural education provided by the university of Louvain was not held in very high esteem by partisans of the Enlightenment. Reports from government officials repeatedly claimed that the whole educational system of the university was totally outdated. One even went so far as to say that 'it does not come as a surprise that outside the Netherlands one has almost completely forgotten the existence of this university.' Another contemporary observed that it was 'enraging to see philosophy [in Louvain] so badly taught by people so well paid'.

These and similar remarks have created the strong impression that the general level of academic learning at Louvain was low, or at least not up to the standards expected by an enlightened cultural elite. This impression is further enhanced by the important role played by Patrice François de Nény (1716–1784), royal commissioner for the university and chief-president of the Privy Council. Nény was an indefatigable advocate of academic reform, keen to counteract the influence of the powerful Faculty of Theology in the Southern Netherlands.[2] His interference in university affairs became particularly apparent in the Faculty of Arts, which offered a propaedeutic philosophical instruction for all students, but where courses were mostly followed by future theology students. On several occasions Nény furthered the novel study of an experientially orientated natural science to support the rise of a more independent philosophy course. Among other things he initiated in 1764 a grand reform of the philosophy curriculum.

However, this emphasis on the individual contributions of one man has tended to obscure the position of the university itself and its own internal evolution that stimulated or opposed possible reform. In particular with regard to the natural science curriculum it is highly misleading to explain the changes during the last decades of the eighteenth century exclusively as the result of an unwelcome pressure from an outside authority on a recalcitrant institution. This would be to underestimate the fact that the study of natural philosophy itself was undergoing rapid changes, imposing new demands on the curriculum and on the expertise of the professors. Even without the meddling of Nény, the traditional educational system of the university was already under great strain because of the changing character of the disciplines in which it provided instruction.

The question of reform cannot then be settled by a mere reference to the political aims of the local government. Nény certainly supported the expansion of natural science teaching in the university and probably advocated that expansion to obtain some influence in the institution for himself. Nevertheless, he was only the heir to a movement which had taken root over the previous century and had already introduced a series of reforms.

To make more explicit the profound changes that were necessitated in the method and structure of the traditional teaching habits of the university, we propose to look at the rise of experimental physics as a new academic discipline in the philosophy curriculum. It should be stressed, however, that the expression experimental physics will not be used to indicate a method of research or the spreading of experimental discoveries in the university courses. Experimental physics as an academic discipline refers in our view primarily to a particular way of teaching, involving the demonstration of experiments and the illustration of natural phenomena to permit closer study. In this sense experimental physics did not necessarily have to alter the content or character of physics as it was taught, but it did change very deeply the habits of the teachers who had to cope with such new problems as defective instruments or talking rather than dictating to an audience.

Louvain did not produce any great scientists during the eighteenth century. The professors' courses in natural philosophy are rather mediocre and, in most cases, a simplified copy of what was available in standard textbooks. But like other science professors in Europe, the Louvain professoriate was forced to come to terms around the middle of the century with the vogue for experimental demonstrations and everything that came with it. This forced them to become acquainted with a kind of knowledge that was not be found in any book, but was learned through personal experience with manipulating the instruments. I will argue that the reform of the natural science curriculum was not brought about by any pressure to conform to new scientific or political ideologies. Rather it was the result of the tedious and exacting care imposed on the Faculty staff in the maintenance and development of its *Cabinet de physique*. The evolution of the natural science curriculum in the eighteenth century should be understood in the first place against the background of the internal scientific challenge presented by the teaching of experimental physics.

The Meaning of Experimental Physics

The one single event which caused the rise of experimental physics in the Louvain philosophy curriculum, was the publication from 1743 onwards of the *Leçons de physique expérimentale* of the French abbé J.A. Nollet (1700–1770).[3] This does not mean, however, that the professors had never mentioned any experiment to their students before they had read Nollet. In fact, experimental physics had been a substantial part of their teaching since the end of the seventeenth century. This was due in the first place to the influence of Jacques Rohault (1618?–1672), a leading French Cartesian who presented in his famous *Traité de physique*, issued in 1671, a new kind of Cartesian natural science.[4]

Descartes' original doctrine with regard to physics formed a rather rigid system. The logical foundation was deduced from Descartes' metaphysical system, which never really caught on in Louvain or in any other Catholic university. The fact that Descartes pretended to explain the natural world and even prove the existence of God from only a few rational *a priori* statements, squarely put Cartesianism in opposition to the orthodox theological dogmas. In particular the problem of transubstantiation could not be rationally comprehended if matter was essentially defined as extension. Rohault offered a solution in separating the physical from the metaphysical. In his view, Cartesian science had no need to be based on metaphysical *a priori* truths, but could conclusively be proven *a posteriori* by the sheer multitude of observations and experiments that it could explain. The philosophy professors in Louvain appreciated very much this new approach to Cartesianism and borrowed extensively from the many apposite experiments described in the *Traité*.[5]

In the preface to his book, Rohault had summed up the various benefits to be expected from the use of experiments in natural philosophy. Instead of reasoning and disputing only on the most general notions, experiments made it possible, Rohault claimed, to descend from these abstract discussions to an 'extensive and certain knowledge' of particular phenomena. Experiments could also yield new insights, but this was not really the aim of Rohault's physics. Throughout his work he remained faithfully within the boundaries of Cartesian principles, which were confirmed by but not deduced from the experimental evidence.

The Louvain professors followed Rohault quite literally in his exposition of the Cartesian System. A rather surprising consequence was that the traditional university disputations, so much despised by Descartes, now flourished again. Indeed, the dispute was found to be very well suited to establishing the superiority of Cartesian principles of natural science against the scholastic or Aristotelian viewpoint. During the first half of the eighteenth century these disputes grew ever larger, treating not only the principles of natural science but also and increasingly the many observations and experiments related by Rohault and others. By far the largest part of the lecture notes was taken up by disputes. To the professors the invariable outcome of every dispute in favour of Descartes' position was ample proof, as they were always keen to point out to their students, that the New Science had definitely superseded the Old. The reason for this was, they said, the novel deployment of experiments.

Yet, the experimental approach of the Cartesians was still far removed from what came to be known in the eighteenth century by the name of experimental physics. First of all, there was no clear definition of the word experiment. Anything that could be experienced by the senses was given the qualification *experientia* or *experimentum*. Some of these observations were indeed genuine experiments in a modern sense. There is no doubt that the usual stock of classroom experiments was performed in the Louvain curriculum. A list drawn up in 1754 of the instruments used in the various colleges of the Faculty shows that each of them possessed a collection of standard equipment, consisting of airpumps, telescopes, electrical machines, mirrors and globes.[6] A detailed description of many of these pieces of equipment can still be found in the extant student note–books. But these experiments (with the possible exception of the pneumatic experiments) did not lay at the core of the natural philosophy course. They were part of a subset of treatises on practical science, the so called physico–mathematical disciplines, including mechanics, hydrostatics, pneumatics and optics. Even in the Cartesian view of natural philosophy, these topics were merely of a secondary nature.

The disputes on the other hand were concerned with the more speculative principles of natural science, and appear not to have relied very much on real experimental demonstrations. They were in the first place meant to be rhetorical exercises for the students, who were asked to explain a wide class of 'experiences', ranging from the double image seen by a drunk person to the horrible taste of vapid beer. But since there was in fact no limit to the range of phenomena that could be studied in this way, the scope of natural philosophy became indefinitely large and nearer perhaps in some respects to the scholastic *quaestiones* than to the eighteenth century definition of physics. The professors' stress then on the 'use of experiments' as it was heralded by many professors merely reflected their empirical outlook in studying scientific matters, not their actual commitment to performing experiments, nor their understanding of contemporary experimental research.

Another characteristic of Cartesian empiricism in the Louvain curriculum was the absence of any attempt to link different observations and experiments into some logical chain of reasoning. Opportunities to do this were constantly swept aside. Gravity was explained after Huygens by a vivid and confused movement of tiny particles in a vortex around the earth. But when it was argued that this movement should produce heat, or that gravity should change with temperature, the explanation was simply dropped and replaced by a far less accurate version. This tendency to view a disputation as an isolated argument appears all too frequently in the Louvain course of philosophy. When it was established that the tides on earth did not correspond exactly with the motion of the moon, there was no effort made to compare the real occurrences of the tides with what was taught about the moon's eclipses. And although it was concluded at the end of one disputation that the movement of invisible particles obeyed the same rules as could be inferred from visible bodies, in another it was just as easily agreed that the behaviour of light particles in optical refraction was exactly the opposite from the usual movement of macroscopic particles.

Such an *ad hoc* changing of arguments sharply contrasts with the tight logical structure that was maintained throughout the disputations. But experiments were not considered to settle a dispute, nor were they used to test the truth of statements that were initially introduced to explain other experiments. Disputes were not guided by the experimental evidence. They were in many cases simply about the experiments, regarded as any other phenomenon to be explained. Conclusions reached at the end of one discussion had no influence on the next one. In this way experiments, although omnipresent in the curriculum, were only pretty illustrations of the impressive explanatory powers of the Cartesian doctrine.

The procedure, followed by Nollet in composing his *Leçons* was entirely different. It was not his aim, he proclaimed, to offer another *cours d'expériences,* but rather a course in experimental physics. As a teacher he knew that the best way to catch the attention of his audience was to 'speak to their eyes' by avoiding any tiresome exposition of doctrine and performing instead as many experiments as possible. Yet, Nollet wanted to teach philosophy, not to amuse. In this, he differed from most of his learned colleagues, who often looked upon their experiments as complementary illustrations of their philosophical views. Nollet not simply invented entertaining experiments; his whole reasoning was built on experiments.

Nollet was a master in thinking up original devices, with which even the most abstract principles could be clarified. When his *Leçons* were completed, he had succeeded in treating the whole of natural philosophy through a long uninterrupted chain of agreeable experiments and without help of metaphysics or loose speculations. Through his teaching (which proved an enormous success) the traditional standards of philosophy instruction were suddenly changed. Nollet's lively style and his remarkable apparatus showed that it was possible to teach physics in a practical, appealing way. As a confirmation of his impact on university education, Nollet became in 1753 the first professor of experimental physics in the university of Paris. In a very short time, other chairs would be installed in most of the European universities.[7] Experimental physics as a philosophical discipline in the academic curriculum had finally come of age.

Building Up the Cabinet

Essential in the rise of experimental physics as an academic discipline was the building up of a *Cabinet de physique*. Instruments were often expensive, so that even a modest set of equipment would very soon outgrow the resources of a philosophy professor. In particular Catholic universities, such as Louvain, met with great difficulties since their professors received only a very moderate salary, often largely based on student attendance. For them, the acquisition of large private collections by one professor, as was sometimes seen in Protestant universities, was generally impossible.[8] The *Cabinet* could only be built after enough money had been collected by the university.

In fact, most of the Catholic universities did not have an instrument collection before 1750. At best, there were some essential pieces of equipment, such as an air pump, a few mirrors and probably an electrical machine. This general view corresponds very well with the situation at Louvain, where the Faculty of Arts was divided into four separate colleges, another handicap in collecting together the necessary funds. We have already mentioned the existence of an instrument collection in every college of the Faculty. We have no idea as to the quality or price of the items. It was said that the instruments were made 'by the hand of good craftsmen'. But the main thing to note is that by 1754 most of them were out of order.

This apparent neglect of the instruments was probably caused by a lack of money to take care of the maintenance and renewal of the apparatus. The existence of four separate colleges, each with its own resources, was certainly not beneficial in constructing a viable Cabinet. In 1743 the Faculty petitioned the Austrian government in Brussels to obtain a subsidy of fl. 10,000 for the purchase of new instruments. The request was refused.[9] It seems that the colleges were in the first place reliant on gifts from their professors and students for the upkeep and acquisition of instruments.

The question of raising funds for the Cabinets was tackled again in 1754, this time by Nény. He ordered the Faculty to sell all the books in the college libraries, which did not deal directly with philosophy, and to use the proceeds of the sale to improve the instrument collections. The Faculty, understandably, took a firm stand against the decree. In the end, Nény had to abandon his project, but during the negociations it was agreed that the four separate collections of the Faculty were to be amalgamated and that a proper course in experimental physics after the example of Nollet was to be prepared. A list of instruments urgently needed for the new course was drawn up and Nény saw to it that 22 items on the list were donated to the Faculty by the governor of the Southern Netherlands, Charles of Lorraine. The gift amounted to about fl.1,600.[10]

The new course started on 17 March 1755. There were to be 24 lectures of two hours each, taking place on Tuesday and Friday for three consecutive months. The course was considered part of the regular philosophy curriculum and had to be attended by the students of the Faculty of Arts at the end of the two-year course. The lessons were given by four professors of the Faculty (one from each college), who were each year assigned to the job. Since spectators from outside the Faculty were also allowed in the audience, the course was regarded as public. The only building suitable for the course was the main building of the Faculty, the *Vicus*. Both building and course were often referred to as the School for Experimental Physics.

The establishment of the School was clearly a result of Nény's perseverance to impose his will on the Faculty, not used to such an interference with its affairs. The colleges were not happy to give up their private instrument collections but they complied. The action of Nény appears not to have been taken as an encroachment on university priviliges. The professors had to rearrange their curriculum and to learn the necessary operations with the unfamiliar equipment. A young professor, still in his first year of teaching, volunteered(?) to work out all practical arrangements and to take on the administration of the School. This professor, J. P. Sauvage (1725–1771), was described by the dean of the Faculty as 'one of the most zealous among us for this establishment [*i.e. the School for Experimental Physics*] and the most versed in these matters'. Sauvage personally assisted his colleages with the demonstrations and appears to have assumed the responsibility for the maintenance of the instruments. Most important, he was the author of the curriculum for the course. It was taken almost without alterations from Nollet's *Leçons*.

Yet the introduction of the course on experimental physics in Louvain was not a success. Already after a few years the Faculty complained that several instruments could only be partially used and that others were out of order. It was impossible to find some one to make the essential repairs. Local craftsmen often lacked 'the delicacy, the precision and the extreme exactitude' to refurbish the instruments. The Brussels instrument maker H. J. de Seumoy, who had manufactured the apparatus ordered by Nény, suddenly refused to take care of his own constructions. For its financial resources, the School was entirely dependent on the generosity of the Faculty. Originally Nény had advised the Faculty to charge the students for the extra instruction they received, but the Faculty had rejected the suggestion. As a result, there was barely enough money to secure the continuation of the demonstrations and the proper maintenance of the collection.

There was also a storage problem. In 1759, the English priest J. T. Needham (1713–1781) inspected the instruments and found that they were 'dispersed (. . .), piled in granaries or garrets, and exposed to air, and humidity'. His judgement on the Cabinet was devastating, dismissing it as 'a certain collection of instruments, mostly constructed in wood, where metal is absolutely necessary for the entire success of an experiment, selected without knowledge, tast, order or principles, ill modelled many of them by aukward work-men from *abbé* Nollet, who is himself an author more brilliant, than scientifical, chosen here and there from scattered lessons indeliberately, more because they strike the senses, than the understanding, some of them merely of a secondary nature, pretty, if you please, but merely accessory, while the less expensive essentials are wanting'.[11]

The most pressing problem, however, was the incompetence of the professors to handle the instruments. Sauvage complained to Needham that 'the state of a professor here is but a transitory state, and so employed in other occupations, that it is impossible, that either he [Sauvage] or any professor should make themselves masters of the experimental part of philosophy; consequently I [Needham] was to excuse, and this was his apology, the very imperfect collection of instruments, and his incomplete knowledge'. Indeed, a professorship at the Louvain Faculty of Arts averaged about ten to fifteen years, in which most of the professors completed their studies in one of the higher faculties. The natural end of a professorship was reached when the professor was given a Church office or promoted to another faculty. Moreover, teaching philosophy was an absorbing occupation, logic, physics and metaphysics being treated by each professor. Also the preparation of students for the public examinations at the end of their two-year course was always an exhausting experience for the students as for the professors. Experimental physics was just another of the many duties a professor had to attend to. Needham concluded that there was an 'absolute necessity, of appointing persons, whose sole employment, as in every other university, should be an entire attachment to the experimental part of philosophy, which is in fact, and ought to be a separate science not in the Theoretical, but practical part'.

Sauvage was not the right man. He had been a brilliant student, but now he was building up a university career, which probably did not leave him much time for experimental physics. In 1760 he was raised to a (small) professorship in the Law Faculty, still retaining his full-time lecture commitment in the Faculty of Arts. He presumably also kept his position in the School for Experimental Physics (by lack of other candidates?), since less than a month after his death in 1771 Nény wrote a letter to the Faculty on the urgent question of appointing a proper director for the School. The Faculty apologized by pointing out that Sauvage had always been responsible for the School, but had never submitted any report about the state of affairs. It was clear to everyone that the School needed a director.

On at least two previous occasions, Nény had tried to find someone capable of taking the responsibility for the lectures on experimental physics and for the maintenance of the instrument collection. Already in 1754 he had asked Seumoy, the instrument-maker, to instruct and assist the university professors in their new task, but Seumoy declined, maybe because he didn't want to leave Brussels. In 1759, Nény hoped to engage Needham at the School, but this time his plan was frustrated at the Imperial Court in Vienna. Finally, in 1771, Nèny would have his way.

The Reform of Philosophy

Before entering the next phase in the history of the School, it is worthwhile to consider the influence of the experimental physics course on the philosophy curriculum of the Faculty. Obviously, the course itself as part of the curriculum can be seen as just another new discipline to be added to the total spectrum of natural philosophy. In this way it may be compared with the introduction of a formal mathematical education into the curriculum by a decree of 1702. But the introduction of elementary mathematics did not interfere with any previously taught treatise, nor did it cause another approach to teaching in general.

The discipline of experimental physics on the other hand was different in that it affected not so much the content but rather the habits of teaching. It was a practical, not a speculative discipline, so that although it often treated the same topics which were also discussed in the main philosophy course, it followed an entirely different method, and a very appealing one to eighteenth century audiences. Would not traditional instruction in the natural sciences in turn adopt some of the novel approaches expounded so elegantly by this latest adjunct to the philosophy curriculum?

There are some reasons to believe that this was not the case. On a personal level, it is obvious that not many professors showed great enthusiasm for learning how to handle the instruments. If so many instruments were put out of action, this was due in the first place to the careless and clumsy manipulation by people with a rather 'incomplete knowledge' of experimental physics. From the start of the course, the professors assigned to do the demonstrations were invariably *secundarii*, i.e. younger professors with less experience and a lower status than their colleagues, the *primarii*. Until 1759, they were assisted by Sauvage but from that date on they apparently were left to their own devices. There was not much time to gain proficiency, either. The philosophy course lasted for two years and since the professors followed their students, a *secundarius* only at the end of every second year had the chance to work with the apparatus. (It may be assumed that they had no interest to visit the Cabinet outside their regular duties—which were many). When after a few years a *secundarius* was promoted *primarius* (or left the Faculty), he probably was very happy to leave the job to his successor, who had to start all over again.

An important divide between traditional natural philosophy teaching and experimental physics was their mutual separation in place as well as in time. The traditional instruction was given in the colleges, where professors and students lived and worked together. The course in experimental physics on the other hand was given in the *Vicus*, the only building large enough to accommodate an audience of at least 100 students. Given the theatrical character of a course with so many demonstrations, it can be imagined that students (and professors) would not take it as seriously as their cumbersome dictations and refined disputes, which made up the bulk of their student years. Moreover the course in experimental physics was placed at the end of the whole philosophy curriculum, a time when most students may have thought that there was nothing more to learn, and in any case were already preparing themselves for their final examinations. Adding all these elements together, it may be wondered whether the experimental physics course was indeed regarded as a regular part of the instruction, or rather as an attractive but futile show-piece.

Somehow, however, the presence of a course on experimental physics must have had an impact on the philosophy curriculum. Even if the traditions of the Faculty did not facilitate a proper integration between the old and the new approaches, it did start an awareness among the university's professors and students that the subject-matter of natural philosophy was gradually changing. To be sure, the Louvain course of experimental physics was nothing more than a series of demonstration experiments. Its objective was to teach, not to investigate. Yet these experiments, well devised, could make visible and understandable physical reasonings that were otherwise much too difficult to be inserted in a natural philosophy course. The use of elaborate mathematical techniques put many eighteenth century natural philosophy treatises outside the intellectual range of the Louvain professors. What was really so appealing in experimental physics was that it could do away with the mathematics and directly show the workings of the laws of nature. Nollet, like many other authors on experimental physics, pictured his audience mainly as 'incapable of understanding algebraic or geometrical expressions'.[12] With his ingenious devices he was able to explain to students, using only rude quantitative measurements, phenomena that would otherwise have been well beyond their understanding.

In the Louvain curriculum this can be best demonstrated by the science of motion. In the traditional treatises, this science dealt with speculative questions such as the definition of movement, place, vacuum and time; the primary and secondary causes of movement; and the general laws of motion, of which the first stated that the quantity of motion in the universe was always preserved. The rules of impact, on the other hand, initially introduced as part of the Cartesian Revolution of the late seventeenth century, had disappeared again before 1750. Their study was only reintroduced into the curriculum through the course in experimental physics, where the mathematically complex rules were experimentally examined for elastic as well as inelastic collisions. Furthermore, experimental physics could demonstrate the laws of projectile motion and centrifugal force, which were hardly ever mentioned in the regular course, due to their intricate mathematical difficulty. Now, if complex mathematics could not be used in the regular physics course, it was hardly to be expected that phenomena such as these would be regarded as an important part of the study of nature's laws. The fact that at last some of these notions had become visible and even accessible to detailed study, effectively removed the most important barrier to the professors regarding them as part of natural philosophy.

Proof of this growing awareness was given at the occasion of the curriculum reform starting in 1764. The reform was initiated by a letter from Nény, urging the Faculty to drop the old-fashioned *materiae promotionis* and to replace them with treatises summed up in the letter. Nény's reforming zeal was not primarily directed at the teaching of natural science, although he certainly called for a more practical mathematical training and a more thorough exposition of such disciplines as astronomy, botany, anatomy, physiology, geography and zoology. More imperative in Nény's eyes were changes in the teaching of logic, metaphysics and moral philosophy. Here he knew to expect resistance from the Faculty, and supporting its stance, the conservative Faculty of Theology.

Surprisingly, Nény found the Arts Faculty very co-operative: it merely wished to consult the theologians on the proposed reform of moral philosophy. With regard to natural science, the suggested reform was favourably received by everyone. The professors immediately began to write new treatises. In fact, the Faculty readily admitted that the old treatises 'were not made with all the exactitude, nor at the same time with all the comprehensiveness, which are required by the new discoveries of the *physique expérimentale*'. When the professors came up with a *Prospectus* of the new curriculum of natural philosophy, they had reworked their lecture-notes to allow for a simultaneous discussion of demonstrations and experiments in connection with the normal theoretical exposition of principles and definitions.

Thus with regard to the natural science curriculum, the reform of 1764 can be viewed as an overdue adjustment of the traditional education to the style and influence of experimental physics. The scope of natural philosophy was narrowed and became much more in tune with the enlightened view of the subject, albeit that mathematics was still neglected or naively (mis)used in the study of phenomena. Yet, paradoxically, despite the professors' apparent enthusiasm for experimental physics evinced in their response to Nény's call for reform, the situation of the Cabinet deteriorated.

The general neglect and mismanagement of the instrument collection aptly portrays, in reality, the continual lack of interest and hence the ignorance on the part of the very professors, who were writing the new treatises and adapting them to the requirements of the *physique expérimentale*.

The lasting success of the reform could only be secured if some members of the Faculty could be persuaded to take the new physics to heart. This was not the obvious thing for them to do, since they usually aspired to a career in the Church, where theology would be of more use to them than experimental physics. Besides, the more natural philosophy developed into a physical science based on experiments, the more the difference between logic, metaphysics and natural philosophy became accentuated. Since every professor was to lecture on all three disciplines, this increasingly imposed an intolerable burden. Professors were bound to specialize and for career reasons few would choose natural philosophy.

At this point, we can return to Nény's letter of 1771 in which he proposes to appoint a director for the School for Experimental Physics. The choice fell on Jan Frans Thijsbaert (1736–1825), professor of philosophy since 1759, about whom very little is known prior to his nomination. However, the choice turned out to be a very fortunate one.

A Career in Natural Science

When Thijsbaert became director of the School in 1771, he was given full responsibility for the acquisition, maintenance and repair of the instruments in the Cabinet. He received no salary but could dispose of some funds, originally destined for the then vacant chairs of French and mathematics, later to be supplemented by the income from the vacant chair of Latin History. From the Faculty he received a fund of fl.700 and even managed to obtain a loan of fl.800, which he never seems to have paid back. As another means of income for the School, he could use part of the proceeds from the sale of didactic engravings and textbooks, an initiative for which he himself was largely responsible.

Already after two years, Thijsbaert reported the purchase of some fifty new instruments, to which was appended a second list of equal length of instruments still required. Most of the apparatus he bought in these years can be divided into three groups. The first group contained the typical demonstrations instruments, still much in the style of Nollet. In a second group we find small scale models of machines, such as cranes, mills and steam-engines. The third group consisted of a very diverse stock of spectacular devices intended for popular entertainment rather than strictly for teaching.

Over the years, Thijsbaert's choice of instruments shows a decisive change. Very soon he had made contacts with the English instrumentmakers, who at the time were the best in Europe. In 1778 Thijsbaert wrote proudly that his Cabinet had been enriched with 'several first class instruments, made by the best craftsmen of London'. The most expensive instrument he ever bought was an orrery made by George Adams (1750–1795). It cost 85 guineas or about fl.1,000. Thijsbaert purchased several telescopes, a good quadrant, a barometer from Jesse Ramsden (1735–1800), a compound pendulum clock and many other precision instruments, which could be used for accurate measurements, as indeed they were.[13] But in a course on experimental physics they were only accessory pieces. The students were not trained to do any research, nor would they have been able to appreciate the value of the costly apparatus. So why did Thijsbaert spend so much money on instruments so alien to his purposes? The answer is that Thijsbaert had changed his orientation: from demonstrator he had become a collector. If teaching had been his original profession, the pursuit of science itself, or at least participation in the scientific enterprise, lay now at the centre of his interests.

The first step in this direction was probably caused by his contact with the travelling Portuguese scientist J. H. de Magellan (1722–1790). Thijsbaert may have met Magellan already one month after his appointment as director. Magellan offered to help Thijsbaert with the Cabinet and served as an intermediary between London and Louvain. On at least one occasion, Magellan also instructed Thijsbaert how to adjust and repair some of his instruments, even providing him with the necessary materials. Through Magellan, Thijsbaert came in contact with the growing community of scientists and instrument-makers, which in the 1770's was directly responsible for 'the rising standards and improving accuracy of physics'.[14]

Thijsbaert soon developed other habits, which were typical for the eighteenth century scientist-collector. He bought books and subscribed to scientific journals, such as the very popular *Journal de*

Physique. He started a collection of natural history objects. He received renowned visitors in his Cabinet (P. Camper, M. van Marum, A. Volta, N. Pigott, . . .) with whom he sometimes carried on a stylish correspondence. And inevitably, he set himself to do some rather amateurish scientific research.

He was not a great scientist, though. When in 1773 he applied for membership of the recently founded Academy of Brussels, he submitted a paper on how achromatic vision was obtained in the eye and the telescope.[15] Probably the paper had no originality or went no deeper into the subject than in the textbook on optics Thijsbaert was writing at that time. It was declined even before being presented to the whole assembly. Thijsbaert offered to work it over, or to submit another paper on the improvement of some of the demonstration apparatus in his Cabinet. Nothing came of it, but it shows the kind of work he was doing in the School.

His efforts did, however, have a favourable influence on the philosophy curriculum. Early in the 1770s he initiated a novel interest in the writing and publishing of manuals for the use of the students. This had not happend in the Faculty for some 150 years. Thijsbaert himself wrote the *Geometria elementaria et practica* and the *Elementa opticae et perspectivae*. Another professor wrote a book on arithmetic and algebra and a third colleague a new book on geometry, after Thijsbaert's went out of print. These books obviously changed the traditional teaching methods of the Faculty, which were still based on *verbatim* dictations, but more importantly they proved that it had become worthwhile for at least some professors to devote a considerable part of their time to the study of an exclusively scientific discipline.

The most conspicuous representative of the scientific spirit spread by the School for Experimental Physics among the professors was Jan Pieter Minckelers (1748–1824), who became a professor of philosophy in 1771. Minckelers became something of an assistant to Thijsbaert, sharing his interest in natural science and delicate instruments. Together with Thijsbaert he introduced the newest discoveries in chemistry to Louvain, producing the only scientific publication by a member of the Faculty during the eighteenth century.[16] Later Minckelers would recall that he had rewritten all the treatises on natural science in the curriculum, so as to incorporate the evolving contemporary conception of the correct approach to physical science. These treatises had outgrown the

stage of the casual demonstration of principles through experiments. Minckelers instructed his students how to perform scientific
research, providing them with tables of numerical values or with
mathematical formulae, even discussing recent work of contemporary scientists. In particular the rapid appearance of an account of
Lavoisier's research in his lecture-notes indicates the alertness and
the understanding of the Louvain professor with regard to what was
going on at the very frontiers of science.[17]

The School for Experimental Physics under the guidance of
Thijsbaert succeeded in convincing the Faculty that the study of
natural science should be based on a thorough experimental knowledge and, in addition, a suitable mathematical education. The old
disputes disappeared and were replaced by detailed descriptions of
experimental apparatus and procedures, such as the different ways
of producing inflammable air. Several features of the traditional
medieval Faculty structure were affected by this evolution. We
have already mentioned the change in teaching methods and the
growing specialization of the professors. Allusion should also be
made to a reform of the examination system, more adapted to the
kind of knowledge the students were supposed to have attained.
Furthermore, the Faculty of Theology took an interest in the
development, its members naturally concerned at the 'materialist'
philosophy being taught in a faculty considered to be its 'nursery'.

Some of the consequences to which this evolution would lead
were made apparent in the short-lived University of Brussels, to
which all Louvain Faculties except Theology were transferred.[18]
The University was founded in 1788 by the Austrian government as
a part of the grand reform undertaken in the universities of Austro-
Bohemia. Only five of the sixteen Louvain professors of philosophy
were invited (and agreed) to teach in Brussels, among them
Thijsbaert and Minckelers. Thijsbaert designed the new philosophy
curriculum. It comprised three years of study with elementary
mathematics and natural history in the first year, and physics and
applied mathematics in the second. Every course was taught by an
individual professor, who no longer followed his students through
the curriculum. Since the Brussels institution had completely broken with the old college system of Louvain, a closer study of its bare
two years of existence could yield invaluable information on the
Enlightenment ideal of natural philosophy teaching, an ideal which
obviously could never be fully realised at traditionalist Louvain.

The history of the Brussels University is however so completely immersed in the tense political situation in the Southern Netherlands in these years that a satisfactory judgement about its educational activities cannot yet be reached.[19]

When in 1790 the university was reinstalled at Louvain, it refused to admit Thijsbaert and Minckelers because of their role in the Brussels institution.[20] Louvain returned to its old traditions. The restoration did not last very long, however: in 1797 the University was abolished by the revolutionary French authorities as a part of their general reform of education. The intellectual history of the Southern Netherlands had reached a highly important hiatus.

Conclusion

The natural science curriculum at eighteenth century Louvain travelled a long way, from the 'Cartesian' disputations of the first half of the period to the mathematical analysis of experimental phenomena at the end. The reforms initiated by Nény may seem to account for these profound changes, but although Nény's support was helpful in breaking through the academic structures, he did not at any time put forward views on the nature of science and scientific education, which the Faculty would be compelled to adopt. The actual path that reform was to take over the century was determined by members of the Faculty itself. Above all, the poor record of the School of Experimental Physics during its early years shows that heavy government support was not enough to secure whatever the School was meant to attain.

Moreover, the establishment of the School in 1755 with its course on experimental physics should not be taken as the decisive step away from the traditional teaching system. It created some disturbance in as much as it crossed the institutional boundaries between the four colleges, but there was no real opposition to this. The School was generally considered a convenient solution to some of the huge practical problems, recognized by the Faculty for at least a decade. In fact, it excited no particular enthusiasm for experimental physics among the professors, who waited another ten years before adapting their dictations to the 'new discoveries of the *physique expérimentale*'. The course on experimental physics as it was installed by Nény was on the whole nothing more than a formal reorganization of an earlier situation which had grown out of hand.

The real importance of the School for the reform of the natural science curriculum became only apparent later on. It was the need that arose out of the School to appoint an 'expert' in modern physics, who knew what eighteenth century physical science was all about, that made all the difference. By concentrating the instruments of the four colleges in one School, the former difficulties concerning their maintenance were not immediately solved. Although Nény paid for a whole set of new instruments, it was not to be expected that the inexperienced professors would know how to handle them. It was therefore a consequence only of the problems encountered with the Cabinet after 1755 that a permanent appointment was made. But this appointment was crucial. The nomination of Thijsbaert and his ensuing career as a scientist-director was the real decisive point in building the new science curriculum.

It is not our aim, however, to replace the emphasis usually placed on Nény by attaching an exaggerated importance to the personal efforts of Thijsbaert. Rather, we want to point out that the example of Louvain follows a pattern that was common to many other European universities. The introduction of experimental physics in the universities around the middle of the eighteenth century was often not simply a matter of installing a course of demonstrations after the fashion of Nollet. The course had to be supplemented by a Cabinet, whose quality was often decisive in the level of success the course would have with the different audiences for which it catered. But building up a Cabinet proved to be much more difficult than lecturing from Nollet's *Leçons*. If there was no-one with enough knowledge of experimental physics, the fate of the Cabinet (as happened at Louvain) was uncertain. Some universities attracted a qualified professor (e.g. Volta in Pavia, Van Musschenbroek in Utrecht, Nollet in Paris); others appointed a 'mechanic' (e.g. Watt in Glasgow). With this pattern in mind, the actions of Thijsbaert as director of the School for Experimental Physics are clearly not to be treated in isolation. Indeed Thijsbaert's role should be seen as peculiarly illustrative of a significant development hastening changes in the university curriculum generally at the end of the Ancien Régime.

Characteristically, the influence of Thijsbaert did not come about so much through his performance as a scientist, which was mediocre, but rather through his successful fulfilment of a mere technical job. The institutional development of the *Cabinet de physique* created the opportunity and provided the encouragement for students and professors to learn about the nature of contemporary scientific research. As a result this development should be considered the major step in bridging the gap between the philosophical education of the Ancien Régime and nineteenth-century scientific education.

Vanden Bemptlaan 4
B-3030 Leuven,
Belgium

REFERENCES

1. The first quotation comes from a 1768 report by Prince Kaunitz to the Empress Maria Theresia pleading for the foundation of an academy in Brussels. His detailed criticism may be given here in full: 'L'on ne peut pas dire non plus que l'université de Louvain manque entièrement de sujets savants, il y en a plusieurs qui ont des connaissances très-étendues dans leur partie; mais tout leur savoir, toutes leurs études sentent la poussière de l'école et la pédanterie, et comme ils négligent entièrement le talent de s'exprimer avec pureté et précision dans les langues vivantes, et qu'ils ignorent totalement l'art de mettre de l'intérêt dans un ouvrage où il est question de quelque matière abstraite, il n'est pas étonnant que, hors des Pays-Bas, on ait quasi oublié l'existence de cette université'. Published in the *Annuaire de l'Académie* (Brussels, 1838) 151–178. The second quotation is a private observation made in a letter by Noël Paquot, professor of history in Louvain, to Nény in 1764. As in the rest of this paper, we will not include references to manuscript sources. For more information on the evolution of the natural science curriculum at Louvain, the reader is referred to my *Echo's van een wetenschappelijke revolutie. De mechanistische natuurwetenschap aan de Leuvense Artesfaculteit (1650–1797)*, 'Verhandelingen van de Koninklijke Academie voor Wetenschappen, Letteren en Schone Kunsten van België. Klasse der Wetenschappen', 48 (Brussels, 1986), no. 173, especially 18–35, 48–59, 133–160. This study is primarily based on the analysis of student notebooks and Faculty archives.
2. On the political ambitions of Nény, see H. Carton de Wiart, *Nény et la vie belge au 18ème siècle* (Brussels, 1943), and J. Roegiers, 'De jansenistische achtergrond van P. F. de Nény's streven naar een

"Belgische Kerk"' *Bijdragen en Medelingen betreffende de Geschiedenis der Nederlanden* 91 (1976), 429–454.

3. J. A. Nollet, *Leçons de physique expérimentale* (6 vols.; Paris, 1743–1748).

4. J. Rohault, *Traité de physique* (Paris, 1671). On Rohault, see P. Clair, *Jacques Rohault (1618–1672)*. *Bio-bibliographie avec l'édition critique des Entretiens sur la philosophie* (Paris, 1978).

5. G. Vanpaemel, 'Rohault's *Traité de physique* and the Teaching of Cartesian Physics' *Janus* 71 (1984), 172–182.

6. The Faculty of Arts consisted of four colleges, called *pedagogia*, each with its own resources and staff. In each college were two *primarii* and two *secundarii*, making the total number of philosophy professors in the Faculty sixteen. The colleges were independent institutions, though their philosophical courses were actually rather similar. At the end of the two year course in philosophy the students of all four colleges were ranked in a collective examination.

7. J. L. Heilbron, *Elements of Early Modern Physics* (Berkeley/Los Angeles/London, 1982), 132–139. J. Torlais, 'La physique expérimentale', in: *Enseignement et diffusion des sciences en France au XVIIIe siècle*, ed. R. Taton (Paris, 1986), 619–645.

8. J. L. Heilbron, *Elements*, 141–142.

9. F. Claeys Bouuaert, *Contribution à l'histoire économique de l'ancienne université de Louvain*, Bibliothèque de la Revue d'Histoire ecclésiastique 32 (1959), 17–18.

10. The largest of the private instrument collections in the colleges was valued at fl.400. The total value of the Louvain Cabinet should then be taken as about fl.2000. This figure should be compared with the value of 's Gravesande's collection, bought by Leyden University around the same time for fl.3,931. Needham, who inspected the Louvain instruments, estimated in 1759 that a suitable Cabinet would cost at least three to four thousand florins. Many of the university collections in Europe, however, were about the size and value of the Louvain Cabinet. See J. L. Heilbron, *Elements*, 139–144.

11. The negative report of Needham to Nény may have been somewhat exaggerated since Needham was trying to obtain the post of director for himself. Still his information seems accurate enough to be a true description of the actual state of affairs.

12. Nollet, *Leçons*, vol. 1, *Préface*.

13. N. Pigott, 'Observation of the Transit of Mercury over the Sun's Disc, made at Louvain' *Philosophical Transactions* 76 (1786), 384–388.

14. J. L. Heilbron, *Elements*, 70.

15. E. Mailly. *Histoire de l'Académie Impériale et Royale des Sciences et Belles-Lettres de Bruxelles*, 'Mémoires couronnés et autres mémoires

196 *History of Universities*

publiés par l'Académie royale des sciences et des lettres de Belgique',
34 (2 vols.; Brussels, 1883), i. 101–105.

16. J. P. Minckelers, *Mémoire sur l'air inflammable tiré de différentes substances* (Louvain, 1783). A critical edition was published by P. A. Th. M. Jaspers and J. Roegiers in *Lias* X/2 (1983), 217–252.

17. The assimilation of Lavoisier's work, however, from 1783 did not include any of his theoretical innovations. The professor only reviewed (and probably repeated) the Frenchmen's experiments, paying attention in particular to his production of 'inflammable air' from water.

18. The history of the Brussels University is treated by A. Verhaegen, *Les cinquante dernières années de l'ancienne université de Louvain (1740–1797)* (Liège, 1884). A recent study of the reform of the natural science curriculum at Louvain, in which much attention is paid to the Brussels institution is B. Urbain-Van Tiggelen, *La Faculté des Arts de Louvain face au gouvernement autrichien, une institution sclérosée ? Les réformes introduites dans l'enseignement des sciences (1715–1790)*, Mémoire de licenciée en Histoire, Université Catholique de Louvain, (Louvain-la-Neuve, 1987), in particular 120–139.

19. On the Brabantine Revolution see S. Tassier, *Les démocrates belges de 1789* (Brussels, 1930) and J. Craeybeckx, 'De Brabantse Omwenteling: een conservatieve opstand in een achterlijk land ?' *Tijdschrift voor Geschiedenis* 29 (1967), 303–330.

20. Minckelers returned to his native Maastricht, where he continued teaching and set up as a pharmacist. He later became a member of the Brussels academy. See P. A. Th. M. Jaspers, *J. P. Minckelers (1748–1824)* (Maastricht/Leuven, 1983). Thijsbaert appears to have retired completely from the scientific life.

Grandes Écoles, Petite Université: Some Puzzled Remarks on Higher Education in Mathematics in France, 1795–1840

I. Grattan-Guinness

To the memory of Charles Schmitt

This article is divided into two parts. The first provides a survey of the institutions of French higher education in the period, with especial reference to mathematics: the *Ecole Polytechnique* and the various schools devoted to engineering, the re-formed *Université*, and the *Collège de France*. The concluding remarks emphasize the contrast in prestige between these schools and the *Université*, and also doubt that French science declined after 1830 to the extent which historians normally assume. The second part of the article contains two illustrative episodes of policy in mathematical education: the reception of Cauchy's treatment of the calculus at the *Ecole Polytechnique*, and the fate of Monge's descriptive geometry.

Part I. The Panorama of Institutions

1. The new structure

The term 'grandes écoles' was not normally used at this time, and 'petite Université' is my own invention; but while the language is anachronistic, the picture which it conveys is accurate enough. In contrast to the preferred place in their educational structures granted to universities in other countries, France has set its special *écoles* above the *Université* ever since the Revolution, especially for the physical sciences (where the overlap is most marked).

Figure 1 indicates in schematic form the principal institutions of education and of profession pertaining to the physical sciences (or,

Figure 1. Schematic outline of institutions.

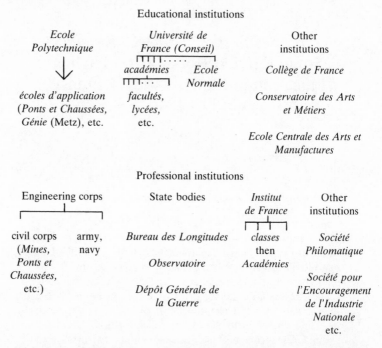

Educational institutions

| *Ecole Polytechnique* | *Université de France (Conseil)* | Other institutions |

↓ *académies*   *Ecole Normale*

écoles d'application (*Ponts et Chaussées,* *Génie* (Metz), etc.   *facultés,* *lycées,* etc.   *Collège de France*

Conservatoire des Arts et Métiers

Ecole Centrale des Arts et Manufactures

Professional institutions

Engineering corps   State bodies   *Institut de France*   Other institutions

civil corps (*Mines, Ponts et Chaussées,* etc.)   army, navy   *Bureau des Longitudes*   *classes* then *Académies*   *Société Philomatique*

Observatoire

Dépôt Générale de la Guerre   *Société pour l'Encouragement de l'Industrie Nationale* etc.

as they were then called, 'mathematical sciences'). This paper will deal entirely with the first row, although those in the second row will be mentioned on occasion, mainly in Section 7.

After the Revolution of 1789 virtually all educational institutions of the *ancien régime* were either suppressed or suspended. Some were restarted without major alteration, but many of them were eliminated, so that either a gap was left in the structure or new institutions were put into place.[1] In the next Sections I shall briefly review some of the most important ones for mathematics.

2. On the Ecole Polytechnique

The early history of this school is extremely complicated, and I shall pick out only some principal features.[2] It was rapidly formed in 1794, and opened at the end of that year (more precisely, in month *nivôse* of Revolutionary *an* 3). Originally called the 'Ecole Centrale des Travaux Publics', it was conceived as *the* institution for the

Figure 2: Topics at the Ecole Polytechnique, 1795; teaching structure.

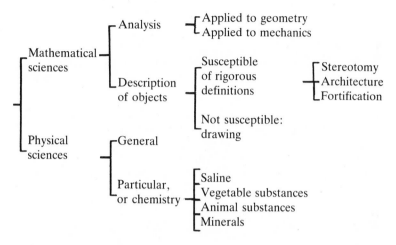

training of engineers—not only for public works (civil and mechanical engineers as we would recognize them) but also for the army and navy.

Soon it was realized that this conception would not work: for example, naval engineers could not be properly taught in a city where the Seine river was the only available water-way. So the school quickly evolved into the 'Ecole Polytechnique', a *preparatory* school where many techniques (hence the name[3]) would be studied. Mathematics was given a prominent place from the start, and chemistry, physics[4] and various branches of engineering joined the other main subjects. (Minor ones included grammar and literature, some foreign languages, and personal hygiene.) Figure 2 shows an early presentation of the main courses, in the form of a synoptic table.[5] This was a favoured mode of representation at the school, evidence of the positive influence of 18th-century *encyclopédisme* on the institution.

The founding *promotion* of students was nearly 400, enrolled in several stages in 1794 and 1795. This proved to be far too large, and the student body was reduced to between 100 and 160 until the Restoration. Then it fell further, often down to around 100 until after the 1830 Revolution, when it climbed back towards 150. Students at the school were (and are) known as *polytechniciens*.

The enrolment of students was effected by the work of the admissions examiners, who visited principal towns in the various parts of provincial France and interviewed students in the June and July before the new academic year; the same procedure was also conducted in Paris. There was also a senior grade of examiner, in two posts; these passed or failed the students from one year to the next and then upon graduation. Both founder *examinateurs* were mathematicians (Bossut and Laplace); their post became qualified with the adjective 'permanent' when in 1798 two *examinateurs temporares* were added, to examine respectively in descriptive geometry and 'graphic arts' and in physics and chemistry. (In the following year the length of the course was reduced from three years to two, so more *examinateurs* had less to do!) One purpose of these *examinateurs* was to act as checks on policies of the teaching body, for nobody could be *professeur* and *examinateur* (in this senior grade) at the same time. The effectiveness of this strategy collapsed during the 1820s, as we shall see in Section 8.

Table 1 lists the *examinateurs* and main *professeurs* for mathematics. The dates given for these offices mask some complications (absences for illness, and so on). In addition, the junior posts of *répétiteurs* are omitted: some of them were promoted to *professeur*, when they are listed here.

From the start the school had the *Journal*, in which lecture notes were printed. However, in a sign of things to come, it rapidly became a forum for research articles (especially in mathematics); so Monge's assistant Hachette started in 1804 a *Correspondence sur l'Ecole Polytechnique*, which contained articles more suitable for students, problems to solve, and news of the school. This valuable publication lasted through three volumes until 1816, when Hachette was forcibly retired (on this, see Section 9).

Some important changes in organization came in during the 1800s. A governing body, the *Conseil de Perfectionnement*, was instituted in 1800: its role, especially in Laplace's hands, will be noted in a moment. Then in 1804 the school was militarized, bringing a marked change of atmosphere:[6] a somewhat free and easy style was replaced by regimentation. The directorship was made a permanent post and given to a solder, Lacuée; previously the post had rotated among the *savants*, including Monge. A new post of *Directeur des études* was instituted, and for some periods the incumbent was officially the second in command. Distinguished holders

Table 1: *Professeurs* and *examinateurs* for mathematics at the *Ecole Polytechnique*, 1795–1840. The date after a name indicates his *promotion* as a student at the school.

Analysis and Mechanics *Professeurs*		Descriptive Geometry *Professeur*	Machines *Professeur*
1794–1814 de Prony	1794–1799 Lagrange	1794–1810 Monge	1806–1816 Hachette
1814–1828 Ampère	1799–1808 Lacroix	1799–1815 Hachette	1817–1818 Petit (1807)
1828–1839 Mathieu (1803)	1808–1815 Poisson (1798)	1810–1816 Arago (1803)	(Machines, geodesy)
1839–1850 Liouville (1825)	1816–1830 Cauchy (1805)	1816 Duhays	1818–1831 Arago (1803)
	1831–1836 Navier (1802)	1817–1849 Leroy	1832–1841 Savary (1815)
	1836–1839 Duhamel (1814)		
	1840–1855 Sturm		

Examinateurs		*Examinateur*	
1794–1808 Bossut	1794–1799 Laplace	1799–1804 Ferry	1817–1821 Lefebure de Fourcy
1808–1815 Lacroix	1799–1816 Legendre	1805–1811 Malus (1794)	1821–1824 Fresnel (1804)
1815–1840 Poisson (1798)	1816–1838 de Prony	1811–1814 Ferry	1825–1841 Demonferrand (1812)
	1838–1863 Mathieu (1803)[a]	1815 Binet (1804)	1831–1864 Babinet (1812)

[a]Mathieu deputized from 1831, although he was also a *professeur*!

included the *polytechniciens* Malus (1812), Binet (1816–1830), Dulong (1830–1838) and Coriolis (1838–1843), who closes our story in this post in Section 10.

At the restoration of 1816 the fate of the school was in the balance for some months; but in the end the major changes were of staff rather than curriculum or general structure (revolutionaries Monge and Hachette were ejected; Catholics Binet and Cauchy promoted). Similarly, after the revolution of 1830 changes in personnel were the most notable consequences (Catholics Binet and Cauchy both left, the latter into self-appointed exile, while Navier became a *professeur*). The new generation of mathematicians held the main posts (*professeurs, Directeur des études* and *examinateurs*) for many years, especially Duhamel, Lamé, Liouville and Sturm.

Looking over the history of the school over its first four decades, three issues stand out. They are of rather different character, and are not presented in any special order.

Firstly, there was some tension between the needs to provide civilian public works engineers and military engineers. This is reflected in the struggle between the Ministries of the Interior and of War to be the controlling influence: even after the school was militarized, the former ministry still exercised considerable authority until the other took over exclusively in 1831.

Secondly, there were severe disputes about the type of mathematics taught at the school, especially concerning the relationship between 'orthodox' applied mathematics and engineering mathematics. At first, when Monge was prominent in its direction, the curriculum was oriented towards practical engineering needs; but after 1800 Laplace in particular nudged the courses towards the more theoretical and general applications of the subject, arguing that the special needs of engineering would be more appropriately carried out in the other schools. We shall see some examples of this tussle in Sections 8 and 9—and also complications to this rather over-simplified form of the difference.

Thirdly, the school gained a high prestige, to such an extent it became a glory place; and yet it was a *preparatory* school for engineers, and not particularly oriented towards research. Its high status was doubtless due to the fact that it was created in an educational near-vacuum, and so was surrounded by (next to) nothing; but the degree of mis-match between status and function is remarkable. One has only to compare the list of illustrious names of its staff in Table 1 with the minor figures who composed the staff at the more specialist, and therefore more advanced, schools to which the *polytechniciens* passed.

3. The 'écoles d'application'

This was the name soon given to this group of specialist schools. Eight were in place by the 1800s, and others were added from time to time later.[7] Some were strictly military and others civilian. The majority were away from the capital, but three were in Paris, and two of those—*Mines* and *Ponts et Chaussées*—had been founded in the mid 18th century and suffered little change after the Revolution. The system of schools was very important; many of the (later) 'grandes écoles' belonged to it. Nevertheless, none of them has been well studied by historians, and indeed the majority not at all; even the existence of the system is little known.[8]

Two of the schools stand out in importance here. One, the *Ecole des Ponts et Chaussées*, was something of a midwife to the birth of the *Ecole Polytechnique*. The connection was strengthened in 1798 when its directorship passed to de Prony, who was already a founder *professeur* of mathematics at the new school. He kept both connections for 40 years, practically to the end of his life.[9] However, while he was diligent as teacher and examiner at the *Ecole Polytechnique*—we shall see some evidence of this in Section 8—his control of the other school was rather negligent. His *professeurs*, such as Eisenmann and Bruyère, were not exactly among the leading *savants* of Paris, and the teaching of applied mathematics was put on a sound footing only in 1819 when Navier, *polytechnicien* and also graduate of this school, was appointed to a supplementary chair.

This appointment is a remarkable example of research and education working together; in the following decade Navier not only prepared important lecture notes but also published a suite of researches on elastic bodies and viscous fluids (hence the 'Navier-Stokes equations') which contributed to the founding of linear elasticity theory.[10] Yet still the school was not running well; so a substantial reform was effected around 1830, in which Coriolis joined the staff. In a related reform of the professional *Corps de Ponts et Chaussées*, a new journal was launched: its *Annales*, an important source both of technical articles and of pertinent laws and decrees.[11]

The other school which deserves description here is the *Ecole de l'Artillerie et du Génie* at Metz in Alsace. Its name reflects its constitution, for it was composed of the famous military school at Mézières (moved in 1794 to Metz in order to be further away from the British) and the artillery school at Chalons-sur-Marne (about half way between Paris and Metz), which was transferred there in 1802.[12]

This school is of interest relative both to educational policy and to research. Although its mathematical *professeurs* were again minor (though interesting) figures—the *polytechnicien* J. F. Français, Ferry and Servois among them—it was quite ready to criticize the *Ecole Polytechnique* over the inappropriateness of the teaching there. (An example is cited in Section 8 below.) And its own teaching received a stimulus in 1824 when Arago, who was a graduation examiner there, persuaded Poncelet to begin a course in machine theory.

At that time Poncelet had hardly done any teaching: *polytechnicien* and graduate of the Metz school, he had pursued a military career (including imprisonment after the failure of Napoleon's campaign to Russia) and was then based with the garrison at Metz. But soon he began to develop a very general theory of mechanics, based in part on Navier's teaching at the *Ecole des Ponts et Chaussées*, in which shock and impact was included and conversion between kinetic energy and work (to use the modern terms) took place. He published a textbook on these ideas in 1829,[13] and thereafter issued suites of lithographed lecture notes and two different textbooks drawn from the first.[14] He also applied these ideas to specific engineering problems, especially the design of water-wheels; and he inspired at Metz a quartet of *polytechniciens* (Lesbros, Didion, Piobert and especially Morin) to a wide variety of researches in friction effects in large equipment, the motion of large bodies of water, the performance of water-wheels and turbines, and so on.

This suite of researches, many of which were also taught at Metz and elsewhere, is of especial note for having taken place largely in the provinces. However, Paris would not be left out: simultaneously with Poncelet's original researches in the 1820s, *répétiteur* Coriolis at the *Ecole Polytechnique* was developing broadly the same approach to mechanics (more as a research than an educational enterprise) and published his own book on the matter, also in 1829.[15] In fact, the word 'work', as a technical term, was introduced by him here.

4. *Two other schools for engineers*

The *Conservatoire des Arts et Métiers* was set up in 1799 in a disused church in Paris (where it still exists) both as a repository for instruments and equipment and also as a teaching institution at a relatively elementary level (corresponding roughly to a modern technical college). Its educational activity was rather low key until 1819, when a reform took place, initiated partly by Arago. Three new chairs were set up, and one of them dealt with 'geometry and mechanics'. This post was taken by Dupin, *polytechnicien* and naval engineer, and he held it for the remaining 55 years of his long life. Dupin taught many of the current theories—for example, the ideas of Poncelet and Coriolis just described—at a simple level; but he began his lecture course each November or December with a public address on some current question in education, science, engineering or economics. The addresses were famous in their time, widely reported in the newspapers and both printed there and as journal articles and pamphlets. In particular, his concern with work brought him via work-rate and ergonomics to questions of working conditions of the working class, and so to social questions, which he pursued with still more vigour when he was elected a *député* to the lower *Chambre* in 1828.[16]

During the following year a new school was founded. It was of a new type, and filled a serious and strange gap in the institutions for higher education. The *écoles d'application* were directed towards public works and military engineering: no effort was made to create comparable schools for commercial and industrial engineering. Despite this, a vast amount of activity went on in these areas, especially with the *Société pour l'Encouragement de l'Industrie Nationale*, founded in 1801 by the chemist Chaptal while he was *Ministre de l'Intérieur*; a variety of small societies and journals was also in operation, in Paris and elsewhere, and the *Conservatoire* (with similar *écoles* at Angers and Chalons-sur-Marne) gave some instruction.[17] But the educational base was inadequate, and so the *Ecole Centrale des Arts et Manufactures* was launched in 1829.[18]

Several features of this school are worth noting. Firstly, it was a private enterprise venture, of five men in their twenties and thirties. The most important were a rich landowner called Lavallée, who bought their first premises in Paris and was the *Directeur* until his death in 1862; and Dumas, then a young chemist, who began his great career in laboratory instruction with this school. Secondly, its founding was permitted only through the strong support of the *Ministre de l'Instruction Publique*, who had to oppose official indifference even at that time. Thirdly, the name of the school was undoubtedly chosen in imitation of the original name of the *Ecole Polytechniqe*, the 'Ecole Centrale des Travaux Publics', and with the original aims of founders such as Monge still in mind. An influence here is likely to have been one of the minor founders, the mathematician Olivier; he was one of the most devoted disciples of Monge's descriptive geometry, and in the 1840s he attacked the drift towards theorization at the *Ecole Polytechnique* with a venom remarkable even by Parisian standards ('the *Ecole Monotechnique*, a school of algebra', and so on).[19]

As far as the teaching of mathematics is concerned, the emphasis fell on mechanics and engineering mechanics, and descriptive geometry—rather similar in context to the *Ecole Polytechnique*, in fact. (The differences between the two schools is evident in the far less attention paid to mathematical analysis, for example, and in the teaching of chemistry and chemical technology.) The teachers of mathematics included not only Olivier but also Coriolis,[20] Liouville, the Swiss engineer Colladon (who spent the years 1825–1835 largely in Paris) and Perdonnet (who succeeded Lavallée as *Directeur*). The early years of the school were difficult—in addition to the lack of public support, it was struck particularly hard by the cholera epidemic of 1832—but it picked up well, and was receiving some subvention by the mid-1830s. By mid-century it was another *grande école*.

5. The so-called 'Université'

The *Ecole Polytechnique* was not the only new school which opened in the mid 1790s; for early in 1795 the *Ecole Normale* began work, in the buildings of the *Muséum*. It was an 'instant' teacher training college of 1200 students chosen from around the country; the idea was that they would return to their local areas after some months' tuition and help found similar schools there.

The basic conception was rather absurd; and the severity of the winter weather helped the school to its early demise.[21] The most durable residue of its existence was an edition of lectures given by the *professeurs* (who included Lagrange, Laplace and Monge) under the title *Séances des écoles normales*. Various versions appeared between 1795 and 1800, the later ones including related articles by others (for example, *polytechnicien* Biot).[22]

No school was set up to replace the *Ecole Normale*; and furthermore, nothing comprehensive was done to compensate for the suppression of the universities in 1793. As a result, the training of several professional classes was falling into desuetude; for example, the system of *écoles centrales* (supposedly models of Enlightened education) had to be converted in 1803 into the more traditionalist *lycées* in part for a lack of qualified teachers of science.[23]

Eventually, in 1808, a new system was introduced. After pressure from various *savants*, in particular the chemist Fourcroy, Napoléon issued a decree creating the *Université Impériale*, and it began to function in 1810. The word 'Université' is misleading, as the system did not resemble a university in any normal sense of the term. It was a monopolistic structure for school education, in which the Empire was divided into about 30 *académies* (another word used in a misleading way!). Each one was composed of several *départements*, and was named after the town in which the administrative headquarters was located (for example, 'Académie de Montpellier', which had no connection with the learned society in that town!).[24]

In addition, higher-level teaching was carried out in *Facultés* of theology, law, letters, medicine and science. They were also placed under the academies, but only the *Académie de Paris* possessed all five. Naturally, the *Faculté des Sciences* in Paris was the most important such faculty, and its *professeurs* were drawn from the *Ecole Polytechnique*, the *Muséum*, and other institutions in the city: Lacroix (who was also the founder *Doyen*), Hachette, Francoeur and Poisson for various branches of mathematics, Biot for astronomy, and Haüy for physics.[25]

In addition to *professeurs*, the *Université* employed *inspecteurs* to supervise courses and examinations, advise on staff appointments, and so on. There were two grades: the lower one for a particular *académie*, and an *inspecteur genéral* with jurisdiction over several *académies*. (In between these two grades in rank was the post of *recteur* of an *académie*.) Ampère and Poinsot were among founder *inspecteurs*, and in due course they gained promotion; but most of their colleague scientists were fairly undistinguished.

Also in the *Université*, but outside the *académies*, the *Ecole Normale* was started again in Paris. It was the elite institution providing accelerated education to gifted students, who should later become major bureaucrats, or *professeurs* for the *Université* or elsewhere. Its first twenty years, however, were disappointing, especially for science, and it was even closed for four years in 1822 for political 'unreliability' and only opened again as a preparatory school. After the Revolution of 1830, however, it began to improve its status; and among the sciences, mathematics was the first to show some prowess.[26] The best remembered *normalien* is Galois (who devised group theory, and promptly got shot), but he is not a typical case. Perhaps the most interesting graduate from the early years is Cournot, who studied there in 1821 and later was to rise through the *Université* system as *professeur, recteur* and *inspecteur*, and also to gain eminence as an economist.[27]

The overall direction of the *Université* was placed in the hands of a *Grand-Maître*, with a supervisory *Conseil* of around 30 members (including Legendre, and Delambre as treasurer until 1815). With the Restoration, the *Conseil* and *Grand-Maître* were replaced by a five-man *Commission*, which became a seven-man *Conseil* in 1820. Poisson joined it when it was enlarged, and stayed in post until his death in 1840. It was an arduous job, for when the body had been reduced in number the duties of each officer were made more specific and considerable.

6. The 'Collège de France'

Last, and to some extent least relative to the concerns of this paper, comes the *Collège de France*. Founded in 1530, it has enjoyed a relatively undisturbed history. In particular, it was not shut for long after the Revolution, and the main change then effected was to give it the current name (previously it had been the 'Collège Royal').

The role of this institution was (and is) very unusual in higher education: knowledge for its own sake, without entry qualifications or examinations for the students, its *professeurs* appointed often within a general academic area but free to give courses on topics of their own choice. 'It is as if the *Institut de France* gave classes', a Parisian friend described it to me, capturing very well by this analogy the chic status of the *professeurs*.

However, there is (at least) one smudge in this distinguished record of teaching and scholarship—namely, mathematics in the period from 1795 and 1840 (indeed up to the 1850s). The *professeur* of mathematics during the Revolution and Empire was one

Mauduit, who wrote a few very elementary textbooks. Poisson assisted him from 1809 to 1812, but with so many other duties to fulfil at the *Ecole Polytechnique* and the Paris *Faculté*, he was not able to make a substantial impact. Upon Mauduit's death in 1815 he was succeeded by Lacroix, one of the great textbook writers of all time but not a researcher. His successor, in 1843, was the Italian immigrant Libri, whose main claim to fame was the theft of manuscripts from French libraries, an activity detected four years later.[28] He had already gained a chair in the *Faculté*, as is recorded in Section 9.

In applied mathematics and related topics the *Collège* had a better record. In Mauduit's day the best mathematician on the staff was Cousin, although his chair was in 'general and mathematical physics'. His successor was Biot, who held the chair from 1800 to the end of a long life in 1862. While Biot had some mathematical talent, his research interests lay largely in astronomy and geodesy, and aspects of experimental physics and chemistry.

There was another chair for physics at the *Collège*, of the 'general and experimental' variety. For nearly 40 years it was held by the undistinguished Lefèvre-Gineau; but he was ousted in 1824 and succeeded, after a somewhat controversial election, by Ampère. This appointment was a recognition of Ampère's achievements since 1820 in the new science of electrodynamics; but one of the (few) other *savants* in Paris who worked in this area was Biot, who studied certain aspects of electromagnetism, and with a quite different basic approach. For once there was no open clash between the two: Biot was often away from France at this time (when Cauchy deputized, with lots of *recherché* mathematics); Ampère, in an example of the *Lehrfreiheit* possible at the *Collège*, largely dropped his interest in electrodynamics around 1827 and switched his course to the philosophy of science.[29]

At the time of the (small) changes in 1795, the top post of the *Collège*, the *inspecteur*, was held by Lalande, who was also the *professeur* of astronomy. Upon his death in 1807 his chair went to Delambre, who produced a large textbook and a comprehensive summary version of the teaching.[30] When he died in 1822, his assistant Mathieu was unanimously proposed to succeed; but the Catholic Bourbon government substituted the Catholic Binet, whom they had made *Directeur des études* at the *Ecole Polytechnique* six years before (as was recorded in Section 2). While Binet was a very capable mathematician, his appointment, like a good many others in the various parts of the turbulent period 1795–1830, also carried some political connotations.

7. *Summarizing remarks*

Conclusions of various kinds could be drawn. I shall group them together in four sub-sections. I concentrate on institutional aspects, and refer to the research achievements only in passing and without supporting evidence: two of these will be explored in a little detail in Sections 8 and 9.[31]

7.1 There is a general feature underlying the structure described above which is of considerable importance: *the growth of the professionalization of science* during these years. Indeed, here are the origins of much of the modern sense of the term: men making a living by means of state-funded appointments rather than the personal decisions of kings, princes or *Herzogen*. France was not unique in this change; but it was the leading country in most areas of science and engineering at that time, and achieved a degree of institutional development far in excess of that evident elsewhere.

These transformations took place in different ways in different countries. The French evolved a system which foreigners had the good sense to avoid: *cumul*, as it was called, the accumulation of several appointments simultaneously. These posts were held not only in the educational institutions but also in the professional bodies listed in the second row of Figure 1: the various engineering corps; the *Bureau des Longitudes* (navigation, geodesy); the *Observatoire* (astronomy); the *Dépot Général de la Guerre* (topography, cartography); and above all for power and patronage, the *Académie des Sciences* (or during the Revolutionary period the *classe* of 'mathematical' and 'physical' sciences of the *Institut de France*). In addition, societies such as the *Société Philomatique* could aid professional advancement by rapid publication of research work; there were various others such as the *Société d'Encouragement* mentioned in Section 4, and indeed further ones in the world of engineering.[32]

This is why some *savants* have been named several times above (and would have appeared still oftener in a more detailed account): Poisson at the *Bureau*, the *Ecole Polytechnique*, the *Université*, and briefly at the *Collège de France* with a supplementary chair; Ampère at the last three (and at the *Collège* with a full post); de

Prony, Coriolis and Navier at the *Ecole Polytechnique* and the *Ecole des Ponts et Chaussées* for some years; almost everybody elected to the *Académie* (or the *classe*) at some stage, and so on. Admittedly, not everybody had all these posts all the time; indeed, there were various successions and replacements.

Cumul made all personal relations very complicated: 'A' might be above 'B' when at the *Ecole Polytechnique*, say, but on a par with 'B' in the *classe* and less powerful in the *Société Philomatique*. No wonder the atmosphere was explosive at times, like a steam engine.

7.2 A related feature should be registered here. It is well known that the atmosphere was very competitive, and indeed pursuit by many men of the same post was often a cause; but one should also note that *the institutions themselves were not much in competition with each other*. The *Ecole Polytechnique* was unique in its preparatory role, and the *écoles d'application* largely divided up by discipline, even if there was some overlap among the military schools, and they were all competing for the attentions of the *polytechnicien*. Again, within the *Université*, Paris was unique in its prestige for appointments; similarly, the *Académie* or *classe* was alone in its *caché*; the *Collège de France* fulfilled a unique role in the whole system.

Above all, there emerged a division of prestige which is expressed in my title. The *Université* was second rate relative to the *grandes écoles* (the *Ecole Polytechnique* and the *écoles d'application*, to be joined by the *Ecole Centrale*; the *Ecole Normale* did not 'arrive' until late in the 19th century for science). Despite many changes since that time—the break-up of the *Université* into *universités*, and the emergence of other schools such as the *Ecole Pratique des Hautes Etudes*—there is still a notable residue of this distinction. It is worth remarking that in recent times the riots occur in the *universités*; and it is important to understand that these riots *only* occur there, never in the *grandes écoles*.

7.3 One result of the educational reforms, although not the principal one, was to produce researchers—often *polytechniciens*, who then went back into the teaching industry (there and/or elsewhere) instead of, or sometimes in addition to, taking posts in a professional body. When the suppressions and reforms took place in the mid-1790s, profound changes took place in the institutional and educational structure; but the intellectual and academic sides continued largely unchanged, and the many textbooks and treatises which began to appear were mostly filled with the knowledge accrued over past and recent decades. The principal changes at the research level occurred in great measure twenty years later, with most of the main work published between 1815 and 1827 (and most researched during this period also): mathematical analysis, heat theory, waval optics, elasticity theory, engineering mechanics, and electrodynamics and electromagnetism.

7.4 After this time, specifically during the 1830s, French science is 'well known' to have fallen into decline, and historians have sought explanations.[33] My own study of pure and applied mathematics calls severely into question the extent to which this decline occurred.[34] Some of it is only optical illusion, in as much as it is *other* countries which *rise*; some is dazzle, from the spectacular character of the *initial* breakthrough which leads one to underrate later stages. In part it is due to historians' own ignorance of French science, especially the central place in it of engineering; for example, the history of the *Ecole Centrale* (Section 4) and the activities of Ponce-let and his circle at Metz (Section 3) actually show an increase and improvement in the quality of work in succeeding decades.

Undoubtedly decline did occur for several reasons. I will stress three, not in any particular order: the excessive amount of time spent by the *savants* in their *cumul* of teaching and administration; the partial ossification of the *Ecole Polytechnique*, which entered an era of social glory but also a staid period of largely unchanging courses; and the strange and continuing uninterest of the government in industrial and commercial engineering, with the result that the *Ecole Centrale* came into being only through private enterprise. Above all, though, the story of the decline was invented by the French themselves, especially the *savants* of mid-century who partly exaggerated or misrepresented the international changes of recent decades. But that is another story—in which educational policy once again played a major role.

Part II. Two Episodes

Up to now the paper has had to be presented in broad strokes: to finish, here are summarized two specific issues in mathematics education which illustrate some of the points already made.

8. Cauchy versus the 'Ecole Polytechnique'

Broadly speaking, there have been three traditions in developing the calculus: one based upon limits, of which Newton's 'fluxional' variety was the first fully-fledged version; one based on differentials (that is, infinitesimally small variable increments on the values of variables), created by Leibniz and developed by the Bernoullis and Euler; and a purely algebraic version due to Lagrange, grounded upon the assumption that a mathematical function could always be expanded in a power series. In all these traditions, some version of the differential calculus (construction of tangents) was developed first, and the integral calculus (evaluation of areas) was taken automatically to be the inverse of the differential version.[35]

When the *Ecole Polytechnique* opened, all these traditions were evident in the teaching within a few years. Lagrange taught his own approach, of course, but de Prony preferred differentials and especially the related topic of difference calculus. When Lacroix took over from Lagrange, he taught all methods, for he adhered to the *encyclopédiste* philosophy of a plurality of methods (and maybe their classification also). By contrast, when Ampère joined the staff (in 1804, as a *répétiteur*) he started out from Lagrange's approach but nudged the theory, none too clearly, towards limits. The students became understandably confused and rather inexpert in the subject, and the military school at Metz complained about this and many other matters in 1812;[36] so a return to infinitesimals was agreed, whereupon *répétiteur* Poinsot came up with an odd course in 1815, which managed to work in elements of all three traditions.[37]

At that time Cauchy had also done some work as *répétiteur*, and when he was made *professeur* in 1816 he developed a fresh approach, based on limits as with Newton but with a far clearer theory of limits themselves and whole network of general definitions designed to cover not only the calculus but also functions and infinite series. His general aim was to raise the level of rigour in the subject; and he succeeded not only by his new treatment of limits but especially by strengthening the logic of necessary and sufficient conditions under which theorems could be proved to be true. In particular, his definitions of the basic notions of the differential and the integral calculus were independent of each other, so that the inverse relationship between the calculi became a theorem, holding only under certain sufficient conditions upon the mathematical function.

For Cauchy this increase in rigour in mathematics was part of his general view of life under the Bourbons and religion under the Pope. His textbook on the calculus of 1823 shows this unity even in its impression: forty lectures, each one printed so as to end on the bottom line of the fourth page, and presenting a theory based on a theory of limits! Now this book was entitled as a *résumé* of his teaching at the *Ecole Polytechnique*, and the four-page signatures were distributed to the students at his lectures.[38] This is an example, and moreover an important one, of mathematics being influenced in its development by mathematical education.

However, one cannot assume that *professeur* Cauchy was really tailoring his pedagogical method to the needs of a preparatory engineering school. On the contrary, right from the beginning of his teaching in 1816 objections were raised by colleages and students: too difficult for the students, inappropriate for the course, too much analysis and not enough mechanics (in the integrated course), too much lecturing and not enough discussion, and so on.

A farcical climax occurred in April 1821, when Cauchy was delivering the 65th of his alotted 50 lectures in analysis. The lectures were scheduled as 30 minutes of questioning followed by 60 minutes discourse; but 90 minutes for Cauchy meant 90 minutes of Cauchy, and on this occasion he even went on for 110 minutes without stopping. So some students go fed up, whistled and walked out.

This constituted an event in the military school, and memoranda passed between the *Directeur* and the *Ministère de l'Intérieur*. The students were sent to their barracks; but in addition the *professeur* was criticized for his manner of teaching, the content of his lectures, and also for turning up ten minutes late for the next lecture (when at last he started on mechanics).[39] His *Cours d'analyse* was in press at the time and came out a few weeks later:[40] it contained his theory of limits and other material preparatory for the calculus, and was also partly based upon his teaching at the school. But it was never used as a text, and even the *Résumé* of 1823 seems to have had little life there.

The protests against Cauchy's teaching continued during the 1820s, but only once was it effective: the *Conseil de Perfectionnement* ordered him in 1824 to cease teaching the latest extension of his theory to the (new) problem of proving the existence of a solution to ordinary differential equations.[41] Otherwise little success was achieved: in particular, *examinateur permanent* de Prony wrote lengthy criticisms of the teaching of his former student and now *professeur*, between 1826 and 1829, but hardly any changes were made in the ways suggested.[42] The personal problems were solved by the Revolution of 1830, when the *professeur* followed the Bourbons into exile; but his ideas stayed in the course, and gradually became standard world-wide. The non-control of Cauchy shows that the principle of *examinateurs* checking the practices of the *professeurs* (see Section 2) had fallen into some decline, which in turn effected the intellectual *élan* of the school to some extent, as was mentioned in sub-section 7.4.

9. The Tragicomedy of Descriptive Geometry

As was mentioned in Section 2, when Monge was prominent in the direction of the *Ecole Polytechnique* his descriptive geometry was given much time in the curriculum. This theory was a mathematical means of representing a three-dimensional object or situation in various two-dimensional sections, and conversely (re)constructing the object from these sections. Of the various theories of this kind, Monge's was a good case, because it worked with real and not apparent sections.

Monge had developed his theory before the Revolution; but since it had military uses, it was classified for a time. When it became public in the 1790s at the *Ecole Normale*, the *Ecole Polytechnique* and the *écoles d'application*, he gave it great publicity with a textbook and papers, many written with his fervent disciple Hachette. He clearly wanted to build it up as a Branch of mathematics, to sit alongside Euclidean geometry, algebra and the calculus.

But this is where the tragicomedy began, for the subject did not have a content equal to the others; so it neither became such a Branch nor remained as practical engineers' mathematics. His main textbook was full of boring questions about the number of (say) ellipsoids which were tangent internally or externally to a given set of spheres, the numbers of related tangent planes, and so on. When he came round to case studies, they were hopelessly impractical constructions to determine the heights of neighbouring points (as in a map).[43] Hachette edited a supplement to the textbook in 1811, and began it with a few pages listing contents where the theory was actually useful.[44] A few of the followers, such as Dupin, managed to make some interesting uses of the theory, but by and large it stagnated, and its decline in importance at the *Ecole Polytechnique* is quite understandable.[45] In fact, the more durable but less advertized part of Monge's approach was the companion discipline of the calculus (in its literally differential tradition) applied to the geometry of curves and surfaces. He also produced a textbook on this topic, and it lasted until a heavily annotated edition of 1850 was produced by Liouville.[46]

The fate of descriptive geometry is well illustrated by the case of Hachette. When Napoléon fell and the Restoration occurred, Hachette was forcibly retired from the *Ecole Polytechnique* (but was never given his pension[47]). By contrast, however, and an example of the lowly status of the *Université*, he was allowed to retain his supplementary chair in descriptive geometry at the Paris *Faculté* until he died in 1834. A debate then took place among the *professeurs*, including Biot, Francoeur, Lacroix and Poisson, about the successorship; and clearly the principal issue was that of the subject. Only Francoeur pressed for descriptive geometry; 'experimental mechanics', 'higher geometry', 'mechanical physics' and probability were the main topics proposed. Eventually Poisson suggested that an *adjoint* post in analysis be filled without specification of topic; and doubtless it was his machinations which let the choice fall upon probability, for the subject (which included parts of what we now recognize as statistics) was growing in importance at that time, and he himself was developing his own ideas. The post was assigned to Libri, whom we met in Section 6;[48] so the result was unhappy in the end. However, the change in subject for the *Faculté* chair was a sensible move.

A happier consequence followed from the more general discussion which ensued on Hachette's death in 1834. The chemist Thenard, as a member of the *Conseil* of the *Université* (and also currently *Doyen* of the Paris *Faculté*), wrote a report on the teaching of science. He asked for more chairs in all *facultés*, a special library for the one in Paris, strengthening of the *Ecole Normale*, and various other things;[49] and while little was done, one of the Paris chairs was quickly instituted. The promotion of 'mechanical physics' led to the creation of a post in 'physical and experimental mechanics'; and it was given to Poncelet, who had moved to Paris in

1833 as a member of the *Comité des Fortifications* (a military organization, similar in status to the *Bureau des Longitudes*).[49]

Poncelet held the job until 1848; but then he retired, giving as the main reason the poor attendance at his lectures. Generalizing upon this detail, he went on to complain of the 'deplorable scission' in science education in France between the applied and the theoretical sciences.[50] Thereby he identified precisely one of the main schisms of this partitioned system: the *grandes écoles* supposedly (though in fact not always) directed their attention towards applied sciences and mathematics, while the *facultés des sciences of the Université* restricted themselves to more general and theoretical areas, and often at a lower level.[51] Such divisions can be seen in many nations; but the structure of the French system gives their case a special *piquant*.

10. Two concluding opinions

In making allowances for man and his weaknesses, will one not eventually find that *cumul* must also tend to substitute small passions: egotism, cupidity, jealousy, intrigue, etc., for generous, elevated sentiments, to the love of glory and of celebrity? One must not admit that the love of money, which alone degrades and cramps ideas, may find a place, nor that one may even imagine it: public instruction may offer broad careers to ability, but it must not be the object of speculations.

Anonymous comments, 1831[52]

A short time before his death [in 1843, Coriolis] declared to us that he would have liked to devote the remainder of his powers to the reform of mathematical teaching, in this same direction. To bring everything into relation with the infinitesimal method was, he told us, the chief aim of his entire life, as a professor and as the director of studies. As he saw it, the teaching of mathematics in France today was the dullest, most pedantic, most tiring exercise for pupils and teachers alike that it was possible to discover, and presented the most peculiar example of deadly routine that any teaching in any period could offer. 'When men talk', he said, 'as they often do, of routine in the teaching of theology in the seminaries, they are far from suspecting that the teaching of mathematics is prey to an incomparably duller and more cruel routine'.

Gratry, 1855[53]

Middlesex Polytechnic
Enfield
Middlesex EN3 4SF

Acknowledgements

The expenses of archival research have been partly met by grants from the British Academy and the Royal Society. Thanks are due to the librarians in Paris for their assistance.

REFERENCES

1. There is a large literature, very variable in quality and degree of relevance, in and around the themes of this paper: the better, or the irreplaceable, items are cited in those footnotes. Some indications of archival sources are also given. For the general institutional and cultural context, see M. P. Crosland. *The Society of Arcueil* . . . (London, 1967); T. Bugge, *Science in France in the Revolutionary Era* . . . ed. M. P. Crosland (Cambridge, Mass., 1969); and the report on education published in *Bulletin universel des sciences et de l'industrie, sciences géographiques, canaux, voyages,* 24(1830), 267–310 (English translation in *Quarterly Journal of Education,* 2(1831), 83–113). The following abbreviations are used for journals cited often: *Ann. sci.: Annals of science; Brit. J. Hist. Sci.: British Journal for the History of Science; J. Ec. Polyt.: Journal de l'Ecole Polytechnique,* 1st series; *Mon. univ.: Moniteur universel* [the official newspaper]; *Rev. hist. sci.: Revue d'histoire des sciences.*

2. On the *Ecole Polytechnique,* see especially A. Fourcy, *Histoire de l'Ecole Polytechnique* (Paris, 1828: repr. Paris, 1987, with extensive introduction, notes and bibliography by J. Dhombres); J. Langins, *La République avait besoin des savants* . . . (Paris, 1987); his 'Sur l'enseignement et les examens à l'Ecole Polytechnique. . .', *Rev. hist. sci.,* 40(1987), 145–177; M. Bradley, 'Scientific education for a new society. The Ecole Polytechnique 1795–1830', *History of Education,* 5(1976), 11–24; [U. J. J. Leverrier], *Rapport sur l'enseignement de l'Ecole Polytechnique. . .* (Paris, 1850); G. Pinet (ed.), *Ecole Polytechnique, Livre du centenaire 1794–1894* (3 vols, Paris, 1894–97). The archives of

the school have recently been put in proper order; information from them underlies a variety of points made in this paper. See C. Billoux and N. Bayle (the heroines involved), 'Les Archives de l'Ecole Polytechnique. . .', *Rev. hist. sci.*, 38(1985), 73–82; and my 'On the Transformation of the *Ecole Polytechnique* Archives', *Brit. J. Hist. Sci.*, 19(1986), 45–50.

3. The name 'Ecole Polytechnique' was apparently proposed by the politician Prieur: it seems to be first in print in his *Mémoire sur l'école centrale des travaux publics. . .* (Paris, *an* 3), 29; see also his letter in *Mon. Univ.*, (1818), 1147, reprinted in G. Pinet, *Histoire de l'Ecole Polytechnique* (Paris, 1887), 450–451.

4. Around 1800 physics was in a relatively poor state; the teaching at the *Ecole Polytechnique* until the late 1810s reflected its status well. The raising of physics among the sciences was a major concern of the *Société d'Arcueil* led by Berthollet and Laplace; Crosland (note 1) is centred on this group.

5. The figure is based upon one in *Programme de l'enseignement polytechnique de l'Ecole Centrale des travaux publics* (Paris, *an* 3), preface. The 'programme' came out each year, with slightly varying titles usually beginning 'Programme générale de l'Ecole Polytechnique'.

6. See M. Bradley, 'Scientific Education versus Military Training: the Influence of Napoleon Bonaparte on the *Ecole Polytechnique*', *Ann. sci.*, 32(1975), 415–449.

7. For an early statement of the range and role of the *écoles d'application*, see L. Carnot, 'Loi concernant les écoles de services publics', *J. Ec. Polyt.*, 1, *cah.* 4 (*an* 4), xii–xxviii.

8. For a general survey, see F. B. Artz, *The Development of Technical Education in France 1500–1850* (Cambridge, Mass., 1966). More details, though largely appropriate for the mid-19th century, are given in two similar works by H. Barnard: *Military Schools and Courses of Instruction. . .* (Philadelphia, 1862), pt. 1, 1–274; and *Systems, Institutions and Statistics of Scientific Instruction. . .* (New York, 1872), 401–606.

9. See especially de Dartein, 'Notice sur le régime de l'ancienne Ecole des Ponts et Chaussées. . .', *Annales des ponts et chaussées*[8], 22(1906), 5–143; and M. Bradley, 'Gaspard-Clair-Francois-Marie Riche de Prony. . .' Ph.D. thesis (Council for National Academic Awards, 1984), i. chs. 2 and 3, and related manuscripts transcripts transcribed in vol. ii from the school's rich but chaotic archives. Some of this thesis is distilled in her 'Civil Engineering and Social Change: the Early History of the Paris Ecole des Ponts et Chaussées', *History of Education*, 14(1985), 171–183.

10. C. L. M. H. Navier, *Résumé des leçons données à l'Ecole Royale des Ponts et Chaussées. . .* (1st ed. 1826, 2nd ed. in 3 parts 1833–38, Paris).

11. The documents on this reform are kept in the archives of the *Ecole des Ponts et Chaussées*, esp. MS 2629 *bis,* parts 15–16; see also *Archives Nationales*, F^{14} 11057. Some manuscripts are transcribed in Bradley, 'De Prony', ii. 83–99.

12. No work of note has been done on the Metz school. The courses of the 1830s are listed in *Journal des sciences militaires* 2nd series, 2(1833), 208–224; those in operation in mid-century are given in Barnard, *Schools*, pt. 1, 137–220. Its excellently organised archives await detailed attention in Paris at the *Chateau de Vincennes, Service Historique de l'Armée de la Terre,* X⁰50–100.

13. J. V. Poncelet, *Cours de mécanique industrielle.* . . (Metz, 1829). An account of this and related matters is given in my 'Work for the Workers: Advances in Engineering Mechanics and Instruction in France, 1800–1830', *Ann. sci.,* 41(1984), 1–33.

14. J. V. Poncelet, *Cours de mécanique appliquée aux machines* (1st ed. lithographed, 1836; 2nd ed., 2 vols. [ed. X. Kretz], Paris, 1874–76); *Introduction à la mécanique industrielle, physique ou expérimentale* (2nd ed. 1841; 3rd ed. [ed. X. Kretz], Paris, 1870). Kretz was a *polytechnicien* who seems to have given Poncelet's surviving *Nachlass* to the *Ecole Polytechnique*: parts of this very interesting collection only came to light during the recent organisation of the school's archives (see footnote 2).

15. G. G. Coriolis, *Du calcul de l'effet des machines* (Paris, 1829); 2nd posthumous ed. published as *Traité de la mécanique des corps solides, et du calcul de l'effet des machines* (Paris, 1844).

16. Dupin published several of these opening lectures together as his *Discours et leçons sur l'industrie* . . . (2 vols., Paris, 1825); see also especially his *Forces productives et commerciales de la France* (2 vols., Paris, 1827). M. Bradley and F. Perrin are working on a biography of Dupin: in the meantime, this aspect of his career is briefly surveyed in my 'Work for the Workers', 25–28.

17. Secondary literature is again sparse and rather disappointing. See R. Tresse, 'La Conservatoire. . . et la Société. . .', *Rev. hist. sci.,* 5(1952), 244–264; and R. Fox, 'Education for a New Age: the Conservatoire des Arts et Métiers, 1815–1830', in D. Cardwell (ed.), *Artisan to Graduate* (Manchester, 1974), 23–38. On the general context of technical education, see C. R. Day, 'The Making of Mechanical Engineers in France. . .', *French Historical Studies,* 10(1978), 439–460.

18. The best history of the early years of the *Ecole Centrale* was written by its third *Directeur* (and son-in-law of Lavallée): F. Pothier, *Histoire de l'Ecole Centrale.* . . (Paris, 1887). The recent book by J. H. Weiss, *The Making of Technological Man.* . . (Cambridge, Mass., 1982) deals only (but usefully) with teaching and training of industrial science in France at this time, and principally with the *Ecole Centrale*; but here it is most disappointing, for principal manuscripts have been missed (the lecture notes catalogued under the names of the *professeurs* in the *Bibliothèque Nationale*; student notes in *Bibliothèque de la Sorbonne,* MSS 616–622; and files in the *Nachlass* of Colladon in *Bibliothèque*

Publique et Universitaire [Geneva], MSS Français 3741, 3743, 3746 and 3747 all *passim*). The school's own archives are very meagre.

19. T. Oliver, 'Monge et l'Ecole Polytechnique', *Revue scientifique et industrielle*, no. 128 (September, 1850), 64–68; and the preface to his *Mémoires de géométrie descriptive.* . . (Paris, 1851).

20. Coriolis's sister was married to the *normalien* Péclet, a physicist who was another of the founders of the *Ecole Centrale*. The three are buried together in the cemetry at Montparnasse.

21. See P. Dupuy, 'L'Ecole Normale de l'an III', in *Le Centenaire de l'Ecole Normale* (Paris, 1895), 1–209.

22. A new annotated edition of the *Séances des écoles normales* is in preparation for the bicentenary celebrations of the Revolution in 1989. The leadership of the project has been entrusted to J. Dhombres: see his 'L'Enseignement des mathématiques. . . Les leçons de Laplace à l'Ecole normale de l'an III', *Rev. hist. sci.*, 33(1980), 315–348.

23. Lucien Bonaparte, as *Ministre de l'Intérieur* but probably not the author, sent in 1800 a very interesting letter to the teachers of mathematics in *écoles centrales:* see *Recueil des lettres, circulaires . . . emanés des C^{ens} Quinette, Laplace, Lucien Bonaparte. . .* (Paris, 1802), 135–139. Pertinent material is to be found *passim* in S. F. Lacroix, *Essais sur l'enseignement en général, et sur celui des mathématiques en particulier*, 1st ed. (Paris, 1805); further eds. in 1816, 1828, 1838.

24. One of the best sources on the origin of the *Université* is still F. V. A. Aulard, *Napoléon 1er et le monopole universitaire* . . . (Paris, 1911). For original decrees and other valuable information, see *Mon. univ.*, esp. (1806), 644–646, 660–661; (1808), 309–312; (1809), 723–724, 1296–1298, 1406–1408 (but misnumbered 1386–1388); (1811), 419–420, 1233–1236; (1814), 728; (1815), 206–208, 757, 877, 918; and (1816), 353–354, 661–662, 684, 1021–1022, 1029, 1048, 1105.

25. Mathematics education in the Paris *Faculté* was lightly but pleasantly surveyed by C. Hermite in *Inauguration de la nouvelle Sorbonne.* . . (Paris, 1889), 30*ff.* (also in Hermite's *Oeuvres*, vol. 4, 283–313). For a broader perspective, see T. Shinn, 'The French science faculty system, 1808–1914. . .', *Historical Studies in the Physical Sciences*, 10(1979), 271–332. Among materials in the *Archives Nationales*, see especially AJ^{16} 5120-5828 and F^{17} 20001-21894.

26. See especially P. Dupuy, 'Notice historique', in *Ecole Normale (1810–1883)* (Paris, 1884), 1–79. C. Zwerling, 'The Emergence of the Ecole Normale Supérieure as a Center of Scientific Education in Nineteenth Century France' (Ph.D. thesis, Harvard University, 1976) has good information on social aspects, but rather overlooks the growth of mathematics. The archives of the school are held mostly in the *Archives Nationales*: see especially 61 AJ 1-432, AJ^{16} 48–49 and F^{17} 4149–4265.

27. Cournot's posthumous *Souvenirs* ed. E. P. Bottinelli (Paris, 1913),

itself contains valuable impressions of the *Université* and several of its personalities. An important figure in both the *Université* and the *Ecole Normale* was the philosopher Cousin, a founder *normalien* and *Directeur* of the school between 1834 and 1840 when he became *Ministre de l'Instruction Publique*. His familiarity with German and Scottish philosophy stimulated his desire to raise the level of science education at the school.

28. After Libri the teaching of mathematics improved at the *Collège de France*, with Liouville and then Jordan taking office. The only useful item of secondary literature is L. P. E. A. Sédillot, 'Les Professeurs de mathématiques et de physique générale au Collège de France', part 4, *Bollettino e bibliografia di storia della matematiche e fisiche*, 3(1870), 107–170. Particular details are disclosed in B. Belhoste and J. Lützen, 'Joseph Liouville et le Collège de France', *Rev. hist. sci.*, 37(1984), 255–304. The archives of the college are modest: the majority of the materials are held in the *Archives Nationales*, F[17], esp. 3849-3879 and 13550-13557.

29. A.-M. Ampère, *Essai sur la philosophie des sciences*. . . 2 pts. (Paris, 1834–43). The second part was edited posthumously by his Jean-Jacques, who was also a *professeur* (in humanities) at the *Collège*. André-Marie was succeeded by Biot's assistant, Savart, in 1836, who was followed by Regnault in 1841; both were *polytechniciens*.

30. J. B. J. Delambre, *Abrégé d'astronomie*. . . (Paris, 1813); *Astronomie théorique et pratique* 3 vols. (Paris, 1814).

31. The technical issues are exceedingly complicated from all points of view. I have examined them from several of those perspectives in these articles: 'Mathematical Physics in France, 1800–1840: Knowledge, Activity and Historiography', in J. W. Dauben (ed.), *Mathematical Perspectives*. . . (New York, 1981), 95–138; 'How it Means: Mathematical Theories in Physical Theories. . .', *Rendicont dell' Accademia del XL*, (5)9, pt. 2 (1985: publ. 1987), 89–119; 'From Laplacian Physics to Mathematical Physics, 1805–1827', in C. Burrichter *et al.* (eds.), *Zum Wandel des Naturverständisses* (Paderborn, 1987), 11–34; 'Small Talk in Parisian circles. . .', in G. König (ed.), *Konzepte des mathematisch Unendlichen im 19. Jahrhundert* (to appear, Göttingen); and 'Work for the Workers'. A full account is given in a large book in a press: *From the Calculus and Mechanics to Mathematical Analysis and Mathematical Physics. French Mathematicians and their Institutions, 1800–1840* (Basel, 1989).

32. Crosland, *Society of Arcueil*, provides information on several of these organisations, but none of them has been fully described. Meanwhile, rest content with a few articles in R. Fox and G. Weisz (eds.), *The Organisation of Science and Technology in France 1808–1914* (Cambridge, 1980); G. Bigourdan, 'Le Bureau des Longitudes. . .',

Annuaire du Bureau des Longitudes, esp. (1928), A1–A71, (1929), C1–C92 and (1930), A1–A110; H. M. A. Berthaut, *Les Ingénieurs géographes militaires. Etude historique*, ii (Paris, 1902); and P. E. M. Bertholet, 'Notice sur les origines et sur l'histoire de la Société Philomatique', in *Mémoires publiés par la Société Philomatique*. . . (Paris, 1888), i–xvii (also in *Journal des savants*, (1888), 477–493). Some of the archives of the *Bureau* are held in the library of the Observatoire; those of the *Société* are in the Bibliothèque de la Sorbonne, MSS 2081–2099 and carton 133.

33. The two best regarded studies are J. Ben-David, 'The Rise and Decline of France as a Scientific Centre', *Minerva*, 8(1970), 160–179 (where all the 'factual' statements about the institutional structure contain errors); and D. Outram, 'Politics and Vocation: French science 1793–1830', *Brit. J. Hist. Sci.*, 13(1980), 27–43 (which contains valuable information in and around the life sciences and chemistry but where four of the main figures for mathematics are treated only in passing and the other 28 passed over in silence).

34. The first hint of revisionism was given in H. Paul, 'The Issue of Decline in Nineteenth-Century French Science', *French Historical Studies*, 7(1971–72), 416–451; few have followed since, though examples are contained in the works of mine cited in notes 13 and 31.

35. Although there are various histories of the calculus, the fundamental importance of the different traditions is not brought out. A brief survey of the historical development is given in my 'What was and What should be the Calculus?', in I. Grattan-Guinness (ed.), *History in Mathematics Education* (Paris, 1987), 116–135.

36. See *Ecole Polytechnique, Programmes*. . . (as in footnote 5), (1812), 5; or Fourcy *Histoire*, 299–316.

37. L. Poinsot, 'Des principes fondamentaux. . .' and 'Sur le changement de la variable indépendante. . .', *Correspondence sur l'Ecole Polytechnique*, 3(1814–16), 111–131.

38. A. L. Cauchy, *Résumé des leçons données à l'Ecole Royale Polytechnique sur le calcul infinitésimal*. . . (Paris, 1823), (also in *Oeuvres complètes*, ser. 2, vol. 4, 5–261). Two additions were made to the text, of exactly four and 12 pages respectively. I found the unpublished proofs of a later third addition in the archives of the school; it is *not* so exactly calculated!

39. Some of the these documents are transcribed in my 'Recent Researches in French Mathematical Physics of the Early 19th Century', *Ann. sci.*, 38(1981), 663–690 (pp. 680–681).

40. A. L. Cauchy, *Course d'analyse*. . . (Paris, 1821) (also in *Oeuvres complètes*, ser. 2, vol. 3).

41. The proofs vanished until a set (possibly not complete) was discovered in the *Bibliothèque de l'Institut* and published as A. L. Cauchy,

Equations différentielles ordinaires. Cours inédit (fragment) (Paris and New York, 1981). The introduction by the discoverer, C. Gilain, is very informative.

42. Extracts from de Prony's reports are transcribed in my 'Recent Researches', 684–690. Strangely, when de Prony died in 1839 Cauchy ended a paper with a warm tribute, quite out of normal character!: 'Mémoire sur l'intégration. . .', *Comptes rendus de l'Académie des Sciences*, 9(1839), 184–190; also in *Oeuvres complètes*, ser. 1, vol. 4, 483–491.

43. G. Monge, *Géométrie descriptive* 1st ed. in *Séances des écoles normales*, (1795), *passim*; later eds. in 1799 and 1811 (ed. J. N. P. Hachette), 1820 (ed. B. Brisson), and further reprints. See arts. 95–102 of the 3rd ed. for the 'practical' cases.

44. J. N. P. Hachette, *Supplement à la géométrie descriptive* (Paris, 1812), iii–viii.

45. The history of descriptive geometry has been well treated by historians. See especially G. Loria, *Storia della geometria descrittiva . . .* (Milan, 1921); P. J. Booker, *A History of Engineering Drawing* (London, 1963, repr. 1979); and M. Paul, *Gaspard Monges Géométrie descriptive und die Ecole Polytechnique* (Bielefeld, 1980).

46. G. Monge, *Feuilles d'analyse appliquée à la géométrie à l'usage de l'Ecole Polytechnique* 1st ed. 1795; 2nd ed. (Paris, 1801); further eds. as *Applications de l'analyse à la géométrie. . .* 3rd ed. 1807, 4th ed. 1809; 5th ed. (ed. J. Liouville. Paris, 1850). Monge's role in education is brought out in R. Taton, *L'Oeuvre scientifique de Monge* (1951, Paris).

47. An interesting file of letters concerning Hachette's pension, and also information on the careers of other *savants*, is held in the D. E. Smith Collection, Butler Library, Columbia University, New York.

48. The minutes of this professional discussion are held at the *Archives Nationales*, AJ[16] 5120, fos. 39–48 *passim*. Libri's own scruffy notes of his *Faculté* lectures exist in a notebook at *Bibliotheca Moreniana* (Florence), *Fonds Palagi*, MS 435. Poisson's concern with probability and statistics emerged in print mainly in his book *Recherches sur la probabilité en matière criminelle. . .* (Paris, 1837); on this part of his research, and on his work in the *Conseil* of the *Université*, see B. Bru, 'Poisson, le calcul des probabilités et l'instruction publique', in M. Metivier *et al.* (eds.), *Siméon-Dénis Poisson et la science de son temps* (Paris, 1981), 51–94.

49. Thenard's report was published, among other places, in *Mon. univ.*, (1838), 138–139.

50. Poncelet's appointment is recorded in the *Faculté* minutes for 31 November 1837 and 5 March 1838 (see note 48). See also *Mon. univ.*, (1837), 2467; and *Journal général de l'instruction publique*, 7(1837),

241–244. Incidentally, Poncelet had succeeded Hachette at the *Académie des Sciences* in 1834.

51. Poncelet's letter is held in a file on his *Faculté* career in *Archives Nationales*, F[17] 21574; see also letters in box 1 of his *Nachlass* at the *Ecole Polytechnique* (see note 14). He was also appointed to a new chair of mechanics at the *Collège de France* after the revolution of February 1848; but he did not take it up, because Arago came into his life again (compare section 3), this time as the new *Ministre de l'Armée et de la Navée* and appointed him the *Commandment* (then the name of the top post) of the *Ecole Polytechnique*. He held the post only until 1850. In 1848 he was also elected to the new *Assemblée Nationale*, where he remained until 1852. On all this, see *Mon. univ.*, (1848), 793, 866, 868 (his letter), 903, 911, 918, 950.

52. 'Sur le cumul des emplois scientifiques', *Journal du génie civil*, 11, pt. 1(1831), 170–186 (p. 174). The paper was occasioned by a proposal of the lower house, the *Chambre des Députés*, to limit *cumul* throughout public service: the upper *Chambre de Pairs* rejected it (see *Mon. univ.*, (1831), esp. pp. 171–175, 586–588, 593–595, 803). Ampère also wrote on *cumul*, in a manuscript held in ch. 313 of his *Nachlass* in the archives of the *Académie des Sciences*.

53. A. J. A. Gratry, *Philosophie. Logique* (1st ed. 1855, Paris), ii. 373: quoted from the English trans. of the 5th ed. (1868) by H. and M. Singer (La Salle, 1944), 566. Gratry was a *polytechnicien* of the *promotion* of 1825 (with Liouville), when Cauchy was a *professeur* and Coriolis his *répétiteur*. At the time of the quotation, Coriolis was the *Directeur des études*. In 1850 a reform partly consistent with Coriolis's hopes was inspired by Leverrier (see his *Rapport* referred to in note 2); but various *professeurs* then resigned in protest. . .

The Medical Curriculum at Glasgow in The Early Nineteenth Century

*Derek Dow and Michael Moss**

I. The Emergence of the Medical School and Curricular Development

Roused from torpor by the appointment in 1751 of William Cullen as Professor of Medicine, the Glasgow Medical School promised for a short time to develop as a serious rival to its Edinburgh counterpart. Such hopes were dashed in 1756 when Cullen—who had personally introduced courses in medicine, *materia medica,* botany and chemistry—was enticed to accept the Chair of Chemistry at Edinburgh University. Cullen's distinguished successor at Glasgow, Joseph Black, is now best remembered for his chemical discoveries, yet contemporaries were equally impressed by his skills as a medical teacher; on Black's departure in 1766 to succeed Cullen in the Edinburgh Professorship he allegedly took with him the majority of the Glasgow medical students.[1]

Despite this setback the number of MD degrees awarded by the University of Glasgow rose steadily. A mere 35 were granted during the fifteen year tenure of Cullen and Black but the next two decades saw the award of a further 112 MDs. Significantly, almost exactly half of these were given in the four years from 1784 to 1787. For the first time in the history of the University, medical degrees outnumbered those gained in arts, theology and law combined (57 from a total of 104), an achievement which was not repeated until the halcyon days of the 1820s. Anxious to build on this platform, Alexander Stevenson, Professor of Medicine from 1766 to 1789, asked his colleagues on 7 November 1786 to consider how best the University might support a scheme to erect an Infirmary in Glasgow.[2] Less than two months later the University agreed to contribute £500 to the proposed institution, a considerable outlay in view of the stretched nature of its resources. The success of the Edinburgh School, whose reputation depended in no small measure on the parallel emergence and growth of the Royal Infirmary of Edinburgh after 1729, rendered such an institution vital to the anticipated development of medical education in Glasgow.

Although the proposal to erect Glasgow's first voluntary hospital was endorsed at a public meeting in June 1787, difficulties about the acquisition of a site, and the desire to obtain a Royal Charter prior to construction, delayed matters for a number of years, and the Glasgow Royal Infirmary (GRI) did not admit its first patient until December 1794. Stimulated by this pending event, however, the University had already taken steps to place itself on a sounder footing. The success of William Smellie and William Hunter in London had encouraged Thomas Hamilton, Professor of Anatomy and Botany after Black resigned that post in 1757, to offer courses on midwifery from the late 1760s. His efforts were matched by a succession of extra-mural teachers, about whom shamefully little research has been conducted.[3] Appointed to his father's Chair in 1781 at the age of twenty-three, William Hamilton showed every sign of raising Glasgow's reputation until his untimely death in 1790.

Although Hamilton's death was a severe blow, it opened the way for a more radical reorganization of the medical curriculum in Glasgow. James Jeffray, who occupied the Chair of Anatomy for the extraordinary period of fifty-eight years and dominated the Medical Faculty for most of this time, was instrumental in bringing about these changes. In addition to his courses on anatomy and midwifery, William Hamilton had lectured in surgery and botany, a course of action which almost certainly hastened his death. Jeffray adopted a more cautious approach from the outset. He raised no objection when, with almost indecent haste, William's erstwhile partner approached the University Principal seeking permission to replace Hamilton as University lecturer in midwifery for the ensuing winter session.[4] In later years Jeffray was equally supportive of the disjoining of surgery and botany from his remit as Professor of Anatomy.[5]

At this time the University medical classes bore something of a resemblance to a merry-go-round, indicative of the relatively unspecialized nature and limited medical knowledge of the era. T.C. Hope lectured successively on *materia medica* and chemistry in the late 1780s before his elevation as Professsor of Medicine in 1789; five years later he returned to Edinburgh to fill Joseph Black's chemistry Chair. Robert Cleghorn followed Hope as lecturer in *materia medica* and then in chemistry, while Richard Millar filled the vacancy left by Cleghorn's transfer from the former Chair. By 1791 this frenetic activity had come to a halt, and Glasgow University had the nucleus of a more comprehensive, though still incomplete, Medical School.[6] It was unfortunate, if perhaps inevitable, that little new blood was brought into the system during the next quarter century. Consequently the School was hampered towards the end of this period by the existence of an ageing and rigid professoriate, all of whom had been born in the mid eighteenth century. Cleghorn demitted office in 1818, Towers in 1820, Robert Freer (who succeeded Hope as Professor of Medicine in 1796) in 1827 and Millar in 1833, while Jeffray remained in post until 1848.[7] Sadly, relations within the group, and with the successsors of the first to depart, became less rather than more harmonious with the passage of time.

These tensions, which came to a head in the late 1820s and 1830s, had their origins in a wide range of disparate factors. The establishment of additional Regius Chairs of Midwifery, Surgery, Chemistry and Botany between 1815 and 1818 broadened the base of medical education in the University.[8] As the Royal Presentation for the first of these stated' . . . it would be of Importance in Education of Youth, and for the Public Advantage, . . .' In the case of surgery, the preamble emphasized the special need for a closer study of wounds and of diseases incidental to military and naval service. The derivation of such a concept was not hard to explain in the immediate aftermath of Waterloo. For the incumbents of these new positions the real battlefield lay within the University itself. The Professors appointed under the Old Foundation (known collectively as the Faculty), which included only the Chairs of Medicine and Anatomy in the medical sphere, were particularly jealous of their historic rights and privileges, and spent much time and effort in resisting the claims to equality of the Regius intruders, whose influence was limited to Senate affairs.

This strife was further heightened by other rivalries which existed within the Glasgow medical community. The principal dispute lay between the University and the Faculty of Physicians and Surgeons of Glasgow (FPSG). Founded in 1599, the FPSG claimed the sole right to license surgeons within an extensive area of West and Central Scotland. Matters were not eased by the election of the aged and increasingly irascible Richard Millar as President of the FPSG in 1818–20 and again in 1826–8, at moments of particular stress.[9] The GRI became caught up in this crossfire between the two bodies when attention was focussed on the right of appointment of medical staff, where both sides attempted to impose a monopoly. To complicate matters further, it is clear that the political turmoil of the 1820s and 1830s, at the height of the agitation over the Reform Bill, had a profound effect on relations between colleagues and on appointments to Chairs.[10]

Affairs in the east, where the University of Edinburgh was determined to rid itself of the traditional controlling interest of the Town Council, were no more harmonious. Faced with mounting conflict on two fronts the Home Secretary, Sir Robert Peel, advised King George IV to accede to Edinburgh University's 1825 request for a Royal Commission and appoint such a body to enquire into the current situation and bring forward suggestions for reform.

Many of these deep-rooted antagonisms were fully aired in the evidence given before the Commissioners appointed to visit the Universities of Scotland in 1826. Their Report was ordered to be printed by the House of Commons in October 1831 but the volumes containing the evidence itself did not appear until six years later, by which time many of the most outspoken protagonists were dead. The bulky document relating to Glasgow, read in conjunction with those compiled through a similar exercise in the other Scottish University Medical Schools, offers a fascinating and detailed insight of current views and practices.

Quite apart from a natural desire to emphasize the value of their own particular subjects to the Commissioners (an exercise which sometimes involved direct or indirect attacks on other University medical teachers), several of the interviewees expressed considerable concern about the nature of the curriculum. Many of these comments were unflattering. Reviewing the Report, though not yet in possession of the printed Evidence, the *Quarterly Journal of Education* concluded in 1833 that:

Considered as seminaries of learning, the Scottish Universities, in their present state, may probably be regarded as occupying a lower plane than those of any other country in Europe.[11]

The *Journal* was especially critical of the poor standard of Latin and Greek scholarship amongst Arts students, an issue which also occasioned extensive debate within the Glasgow University community. Some conflicting views were expressed when members were interviewed by the Commissioners in 1827. Not surprisingly, in a vocation where income was largely dictated by the *per capita* fee income from students, self-interest played a part. Thus the Professor of Greek was in favour of compelling candidates for the MD to first gain an Arts-based certificate of education;[12] he was supported in this view by the Professors of Divinity, who argued that 'in short, a physician should have the education of a gentleman'[13], and of Moral Philosophy. The latter believed many of the Scotch medical students who graduated from Glasgow (as opposed to those of other nations) had a very limited education, an observation based in part on the Latin theses read aloud prior to graduation. Having listened to those, Professor Mylne was of the opinion that many of the candidates were incapable of translating the dissertations which they had supposedly penned.[14] Initially, the medical teachers broadly supported this view. Richard Millar (*Materia Medica*) and John Towers (Midwifery) both wished an improved grounding in the classics and in languages,[15] an attitude neatly summarized in the statement by Thomas Thomson (Chemistry) that medical men should have the same literary education as clergymen.[16]

John Burns, whose appointment to the new Chair of Surgery in 1815 led directly to the introduction two years later of degrees in surgery,[17] sounded a cautionary note in his evidence. He readily agreed a preliminary education was a good thing in principle, especially for physicians, but he warned that its introduction would merely drive students of surgery away from the University and into the private schools.[18] In his first appearance before the Commissioners, James Jeffray expressed his conviction that physicians ought to have MA degrees, but he saw no point in surgeons devoting six to eight years to Latin and Greek which might be of little use to them. Like Burns, he had reservations about any unilateral tightening of regulations at Glasgow since this would merely encourage students to attend another University with less demanding standards.[19] Questioned a second time, nine months later, Jeffray retreated from his original stance. The requirement for physicians to obtain the MA, be explained, would unfairly restrict practitioners with thirty or forty years experience as surgeons or apothecaries from proceeding to the coveted MD.[20]

The provisional resolutions of the Commissioners paid scant

heed to these fears, recommending that MD candidates should have a liberal education in classics, mathematics, natural philosophy and French, all to be tested by examination. They also outlined the proposed new curriculum.[21] The Glasgow Medical Faculty (in the shape of Jeffray, Burns, Thomson and Towers) was deeply disturbed by these proposals. In a lengthy submission to the University Senate (forwarded without comment by that worthy body, which felt unqualified to judge its conclusions, despite the earlier testimony of members to the Commission) the Medical Faculty outlined its opposition.[22] Priority was given to an exposition of the damage which would be done by the introduction of a preliminary examination in Latin, Greek and mathematics. Most students, apart from some elderly English apothecaries seeking the enhanced status of an MD, already had Latin, but Greek and mathematics were an entirely different story. Compulsory attendance on these would, it was feared, result in the loss of 90 per cent of Glasgow University medical students, who came from a poorer stratum of society than those attending classes in Edinburgh and London, and could not afford an expensive education. This would in turn render Glasgow professorships unattractive to those of superior attainments, thus hastening the downward spiral. In support of this argument Jeffray and his companions cited the example of the University of Copenhagen, where the introduction of a preliminary examination created a situation where few students came to study and the quality of teaching was unsatisfactory.

A second major concern of the professoriate was the future structure of the medical curriculum proper. Glasgow was rightly praised for its foresight in obtaining a Chair of Surgery, an example which Edinburgh was urged to follow. In other important new subject areas Glasgow was reckoned to be markedly deficient, an accusation which revealed fundamental differences of opinion within the University itself.

James Jeffray denied the necessity of creating a Chair of Medical Jurisprudence on the grounds that the various component parts were already taught by the existing Professors. He was little impressed by the Continental model, where four professors were required to do the work of one Glaswegian, thus leading to repetitive and time-consuming practices.[23] He was supported in this attitude by John Towers, who claimed that he already taught medical jurisprudence as it bore on midwifery, while Professors Thomson and Burns were quite capable of covering poisons and wounds respectively.[24] These views were refuted by John Burns, himself a widely-acclaimed obstetric author, who believed a separate Chair should be instituted.[25] Backing for this stance came also from Dr James Corkindale, a regular medico-legal examiner who probably harboured an ambition to fill the new Chair.[26] This debate was finally resolved with the appointment of Robert Cowan to the new Regius Chair of Forensic Medicine in 1839.[27]

An even more acrimonious dispute occurred in this decade over the separation of the Theory and Practice of Medicine. After the death of Robert Freer in 1827 the University experienced some difficulty in finding a suitable replacement for the Chair of Medicine. The eventual appointment was not a happy one. Writing to Principal Macfarlan in April 1827 the University Chancellor, the third Duke of Montrose, reported his failure to persuade either of two good candidates to leave their assured positions in London. His choice instead fell upon Charles Badham, a London physician whose income had recently fallen from £800 to £400, 'So he must work, and trust to his labors!'[28] Montrose's plea to Macfarlan to let him know of any impediment came too late. By the time Macfarlan wrote on 3 May to express his doubts about Badham's 'Temper, Prudence and Professional Knowledge', the appointment had been confirmed by the Home Secretary.[29] Subsequent developments did nothing to refute accusations that Badham's was an ill-judged political appointment.[30]

During Robert Freer's tenure of the Chair of Medicine two distinct courses had been offered. The practice of medicine was taught on five days of the week, according to Cullen's *Nosology*. In addition, Freer delivered three lectures each week on the institutes of medicine, in conformity with Dr Gregory's *Conspectus Medicinae Theoreticae*.[31] Freer's death gave his colleagues the opportunity to advocate the introduction of a second Chair, agreed to by the Government and accepted in principle by Badham, prior to his appointment.[32] When he appeared before the University Commissioners in October 1827 Badham's attitude must have caused a certain unease, as he expressed his ignorance of the Scottish system and his refusal to deliver two courses during the pending session because of the demands this would make upon him.[33] In the following September, shortly before the opening of the new session, Principal Macfarlan was obliged to write to Badham, warning that his continued refusal to provide lectures in the theory or institutes of medicine would damage the Glasgow School, thus reducing Badham's own income. He would not like, Macfarlan continued, to bring in another lecturer or to see the formation of another Chair, a sentiment clearly at odds with prevailing opinion. Suggesting that Badham need only give two lectures each week, the worried Principal concluded that 'I think it would pass for a course'.[34]

Badham's performance did not improve over the next few years, and contributed to the unfavourable publicity which appeared in the medical press. Refusing Badham permission to absent himself from the beginning of the 1833–4 session, Principal Macfarlan explained that his absence would be 'deeply injurious' to the medical curriculum as a whole.[35] Pleading ill-health, Badham was given permission to enlist Dr Harry Rainy to teach the theory of medicine, a move which undoubtedly made it easier for the Crown to appoint Dr Andrew Buchanan as Professor of the Theory of Physic or Institutes of Medicine in 1839.[36]

Although the Report of the Royal Commission stated that the Glasgow Medical School had recently 'risen into great eminence'[37] there were still obvious gaps in the curriculum, only partially filled by the creation of two additional Chairs in 1839. No further extension of the medical teaching staff occurred for more than three decades. Some of the responsibility for this can be laid at the door of the Medical Faculty Report of 1829, which claimed that the existing curriculum of twelve classes in four years was already at saturation point. The proposed addition of a Chair of Pathology would merely overburden the students, with no obvious benefit. As a result of such entrenched attitudes, Glasgow did not acquire a Professor of Pathology until 1893.[38]

Not all of this failure to expand can be laid at the door of the University teachers. Other interested parties sometimes conspired to hinder development. One of the principal motives behind the foundation of the Glasgow Royal Infirmary had been the desire to provide clinical experience for medical students. In discussing the administration of the new hospital, three months prior to the admission of patients, the Managers granted permission to Drs Cleghorn and Hope to deliver clinical lectures on Infirmary cases in order to encourage medical students and improve the Glasgow Medical School.[39] The regulations for students attending the Infirmary, drawn up in November 1794, made provision for them being allowed to take copies of cases in the Infirmary books. Strict rules were introduced to ensure that those attending ward rounds behaved in a manner befitting the hospital environment:

Students. . .are to study a composed and decent carriage, and are not then to stroll about the Wards, converse together, stand upon benches, beds or do any thing that may be disturbing to the Physician, Clerk or Patients.[40]

The system of clinical lectures given by the hospital physicians continued without demur for more than a decade. In February 1810, however, the Infirmary Managers received a petition signed by a great number of medical students[41] requesting the introduction of a course of lectures in clinical surgery, to complete the system of medical education in the Glasgow School. After lengthy deliberation their request was denied, with an explanation from the Medical Committee that, based on the experience of Edinburgh and London, clinical lectures on surgery would not attract sufficient numbers of students to make the practice financially attractive for the lecturer.[42]

In their 1827 evidence to the Royal Commission a number of the medical teachers referred to the unsatisfactory provision for clinical lectures in Glasgow. There was general agreement that an improvement was long overdue, especially in surgery. Professor Thomson went so far as to describe the current situation as 'an almost intolerable defect'—adding in a later examination that he was currently the only individual in the University who would be prepared to undertake this task![43] Thomas Campbell, Lord Rector of the University, supported this view in his claim that clinical lectures were not compulsory in the University curriculum 'because there are no clinical lectures given here, on the efficiency of which we can repose confidence.'[44] Richard Millar, Lecturer in *Materia Medica* and an influential figure in the GRI, emphasized the value of compulsory courses in clinical medicine and surgery, to be held in either the Infirmary or University. The real problem, he claimed, was the reluctance of students to avail themselves of such opportunities— 'the truth is, they are rather a poor class of students, and they will not attend any class unless they are forced to do so.' Millar was currently President of the Faculty of Physicians and Surgeons of Glasgow, a position which obliged him dispute the University's right to appoint clinical lecturers to the Infirmary since the Faculty 'furnishes all the surgeons to the Infirmary'.[45]

This disagreement was part of the long-standing dispute between the two bodies which soured relations for most of the first half of the century and made it hard to achieve the desired degree of co-operation between the University and the GRI. As the latter's Committee on Clinical Lectures ruefully concluded in November 1825, there were great problems in reconciling the conflicting views of 'two such respectable parties' as the University and the FPSG.[46]

In 1829 the Infirmary Managers resolved that all students seeking class tickets for the Infirmary should be obliged to fee the courses of clinical medicine and surgery, to be given by the hospital physicians and surgeons. In reporting this development Dr Moses Buchanan, surgeon to the GRI and its first historian, acknowledged the need to further increase the number of such lectures; despite this reservation, he still felt able to claim in 1832 that these new regulations gave the Infirmary a 'decided superiority over every other Institution in the Empire'.[47]

Given these stated views, there is a certain irony in Buchanan's later actions. It was not until 1874, and the opening of the rival Western Infirmary, that the University was able to appoint Professors of Clinical Medicine and Clinical Surgery, thus increasing the size of the Medical Faculty which had remained unchanged since 1839. The money to endow the Chair of Clinical Surgery at the Western was provided by the Buchanan family in memory of their father (Moses himself had died in 1860) and the first incumbent was his own son, Dr George Buchanan.[48] Almost ninety years after agreeing to support the establishment of a hospital for the City, the University had finally achieved one of the prime objectives of the exercise, but only through the medium of a second and separate institution.

II. Student Numbers: An Interpretation

In assessing the number of students attending European Universities in the early nineteenth century, it has generally been assumed that records of matriculations can be used to indicate approximately the number of students pursuing courses of study.[49] Although non-matriculated students are known to have attended lecture series and completed sufficient of the syllabus to qualify for degree examination, it is usually reckoned that their numbers will not greatly distort the overall pattern derived from matriculation information.

These assumptions do not hold good for the University of Glasgow and are completely misleading in any analysis of the number of students enrolling for medical classes.[50] Matriculation was mandatory in the mediaeval University and usually took place at the close of the student's first year, at the time of the annual election of the Rector. By the close of the seventeenth century the practice seems to have fallen into disuse and only those students in the '*togati*' or 'gown' class who intended to present themselves for degrees or those wishing to vote in the rectorial elections troubled to go through the formality.[51] The gown students were confined to those taking degree or public classes in Latin, Greek, Logic, Moral Philosophy and Natural Philosophy.[52] This practice was confirmed by the Commission of Visitation of 1727 and continued until 1853-4.[53] It was, therefore, not necessary to matriculate in order to take the degree of MD, although from 1755 candidates had to present themselves at the University for examination.[54]

Since there was neither a fee nor a requirement for attestation of faith or allegiance to the Crown, there was nothing to prevent students matriculating if they wished, but the majority for most of this period would seem to have neglected to do so. Consequently the very complete matriculation records for the University, published in 1913, provide an imperfect guide to the number of students at the University at any one time.[55] This was readily admitted by contemporaries. The University *Calendar* for the session 1826–7 stated:

All other students of the University may be classed under the general name of *Non Togati*, or ungowned; a large, mixed, and somewhat fluctuating body whose numbers it is not easy to ascertain.[56]

It is possible, however, to make a guess at the total number of *togati* students using the evidence from the class catalogues printed annually from 1794. These contain the names of all *togati* students, whether matriculated or not, who attended those public lectures which constituted part of the MA degree course.

Records relating to medical students are, thankfully, more comprehensive. One consequence of the revival of the Glasgow Medical School in the 1790s was a considerable increase in student numbers. Jeffray's anatomy class, which attracted 54 students in the first year of his appointment, had more than doubled by the end of the decade. This expansion coincided with a growing concern about the laxness of the regulations governing the award of MDs by Scottish Universities. Towards the end of 1801 the Senate of Glasgow University established a committee to review procedures. On the basis of its findings, the Senate introduced new ordinances in the spring of 1802 requiring intending graduates to study for three years (one of which had to be in Glasgow) in a reputable Medical School; to show that they had attended classes in Anatomy, Surgery, Chemistry, Pharmacy, Theory and Practice of Physic, *Materia Medica* and Botany; and to undergo *viva voce* examinations in Latin in these subjects. They are not allowed to graduate as MDs until they reached twenty-one years of age.[57]

These new regulations were then used as a springboard from which to launch an attack on current practices in other Scottish Medical Schools. Acting on a suggestion from Professor Freer, a Medical Committee was appointed by Faculty to consider the current position. Its report, submitted in May 1804, was sharply critical of the Universities of St Andrews and Aberdeen, whose award of medical degrees without examination or 'any personal knowledge of the candidates' was described as 'a flagrant, disgraceful and hurtful abuse.' Proposals to introduce a degree of uniformity throughout Scotland were discussed during the following year, but ultimately came to naught.[58]

In the wake of the 1802 reforms at Glasgow a committee was appointed to consider the most appropriate method of maintaining a Register of Medical Students. Some Professors, like James Jeffray, already kept individual class registers[59] but it was now agreed to institute a central register, to be compiled by the University Librarian from class lists submitted by each of the lecturers. In order to ensure accuracy, students were ordered to attend a meeting midway through the session to check their own entries, and to pay one shilling to the Registrar. They were then entitled, on payment of a further five shillings, to a vellum certificate recording their attendance on all classes shown against their names, for which they had, presumably, paid the class fee.[60]

The first volume of the register, covering the period 1803–20, is written throughout in the same hand and appears to have been consistently and accurately maintained. Unlike the matriculation albums, it contains no details of place of origin, father's name and occupation, or year of study. Entries are limited in the majority of cases to the student's name and the classes attended. If there were two students of the same name in a year, then one or both are normally differentiated by an indication of geographical origin.[61]

The second volume, embracing the years 1822–43, is much more comprehensive and contains both father's name and place of origin. It is, unfortunately, less reliable from a statistical standpoint, particularly after the retirement on health grounds in 1827 of the original Registrar, Dr Muirhead. The number of entries for the early 1830s is clearly deficient, falling below the recorded figures for the anatomy class alone; several pages have also been lost when the volume was rebound at some unrecorded time in the past 140 years.[62]

In the opening session of the first register (1803–4), 141 students enrolled; by 1805 there were over 200 students in attendance and by 1809 the number had climbed to 318. Such a big enrolment caused an accommodation crisis in the University's lecture halls, forcing the Principal and the Professors to appeal to the Government for funds to extend the College buildings.[63] The intake continued to grow until 1813 when it reached 500; thereafter it fell away to 296 in 1816 before recovering in the next three years. During the mid 1820s the population of medical students remained relatively constant. The reduction in the late 1830s, unlike that of the earlier part of the decade, is confirmed by other evidence and suggests a real decline in medical student numbers in Glasgow.[64] It is possible, nevertheless, to make some assessment of the relative importance of the Medical School to the University as a whole. If the 256 medical students in session 1827–8 are added to the 616 *togati* students recorded in the class catalogue, the total is 972. As some of the medical students were also *togati*, it is probably safe to assume that about 900 students are covered by these lists. Since other students are known to have been at the University, the total number attending classes was possibly upwards of 1,000, making the medical students about 25 per cent of the undergraduate community in that year.[65]

As the University *Calendar* for 1827–8 explained, the *non-togati* students were a very disparate group:

Under this description are comprehended all those who having finished their course of instruction in Arts, are prosecuting their studies in the other Faculties with a more immediate view to their intended professions; and it comprised also many persons of maturer age who are resident in the city or its vicinity; and who, though engaged in other avocations, are still disposed to cultivate the literary pursuits of their earlier years, or to extend their acquaintance with some favourite branch of learning or science by attending the lectures given at the University.[66]

This claim is substantiated time and again by information abstracted from the medical student registers and other contemporary sources.

Apart from those students attending medical classes with a view to entering the profession, there were many who enrolled to gain some smattering of medical knowledge. Some took classes as they believed it would be helpful in their chosen profession, notably those intending to enter the church. Norman Macleod, who was later to become a famous Church of Scotland minister, matriculated in 1827 and then left to pursue his studies at Edinburgh. He returned to Glasgow in 1836 with the avowed intent to rise every morning at 6am to pursue his academic work—'I study Hebrew, Greek, and Church History every morning before breakfast; chemistry, anatomy, and natural history (my favourite study next to divinity) during the day; logic; theology, reading and writing in the evening.' He was registered in the anatomy class in that session.[67] John Kenrick, a *togati* student who matriculated in his second year in 1807, took the chemistry class in 1807 and 1808, and those of anatomy and private dissection in 1809. He graduated MA in 1810 and was, by the end of his career, Professor of History in the Unitarian College at Manchester.[68] James Finlay Weir Johnston, who matriculated in 1819 and graduated in 1826, was a divinity student between 1823 and 1828 and attended the antomy class in the session 1825–6. He never entered the church, but was appointed Reader in Chemistry and Mineralogy at the University of Durham in 1833.[69]

Others, as the *Calendar* suggested, came as mature students in order to extend their knowledge, a tradition extending back into the eighteenth century. Thomas Reid, Professor of Moral Philosophy at Glasgow from 1764 to 1796, had attended Joseph Black's lectures on chemistry at the age of fifty-five, shortly after taking up his appointment.[70] In 1806 the Revd Dr Alexander Ranken, the minister of St David's Church of Scotland in Glasgow, registered to study botany. He was then fifty-one years old and had already begun work on his monumental but inaccurate History of France, published in nine volumes between 1802 and 1822.[71] With the opening of the

GRI in 1794, such men may have enrolled as part of a conscious and conscientious commitment to the new institution. The Established Clergy of Glasgow nominated one representative each year to serve as an Infirmary Manager. Ranken acted in this capacity on four separate occasions between 1800 and 1826. At least two of his colleagues showed a similar interest. The Revd Dr Stevenson McGill, a Manager for three years in the period 1801–12, attended the botany class in 1803; the Revd Dr Lockhart did likewise in 1808 and 1812, and was elected an Infirmary Manager in 1796, 1807, 1819 and 1827.[72]

Admittedly, in early nineteenth century Scotland, it was possible to enter medical practice by a period of apprenticeship, there being no legal requirement to attend formal classes. Even for those who decided to obtain a University education at Glasgow, there was no prescribed course of study. The three-year minimum course of six sessions of study, required of intending graduates under the 1802 regulations, did not stipulate the order in which classes had to be taken; neither did the regulations require students to complete their studies in consecutive years unless they held University bursaries. In some cases the periods of attendance were far apart. David Henry Wilsone, who matriculated in the third year of his Arts course in 1805, took eighteen medical classes between 1807 and 1811, and was licensed by the FPSG in that year. He returned to the University in 1816 and 1817 to study botany and eventually graduated MD in 1834, shortly before emigrating to Australia.[73]

In some instances such breaks were dictated by financial necessity. It is probable that the Robert Davidson who studied anatomy, chemistry and private dissection in 1809–10 was the same Robert Davidson who attended anatomy, surgery, medicine, clinical lectures, private dissection, *materia medica* and the Infirmary in 1812–13, a punishing schedule which was rewarded by the FPSG licentiateship on 7 June 1813. In the intervening years, from October 1810 until October 1812, Robert Davidson had acted as apothecary to the Paisley Dispensary and House of Recovery at a salary of £40 p.a., resigning on 4 September 1812 in order to pursue his University studies.[74]

In many cases the disruption in attendance was caused by the protracted conflict with France, which lasted from 1793 to 1815. James McArthur, the eldest son of a Perthshire farmer, matriculated in his third year in Arts in 1808 before proceeding to the study of medicine in three consecutive sessions from 1810–13. In January 1814 he entered the Army Medical Service as a hospital assistant, being promoted to the role of assistant surgeon in the following year. Placed on half pay in December 1818, McArthur registered as a medical student for the sessions 1818–19 and 1819–20. He returned to his Regiment (the 90th Foot) on Christmas Day 1819, becoming a full surgeon in April 1825. He finally gained the Glasgow MD in 1828, retiring to civilian practice three years later.[75]

Similar occurrences took place in other branches of the Armed Forces. Marcus Dill, who attended medical classes between 1805 and 1807 in anatomy, botany, chemistry, *materia medica*, medicine, midwifery and at the Infirmary, joined the Navy in 1808 and returned to complete his studies in 1816. He graduated MD in 1817 and CM in 1852.[76]

The database from which these examples are drawn contains 5,231 entries for the period 1803–20, each entry denoting a single year of study (containing 1–11 separate courses) for one student. The analysis of this data is a complex and difficult task, as indicated by the highly individual nature of some of the courses of study quoted above. (See Figures 1–3 on pp. 243, 245, 246). Figure 1 represents the annual returns of medical students and of matriculated students for the period 1803–43. As already explained, the figures for the post–1822 medical students are suspect, but there appears to be some degree of correlation between the two graphs. It would be unwise, however, to read too much into these figures since matriculation offers no accurate guide to the total student population at any given time. The increasingly close relationship between the number of medical students and the medical degrees awarded each year (also shown on the graph) does suggest a fundamental change in the nature of medical education at Glasgow University by the 1830s, a trend which will be explored in the next phase of this research.

Figure 2, which aggregates attendances in those components of the curriculum which appear consistently throughout the period 1803–20, perhaps offers a more meaningful picture of the University's teaching role, supporting the view that Glasgow had a cohesive Medical School by this time. The pattern is one of steadily rising demand until 1813, succeeded by a sharp decline in the succeeding three years. The steady revival from 1816 clearly co-incides with the institution of the new Regius Chairs. Of equal

Figure 1: Glasgow University medical students, 1803–1842

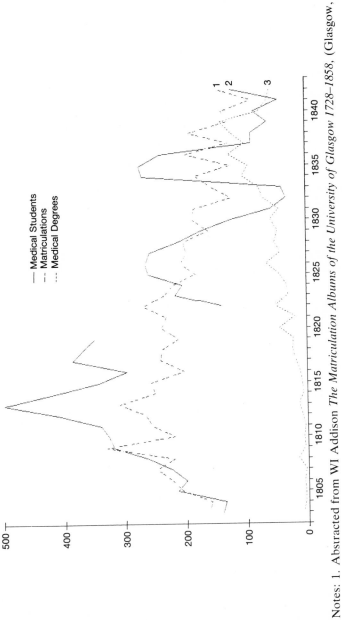

Notes: 1. Abstracted from WI Addison *The Matriculation Albums of the University of Glasgow 1728–1858*, (Glasgow, 1913) p. 538.

2. Calculated from Registers of Medical Students 1803–1843 (GUA 19089 and 31247). The break in the graph between 1819 and 1822 is due to a gap in the surviving data.

3. Abstracted from WI Addison, *Roll of Graduates of the University of Glasgow 1728 to 1897*, (Glasgow, 1898) pp. 678–681.

interest, however, is the fact that the graph as a whole mirrors almost exactly that for anatomy alone, offering further proof of Professor Jeffray's importance to the Medical School as a whole. It would seem, on this evidence, that anatomy was the key factor in the fortunes of medical teaching in the University. One major difficulty in trying to assess the importance of these changes over time is the lack of comparable evidence for the independent extra-mural schools in the City. It has been claimed that the total number of anatomy students in Glasgow in 1814 was not less than 800, yet Jeffray's University class accounts for only 248, less than a third of that number.[77]

Figure 3, which shows the number in each class as a percentage of the total attendance in each year, is also most revealing. The relative popularity of specific classes is more easily seen than in the format adopted for Figure 2. The data shown in these three graphs will, it is hoped, form the basis of a comprehensive assessment of the Glasgow Medical School in the first quarter of the nineteenth century and will, when placed in conjunction with similar data from the Register for 1822–43, allow an analysis of events over a longer timespan. As a preliminary exercise two individual years, and one particular element in the curriculum, have been investigated in detail.

An examination of the 1806 and 1817 classes shows the patterns of attendance set out in Table 1. These results must be treated with some caution. Although students who attended for only one session can be identified, it is much more difficult to distinguish with accuracy those who continued their studies for two or more years, unless they have unusual or distinctive names.[78] Despite this reservation the figures are heavily weighted towards those who enrolled

Table 1 Years in attendance at Medical Classes
(percentages in brackets)

Date	1	2	3	4	5	6	7	8	Total
1806	53	45	35	40	12	11	2	1	200
	(26.5)	(22.5)	(17.5)	(20.0)	(6.0)	(5.5)	(1.0)	(0.5)	
1817	113	100	74	50	29	11	6	2	386
	(29.3)	(25.9)	(19.2)	(13.0)	(7.5)	(2.8)	(1.6)	(0.5)	

Note: In both years the number of years of attendance of one student cannot be identified

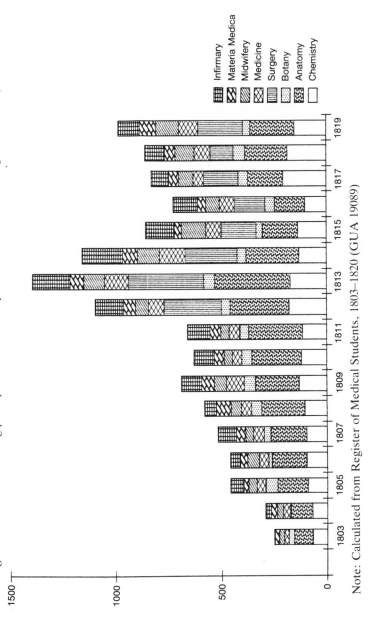

Figure 2: Bar chart showing principal classes taken by medical students at Glasgow University, 1803–1819

Note: Calculated from Register of Medical Students, 1803–1820 (GUA 19089)

Infirmary
Materia Medica
Midwifery
Medicine
Surgery
Botany
Anatomy
Chemistry

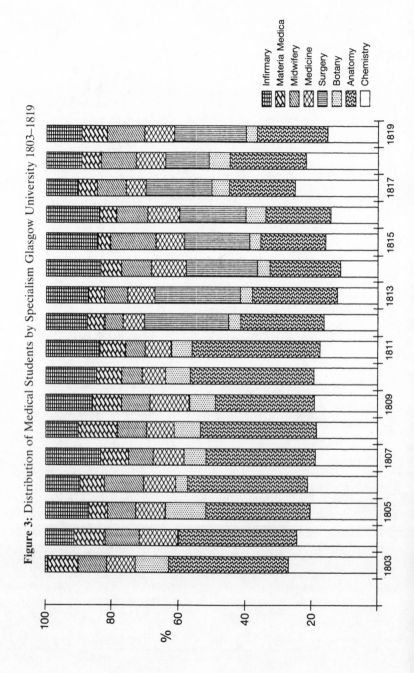

Figure 3: Distribution of Medical Students by Specialism Glasgow University 1803–1819

for only one or two years—49 per cent in 1806 and 55.2 per cent in 1817. This suggests that the bulk of the students were not contemplating completing their medical curriculum at Glasgow. Of the residue, the majority (over 30 per cent of the total in both cases) appear to have come for either three or four years, probably representing those intent on medical careers. In both years 11 per cent of the students were present for between five and eight years.

Some of these, like David Henry Wilsone and James McArthur, returned to University as students after establishing themselves in a medical career. Since no distinction was made in the classes between undergraduate and postgraduate students, such attendance may have been in the nature of a refresher course. Other more worldly motives may also have entered their calculations. William Richardson Gibb matriculated in 1800, graduated MA in 1806 and attended the University medical classes from 1809–11. Equipped with an MD, he then joined the Army Medical Service as a hospital assistant on 8 July 1811. Transferring in May 1816 from half pay service in the 81st Foot to full pay in the 88th Foot, he returned to take classes in anatomy, chemistry, surgery and Professor John Burns' separate surgery class in the autumn of 1817. Retiring from the Army in 1819, Gibb's recent contacts with his *Alma Mater* may have helped him obtain a coveted position as one of the four surgeons to the GRI in 1821 and 1822.[79]

Unlike the *togati* students who were restricted to one regular or public class each year to qualify for the MA degree, it was possible for medical students (whether *togati* or not) to enrol in as many classes as they wished in a session.[80] The results of our investigation of the number of classes in which each student enrolled in the years 1806 and 1817 are shown in Table 2. The greater number in both years enrolled in only one or two classes, 60 per cent in 1806 and 58.6 per cent in 1817. Of the rest most took only three or four

Table 2. Number of courses taken in the Medical Classes
(percentages in brackets)

Date	1	2	3	4	5	6	7	8	9	10	11	Total
1806	80	40	34	31	13	2	–	–	–	–	–	200
	(40.0)	(20.0)	(17.0)	(15.5)	(6.5)	(1.0)						
1817	169	57	47	35	30	26	11	6	3	1	1	386
	(43.8)	(14.8)	(12.2)	(9.1)	(7.8)	(6.7)	(2.8)	(1.6)	(0.8)	(0.3)	(0.3)	

Table 3. Number of classes enrolled in by those who attended medical classes for only one year
(percentages in brackets)

Date	1	2	3	4	5	6	7	8	9	10	Total
1806	29	9	6	4	4	1	–	–	–	–	53
	(54.7)	(17.0)	(11.3)	(7.5)	(7.5)	(1.9)					
1817	79	12	7	4	7	1	1	1	0	1	113
	(69.8)	(10.6)	(6.2)	(3.5)	(6.2)	(0.9)	(0.9)	(0.9)	–	(0.9)	

classes, but by 1817 twice as many students proportionately were taking more than four classes. We have still to explain this transformation but it seems reasonable to attribute it, at least in part, to the increase in the number of lecturers in the Medical School. A further examination of those who attended for only one year reveals that in both years, more than half attended only one class (see Table 3). Those who fit this pattern had clear preferences as can be seen from Table 4.

Some of these single class students, like John Hooper (later a dissenting minister at Old Gravel Lane, Wapping),[81] were *togati* students pursuing MA degrees, while others were 'irregular' or 'voluntary' students taking classes for pleasure (as previously described); a third category were clearly present to gain a theoretical basis for their manufacturing interests. This was especially true of those enrolled in chemistry. The tradition was long established in Glasgow. Dr William Irvine, lecturer in chemistry from 1769 to 1787, had founded a Chemical Society shortly before his death; one of the early members was Charles Macintosh, a pioneer of the chemical industry and inventor of the waterproof coat which bears his name.[82] During the 1790s Robert Cleghorn's class attracted one Josias Gamble. The Irish theological student was so impressed by

Table 4. Classes attended by those who attended medical classes for one year and enrolled in one class

Date	Ana-tomy	Botany	Chem-istry	Infir-mary	*Materia Medica*	Mid-wifery	Prof. Burns' Surgery	Total
1806	14	3	11	–	1	–	–	29
1817	–	–	71	2	1	1	4	79

this experience that he later abandoned his Irish Presbyterian Church ministry to become one of the founders of the alkali industry.[83] The peak of such activity in the early nineteenth century occurred in 1817, when the celebrated Dr Thomas Thomson, newly appointed to the lectureship in chemistry, delivered his first lecture series in Glasgow. Of the 79 Glasgow medical students who attended a single course in that year, a staggering 71 elected to join Thomson's class.[84] Thomson, although an MD and voluble in his claims to be the only willing clinical teacher in Glasgow, had views on the future of chemistry teaching which made it especially attractive to such men. In his 1827 evidence to the Royal Commission he stressed his desire to raise up a race of practical chemists, and emphasised that he did not lecture on chemical pharmacy which he regarded as a trade and not a science.[85]

Quite clearly, chemistry and botany—on the evidence presented in this paper—were not solely the pursuit of intending medical men in this period. It is possible that the same may have been true of a minority of anatomy students, enrolling in order to seek knowledge for artistic purposes as Da Vinci had done in earlier times or as part of their general education. Our knowledge of the motivation and curricula of registered medical students is still incomplete, although additional analysis of this database should bring further enlightenment. It is, however, only prudent to end on a cautious note. When he first appeared before the Royal Commissioners in January 1827, Principal Macfarlan admitted his inability to comment in detail on recent changes in the medical curriculum: 'I cannot state all of them, as medicine is, of all branches, most foreign to my department.'[86] A century and a half later, historians are still hampered by some of the same difficulties, compounded by the irreversible factors of time and distance.

University of Glasgow
Glasgow G12 8QQ

REFERENCES

* Derek Dow is archivist of the Greater Glasgow Health Board and Michael Moss is archivist of the University of Glasgow.
1. J. Coutts, *A History of the University of Glasgow* (Glasgow, 1909), 494.

2. Glasgow University (hereafter GU) Faculty minutes, 7 November 1786. The Faculty, the governing body of the 'College', consisted of the Principal and the incumbents of the 13 Chairs founded prior to 1761. it claimed the sole right to administer the 'College' revenues until it was replaced in 1858 by the University Court. The Crown appointed the Principal, who was required to be a Professor of Divinity, and the Professors of the Practice of Medicine, Hebrew and Semitic Languages, Law, Ecclesiastical History, Anatomy and Astronomy. Appointments to the other seven Chairs in the Faculty were made by the Faculty itself. The Senate, concerned primarily with the teaching functions of the University, included the members of the Faculty and those Regius Professors appointed after 1807 (see 8 below). There was constant friction between the two bodies in the half century prior to 1858 over the Faculty refusal to accord Regius Professors equal rights with its members.

3. See D. A. Dow, *The Rottenrow. The History of the Glasgow Royal Maternity Hospital 1834–1984* (Carnforth, 1984), 125–7 for an account of early midwifery teachers in Glasgow. By the early nineteenth century extra-mural teaching had been established on a more formal footing at the Andersonian University, College Street School and, in the 1820s, the Portland Street School. See A. Duncan, *Memorials of the Faculty of Physicians and Surgeons of Glasgow* (Glasgow, 1896), 178–86.

4. GU Faculty minutes, 19 March 1790. Copy of letter from James Towers, who later became the first incumbent of the Regius Chair of Midwifery, 1815–20.

5. *Evidence, Oral and Documentary, taken and received by the Commissioners appointed for Visiting the Universities of Scotland* (1837) Vol. II, University of Glasgow, 128, 136, (hereafter cited as *Evidence*).

6. Writing in 1804, Joseph Frank recorded disparagingly that the University contained no complete Medical Faculty since medical science was taught by two Professors and two lecturers who were not 'proper professors.' Quoted in A. Kent (ed), *An Eighteenth Century Lectureship in Chemistry* (Glasgow, 1950), 166.

7. Professors at this time were appointed *ad vitam aut culpam*. Substitutes were often required when the appointees became too old or infirm to continue teaching, a practice which brought sharp criticism of the University Medical School in the medical press in the early 1830s. See *Glasgow Medical Examiner* (January 1832) 227–8.

8. These Regius Professors, as the name suggests, were presented by the Crown but, unlike their eighteenth century predecessors, excluded from membership of the Faculty and therefore a share in the endowment of the 'College' (see 2 above). In Edinburgh such patronage was still in the hands of the Town Council. Sir William Hamilton, the distinguished metaphysician, believed the Edinburgh system to be

infinitely preferable to either of the current Glasgow practices. Sir W. Hamilton, 'Patronage of Universities', *Edinburgh Review, 59* (April 1834), 217–26. Hamilton could speak with some authority on the subject. His grandfather, great-uncle and father had each filled the Chair of Anatomy and Botany at Glasgow. Sir William himself had originally intended to enter the medical profession and had studied medicine successively at Glasgow, Edinburgh and Oxford before electing for a legal career. See W. I. Addison, *The Snell Exhibitions* (Glasgow, 1901), 83–6.

9. i.e. the introduction of surgical degrees (see 17 below) and the rift within the Professoriate at the time of the Royal Commission which began to take evidence in 1827. For an account of the latter dispute, seen largely in the context of one of the major protagonists, see J. B. Morrell, 'Thomas Thomson: Professor of Chemistry and University Reformer', *The British Journal for the History of Science,* Vol. 4 No. 15 (1969), 245–65.

10. For one notorious incident, involving the presentation of Robert Lee to the vacant Chair of Midwifery in 1833, see D. A. Dow, 'Rival Conceptions', *The College Courant. The Journal of the Glasgow University Graduates Association,* No. 74 (March 1985) 11–15.

11. *Quarterly Journal of Education,* Vol. V. (1833), 75. The *Journal,* founded in 1831, ceased publication after 10 issues because sales were insufficient to cover expenses. It aimed to give a comparative picture of education throughout Europe.

12. *Evidence,* 79.

13. Ibid., 71.

14. Ibid., 103.

15. Ibid., 132, 154.

16. Ibid., 152.

17. This innovation, the first such qualification in the UK, led to a protracted lawsuit with the FPSG and to bitter divisions within the Medical Faculty itself. See Coutts, *History,* 546–54 and Duncan, *Memorials,* 161–70. The University actually introduced two degrees in 1817—the master of surgery (CM) at a cost of 10 gns. and the bachelor of surgery (ChB) for 6 gns. A total of seven ChBs were awarded between March 1819 and March 1822, after which the degree was abandoned in favour of the CM. All seven ChBs were natives of Ireland. By 1816 a hospital for clinical teaching had been opened in Dublin and the Glasgow degree seems to have been a conscious effort to maintain the University's attraction for the large numbers of Irish students who came to study in Glasgow each year.

18. *Evidence,* 128–9.

19. Ibid., 140.

20. Ibid., 179.

21. Ibid, 558. Describing similar requirements in the Medical School of

Paris, the *Quarterly Journal of Education* concluded that many of the French requirements might be profitably adopted in the UK. *QJE*, I (1831), 44–8. The infamous Glasgow-born and -trained anatomist, Granville Sharp Pattison, was appointed inaugural Professor of Anatomy in the University of London in 1827. Four years later he was dismissed as the result of a campaign orchestrated by a number of his students; heading their list of Pattison's defects was 'An evident want of a liberal education, frequently evinced by the commission of flagrant classical errors.' See F. L. M. Pattison, *Granville Sharp Pattison, Anatomist and Antagonist 1791–1851* (Edinburgh, 1987), 169.

22. GU Senate minutes, 22 April 1829. The Report was later printed in the *Evidence*, 562–5.

23. *Evidence*, 137–8.

24. Ibid., 200–1.

25. Ibid., 130.

26. Ibid., 218; Duncan, *Memorials*, 269; *Testimonials in favour of James Corkindale. LLB* (1832). The Portland Street School appointed a lecturer in medical jurisprudence in 1826. Both the lecturers prior to 1840 (James Armour 1826–8 and J. M. Pagan 1830–40) left to fill Chairs of Midwifery, at the Andersonian and Glasgow Universities respectively.

27. GU Senate minutes, 7 August 1839. On the same date the Senate appointed Allan Burns, son of Professor John Burns, lecturer in forensic medicine during its pleasure. Burns' rejection of the appointment in the light of Cowan's appointment was recorded in the Senate minutes of 10 October.

28. Principal Macfarlan's Papers (hereafter DC9), DC9/129, Montrose to Macfarlan, 25 April 1827. The papers are housed in Glasgow University Archives (GUA).

29. DC9/131, Macfarlan to Montrose, 3 May 1827. The Chair of the Practice of Medicine was the oldest of the University's Regius Chairs. First instituted in 1637, it was allowed to lapse nine years later. It was revived in 1712 and endowed by Queen Anne in the following year.

30. *Evidence*, 210–1. See 'Medical Jobbing in Glasgow', *The Lancet*, 9 February 1833, 634–6 and 'Chair Jobbing', ibid., 12 April 1834, 83. Badham had been recommended to Montrose by Sir Henry Halford, President of the Royal College of Physicians, to whom Badham dedicated his 1831 edition of a translation of Juvenal. The new Professor seems to have been more interested in his poetic and classical studies than in medical teaching. See J. Finlayson, 'Dr. Charles Badham' in *Glasgow Medical Journal*, Vol. 53 (May 1900), 321–31.

31. GU *Calendar*, 1826–7, 27. William Cullen's *Synopsis Nosologiae Methodicae*, first published in 1769, was translated into English in 1800. James Gregory's *Conspectus* appeared in two parts between 1780 and

1782, but was not translated from the Latin until 1823. Glasgow University Library possesses copies of most of the editions, Latin and English, of these two works, whose use was widespread. The British Library catalogue records an 1831 'literal translation' of those parts of the *Conspectus* which had been fixed upon by the Society of Apothecaries for the examination of candidates for the licentiateship.

32. DC9/136, Montrose to Macfarlan, 14 May 1827.

33. *Evidence*, 190.

34. DC9/166, Macfarlan to Badham, 27 September 1828.

35. DC9/270, same to same, 12 October 1833.

36. The appointment was not without irony. Five years earlier Buchanan had been one of the bitterest critics of the monopolistic nature of University education. See A. Buchanan, *Of Monopolies in Learning: with remarks on the Present State of Medical Education, and on the constitution of the Scotch Universities* (Glasgow, 1834).

37. *Report made to His Majesty by a Royal Commission of Inquiry into the State of the Universities of Scotland* (1830), 55.

38. The 1829 Report of the Medical Faculty was transmitted in its entirety to the Royal Commission, since many of the Senate members did not feel themselves qualified to comment on its suggestions. The Report claimed that pathology was too limited a subject to justify an independent existence and would not attract students, despite its admission that such courses were well attended on the Continent. Edinburgh University did appoint a Professor of Pathology in 1831, on the advice of the Commissioners.

39. GRI minutes, 29 September 1794.

40. Ibid., 25 November 1794.

41. The Register of Medical Students shows a significant rise in University students attending Infirmary classes at this time. The figure rose from 56 in 1808 to 93 in 1809 and to 131 in 1812.

42. GRI minutes, 5 February 1810 and 13 August 1810. In this same year the Managers agreed to pay salaries of £50 p.a. to the Infirmary Physicians and £20 to the Surgeons, the cost to be covered by the income from students' fees.

43. *Evidence,* 150–1, 204.

44. Ibid., 166.

45. Ibid., 213.

46. Since the GRI Managers were subject to annual re-election, they also found it difficult to implement any long-term policy, a point conceded by the Commitee in its Report. William Hamilton, Lord Provost of Glasgow and an *ex officio* Manager, made this point to the Commissioners, claiming that there had recently been 'an overthrow of the Managers very much' inspired by Dr Richard Millar in support of the FPSG position. *Evidence*, 221.

47. M. S. Buchanan, *History of the Glasgow Royal Infirmary* (Glasgow 1832), Preface, 31.
48. GU Court minutes, 25 February 1874. Copy of letter dated 14 February stating terms on which endowment of £2,200 would be handed over to the University. The gift was wholly conditional upon George Buchanan being appointed as 'The first professor under this foundation'.
49. See N. Hammerstein, 'University Development in the Seventeenth and Eighteenth Centuries: A Comparative Study', in *Town and Gown: the University in Search of its Origins*, CRE Information No. 62 (1983), 86.
50. This difficulty was well understood by W. I. Addison, Registrar of the University of Glasgow for 1911–12, who, from the time he joined the staff in 1887 until his death in 1912, compiled rolls of graduates and matriculated students. In a posthumous preface he commented: 'It is necessary to presume that these Matriculation Albums do not contain a record of all who actually attended the University during the periods covered'. W. I. Addison, *The Matriculation Albums of the University of Glasgow 1728–1858* (Glasgow, 1913), vii.
51. J. Durkan and J. Kirk, *The University of Glasgow 1451–1577* (Glasgow, 1977), 365; Addison, *Matriculation Albums*, vii; GU *Calendar* (1826–7), 16. The process of matriculation took place on 14 November each year, in the presence of the professors of the 5 public classes and the Clerk of the Faculty. Students were required to matriculate only once, and could do so at the beginning of any one of their sessions of attendance. It is therefore impossible to calculate how many intending graduands abandoned their studies prior to formally matriculating.
52. GU *Calendar* (1826–7), 15.
53. Coutts, *History*, 205.
54. Ibid., 505.
55. Addison, *Matriculation Albums*. Each student was denoted by a unique number and these have been used in subsequent references where individual students are mentioned. Earlier matriculations can be found in C. Innes (ed.) *Munimenta Alme Universitatis Glasguensis* (3 vols. + Appendix; Glasgow, 1854).
56. GU *Calendar* (1826–7), 17. This was the first year in which the University authorities saw fit to publish a Calendar. Annual publication did not commence until the 1860s.
57. Coutts, *History*, 541.
58. Ibid., 542–3.
59. Two of Jeffray's Registers survive. The first covering the period 1790–1811, is GUA 19057. The second, GUA 19039, covers the period 1811–48.
60. GU Faculty minutes, 7 February 1803.

61. Register of Medical Students, 1802–20, GUA 19089.
62. Register of Medical Students, 1822–43, GUA 31247. The missing pages had already disappeared when the volume was indexed in 1895. We have not yet found any explanation for these discrepancies.
63. 'Memorial and Petition of the Principal and Professors of the College and University of Glasgow' to the Treasury, 1809, PRO T1/1126.
64. These figures tend to confirm the damage done to the reputation of the University by the internecine warfare described earlier, and by Jeffray's declining prowess as a lecturer. The Portland Street School shows a corresponding rise in fortunes at this period. See attendance figures in Duncan, *Memorials*, 184.
65. PRO T1/1126 stated that during the session 1808/9 'upwards of 1100 students ought to assemble in the Common Hall which can hold no more conveniently than 334'.
66. GU *Calendar* (1826–7).
67. Addison, *Matriculation Albums*, No. 12091 and, Revd D. Macleod, *Memoir of Norman Macleod DD* (London, 1876), 102. Three years earlier Macleod had recorded in his Journal his intention of taking anatomy, botany and chemistry while studying at Edinburgh University. Much later, in 1848, he expressed the view that the choice of a profession lay specifically between the Church or medicine. Ibid., 102,298. Detailed accounts of the medical curriculum of individual students are surprisingly hard to trace. One of the few known to us appears in J. H. Alexander, 'Student Life at Glasgow University about ninety years ago' in *Glasgow Medical Journal* (January 1925), 37–44. Alexander's father (William Alexander) attended the University of Glasgow from 1831–5 and graduated CM (1834), MD (1836). The son's description of his undergraduate career lists the courses undertaken, together with the prescribed books for each. Thomas Lyle, a student from 1812 to 1815, left a manuscript volume of 'University Reminiscences' which has been transcribed and will be published by its owner, Dr L. R. C. Agnew of the University of California. See Pattison, *Pattison*, 241, 259.
68. Addison, *Matriculation Albums*, No. 7223 and Mrs. W. B. Kenrick, *Chronicles of a Nonconformist Family* (Birmingham, 1932).
69. Addison, *Matriculation Albums*, No. 10305 and Sir E. J. Russell, *A History of Agricultural Science in Great Britain, 1620–1954* (London, 1966), 130.
70. Coutts, *History*, 494.
71. *Dictionary of National Biography*, xlvii, 289.
72. M. S. Buchanan, *History*, contains a list of Directors of the Glasgow Royal Infirmary from 1793 to 1832. Botany was then a three month course, taken during the summer session.
73. Addison, *Matriculation Albums*, No. 6876 and Duncan, *Memorials*, 273.

74. Paisley Dispensary and House of Recovery minutes, 5 October 1810, 4 September 1812 and October 1812. Davidson received a 10gns. bonus on his departure as a mark of the Directors' satisfaction. The Dispensary Movement in Britain had its origins in the foundation of the General Dispensary in Aldersgate Street, London, in 1770. Intended to provide medicines and outpatient attendance, there were almost 40 dispensaries in England by 1800. See I.S.L. Loudon, 'The Origins and Growth of the Dispensary Movement in England', *Bulletin of the History of Medicine,* (1981), 322–42. The Paisley Dispensary was founded in 1786. See D. A. Dow, *Paisley Hospitals: The Royal Alexandra Infirmary and Allied Institutions, 1786–1986* (Paisley, 1988), Chapter 1.

75. Addison, *Matriculation Albums,* No. 7416 and A. Peterkin and W. Johnston, *Commissioned Officers in the Medical Services of the British Army 1660–1960* (London, 1968), Vol. I, 250.

76. Addison, *Matriculation Albums,* No. 7416.

77. GUA 19039 and Duncan, *Memorials,* 177.

78. For example, the name John Bell is recorded sixteen times between 1803 and 1817. The appearance of two entries in 1808 and three in 1812 suggests there were probably four individuals involved. There may have been others since five students of this name matriculated between 1805 and 1817.

79. Addison, *Matriculation Albums,* No. 6155 and Peterkin and Johnston, *Commissioned Officers,* 211.

80. It was possible for *togati* students to attend these other classes as private students but these were not taken into account in assessing their qualification to take a degree.

81. Addison, *Matriculation Albums,* No. 6987.

82. Kent, *An Eighteenth Century Lectureship in Chemistry,* 154.

83. Ibid., 167. Gamble is a very good example of the difficulties encountered in tracing accurate details of individual students. The *Matriculation Albums,* No. 5518 (matriculated 1794) claim that Josias Christopher Gamble graduated MD in 1787 and MA in 1797. This appears to be confirmed by the manuscript volume in which medical graduates were required to inscribe their names (*Nomina Medicinae Doctorum Universitatis Glasguensis ab Anno 1769,* GUA 26677, 15. Josias Gamble, Hibernus, 13 August 1787). J. C. Gamble was born in 1776, see J. F. Allen, *Some Founders of the Chemical Industry* (London and Manchester, 1906) 43, or in 1778, see Burke's *Peerage and Baronetage* (London, 1912) 816. He coud not, therefore, have obtained an MD in 1787, leading to the conclusion that there must have been two Josias Gambles. W. I. Addison's previously published *A Roll of the Graduates of the University of Glasgow* (Glasgow, 1898), 211 had been much more cautious than his *Matriculation Albums,* claiming only that Josias Gamble, MD 1787, MA 1797 was 'possibly' the same Josias

Gamble as the Presbyterian Minister/manufacturing chemist. He still made the error of assuming that the two degrees were awarded to the same individual. The plot thickens further with the discovery that 'Josias Gamble, Ireland' was a student in Jeffray's anatomy class in 1795 and 1796, GUA 19057.

84. Robert Cleghorn's resignation was accepted by the Faculty on 8 August 1817 on the grounds of ill-health, when the Faculty agreed to meet on 5 September to appoint 'a fit Person to lecture on Chymistry, an Office peculiarly important to the University'. The meeting of 5 September duly appointed Thomson, then resident in London, on the same terms as his predecessor and asked the Principal to inform him of his election. The GU *Calendar* wrongly gives his date of appointment as 1818.

85. *Evidence*, 151. For a comprehensive account of Thomson's influence See Morrell, 'Thomas Thomson', passim and J. B. Morrell, 'The Chemist Breeders: The Research Schools of Liebeg and Thomas Thomson', *Ambix*, XIX (1972), 1–46.

86. *Evidence*, 31.

The Edinburgh Medical School and the End of the 'Old Thing' 1790–1830*

Christopher Lawrence

Measured by student numbers, Edinburgh University and its medical school apparently enjoyed a golden age during the near twenty-five years of the French wars. University attendance doubled from one to two thousand and, during the second decade of the new century, medical student numbers consistently remained above 700 a year. Usually more than half of this number were Scots. There was also a consistently high proportion from Ireland.[1] After 1826 there was a slow decline in the popularity of Edinburgh as a centre for the study of medicine and, over the next forty years, student numbers fell from around 900 to about 400 a year.[2] Measured by anything other than numbers, however, this golden age turns out to have had baser metals in its composition. Behind its sizeable carapace, its new Adam buildings, the University was the home of faction and intellectual and political division. The University's historians, however, have not been forthcoming about such things. The valuable older histories of Bower and Grant offer a number of intriguing hints about political difficulties but never fully expose or explore them.[3] This neglect was not remedied in the useful short history by Horn, and the issues are avoided by Chitnis, whose work specifically addresses this period.[4] J. B. Morrell, however, has been bold enough to grasp the thistle and, in a number of illuminating studies, has explored the politics of the University in terms of its peculiar institutional infrastructure.[5] Morrell, in turn, has used his findings to define the local character of Edinburgh intellectual products. Morrell has also employed the same method in order to explore the history of the University in the mid and late eighteenth century.[6] This was a time when student numbers were smaller but, because of the relative absence of strife, it has more often been perceived as a golden age.

Until the 1830s the administration of Edinburgh University was unique in Scotland. It was directly controlled by the Town Council, a self-perpetuating mercantile interest who were by no means unmindful of the wishes of the Kirk, the local landed gentry and, ultimately, the Court.[7] Appointments to University chairs therefore were the end point of a complicated patronage network of which the University's Senate was a relatively ineffectual part.[8] During the mid-eighteenth century the use of this network effected the appointment of a series of extremely able professors to medical and other chairs. This was not simply fortuitous. In general, those who operated within the patronage web were the creators of the Scottish ideology of 'improvement', and they endeavoured to select energetic candidates with modernizing ideas and ideals. Despite intellectual diversity among Scottish professors and the Edinburgh literati generally, they shared, at the broadest level, a common account of Scotland's past and future. This account valued a number of things: the English connection, civic virtue with its roots in the land, elitism, small scale commerce, agricultural reform, cosmopolitan refinement, and the application of science to practical affairs.[9] This account can be traced not only in works on moral philosophy and history, but in texts on medicine and natural philosophy.[10] The most celebrated products of the Scottish Englightenment—in philosphy, medicine, the sciences and the arts—were, ultimately, built by the interests of those high in the patronage chain. These were, primarily, the Scottish landed magnates.[11] The golden age was predicated on a powerful allegiance of social and intellectual elites which maintained order in Scotland during a period of substantial social and economic change.

Within the University at mid-century intellectual innovativeness, daring speculation, scepticism and a relative indifference to religion were quite compatible with the preservation of order and the legitimation of gradual change. The professors who constituted the core of the medical school, especially Alexander Monro *primus* and *secundus*, William Cullen, and Joseph Black, were the soul-mates of the Moderate Churchmen, notably the University's Principal, William Robertson, and the city's other great intellectual stars, for example David Hume, Adam Smith and James Hutton.[12] Within the tradition of the history of ideas it has been customary to represent the works of these men as innovative; revolutionary even. Yet, when analysed at the local level, the Scottish literati spoke with the voice of the Court.[13] In word and deed they promoted the modernization of Scottish farming, the Anglicization of Scottish culture and the cultural and material subjugation of the Highlands. It would be improper, however, to see large scale industry and commerce as the goal of these transformers of Scottish life. By and large, the literati and gentry were advocates of limited agrarian reform and small scale industrial innovation. Change of a radically different variety, in any sphere, was not envisaged. The overwhelming conservativism of the Scottish landed classes after 1789 is a matter of record.

The halcyon days of common intellectual concern and social stability in Scotland were relatively transient, and, at the end of the century, dissent replaced consensus and social disorder displaced harmony. The French wars saw a comparative fragmentation of the political, social and intellectual solidarity of the Edinburgh landed and professional classes. During these years Edinburgh grew massively in size, and mercantile and manufacturing elements began to challenge the old cultural leadership. The increasingly clamorous cry of 'Reform' which was heard during this period was directed not only at Edinburgh's overt political machinery, but all the institutions which served the elite, including the University, the medical school and the College of Physicians.

Politically the French wars saw the apogee of the ascendancy of Henry Dundas, and the almost total support by the traditional elite for Tory policy. Moderatism, the ascendant party of the Kirk, became the 'Dundas interest at prayer'.[14] Scots Whigs were in a minority both in parliament and in Scotland.

The pulpit, the bench, the bar, the colleges, the parliamentary electors, the press, the magistracies, the local institutions were . . . completely at the service of the party in power.[15]

The University was predominantly Tory, with only a handful of distinguished Whigs in post: Dugald Stewart, Andrew Dalzel, John Leslie and John Playfair.[16] Conflict between the Edinburgh Tories and their opponents erupted in the University several times during these years, the most famous episode of which was the so-called Leslie affair.[17]

What is striking about the natural philosophy and medicine taught in and around Edinburgh University 1790–1830 is how difficult it is to draw out a common, intellectual thread. Diversity notwithstanding it is a fairly easy task to characterize the new Paris medicine and map it onto the hospitals and the University.[18] But at Edinburgh, in spite of an institutional focus, medicine evades precise definition. By 1800 the shared and uniquely Scottish account of the body, which described the nervous system as binding the organism together by sympathy, had disappeared.[19] In place of a common model teachers and practitioners employed a variety of English and, later, French ideas. At least one of the reasons for this medical fragmentation was the expanding power of the surgeons, who in some instances aligned themselves with the local Scottish landed interest but in others identified with a wider surgical *profession*. This, however, is only one typical example of a general breakdown of allegiance to the old order. The characteristic feature of Edinburgh intellectual life in these years is the way that different issues repeatedly divided the medical and wider community in different ways. Some issues, such as the question of Infirmary attendance, divided the surgeons among themselves, but on the question of the oppressive monopoly of physicians in the city, they were united. Over the threat of phrenology, extramural teachers stood with the University professoriate; in other instances, however, they stood against them. In the end, this fragmentation and regrouping were measures of how difficult it was for the old order to marshall virtually total support, consistently, in the way it had done at mid-century. The difference perhaps is less one of a shift from order to relative chaos but a move from containable to uncontainable conflict. In what follows I shall exemplify this breakdown in a number of ways, while concentrating principally on the cognitive and institutional crises forced by the new power in medicine: the surgeons.

Within the University it was the very structural features which had been the basis of cohesion and intellectual eminence in the earlier period which were the source of division and mediocrity in the new century. In the mid-eighteenth century the University professors had welcomed the burgeoning demand for medical education. By 1800, however, the hosts of students who flocked to Edinburgh were seeking a medical training which the University professoriate seemed unable to provide. In turn, a host of extramural teachers began to offer alternative courses. Edinburgh professors had a legal monopoly over their subject, and the was no intramural competition.[20] Until 1858 the medical professors received no salary, their remuneration coming solely from students paying individual course fees. The students had no obligation to attend any course or courses in any order. In the eighteenth century this *Lehrfreiheit* encouraged professors to maximize the attraction of their courses. Black, Cullen and the first and second Alexander Monro had made their classes a great success. More spectacularly, in the revolutionary years Thomas Charles Hope, 'the showman', transformed the chemistry course.[21] But elsewhere the system failed. The professorial monopoly opposed the formation of chairs in new subjects. Similarly the close control which professors retained over their successors' appointments encouraged nepotism of a flagrant variety. The Rutherfords, Monros, Humes, Gregorys, Hopes, Duncans and Hamiltons virtually carved up the University's medical chairs in the period 1780–1830.[22]

Elsewhere in Europe, and particularly in Paris, medicine was being transformed. New disciplines were being created and institutionalized. These new subjects included comparative anatomy, surgical anatomy, physiology, general and special pathology and clinical surgery. The Edinburgh professoriate, by contrast, claimed that all these subjects were already taught by the incumbents of the traditional chairs of Anatomy the Institutes of Medicine and the Practice of Physic. These new subjects, however, which were being shaped by the new surgical interest were, in many ways, cognitively quite different from the traditional bodies of knowledge over which the Edinburgh professors presided.

If, as contemporaries observed, there was a decline in the standard of teaching at Edinburgh other factors had a beneficial effect on student numbers in the city. Increasingly, students went to Edinburgh to obtain qualifications from the Edinburgh Royal College of Surgeons and, after 1815, to attend courses required by the Apothecaries Act.[23] The Edinburgh MD was not a particular attraction; in 1805 only 21% of the students took the degree.[24] In the late seventeenth century the surgeons had been one of the most powerful corporations in Edinburgh, and the physicians in their newly founded Royal College rather insecure outsiders.[25] The next hundred years saw a reversal of this power balance as the physicians organized a number of strong political allegiances. By mid-century the physicians were extremely well-placed in the Edinburgh patronage network. They controlled the teaching of medicine at the University, and had an important voice in the running of the Royal Infirmary. The physicians remained extremely jealous of their privileges and well into the third decade of the nineteenth century they used their power to maintain distinctions between themselves and the Edinburgh surgeons. The Edinburgh surgeons, on the other hand, like their brethren elsewhere in Europe, sought to erode the physicians' privileges. They increasingly took medical as well as surgical qualifications and treated internal as well as external disorders.[26] Not surprisingly, the eighteenth century saw numerous boundary disputes between Edinburgh physicians and surgeons. No doubt future work will show that many of these disputes can be analysed at the local level in terms of competition for practice. By the end of the century the New Town offered a rich market for the increasing numbers of polite young surgeons and physicians. In this situation extramural medical and surgical teaching became an important resource for those outside the University attempting to advertise themselves as practitioners.

During the Napoleonic Wars, by exploiting the demand for military surgeons, the Edinburgh surgeons increasingly wrested from the London College its monopolistic control of surgical licensing. In 1789, with the assistance of Henry Dundas, the Edinburgh College (since 1778 a Royal College) was empowered to examine surgeons for the African slave trade. In 1797 they obtained the right to examine navy mates or assistant surgeons, and in 1799 to examine surgeons for the East India Company. In 1803 they were empowered to examine army hospital mates, in 1805 assistant surgeons, and, in 1813, regimental surgeons.[27] During the 1790s the requirements for entry to these examinations were laid down. They included attendance at various academic courses, although not necessarily at Edinburgh. In 1808 the regulations required three years study for the unapprenticed and two for those who had served an apprenticeship. The three years of study had to include attendance at classes in anatomy, chemistry, medical theory and practice, principles and practice of surgery, clinical surgery, midwifery, and *materia medica*.[28]

The University professoriate, more jealous of its rights than alert to opportunity, did not respond to this new situation. Not surprisingly, extramural lecturers appeared in profusion and exploited the deficiencies in the system. The history of extramural teaching at Edinburgh has long been neglected and the following is not intended to be anything other than a sketch of some of the ways in which extramural lecturing may have moulded the intellectual shape of Edinburgh medicine. One thing seems clear: the new teachers flourished because they offered courses in new subject areas.

The failure of Alexander Monro *tertius* to teach anatomy within the University with as much success as his father and grandfather, who held the chair before him, is often recounted by historians of science and medicine.[29] This putative failure is usually attributed to the incapacity of nepotism to work as a system for selecting able candidates. This received tale is in need of re-examination, for at least two reasons. First, Monro *tertius*, whatever his rhetorical failings, may have been teaching an anatomy no longer demanded by Edinburgh surgical students. Second, and related, the mythology of his inadequacy may have been created by the extramural teachers, who were teaching anatomy of a different sort. There seems little doubt that *tertius* was teaching anatomy in much the same manner as his predecessors. The course was given on a couple of corpses in a large amphitheatre. The classes began with comparative anatomy, and closed with lectures on the operations of surgery. The core of the course was an animated anatomy, that is, it was, simultaneously, a discourse on form and function.[30] Design ensured that form and function were perfectly matched, and hence the course was a demonstration in natural theology. Although surgical students had always sat in the University anatomy classes, these classes were not simply a utilitarian training for surgical practice. The anatomy course put on by the Monros was also aimed at a local audience. It spoke to the concerns of the literati (for instance in the use of the Great Chain of Being) and to the interests of the physicians (for instance, in the natural philosophical emphasis).[31] Monro *tertius*, like his father, was a *physician*.

The 'sort' of anatomy taught by the Monros was radically transformed during the late eighteenth and early nineteenth century. Once again, those who were effecting this transformation were chiefly surgeons, to a great extent in France, but also in London. During the eighteenth century surgeons increasingly came to view internal disorders, formerly the province of physicians, in the way that they regarded external disorders, that is as local pathological changes. This, of course, was the cognitive dimension of the increasing exploitation of the medical market by the surgeons. The corollary of this new pathology, however, was the dismantling of the old anatomy and its recreation as a number of distinct subjects. These were: comparative anatomy, based on the concept of organization rather than natural history; experimental physiology, increasingly divorced from anatomy; and an anatomy that was less and less functional and increasingly morphological or surgical. The practice of this new anatomy was based on individual dissection rather than demonstration.

These new, surgically-orientated disciplines were those which were provided by the Edinburgh extramural teachers. *Tertius,* apparently, devoted less attention to comparative anatomy than his father. On the other hand, the extramural lecturers John Barclay and, later, Robert Knox gave special courses devoted to the subject.[32] Barclay began lecturing on anatomy and surgery in 1797 and his lectures were recognized by the College of Surgeons in 1804. Barclay provides yet another case history of the difficulty of discovering in turn of the century Edinburgh consistent and coherent interest groups. Barclay was not, as might be guessed, a surgeon but an Edinburgh MD who eventually became a Fellow of the College of Physicians.[33] Besides his anatomy course Barclay also taught comparative anatomy, but this course was not simply an elaborate version of an eighteenth-century comparative anatomy based on natural history. Barclay's teaching was based on the new transcendental doctrine of unity underlying the diversity of forms, 'All living bodies', he taught, 'are constructed on one general plan'.[34] Further, it seems that the extramural classes in anatomy differed not only in the substance of the anatomy that was taught, but in the form the classes took. Practical classes in dissection were increasingly available in London in the second half of the eighteenth century. They were advertised as the only manner for aspiring surgeons to learn the subject.[35] Evidence suggests that the Edinburgh extramural lecturers began to teach in this manner and were well provided with corpses while Monro was content to use perhaps one or two.[36] Bodies, however, were not cheap.[37] During the first twenty years of the new century Monro's class fell from 400 to 200 while Barclay built up a class of 300.[38] This success notwithstanding, the attempt to erect a University chair of comparative anatomy for Barclay was blocked by the two men most likely to be affected: Monro and Robert Jameson, the professor of natural history.

John Bell, another extramural lecturer, stigmatized Monro *tertius'* course in the following manner:

In Dr Monro's class, unless there be a fortunate succession of bloody murders, not three subjects are dissected in the year. On the remains of a subject fished up from the bottom of a tub of spirits, are demonstrated those delicate nerves which are to be avoided or divided in our operations; and these are demonstrated at a distance of 100 feet!—nerves and arteries which the surgeon has to dissect, at the peril of his patient's life.[39]

Now Bell of course, as an extramural lecturer, had every reason to denigrate Monro's course. But the accusation that he was not teaching with enough corpses, nor teaching surgical anatomy, suggests that Bell employed a different approach. John Bell was a surgeon, who had begun lecturing at the College of Surgeons, on midwifery, in 1787.[40] Bell was probably the most vociferous campaigner in Edinburgh for a *science* of surgery based on anatomy and physiology. He was at the centre of numerous pamphlet wars, most notably with the professor of medicine, James Gregory.[41] The dispute with Gregory, ostensibly about the admission of surgeons to the Infirmary, has been analysed by Michael Barfoot.[42] Barfoot has concluded that the language used in these debates appears to be the reverse of what might at first be expected. Bell employed a language which identified an academic education as important for the surgeon, concluding that all surgeons thus educated were competent to attend the Infirmary. Gregory, however, used a rhetoric which singled out experience as the most important qualification in any branch of medicine, concluding therefore that the most successful practitioners were *ipso facto* the best. In context, however, Bell's language was an attack on elitism and patronage and a defence of equality in the medical world, and Gregory's the reverse. But these were not simply educational issues being discussed by enraged medical men. They were disputes about the control of one of the most prestigious, elite-run institutions in Edinburgh, the Royal Infirmary. Such control, of course, ultimately gave the victors access to *practice* in the city at large.

The controversy, however, cannot be reduced to one which identifies surgeons as the outsiders aligned against the physicians of Edinburgh. The surgeons themselves were divided between those who were integrated into the old order, and those whose allegiances lay outside of it. Taking Gregory's side in the dispute were the senior and well-connected surgeons already associated with the Infirmary, Benjamin Bell, James Russell and John Thomson. Not surprisingly, perhaps, Benjamin Bell's surgical texts were attacked by John Bell (they were not related). From a nineteenth-century viewpoint, John Bell was defending a position 'which no man will now dispute, that surgery must be based on anatomy and pathology', and he was, from this perspective, 'the only true surgeon in Edinburgh'.[43] It is tempting to construe this and other Edinburgh controversies in terms of the interests of the extramural versus those of intramural teachers. Any attempt to do this, however, consistently fails. John Thomson, Gregory's ally in this matter, was one of the most important extramural lecturers in Edinburgh (see below). Similarly, in 1799 John Barclay, the extramural lecturer who was later to become a Fellow of the College of Physicians, launched a savage assault on John Bell's anatomical work. Nor do other distinctions such as between Whig and Tory help to characterize the Edinburgh medical scene. The Edinburgh Whigs could be as much a part of the old order as the Tories. John Thomson, surgeon and stout Whig, stood with the Tory establishment in the Infirmary dispute.

Thomson's career nicely illustrates the complex relations between extramural and intramural teachers. Thomson is best known as the biographer of William Cullen, but his own life, of which there is a valuable account by his son, deserves further study.[44] Thomson was apprenticed as a surgeon in 1785, and in 1789–90 attended lectures at the University. Thomson moved in Whig circles and was a close friend of John Allen, a medical man, but for most of his career private secretary to Lord Holland, nephew of Charles James Fox and one of the leaders of the Whigs. Later in his life Thomson was accused of having been too democratic in his sympathies in the 1790s. From the winter of 1803 onwards Thomson gave an extramural course on military surgery in Edinburgh. The College of Surgeons had long been dissatisfied with the University teaching of surgery. Monro *tertius* taught it as part of or subsidiary to his anatomy course and resisted, as his father had done, all attempts by the surgeons to have a separate University chair created.[45] In 1806 the surgeons appointed Thomson professor in their college. Immediately, Monro and the other University professors objected and pressurized the Town Council who attempted to prevent Thomson lecturing. Thomson, however, was favoured by the brief Whig interlude, the 'Ministry of all the Talents' of 1806, when the King created a Regius Chair of military surgery in the University which Thomson was chosen to fill.[46] The University Senate, however, under pressure from the medical professoriate, had even tried to block this, but the Town Council knew where their best interests lay and 'declined to transmit to His Majesty's Ministers the Memorial of the Medical Faculty'.[47] After this, the surgeons made no further attempt to create a separate chair of surgery, being satisfied with 'distinct and full' extramural courses and a regulation that Monro's course was insufficient to admit a student for a surgical diploma.[48]

Thomson used his lectures on military surgery to attack what he saw as spurious distinctions between surgery and physic. In the preliminary lecture to his course Thomson gave a glowing account of the history of surgery in Paris. In France, he noted, the surgeons had once been persecuted by the physicians with the help of the Pope. But, after liberating themselves from this oppression in the later seventeenth century, they made Paris into the surgical centre of the world.[49] At the same time that Thomson was delivering his lectures asserting the unity of physic and surgery, James Gregory revised and republished his father's *Lectures on the Duties and Qualifications of a Physician*. In this work, which originally appeared in 1772, John Gregory had asserted the intellectual unity of physic and surgery. This argument, however, was advanced to show that physicians should possess knowledge of external disorders, and that surgery should be in the hands of simple operators controlled by physicians. The argument was republished, unchanged, by his son in 1805.

If surgery was confined to a set of men who were to be merely operators, it might justly be expected that the art would be more quickly brought to perfection by such men, than by those who follow a more complicated business, and practise all the branches of medicine.

This, however, had not happened and:

the consequence is, that in many places physic is practised by low, illiterate men, who are a disgrace to the profession.[50]

In the 1790s James Gregory had taken a strong line against the inclusion of a mandatory midwifery class for students intending to obtain the MD; 'physic and midwifery' he argued 'are two very different things'.[51] He acknowledged that, since many students who came to Edinburgh eventually practised midwifery, it was proper that there should be a professor of the subject, 'But, as many of our students never mean to practise midwifery, it would be unreasonable and unjust to compel them to learn it more especially, as, there are many young men to whom it is particularly disgusting'.[52]

Gregory, notoriously, was involved in a large number of feuds with his colleagues. But in many ways his polemical career was only a florid version of the disputes which were wreaking havoc within the medical school and College of Physicians. The College, for instance, was divided over the issue of whether its members, (Fellows and Licentiates) should be allowed to dispense drugs. One of the legal rights which the Edinburgh physicians treasured was that of examining apothecaries' shops. To have permitted dispensing would have been an ackowledgement of the breakdown of boundaries between physicians, who did not dispense, and surgeon-apothecaries, who did. The College, or at least many members of it, remained committed to divided medical practice well into the 1820s. In 1815, for example, the President had complained that the Edinburgh surgeons had 'managed to impress the minds of the people here, that it is impossible to separate the two departments of the profession'.[53]

Thomson, for one, denied that physic and surgery could be separated either in practice or in theory. This was the thrust of his *Lectures on Inflammation* of 1813 (which, he stated, were originally given as lectures in 1804). In these lectures Thomson began by quoting with approval the French surgeon, Quesnay: 'the external diseases which form the object of surgery are essentially the same with the internal diseases'.[54] Thomson argued that, since this was so, there should be a single medical education. After this, practitioners in towns should be able to choose whether to specialize in physic or in surgery. Once again Thomson favourably compared the eighteenth-century French experience. Thomson also used the theory of inflammation to show that there was no basis in nature for the separation of physic and surgery. Discussing the relation of constitutional and local symptoms he noted:

It is in the knowledge and treatment of these, and similar morbid phenomena, that the boundaries which divide surgery from physic meet and are lost in each other; for whatever distinctions convenience or custom may have introduced among the practitioners of the healing art, there is no foundation for these distinctions, either in the nature of disease, or in the knowledge which every medical practitioner should possess of the appearances which different diseases exhibit, and of the means by which they are to be removed.

He pointed out that physicians had made a distinction between a local inflammation associated with symptomatic fevers (the surgeon's province) and constitutional or essential fevers (the physician's territory). But, he added, it was often impossible to tell the difference between these disorders. Moreover, they often required the same therapy 'The terms Fever in physic and Inflammation in surgery are . . . general abstract terms'. In practice the distinction was useless:

as local inflammation gives rise to constitutional febrile symptoms, so idiopathic fevers of all kinds, in their turn, often give rise to, or at least are accompanied by local inflammatory affections.[55]

Thomson, in other words, was arguing that pathological knowledge showed there should be no distinction between physicians and surgeons. This was polemical stuff which reached a large audience. Thomson, an observer estimated, attracted 250–80 students to his military surgery course in 1815.[56]

A pupil and close friend of Thomson's, who later lived with his family for many years, was the surgeon and physician John Gordon. Gordon, like Thomson, was an extramural lecturer and almost certainly a Whig. He is perhaps best known now for his vehement opposition to the phrenologists. Phrenology fired off a controversy in Edinburgh which, as analysed by Steven Shapin, was a conflict beween the old landed establishment and the new, and relatively powerless, bourgeois mercantile interest. Phrenology nicely exemplifies how the old order, so often divided amongst itself, could in the face of a radical threat close ranks. Against the phre-nologists, Whigs and Tories, extramural lecturers and university professors stood full square.[57] Apart from his involvement in this controversy and a short contemporary biography, Gordon has received no attention.[58] Gordon, however, was responsible for instituting a new medical course in Edinburgh: physiology. Physiol-ogy existed as a distinct subject in France, but in Edinburgh, in one sense, it did not exist at all. Animal function was taught as part of the Institutes of Medicine and as part of anatomy. The Institutes was taught by the Tory physician, Andrew Duncan senior.[59] Dun-can held the chair from 1789 until his death in 1828, aged 84. Although after 1819 he shared the teaching, first with his son and then with William Pultney Alison. The Institutes, said Duncan, was 'the philosophy of the human body'.[60] Duncan divided the course into 'Pathological Physiology' and 'General Therapeutics'. In 1823 his introductory lecture to this course was published. It evidenced relatively little interest in recent medical innovation, which is all the more striking since in practical matters Duncan was one of Edin-burgh's most innovative physicians.[61] In his lectures, however, he noted 'if the conjectures . . . which have lately been thrown out by Beddoes, Trotter, Patterson and others shall even, in part, be established . . . medicine will be improved'.[62] Thomas Beddoes had died in 1808. Robert Christison recorded that Duncan 'contrived to make it appear as if the physiology, pathology and therapeutics of Gaubius and the previous century were the physiology, pathology and therapeutics of the present day'.[63]

In 1807 Gordon began to teach a combined extramural course in anatomy and physiology. Ellis, Gordon's biographer, records that Gordon later separated the subjects.

> Dr Gordon, from the time he began to lecture, taught Anatomy and Physiology in conjunction; and this he continued to do till the summer of 1813. By experience, however, he became convinced that this plan could not be pursued with advantage to either of the sciences which it professed to teach;—that the simplicity and precision of anatomical demonstration, which is addressed directly to the eye, were embarrassed and overlaid by the introduction of physiological reasoning, the principles of which must often be sought in other sciences, and addressed to other senses.[64]

Such a separation of physiology and anatomy was also being effected in France, notably by François Magendie. The separation was equally important for both subjects. On the one hand it was a redefinition of the concerns of anatomy, on the other it was the creation of a new subject, *general* physiology.[65] In 1817 Gordon produced a physiology text book for his students. Duncan's last edition of his *Institutes* had appeared in 1809.[66] Gordon's work was only an outline, which virtually obliged the student to attend his lectures to make sense of it. His text indicates extensive reading among continental authors, especially French physiologists. Gordon's course, from the evidence of the texts published after the wars, described life in much the same way that Xavier Bichat had done.[67] Like Bichat, Gordon identified three great systems, the circulatory, absorbent and nervous.[68] In addition to these he detailed the common textures. His division of these was similar to Bichat's enumeration of the tissues or membranes. Gordon, however, unlike some of the French authors, was not making a methodological commitment to an autonomous physiological science which also regarded the mind as its proper object of study. Such an approach was associated with irreligion, radicalism and materialism—the charges laid against the phrenologists.[69] In Edinburgh physiology served the interests of a traditional establishment. Not surprisingly, in his course Gordon dilated on the role of the Creator, and the 'immaterial and spiritual mind'.[70]

Throughout the second decade of the nineteenth century new

divisions kept appearing within the Edinburgh medical world. In 1815 Thomson and others established a Dispensary in the New Town. Its establishment was vigorously opposed, principally by Andrew Duncan senior.[71] Duncan and others ran a dispensary in the old town and, in the words of Thomson's biographer, the new dispensary was seen as being 'calculated to be prejudicial to them'.[72] In other words, it was another dispute about opportunities for practice. As Cockburn put it, 'All the existing establishments had the usual interest to suppress a rival'.[73] In 1817 the College of Physicians considered a *Bill for the Reglation of Surgery*. It proposed an examination for everyone practising medicine in Edinburgh excepting those with an MB or an MD, with the College of Physicians having 'an equal share in the business'.[74] Since nearly all the examining done in Edinburgh at this time was done by the surgeons, this was not an attempt by the physicians to compromise with the surgeons. Rather it was a move intended to extend the physicians' prerogatives.

By the 1820s, the Town council, which had occasionally in earlier years acted to appoint able Whig candidates to chairs, became overtly Tory. In the first two years of the new decade it made two overtly political appointments, overlooking what seemed to many, much more suitable candidates. In 1820 the Tory John Wilson was appointed to the chair of moral philosophy in a bitter contest. In 1821 the chair of the practice of physic was made vacant by the death of James Gregory. The chair was a lucrative one, since there seems to have been little or no extramural competition, most of such teaching being on surgical subjects. To some, the standards of Gregory's teaching in his later years had left much to be desired. One critic, in 1821, wrote that Gregory 'scarcely thought it worth his while to change any of his lectures for the last thirty years', a fact which had set 'the tone of medical thinking throughout the country'.[75] Thomson, by now a licentiate of the College of Physicians, received massive support for the 1821 Chair but testimonial letters from the University professors came only from Robert Jameson and Dugald Stuart, who had, by then, retired. On the other hand, 'a declaration of the high qualifications of James Hume' was obtained from several of the members of the Medical Faculty.[76] Hume was a Tory. He was over sixty and had held his father's Chair of *Materia Medica* since 1798. He was elected to Gregory's chair. He published nothing and his medical classes became 'a scene of negligence, disrespect, noise and utter confusion for a few years before his death in 1842'.[77] Earlier, in 1818, Thomson had upset the Royal Infirmary managers by instituting 'an inquiry . . . as to certain defects in the economical treatment of the patients in the Royal Infirmary'. His biographer considers that it was this snub to the establishment that cost him the University Chair.[78] It should be noted that this method of choosing professors had its public defenders. In 1819 (anonymously) William Foster published *An Answer to the Several Attacks which have appeared against the University of Edinburgh*. Opposing the fashion for 'Reform' he declared Edinburgh's institutional arrangements were perfectly adequate. The University was managed on a system whch ensured 'that none are chosen to the professorial chair but such as have talents competent to fulfill it'.[79]

Early in 1821 Thomson resigned his Chair of Surgery at the College of Surgeons. The following year he resigned his appointment as Professor of Military Surgery. Because of the professorial monopoly, while Thomson occupied a University chair he was debarred from lecturing on any subject which encroached on the territory of his colleagues. Freed from this imposition Thomson began to deliver extra-faculty courses on the practice of physic. Thomson, a surgeon, was by now teaching a medical course from a surgical perspective. In this course he 'put aside the arrangement of diseases which nosologists had adopted' and substituted an anatomico-physiological arrangement'.[80] In his classes, according to his son, he embraced 'the most recent researches of the continental . . . pathologists . . . especially those of M. Laennec'.[81] Thomson also advocated therapeutic scepticism, another characteristic of French clinical medicine. Thomson was not alone in drawing on French material. By the 1820s French comparisons were being used extensively by those agitating for the reform of medical education. Daniel Ellis, Gordon's biographer, writing in 1823, unfavourably compared Edinburgh with other universities:

In most of the Universities of Europe . . . in which Medicine is scientifically taught, both Surgery and Physiology had been separated from Anatomy, and treated as distinct sciences.[82]

Ellis noted that the nervous system seemed to be the proper place to start a physiology course. This was the plan adopted by Gordon 'and a similar preference, I observe, is assigned to it in the recent elementary work of M. Magendie'.[83]

The 1820s, however, saw little overt change in the power structure of Edinburgh. During the Romantic Tory twilight the University medical school probably became increasingly less attractive to students. The only exciting new appointment, perhaps, was that of the dynamic William Pultney Alison to the chair of the Institutes of Medicine in 1821. All the sparkle lay with the extramural teachers. In 1824, 'it having been rumoured' that the Senate was considering changing the MD regulations, Thomson produced a pamphlet on the subject. Thomson argued as he had done before, for a single medical education, preceded by a mandatory broad general education. He cited Cabanis to show that medicine was a pivotal science, lying between moral philosophy and physics.[84] Thus medical men had a crucial role in the reform and running of society. Although Thomson argued that the study of mind was the province of medicine, his work produced no accusations of materialism, as had the works of the French authors, and, in London, those of the surgeon William Lawrence.[85] In Edinburgh this accusation seems to have been reserved for the phrenologists. By the 1820s Thomson was beginning to shift his ground in the arguments he used for advocating a single medical education. Ten years earlier he had argued that such an education was necessary because there were no important distinctions among physicians, surgeons and apothecaries. Now he was arguing that a single education was essential because there were important distinctions between those regularly educated in medicine and irregular practitioners: herbalists, homeopaths and so forth. This change of tack can probably be taken as a measure of how far *de facto* if not *de jure* a tribe of general practitioners had come into existence in the years 1800–20.[86] Thomson, citing at length from his own *Lectures on Inflammation* on the unity of medicine and surgery, argued that the University should create new chairs of pathology, surgery and physiology and dismantle the outdated chairs of the Institutes of Medicine and anatomy. He supported his argument by a comparison with universities in Austria and France, where such subject areas existed and where a broad general education was a prerequisite for medicine.[87]

Thomson's *Hints*, however, prompted a reply, *More Hints*, by a 'New'un' who saw in Thomson's work the ubiquitous voice of reform. The author began by noting that he lived in an age which 'teems with some new and vast design' and where the collective wisdom of centuries, and institutions of approved efficacy, are scrupulously arraigned and flippantly decried, by myriads of ephemeral babblers.[88] He noted, therefore, that it was not surprising to find the Edinburgh Medical School under attack. Reforms which had recently been proposed from within the University filled the author with disgust. They were proposals, he said, which obviously originated with the 'youngest' in the Faculty or those who had no business with the subject. The object of *More Hints* was to defend the distinction between physician and surgeon. Latin theses, which the Faculty were considering abolishing were, the author argued, 'the chief and almost only distinction between a physician and a surgeon or apothecary and constitute his principal claim to take precedence of these, and to be considered a liberally educated man'.[89]

By 1826, so controversial had the question of the Edinburgh curriculum become that a Royal Commission for visiting the Universities and Colleges of Scotland was set up by Peel. The origins of this Commission in the controversies generated by institutional arrangements of the University and the relation of the Commission to reform agitation in general have been admirably analysed by J. B. Morrell.[90] The particular origin of the Commission lay in a dispute about the teaching of midwifery. This is an issue which cannot be analysed here. Once again, however, a history of the divisions within the Edinburgh medical community over the teaching and examining of midwifery would be instructive. Such a history would almost certainly reveal familiar antagonisms over access to practice. Addressing the Commission, Thomson published two more pamphlets on the subject of University reform. The first of these again argued that a liberal education should be prerequisite for medical study. He once again referred to foreign universities, and the 'new regulations' for the teaching of medicine in Prussia, where students had to be examined in 'Languages, Logic, Philosophy, History and Natural Sciences'.[91] In the Netherlands, he noted, attendance at medical lectures required evidence of knowledge of mathematics, Greek, Latin and logic.

Thomson used the French example to criticise the clinical and pathological teaching at Edinburgh.

In France, no provision seems to have been made for having Clinical Lectures regularly delivered, before the creation of the new Schools of Medicine, at the commencement of the Revolution. But, if the French were tardy in availing themselves of this mode of instruction, it must be allowed that they have recently pursured it with more vigour, ability, and success, then has hitherto been done by the Clinical Professors in the Medical Schools of any other country. In addition, the study of Pathologial Anatomy, it is interesting to observe, formed a primary object with those by whom the practice of giving Clinical Lectures was originally set on foot.[92]

It is doubtful whether students gained a great deal of clinical experience in Edinburgh at this time. In the 1820s clinical lectures in Edinburgh were shared by those in the Medical Faculty willing to undertake them. But the Faculty seem to have found it a rather onerous task. There was no separate professorship of clinical medicine, and lectures were given in a ward set aside from the rest of the hospital. Only in 1829 were four physicians in ordinary given permission to give lectures on the main wards.[93]

Edinburgh students, on the other hand, found much to excite them in Paris. Thomson noted that there were sixteen medical professors in Paris, two each for the practice of physic and surgery, and four separate professors of clinical medicine. The Edinburgh system of clinical teaching he held had caused a loss of 'reputation' of the School:

It is impossible for those who take an interest in the maintenance of the reputation of the Medical School of Edinburgh, to conceal from themselves the fact, that the greatest advantage, possessed by the rival schools of Medicine in the sister metropoles, as well as by some of those on the Continent, consists in the immense facilities for the practical study of their profession afforded to Students of Medicine, by the numerous and extensive hospitals which these cities contain. The Medical School of Edinburgh, therefore, can ill afford to lose such opportunities of this kind as are within its reach. It can only be by the whole of its hospital being converted into a school of instruction, that it can hope to contend with rivals who are every day becoming more formidable. If, in addition to the comparatively greater facilites for dissection afforded in the schools of London and Dublin, these schools should, by a judicious system of Clinical Instruction, turn to the best account, the practical opportunities which they undoubtedly enjoy, whilst opportunities of this kind continue in Edinburgh to be as limited as they at present are, it cannot but happen that the Students of your University will resort to these schools for the study of Practical Medicine, as many of them now do for that of Practical Anatomy.[94]

Resort to these schools the students eventually did.

By the time Edinburgh reformed its medical curriculum, its leadership of the medical world had been lost. Various new chairs were gradually created, Thomson himself being appointed professor of pathology in 1831. In the same year a chair of surgery was created.[95] By then, however, University College had been founded, ironically, with the help of the Edinburgh Whigs. The London hospitals were also flourishing, as were those of Dublin, and new schools were burgeoning in the provinces. More locally, Glasgow had found its feet.

The origins of the flourishing Edinburgh medicine during the revolutionary years did not lie in the University, but among the extramural teachers. Much of the success of this school was a consequence of war, the ability of the teachers to exploit the changes produced by a new demand for surgeons and the inability of students to study abroad. This exploitation, however, created tensions in every aspect of Edinburgh life. The forty years 1790–1830 saw the draining of power and patronage from the old order of physicians, lawyers, landed gentry and literati. New social groups, or newly powerful old ones, had interests which often conflicted with those of the 'Old Thing'.[96] The consequence was that although within the University the old order reigned, behind the scenes it was being dismantled. This was a slow and turbulent process, for on some issues the establishment could muster support, and on other it could not. Whence the patchwork appearance of allegiences in the Edinburgh disputes of these years. By the 1830s, overt reform in politics as well as medicine in Edinburgh was only the vestigial sign of a collapse of the culture that had created a Scottish Englightenment seventy years before. 'Old Edinburgh', as Cockburn put it, 'was no more'.[97]

The Wellcome Institute for the History of Medicine
183 Euston Road,
London NW1 2BP

REFERENCES

* I would like to thank Mike Barfoot, Laurence Brockliss, Stephen Jacyna, J. B. Morrell, Malcolm Nicolson and Roy Porter for commenting on an earlier draft and Sally Wood for typing the paper.

1. J. B. Morrell, 'Science and Scottish University Reform: Edinburgh in 1826', *British Journal for the History of Science,* 6 (1972), 39–56; Anand C. Chitnis, *The Scottish Enlightenment and Early Victorian English Society* (London, 1986), 36.

2. J. B. Morrell, 'The Patronage of Mid-Victorian Science in the University of Edinburgh', in G. L'E. Turner (ed.), *The Patronage of Science in the Nineteenth Century* (Leyden, 1976), 53–93; Sir Alexander Grant *The Story of the University of Edinburgh* (2 vols.; London, 1884), ii, 68.

3. Grant, *History*; Alexander Bower, *The History of the University of Edinburgh* (3 vols.; Edinburgh 1817–30).

4. D. B. Horn, *A Short History of the University of Edinburgh* (Edinburgh 1967); Chitnis, *Scottish Enlightenment*; see also his 'The Edinburgh Professoriate 1790–1826 and the University's Contribution to Nineteenth Century British Society', Ph.D. Thesis, University of Edinburgh (1968).

5. Morrell, 'Science'; 'Patronage'; 'The University of Edinburgh in the Late Eighteenth Century; its Scientific Eminence and Academic Structure', *Isis*, 62 (1970), 158–71; 'Practical Chemistry in the University of Edinburgh', *Ambix* 16 (1969), 66–80; 'Professors Robison and Playfair and the *Theophobia Gallica*: Natural Philosophy Religion and Politics in Edinburgh 1789–1815', *Notes and Records*, 27 (1972–3), 43–63; 'Individualism and the Structure of British Science in 1830', *Historical Studies in the Physical Sciences*, 3 (1971), 183–204.

6. J. B. Morrell, 'Reflections on the History of Scottish Science', *History of Science,* 12 (1974), 81–94; 'The Edinburgh Town Council and its University 1717–1766', in R. G. W. Anderson and A. Simpson (eds), *The Early Years of the Edinburgh Medical School* (Edinburgh, 1976), 46–65.

7. Bruce Lenman, *Integration, Enlightenment and Industrialization, Scotland 1746–1832* (London, 1981).

8. On the patronage network see Alexander Murdoch, *The People Above: Politics and Administration in Mid-Eighteenth Century Scotland* (Edinburgh, 1980); John Stuart Shaw, *The Management of Scottish Society 1707–1764* (Edinburgh, 1983).

9. Nicholas Phillipson, 'The Scottish Enlightenment', in Roy Porter and Mikulas Teich (eds.), *The Enlightenment in National Context* (Cambridge, 1981), 19–40.

10. J. R. R. Christie, 'The Origins and Development of the Scottish Scientific Community', *History of Science,* 12 (1974), 122–141; see also his, 'The Rise and Fall of Scottish Science', in M. P. Crosland (ed.), *The Emergence of Science in Western Europe* (London, 1975), 111–26; Christopher Lawrence, 'The Nervous System and Society in the Scottish Enlightenment', in Barry Barnes and Steven Shapin (eds.), *Natural Order* (Berverley Hills, 1979), 19–40; Steven Shapin, 'Science' in David Daiches (ed.), *A Companion to Scottish Culture* (London, 1981), 318–22. There were, of course, social and intellectual challenges to this account of the natural order. In medicine the most important was that of Brunonianism. See Michael Barfoot, 'Brunonianism under the Bed: an Alternative to University Medicine at Edinburgh in the 1780s', in W. F. Bynum and Roy Porter (eds.), *Brunonianism in Britain and on the Continent* (London, 1988) forthcoming.

11. S. Shapin, 'The Audience for Science in Eighteenth Century Edinburgh', *History of Science,* 12 (1974), 95–121.

12. N. T. Phillipson, 'Culture and Society in the Eighteenth Century Province', in L. Stone (ed.), *The University in Society* (2 vols.; Princeton, 1974–5), ii, 407–448. On the Moderates, see Richard B. Sher, *Church and University in the Scottish Enlightenment* (Princeton N.J., 1985).

13. The great Scottish intellectuals, it should be noted, did not, by and large, side with the American Revolutionaries. See Lenman, *Enlightenment,* 56–72.

14. W. Ferguson, *Scotland 1689 to the Present* (Edinburgh, 1968), 227, cited in Morrell, 'Robison', 44.

15. Alexander Cockburn, *Memorials of his Time* (Edinburgh, 1856), 86. The Whig journal the *Edinburgh Review* was founded in 1802, although it only became political after 1808

16. All these appointments, however, were made by a Tory Town Council, which in the early 1790s at least seems to have acted with some consideration for intellectual aptness as well as political propriety. This sense of intellectual aptness, Morrell suggests, was based on calculations of the financial reward to the city. See Morrell, 'Robison', 44.

17. Briefly the Leslie affair involved a contest for the vacant chair of mathematics in 1805. John Leslie was the Whig candidate who was opposed by the Moderate party of the Church and the Tories. The Whigs were successful. Morrell, 'Robison'; John G. Burke, 'Kirk and Causality in Edinburgh 1805', *Isis,* 61 (1970), 340–353.

18. E. H. Ackerknecht, *Medicine at the Paris Hospital 1794–1848* (Baltimore, 1967); J. Lesch, *Science and Medicine in France 1790–1855* (Cambridge Mass., 1984).

19. For this model see Lawrence, 'Nervous System' and also his 'Ornate Physicians and Medical Artisans' in W. F. Bynum and Roy Porter (eds.), *William Hunter and the 18th-century Medical World* (Cambridge,

1985), 153–76. More generally see his 'Medicine as Culture: Edinburgh and the Scottish Enlightenment', Ph.D. Thesis, University of London (1984).

20. Morrell, 'Structure'.

21. Morrell, 'Science', 48.

22. J. Comrie, *History of Scottish Medicine* (2 vols.; London, 1932), ii, 473.

23. The Apothecaries Act of 1815 essentially empowered the Society of Apothecaries in London to license all 'general practitioners' (i.e. apothecaries) in England and Wales. In order to obtain a license candidates had to have served an apprenticeship. The Diploma of the Edinburgh College of Surgeons entitled the holder to practise as a surgeon and apothecary in Scotland. It was not recognized by the Act. Moreover, many diplomates had not served an apprenticeship. These differences were a cause of bitterness for some years. See S. W. F. Holloway, 'The Apothecaries Act of 1815: A Reinterpretation: Part II: The Consequences of the Act', *Medical History,* 10 (1966), 221–236.

24. It had in fact increased in significance since mid-century when very few students graduated, see Lisa Rosner, 'Students and Apprentices: Medical Education at Edinburgh University, 1760–1810', Ph.D. Thesis, The Johns Hopkins University (1985).

25. On the surgeons in the late seventeenth and early eighteenth century see Rosalie Stott, 'The Incorporation of Surgeons and Medical Education and Practice in Edinburgh 1696–1755', Ph.D. Thesis, University of Edinburgh (1984).

26. For the French situation see Toby Gelfand, *Professionalizing Modern Medicine* (Westport, Conn., 1980). On England see his 'Invite the Philosopher as well as the Charitable': Hospital Teaching as a Private Enterprise in Hunterian London', in Bynum and Porter, *Hunter,* 129–52.

27. Rosner, 'Students', 227–8. On the organization of medical services in the army and navy see Sir Neil Cantlie, *A History of the Army Medical Department* (2 vols.; London, 1974) i, 170–209; Christopher Lloyd and Jack L. S. Coulter, *Medicine and the Navy* (4 vols.; London, 1961) iii, 10–37.

28. Rosner, 'students', 237.

29. R. E. Wright-St Clair, *Doctors Monro. A Medical Saga* (London, 1964), 109.

30. On the meaning of *anatomia animata* see Lloyd G. Stevenson, 'Anatomical Reasoning in Physiological Thought' in Chandler McC. Brooks and Paul F. Cranefield (eds.), *The Historical Development of Physiological Thought* (New York, 1959), 27–38.

31. On the local meanings of Edinburgh medical knowledge see Lawrence, 'Medicine as Culture'.

32. On traditional Edinburgh anatomy see Christopher Lawrence, 'Alexander Monro *primus* and the Edinburgh Manner of Anatomy', *Bulletin*

of the History of Medicine (forthcoming). Michael Barfoot has suggested to me that, paradoxically, Monro *tertius* was teaching a great deal of pathological anatomy related to disease diagnosis at a time when the students were demanding more metaphysical and comparative studies as the basis of surgical practice. There is no doubt, however, that one of the main attractions of the extramural teachers was their provision of abundant corpses.

33. G. R. Waterhouse, 'Memoir of John Barclay M.D.' in *The Naturalists Library* (Edinburgh, n.d.) xi, 17–44.

34. John Barclay *Introductory Lectures to a Course of Anatomy* (Edinburgh, 1827), 30; on Transcendentalism in Edinburgh see Stephen Jacyna, 'John Goodsir and the Making of Cellular Reality', *Journal of the History of Biology*, 16 (1983), 75–99.

35. On this, a French innovation, see Toby Gelfand, 'The "Paris Manner" of Dissection; Student Anatomical Dissection in Early Eighteenth Century Paris', *Bulletin of the History of Medicine*, 46 (1972), 99–130; On anatomy teaching in London see Susan Lawrence 'Science and Medicine at the London Hospitals: the Development of Teaching and Research', Ph.D. Thesis, University of Toronto (1985).

36. Henry Lonsdale, *A Sketch of the Life and Writings of Robert Knox the Anatomist* (London, 1870), 56.

37. In 1819 William Foster noted: "It is true that subjects cost more money here than in Dublin, but there is no actual want of them. They mostly come from London, and consequently there is often delay in their arrival. But every student is at length supplied with as many as he wants. A body in . . . [London] . . . costs four guineas, in Paris about four shillings, and in Edinburgh six guineas; what is the price in Dublin we are not informed". William Foster, *An Answer to Several Attacks which have appeared against the University of Edinburgh* (Edinburgh, 1819), 19.

38. John Struthers, *Historical Sketch of the Edinburgh Anatomical School* (Edinburgh, 1867) 60.

39. John Bell, *Letters on the Professional Character and Manners on the Eduction of a Surgeon and the Duties and Qualifications of a Physician* (Edinburgh, 1810), 579.

40. Struthers, *Historical Sketch*, 40.

41. He also fell out with John Barclay and the surgeon Benjamin Bell. See Struthers, 40–41.

42. Michael Barfoot, 'Pedagogy, Practice and Politics: the Edinburgh Medical Community in the Eighteenth Century' in Malcolm Nicolson (ed.), *Scotland's Health and Medicine* (London, forthcoming).

43. Struthers, *Historical Sketch*, 41.

44. The Life is in John Thomson, *An Account of the Life, Lectures, and Writings of William Cullen M.D.* (2 vols.; Edinburgh, 1859), i, 5–92.

45. [John Thomson], *Additional Hints Respecting the Improvement of the*

System of Medical Instruction Followed in the University of Edinburgh [1826], 27.

46. *Ibid.*, 46. It was the patronage of Earl Spencer, who advised the King on Thomson's suitability. Thomson was also quite active on his own behalf in this matter.

47. *Ibid.*, 28–29. Even the Faculty opposition to Thomson was divided, however. James Gregory supported Thomson in his attempt to get the chair. The link here lies with the Commonsense Philosophy. Thomson and Gregory were both close to Dugald Stewart. Gregory's father, John, had been a founder, with Thomas Reid, of this philosophy.

49. *Ibid.*, 24.

50. John Gregory, *Lectures on the Duties and Qualifications of a Physician. Revised and Corrected by James Gregory* (Edinburgh, 1805), 43.

51. [James Gregory], *Answer to James Hamilton Junior by Dr Gregory* (Edinburgh, 1793), 77.

52. *Ibid.* For his pains, Gregory was attacked by the professor of midwifery, James Hamilton, in a pseudonymous work, *J. Johnson, A Guide for Gentlemen Studying Medicine at the University of Edinburgh* (London, 1792).

53. Royal College of Physicians of Edinburgh, General Correspondence, 17.v. 1815, cited in W. S. Craig *History of the Royal College of Physicians of Edinburgh* (Oxford, 1976), 230.

54. John Thomson, *Lectures on Inflammation* (Edinburgh, 1813), 4.

55. *Ibid.*, 100–1.

56. Thomson, *Life,* i, 42. For an account of pathological anatomy and its use by French physicians and surgeons to unify the profession, and for the employment of French pathological models in British medicine see Russell C. Maulitz, *Morbid Appearances: The Anatomy of Pathology in the Early Nineteenth Century* (Cambridge, 1987).

57. G. N. Cantor, 'Phrenological Knowledge in Early Nineteenth Century Edinburgh: an Historical Discussion' *Annals of Science,* 32 (1975), 195–218; Steven Shapin, 'Phrenological Knowledge and the Social Structure of Early Nineteenth-Century Edinburgh', *Ibid.*, 219–43; G. N. Cantor 'A Critique of Steven Shapin's Social Interpretation of the Edinburgh Phrenology Debate', *Ibid.*, 245–56; Steven Shapin, 'The Politics of Observation: Cerebral Anatomy and Social Interests in the Edinburgh Phrenology Disputes', in Roy Wallis (ed.), *On the Margins of Science: The Social Construction of Rejected Knowledge* (Keele, 1979), 139–78; see also his 'Homo Phrenologicus: Anthropological Perspectives on an Historical Problem' in Barnes and Shapin, *Natural Order,* 41–72.

58. David Ellis, *Memoir of Life and Writings of John Gordon, M.D. F.R.S.E.* (Edinburgh, 1823).

59. Duncan exemplifies the difficulty of using the distinction Whig and Tory. In many ways, especially in his youth and when an outsider,

Duncan was associated with Whig tendencies. He was, in addition, one of the first extramural lecturers at Edinburgh. In later life, however, his opinions and allegiances seem more Tory. A similar move can be identified in James Gregory's career.

60. Andrew Duncan, *Observations on the Office of a Faithful Teacher and on the Duty of an Attentive Student of Medicine* (Edinburgh, 1823), 12.

61. Duncan founded, amongst many other societies: the Aesculapian Club, the Harveian Society, the Medicochirurgical Society and the Gymnastic Club. He was also 'instrumental in obtaining charters for no fewer that four royal institutions', see Comrie, *History*, i, 481.

62. Duncan, *Observations*, 20.

63. Robert Christison, *Life of Sir Robert Christison, Bart.* (2 vols.; London, 1885) i, 75.

64. Ellis, *Life*, 104. By this time *tertius* had droped the additional physiology lectures from his course.

65. On the constitution of 'classical' physiology see W. R. Albury, 'Experiments and Explanations in the Physiology of Bichat and Magendie', *Studies in the History of Biology*, I (1977), 47–131; J. V. Pickstone, 'Bureaucracy, Liberalism and the Body in Post-Revolutionary France', *History of Science*, 1981, 115–42; Lesch, *Physiology*. No-one in Edinburgh taught a course of 'pure' experimental physiology until later in the nineteenth century. But there is plenty of evidence for the gradual disassociation of a separate subject, physiology, from anatomy in the first three decades of the nineteenth century. Indeed, John Allen first taught a separate course of physiology in Edinburgh in 1794. See Thomson, *Life*, i, 13.

66. John Gordon, *Outlines of Lectures in Human Physiology* (Edinburgh, 1817). The last edition I have traced of Duncan's text is the 6th, in the Edinburgh Univesity Library, *Heads of Lectures on the Institutions of Medicine* (Edinburgh, 1809).

67. On Bichat see Elizabeth Haigh, *Xavier Bichat* (London, 1985) and, more importantly, John Pickstone, 'Bureaucracy'. Also Lesch, *Physiology* and Albury, 'Magendie'.

68. John Gordon, *A System of Human Anatomy* (Edinburgh, 1815), 25.

69. On the materialistic implication of the new physiology see Owsei Temkin, 'Basic Science, Medicine and the Romantic Era', *Bulletin of the History of Medicine*, 37 (1963), 97–129; J. Goodfield-Toulmin, 'Some Aspects of English Physiology: 1780–1840', *Journal of the History of Biology*, 2 (1969), 283–320; Karl Figlio, 'The Metaphor of Organization: an Historiographical Perspective on the Bio-Medical Sciences of the Early Nineteenth Century' *History of Science*, 14 (1976), 17–53. On the radical associations of phrenology see Roger Cooter, *The Cultural Meaning of Popular Science. Phrenology and the Organization of Consent in Nineteenth Century Britain* (Cambridge, 1984).

70. Gordon, *Anatomy,* 2.
71. Thomson, *Life,* i, 50. Dispensaries were charitable institutions, usually organized and run by physicians and/or surgeons. They had no beds but provided outpatient treatment.
72. Thomson, *Life,* i, 50.
73. Cockburn *Memorials,* 283.
74. Craig, *History,* 230.
75. Peter Reid, *Letter addressed to the Right Honourable the Lord Provost, Magistrate and Town Council of Edinburgh Regarding the Institutes of Medicine* (Edinburgh, 1821), 6–7.
76. Thomson, *Life,* i, 60.
77. Comrie, *Scottish Medicine,* ii, 489.
78. Thomson, *Life,* i, 50–8.
79. [Foster], *Answer,* 13.
80. Thomson, *Life,* i, 61.
81. *Ibid.* It was in these years that Thomson, a lifelong champion of the unity of physic and surgery began compiling a biography of one of the greatest Edinburgh physicians of the eighteenth century: William Cullen. There were many reasons for this, including the fact that Cullen could be represented as a profound meditator on general pathology, Thomson's own favourite sphere, and the intellectual area that could be used to link physic and surgery. It was also an attack on Brunonianism and its repudiation of the importance of local pathology. See Christopher Lawrence, 'Cullen, Brown and the Poverty of Essentialism' in Bynum and Porter, *Brunonianism.*
82. Ellis *Life,* 106–7.
83. *Ibid.,* 124.
84. Thomson, *Hints,* 80.
85. Temkin, 'Romantic Medicine'.
86. The term General Practitioner came into wide use in the 1820s. See Irvine Loudon, *The General Practitioner 1750–1850* (Cambridge, 1986), 1.
87. Thomson, *Hints,* 15–20.
88. New'un, *More "Hints" and More to the Purpose on the Tendency of the Projected Changes in the Requisite Qualifications of Candidates for a Medical Degree in the University of Edinburgh* (Edinburgh, 1824), 3.
89. *Ibid.,* 17.
90. Morrell, 'Science'. I follow Morrell here in seeing the origin of the Commission in the local collapse of effective organization rather than in a full scale assault on Scottish Education by Scottish Anglicizers. For this view see G. E. Davie *The Democratic Intellect. Scotland and the Universities in the Nineteenth Century* (Edinburgh, 1964).
91. Thomson, *Observations,* 16–17.
92. Thomson, *Additional Memorial,* 41. On the introduction of French clinical methods into Edinburgh medicine at this time see Malcolm

Nicolson 'Percussion and Stethoscopy in Early Nineteenth Century Scotland' in W. F. Bynum and Roy Porter (eds.), *Medicine and the Five Senses* (Cambridge, 1988), forthcoming.

93. A. Logan Turner, *Story of a Great Hospital. The Royal Infirmary of Edinburgh 1729–1929* (Edinburgh, 1937), 139.

94. Thomson, *Additional Memorial*, 59–60.

95. These chairs were established 'by a resolution of the Government . . . in accordance with representations from the Town Council'. There was opposition from the Senate. See Grant, *History*, i, 326. The chairs carried no salary.

96. A term widely used at this time to describe the, apparently, harmonious days of mid and late eighteenth-century Edinburgh.

97. Cockburn, *Memorials*, 377. For an excellent account of the anomie of this period see John Dwyer, *Virtuous Discourse: Sensibility and Community in Late Eighteenth Century Scotland*, (Edinburgh, 1987), 168–93.

Military Empire, Political Collaboration, and Cultural Consensus: The *Université Impériale* Reappraised: The Case of the University of Turin

Dorinda Outram

The Napoleonic Empire is usually conceived of in largely military and diplomatic terms, explicable in terms of armed aggression, expansion, negotiation, and renewed conquest. Conversely, the study of France itself during the Napoleonic period has been dominated by a largely socio-political approach, which has concentrated on the history of the economy, on the prosopography of the Napoleonic elite, on religious history, and, to a lesser extent in recent years, on the history of institutions.[1] Missing from both the history of the Empire and the internal history of Napoleonic France, is any investigation of the actual *behaviour* of the political elites. We know who the blokes were; but not what they would tend to do in a given situation, and why. We are very short on discussion of political *mentalités*, either in France, or in the Empire at large. This is all the more surprising in view of the increasing emphasis in the history of the proceeding periods, the French Revolution and Enlightenment, on the description of political culture, and *mentalités* of public life, and the patterns of political behaviour.[2]

I would like to suggest here that one way in which this problem could be approached would be the examination of the Imperial University. Founded by Napoleon by a series of decrees between 1806 and 1808, the University was established as a secular, over-arching body responsible for all aspects of educational administration from the primary to the tertiary level. In French terms, although many of its features were clearly borrowed from Piedmontese and Austrian models, it completely broke with traditional organization in numerous ways.[3] Frist, it was a state organization, explicitly vowed to the control of education by the state, by lay persons, and without explicit religious orientation. Secondly, it replaced the old regime universities, abolished in 1790, by a structure of *Facultés*, university-level institutions situated in major cities with a variety of subject areas offered. Only in the case of Paris was the full range of subjects offered.[4] Lastly, the Imperial University offered the revolutionary innovation of demanding examination success as entry-tickets into its employment, as well as into that of other state-sponsored professions, such as medicine, law, and engineering. It thus played a vital part in the history of the 'professionalization' of French life in the nineteenth and twentieth centuries.[5]

However, my intention here is not to examine the Imperial University from the inside, as a more or less efficient or innovatory organization of education. It is, much more, to look at it from the *outside*, as a civilian institution among many others, and assess its contribution to the way the French Empire sustained itself over the years through the actions, behaviour, and *mentalité* of its governing elites.

This is an important question to consider, because it is all too easy to consider the Napoleonic Empire as a military enterprise inevitably doomed to failure and collapse once concerted action by the armed forces of the Allies could be obtained. Often over-looked is the fact that the Empire, while it might have depended heavily on its armed forces for its short-term objectives of aggression and expansion, also depended equally heavily on its civilian administrations for the vital long-term objectives of consolidation. If the Empire was to survive, it could not be run indefinitely purely as a military operation: the basis of its political support had to be expanded, the conquered territories stabilized, and their ruling classes given an incentive to work with and for the French regime, rather than against it. In all these objectives, the Italian provinces captured since 1796 (Piedmont, Lombardy, Parma, Piacenza, Papal States, and Kingdom of Naples) played a vital role. They *had* to be stabilized, because they were financially and strategically central to the needs of France itself. Their tribute provided the only means of bolstering the shaky mechanisms of French public credit. Strategically, the Italian provinces sealed off Austria's southern outlets; as a source of conscripts for the Imperial armies they were unrivalled. It was not for nothing that Napoleon's finance minister exclaimed that the finances of France were founded on the battlefield of Marengo.[6]

Yet precisely because of their importance, the Italian states of the Empire also posed great problems for France, and could exert great pressures on her. If the Empire was ever to escape from the relentless spirals caused by the pursuit of the short-term objective, she had to accord weight to the desires of those within the conquered territories on whom she depended for the running of the civilian Empire: in other words, a collaborator class had to be produced, and to some degree, allowed to obtain its own objectives. Owing to recent upsurges in interest in modern European empires, and especially that of the Third Reich, the topic of collaboration in twentieth-century history has received increased attention over the last few years.[7] How are links formed between invading powers, and native elites and populations, who, on the face of it, have every reason not to co-operate with their new masters? It is argued here that it is only, and not even most importantly, coercion which produces collaboration: it is, far more, political, and cultural continuities together with patronage and personal relations between *occupants* and *occupés*. It is for these sorts of reasons that educational institutions such as the Imperial University assume a vital role in situations of occupation by fragile, military empires. They are at once, and at the same time, visible expressions of foreign domination, vehicles through which new loyalties may be formed through service, and themselves market places of cultural reconciliation. They provide simultaneously benefits for the new rulers in terms of financial resource to be plundered, and patronage base to be dispensed as required; they can be used, simultaneously, by collaborators, in quite a different sense, to block or modify the demands of the invaders while seeming to fulfil them.

In the case of the Italian provinces, the first pre-requisite for successful collaboration, that of substantial cultural continuities between occupying and occupied, was already present by 1796, and significantly included many of those who were to figure in the administration of the Imperial University in Italy. Under the Enlightenment, personal and institutional cultural contacts between the Italian states and France had abounded. Nearly half a century before, in 1759, a group of young Piedmontese nobles, including Count Giovanni Saluzzo, future vice-president of the University of Turin after 1802, and Prospero Balbo, future Rector of the *Accadémie* of Turin, the regional administration of the *Université* in the former Piedmontese kingdom, together with Louis Lagrange, the great mathematician, and future member of the Paris Academy of Sciences, had together founded the *Accademia delle Scienze* in Turin. They soon attracted royal patronage and began to publish the scientific work of many famous scholars, especially those of French nationality, such as Condorcet and Lavoisier. In this way, the Turin group became part of the contemporary European revival of interest in learned societies.[8] They also placed themselves in contact with the leading figures of the French scientific world, many of whom were to be metamorphosed by the Revolution into propounders and administrators of the new state educational organization. Balbo's involvement with the revival of the Academies would also have allowed him to view with sympathy the ideas put forward by Condorcet, during the revolutionary period in France, on the role of the state in education. Chief among them was the direction of instruction and research at all levels by a master-academy, not very different either from the Imperial University set up by Napoleon, or, indeed, from the Enlightenment University of Turin.[9] Scholarly debate has raged in Italy over the (ultimately unprovable) extent to which the structure of the Imperial University may have been borrowed from Piedmontese models.[10] But it is undoubtedly true that the Piedmontese reforms of 1772, closely following on from the expulsion of the Jesuits from the Kingdom, and largely carried through by Balbo's grandfather Count Lorenzo Bogino, the Minister of the Interior, gave a new body known as the *Magistrato della Riforma*, the surveillance of all levels of education in mainland Piedmont, in exactly the same way that the French *Université* was to do.[11] It is also important to note that the *Magistrato* and the *Université* also operated not just with similar structures of organization, but also with the same fundamental aims: to produce complete control of education and opinion formation within its borders by the secular state. In Piedmont, the manipulation of educational institutions to produce docile citizens was received practice long before 1796. Balbo and his group of friends were thus well prepared by their own experiences in their native Piedmont, as well as by their French contacts, for collaboration with the form that the organization of education was to take under Napoleon.

They were also well-prepared by a whole network of personal

relations between themselves and the French administration. Prospero Balbo's time in Paris as Sardinian Ambassador between 1796 and 1799 left him with many contacts amongst the men who were to re-surface among the educational administration in Italy.[12] There, he had encountered the rising young scientist Georges Cuvier, who was to become Inspector-General of Education in the Imperial University with special responsibilties for the Italian territories from 1806; Balbo also encountered in Paris Jean-Marie de Gérando, *philosophe*, a friend of Cuvier, ex-member of post-thermidorean Convention, who was to become Secretary to the *Junta* which administered the former Grand-Duchy of Tuscany from 1808, with special responsibilities for the incorporation of schools and universities into the *Université*. Common friends between De Gérando and Balbo in Paris were also the family of Baron Pastoret, royalist member of the National Assembly, and entrusted with important responsibilities by Napoleon in the administration of justice after his coming to power in 1799. As Sardinian Ambassador in Paris, Balbo had performed a valuable service for Baron Pastoret by providing him with a Sardinian passport which enabled him to leave France in safety during the left-wing *coup* of *fructidor* 1797.[13] Such personal links worked to bind men like Balbo closer to the institutional structures of the regime. When, for example, Balbo's son Cesare, the future *Risorgimento* hero, left Turin in 1808 to become a junior member of the Tuscan *junta*, he was

raccomandato alle cure dell' ottimo De Gérando, amico di casa, e referendario nella medesima Giunta.[14]

Administrators like De Gérando were not slow to make explicit equivalences between a graceful cosmopolitan acceptance of civilized and friendly relations with the new French possessions, and their ruling elites, and the stabilization of the Empire itself:

Il est remarquable que cette excessive prévention que nous avons connus quelque temps contre les productions étrangères, s'est précisément recontré avec la crise de nos exagérations politiques . . . Nous devons tâcher d'étendre le voile sur ces funestes souvenirs; mais c'est en restaurent qu'on fait oublier les maux qu'on a soufferts. Un héros a presenté l'olivier de la paix aux ennemis qui nous entouraient! Que nos savants, que nos littérateurs tendent la main à des hommes qui ne furent que nos rivaux et dont la plupart demandent à être nos amis! . . . . La France, après avoir réuni tant

de titres de gloire, trouverait encore à s'illustrer par de douces, de pacifi-
ques conquêtes; en rendant cet hommage solonnel aux génies dont
s'honorent les nations étrangères, elle en obtiendrait à son tour une
nouvelle estime, elle conserverait d'autant mieux le rang qui lui est dû, elle
se serait montrée plus juste, plus désintéressée, dans ses communications
avec elles.[15]

It is opinions like this which enable us to trace the very close
relationship within the Imperial University between the cosmopolitan outlook of many French administrators, the personal
relationships with Italians already prominent in educational and
intellectual matters, and the easing of such Italians into positions in
the Imperial administrations. And backing up these links lay
another factor: the operation of patronage.

As mentioned before, the Imperial University, simply because it
was a new institution, offered patronage opportunities which were
far greater than older institutions already colonized by clienteles
firmly rooted in the old regime. The Imperial University offered
golden opportunities for 'new men' such as the scientist Cuvier, the
Inspector-General d'Etudes, to establish their own European
patronage networks; and in doing so, to serve the Imperial purpose
of ensuring that the *occupés* would be bound to the new French
regime by self-interest. Cuvier's hospitality was well-known in Italian academic circles, and produced a multiplicity of contacts which
the academic and the political were inextricably mixed. For
example when Jerolamo Buniva, the professor of medicine in
Turin, introduced the famous physicist Galvani's nephew, Giorgio
Aldini, president of the puppet Cisalpine Republic, he hoped that
Cuvier would welcome Aldini with the 'même facilité que vous avez
bien accordé à moi, et à tant d'autres italiens'.[16] Cuvier also took
care that the dispensation of appointments in the *Université Impériale* should become almost his own private fief, virtually independent from control by the central administration in Paris.
Appointments in Tuscany, in particular, as I have shown elsewhere,
were regularly made by Cuvier in consultation with his Italian
clients, in direct contradiction to the weakly expressed wishes of the
central administration of the University of Paris.[17] A fine example
of how closely this network of patronage could function is provided
by the conflict which blew up over the appointment to the chair of
surgery at the Faculty of Medicine in Pisa. Cuvier's friend the
Italian *savant* Giovanni Fabroni and his patron Prince Neri Corsini,
who was also a friend of De Gérando, recommended a certain

Paolo Ucelli for the post.[18] Ucelli happended to be Fabroni's nephew, and the son of one of his political supporters during the revolutionary upheavals in Tuscany in 1799. Cuvier gave strong backing to the proposal, and the appointment was ratified in November 1812, against the strongly urged claims both of the son of the former holder of the chair, and of a candidate supported by members of the Senate in Paris. Throughout the records of this affair, there is no hint until the ratification of the appointment of any input by the central authority of the *Université* in Paris.[19] It is cases such as this which demonstrate the force of recommendation, originating in Italy rather than in Paris, within a small group of friends and scientific acquaintances, far outweighing the powers of appointment nominally possessed by the Grand-Master of the *Université*. Such links, formed under the Empire, were often to stay in existence long after 1814. To take only two examples: in 1824, the former *Inspecteur-Général* of the *Université* at Genoa, the zoologist Domenico Viviani, was still writing to Cuvier to recommend him promising pupils and report on his latest work, as did the veteran physicist Vassalli-Eandi of Turin, a relative and life-long friend of Prospero Balbo.[20]

In the functioning of the Imperial University, such mechanisms of patronage gave Italians working for and with the French great effective powers of appointment. Patronage, in other words, made it easier for Italians to collaborate and gave them an interest in continuing to collaborate. This is an important point to make, on two grounds: firstly, because there were so many other aspects of the Italians' experience under the French which worked against their co-operation with the regime, that patronage goes some way to explain why any Italians collaborated at all and hence, how it was that the French could build up an Italian collaborator class. The second point is that Italians could use patronage networks to gain much freedom from central direction in Paris. The effect of an efficient and wide-ranging patronage system such as that set up by Cuvier, was to buffer the Italians from the direct impact of demands from the centre. All these points are vital in accounting for the fact that many Italians did actually collaborate with the French: for, after all, they had many reasons not to do so. Chief among these was the fact that the Italian universities, with their massive historic endowments, were tempting prey for the grasping financial institutions of the Empire, as well as for the military, always on the look-out for new resources to finance Imperial expansion. Endowments were ruthlessly cut, state subsidies not paid on time, real estate properties owned by universities confiscated and sold.[21]

The mechanisms are now well understood by which the French liquidated the state debts of the occupied territories, invested the funds so gained for their own profit, and at the same time funded the remaining institutions in these territories from such investments.[22] However, the internal functioning of institutions funded by these methods has received little attention. In the case of the universities in Italy, Napoleon's own statements of policy clearly stated that the universities would as far as possible finance themselves from the interest on their endowments, which the French had invested on their behalf in state loans.[23] Direct subsidies to the universities from government departments were frowned upon. This scheme could only function efficiently given an adequate initial endowment, and a measure of promptitude and honesty on the part of the agencies charged with the payment to the University of its interests. In the case of Turin, these provisos were not met. The university, enormously wealthy before 1796, now suffered a crippling financial burden, and the conduct of the French financial agencies strained the loyalty of Balbo and his colleagues almost to breaking point.[24]

Between 1799 and 1805, the University had administered its own endowments, which provided it with an annual income of about fr.500,000. Such revenues and such independence could not last long. Very early on, Saluzzo expressed his fears that the university would be placed at the mercy of 'la cupidité des financiers'.[25] His forebodings were justified. On Napoleon's initiative, the Minister of the Interior had already decided the University's fate. Its main agency, the Imperial *Domaine*, sold the University's property and invested the proceeds in 5% consolidated shares. From this, it was to pay the University annually the resulting fr.300,000. The Domaine's profit came from delaying payment of the interest and reinvesting it during the delay. Furthermore, of the fr.300,000, one-tenth was to be retained by the University as an endowment fund, so that its real annual revenue was fr.270,000, little more than half the amount obtained before 1805.[26]

Difficulties over payment through the *Domaine* began almost immediately. Delays of up to ten months were common, and left the University with an initial deficit of fr.157,607. When payment was eventually obtained, it was in the form of drafts on the Receveur des Domaines in Turin, and on the Receveur Général for the *départment*. This meant that the University would again be faced with delays in payment, since the Receveurs also depended for their profit on prolonging the period between the receipt and payment of funds so that they could speculate with the money they held.[27] Other drafts, on the Caisse d'Amortissement, were also given to the University. This was just as likely to delay payment, as the Caisse was regularly used by Napoleon to maintain the levels of purchase of state loans at time when confidence in the regime was low. When levels of purchase were high, interest payments tended to be reduced, and no exception was made for the University.

In 1811, the atmosphere became increasingly heated, and Balbo and the governing body of the University accused the Domaine of swindling them by misrepresenting the amount of revenue obtainable from the University's endowment. In August, part of the missing sum was ordered to be paid, but no cash ever materialized, and unpaid arrears continued to cripple the University's finely-balanced finances. By 1813, functionaries of the central educational adminstration in Paris regarded their defeat at the hands of the financial agencies as inevitable. Attached to one of Balbo's letters of complaint is a despairing comment:

Voici une note de M. de Balbe sur la manière dont l'Académie de Turin est payée des rentes qui lui appartiennent. Comme l'expérience m'a prouvée que toute réclamation relative aux finances est inutile et de nul effet, je me borne à vous transmettre cette note, sans y joindre aucune observation, et seulement pour l'acquit de ma conscience.[28]

Financial transactions such as these, unpleasant, frustrating, and with disturbing implications for long-range planning, made up the greater part of the day-to-day administration of the University. This renders even more pressing the need to explain what made continued collaboration worthwhile for the Italians. The answer is overwhelmingly to be found in the political sphere, and the role of the Imperial University in Italy casts new light on the operation of the French Empire as a political system, and therefore on many recieved ideas about the nature of the powers wielded by Napoleon. First Napoleon himself, and then the French Right, have presented the view that the *coup* of *brumaire* 1799 was the work of a successful general, who, by 1802, had rescued France from internal political chaos by quelling civil war in the Vendée, allowing the *emigrés* to return, and re-establishing friendly Church–State relations. Social and political policies swung firmly to the right, in reaction to what were perceived as the populist excesses of the Jacobin era. But examination of the way that the French government, including the Imperial University, operated in the annexed territories, suggests that this is too simple a picture. There were, for a start, too many powerful forces of opposition to Napoleon. It took him four years to remove his liberal critics in the *Sénat*; powerful groups in the army itself, including the military government in Piedmont, did not bother to hide their continuing allegiance to republicanism, while royalists gave the regime only a surface acquiescence.[29] I would argue that just as much as France's internal direction, the surrounding conquered territories contributed to France's swing towards conservatism. It is no coincidence, for example, that the concordat of 1802 which restored the Catholic Church in France, took place in the same year which saw the formal integration of the most important Italian territory, Piedmont, into full amalgamation with France. The maintenance of that relationship with France rested on the collaboration of the Italian ruling class, a ruling class drawn from conservative sections of the nobility, rather than the middle-class radical republicans who had fuelled the Italian revolutions of the 1790s which allowed her first toe-hold in the region.[30] By 1802, the surviving Italian radicals had long before been disowned by the French, who preferred to recruit the nobility into administrative positions, in order to confer an aura of legitimacy and stability upon the regime; in turn the nobility looked to the French to hold down the former radicals and the threat of political and social instability which they were perceived to represent. This was the nature of the political bargain on which the Empire rested. It was an important one for the Italian universities, because it had been from their ranks that many of the Italian revolutionaries of the *triennio* (1796–99) had been drawn, and after 1800, on return to their University employment, such men constituted the major part of those under the authority of conservatives like Prospero Balbo.[31] In order to gain the co-operation of such men, the French had to promise to hold down the former radicals in the subject territories, and it is at least arguable that the conservative swing visible under the Empire was not so much imposed on, but actively desired by Napoleon's Piedmontese collaborators, and was virtually imposed on the French as a necessity if they were to retain the support of the collaborators. The famous policy of '*amalgame*', practised in France, could not have worked outside.[32]

But in what way was the Imperial University any different in these respects from any other of the civilian institutions of the

Empire? The answer must be that first of all the *Université* was the only wholly new institution of *central* government established by Napoleon. It thus offered unique opportunities to make appointments and keep patronage free of long-standing Ancien Regime clienteles. It is thus virtually a laboratory-site for the operation of patronage in a way which is *specifically* Napoleonic. Secondly, as an educational system, it exemplified, as does every other such organization, stresses between financial objectives, and long-term objectives of stabilization and the inculcation of cultural values. Within each of the Italian universities, the same conflicts ground themselves out, more visibly than in any other place, because no other institutional setting was more *visibly* devoted to the promulgation of ideals which its institutional existence daily undermined.

And finally, what of the future? Was the Napoleonic period a mere *cesura* in the history of the Italian university, or did it show at once deep continuities with the past and considerable importance for the future? The answer must be the latter.

The paradoxes on which the working of the Imperial system in the Italian universities was based did not vanish with the collapse of the Empire in 1814; in fact they became increasingly important during the succeeding decade. A substantial part had been played in revolutionary politics in Piedmont by men engaged in academic life. The new importance of this occupational group in political life has only recently been realized, and never fully explored. This is partly due to the surprising lack of biographical analysis of the protagonists of the revolutionary period. It is also only recently that the Napoleonic period in Italy has ceased to be dismissed as a sterile interlude between revolution and Risorgimento, and little attempt has been made to establish continuities between all three periods. One such linking thread is provided by the gradual rise of professional men and university teachers as a political force to be reckoned with. Between 1814 and 1830, great changes took place in the organization of the institutions of learning and science and their relation to the state. At the same time, it became possible as never before, due to the spread of literacy, and the rise of a larger reading public, and the expansion of the newspaper press, to diffuse facts and opinions fast and effectively to most classes of society. The control of the diffusion of knowledge thus became a newly acute political problem, and educational institutions became new political battlegrounds. In Italy, those who were involved with these problems, as Balbo was during the upheaval in Turin in 1821, faced a political situation moulded by the actions of the previous regime.[33]

The early Risorgimento held many contradictory ideas on the subject of the Napoleonic regime. The Empire had brought with it a high degree of the very territorial unification and administrative rationalization demanded by liberals in the 1820s. Former employees of the French were to the fore in many of the revolts of 1821.[34] Yet at the same time the subordination of the Italian people within the Empire was repugnant to aspirations of national unity and independence. The Empire had also established new lines of political cleavage. Conservative collaborators had had to turn to the French to restrain the university radicals. In the period of the Enlightenment, things had been very different. The Italian ruling houses and the intelligentsia had worked together for reform.[35] In the 1790s the position had started to change. Fearful that events in revolutionary France would spread to their own territories, the monarchs drew back from their support of reform and, in doing so, isolated many of the intellectuals who had been their strongest supporters.[36] When the French began to invade they provided the impetus behind the revolutions which paved the way for the final collapse of many of the old monarchies. But the French were not grateful allies. The radicals and republicans found themselves exiled or relegated to the obscurity of the classroom. When Napoleon reinforced the position of the conservative nobility in administration, he did nothing to quieten the hostility of the moderates. No real policy of *amalgame* was put into effect. The disaffection of the republican intelligentsia within the University from the ruling authority was thus maintained, and carried over without difficulty after the restoration of the ruling houses once so gladly served by the universities.

It was in the light of this development that conservatives and liberals were to face each other in the 1820s.[37] Few of the governments of the Italian states restored in 1815 carried out widespread purges of those who had collaborated with the French. But almost everywhere, movements of reform associated such collaboration with fidelity to Enlightenment progress in the past, and to modernization in the future, accompanied by greater or lesser degrees of political change. As governmental politics tended to become more conservative during the 1820s, even men like Balbo began to be viewed as 'liberals' due to their previous association with the French regime. At the same time, particularly in conservative states such as Naples and Piedmont, the increasing isolation of the former collaborators in government, bureaucracy, and armies, led them into desperate measures to retain their hold on power, such as the Neapolitan revolution of 1821–1822.[38] As the century progressed, such attempts to seize power by disaffected middle-class groups became associated with one strand or another of the movement for national unification. The 'French experience' thus gave two crucial inputs into the Risorgimento: it made visible collaborator groups, and underlined the differences between restored regimes and reforming bourgeoise; and it also meant that the major political experience of the late eighteenth century in Italy, the French occupation, left a legacy both attractively reformist and 'Enlightened', and disturbingly non-national. In this complex process, which lies at the origins of the Risorgimento, the Italian universities of the French occupation had been very visible arenas of the beginnings of such conflicts.

Department of Modern History
University College Cork
Eire

REFERENCES

1. E. g. D. G. Wright, *Napoleon and Europe* (London and New York, 1984); E. E. Y. Hales, *Napoleon and the Pope* (Eyre and Spottiswood, London, 1962); P. Latreille, *Napoléon et le Saint-Siège, 1801–1808* (Paris, 1935); G. Chaussinand-Nogaret, L. Bergeron and R. Forster, 'Les notables du Grand-Empire en 1810', *Annales ESC* 1971; L. Bergeron and G. Chaussinand-Nogaret (eds.), *Grands Notables du Premier Empire* (Paris, 1978—(in progress)); L. Bergeron, 'Problèmes économiques de la France napoléonienne', in L. Bergeron, ed., *La France à l'époque napoléonienne* (Paris, 1970); J. Godechot, *Les institutions de la France sous la Révolution et l'Empire* (2 vols.; Paris, 1951); Marcel Marion, *Histoire financière de la France depuis 1715* (6 vols.; Paris, 1927); J. Godechot, 'Sens et importance de la transformation des institutions revolutionnaires à l'époque napoléonienne', *Revue d'histoire moderne et contemporaire* 17 (1970), 795–813.
2. E. g. F. Furet, *Penser la révolution* (Paris, 1978); translated as *Interpreting the French Revolution* (Cambridge and London, 1981); Lynn

A. Hunt, *Politics, Culture and Class in the French Revolution* (Berkeley, Los Angeles and London, 1984).

3. For comparison with Enlightenment models, see M. Viara, 'Gli ordinamenti della Università di Torino nel secolo XVIII', in *Bollettino storico-bibliografico subalpino*, 40 (1942), 42–54; E. Rota, 'Per la reforma degli studi ecclesiastici nell'università Pavese al tempo di Guiseppe II', *Bollettino della Società Pavese di Storio Patria*, 7 (1907), 402–412; Greta Klingenstein, 'Vorstufen der theresianischen Studienreform in der Regierungszeit Karls VI', *Mitteilungen des Instituts fur österreichische Geschichtsforschung* 66 (1968), 343–77.

4. Aulard, *Napoléon I et le Monopole universitaire* (Paris, 1911); C. Schmidt, *La réforme de l'Université Impériale en 1811* (Paris, 1905); M. Vaughan and M. Scotford-Archer, *Social Conflict and Educational Change in England and France, 1789–1848* (Cambridge, 1971); L. Liard, *L'enseignement supérieur en France 1789–1889* (2 vols.; Paris, 1894); P. Gerbod, *La condition universitaire en France au dix-neuvième siècle* (Paris, 1965); *Annales historiques de la révolution française*, 243 (i) (1981); special number on education.

5. D. Outram, 'Politics and vocation: French science 1793–1830', *British Journal for the History of Science*, 13 (1980), 27–43.

6. Martin-Michel-Charles Gaudin, duc de Gaëte, *Mémoires, Souvenirs, Opinions et Ecrits* (2 vols.; Paris, 1826) 1, 170–71; Marion, *op. cit.*, note 1, IV, 6, pp. 8–9; O. Connelly, *Napoleon's satellite kingdoms* (New York and London, 1965).

7. R. O. Paxton, *The Vichy Regime: Old Guard and New Order* (New York, 1972); S. Hoffman, 'Collaborationism in France during World War II', in S. Hoffman (ed.), *Decline or Renewal? France since the 1930s* (New York, 1974).

8. E. W. Cochrane, *Tradition and Enlightenment in the Tuscan Academies 1690–1800* (Rome, 1961); D. Roche, *Le Siècle des lumières en province: académies et académiciens provinciaux 1680–1789* (2 vols.; Paris and La Haye, 1978); G. Torcellan, 'Un terra di recerca: le academie agrarie del settecento: la società agraria di Torino', *Rivista storica Italiana*, 66 (1964), 530–52; Accademia delle scienze de Torino, *Il primo secolo della R. Accademia delle Scienzi di Torino* (Turin, 1883); J. E. McClellan III, *Science reorganised: scientific societies in the eighteenth century* (New York, 1985).

9. K. M. Baker, 'Les débuts de Condorcet au Secretariat de l'Académie Royal des Sciences, 1773–1776', *Revue d'histoire des Sciences*, 20 (1967), 229–80; *Condorcet: From Natural Philosophy to Social Mathematics* (Chicago and London, 1975).

10. Viara, *op. cit.*, note 3.

11. G. G. Quazza, *Le reforme in Piemonte nella prima metà del settecento* (2 vols.; Modena, 1957), 2, x, *passim*; F. Venturi, 'Il Conte Bogino, il

Dottor Cossu, e i Monti Frumentari', *Rivista Storica Italiana*, 66 (1964), 470–506.

12. The best modern biography of Balbo is the entry by F. Sirugo in *Dizionario degli Italiana* (Rome, 1963), 5; there is also material relevant to his career in the Napoleonic administration in E. Passamonti, 'Prospero Balbo e la rivoluzione del 1821', *Biblioteca di Storia recente*, 12 (1926), 190–347. There have been few studies of the Italian colaborators as a group since T. Corsini, 'De alcuni cooperatori italiani di Napoleon I', in his *Ritratti e studi moderni* (Milan, 1914), 397–459, with the execption of R. Davico, *Peuples et notables, 1750–1816 Essai sur l'Ancien Régime et la Révolution en Piémont* (Paris, 1981). F. Bassan, *La famille Pastoret d'après leur correspondance 1788–1856* (Paris, 1969); Sirurgo, *op. cit.*, note 12.

14. E. Ricotti, *Della vita e degli scritti del conte Cesare Balbo* (Florence, 1856), 12. The extent to which Balbo was able to find positions in the administration of education for many members of his family has been chronicled in D. Outram, 'Education and Politics in Piedmont 1796–1814', *Historical Journal*, 19 (1976), 611–33.

15. Quoted in R. Mortier, 'Les *Archives littéraires de l'Europe* (1804–1808), et le cosmopolitisme littéraire sous le Premier Empire', *Mémoires de l'Académie Royale de Belgique, Classe des lettres et des sciences morales et politiques* 4 (1954), 1–251; 17–18; D. Outram, *Vocation, Science and Authority in Post-Revolutionary France: Georges Cuvier* (Manchester, London and Dover, New Hampshire, 1984), 69–92. The *héros* referred to is of course Napoleon.

16. Fonds Cuvier, Library of the Institut de France, Paris, 3299, fol. 14, letter of 25 *messidor*, an IX.; Jean Théoridès, 'Quelques documents inédits ou peu connus relatifs à Georges Cuvier, à sa famille et à son salon', *Stendhal Club* 9 (1966–1967), 55–64, 179–188.

17. Outram, *op. cit.*, note 15, 69–92.

18. D. Outram, 'Politics, publicisation and natural history: the correspondence between Georges Cuvier and Giovanni Fabroni', *Ricerche Storiche* 13 (1982), 412–40; see also Renato Pasta, 'The Making of a Notable: Giovanni Fabroni (1752–1822) between Enlightened Absolution and Napoleonic Administration' (Princeton University Ph.D. thesis, 1985: NBM 85–04419).

19. Archives Nationales, Paris, F[17] 1601, Dossier, Faculté de Médicine; G. Turi, *'Viva Maria': La reazione alle riforme leopoldine* (Florence, 1969); L. Neppi Modona, 'Il diario delle persecuzioni di Ferdinando Fossi', *Rassegna Storica Toscana*, 15 (1969), 151–201.

20. Fonds Cuvier, Library of the Institut de France, Paris, 3248, fol. 49, letter of 20 April 1824; 3246, fol. 31, letter of 18 February 1824.

21. For a more detailed account, see D. Outram, *op. cit.*, note 14, 611–33.

22. Marcel Marion, *op. cit.* (note 1), IV, 6, passim.

23. *Correspondence de Napoléon I . . . publiée par l'ordre de l'Empéreur Napoléon III* (32 vols.; Paris, 1855–70), 18, p. 89, No. 14503.

24. E.g., financial difficulties forced Balbo to suspend the opening of projected departments of art, pharmacy, and veterinary medicine. No salaries could be paid to the professors of music, the keeper of the botanical gardens, or to the staff of the University Museum of Natural History. It was impossible to open a new anatomy theatre, establish an extra chair of medicine, or a new student hostel, all of which had been promised in the plans for university reconstruction produced by the French in 1802. Salaries of teaching staff were paid at least three, and often nine months in arrears. Cp. Archives Nationales, Paris, F[17] 1605, letter of 24 April 1807; F[17] 1603, report of 28 April 1811.

25. *Ibid.*, F[17] 1607, unpaginated dossier 'Personnel et notes diverses', letter of Saluzzo to Fourcroy, 12 Messidor au XI.

26. *Correspondence, op. cit.,* note 23, 8, 278, no. 6593; 9, 651, no. 8008; Archives Nationales, Paris, F[17] 1607, Minister of the Interior to Ministry of Finance, 13 prairial XIII; F[17] 1603, fol. 36, 18 germinal XI.

27. *Ibid.*, F[17] 1605, *procès-verbal* du Grand-Conseil de l'Université de Turin, 11 July 1811, 51: 'Le Directeur du Domaine du Pô, à force de subterfuges et de prétextes évasifs a réussi jusqu'à présent à contrarer et rendre inutile toute espèce de démarche'.

28. *Ibid.*, F[17] 1613, dossier Domaine, letter of Coiffier to Cuvier, 30 August 1813.

29. For the links between army and republican opposition, and their crystallisation round the 1802 reorganisation of education in Piedmont, see F. Boyer, 'Les institutions universitaires en Piémont de 1800 à 1802', *Revue d'histoire moderne et contemporaire*, 17 (1970), 913–17; Outram, *op. cit.*, note 14.

30. G. Vaccarino, 'L'inchiestà del 1799 sui Giacobini in Piemonte', *Rivista Storica Italiana* 67 (1965), 27–77; *id.*, 'La classe politica piemontese dopo Marengo, nelle note segrete di Augusto Hus', *Bolletino storico-bibliografico subalpino*, 45 (1953), 5–74.

31. The ensuing, inevitable, conflicts are recounted in more detail in Outram, *op. cit.*, note 14; P. Balbo, *Lezione accademiche . . . intorno alla storia della Università di Torino* (6 vols.; Turin, 1825), 2, 194 ff.; G. Brayda, C. Botta and G. Giraud, *Vicissitudes de l'Instruction publique en Piémont depuis l'an VII jusqu'au mois de ventôse an XI* (Turin, 1803).

32. Significantly, disappointed candidates for Balbo's position of Rector were nearly all drawn from republicans prominent between 1796 and 1799. One of them, the leading radical Carlo Botta, ascribed his failure to gain the appointment to French fears 'de déplaire à la noblesse piémontaise': quoted in A. Bersano, 'Il fondo Rigoletti dell' epistolario Botta', *Bolletino storico-bibliografico subalpino*, 46 (1958), 351–79; letter 221; for similar sentiments, see A. Neri, 'Una lettera

apologetica di Carlo Botta', *Archivico Storica Italiano*, 5th series, 9 (1982), 76–87.

33. P. Egidi, *I moti studenleschi di Torino nel gennaio 1821* (Turin, 1923); Passamonit, *op. cit.*, note 12.

34. E.g. G. T. Romani, *The Neopolitan Revolution of 1820–1821* (Evanston, Illinois, 1950).

35. Turi, *op. cit.*, note 19; N. Carranza, 'L'università di Pisa e la formazione culturale del ceto dirigente toscano del settecento', *Bollettino storico pisano*, 33–35 (1964–1966), 469–537; Cochrane, *op. cit.*, note 8.

36. For a specific instance see Outram, *op. cit.*, note 18.

37. All the more so because of the high degree of continuity in university administration between Napoleonic and restoration regimes in Italy: A. Carraresi, 'La politica interna di Vittorio Fossombroni nella Restaurazione', *Archivio Storico Italiano*, 129 (1971), 267–355; Egidi, *op. cit.*, note 33; R. Boudard, *L'organisation de l'Université . . . dans l'Académie Impériale de Gênes entre 1805 et 1814* (Paris and The Hague, 1962); A. Zobi, *Storia civile della Toscana dal MDCCXXXVII al MDCCCXLVIII* (5 vols.; Florence, 1850–52), 4, *passim*. Appointments in the Dutch territories of the Empire also showed a high degree of continuity: S. Schama, 'Schools and Politics in the Netherlands, 1796–1814', *Historical Journal*, 13 (1970), 589–610.

38. For another perspective on this problem, L. O'Boyle, 'The problem of an excess of educated men in Western Europe, 1800–1850', *Journal of Modern History*, 4 (1970), 471–95; C. Graña, *Bohemian vs bourgeois: French society and the French man of letters in the nineteenth century (New York, 1964).*

Research in Progress

The International Commission for the History of Universities: A Note

John M. Fletcher*

The Commission operates as a section of the International Committee of Historical Sciences. It was formed after the Second World War by historians who were mainly inspired by a regard for the unity of academic life that they believed characteristic of medieval and early modern Europe. The early activities of the Commission, therefore, attempted to encourage research and publications related especially to medieval and renaissance Europe. With a growing concern for the history of later universities and of those established outside Europe, the Commission has tried to expand its assistance to all areas of university history.

The composition of the Commission is determined by the members themselves who elect one, or in exceptional cases, two representatives from countries where there is a lively interest in the history of universities. Such elections are made after consultation with the learned societies of the particular countries. The Commission meets usually in formal session once each year, but the members retain close and regular personal contact with each other. Since the Commission has no funds at its disposal beyond those required to cover secretarial expenses, its function is to encourage and advise rather than itself to sponsor activities. For instance, members regularly advise on the organization of relevant conferences, the provision of speakers and the choice of topics. They especially attempt to encourage the production of bibliographies and other such aids to research. At each meeting representatives report on activities in their own countries and so members are well informed of the progress of research and publications generally in this field. Individual representatives are always happy to receive enquiries from those working in the field of university history and to offer what help they can.

The Commission has recently seen the retirement of its energetic President, Prof. A. L. Gabriel of the United States, who was responsible for strengthening the Commission and seeing it gain greater international recognition. The present President is Prof. Robert Feenstra of the University of Leyden, himself a distinguished historian of the legal faculties of the European universities. The Secretary is Dr. Hilde de Ridder Symoens who can be contacted at the University of Ghent, Blandijnberg 2, B 9000 GHENT, Belgium. She is able to supply up to date information about the work and membership of the Commission.

The last session of the Commission was held at the University of Prague in June 1987. The next meeting will take place at the University of Siena in May 1988. The Commission will also make its contribution to the International Congress of Historical Sciences at Madrid in August 1990.

Department of Modern Languages
University of Aston
Birmingham B4 7ET

*Representative for the British Isles on the International Commission for the History of Universities.

Charles Samaran's Dream for Paris: Fifty Years After. With Special Reference to the Faculty of Theology*

James K. Farge

Fifty years ago, Charles Samaran was taking stock of the archives of the University of Paris, with a view—or rather a vision—of making available for the first time to historians of the University those records which still remained unpublished and, practically speaking, largely inaccessible to all but trained paleographers.[1] He was optimistic about the prospects, because a formidable record of publication had already been achieved during the preceding half-century.[2] He could not have known in 1938, however, the extent to which the ensuing war, the post-war economy, and, perhaps even more decisively, a shift in orientation in the concerns and priorities of French historians would delay the fulfillment of his hopes.

Indeed, during the ensuing fifty years—and especially during the past twenty-five—the pace of the publication of Paris University records has slackened considerably.[3] Today, however, Charles Samaran's hopes for further published editions of Paris archives once again have a realistic prospect of fulfillment.

Before elaborating on this venture and specifically on the records of the Faculty of Theology of Paris, two preliminary observations merit attention. The first is that the editing of the records of any single faculty, nation, or college of the University requires frequent reference to the archives of the other faculties, nations, and colleges, as well as to a wide range of public and private documents. The doctors of the Faculty of Theology, for example, participated collectively and individually in the affairs of the colleges, of the nations, of the nations assembled together in the Faculty of Arts, and in the general assemblies of the four faculties. Furthermore, they were consulted in an official capacity by prominent persons and institutions of Church and state. It is clear, then, that anyone who wants to annotate the documentation on such wide-ranging activity must be prepared to work with the records—most of them presently unpublished—of several other institutions and of private parties both within and without the University. César-Égasse Du Boulay must have known this intuitively, since his seventeenth-century history of the University is more a string of documents from many sources than a synthetic history.[4] Charles Jourdain likewise pursued the same course in giving us, in mid-nineteenth century, a list of documents *pertaining*—I stress that word because he uses it in his title[5]—*pertaining* to the history of the University. In the same way, had Heinrich Denifle and Émile Chatelain restricted their sights to documents emanating solely from the enclave bounded on the North and South by the Ile-de-la-Cité and the abbey of Sainte-Geneviève, and on the East and West by the abbey of Saint-Victor and the Pré-aux-Clercs, their *Chartularium*[6] would have filled perhaps one or two volumes—but certainly not four—and our knowledge of the medieval University of Paris would be correspondingly small.

The second general observation concerns the process of selection among all these documents. Denifle tells us that he gleaned 8,000 notes about the University from over 300,000 papal documents—and from just two papacies alone![7] It is no discredit to such indefatigable energy and scholarship if we nonetheless wonder about the thousands of notes from just those 8,000 which he chose not to include in the published *Chartularium*. In still another place he tells us that he selected from the registers of the Parlement of Paris and from the financial accounts of the Faculty of Theology only certain materials which he considered to be the most important.[8] But just as his own criteria of selection differed from those of Du Boulay and of Jourdain, so today, a hundred years later, our criteria may likely vary from his. While such a reappraisal should not take priority over more obvious needs, historians today and in future nevertheless have a valid interest to re-examine the documents about the University which Denifle and Chatelain passed over.

With these preliminary observations recorded, let us now survey the state of the documentation on the Faculty of Theology of Paris. Several major projects of publication of the archives of this Faculty require the attention of editors. Certainly the most demanding of all is the continuation of the *Chartularium* beyond 1452. Denifle and Chatelain had intended this *terminus ad quem* of their fourth volume to be only a temporary one, but Denifle's death in 1905, Chatelain's increasing administrative duties, and the Great War of

1914–1918 intervened. As a result, some historians seem to have presumed that nothing about the University of Paris after 1452 is worth knowing. Others, lacking access to documentation necessary for solid analysis and synthesis, have drawn unfounded conclusions about the University and especially about its Faculty of Theology. But the hundreds of disparate documents from post-1452 which concern the internal matters of the Faculty (indeed of the whole University) and its relations with other faculties, with the king, the Parlement of Paris, the chancellor, the papacy, bishops, mendicant orders, privileges and exemptions—in short all the kinds of things gathered by Denifle and Chatelain for the previous centuries—are extant either in original in the several series H, J, L, M, S, and X of the Archives Nationales or in the voluminous copies made in the seventeenth century by Jacques Quintaine and Philippe Bouvot[9] and by the abbé Henri Baudrant.[10] Nor can one ignore the Vatican Archives and the archives of religious orders, all of which Denifle had assiduously mined for the earlier period. To collate and edit this vast array of scattered records is probably the most important task of all. It is undoubtedly the most demanding, requiring skills and resources that may indeed be difficult to recruit.

The *Chartularium* had likewise relegated to a future volume the vast documentation, much of it in the Vatican, dealing with the University's earlier role in the schism in the West and the Councils of Constance and Basel. Samaran thought that these materials might have to be left to monographs on these subjects, but we know that this kind of selection of materials is surely not a satisfactory solution to the needs of the historian.

Unlike the *Chartularium*, which gathered together disparate documents from many sources, the *Auctarium chartularii* series was launched to publish materials which exist in the form of registers, and it published several registers of the University's nations. The Faculty of Theology kept several different registers: financial accounts, doctrinal decisions, conclusions of its regular meetings, and records of the bachelors' academic disputations. Denifle selected certain excerpts from the single extant pre-1452 Faculty document, comprising the financial accounts for 1421 to 1439,[11] for publication in the *Chartularium*. The accounts for 1449 to 1465 have been edited in a recent, but unpublished thesis.[12] Lamentably, all succeeding financial records between 1465 and 1549 have been lost. The register of accounts for 1549–1550,[13] has been analysed in our recent monograph on the Faculty of Theology,[14] but it and a series of later financial accounts merit an editor's attention.

A more critical need is a modern, annotated edition of the registers and other manuscripts containing the Faculty of Theology's doctrinal decisions which Charles DuPlessis d'Argentré published in the eighteenth century in his *Collectio judiciorum de novis erroribus.*[15] This monument in its time, still the principal source for many historians of the medieval Faculty of Theology, is based largely on the two parchment registers created by the Faculty's decision in October 1523 to gather together all its past and future judgments about faith and morals.[16] Both these registers are conserved today in the Bibliothèque Nationale.[17] Doctor Noël Béda, probably the founder of the registers, claimed in 1526, however, that they contained errors and omissions, and wanted them corrected according to the original decisions conserved in the Faculty archives.[18] But since few corrections and insertions as such are to be seen in them, we must suspect that d'Argentré unknowingly reproduced those errors—or, at least, what Béda thought were errors. After 1540, although the Faculty continued to record the *procès-verbaux* of its meetings, it abandoned the parallel register for its doctrinal determinations. Therefore, for anything after this date, d'Argentré had to rely on scattered documents, and here he himself introduced not a few mistakes. Thus today we depend entirely—and sometimes perhaps perilously—on d'Argentré for this critical area of Faculty pronouncements in faith and morals. A new edition of the manuscripts utilized over 250 years ago by d'Argentré, an edition which would set the decisions of the Faculty of Theology in the light of more recent scholarship, would greatly help to establish more firmly the true significance of those decisions and of the authority of the Faculty of Theology in theological questions in the Middle Ages and in the early modern era.

The one project for which work is currently under way is the editing of the series of thirteen registers of conclusions, or *procès-verbaux*, of the assemblies of the Faculty of Theology from 1505 until 1790. It would be difficult to overestimate the importance of these documents for the history of the University of Paris and for the intellectual and religious movements of those three centuries; yet only one-half of the first *one* of the thirteen registers has been published to date.[19] This first register, confiscated in December 1533 and not seen again by any historian until 1898,[20] not only allows us to examine the Faculty's involvement in the extraordinary issues of its time—the scholastic-humanist controversies, the onset of the Protestant Reformation, the censorship of printed books, relations with kings and the Parlement, with bishops and other universities—but also offers the most detailed view we have of the day-to-day institutional and academic concerns of the Faculty of Theology. Alexandre Clerval's publication in 1917 of the first half of this register, for the years 1505 to 1523, has not been adequately exploited by historians, perhaps the fault of his failing to index the work.[21] However, an annotated and indexed edition of the second half of the register (for the years 1524 through 1533) has now been submitted to press and should appear by mid-1988.[22] The transcription by the same editor of the subsequent register, for the period 1534 to 1549, is well under way.[23] These editions, with annotations based on extensive use of the registers of the Parlement of Paris and of notarial and other archives of the period, will give access for the first time to a wealth of information about the Faculty of Theology and provide opportunity for concrete documentation for the pronouncements of historians about the Faculty and its position in French religious and socio-politcal life during the first three decades of the French Reformation.

Happily, prospects are strong for the publication of the subsequent Faculty registers. Professor André Godin of the CNRS and the University of Paris has already begun putting students to work on the registers of the Faculty for the second half of the sixteenth century.[24] Professors Bruno Neveu of the École des Hautes Etudes (Paris) and Jacques Gres-Gayer of the Catholic University of America (Washington, DC) are turning their attention to the registers of the Faculty of Theology for the seventeenth century, the period of great theological debates. These efforts to make available for the first time the proceedings of the Faculty of Theology of Paris hold great promise not only for the history of the University but also for our understanding of the major intellectual, religious and political currents of Reformation, Counter-Reformation, the Wars of Religion, Gallicanism and neo-Scholasticism in France.

The projected publication of these registers will take place under the auspices of the Centre de Recherche et de Documentation sur l'Histoire des Universités, created in 1982 by the CNRS[25] under the direction of M. André Tuilier, now director *emeritus* of the Bibliothèque de la Sorbonne, and with the collaboration of the Paris publisher Alain Baudry of Aux Amateurs de Livres. The Centre sees its proposed collection as successor to the *Auctarium* series. Its scope embraces the documents of all the faculties, nations and colleges, the first volume in its series, 'Collection de Textes et de Documents sur l'Histoire des Universités, publiée sous les auspices de la Bibliothèque de la Sorbonne', is Robert Marichal's edition of the Prior's Book of the Collège de Sorbonne for 1430–1483.[26] Charles Samaran would doubtless be pleased at the start of this venture and at its prospects for the near future.

In conclusion, we should mention one further area of strategic importance for the documentation of the Faculty of Theology of Paris: bio-bibliographical notices. No one would deny the solid contribution to medieval studies made by Monseigneur Palémon Glorieux's *Répertoire* of 425 thirteenth-century theologians[27] or of the *Bibliographical Registers* of Oxford and Cambridge graduates produced by A. B. Emden.[28] Indeed, some pioneering work in this regard has been done for Paris by Pierre-Yves Féret, but he treats only the most prominent doctors of theology and relies for the most part on older, printed sources.[29] We need instead complete bio-graphical registers of the Paris theologians for the fourteenth and the fifteenth, for the seventeenth and most of the sixteenth centuries. Even though Paris never had real matriculation rolls, such biographical registers are not beyond our reach. One of the many debts we owe to Philippe Bouvot, a long-time bedel and archivist of the Faculty of Theology in the seventeenth century, is an authentic reliable list of all those candidates who completed the licence and doctorate in theology in Paris between the years 1373 and 1694.[30] Denifle and Chatelain included parts—but only parts—of this pre-cious register in the *Chartularium*. Henri-Bernard Maître published the names of graduates for the years 1494–1536.[31] But the vast majority of the theologians on Bouvot's list remain mere names. True biographical registers, established on manuscript as well as printed sources, would be tremendous research tools! Let us not say, as one eminent scholar in Paris advised in 1971, that we would look in vain for the materials required to produce such a register of theologians of the sixteenth century. Nine years after that dis-couraging but greatly mistaken advice, the Pontifical Institute of Medieval Studies published our *Biographical Register* of 474 Paris theologians for the period 1500 to 1536 which is now serving a wide range of scholars interested in this period.[32] For those who would make similar biographical registers for the period before or after, the materials are indeed at hand: benefice rolls, diocesan archives, notarial documents, registers of the Parlements, catalogues of manuscripts and printed books, book dedications, archives of cathedrals, of monasteries and mendicant orders, financial records of Paris colleges, proctors' and receivers' books of the nations, quarterly reports by records, certificates of study, etc.[33] None of these are records of the Faculty of Theology per se, and many of them are not easy to exploit; but all of them hold materials which help to turn mere lists of anonymous theologians into elite, influential groups of historical persons who taught, argued, and acted in and for the Faculty of Theology. Only after such bio-bibliographical studies have been achieved, along with the publication of the documents and registers of which Charles Samaran dreamed, can historians produce the solid and authoritative history of the University of Paris which the subject so richly deserves.

University of St Thomas
Houston, Texas 77006

REFERENCES

*An earlier version of this article was presented in Toronto on 23 April 1987 at the annual meeting of the Medieval Academy of America.

The present article is not intended to serve as a complete bibliography of the subject. For a bibliography on the whole University, at least for works prior to 1979, the reader should consult Simonne Guenée, *Bibliographie de l'Histoire des universités françaises*. I. *Généralités—Université de Paris* (Paris, 1981). For the Faculty of Theology, see the reference in note 33 below.

1. Charles Samaran, 'Pour l'histoire de l'Université de Paris,' *Annales de l'Université de Paris*, 13ᵉ année, no. 4 (juillet-août 1938), 300–319.
2. The four volumes of the *Chartularium universitatis parisiensis*, ed. Heinrich Denifle and Émile Chatelain (Paris, 1889–1897); the first four volumes of the *Auctarium chartularii universitatis parisiensis*, ed. Heinrich Denifle, Émile Chatelain, Charles Samaran and Émile van Moé (Paris, 1894–1938); the *Commentaires de la Faculté de Médecine de l'Université de Paris (1395–1516)*, ed. Ernest Wickersheimer (Paris, 1915); the *Commentaires de la Faculté de Médecine de l'Université de Paris (1377–1586*, ed. G. Steinheil (2 vols.; Paris, 1903); the deliberations of *La Faculté de Décret . . . au XCᵉ siècle*, ed. Marcel Fournier (3

vols.; Paris, 1895–1913); the *Registre des procès-verbaux de la Faculté de Théologie, 1505–1523*, ed. Alexandre Clerval (Paris, 1917); the cartularies of the Nation of France for 1507–1537 and of the Nation of Normandy for 1266–1467, edited respectively in 1915 and 1917 by Henri Omont. The same period produced a significant number of studies, many with published documents, about the colleges of the University, several of which originated as theses at the École Nationale des Chartes.

3. The following have appeared since 1938: volumes 5 and 6 of the *Auctarium* series, comprising Samaran's own edition of the *Liber procuratorum nationis gallicanae (franciae), (1443–1466)* (Paris, 1942) and Astrik L. Gabriel and Gray Cowan Boyce's edition of the *Liber receptorum nationis anglicanae (alemaniae), (1425–1494)* (Paris, 1964); Marie-Louise Concasty's edition of the *Commentaires de la Faculté de Médecine . . . (1516–1560)* (Paris, 1964); and Palémon Glorieux's *Aux origines de la Sorbonne,* (2 vols.; Paris, 1965–1966). Astrik L. Gabriel and some of his students at the University of Notre Dame (Indiana) have edited the statutes or cartularies of several of the Paris colleges, and Professor Gabriel is currently working on the *Liber procuratorum nationis anglicanae (alemaniae)* for 1494–1530.

4. *Historia universitatis parisiensis*, (6 vols.; Paris, 1665–1673; reprint Brussels, 1966).

5. *Index chronologicus chartarium pertinentium ad historiam universitatis parisiensis* (Paris, 1862).

6. *Chartularium universitatis parisensis,* (4 vols.; Paris, 1889–1897).

7. *Chartularium universitatis parisiensis,* 2, xviii.

8. See *Chartularium universitatis parisiensis,* 4, x–xi; the financial accounts are Bibliothèque Nationale MS Lat 5494.

9. For example, Bibliothèque Nationale MSS Lat 12846–50, 13884, 15445, 16576.

10. Paris, Bibliothèque de Saint-Sulpice, MS 25 (5 vols.).

11. Bibliothèque Nationale MS Lat 5494.

12. Bibliothèque Nationale MS Lat 5657-C. Ed. by John Barry Weber, 'The Register of the Beadles (receipts and expenses) of the Faculty of Theology of Paris for 1445–1465', (Ph. D thesis; Notre Dame, 1975); available on microfilm or Xerox reproduction (Ann Arbor, MI: University Microfilms, 1984).

13. Archives Nationales M 69-A #47.

14. *Orthodoxy and Reform in Early Reformation France: the Faculty of Theology of Paris, 1500–1543,* (Studies in Medieval and Reformation Thought, 32; Leiden, 1985), especially 43–46.

15. (3 vols.; Paris, 1725–1736; reprint Brussels, 1963).

16. See [Jules-] Alexandre Clerval, ed., *Registre des procès-verbaux de la Faculté de théologie de Paris,* I (1505–1523), (Paris, 1917), 399.

17. Bibliothèque Nationale MS Nouv Acq Lat 1826 (for 1210 to 1523), and

MS Lat 3381-B, (for 1524 to 1532). A third, paper register for the period 1534 to 1540 (Archives Nationales M 67-B #58)—mistakenly thought by some historians to be lost—reflects by its inferior condition the absence of Noël Béda, syndic of the Faculty, who had insisted on the high standards and strict care of these registers.

18. Bibliothèque Nationale MS Nouv Acq Lat 1782, f° 188v° (7 March 1526 n. st.); cf. séance 144 E in our forthcoming edition (see note 22).

19. [Jules-] Alexandre Clerval (ed.), *Registre des procès-verbaux de la Faculté de Théologie de Paris*, 1 (1505–1523), (Paris, 1917).

    We have drawn extensively from the first three of these registers in our *Biographical Register* (see note 31) and our *Orthodoxy and Reform in Early Reformation France* (see note 14).

20. Léopold Delisle, 'Notice sur un registre des procès-verbaux de la Faculté de Théologie de Paris pendant les années 1505–1533', *Notices et extraits des manuscrits de la Bibliothèque Nationale et autres bibliothèques*, 36 (1899), 315–407. This register is Bibliothèque Nationale, MS Nouv Acq Lat 1782.

21. [Jules-] Alexandre Clerval (ed.), *Registre des procès-verbaux de la Faculté de Théologie de Paris*, I (1505–1523), (Archives de l'Histoire religieuse de la France; Paris, 1917). A reprint of Clerval, with index, is currently under consideration.

22. James K. Farge (ed.), *Registre des procès-verbaux de la Faculté de Théologie de l'Université de Paris,* 2 (1524-novembre 1533), (Collection de Textes et de Documents sur l'Histoire des Universités, publiée sous les auspices de la Bibliothèque de la Sorbonne; Paris: Aux Amateurs de Livres, 1988).

23. Archives Nationales MM 248: 'Regestum conclusionum sacrae facultatis theologiae in universitate parisiensi' (27 November 1533–March 1549).

24. Yves Tatarenko, a student at Paris XI, submitted an annotated transcription of the *procès-verbaux* for the period 1552–1553, found in Archives Nationales MM 249, for his *mémoire de maîtrise* in the Fall of 1987.

25. See the *Annuaire CNRS des Sciences de l'homme* (1982).

26. *Le livre des prieurs de Sorbonne (1431–1485),* Texte critique avec introduction, notes et index par Robert Marichal, membre de l'Institut (Paris: Aux Amateurs de Livres, 1987).

27. *Répertoire des maîtres en théologie de Paris au XIIIe siècle,* (2 vols; Paris, 1933).

28. A. B. Emden, *Biographical Register of the University of Oxford,* to A. D. 1500 (3 vols; Oxford: 1957–59); 1500 to 1540 (Oxford, 1974); Idem, *Biographical Register of the University of Cambridge to 1500* (Cambridge, 1974).

29. *La Faculté de théologie de Paris et ses docteurs les plus célèbres,* Moyen Age, (4 vols; Paris, 1894–1897); and Époque Moderne, (7 vols; Paris, 1900–1910).

L. W. B. Brockliss' biographical register of about 1000 Irish students who studied at the University of Paris in the early modern period has remained in manuscript, a copy of which is held in the library of the Royal Irish Academy.

30. B. N. MS Lat 5657-A. (A few years in the early 15th-century are lacking.) Bouvot compiled these lists from other registers which he called 'Libri actuum', which, now missing for the 15th and 16th centuries, are still extant for the 17th century. A tantalizing entry in Bibliothèque Nationale MS Lat 15445, 158 (17th century) evokes the 'Primus liber actuum sacrae facultatis theologiae parisiensis qui extant, incipit 22° Septembris 1469; hic scribuntur omnes actus scholastici qui fiunt in praeclara facultate theologiae per bacalaureos formatos in dicta facultate, et nomina baccalaureorum formatorum, in quolibet dictorum actuum. . .' This register is no longer extant.

31. 'Les "Théologastres" de l'université de Paris au temps d'Érasme et de Rabelais (1496–1536)', *Bibliothèque d'Humanisme et Renaissance,* 27 (1965), 248–264.

32. James K. Farge, *Biographical Register of Paris Doctors of Theology, 1500–1536,* (Subsidia Mediaevalia, 10; Toronto, 1980).

33. See ibid., 443–464: 'A Bibliographic Essay on the Sources for the Study of the Faculty of Theology of Paris in the Sixteenth Century', and the Bibliography, 465–495.

Aberdeen University's Quincentennial History: A Report

Jennifer Carter

Anniversaries provide historians with a stimulus and opportunity, but one beset by many potential traps. Historians at Aberdeen University, seeking to honour the five hundredth anniversary of their institution, are well aware of the hazards, amongst which the worst are probably parochialism and hagiography. We have sought to avoid these hazards in several ways. When we began work we took advice from others experienced in the field, a process which included a seminar to which a number of colleagues came to tell us (for instance) about the pleasures and perils of writing the history of the University of Oxford, and about the wider work on European universities now in progress. We took an early decision to involve non-Aberdeen scholars in our enterprise, and have been particularly grateful for the continuing interest of Dr John Fletcher from Aston, and of the two historians who serve as outside assessors on our governing committee—Dr Robert Anderson of Edinburgh and Professor Donald Watt of St Andrews. Of the studies in the history of the university so far commissioned, half will be written by historians from outside Aberdeen, including two from Canada. We have tried also, as a matter of policy, to involve younger historians in our work, and are pleased to have attracted the help of such as Dr Christine Shepherd, Dr Peter Slee and Dr Paul Wood. In briefing our prospective contributors we have laid emphasis on the need for them to present the history of this university in the widest national and international context. We have also made the stipulation that contributions must be approved by external assessors before publication.

The attitude of the university's governing body, the University Court, has been supportive. Even in such difficult times as these, a measure of financial support has been promised to assist publication of our work, and very free access has been granted to the records of the university, to make it possible for those dealing with the twentieth-century history of the institution to do a proper job. The only embargoed categories of material are the records of living members of staff, past and present, and the files of the Principal and Secretary of the University covering the last fifteen years. While encouraging the work of the 'Quincentenary History Project' (QHP)—as it has come to be known—the University Court has not sought to interfere with it or dictate its direction in any way. There has been no attempt to persuade us to write 'official' history in the pejorative sense of that term.

Another advantage which the QHP enjoys is that of operating at a time when there is (for obvious contemporary reasons, as well as from longer-acting causes) a widespread interest in the history of universities. The existence of this journal, *History of Universities*, is one example, as is the ongoing work on the history of Oxford. In 1986 the London University Institute of Historical Research devoted its annual Anglo-American Conference of Historians to the topic: 'The University in Society', and that occasion also marked the one hundred and fiftieth anniversay of the foundation of the University of London. The climate of professional interest in the history of universities, and the many good publications which it is helping to produce, are a great encouragement to the Aberdeen project.

In 1995 Aberdeen will celebrate the five hundredth anniversary of the foundation of King's College, one of the two colleges which united in 1860 to form the University of Aberdeen. The second college, Marischal College, founded in 1593, enjoyed the status of an independent degree-giving university for 267 years before the union of the two colleges produced the modern university in 1860. It was on 10 February 1495 that a papal bull authorized the foundation of King's, or as it was originally called the College of St Mary in the Nativity.[1] Aberdeen thus combines a late-medieval with a Reformation origin, King's being an episcopal and Catholic foundation, the creation of Bishop William Elphinstone, whereas Marischal was founded by a vigorous Protestant reformer, George Keith, fifth Earl Marischal of Scotland, under a charter dated 2 April 1593. It is striking that at such early dates, and in so remote and relatively unprosperous a part of the world, two universities should have been founded, and perhaps more surprising still that they managed to survive. Both were, of course, very small institutions at the beginning, each starting with fewer than three dozen staff and students, and neither passing the hundred mark until nearly the eighteenth century. At the beginning of the nineteenth century King's still had only about 100 students, and Marischal about double that number; in 1861 the joint university numbered 634; by the end of the nineteenth century there were 800 students; by 1980 the population was just under 6,000.[2]

Although there have always been historians on the staff of the university from the time of the first Principal, Hector Boece, no anniversary until the quatercentenary in 1895 seems to have been celebrated by publications that survive. The quartercentenary produced two histories, by Bulloch and Rait, as well as a book of essays on the teaching of various subjects in the university since its beginning, edited by P. J. Anderson.[3] Librarian of the university, Anderson was the scholar who, more than any other, drew attention to the history of this university (at a time when university history was less fashionable than it is now) both by his own writings, and by his extensive publication of materials from the university archives. Aberdeen is indeed fortunate in the amount of its record materials which has been published—perhaps the most lasting kind of work on university history—though the task that Anderson set himself has never been completed. Besides collections of charters and other documents, there are lists of office-bearers and graduates, and there are also biographical dictionaries of graduates running from 1860 to 1970.[4] In 1960, the centenary of the 1860 union of the colleges produced a book of reminiscences, together with short histories of the university and of its General Council since the 'fusion'.[5] There has also been sporadic coverage of different aspects of the university's teaching, published mainly in the *Aberdeen University Review*;[6] and there are short works on the early history of Marischal College,[7] and on the late eighteenth-century disputes about college union.[8] Much good work has thus already been done, but with changing perspectives it is clear that there is still much to do.

In the summer of 1984 the University Court appointed an Editorial Board to produce a number of studies in the history of the university.[9] It is from the Editorial Board, with the advice of its governing committee, that the QHP has grown. There are four separate but inter-linked aspects of our current programme of work, which may be described as follows:

(1) In line with the original intention of those involved with launching the QHP, we intend to publish a series of short studies of different aspects of the history of the university. Each will focus on a

theme or episode of special local or wider significance, which either has not been covered by earlier work, or perhaps demands modern reinterpretation. Each study will be short (50,000 words or less) and will be published individually, while conforming to a common format. The studies so far commissioned fall into four groups. First are a number which seek to elucidate puzzles and reinterpret the more familiar aspects of the early history of the university. Thus Leslie J. Macfarlane and John M. Fletcher will look at *The Foundation of King's College Aberdeen in its European Context*, attempting for the first time to look thoroughly at the European university scene to discern what was routine and what was unusual in the form of the foundation of King's. Similarly, David Stevenson will examine the question: *New Foundation or Old? The Dispute over Reform at King's College Aberdeen 1569–1641*, seeking to untangle how far and how fast King's adapted to the Reformation. The alleged failure of King's to reform quickly enough is the supposed reason for the founding of Marischal College, but this claim will be re-examined by James Kirk when he writes about the early history of Marischal College, a subject full of unresolved ambiguities. The year 1641 is the stopping point for both Stevenson and Kirk because this was the date of a royal attempt to unite the two colleges into one 'Caroline' University of Aberdeen—an attempt which failed, as did several other attempts at union until the mid-nineteenth century. Also dealing with the early history is a study of *King's College Aberdeen in the Age of the Reformation*, by John Durkan and Allan White, which will explore the humanistic background to the early university, and also its links with the town of Aberdeen.

A second group of commissioned studies seeks to establish what was being taught at the university at various times. Thus Christine Shepherd and David Stevenson will write about what was happening in the seventeenth and early eighteenth centuries, while Paul Wood will take the story forward by exploring the curriculum and the way in which teaching was carried on in the period of the Enlightenment. Peter Slee will look at the new undergraduate curriculum, 1878 to 1914, a time which saw sweeping and controversial reforms at Aberdeen, as elsewhere in Scotland, reforms which might be viewed either as the updating of the curriculum to take proper account of expanding knowledge and growing specialization, or as the culmination of that anglicization of Scottish universities deplored by G. E. Davie.[10] It is often surprisingly difficult to establish exactly what was being taught in universities, by whom and to whom, and with what ends in view. Especially in periods before the late nineteenth century—when classes often contained 'ungowned' students (those attending only one particular class), when non-graduation for a variety of causes was common, and when not all professors taught—it is by no means simple to explain the content and intention of the curriculum. Aberdeen is fortunate in having a good collection of students' notebooks for the early modern period, and a wealth of manuscript class lists which, if they can be pieced together, will reveal much about the structure of teaching.

If curricular matters need illumination, so too does the day-to-day life of students, and this will be the subject of a third group of studies. Fragments of knowledge survive about student life in the first three and a half centuries of the university's history, and these will be analysed by Colin McLaren in his study of *The Aberdeen Student Community 1600–1860*. In *Student Life at Aberdeen 1860–1939*, Robert Anderson will examine a topic which has received little academic consideration, the subject of student culture and sporting and other communal activites. Some aspects of student communal activity were doubtless encouraged by the survival in Scottish universities of the office of Rector. At Aberdeen this office was revitalized in the nineteenth century, becoming once more student-elected, and it was often at the heart of internal and extra-mural political controversy. Controversy ran high over the admission of women to full academic status in the later nineteenth century. An Ordinance of 1892 granted them almost full admission to the Scottish universities,[11] but Aberdeen is said to have been the first university in Scotland to accord women entry to every Faculty.[12] *Aberdeen University and the Education of Women 1860–1918* is the subject of a study to be made by Lindy Moore.

A fourth theme will be the political history of the university. All work on the earlier history of the university will take account of the turbulent political life of the sixteenth, seventeenth and early eighteenth centuries which in many ways dictated the directions in which the university developed. In 1715, at the time of the first Jacobite rebellion, most of the professors both at King's and at Marischal College were purged for political reasons, and at Marischal the rights of appointment to six out of the eight chairs, which

until then had been in the hands of the family of the Earls Marischal, fell to the crown when the tenth Earl Marischal was attainted
for Jacobitism. Roger Emerson will write about the eighteenth-
century professoriate, and the political world in which King's and
Marischal existed. He will extend an argument he has advanced
already, that the contrasting fortunes of the two Aberdeen colleges
in the eighteenth century owed much to their differing political
orientation and fortunes, not least their contrasted ability to attract
local and national patronage.[13] Allan MacLaren will consider the
interaction of the university and local politics and society, from the
late eighteenth century to 1860, in *The Professors, the Pulpit and the
Press at Aberdeen*; while two very important political events in
Aberdeen University's nineteenth-century history will be examined
by Donald Withrington in two separate studies, one on the Royal
Commissions of the 1820s, and the other on the union of the
colleges in 1860. Like Anderson, Withrington believes that the
extent of government intervention in the university system, particularly in Scotland, in the nineteenth century is often underestimated, and that the reasons for that intervention are not always
understood.[14] Government money was already being sought and
obtained for university buildings and equipment, and for supple-
menting teachers' stipends before the 1820s, and the Royal Commissions of 1826 and 1876 provided a forum of public debate about
how the existing universities ought to be reformed, while the execu-
tive commissions of 1858 and 1889 carried out the detailed changes
which legislation arising from the Commissions' Reports sketched.
Thus, the union of the Aberdeen colleges was strongly recommended by the 1826 Commission, and finally accomplished as a
result of the Universities (Scotland) Act of 1858, and the work of
the special commissioners which it appointed. The reformers aimed
to enhance the public credibility of the univerisities, and to modern-
ize them: to create a 'strong university for a new age'.[15] The creation
in 1860 of the modern medical school at Aberdeen was another
result—in large part—of governmental pressure and subsidy, an
earlier attempt at the joint teaching of medicine, begun in 1818,
having failed in 1839. While the existence of the two Aberdeen
colleges provided one reason for state intervention here, much else
of Aberdeen's experience in the nineteenth and twentieth centuries
reflects a pattern which is common to the Scottish, and even the

British university system as a whole. Iain Hutchison will be examining this theme when he writes about *The University and the State in Modern Times: the Example of Aberdeen.*

Finance was clearly a major issue in university affairs in earlier times as well as today. The QHP has not yet commissioned work on the university's financial history, though two possibilities are under discussion. Several other themes are also at various stages of planning—notably a contribution by John Hargreaves on Aberdeen's extensive overseas links. Work is planned too on the development of the academic profession, and other aspects of professionalization as exemplified by practice in Aberdeen. In all we hope to publish at least twenty *Quincentennial Studies in the History of the University of Aberdeen*, with the intention that some or all of them could be collected and republished at the time of the Quincentenary.[16]

(2) In support of the scholarly enterprise of investigating the university's history, the QHP has already organized three conferences, and will continue this activity over the coming years. In 1985 two small conferences were held—one on the curriculum since the seventeenth century, and the other on the university's overseas connections. In 1986 there was a larger conference, organized in conjunction with the British Society for Eighteenth-Century Studies, on 'Aberdeen and the Enlightenment'.[17] In 1987 a smaller conference will be held on the buildings of the university before 1860. It is intended to supplement this programme of conferences, which has already proved most useful to those involved in the QHP, by a series of seminars on the twentieth-century history of the university.

(3) Another spin-off from the work of the QHP has been the assembling, under the direction of the University Archivist, of an oral history archive. This draws upon the memories of past and present staff, students and others connected with the university, and illustrates many aspects of university life, ranging from the highest policy matters (interviews have been recorded with two former Principals) to the cost of high tea for impoverished students in the 1920s. Some of the interviews with former students were recorded at graduate reunions, and this led to a further initiative whereby the University Archivist appealed in *Gaudeamus* (the graduate newsletter) for written memoirs. About fifty former students have responded, sending most interesting and varied

material. It is envisaged that the development of the oral history archive and the collection of written memoirs will become a permanent part of the activities of the University Archivist, thus providing a useful source of material for future historians, beyond the date of the Quincentenary.

(4) From the beginning, one of the highest priorities of the QHP has been the compilation of a computerized student database. Aberdeen has a rich holding of manuscript class-lists and other records, as well as the published lists and rolls of graduates, and it is clear that if all the material could be brought together in a database, much valuable information could be extracted, both about the organization of the curriculum, and about the make-up of the student community and the shape of student careers—in many cases the records show a student's place of origin, school attended, and parental profession. Dating back to the 1780s at least, this material could be made to yield the most interesting results for social as well as university history. The task is, however, too large to attempt without full-time research assistance. A bid for this has been approved by the Economic and Social Research Council, but at the time of writing has not yet been funded.

These, then, are the plans in which the Aberdeen QHP is engaged. There is some comfort in difficult times to reflect on the battering this university has withstood in the past: ironically, two of its best periods academically were times of great political tension, external or internal, namely the earlier seventeenth century when the university was famous for a group of scholars known as the 'Aberdeen doctors'; and the period of the Enlightenment and the Aberdeen invention of Common Sense philosophy. Despite such comforting reflections, however, present-day problems are such that we sometimes feel like the characters in Robert Musil's novel, *The Man Without Qualities*,[18] who comprised a committee appointed to arrange official celebrations of the seventieth anniversary of the Austro-Hungarian Emperor's accession, a jubilee which unfortunately fell on 2 December 1918.

University of Aberdeen
Aberdeen AB9 2UB

REFERENCES

1. The date of the foundation bull has sometimes been taken to be 1494, but this ambiguity is resolved by L. J. Macfarlane, *William Elphinstone and the Kingdom of Scotland 1431–1514. The Struggle for Order* (Aberdeen, 1985), 295.

2. Precise numbers are hard to establish, but Emerson puts King's at 100 in 1700, and 80 in 1800; Marischal at 90 and 200 at the same dates: see Roger L. Emerson, 'Scottish universities in the eighteenth century, 1690–1800', *Studies on Voltaire and the Eighteenth Century*, CLXVII (1977), 473. The 1861 and 1900 figures are from tables in R. D. Anderson, *Education and Opportunity in Victorian Scotland. Schools and Universities* (Oxford, 1983), 348, 352. The 1980 figure of 5590 is given in University Grants Committee, *University Statistics 1980*, vol. I, *Students and Staff*, 36, and the size of the population has increased since then.

3. J. M. Bulloch, *A History of the University of Aberdeen 1495–1895* (London, 1895); R. S. Rait, *The Universities of Aberdeen. A History* (Aberdeen, 1895); P. J. Anderson (ed.), *Studies in the History and Development of the University of Aberdeen. A Quatercentenary Tribute* (Aberdeen, 1906), which includes Anderson's 'Collections towards a bilibiography of the Universities of Aberdeen 1522–1906', 385–525. Anderson had prompted both Bulloch and Rait into publishing their histories: see C. A. McLaren, 'P. J. Anderson and the history of the University', *Aberdeen University Review*, LI (1985/86), 90.

4. C. Innes (ed.), *Fasti Aberdonenses. Selections from the Records of the University and King's College of Aberdeen 1494–1854* (Aberdeen, 1854); P. J. Anderson (ed.), *Officers and Graduates of the University and King's College Aberdeen 1495–1860* (Aberdeen, 1893), *Fasti Academiae Mariscallanae Aberdonenses. Selections from the Records of Marischal College and the University 1593–1860* (Aberdeen, 1889–98—vol. I, *Endowments*, vol. II, *Officers, Graduates, and Alumni*, vol. III, index to vol. II compiled by J. F. K. Johnstone), *Roll of Alumni in Arts of the University and King's College of Aberdeen 1596–1860* (Aberdeen, 1900); William Johnston (ed.), *Roll of Graduates of the University of Aberdeen 1860–1900* (Aberdeen, 1906); Theodore Watt (ed.), *Roll of Graduates of the University of Aberdeen 1901–1925, With Supplement 1860–1900* (Aberdeen, 1935); John Mackinnon (ed.), *Roll of Graduates of the University of Aberdeen 1926–1955, With Supplement 1860–1925* (Aberdeen, 1960); Louise Donald & W. S. Macdonald (eds), *Roll of Graduates of the University of Aberdeen 1956–1970, With Supplement 1860–1955* (Aberdeen, 1982). On what remains to be finished of Anderson's work, see McLaren, 'P. J. Anderson', 95.

5. W. Douglas Simpson (ed.), *The Fusion of 1860. A Record of the*

Centenary Celebrations and a History of the United University of Aberdeen 1860–1960 (Edinburgh, 1963).

6. E.g. J. D. Matthews, 'Department of Forestry, University of Aberdeen, an account of 1908–1945' and 'Department of Forestry, University of Aberdeen, an account of the period 1945–1960', *Aberdeen University Review*, XLVI (1975/76), 117–31 and XLVII (1977/78), 1–18; J. Durkan, 'Early humanism and King's College', *ibid.*, XLVIII (1979/80), 259–79; B. Ponting, 'Mathematics at Aberdeen: developments, characters and events, 1495–1717' and '1717–1860', *ibid.*, XLVIII (1979/80), 26–35 and 162–76; G. P. Edwards, 'Aberdeen and its classical tradition', *ibid.*, LI (1985/86), 410–26; C. A. McLaren, 'The process of curricular change: "the Pathology Question at Aberdeen" 1875–1884', *ibid.*, LI (1985/86), 474–84. See also Alexander Findlay, *The Teaching of Chemistry in the Universities of Aberdeen* (Aberdeen, 1935); Christine Shepherd, 'The Arts curriculum at Aberdeen at the beginning of the eighteenth century' and John S. Reid, 'Late eighteenth-century education in the sciences at Aberdeen: the natural philosophy classes of Professor Patrick Copland', in Jennifer J. Carter & Joan H. Pittock (eds), *Aberdeen and the Enlightenment* (Aberdeen, 1987), 146–54 and 168–79; Roger French, 'Medical teaching in Aberdeen: from the foundation of the university to the middle of the seventeenth century', *History of Universities*, III (1983), 127–57.

7. G. D. Henderson, *The Founding of Marischal College Aberdeen* (Aberdeen, 1946).

8. W. R. Humphries, *William Ogilvie and the Projected Union of the Colleges 1786–1787* (Aberdeen, 1940).

9. Members of the Board are: Dr Jennifer Carter (General Editor), Dr N. W. Fisher, Dr L. J. Macfarlane, Dr David Stevenson, Mr Donald J. Withrington, Mr Colin A. McLaren (Bibliographical and Archives Services Adviser), Mr W. Jamieson (Business and Marketing Manager) and Professor John D. Hargreaves (Secretary). Correspondence about the QHP may be directed to the General Editor, QHP, Department of History, University of Aberdeen AB9 2UB.

10. G. E. Davie, *The Democratic Intellect. Scotland and her Universities in the Nineteenth Century* (Edinburgh, 1961), and *The Crisis of the Democratic Intellect. The Problem of Generalism and Specialism in Twentieth-Century Scotland* (Edinburgh, 1986).

11. R. D. Anderson, *Education and Opportunity in Victorian Scotland. Schools and Universities* (Oxford, 1983), 275–76.

12. Simpson, *Fusion*, 66.

13. Roger L. Emerson, 'Aberdeen Professors 1690–1800: two structures, two professoriates, two careers', in Carter & Pittock, *Aberdeen and the Enlightenment*, 155–67.

14. Anderson, *Education and Opportunity*, 1.

15. D. J. Withrington, *'A Strong University for a New Age': the Union of the Aberdeen Colleges,* forthcoming in the QHP *Studies* Series.

16. The QHP intends also to publish three or four short, illustrated pieces, including a 'popular' history of the university.

17. The proceedings of this conference have just been published: Jennifer J. Carter & Joan H. Pittock (eds), *Aberdeen and the Enlightenment* (Aberdeen, 1987).

18. Robert Musil, *The Man Without Qualities,* translated by Eithne Wilkins & Ernst Kaiser, vol. I (London, 1953). My colleague, Dr David Longley, kindly drew my attention to this work.

Conference Reports

Editorial Note: It is intended that in future each volume of the Journal will carry a brief notice about conferences held on the history of universities in the previous year. As not every such conference is attended by a member of the editorial board, the editor would welcome the assistance of conference organizers in compiling future reports.

Universities, Learning, and Society *Twelfth Anglo-American Conference of Historians:* The Institute for Historical Research, London, 1–4 July 1986

Plenary papers were given by Sir Richard Southern ('The Changing Role of Universities in Medieval Europe') and Professor L. Stone ('The Rise and Fall of the Oxbridge Tutorial System, 1550–1750: Institutional Response to Social Change or Independent Variable?'), and 21 papers were given at section meetings. The closing session of the conference was a panel discussion on 'Universities and Late 20th-Century Society: Does the Past Matter?'. Five of the papers were published in a special issue of the *Bulletin of the Institute of Historical Research* (1987), which will be reviewed in the next issue of this journal.

Peter Denley
Westfield College
London NW3 7ST

Continuity and Change in the European University in the Age of the Liberal Revolution: Magdalen College, Oxford, March 27–29 1987.

The conference brought together some thirty-five people with a variety of academic interests. Besides a hardcore of social and educational historians (many of them contributors to the early-nineteenth century volume of the *History of the University of Oxford*), the meeting attracted a number of historians of science, mathematics and medicine, a legal historian and several students of English literature. The presence of such an impressive assortment of scholars was reminder enough of the importance of the university as an institutional locus of cultural creativity and dissemination throughout this period of political and social upheaval. The aim of the conference was to trace the changes wrought in higher education by the advent of the liberal revolution. Papers were given on a wide variety of aspects of university history, ranging from contemporary theoretical perceptions of the institution to the professionalization of the professoriate. Most speakers limited their analysis to a single institution. Nevertheless, as the conference participants between them possessed a detailed knowledge of the university system in most European countries, individual papers normally proved the starting-point for a wide-ranging discussion. Unfortunately there were no participants working on the universities of Spain, Italy and the Habsburg Empire, so all conclusions about the fate of the European university in this period were necessarily tentative.

With this proviso in mind, two conclusions seemed to emerge from the conference. In the first place, the era 1760–1848 (the traditional age of the liberal revolution) was a transitional period in the history of the university. Broadly-speaking there was only one university typology in 1760. Child of the late middle ages, the mid-eighteenth century university was a self-governing corporation comprising three or four self-regulating faculties. By the mid-nineteenth century, however, there was no longer one but several university typologies as the governments of the era of revolution strove to create a higher educational system that would more adequately meet their ideological, administrative and military needs. Thus, while the British merely reformed what was already there, the French created the *grandes écoles*, and the Germans invented the research university. In 1848 there was no way of telling which, if any, of these various national typologies would become the predominant model for the future. The Humboldtian university only became the eventual paradigm because of the military and scientific prowess of Imperial Germany.

In the second place, despite the fact that this was an era of change, it was also one of continuity. Throughout the late middle ages and the early modern period the hallmark of the educated man was a knowledge of the classics, in particular a written and oral knowledge of the Latin language. Whatever the favoured university typology in the period 1760–1848, great emphasis continued to be placed on the provision of a classical training. Even in the new college and university systems of the United States and Russia, study in the humanities was *de rigueur*. Latin might steadily cease to be the language of the classroom and was certainly no longer the *lingua franca* of Europe's educated elite. Nevertheless, a classical education continued to be promoted everywhere in this era of reform. This commitment to the classics was a reflection of the contemporary educational belief that the university was an institution to broaden the mind, not simply fill it with facts. In this respect, too, the reformers were merely restating a longstanding tradition. The basic thrust of liberal university reform in this period was to construct an institution which catered both for the changing practical needs of the state and society and for the independent promotion of knowledge for its own sake.

Eleven of the papers given at the conference appear in this present volume of *History of Universities*. A further three will appear in Volume VIII (1989). For further information, readers are requested to contact the editor.

Laurence Brockliss
Magdalen College
Oxford OX1 4AU

Students: Social Origins, Behaviour Patterns and Manner of Life from the Middle Ages Until the Nineteenth Century, *The Fifth International Conference on the History of Universities:* University of Cracow, 28–30 May 1987.

Conference organizer: Prof. Mariusz Kulczykowski, Instytut Historii, Uniwersytet Jagielloński, Ul. Gołębia, 31–007 KRAKÓW, Poland, to whom all enquiries about the future publication of the papers given should be addressed.

After a welcome by the university Rector, the conference heard a general introductory paper from Jerzy Wyrozumski. Then followed two papers from Peter Čornej and Jiři Pešek of the University of Prague. The former spoke of the influence of Hussite ideology on students at Prague and the latter applied sociological concepts to an investigation of the social background of Prague students from the fourteenth until the first half of the sixteenth century. Much of the discussion that followed was concerned with the difficulties of identifying 'national' groups, in the modern sense, at earlier universities and with the use of the term 'nation' in these universities, especially with regard to the university of Prague in the fifteenth century.

The afternoon session began with papers by Leszek Hajdukiewicz and Irena Kaniewska, who spoke of students at Cracow in medieval and modern times, and by John Fletcher of the university of Aston who argued that earlier historians have wrongly underestimated the age of entry of students to the English universities before the Reformation. The ensuing discussion was mainly concerned with the problems of interpreting the evidence of the Cracow material.

Before the opening of the second day's session, the conference observed a short silence in memory of Kazimierz Kubik of Gdansk university, whose death prevented the presentation of a paper. Willem Frijhoff of Rotterdam then gave a careful and well illustrated paper showing the impact of university studies in one Netherland's town, Zutphen, from the middle ages until the early nineteenth century. He noted how poorer students tended to study theology and the richer law. Lidia Burzyńska of Gdansk gave a very interesting paper on the problems of integration in this university from the seventeenth to the nineteenth centuries; class differences were accompanied by racial and religious differences, with a dominant German-Lutheran element confronting a Polish-Catholic majority especially after the Partitions. Werner Fläschendräger of Leipzig gave a lively and detailed entrée into the world of student life at Wittenberg and Leipzig in the eighteenth century, showing how the vigour and intellectual life of the latter university outshone that of the former. The discussion was mainly concerned to examine the sources used by Prof. Frijhoff for his work.

The final session of the conference heard a paper by Harald Heppner of Graz who noted how in the second half of the nineteenth century Polish students used Graz as a stepping stone to the more important centres at Prague and Vienna. Françoise Mayeur of Lille gave a detailed account of attempts to reform the study of 'letters' and 'sciences' in nineteenth century France. Finally, Stanislas Brzozowski and Antoni Podraza of Cracow studied the activities of Polish students abroad in the fifty years before the first world war and the recruitment of 'lower class' students by the university of Cracow in the past century and a half. There was some debate about the extent of the political involvement of Polish students after the Partitions in countries abroad and Prof. Podraza produced some interesting figures for the recruitment of the sons of farmers and factory workers to the university of Cracow. He pointed out, however, that 'farmer' was a term to be used with caution as many were holders of a considerable acreage. An energetic discussion centred on the long-standing debate concerning the origins of the Polish intelligentsia in modern times. The role of Vilnius in the spread of learning was emphasised; a very humourous account of the often scandalous activities of the students of Zamość was presented.

A summary of the conference activities was given by Kamila Mrozowska who continues to astonish and delight all by her good health and interest in problems of university history.

Five international conferences have been held in this series and the proceedings of three published by the University of Cracow:

L'Histoire des Universités. Problèmes et Méthodes, 1980

L'Université et l'Enseignement extrauniversitaire XVIe—XIXe s., 1983.

Les grandes Réformes des Universités Européennes des XVIe au XXe s., 1985

John M. Fletcher
Department of Modern Languages
University of Aston
Birmingham B4 7ET

Terminology of the Book and of Writing in the Middle Ages:
Paris, 24–26 September 1987.

The second conference organized by the Comité International du Vocabulaire des Institutions et de la Communication Intellectuelles au Moyen Age (CIVICIMA) was held at Paris with the support of the Comité du Cange and the Institut de Recherche et d'Histoire des Textes.

Many of the papers concerned technical aspects of the subject, but most at least touched on subject matter of some interest to the university historian. Especially valuable here were the papers of Jacqueline Hamesse, who spoke on the role of the oral transmission of texts within the medieval universities and gave a particularly wide survey of the statutory material, and of Prof. L. J. Bataillon who discussed the significance of Exemplar, Pecia and Quaternus to the medieval university historian. Most speakers came from France and the Low Countries, and their interests were largely restricted to these areas, the Iberian peninsula and Italy.

It is expected that the conference papers will published and enquiries may be directed to the Secretary of CIVICIMA, Dr. Olga Weijers, Royal Library, Prins Willen Alexanderhof 5, 2595 BE Den Haag, Netherlands.

John M. Fletcher
Department of Modern Languages
University of Aston
Birmingham B4 7ET

The Low Countries and the British Isles. Academic Relations 1450–1750: Ghent, 30 September–2 October 1987.

The first joint conference of historians of universities from Belgium, the Netherlands and the British Isles took place in Ghent from 30 September until 2 October 1987. Participants from all three regions heard Dr. Roegiers welcome the enterprise of Dr. Hilde de

Ridder-Symoens, who was largely responsible for the organization of the conference.

As a general introduction to the proceedings, Dr. Vandermeersch surveyed intellectual relations between the southern Netherlands and England in the sixteenth and seventeenth centuries; he noted especially the large number of books by English authors printed in the Netherlands and pointed out that the English and the Irish languages were used as well as the more usual Latin. Dr. Frank- van Westrienen spoke about Dutch tourists in seventeenth century England and suggested that there was more interest shown in ceremony and monuments than in academic work. From England, Dr. Upton discussed the collections of poems published by the universities of Oxford and Cambridge on the death of Philip Sydney in the Netherlands. Prof. Luyendijk-Elshout then described the conflicts that troubled the Leyden faculty of medicine as students from Edinburgh attempted to introduce the theories of William Cullen into that university. To end the first day, Dr. Fletcher, replacing a speaker who was unable to be present, gave a comparative account of eating and drinking habits of Louvain and Oxford based on material from college records at both universities.

The second day of the conference heard Dr. Braekman introduce a discussion on the theological training of Reformed ministers in the Low Countries; he showed how difficult it was to reconcile the different traditions supported by the congregations of France, the Netherlands and London before the foundation of Reformed faculties of theology in the new universities. Prof. Feenstra spoke about the influences of Scottish law students in the Netherlands and, finally, Dr. Fletcher illustrated, with new evidence, the career and influence of John Drusius, the Flemish Hebraist, at Merton College, Oxford.

The success and efficient organisation of the lively conference was an excellent beginning to this cooperative venture. It is hoped to publish the proceedings and to hold another conference in the British Isles in 1989. Those interested may contact for the Netherlands, Dr. Hilde de Ridder-Synoens, The University of Ghent, Ghent, Belgium, and for the British Isles, Dr. John M. Fletcher.

John M. Fletcher
Department of Modern Languages
University of Aston
Birmingham B4 7ET

Universitates e Università. University of Bologna, 16–21 November 1987.

However spurious the notion of a foundation date might in practice be, the value of centenaries, in academic, political and historiographical terms, is such that it would be particularly hard on those universities whose origins are shrouded in the mists of time to have to forego such celebrations. For Bologna the principle was in any case established in the celebrations of 1888, and in many respects the events of this year, and this conference, look back to that date as well as to the date of the first sign of law teaching in the town, nine hundred years ago. But the date signifies more than that. On 1088 rests Bologna's claim to be the oldest university and therefore the 'Alma Mater Studiorum'. An indication of the thinking behind the centenary arrangements is the lavish scale and wide range of the programme of events organized by the university in cooperation with municipal, regional and state authorities. A year of special conferences, lectures, seminars, meetings, exhibitions and concerts in Bologna and throughout the universities of the world, research projects, publications, films, records and even sporting events–all serve to emphasize Bologna's historically international and pioneering role. The celebration of Bologna is being presented in the form of the celebration of the university as institution.

It is fitting that the inaugural conference of this enormous programme should be an historical congress, and one not confined to the history of the university of Bologna but on the theme of universities and their contribution generally. As with the centenary programme generally, the congress was mounted on the grandest and most lavish scale imaginable (something which did not escape the attention of the students, whose protests were a running accompaniment to the proceedings, engendering considerable press interest). Six days of papers were held, including parallel sessions, on the universities in history from their origins to the present day. Again, an emphasis on the ceremonial nature of the event was prominent. The congress was inaugurated by a well-managed and indeed moving reenactment of a medieval Bolognese degree ceremony, televised for transmission in Italy and Germany. The recipient of the

Laurea Honoris Causa was Professor Robert Feenstra, both on merits as a scholar and in his capacity as current President of the International Commission for the History of Universities. Other events included a visit to Ravenna which was in a sense offered as Bologna's tribute to its precursor as Roman law school.

Inevitably with such a vast subject area, coverage was uneven and selective, indeed more so than intended due to the fact that a number of distinguished scholars listed on the programme failed to come. Medieval university history was represented by leading scholars in the field such as Girolamo Arnaldi, Manlio Bellomo, Hilde de Ridder-Symoens, Gina Fasoli, Johannes Fried, Jean Gaudemet and Jacques Verger. After that the programme became more fragmented. There was emphasis on specific disciplines, with contributions by specialists such as Paolo Galluzzi, Mirko Grmek, Rupert Hall and Marie Boas Hall, John Heilbron, Wolfgang Mommsen and Abrahm Pais; but also several papers by historians, and others,—Karl Otto Apel, Karl Dietrich Bracher, Umberto Eco, Paolo Prodi—whose expertise was less specific to university history but who in some respects produced the most stimulating reflections on the role of universities in culture and society. The volume of proceedings, to be published shortly, will be of interest above all for the wide range of papers offered. One factor is bound to differentiate it from the mass of celebratory writing generated by the octocentenary. The conference was distinguished by a remarkable absence of campanilism or rivalry. There was a clear sense that that stage had been outgrown, and that there were more important things to worry about. Coming as it did at a time when the role of universities is more uncertain than it has been for centuries, the event produced few confident answers but a great deal of fundamental questioning.

Peter Denley
Westfield College
University of London
Kidderpore Avenue
London NW3 7ST

Other Conferences

Unpublished Records of French Universities in Medieval and Renaissance Period: University of Toronto, 26 April 1987. (Organizer: Professor A. L. Gabriel, University of Notre Dame, Ind., for the United States Sub-Commission for the History of Universities and the Medieval Academy of America).

The Social History of Universities: Chicago, 3 December 1986. (Organizer: Professor William Courtenay, University of Wisconsin-Madison, for the American Historical Association).

Book Reviews

Alessandra Ferraresi, Alberta Mosconi Grassano and Antonia Pasi Testa, *Cultura e vita universitaria nelle miscellanee Belcredi, Giardini, Ticinensia*. Fonti e studi per la storia dell'Uiversità di Pavia, Vol. 8, Instituto Editoriale Cisalpino-La Goliardica, 1986. 405 pp. L.40,000.

This useful handbook will be of interest beyond the circle of those involved in university history. The inventories of three collections of *miscellanee* in the Biblioteca Universitaria di Pavia have been undertaken in tandem, with serial numeration and standardized conventions and criteria, and with an introduction to each inventory by its compiler. The collections were put together mainly by three prominent figures of Pavian life in the late eighteenth and early nineteenth centuries: Giuseppe Gaspare Belcredi, a member of a patrician family going back to the thirteenth century, teacher of law at the university, secretary of the Accademia degli Affidati and leading figure in the municipal administration under Austrian rule; Elia Giardini, teacher of grammar, rhetoric and then law at the university, and librarian of the Accademia degli Affidati, the Collegio Ghislieri and finally the Biblioteca Universitaria; and Siro Comi, municipal archivist. In their introductions the compilers describe the careers of these men and the origins and composition of the collections, and show the significance of their contents to the study of the history of the university. This significance ranges particularly over the intellectual and social history of the university in the seventeenth and eighteenth centuries, but it also includes material on legislation, controversies within the university over precedence, the relationship of the university to the Collegio dei Giudici and to non-university teaching in Pavia (e.g. that of the Jesuits), as well as some earlier material (such as the fifteenth-century statutes of the college founded by Catone Sacco, and material on the first century of theology teaching at Pavia). The inventory is as informative as a short-title catalogue can be, and the introductions are helpful and well-documented. An extremely thorough index completes the volume.

Peter Denley
Westfield College
University of London
Kidderpore Avenue
London NW3 7ST

Giovanni Minnucci, *Le lauree dello Studio Senese alla fine del secolo XV*. Milan: A. Giuffrè Editore, 1981. Quaderni di 'Studi senesi', no. 51. Pp. 123. L.7,000. *Le lauree dello Studio Senese all'inizio del secolo XVI*. Vol. 1: *(1501–1506)*; Vol. 2 *(1507–1514)*. Milan: A. Giuffrè Editore, 1984 and 1985. Quaderni di 'Studi senesi', nos. 55, 58. Pp. 152, 125. L.13,000 and 9,000.

These three volumes transcribe from notarial records found in the Archivio Arcivescovile of Siena the graduates of the University of Siena between 1484 and 1486 plus 1496 through 1514. Each document gives the name of the successful candidate, usually with surname and place of birth, sometimes with a patronymic, and his diocese if a clergyman. Next follow the names of the promoters, the name of the degree, and sometimes an indication of the passage successfully argued. The usual method for choosing the text was simply to open the book at random. Arts graduates had to defend points taken from Aristotle's *Posterior Analytics* or *Physics*, medical graduates from the *Ars medica* of Galen or the *Aphorisma* of Hippocrates, canon law graduates points from the *Decretum* or the *Liber extra*, and civil law graduates points from the *Digest* or *Codex*. Aspiring theology graduates disputed points from Peter Lombard's *Sentences*.

The documents record 389 graduates, an average of twenty per year. Minnucci thoughtfully summarizes the degrees granted in a series of tables. They show that 83 students took degrees in canon law, 93 in civil law, 80 *in utroque iure,* 84 in arts and medicine combined, 25 in theology, 8 in medicine, and 5 in arts. The data also show that a substantial part of Siena's graduates came from afar: 116 Germans, 16 Spaniards, 8 Portuguese, 4 Poles, 1 Englishman, 1 Scot, 1 Frenchman, and 1 Swede. While Italian students came from all parts of the peninsula, the vast majority came from small centres in Tuscany and Umbria. Siena did not have very many famous graduates. Perhaps the best known in this period were Mariano Sozzini il Giovane from Siena who received a degree *in iure civili* in January 1505 and Lancelotto Politi (Ambrogio Catarino), also a Sienese and the future author of tracts against Italian heretics, who received a degree *in iure civili* in May 1502. Minnucci also compiles summary chronological lists of the promoters, in effect, faculty lists. They show that Siena had a stable faculty over many years.

Siena emerges as a small- to medium-sized university which served two different constituencies. Like the more famous Italian universities, it enrolled and graduated a large number of *ultra-montani*, especially Germans, the majority of whom took degrees in civil law. It also served as a regional university for Italian clergymen and laymen in all fields. These points come through clearly, thanks to Minnucci's careful transcriptions of the documents and his summaries. This is a useful documentary source for future study of Italian Renaissance universities.

Paul F. Grendler
Department of History
University of Toronto
Toronto M5S 1A1, Canada

R. B. McDowell and D. A. Webb, *Trinity College Dublin 1592–1952. An Academic History.* Cambridge University Press: Cambridge, 1982. xxiii+580 pp. £35.00.

Ancient institutions, like elderly people, benefit from regular and thorough re-examination, expecially if new approaches can be employed to uncover previously neglected problems. Over the past twenty years, a generation of academic historians has applied the techniques and methodology of the social sciences to compel us to look afresh at many aspects of university history. The authors of this history are aware of this development, but it cannot be said that they pay more than token attention to its significance. One of the most important surveys in this book, Statistics relating to Students, is relegated to an appendix with only an incomplete if interesting discussion of its implications, the problem of interpreting its evidence and its wider ramifications, here and there in the text itself. Even for 'An Academic History' the impact of such statistics on the structure and presentation of the curriculum can hardly be exaggerated.

As Provost Lyons writes in his Foreword, this volume is suffused with 'the gentle glow of an unmistakable nostalgia'. This may attract college *alumni* but can be disturbing to the reader seeking a modern, critical appraisal of aspects of Trinity's history. The authors do not seem at ease with the wider world of university history studies, especially for the earlier period. Indeed, despite its ambitious title, by page 201 we have concluded our examination of college affairs before 1851! The opening sentence of the volume suggests that the foundation of a university marks 'the final emergence of any part of Europe from the barren disorder of the Dark Ages into the fullness of medieval civilization'; it is some time since we came upon such writing in any history of an educational institution! The authors' style, pleasant and urbane can sometimes become over-discursive, lengthening unnecessarily an already long book. Nor do the two Trinity men make much use of comparative material; there are regular references to Oxford and Cambridge, an occasional comment, often derogatory, about Scotland, but hardly any attempt to look at conditions in the continental universities. It is surprising that no awareness is shown, for instance, of the earlier efforts to combine 'university' and 'college', as at Sigüenza, Alcalá and, perhaps more pertinent, at Aberdeen, when the foundation of Trinity is considered.

The virtues and limitations of the authors' approach are well shown in their discussion of the admission of women to the college. In a lively and interesting account we are introduced to the Gilbertian suggestion of the Board for a separate women's university in Ireland and the battle over a second lavatory for the Common Room. But we are also treated to a rather precious view of male student attitudes at the close of the nineteenth century and nowhere allowed to learn how far the prejudices of the Trinity fellows were deeper or less ingrained than those of their continental contemporaries. If college-universities had difficulty in integrating female students into their exclusively male communities, how did, for instance, the university of Aberdeen cope with this problem?

This new study presents a useful survey of the history of Trinity, especially during the late nineteenth and twentieth centuries. It should appeal to the informed general reader who requires a well written and enjoyable account of the vicissitudes of the history of the college. The academic historian will regret that the authors' eyes have been too often fixed almost exclusively on the college itself and will wonder why the Cambridge University Press should, in such a well produced volume, place all the notes at end of the text. In the Trinity parlance of the early nineteenth century, this reviewer would pronounce a 'Judgement' of '*bene*'.

John M. Fletcher
Department of Modern Languages
University of Aston
Birmingham B4 7ET

James McConica (ed.), *The History of the University of Oxford. Volume III. The Collegiate University*. Oxford: Clarendon Press, 1986. xxiv+775 pp. £60.

The title of the third volume of the splendid History of Oxford University indicates one of the keys to the understanding of the sixteenth-century university, but only one of them, and other subtitles could perhaps have been selected. Though the volume is, on the whole, highly satisfactory and contains sections that are both new and far-reaching in their conclusions, it is clear that the authors have met with some difficulties in trying to arrange the material at their disposal.

First of all, the volume enters non-Emdenized territory, so to speak. The fourth volume of A. B. Emden's *Biographical Register* is not so full as the medieval volumes, whilst Foster's dictionary of alumni is somewhat difficult to use. As a result, reliable statistics on both the whole period and the whole university are lacking. The authors have been conscious of this, and they have made attempts to find suitable alternatives: there is, for instance, a secure, useful and stimulating (though rather crude on the statistical side) prosopographical study on the students and fellows of Corpus Christi College, which is presented on pages 666–693 of the editor's chapter on the collegiate society. But it is strangely inserted between thirty pages on disciplinary problems and a section on the teaching of arts in colleges (which duplicates some of the matter found in J. M. Fletcher's chapter on the Faculty of Arts, though from a different standpoint, successful use being made of Carnsew's diaries). If the rise of the colleges is such an outstanding feature of sixteenth-century Oxford—and this is convincingly established by the editor in his own first chapter (pages 2–68)—the Corpus case-study ought to have have been more than just an example, but rather a starting point from which to attempt a sociology of the university, which is conspicuously lacking here. One of the benefits of such a sociology would have been to allow an evaluation of Oxford's part in the fabric of English society at large, a theme on which Lawrence Stone has brought illuminating insights, which have been quoted here (by G. E. Aylmer) but not emulated.

The second problem lies in the articulation between the respective chapters of Claire Cross on the University and the Tudor State, and Penry Williams on the Elizabethan State and Church, and Jennifer Loach's chapter on Religious Controversies. There are no flaws in the individual chapters (Penry Williams's piece being the most satisfactory in my opinion) and the emphasis is rightly put on the state: but to dichotomize state intervention and religious controversies is to set apart flesh and bones. Understandably the authors have been reluctant to do so, and there is a lot of duplication between these chapters and the contribution by S. L. Greenslade on the faculty of Theology, where we have to look for the emergence of Oxford 'Anglicanism'. Another difficulty is that the lack of prosopographical data hinders the study of patronage, though Penry Williams's study of Leicester's patronage is rather successful. Therefore we are not given a clear view of the relative strengths of the religious and political factions, and the reasons why so many of these intellectuals chose voluntarily the hard path of exile or even martyrdom—and this too is as much a distinctive feature of sixteenth-century Oxford as the rise of collegiate society—are not convincingly exposed.

All this, nevertheless, must not distract the reader from the outstanding qualities of the volume: as we all know, it is easier to criticize a plan than to produce a really satisfactory one! There are at least three fields in which the volume is extremely useful, and from now on the indispensable foundation for further study: first, the institutions of the university, both colleges and chairs (J. Barton on the King's Readers and G. D. Duncan on professors and public lectures); second, the life and production of the faculties (arts, with a special note on music by J. Caldwell, medicine by Gillian Lewis, law by J. Barton and theology by S. L. Greenslade) well coordinated and introduced by the editor himself; and thirdly, the question of buildings and furniture (J. Newman). But the two really impressive breakthroughs are the chapter and appendices devoted by Neil Ker—whose last work it probably was—to the provision of books, and the chapter by G. E. Aylmer (partly based upon notes and transcripts by the late J. P. Cooper) on the economics and finances of the colleges and university with two appendices by G. D. Duncan. In fact we find in this chapter (and in C. I. Hammer's chapter on the town and the university) a good deal of sociology which compensates in some measure for the lack of a systematic chapter on it.

J.-P. Genet
Paris 1 University

L. S. Sutherland and L. G. Mitchell (eds.) *The History of the University of Oxford. Volume V. The Eighteenth Century.* Oxford: Clarendon Press, 1986. xix+949 pp. £75.

The volume under review traces the history of Oxford from the accession of James II to the reform of the examination system in the first decade of the nineteenth century. Thanks chiefly to Gibbons's account of his undergraduate days at Magdalen, the eighteenth century has always been seen as the least heroic in Oxford's existence, an age of numerical decline and intellectual torpor. Henceforth, this customary verdict will be no longer tenable. The contributors to Volume V may not have demonstrated that eighteenth-century Oxford was an intellectual powerhouse but they convincingly show that the university was a far more lively and educationally serious institution than has hitherto been thought.

The book is divided into five parts. The first is labelled 'The University and National Politics' and as the title suggests is devoted to exploring the relationship between the university and the state. In traditional historiography Oxford has usually been seen as a Jacobite institution bitterly hostile to the Whig ascendancy and only reconciled to the Hanoverian dynasty with the accession of George III. The present detailed study reveals that such a view is unjust. There were Jacobites in Oxford but the majority of college fellows are better described as High-Anglican Tories indifferent rather than hostile to the Hanoverian succession. Nor did the university suddenly become supinely royalist with the advent of an ideologically sound monarch. Patronage might at last have begun to come the way of the university's senior members, but Oxford valued the independence it had gained by being out in the political cold and was anxious not to become the government's poodle. Government and university only became closely attached with the outbreak of the French Revolution, as Oxford's values increasingly became those of the political establishment.

The second part of the book deals with 'The Social and Administrative Structure of the University'. As an institution Oxford hardly changed at all in the eighteenth century. It remained a university run by its senior members and dominated by a handful of colleges whose large fellowships, if properly organized by the heads of house, formed a formidable voting phalanx. Much of the material in this section is inevitably very familiar. The most interesting details are provided by I. G. Doolittle and J. P. D. Dunbabin in two chapters on college administration and college wealth. Both tell a tale of good management. While not being notable rackrenters or enclosers, the colleges still managed on average to double their income in real terms over the century. As a result fellows' income remained bouyant and rose dramatically in the 1790s.

Section iii deals with 'Oxford and the Church'. Throughout the century almost half of Oxford's matriculands took orders. Although Oxford-educated clerics had little chance of becoming bishops before 1760, there was no way of preventing them becoming parish priests in a country where the Tory gentry controlled the appointment to village cures. As a result, Tory High-Anglicanism became the dominant religious creed of the grass-roots of the Church of England and was not simply limited to the university's dons. Religious indoctrination at Oxford, however, was far from perfect. As R. Greaves in his chapter on 'Religion in the University 1715–1800' is careful to point out, undergraduates, even ordinands, received little serious religious instruction beyond the odd college lecture and directed tutorial reading. Students rather imbibed a religious ambience. Theology as such was only studied by the handful of graduate students (generally fellows) who stayed on after taking their B.A. As a result, many Oxford men proved insufficiently programmed and turned their back on their Alma Mata. Eighteenth-century Oxford produced not only Tory High Anglicans but Whig politicians, like Pitt the Elder, free thinkers and radicals, like Southey, and religious enthusiasts like the Wesleys. John Wesley was a fellow at Lincoln and it is appropriate that the unhappy history of the rise and fall of Methodism in the university is traced in the present volume by the retiring rector, V. H. H. Green.

The longest and most important section of the book deals with 'Academic life in the University'. An introductory chapter introduces the reader generally to the curriculum, then separate chapters are devoted to particular disciplines. This section completely discredits Gibbons's view that the college tutorial system was a farce, by presenting for the first time a detailed picture of undergraduate studies based on the Christ Church Collection books. This unique source, described by P. Quarrie in a specific chapter, lists the authors that students were supposed to have read during the year and on which they were examined within the college. As the Collection Books exist for most of the eighteenth century, it is possible to use them as a standard against which to judge the information provided by other sources, chiefly memoirs. The Collection Books reveal some important developments over the century. M. L. Clarke in a chapter on 'Classical Studies' finds that they suggest a growing importance of Greek in the undergraduate curriculum, while J. Yolton in a chapter on 'Schoolmen, Logic and Philosophy' is able to trace the way in which Locke entered the classroom.

On the other hand, this section tends to confirm the traditional view that there was much amiss with the tuition provided by the university as opposed to the colleges. Oxford in the eighteenth century had a faculty of fifteen to twenty professors. If the professoriate had fulfilled its statutory obligations, then daily lectures would have been given in the three higher sciences of theology, law, and medicine and in a variety of undergraduate and propaedeutic subjects for which there was seldom college provision. In fact, many professors never lectured at all and some made no attempt to find substitutes. Few lectures in medicine, for instance, were given over the century (see the chapter by C. Webster). Admittedly, the tale was not one of unremitting woe. The chair of poetry, founded in 1708, seems to have been a success. Mention, too, must be made of the introduction of the teaching of common-law through the efforts of Blackstone. Nor were the natural sciences neglected, as has often been thought, the Ashmolean museum (founded in 1683) providing a convenient location for extracurricular but popular courses in chemistry and experimental philosophy. Some professors were clearly extremely conscientious. The astronomer James Bradley (1693–1762) was a paragon of virtue, filling the Savilian chair of astronomy with distinction for forty years (1721–62) and finding time in the 1750s to give a highly acclaimed course in experimental philosophy as well (see the chapter by G. L'E Turner).

The final section is devoted to 'Libraries and the Arts'. Under this head, the university's broader cultural role is discussed. The various authors present an exciting picture. Although the Bodleian Library had problems acquiring new books before the colleges agreed to provide an annual subsidy in the 1780s, its manuscript collection was unrivalled. Eighteenth-century Oxford, moreover, was endowed with two other magnificent libraries thanks to the munificence of Codrington and Radcliffe. As a result, Oxford's libraries, together with the Ashmolean museum, provided untold opportunities for archival study. Universities were not yet research institutions, but Oxford thanks to these facilities produced a clutch of scholars, like Thomas Hearne (1678–1735) who beavered away deciphering Iron Age and Romano-British bric-à-brac. According to David Fairer, the university's contribution was particularly important in the development of Anglo-Saxon studies. Although there was no chair of Anglo-Saxon before 1795, it was at Oxford through the efforts of pioneers like William Elstob (1683–1756) that an interest in the language was first created at the turn of the eighteenth century. Admittedly such figures were exceptional, but if the majority of fellows seldom made any positive contribution to the development of English culture themselves, they made sure that others did by their discriminating patronage of the leading architects, painters and musicians of the day. In the opinion of H. M. Colvin Oxford was at the forefront of English eighteenth-century architecture. The university, then, if not always a centre of good learning was certainly one of good taste. Its senior members might not in the main have been able to understand the subtleties of Newtonian physics but they had no difficulty in appreciating the virtuosity of Haydn, duly given an honorary degree in 1791.

Even such a brief survey of the contents of this volume is enough to suggest the mine of information that it contains. No eighteenth-century university has ever been studied in such detail and depth. Moreover, despite its great length, there are few repetitions and the book always remains eminently readable. The one criticism that can be levelled against it is its lack of perspective. Although Oxford was not the intellectually defunct institution we have hitherto assumed, it was also no Edinburgh, Halle or Göttingen, dynamic centres of learning that in the fields of medicine, law, classical languages and history had a European renown. Rather, Oxford in the eighteenth century (despite its great medieval past) was no different from the large majority of the hundred or so universities of Europe. It was small (*c.* 200–300 matriculands per year), drew its students from a narrowly defined geographical radius, and was most decisively confessionally closed: even alternative forms of Anglicanism were deemed beyond the pale. Indeed, given the small numbers of graduates and the uncertainty of the teaching provision in the higher faculties, Oxford could scarcely be called a university at all. It had more in common with a modern college of liberal arts. As a result, its continental counterpart was not a stolidly respectable institution like Paris with its four flourishing faculties, but a paper university like Bourges. The only thing that invalidates such a comparison is Oxford's collegiate provision. Bourges only had the Collège de Sainte-Marie; even at Paris there were only ten colleges providing tuition in arts; Oxford in contrast had twenty.

Nevertheless, the insignificance of eighteenth-century Oxford in European terms cannot be gainsaid. This, though, is nowhere acknowledged. L. G. Mitchell admits in the introduction that Oxford was not in the big league, but no attempt is made thereafter to evaluate the university's standing more closely. Indeed, the book is written as if Oxford was the only university extant. Scarcely any other university, even Cambridge, receives a mention in all the nine-hundred pages. Such an approach seems perverse. One of the chief attractions of this book to the university historian is that it is the most complete study to date of a very ordinary eighteenth-century educational institution. It would be interesting, in consequence, to compare and contrast it with its equally ordinary European counterparts. Were arts students everywhere drawn from similar backgrounds? Did they study the same authors? Were they subject to the same kind of discipline in continental colleges? Did they pursue the same leisure activities? Enough has been published about the French eighteenth-century colleges in particular for a comparative treatment to be possible. The value of such an approach is evident. If nothing else, it would help to throw light on developments at Oxford itself. The university, it seems, witnessed a falling roll throughout the first half of the eighteenth century. As the evidence suggests falling rolls were a problem on the continent, too, it seems unlikely that the explanation simply lies entirely in the bad publicity resulting from Oxford's High-Anglican profile as the present study suggests. A comparative treatment, moreover, would make the book a more useful work for the eighteenth-century social historian. At the moment debate rages over the relative similarity or distinctiveness of eighteenth-century English and continental society. One way of exploring this problem would be to investigate the comparative educational experiences of the English and continental elites. This is not the place to attempt such an exercise. Suffice it to say that on a number of occasions I was struck by the peculiarity of Oxford. What, for instance, should we make of the fact that in the Paris colleges of the eighteenth-century the favourite authors included Tacitus and Plutarch, yet at Oxford neither seems to have been studied at all?

Whatever the conclusions of such a comparative survey, there can be no doubt that Oxford was a singular university in one important respect. Throughout the period 1688–1760 it was a confessional university certainly, but an anti-establishment one. In what other country in Europe would the government have tolerated such behaviour? Universities were supposed to work with the establishment not against it. Had it been anywhere else Oxford would have been abolished (like the French Protestant Academies of the seventeenth century) or at least reformed. Indeed, to a Europeanist (and be it said a Cambridge man) the survival of an unreformed Oxford in the eighteenth century seems extremely peculiar. Oxford not only went against the religious and political establishment grain. Through its early interest in Anglo-Saxon and the Gothic it went against the cultural grain as well. Furthermore, it revelled in its independence, its building programme alone an arrogant testimony to its complacency. That Oxford survived to see a change in establishment values in the late eighteenth century can only be attributed to the political and ecclesiastical power of the Tory gentry, plus the good sense of the university not to push its unorthodoxy too far.

The survival of Oxford, however, is not something the authors of this book find controversial. Again, a wider perspective would have permitted a better understanding of what a strange institution the University of Oxford really was.

Laurence Brockliss
Magdalen College
Oxford

Geert Vanpaemel, *Echo's van een Wetenschappelijke Revolutie. De mechanistische natuurwetenschap aan de Leuvense Artesfaculteit (1650–1797)*. Verhandelingen van de Koninklijke Academie voor Wetenschappen, Letteren, en Schone Kunsten van België, Klasse der Wetenschappen, Jaargang 48, nr 173. Brussels, 1986. 850 Belgian Francs.

This useful study of the mechanical sciences as taught in the faculty of Arts during the seventeenth and eighteenth centuries at the University of Louvain fills a conspicuous gap in the history of universities. Dr Vanpaemel accepts the notion of a continuing 'scientific revolution' in Europe at large, and uses it as a measure of Louvain activity, only to conclude that there are no striking examples of original Louvain science during the period under review (1650–1797). His account of changing intellectual styles is valuable, even so, a story of the gradual replacement of Aristotelian natural philosophy by a significant part of the New Science. Newton never made a direct entry—but after all, even in Britain, the incursion of Newtonian ideas into the curriculum was extremely slow. At least until the middle of the eighteenth century, the most significant Louvain teaching in physics was Cartesian, with a residuum of Aristotle; and for all its theoretical shortcomings, a substantial corpus of experimental knowledge was eventually taught against this background.

Dr Vanpaemel has been able to draw on several excellent studies that have been made of Cartesianism in the Low Countries, north and south. He has made a detailed study of thirty-seven sets of students' Louvain lecture notes, four of them from the period before the *Corpus Aristotelicum* was finally abandoned in 1658, and twenty-four from after the curriculum reforms of 1764. Using these to supplement text-books, he shows that the strongest appeal of Cartesian philosophy lay at first in its cosmological doctrines—compatible with Copernicanism, of course—but that interest in cosmology gradually yielded place to the sort of natural philosophy to be found in the *Traité de physique* of J. Rohault (1620–75), for long the standard of Cartesian orthodoxy. He shows how Aristotle and the newer science were then taught in a dialectical manner, Aristotle being the loser, more or less all along the line. Although he does not go into much detail in the matter of the propositions actually defended, and arguments offered in their support, we can see from Dr Vanpaemel's book that—for all that Aristotle was nominally dead—the topics established by The Philosopher, and their ordering, continued to provide the *structure* of the curriculum right up until the end of the eighteenth century. (It is amusing to consider a series of fifty-one theses proposed in 1732, which include 'Corpora gravitant in loco suo naturali', 'Coeli sunt natura sua fluidi', and 'Vanae sunt astrologorum praedictiones . . .'.)

During the whole of this period, formal disputations continued to be used as academic exercises in natural philosophy—although in reality, the education they were really giving was in rhetoric. Mathematics seems never to have been properly integrated into physics, even after the curriculum took its more experimental direction under the influence of J. A. Nollet's monumental (and in character largely Newtonian) *Leçons de physique expérimentale* (6 vols., 1743-8). The Louvain School of Experimental Physics (part of the Arts Faculty) was established in 1755, with a number of instruments for demonstration. It seems that they were never, or scarcely ever, used for anything that could be called original research.

Dr Vanpaemel's study is a well written and readable book that—for all its trappings of the scholarly monograph—could well be used as an undergraduate text in any Dutch-speaking country. It contains much of general historical importance—it goes without saying that it includes much on the reconciliation of science and religion. It would be pleasant to think that it will stimulate a greater interest, within the universities of the Netherlands generally, in their own cultural history.

J. D. North
Filosofisch Instituut
Rijksuniversiteit Groningen

J. Roelevink, *Gedicteerd Verleden. Het Onderwijs in de Algemene Geschiedenis aan de Universiteit Te Utrecht, 1735–1839.* APA-Holland Universiteits Pers Amsterdam & Maarssen 1986. xiii+378 pp.

This noteworthy thesis takes the University of Utrecht as a model for the examination of the transition from an inter-disciplinary approach to the study of history in Holland to a more Enlightened one. After Leiden, Utrecht was the second most important university in the country. In the eighteenth and early nineteenth century posts were held there by outstanding historians who are the focus of this study. The three foremost scholars were Petrus Wesseling, who taught history in the Faculty of Arts from 1735 to 1764, Christopherus Saxe, 1753 to 1803, and Philip Willem van Heusde, 1803 to 1839, and working alongside them there were figures of lesser importance such as Michael van Goens and Johann Frederik Reitz. Publications, students' transcripts of lectures and a generally favourable documentary basis make possible a comprehensive analysis of the conditions in the universities in this period, and of the particular conditions in the Faculty of Arts with respect to the actual contents of lectures and classes.

An introductory chapter outlines the provisions for history teaching and the role of history within the Faculty in the period to 1815. Chapter two then covers the period from 1815 to 1839. The new political structure of the Dutch state, and the period after the Congress of Vienna which saw the reordering of Europe also necessitated changes in the structure of the universities. The new state took considerably more interest in its universities, completely rearranged the pattern of studies, and thenceforth gave the minor, subordinate faculty of arts equal status to the higher faculties.

The third chapter describes the forms of academic teaching, lectures, disputations and graduation. Chapter four gives a survey of the history of the professorial chairs within the faculty. Initially it was the State that advised on appointments; after 1815 it was the provincial government. Here the sources proved less favourable, with the result that the specific aims intended when professors were nominated are not always clearly identifiable.

In the fifth chapter the content of history teaching is described. Since the superior faculties kept control of the historical lectures that suited their needs, the historians from the Faculty of Arts were left with traditional Universal History. It is interesting that throughout the eighteenth century the basis was always Horatius Tursellinus' handbook. The emphasis was on things from antiquity, from ancient history in particular. Besides this, national—that is, Dutch—history might also be taught. After 1815 the character of this pragmatic form of history teaching was not substantially altered except that now, in place of veneration of the Ancient World came Humanity in the Enlightenment sense, and progress towards improvement.

The sixth chapter describes the methodical transition from an interdisciplinary, polymathic, approach to history and its teaching to a more pragmatic, Enlightenment approach. In the seventh chapter this is, as it were, refined, in that Roelevink attempts a precise analysis of the methodological principles of this view of history. This scholarly book is rounded off by a summary in English, an extensive bibliography and an index.

All in all, it is astonishing how outdated the teaching of history was in the Netherlands. History, and ultimately Jurisprudence too, seem as undeveloped as philological studies were important and prominent. It is indeed very remarkable that the Enlightenment on the model of Göttingen only took hold in the nineteenth century, and that until the late eighteenth century polymathy determined the conception of scholarship. Here, I think, a comparison, particularly with the situation in Germany, could have helped to give this study even sharper definition, since the reader has ultimately no clear idea of the singularity of the Utrecht experience. It is also extremely striking that when the universities were restructured after 1815 there was established what was fundamentally an antiquated understanding of the universities and of scholarship. Naturally this was connected with the political situation of the country and with the criteria for evaluation applied to the individual academic disciplines. History never acquired more than a subordinate, auxiliary function. This book demonstrates that very well; likewise it shows how, in this manner, extraordinary contributions to scholarship found their way into this environment. I also find very convincing the way in which the author combines general university history, traditional institutional history and the study of the curriculum to uncover the contextual significance of a particular academic discipline. This book is exceptionally successful in illuminating an important period of Dutch academic history that has hitherto received little attention. Further studies like this are to be hoped for.

Notker Hammerstein
Frankfurt am Main

J. L. Black, *G.-F. Müller and the Imperial Russian Academy*. McGill-Queen's University Press, Kingston and Montreal, 1986. xi+290 pp. $34.00 (cloth).

Professor Black's goal in this work, as he describes it in his preface, is 'to study Müller's career at the Imperial Russian Academy of Sciences in general, and to outline his contribution to the development of Russian historical sciences in particular'. Müller had a long and multi-faceted career, but Black chooses to emphasize 'the historian because that was his chosen profession . . . and the Academy of Sciences because that was his place of work'. The organization is a straightforward chronological one, from Müller's birth in Westphalia in 1705 to his death in 1783 in Moscow, in eight chapters and an extended 'epilogue' that assesses Müller's contribution, and place, in Russian historiography. The sources are entirely published ones, but Black's research is so thorough as well as extensive that it is impossible to imagine that anything of significance bearing on his subject has escaped his attention. The notes and bibliography are complete and rich. Though some important recent works (e.g. Cracraft and Garrard) do not appear in the bibliography, they are cited nonetheless in footnotes (e.g. 227, note 20).

The text that describes the life and work of Müller is both richly detailed and clear. It might go too far to assert that the detail itself is Black's thesis. Nonetheless, while no chapter has an introductory statement of its main theme or a summing up paragraph or two at the end to make a conclusion, the accumulation of detail makes clear not only Müller's contribution in several fields of work, but also the extraordinary difficulty that the Russian social and political situations, not to mention also weather and terrain, placed in his way. For example, his work repeatedly was bitterly attacked by Lomonosov and many others, whose notions of acceptable conclusions for scholarly work differed from those Müller offered. Müller, who on entering Russian service first required 'full immunity from Russian jurisprudence', throughout his career suffered from budget cuts, or simply not being paid for extended periods, and through many struggles and quarrels, some of them scholarly.

Black finds that Müller performed significant service for the Russian state over a long period of time, for the result of his labours was the accumulation of a great deal of accurately observed and carefully recorded information about many aspects of Russian life. Nonetheless, it proved impossible for Müller to achieve his own goal, the production of a 'full' history of Russia. He did accomplish a good deal in gathering and editing materials that proved important to those who, in the next century, were able to produce the sort of multi-volume, thoroughly documented history that Müller sought. Black makes clear the Müller thought that writing 'history was matter of straightforward fact finding' and that he would have been 'astonished' to find himself called a proponent of a 'Norman Theory', or perhaps of any theory. Doubtless, Lomonosov would have been astonished at his astonishment, for Müller clearly did find much room for Varangians in his account of the origins of the Russian state. Nonetheless, Black makes clear that for all his troubles, and lack of success, Müller remained loyal to Russia. Never an apologist for autocracy or serfdom, he also never opposed any 'patriotic party' in the Academy, but simply worked hard to establish the truth about Russia's past as best he could. As an educator, he accomplished even less than as an historian. Catherine the Great, on Müller's death, praised Müller and his contribution to Russia. Within a few weeks of his death, nonetheless, she complained of the lack of a good textbook on Russian history, suitable for students in the public schools, whose foundation she planned to begin quite soon, and appointed a commission of scholars to write one. At the same time, she held up the publication of the text recently completed by one of Müller's colleagues in the Academy, J.-G. Stritter, because Stritter's conclusions differed from her own. In sum, while Black does not explicitly conclude so, it seems that the life story he recounts here indicates quite well that although Müller did fail to achieve the goals he sought, perhaps he succeeded at his scholarly work as well as it was possible for a western academic to succeed in eighteenth century Russia.

James T. Flynn
College of the Holy Cross
Worcester
Massachusetts, 01610
U.S.A.

Jennifer J. Carter and Joan H. Pittock (eds.), *Aberdeen and the Enlightenment.* Aberdeen: Aberdeen University Press, 1987. x+438 pp. £14.90.

The forty-two essays in this bargain volume arising out of a conference held in 1986 fall into three categories. Some deal with aspects of eighteenth century Scottish culture in general: amongst these is Marie Roberts's illuminating discussion of Burns as a freemason. Others focus upon the still vexed question of the nature and origins of the Scottish Enlightenment. Here Donald J. Withrington (fiercely) and Anand Chitnis (politely) register their dissent from the interpretations various advanced by Lord Dacre, J. G. A. Pocock and Nicholas Phillipson, all of whom stress the crucial significance of the Act of Union in precipitating that external stimulus which they regard as essential for transforming backward seventeenth century Scotland into a progressive nation. Withrington in particular counter-argues for continuity and an internal dynamic, seeing Scotland as already undergoing improvement under the Stuarts, and stressing the importance of Scotland's broadly-based educational system. There was far more to the Scottish Enlightenment than a small coterie of Edinburgh literati.

The third group of essays—by far the largest—deals with higher education in Aberdeen itself. As Roger Emerson convincingly demonstrates, Marischal College flourished whereas King's College relatively suffered eclipse, yet between them they supported a professoriate which included Thomas Reid, James Beattie, Colin McLaurin, James and John Gregory, George Campbell, Alexander Gerard, Thomas Blackwell, George Turnbull, William Ogilvie, James Dunbar, Patrick Copland and David Scene—no feeble constellation of luminaries. Many of these are discussed in individual essays of high quality far too numerous to be listed here. John S. Reid offers a particularly eye-opening account of the successful extramural science lectures offered for many years by Patrick Copland, and George Campbell's interpretation of language and rhetoric finds sympathetic exponents in H. Lewis Ulman and Kathleen Holcomb. It is a pity that

Reid and McLaurin are rather neglected, and in general, science and medicine are squeezed to the sidelines by a concentration on ethics and the liberal arts.

Collectively these re-examinations of the Aberdeen colleges remind us that the Scottish Enlightenment was not simply an Edinburgh affair, and that Aberdeen philosophy was not merely a series of negative rejoinders to Hume. We are shown, *inter alia*, the positive contribution of Aberdeen intellectuals to aesthetics, a union of philosophy and poetics which found its finest expression in Beattie and its most ambiguous one in Macpherson. We are left in no doubt about the intellectual vigour of Aberdeen up to around 1780. Its subsequent precipitate decline remains to be explored. Authors and editors alike are to be congratulated for the new light shed by this volume upon a rather neglected dimension of the Scottish Enlightenment.

Roy Porter
Wellcome Institute for the History of Medicine, London

Les problèmes de l'institutionnalisation de l'économie politique en France au XIXe siècle. Special issue of *Economies et sociétés* Tome XX No. 10 (Octobre, 1986) 237 pp. 95 FF.

This special issue of the journal *Economies et sociétés* brings together the French contributions to an international project on 'The Institutionalization of Political Economy. Its Introduction and Acceptance into European, North American and Japanese Universities' which was initiated by Professors Istvan Hont (then King's College, Cambridge; now Columbia University, New York) and Piero Barucci (University of Florence). There are nine case studies: Jacqueline Hecht, 'An Offspring of Enlightenment, Physiocracy and Ideology: The First French Chair of Political Economy (1795)' (pp. 5–48); D. Damamme, 'Political Economy under the "Consulate" and "Empire" Misery of Economy, Science of Wealth' (pp. 49–62); Philippe Steiner, 'J. B. Say and the Teaching of Political Economy in France' (pp. 63–95); Madeleine Ventre-Denis, 'The First Chair of Political Economy in a French University' (pp. 97–102); Francis Demier, 'Economic Vanguards and the Diffusion of Political Economy in France (1815–1914)' (pp. 103–142); Yves Charbit, 'The Statistical Institute, Political Economy and Demography' (pp. 143–57); F. Etner, 'Economic Teaching in the French 'grandes écoles' in the 19th century' (pp. 159–74); Annie Vinokur, 'Political Economy between Faith and Works: Saint-Simonism and the case of Michel Chevalier' (pp. 175–202); R. F. Hébert, 'Emile Cheysson and the Birth of Econometrics' (pp. 203–22); plus a foreword and an overview by the French convener of the international project, Professor Lucette Levan-Lemesle, 'From "Societies of Political Economy" to Law Schools. Characterizations and Paradoxes of the Institutionalization of Political Economy in France' (pp. 223–37).

Taken together, the ten essays provide a most useful survey of a neglected aspect of the history of French universities. As the contributors approached their common topic from different backgrounds (economics, demography, law, and history), the tunnel perspective, i.e. to look only at those aspects of economic teaching that have survived to the present day, has successfully been avoided. Another valuable feature of the volume is that a number of contributions have appendices documenting the curricula and their development.

I was particularly impressed by the contributions of J. Hecht, tracing the various intellectual influences that led to the foundation of the political economy chair at the "école normale", and of Annie Vinokur, clarifying the division of labour in French economics between the "grandes écoles" and the universities.

Norbert Waszek
University of Hannover
Federal Republic of Germany

Negley Harte, *The University of London 1836–1986*. London: The Athlone Press, 1986. 303 pp.
Neville Marsh, *The History of Queen Elizabeth College*. London: King's College, 1986. 336 pp.
G. P. Moss and M. V. Saville, *From Palace to College*. London: Queen Mary College, 1985. 152 pp.

'Why', asked Danie Defoe in 1728, 'should such a metropolis as London be without a University? . . . Would it not add to the lustre of our state and cultivate politeness among us? . . . Knowledge will never hurt us . . .' The pairing of this quotation with Metternich's forecast that the 'foundation of a university of London . . . would bring about England's ruin' is but one example of the liveliness and wit which adorns Negley Harte's historical survey of the University of London, published to coincide with the one hundred and fiftieth anniversary of its eventual foundation. Apart from H. Hale Bellot's brief account (1969), written originally for the *Victoria County History of Middlesex*, there has been no work the enquirier can conveniently refer to for factual information regarding England's largest university, and none to approach the present offering in the fullness of its scope and the attractiveness of its presentation. Insiders, no less than outsiders, will be enlightened on many points by Harte's authoritative exposition, in which he modestly sets out to portray 'some of the complexity of the University's development': to say that he succeeds is intended as a compliment. Harte's system of referring to successive variants of the University as Marks I, II and III helps the reader to keep his bearings and reduces the need for clumsy circumlocutions. Mark I is identified as the self-proclaimed 'London University' which was opened in 1828 in Gower Street and obliged shortly afterwards to change its name to University College. Mark II, whose inception was intimately connected with the burgeoning success of Mark I and of its near co-eval, King's College in the Strand, was founded by government under Charter in 1836; although restricted to examining and the award of degrees, its competence was not limited to London, with the result that the syllabuses devised by the government-appointed examiners, persons distinguished by their practicality as well as by their learning, came close to acquiring the status of a national curriculum. Towards the end of the century, mounting dissatisfaction with a University which, in the words of W. H. Allchin was no more than 'an Examining Board *urbi et orbi*', led after stormy debates to the patenting in 1900 of Mark III: a more orthodox model, and more positively linked with the metropolis, but one which continued to honour, through the arrangements made for 'external' candidates, its predecessor's commitment to the invisible body of students at home and overseas who wanted a London degree. In London itself, the teaching force for the reconstituted University was recruited from pre-existing foundations where students were already being prepared for London degrees. A number of these institutions, in which the ten Medical Schools were included, received the designation 'School' of the University, although only University College and King's College were admitted to all eight of the Faculties. Shortly afterwards the Government relinquished direct control of the University's finances. Thereafter public funding took the form of a modest but fixed grant-in-aid similar to those already being received by other places of Higher Education, some of the University's own Schools included. Nevertheless, the standards of efficiency expected from the reconstituted University, not least by politicians such as R. B. Haldane, who had done much to engineer the reform, ensured that its workings were subjected to continuing public scrutiny. In consequence there have been two further revisions of the University's Statutes, in 1929 and 1981, preceded in each case, as in 1900, by legislation; but in Harte's judgement these were not sufficiently far-reaching to a constitute a University of London Mark IV. Under the 1929 Statutes, however, a newly created body, the University Court, (reinforced by a proportion of outside members), became the channel through which the increasingly necessary and substantial grants-in-aid from central government were distributed to the Schools, while at the same time measures where taken to strengthen the representation of the Schools in the higher counsels of what was now more clearly than before a 'federal' university.

While dealing conscientiously with these constitutional aspects of the University's development, Harte is equally alert to the issues that will interest historians of educational change, beginning with the economic, social and cultural factors which stimulated demand in the early nineteenth century for a new kind of degree. The appeal of the London degree was twofold: the absence of religious discrimination (a feature inherited from the University of London Mark I), and the inclusion of subjects—modern languages and the experimental sciences, for example—which continued to be ignored by the ancient English universities, whose degree-giving monopoly had now been breached. The response in quantitative terms can be judged from tables Harte provides which show an uninterrupted rise in the number of candidates who were undeterred, it seems, by failure rates sometimes verging on fifty per cent. It would be interesting to know how the many thousands of students who presented themselves for first degrees between 1838 and 1900 were distributed between London, the provinces and places overseas, and also whether, as Bellot maintained, the proportion based on University and King's Colleges markedly declined in the last quarter of the century. However that may be, after 1900 the reconstituted University was never short of 'internal' students and indeed almost immediately surpassed in size both Oxford and Cambridge. The disparate nature of the student experience pre- and post-1900 makes it difficult for the historian to comment meaningfully on changes of habits and attitude, even if the sources were available; in regard to the latter, Harte's suggestion that novels (and surely memoirs?) might help to fill the gap is well worth pursuing.

For all its modernity, the University of London Mark II did not fail to imitate the customs of more venerable academic institutions, starting with the grant of a coat of arms in 1838. The impetus behind the adoption of an 'academical costume' (based on that of Cambridge) in 1844 and the staging from 1849 of a degree ceremony came from the graduates, who in 1858 achieved collective recognition in the body known as Convocation—a force to be reckoned with in all future debates. Still lacking, however, was an 'appropriate Edifice' which was needed, as Harte puts it, for 'reasons both of space and image'. His account of how, in the 1930s, these two desiderata were at last achieved in Bloomsbury is of more than architectural interest: while it gives him opportunity to resurrect one or two heroes, his survey also lays bare some of the internal conflicts, not tending to 'cultivate politeness', which time and again have dimmed the University of London's contribution to 'the lustre of our state'.

In evaluating the University's historical contribution to the essential task of advancing and disseminating knowledge, Harte is handicapped not only by the usual difficulty of having to cope with a wide range of disciplines (embracing at the present time 'seventy-five fields of academic endeavour') but still more by the multiplicity of institutions involved. The pioneering achievements of the nineteenth century had included the timely boost given to scientific studies by the introduction in 1859 of the B.Sc. (like the B.A. a broadly-based degree) and the admission of women to London degrees in 1878 on the same terms as men. Less well-known is the encouragement already being given in the 1880s to original research (an aim only formally added to those of the University in 1900) through the joining of a dissertation to the requirements for higher degrees. In the twentieth century, as the largest, most cosmopolitan and in some ways the most flexible of British universities, London has been in an position, through Institutes under the direct control of the Senate, to promote research and specialized teaching in fields such as medicine, archaeology, history and a variety of regional studies. But the bulk of the academic work has been carried on, admittedly to an agreed pattern, in the constituent Schools, some of which were already flourishing and famous when they came under the University's umbrella in 1900, although others still had their way to make.

Founded with varying intentions and in some instances, as with the former women's colleges, for a specific clientele, the Schools retained their separate governing bodies along with a strong sense of their own identity and worth. Harte finds a place for all of them on his crowded canvas but for full-length portraits (perhaps one should say self-portraits) reference should be made to the individual histories listed in Harte's up-to-date and comprehensive bibliography in which every School will be found to figure, some more than once. The definite article in the title of *The History of Queen Elizabeth College* is all too accurate since this attractive and thoroughly researched study, the first to be attempted, was completed by Neville Marsh, with understandable feelings of sadness, on the eve of the College's absorption (or re-absorption) into King's College in 1985. Co-educational since 1953 and since then biased towards the biological and physical sciences, Queen Elizabeth college had previously been a women's college specializing in Household and Social Science, the money for which had been raised by Sir John Atkins, and before that the women's branch of King's College. Marsh's book, which is well-furnished with references, lists and tables, therefore forms a notable and unusual addition to the history of the higher education of women; furthermore, with its detailed accounts of the scientific and educational work done in the various departments (which included distinguished contributions to Physiology, Food Science and Nutrition), and its chapters on students, it brings us close to the actualities of university life, at any rate in Kensington. Changes of name and function also enter into the history of Queen Mary College, which is the subject of Moss and Glanville's *From Palace to College*. The 'Palace' part of the title comes from the 'People's Palace', erected in 1887, with support from City charities and public donations, in order to provide facilities 'amidst the dense populataion of East London for rational amusement and technical education'. In pursuit of the latter aim, the staff on the technical side began to prepare students for London degrees, with the result that in 1907 the East London College, as this branch of the People's Palace was now called, gained admission to the (reconstituted) University in the Faculties of Arts, Science and Engineering, reference again being made to the 'very large population of the East End of London'. Since it would have been out of keeping with the format of this 'pictorial history' for the authors to delve into the geographical and social origins of successive generations of students, the extent to which the College succeeded in meeting a local need remains unclear, though we are told that the change of name when the College received its royal charter in 1934 was designed to discourage the idea that 'its work was intended for, or should be confined to, those resident in the immediate neighbourhood'. Against this rather bleak statement can be set the many recent examples given by the authors of the College's close involvement in local affairs and of its attempts, illustrated by maps, plans and photographs, to improve the environment. The space and buildings needed for the College's academic expansion, which has been especially marked on the engineering side, were achieved in large measure through the good offices and munificence of the Drapers' Company, whose fruitful association with the Governing Body dates back to the People's Palace era.

In these household chronicles the university plays an ambivalent role. Speaking of the period after 1900, Harte warns us not to mistake the 'central offices' of the University for the whole. But the error has been hard to avoid, and never more so than in the past few decades when the University's central machinery has been very much in evidence, driving the Schools forward in the heady days of pre- and post-Robbins expansion, and most recently, in response to the severe crisis affecting all British Universities in the 1980s, applying the brakes or going into reverse. Perhaps after all the 'arranged complexity' (to use Harte's expression) of the constitution devised for the reconstituted University in 1900 was too artificial to nourish a corporate spirit, although the disruptive effects of two world wars are not to be discounted, especially since each occurred at a moment when the University seemed on the verge of consolidating its identity. There is also the matter of geography. Any aspiring member of the university who contemplated the 1906 map of London reproduced by Harte pp. 168–9, on which the University's settlements and outposts were originally shown in an appropriately imperialistic red, would have been warned not to expect the easy intellectual and social intercourse characteristic of more traditional universities. A focal point for junior members has been provided since the early 1920s by the University of London Union and its affiliated clubs, but there appears never to have been anything comparable for senior members, whose academic and personal loyalties have tended to remain with their Colleges or specialist institutions. Whether this particular problem will be solved by the current programme of mergers, which aims to concentrate the University's rich scholarly resources on a smaller number of still scattered sites, remains open to doubt. Finally, in so far as public prestige is important, it may be relevant that the capital's great museums and art galleries, not to mention its copyright library, grew up independently of the University and have no organic connection with it: this is not to belittle the efforts made by the University, beginning in the 1870s and helped initially by private benefactions, to build up the collections of books, pamphlets and manuscripts now contained in the Senate House libraries, nor to deny the cultural value to the metropolis of the paintings and other objects housed in the Courtauld Institute Galleries and the neighbouring Percival David Foundation of Chinese Art.

Each of the histories discussed here is enlivened by a rich assortment of well-captioned illustrations, ranging far beyond the expected formal portraits, group photographs and shots of buildings. Harte in particular is to be congratulated on presenting us with so many visual emblems of the University in the exercise of its ceremonial, examining and administrative functions, though this reviewer would have liked a close-up of the mace, said by a Westfield source in 1902 to symbolize 'the rush and whirl of modern life'. In all three there is a generous helping of formal and informal likenesses (caricatures included) to enhance the necessarily brief sketches of leading personalities given in the text. Each has an index, but it would have been helpful if the others had followed Marsh's example in providing dated lists of functionaries (Harte's index, which is not wholly dependable, is of no help in tracing the succession of Vice-Chancellors and Principals). In one way or another, they are all commemorative in intention and adhere to a chronological framework. Historians wanting to explore in greater depth or across the board some of the wider themes hinted at in passing will be helped by the authors' references to archival and other sources—always supposing they can find them. While it is satisfying to hear of the work being done to put the University's central archives in order and to make them more accessible, it is disconcerting, especially at this time of flux, that *From Palace to College* is dedicated to 'someone who does not exist—the College Archivist'.

Janet Sondheimer
Archivist
Westfield College
University of London

Peter R. H. Slee, *Learning and a Liberal Education. The Study of Modern History in the Universities of Oxford, Cambridge and Manchester, 1800–1914*. Manchester University Press, 1986. x+181 pp. £25.00.

This brief but challenging book is presented as 'a contribution to the history of higher education'; that is to say, it is not primarily about the history of historiography or of historical scholarship but about the redefinition of the university curriculum in nineteenth and early-twentieth century England. The processes of university reform are, Slee suggests, too often interpreted in crudely functionalist terms or, alternatively, as simple translation into practice of the ideas of educational theorists. Whereas, given the highly complex and diverse character of English universities and their autonomy for academic purposes, there can be no short cuts to an understanding of how and why the *practice* of higher education changed in response to the social and intellectual pressures of the Victorian and Edwardian eras. What is needed, and what is offered here, is the patient, archivally-based reconstruction of what was actually going on in universities, set within a comparative analytical framework. By way of a comparative case-study in modes of change in higher education we are given an account of the introduction of modern history to the curriculum of Honours degree subjects at Oxford and Cambridge in the mid-nineteenth century and at Manchester (then part of the Victoria University) in 1882, and of the manner in which history was treated as a medium of undergraduate education in the years before the First World War. The book falls into three sections dealing, respectively, with the background to the adoption of history courses at Oxford and Cambridge, the way in which these courses assumed distinctive academic styles that resisted further modification, and the efforts of Bury, Firth and Tout, successful at Manchester but largely frustrated at the ancient universities, to introduce into undergraduate studies some training in historical research.

Slee's central conclusion is that the study of history at Oxford and Cambridge, while it differed in significant respects, was conditioned by the idea of the 'liberal education' which, by common consent among dons, those universities existed to purvey. This idea originated not as normative theory but as a defensive justification of the classical and mathematical studies whose dominance at Oxford and Cambridge had been accentuated by early reforms of the examination system. Under fire for their narrowness and lack of contemporary or vocational relevance, these disciplines found persuasive advocates in Bishop Copleston's generation: the accepted criteria for higher education became its value as rigorous mental training, its 'general' rather than specialized content and its remoteness from modern controversies and the materialist requirements of the professions. When it became impossible to avoid broadening the curriculum to include science and some modern arts subjects, they were admitted only on terms that did nothing to undermine the pre-eminence of traditional studies or challenge received pedagogical notions. Thus the study of history was yoked to Jurisprudence at Oxford and combined with other 'Moral Sciences' at Cambridge as a safeguard against specialization; even so, it qualified for a degree at Oxford only in combination with Literae Humaniores while at Cambridge Moral (and Natural) Sciences were merely offered as an optional extra to graduates in the Mathematical Tripos. The syllabuses initially adopted had less to do with the historical-mindedness of the mid-Victorians, or the manifold uses they found for the past, than with examinability and institutional convenience. Cambridge students were set factual questions on the professor's lectures while Oxford examined set books, easily got up by tutors and treated, by analogy with classical texts, as 'authorities'.

The growth of confidence in the educational value of history as a discipline in its own right in the 1860s and after did something to emancipate it from these constraints, bringing single-honours degree courses, a shift from the study of authorities to the study of periods, a proliferation of teachers and more specialized teaching. And a new sense that the critical study of original sources had particular value in training the mind arose with the growth of university interest in historical research—influenced, Slee argues, less by direct emulation of contemporary German scholarship than by the example of disciplines like philology and the sciences in which there had been earlier moves towards the continental view that research was a proper function of the universities. Yet Oxford and Cambridge showed a common reluctance to take the logical next step and introduce their students to the process of research itself: the training of professional historians, specialized vocational training, was alien to their function as places of liberal education. In Manchester, by contrast, T. F. Tout was able to make the writing of a dissertation, personally supervised by him, a compulsory element in the syllabus; and his was a school that produced a much higher proportion of writers of history.

A secondary theme is the importance of institutional factors in shaping the curriculum within each of these three universities. The prominent place of political science and economics in the Cambridge Tripos owes less, it is argued, to Seeley's notion of history as a 'school for statesmen' than to the shortage there of college history teachers, which encouraged historians to take advantage of lectures offered by professors in 'cognate sciences'. At Oxford, by contrast, the strength of the tutorial body, organized from 1868 in the Modern History Association, entrenched a regime of continuous English history, epochal European history and intensively taught special subjects that defied professorial influence. In the Modern History Association Slee sees a distinctively English concept of the professional historian as *teacher* of history; critics of Oxford's complacency in failing to appoint and train researchers rather missed the point, he suggests, that tutors saw their role as trainers of men for the Schools, which tested qualities that were judged desirable for England's future elite: clarity, agility and the capacity to argue an informed case. On the whole, it seems, the Oxford system did what it set out to do, although the result was that research was marginalized as an activity suitable for mere professors. Manchester, on the other hand, did not aspire to educate England's elite—most of Tout's pupils became schoolteachers—and in its tiny history department the values of the committed research could reign unchallenged.

This book should give pause to anyone inclined to treat the peculiarities of English university history as reflections of a generalized 'English culture' or to assume that the ideas of history professors necessarily conditioned what history students were taught. It does, however, leave some questions unresolved. How are we to reconcile the alleged dominance of the liberal education ideal with the fact that the ancient universities did introduce some explicitly vocational courses before 1914—in Law, Theology, Medicine and Engineering, for instance? And how far-reaching are the implications of Slee's institutional account of curriculum development for our understanding of the rise of academic history in England? Were the *writings* of academic historians, which he hardly considers, influenced by the ecology of the departments they worked in? These are important issues: a much longer book would have been needed to examine them fully.

Janet Howarth
St Hilda's College, Oxford

Ludwig Hatvany, *Die Wissenschaft des nicht Wissenswerten. Ein Kollegienheft*, edited by A. Grafton. Oxford: Pergamon Press, 1986. xxvi+118 pp. £20.

Hatvany's sardonic view of classical philology caused a flutter in German academic dovecotes when it was first published in 1908. This facsimile reprint—from the second edition of 1911—demonstrates that it can still amuse and stimulate. The target of the lampoon, imaginatively presented as the private lecture-notes and musings of a disenchanted student, is a professoriate which the author claims to have progressively perverted the true legacy of the ancients by embalming it in pedantic exegesis. What was once, in the age of Winckelmann, a vehicle for liberation and creativity, has degenerated into thesis-fodder for the 'barbarians of a second Völkerwanderung' and their 'slavery of the fact': an obsession with historical context, trivial detail, and grammatical explication. Hatvany was not afraid to name names, prominently among them that of Wilamowitz-Moellendorf (and Wilamowitz—under whom Hatvany studied—has often been thought the model too for the execrable pedagogue 'Woepke', at whose feet the writer is purported to sit). That in itself suffices to show how far his ridicule, in its lack of measure, condemns good learning along with bad. But Hatvany's text abounds in finely-honed *aperçus* on (neo-)humanism and on the (ir)relevance of classical studies generally. He is full of scorn for much of the contemporary Gymnasium syllabus (which included, so we learn, the translation of Chancellor Bülow's speeches into Greek), and even prepared to argue that Goethe's immersion in the ancients yielded him nothing more than 'a certain affectation'.

The finesse and power of its writing, and the beautiful evocations of the spirit of the classical world, earn for this little book a modest place in the annals of German literature. As such it stands in a long tradition of satire on university learning: Grafton cites Hutten and Mencke as earlier exponents; among more recent ones Heinrich Mann and Canetti may come to mind. Yet the book was not written by a German. Hatvany (1880–1961), son of an industrialist ennobled in the very year 1908, was an outstanding member of that pre-war Hungarian Jewish intelligentsia which could achieve a close personal identification with German culture (not for nothing was the family's original name Deutsch, Hatvany being a Magyarized form derived from the site of its sugar refinery), yet at the same time exhibited a growing intellectual alienation from it—the young György Lukács provides another good example. Hatvany's comprehensive programme of *docta ignorantia* would not have left room for much more than an intuitive and aesthetic appreciation of the ancients. It can be no coincidence that this passionate plea for the individual, evanescent, and spontaneous, inspired in part by the Switzerland of Burckhardt and Nietzsche, also appeared only a year after Bergson's *Evolution créatrice*, and simultaneously with Sorel's *Réflexions*. Such ideals, which Hatvany pursued in Hungarian-language work too (*Én és a könyvek*, 1910), found poetic embodiment for him in his great compatriot and friend, Endre Ady, whose biographer Hatvany became; and they possessed a socio-political dimension, which led him to revolt against the Hungarian establishment and endure a life rich in exile and deprivation. The modest editorial apparatus of this welcome reprint does not extend to wider evaluation of Hatvany's *oeuvre*, though Nicholas Kurti —who knew Hatvany in Oxford during the last war—has assembled no less than three other distinguished scholars to pay tribute to him. The Hatvany of 1908 might have found such erudition quaint, while registering satisfaction that the name of one of them is misspelt on the cover.

R. J. W. Evans
Brasenose College, Oxford

Robert C. Alberts, *Pitt: The Story of the University of Pittsburgh 1787–1987* Pittsburgh: University of Pittsburgh Press, 1986. xvii+537 pp. $24.95.

This well written narrative history of coffee-table format is a delight to the eye. Intended for a wide public of alumni and friends of the university, it abounds with illustrations, places the emphasis on people throughout, and relates the history of the university through glimpses into lives of its chancellors, professors, and students. The author has made good use of archival sources and has supplied notes and a bibliography. Still, the book is bound to disappoint the historian as it short-changes the past and gives a disproportionate emphasis to the years after 1921: 70 pages of text are devoted to 134 years of university history; the remaining 71 years have 356 pages at their disposal.

Jurgen Herbst
Departments of Educational Policy Studies and History
University of Wisconsin-Madison

David O. Levine, *The American College and the Culture of Aspiration 1915–1940* Ithaca and London: Cornell University Press, 1986. 281 pp. $32.95.
Roger L. Geiger, *To Advance Knowledge: The Growth of American Research Universities, 1900–1940* New York and Oxford: Oxford University Press, 1986 x+325 pp. $27.50.

These two volumes are welcome additions to the historiography of higher education in the United States. Together they provide a first general survey of this subject that carries on where Laurence Veysey left off with his *The Emergence of the American University*. While the two authors differ in their choice of subject—Levine emphasizes students and teaching whereas Geiger places the spotlight on research and the faculty—they nonetheless share many overlapping topics of interest. Both also strive to place the universities and their affairs into their wider social, economic, and political context. As a result, the two books give us a good overview of the place of higher education in twentieth century American life.

World War I and the Great Depression are given prominent place by both authors. During the war years American colleges and universities came to occupy a more central place in the affairs of the nation. Levine portrays the Student Army Training Corps as 'a rite of passage for American higher education from carefree adolescence to manhood', (p. 27) and Geiger credits it with having brought to college many young men who would not otherwise have considered attending (p. 108). Nonetheless,

Geiger feels, because of its short duration the Corps was 'a truncated experience in academic organization' (p. 104). Faculty members found in groups like the Intercollegiate Intelligence Bureau or the Inquiry instruments for their enlistment in the war effort, and 'campuses were nationalized,' writes Geiger, 'almost as completely as the railroads had been . . .' (p. 102). Still Geiger concludes that with the passing of the war the role of the federal government receded and research coordination was left to decentralized efforts of largely autonomous institutions. Levine sees it differently. 'World War', he writes, 'was the take-off point in the history of American higher education' (p. 38). It brought 'the college-educated man' as a new privileged class into American life. From now on the college-trained and socialized experts were to run American government, business, and the professions.

In their discussions of the depression both authors assign central importance to the role of the federal government in higher education. Levine describes how through work-study programmes the federal government sought to maintain a supply of trained persons and to keep students out of the labour market. As a result the public sector of higher education grew faster than the private, and the growth of teachers and junior colleges contributed to a more heterogeneous student body and a more differentiated system of higher education. The research universities suffered from shrinking private resources and many of their spokesmen were hesitant to become dependent on the federal government. 'They tended to fear government interference with the autonomy of science more than they welcomed its succor', writes Geiger (p. 257). The problem, then, was to find ways in which federal support could be channelled through the existing science and university network—a problem that was to remain into the fifties and later.

When it comes to their different subjects, Levine keeps his attention centred on the student and on what one might well consider the single most important demographic fact of rapidly increasing college attendance among American young people after World War I. He writes of curricular experimentation and new institutions like urban universities and junior colleges. He probes the meaning of what he calls 'the emergence of the American post-secondary school as a central economic, social, and cultural institution . . .' (p. 7). He intends to challenge head-on Veysey's contention that innovation ended in American higher education around 1910. For Levine academic growth and ferment only began and, he argues, 'it was during the 1920s and 1930s that American schools of higher education moved into the mainstream of American . . . life' (p. 17).

By the very nature of his subject Geiger clings a bit more closely to Veysey's modern university and argues that Veysey's emergence never stopped. It continued unabated after 1910. And it was research rather than teaching, the graduate students rather than the undergraduates, and a slowly consolidating nation-wide system of research universities rather than individual colleges that became most characteristic for American higher education in the twentieth century. In a detailed account of universities and associations, of individual donors and foundations, of debates and position papers Geiger discusses the fortunes of the research and science sector of American higher education and lets us see how the opportunities and demands of research have affected faculty members in their departments and universities.

Though Geiger's book centres on research, it offers some fascinating observations on what Geiger calls the 'collegiate syndrome', a kind of student side-show to the main act played by the faculty. The collegiate syndrome concerns the residential college on the Oxbridge model with its tutors, honours programmes, fraternities, athletics, and extra-curricular activities. It entails as well the numerically impressive growth of business programmes, urban universities, teachers and junior colleges. It comprises a social atmosphere of peer pressure that undermined democracy and encouraged anti-intellectualism, in turn alienated the faculty and provoked the rise of an administrative bureaucracy of student counsellors, deans, and personnel workers. The pressure of the collegiate syndrome against the values of the research university, argues Geiger, fed the discrimination against Jewish students and the opposition to meritocratic college admissions. Levine writes about the same developments at much greater length, adds some equally fascinating observations on the fear of feminization in the colleges of the twenties, and on the social as well as religious and ethnic discrimination in admission policies.

The two books also differ in approach and style. Geiger's presents an 'account of the growth of American research universities . . .' It reports and discusses the acquisition and use of resources for research and the extra-mural sources needed to keep the research enterprise going. Except for the chapter on the period for World War I to 1930 which contains the section on the collegiate syndrome, the book remains faithful to the research theme. Geiger writes from the inside, as it were; discusses the strengths and weaknesses of research and funding policies from either the grantor's or the grantee's point of view. His is no critical voice; terms like big business and big research are absent. Strange to say, Thorstein Veblen or academic freedom do not occur in the index. Information on projects, agencies, and institutions, however, crowds the pages, and the book serves well as a reference source on many an aspect of research policy. By comparison with Levine's Geiger's narrative is painstaking, detailed, and withall a bit dull.

In its title, *The Culture of Aspiration* already indicates the interpretive direction of Levine's analysis. To him American colleges do more than inform, teach, and educate. By their very diversity they reflect a social hierarchy and as accrediting agencies they act as arbiters of social and economic mobility for their students. The historical point of Levine's argument is to convince us that 'by taking on these varied roles in the twenties and thirties the mission of American colleges became diffuse and ambiguous. College spokesmen were caught between collegiate rhetoric and reality. Americans were of divided mind whether they should support their colleges for social or for intellectual reasons. Students were unsure whether going to college was a privilege or a right.

Issues of this kind provoke thought and argument and enliven the pace of the discussion. From an historical point of view one might ask whether Levine is not loading too heavy a freight onto the decades under discussion. The nineteenth century college already stressed character education as much as mental training. It was in the nineteenth century that social fraternities replaced the intellectual debating societies, and the question whether colleges were privileged sanctuaries modelled on family governance under *in loco parentis* or small republics of young citizens who were to exercise their rights as freemen had been discussed already during the 1780s and 1790s. Levine overstates his case when he describes as novel the kinds of issues that beset the colleges in the twenties and thirties. He is, however, undoubtedly right when he points to the unprecedented enrollments in both absolute numbers and relative size of the collegiate age cohort. This was new after World War I, and it was, as we now know in retrospect, but a general rehearsal for what was to come after World War II.

Both books, then, leave us with a common unease. As American higher education entered the post-World War II era it faced uncertainty over its mission and ambiguity concerning its prospects. Levine sees that the rhetoric of equal educational opportunity was belied by remaining privileges of social class and race. Geiger stresses the precarious survival of such traditional values as freedom for academic research, peer control, and university autonomy in an era of federally funded research. Even if the two authors can't agree whether the first half of the twentieth century ushered in a new era or did no more than accelerate already existing trends, neither of them denies the magnitude of expansion and the unresolved questions that this presents for the future.

Jurgen Herbst
Departments of Educational Policy Studies and History
University of Wisconsin-Madison

History of Education volume 16, number 3. London: Taylor and Francis Ltd, September 1987.

This special issue of the journal *History of Education* is devoted to papers delivered at the 1986 Annual Conference of the History of Education Society of Great Britain. As the topic chosen for this particular conference required a consideration of some aspects of modern university history, the papers are of interest to readers of *History of Universities*.

Sheldon Rothblatt of the University of California provides a stimulating discussion of the historical role of the federal principle in higher education. He considers the British experience of the nineteenth and twentieth centuries with illuminating use of comparative material from the United States. Fritz Ringer compares the universities of France and Germany around the year 1900 and Brian Simon, president of the National Union of Students of England and Wales in 1939–40, examines the 1930s student movement, suggesting that a critical attitude towards the establishment developed as a result of student reaction to events on the continent and social problems at home. W. H. G. Armytage adds a note on the influence of university trained women on the fall of the birth-rate after 1964 and Noel Annan, beginning with the statement 'Higher education in Britain today is in a mess', discusses the reform of higher education in 1986. Finally, Geoffrey Giles, of Florida, publishes a short abstract of his forthcoming paper on student drinking in the Third Reich.

The contents of this special issue show clearly how the historical developments of the recent past are clearly related to the present European-wide debate on the role of our universities in modern society.

John M. Fletcher
Department of Modern Languages
University of Aston
Birmingham B4 7ET

Publications on University History since 1977: A Continuing Bibliography

Edited by
John M. Fletcher
With the assistance of
Christopher A. Upton

Produced with the co-operation of the International Commission for the History of Universities

Preface

Lists of publications relating to European university history were printed for the years 1977–1981 in five booklets *History of European Universities: Work in Progress and Publications*. Consequent on changes in the editorship and publisher of *History of Universities*, the work of publishing such annual lists has been assumed by this journal. Each future issue will contain a summary of relevant titles reported to the editor. These lists will include any titles published after 1977 that have not previously been recorded and will be extended to cover material relating to non-European universities. Since this work will also require the printing of all titles from the year 1982 and subsequent years, pressure on space compels us to complete this task gradually over the next few issues of the journal. We here begin the work of updating the existing lists for 1977–1981 and of adding certain of the sections for subsequent years. To obtain the complete bibliography from 1977, readers may wish to purchase back numbers of *History of European Universities: Work in Progress and Publications* which are still available on request from the address below.

The following scholars have contributed reports for this issue: membership of the International Commission for the History of Universities is indicated by an asterix: W. Höflechner and H. H. Egglmaier (Austria), H. de Ridder-Symoens* and J. Paquet* (Belgium and The Netherlands), C. A. Upton (British Isles), R. S. Harris (Canada), M. Svatoš (Czechoslovakia), J. Verger* (France), W. Fläschendräger (DDR), R. vom Bruch and R. A. Müller (BRD), L. Szögi (Hungary), D. Maffei* and P. Nardi (Italy), M. Koczerska (Poland), A. Garcia y Garcia* (Spain and Portugal),

W. Rother (Switzerland) and N. G. Siraisi (USA). We are most grateful for their work and also for the contributions received from many individuals. The laborious work of preparing copy in so many languages has been kindly undertaken by Pauline A. Fletcher and Françoise Bannister.

We should be happy to receive notes of any omissions from our lists for future inclusion. Please send details to us at the address below.

Dr John M. Fletcher,
Dept of Modern Languages,
Aston University,
Aston Triangle,
Birmingham B4 7ET
England

Australia

Publication 1985

Bruneau, W.: Opportunism and altruism in official programmes of moral educ.: the cases of France and Canada 1880–1939, *Hist. of educ. rev.,* 14 (1): 39–51. (Discusses contrib. of univ. professors).

Austria

Additions to Earlier Lists

For 1978
Kohler, A.: Bildung u. Konfession. Zum Studium d. Studenten aus d. habsburgischen Ländern an Hochschulen im Reich 1560–1620, in G. Klingenstein, H. Lutz and G. Stourzh eds: *Bildung, Politik und Gesellschaft. Studien zur Geschichte des europäischen Bildungswesens vom 16. bis zum 20. Jahrhundert,* Vienna: 64–123.
For 1980
Egglmaier, H. H.: Das medizinisch-chirurigische Studium in Graz. Ein Beispiel für den Wandel staatlicher Zielvorstellungen im Bildungs-und Medizinalwesen. Thesis. Graz.
For 1981
Herrmann, E.: Beiträge zur Geschichte der Lehrkörpers der medizinischen Fakultät der Universität im 18. Jahrhundert. Thesis. Vienna.
Klingenstein, G.: Der Fall Buresch oder über d. Anfänge d. Polizey-u. Cameral-wiss. in Graz, in G. Pferschy ed.: *Siedlung, Macht und Wirtschaft. Festschrift Fritz Posch,* Graz: 397–409.
Kloiber, I. M.: Studenten aus Deutschwestungarn an der Universität Wien von 1365 bis 1848. Thesis. Vienna.

Körrer, K.: Die zwischen 1938 und 1945 verstorbenen Mitglieder des Lehrkörpers an der Universität Wien. Thesis. Vienna.

Kremsmair, J.: Kath. Univ. u. Konkordat von 1933–34, *Jb. d. Univ. Salzburg*, 1979–81: 37–46.

Putzer, P.: Die Szepter d. Univ. Salzburg, *Jb. d. Univ. Salzburg*, 1979–81: 72–89.

Rinnerthaler, A.: Die Kanonisten an d. alten Salzburger Juristenfak. im 17. Jh., *Jb. d. Univ. Salzburg*, 1979–81: 90–101.

Publications 1982

Bancher, E.: *Aus dem akademischen Leben der Technischen Universität Wien*, 1–4, Vienna, 1979–82.

Baumgart, M.: Die Wiener als Studenten an der Wiener Universität im Spätmittelalter 1365–1518. Thesis. Vienna.

Berghofer, C.: Die Anfäge der Zoologie an der Universität Graz. Thesis. Graz.

Egglmaier, H. H.: Deutsche Studienanstalten aus d. Sicht eines vormärzlich-österr. Akademikers. Ein Bericht Prof. Franz Hruschauers aus d. Jahre 1840 über seine Studienreise, *Mitt. d. österr. Gesellschaft f. Gesch. d. Naturwiss.*, 2: 1–14.

Forster, C.: Die Geschichte der österreichischen Hochschülerschaft 1945–55. Thesis. Vienna.

Heindl, W.: Universitätsreform, Gesellschaftsreform. Bemerkungen zum Plan eines 'Universitätsorganisationgesetzes' in d. Jahren 1854–55, *Mitt. d. österr. Staatsarchivs*, 35: 134–49.

Hoffmann, R.: Salzburger Lycealstudenten im Vormärz, *Mitt. d. Gesellschaft f. Salzburger Landeskunde*, 122: 371–402.

Höflechner, W.: Ludwig Boltzmann, Sein akad. Werdegang in Österreich. Dargestellt nach archivalischen Materialien, *Mitt. d. österr. Gesellschaft f. Gesch. d. Naturwiss.*, 2: 43–62.

Jontes, G.: Zur Gesch. d. polnischen Studentenvereins in Leoben, *Z. d. hist. Vereins f. Steiermark*, 73: 131–39.

Jungwirth, E.: Die philosophische Fakultät der Universität Wien von 1848 bis 1873 unter Berücksichtigung der Thun-Hohensteinschen Universitätsreform. Thesis. Vienna.

Kernbauer, A.: Das Fach Chemie an der Philosophischen Fakultät der Universität Graz von 1850–1906. Thesis. Graz.

Mayerhofer, T.: Der Lehrkörper der Philosophischen Fakultät der Universität Wien von 1848 bis 1873. Thesis. Vienna.

Niederstätter, A.: Grafen von Montfort als Studenten an d. Univ. Europas, *Montfort*, 34: 271–76.

Oberkofler, G.: Die Strafrechtslehrer an d. Univ. Wien u. Prag im Vormärz, *Innsbrucker Hist. Studien*, 5: 47–81.

Pakes, B.: Beiträge zur Geschichte des Lehrkörpers der juridischen Fakultät der Universität Wien zwischen 1918 und 1938. Thesis. Vienna.

Pauli, L.: Kirchenrecht in d. Gesch. d. Jagellonischen Univ. Krakau, *Österr. Archiv f. Kirchenrecht*, 33: 112–122.

Sacher, H. D.: Die Klagenfurter Ärzteschule. Über Klagenfurts medizin. Leyzeum um 1800, *Die Brücke*, 8: 44–49.

Sauer, W.: Universitätsrektor Friedrich Wagl u. d. Grazer Revol. d. Jahres 1848, *Z. d. hist. Vereins f. Steiermark*, 73: 115–29.

Status univ. 1: Zur Charakterisierung d. univ. Entwicklung in Österreich von 1954 bis 1980. 2: Dokumentation sozialwiss. Befunde zur Lage d. Studenten in Österreich, *Arbeitsnummer d. Inst. f. kirchliche Sozialforschung*, 140.

Stranzinger, E.: Gesch. d. Universitätsbibliothek d. TU Graz 1875–1975, *Biblos-Schriften*, 119.

- - - - - Gesch. d. Universitätsbibliothek d. TU Graz 1875–1975, *Biblos*, 31: 12–56.

Wallisch, F.A.: Das höhere Lehramt von 1849–1914. Staatliche Vorstellungen in der Ausbildung von Lehrern für Gymnasien, Realschulen und Mädchenlyzeen. Thesis. Graz.

Weiling, F.: Die phil. Lehranstalt in Brünn 1808–49 u. d. österr. Bildungspol. jener Zeit. Ihre Bedeutung f. d. Entdeckertätigkeit Johann Gregor Mendels, *Mitt. d. österr. Staatsarchivs*, 35: 110–33.

Publications 1983

Cohen, A. E.: Das Universitätswesen in d. Niederlanden um 1780 bis 1880, in R. G. Plaschka und K. Mach eds: *Wegenetz Europäischen Geistes*, Vienna: 206–12.

Klingenstein, G.: Universitätsfragen in d. österr. Monarchie um 1800, in R. G. Plaschka and K. Mack eds: *Wegenetz Europäischen Geistes*, Vienna: 80–87.

Publication 1985

Freisitzer, K. etc. eds: *Tradition und Herausforderung. 400 Jahre Universität Graz*, Graz.

Publications 1986

Apfelauer, R.: Das Archiv d. Univ. Salzburg, *Scrinium. Z. d. Verbandes österr. Archivare*, 35: 214–217.

Bernhard, G., Höflechner, W. and Zach, W.: *Bibliographie. Geisteswissenschaftliche Fakultät. Karl-Franzens-Universität Graz*, Graz.

Brauneder, W.: Emanzipation von d. Pol. Der Aufbruch d. Wiss. vom Öffentlichen Recht, in P. Berner, E. Brix and W. Mantl eds: *Wien um 1900. Aufbruch in die Moderne,* Vienna (henceforth noted as *Aufbruch in d. Moderne*): 243–48.

Egglmaier, H. H.: *Die Gründung der Grazer Medizinischen Fakultät im Jahre 1863,* Graz.

Engelbrecht, H.: *Geschichte des österreichischen Bildungswesens. Erziehung und Unterricht auf dem Boden Österreichs,* 4, Vienna.

Fellner, G.: Athenäum. Die Gesch. einer Frauenhochschule in Wien, *Zeitgesch.,* 14: 99–115.

Hamann, G., Mühlberger, K. and Skacel, F. eds: *100 Jahre Universität am Ring. Wissenschaft und Forschung an der Universität Wien seit 1884,* Vienna.

Hantschk, C.: Technik u. Kunst, in *Aufbruch in d. Moderne*: 81–99.

Hödl, G.: Universitätsreform einst u. heute. Zum 175. Geburtstag Graf Leo Thun-Hohensteins, *Österr. Hochschulzeitung. Magazin f. Wiss., Forschung u. Praxis,* 38 (3): 4–5.

Honek, K.: *Dissertationsverzeichnis der Katholischen Theologischen Fakultät an der Universität Wien von 1831 bis 1984,* Vienna.

Jungreithmayr, A.: Die Handschriftensammlung der Universitätsbibliothek Salzburg. Historische Entwicklung, thematische Gliederung und Beschreibung ausgewählter Codices, unter besonderer Berücksichtigung der deutschen Handschriften. Thesis. Salzburg.

Kattinger, H.: 40 Jahre Studienrichtung Lebensmittel-u. Biotech., *Österr. Hochschulzeitung, Magazin f. Wiss., Forschung u. Praxis,* 38 (1/2): 26–27.

Kernbauer, A.: Das chem. Lab. d. Univ. Prag bis zur Mitte d. 19. Jhs, *Mitt. d. österr. Gesellschaft f. Gesch. d. Naturwiss.,* 6: 10–67.

Leitsch, W.: Wien u. d. Ausbildung von Hist. osteurop. Länder, *Mitt. d. Inst. f. österr. Geschichtsforschung,* 94: 143–58.

Leser, N. ed.: *Die Wiener Schule der Nationalökonomie,* Vienna/Cologne/Graz.

Mühlberger, K.: Juristen in d. Akad. Legion 1848, in *200 Jahre Rechtsleben in Wien. Advokaten, Richter, Rechtsgelehrte. 96. Sonderausstellung des Historischen Museums der Stadt Wien, 21 November 1985 bis 9 Februar 1986,* Vienna (henceforth noted as *200 Jahre Rechtsleben*): 51–53.

- - - - - Juristenpromotionen *sub auspiciis* an d. Univ. Wien, in *200 Jahre Rechtsleben*: 239–42.

- - - - - and Wakounig, M.: Vom Konsistorialarchiv zum Zentralarchiv d. Univ. Wien, *Scrinium. Z. d. Verbandes österr. Archivare,* 35: 190–213.

Oberhummer, W.: Zur Gesch. d. Chem. an d. Univ. Wien 1749–1848, in G. Hamann ed.: *Aufsätze zur Geschichte der Naturwissenschaften und Geographie,* Vienna: 137–53.

- - - - - Adolf Martin Pleischl. Der erste Inhaber eines Lehrstuhles d. Chem. an d. Univ. Wien, in G. Hamann ed.: *Aufsätze zur Geschichte der Naturwissenschaften und Geographie,* Vienna: 155–62.

Ogris, W.: 200 Jahre Rechtswiss. an d. Univ. Wien, in *200 Jahre Rechtsleben:* 221–31.

Preglau-Hämmerle, S.: *Die politische und soziale Funktion der österreichischen Universität. Von den Anfängen bis zur Gegenwart. Mit einem Vorwort von Anton Pelinka,* Innsbruck.

Reiffenstein, B.: Zu d. Anfängen d. Englischunterrichtes an d. Univ. Wien u. zur frühen wiss. Anglistik in Wien, in O. Rauchbauer ed.: *Beiträge zur Englischen Philologie 80. A Yearbook of Studies in English Language and Literature 1985/86. Festschrift für Siegfried Korninger,* Vienna: 163–85.

Roubicek, F.: *Von Basel bis Czernowitz. Die jüdisch-akademischen Studentenverbindungen in Europa,* Vienna.

Spath, F.: *Zur Geschichte der Chirurgie an der Karl-Franzens-Universität Graz. Aus dem Nachlaß hg., ergänzt und fortgeführt von Walter Höflechner,* Graz.

Speiser, W.: *Die sozialistischen Studenten Wiens 1927–38. Mit einem Vorwort von Heinz Fischer,* Vienna.

Streissler, E.: Die Wiener Schule d. Nationalökonomie, in *Aufbruch in d. Moderne:* 77–80.

Sutter, B. ed.: *Die Grazer Juristenfakultät 1945–85. Hermann Baltl. 40 Jahre akademischer Lehrer und Forscher. Würdigung und Erinnerungen,* Graz.

Uiblein, P.: Die Kanonisation d. Markgrafen Leopold u. d. Wiener Univ., *Jb. d. Stiftes Klosterneuburg,* 13 (1985): 21–58.

Vernunft als Institution? Geschichte und Zukunft der Universität. Ed. by the Projektgruppe Kritische Universitätsgesch., Vienna.

Wiesflecker, H.: Wien vor d. Refn. Eine Studentenrevolte im Jahre 1514, in K. Amon etc. eds: *Ecclesia Peregrinans. Josef Lenzenweger zum 70. Geburtstag,* Vienna: 161–67.

Wyklicky, H.: Wiener Medizin um d. Jahrhundertwende, in *Aufbruch in d. Moderne:* 69–72.

Belgium and the Netherlands

Additions to Earlier Lists

For 1980

Bruneau, W.: An untapped resource for the hist. of French higher educ.: the *Enquêtes et documents relatifs à l'enseignement sup. en France*: Introd. and Cat., *Paedagog. hist.,* 20: 381–95.

Spade, P. V.: Richard Lavenham and the Cambridge Logic, in K. Koerner etc. eds: *Studies in Medieval Linguistic Thought Dedicated to Geoffrey L. Bursill-Hall,* Amsterdam: 241–47.

For 1981

Apports de Liège au progrès des sciences et des techniques, Liège. (Material relating to univ. of Liège 19th and 20th centuries).

Bondt, J. de: Hist. overzicht van de dienst stomatologie en tandheelkunde aan de Kath. Univ. te Leuven (Hist. sketch of the dept of stomatology and dentistry at the K.U.L.), *Belg. tijdsch. voor tandheelkunde*, 36: 111–114.

Braakhuis, H. A. C., Kneepkens, C. H. and Rijk, L. M. de eds: *English Logic and Semantics from the End of the 12th Century to the Time of Ockham and Burleigh*, Nijmegen. (Material relating to the teaching of logic in the universities).

Coppens, J: *Les six dernières années des Facultés unitaires de théologie et de droit canonique 1962–68*, Louvain.

Dethier, F.: L'enseignement univ. dans les provs wallonnes, in *La Wallonie, le pays et les hommes*, 4: 253–70.

Kubik, D.: L'univ. dans la ville médiévale: le cas de Louvain 1425–1500, *Assoc. des hists de Louvain. Résumés des mémoires de licence en hist.*, 4: 11–14.

Pushkin, M.: *Raznochintsy* in the univ. Govt pol. and soc. change in 19th cent. Russia, *Internat. rev. of soc. hist.*, 1: 25–65.

Schtickzelle, M: Pierre-François Verhulst 1804–49. La première découverte de la fonction logistique, *Population*, 36: 541–55. (P.-F. V. prof. univ. of Brussels 1835–40).

Simon-Vandermeersch, A. M.: Het archief van de Fac. van de toegepaste wetenschappen van de Rijksuniv. te Gent (The records of the fac. of tech. sciences of the R.U.G.), in *Professor R. L. Plancke 70*, Ghent: 201–28.

Stengers, J.: Une page de l'hist. de l'Univ. de Bruxelles sous l'occupation: l'incident Rolin—De Man de nov. 1940, *Annales de la soc. royale d'archéol. de Bruxelles*, 58: 255–63.

Tender, P. de: Un siècle d'hist. et d'hist. de l'Instit. d'astrophysique, *Liège-Univ.*, 13: 5.

Vanderdonck, R.: De ontwikkeling van de tandheelkunde aan de Rijkuniv. Gent sinds 1930 (The progress of dentistry at the R.U.G. since 1930), *Belg. tijdsch. voor tandheelkunde*, 36: 115–119.

Walckiers, M.: Le médecin belge du 19e s. le plus cité par les auteurs contemporains, *Louvain médical*, 100: 371–79. (Concerns A. van Gehuchten 1861–1914, prof. univ. of Louvain).

Publications 1982

Ansiau, C.: La loi du 21 mai 1929 sur la collation des grades acad. et le programme des examens univ., *Assoc. des hists de Louvain. Résumés des mémoires de licence en hist.*, 5: 37–38.

Ashmann, M.: Willem de Groot 1597–1662 en zijn studie te Leiden in het licht van zijn broer Hugo (The studies of W. de G. at L. as seen by his brother H.), *Tijdsch. voor rechtsgesch.*, 50: 371–401.

Auwera, M. van der: Wetenschappelijke loopbaan aan de univ.: niet zonder problemen voor vrouwen (A scholarly career at univ.: not without problems for women), *Onze alma mater*, 36: 205–217.

Bacq, Z.: Les biologistes et les médecins au 19e s. à Liège, *Bull. de la classe des scs de l'acad. royale de Belg.*, 68, 1982–85: 309–13.

Berkel, K. van: Intellectuals against Leeuwenhoek. Controversies about the methods and style of a self-taught scientist, in L. C. Palm and H. A. M. Snelders eds: *Antoni van Leeuwenhoek 1632–1723*, Amsterdam: 187–209.

- - - - - Wetenschapsgesch. en Universiteitsgesch. nieuwe stijl (The hist. of knowledge and the hist. of univs: new style), *Tijdsch. voor de gesch. der geneeskunde, natuurwetenschappen, wiskunde en tech.*, 5: 89–95. (Review article of W. Frijhoff: *la société néerlandaise et ses gradués 1575–1814*).

Bonte, A.: *Profiel van een Vlaamse Universiteit* (Profile of a Flemish univ. (Ghent)), Ghent.

Bots, H.: Pierre Bayle en de Rotterdamse Illustere schl 1681–93 (P. B. and the 'Illustere Schl' in R.), *Rotterdams jb.*: 176–201.

- - - - - F. J. L. Kraemer: leraar, hoogleraar, archivaris 1850–1928 (F. J. L. K.: teacher, prof., archivist 1850–1928), *Ned. archievenblad*, 87: 219–25.

Broeyer, F. G. M.: William Whitaker 1548–95. Leven en werk van een anglo-calvinistisch theoloog (W. W. Life and work of an anglo-calvinistic theol.). Thesis. Utrecht. (W. W. prof. at Cambridge and Mast. of St John's College).

Catalogus bij de tentoonstelling 'Twee helden die der dingen diept and steilt afpeilen' (Cat. of the exhib. 'Two heroes who sound the depths and the heights'), Amsterdam. (See below under Heesakkers, C. L., etc.).

Ceyssens, L.: Le 'Saint Augustin' du 17e s. L'éd. de Louvain 1577, *18e s.*, 34: 103–120. (Discusses role of Louvain profs in the preparation of the edition).

- - - - - Les voies détournées dans l'hist. du Jansénisme, in J. van Bavel and M. Schrama eds: *Jansénius et le jansénisme dans les Pays-Bas. Mélanges Lucien Ceyssens*, Louvain: 11–26. (Inform. concerning univ. of Louvain).

Clerck, K. de: De vernederlandsing van het univ. onderwijs in Vlaanderen (The devel. of Flemish teaching in univs in Flanders), in *Algemeen— Nederlands Jaarboek 1981*, Brussels/The Hague: 34–39.

Duliere, A.: Herman Meganck 1792–1853, stichter van het kol. en van de fac. Notre-Dame de la Paix (Namur) (H. M. founder of the coll. and facs of N.-D. de la P.), *Het land van Nevele*, 13: 17–24.

Engels, M. H. H.: De Franeker Academiebiblioth. voor 1700 (The library of the univ. of F. before 1700), in *Freonen om Ds J. J. Kalma hinne*, Leeuwarden (henceforth noted as *J.J.K.*): 266–84.

Feenstra, R.: Jacobus Maestertius 1610–58. Zijn juridisch onderwijs in Leiden en het Leuvense disputatiesysteem van Gerardus Corselius (J.M. His juridical teaching at L. and the L. disputation system of G.C.), *Tijdsch. voor rechtsgesch.*, 50: 297–335.

Frijhoff, W.: Deventer en zijn gemiste univ. Het Athenaeum in de socioculturele gesch. van Overijssel (The Athenaeum of D.—almost a univ.—in the soc.—cult. hist. of O.), *Overijsselse hist. bijd.*, 97: 45–79.

Grafton, A. T. and Jonge, H. J. de: *Joseph Scaliger: a bibliography 1852–1982*, The Hague.

Grauwels, J.: Limburgse studenten aan de Luikse univ. 1817–69 (Limburg students at the univ. of L. 1817–69), in *Gedenkboek Michiel Mispelon*, Kortemark–Handzame: 223–54.

Heesakkers, C. L.: The Amsterdam profs and other friends of Johannes Blasius. Amsterdam, univ. library MS VJ 50, *Lias*, 9: 179–232.

- - - - - Rademaker, C. S. M. and Blok, F. F.: *Vossius en Balaeus. 'Twee helden die der dingen diept en steilt' afpeilen: het Athenaeum Illustre en zijn eerste hoogleraren* (V. and B. Two heroes who sound the depths and the heights. The A.I. and its first profs), Amsterdam.

Heyd, M.: *Between Orthodoxy and the Enlightenment. Jean-Robert Chouet and the Introduction of Cartesian Science in the Academy of Geneva*, The Hague.

Idenburg, P. J.: *De Leidse Universiteit tegen nationaal-socialisme en bezetting* (L. univ. against nat. socialism and the occupation), Leyden.

Jong, O. J. de: *Benoemingsbeleid aan Rijksuniversiteiten 1896–1931* (The policy of appointment to the Neths state univs 1896–1931), Utrecht.

Kossmann, E. H. etc.: *De Groninger Vrijwillige Flankeurs en de Belgische Opstand 1830–31* (The G. volunteers and the Belgian revolt), Groningen.

Lanoo, I. de: *Sociale herkomsttrends in de Belgische Leuvense studentenbevolking, periode 1964–80* (Trends in the soc. origin of the students of L. 1964–80), Louvain.

Lieburg, M. J. and Toellner, R. eds: *Deutsch–Niederländische Beziehungen in der Medizin des 17. Jahrhunderts. Vorträge des Deutsch–Niederlaendische Medizinhistorikertreffens 1981*, Amsterdam (henceforth noted as *D.-N.B.*).

Lieburg, M. J.: Deutsche Studenten in Leiden 1628–88 u. d. Einführung d. Kreislauflehre William Harvey's in Holland, in *D.-N.B.*: 39–76.

Luyendijk-Elshout, A. M.: 'Der grosse Kurfürst' u. d. holländ. medizin. Wiss., in *D.-N.B.*: 25–38.

Maesschalck, E. de: Collegemaaltijden te Leuven ten tijde van Erasmus (Coll. meals at L. in the time of Erasmus), *Alumni Leuven*, 13: 12–16.

Meerts, K.: De Leuvense hoogleraar Victor Brants. Een brugfiguur in het soc.-kath. 1856–91 (The L. prof. V. B. A bridging agent for soc. cath. 1856–91), *Bijd. tot de gesch.*, 65: 197–233.

Meulemans, A.: *Farmaceutisch onderwijs te Leuven van 1794 tot 1968* (The teaching of pharmacy at L. 1794–1968), Louvain.

Petry, M. J.: *Wijsbegeerte in Rotterdam in heden en verleden* (Past and present Phil. at R.), Leyden.

Postma, F. and Krikke, A.: Bernardus Schotanus 1598–1652. Een schets van zijn rechtsgeleerd onderwijs aan de hand van een aantal onder zijn leiding verdedigde disputationes exercitii gratia (An outline of the legal teaching of B.S. as shown by some d. e.g. defended under his supervision), in *J.J.K.*: 285–301.

Quarantième anniversaire de la fermeture de l'université libre de Bruxelles, 25 nov. 1941, 2 vols, Brussels.

Ramaekers, A.: De Kruisheren en de Leuvense univ., I (The crusaders and the univ. of L.), *Clairlieu*, 40: 25–136.

Ridder-Symoens, H. de: The Elite of the Neths at the univs of the 16th cent., in M. Boelde and H. van Nuffel eds: *De eeuw van Marnix van Sint-Aldegonde* (The Cent. of M. of S.-A.), Ostende: 51–58.

Robaye, R.: Gabriel Mudée et l'enseignement du droit romain à l'univ. de Louvain au 16e s. 1536–60, *Assoc. des hists de Louvain. Résumés des mémoires de licence en hist.*, 5: 16.

Roegiers, J.: De acad. drukkerij van de oude univ. Leuven (The acad. printing house of the old univ. of L.), *Documentatieblad werkgroep achttiende eeuw*, 53–54: 143–61.

- - - - - Les théols de Louvain contre l'Edit de Tolérance 1781–82, in R. Crahay ed.: *La Tolérance civile*, Brussels: 69–78.

Schenck, F.: De Utrechtse Schl: de gesch. van de Utrechtse psychol. tussen 1945 en 1965 (The U. schl: the hist. of Psychol. at U. 1945–65), *Utrechtse hist. cahiers*, 3 (2): 1–66.

Simon-Vandermeersch, A. M.: *De eerste generaties meisjesstudenten aan de Rijksuniversiteit te Gent 1882–83 tot 1929–30* (The first generation of female students at the R.U.G.), Ghent.

Sottili, A.: Le contestate elezioni rettorali di Paul van Baenst e Johannes von Dalberg all'Univ. di Pavia, *Humanistica Lovaniensia*, 31: 29–75.

Steenmeijer-Wielenga, T. J.: De journalistieke en literaire aktiviteiten fan Pieter Troelstra yn it Groninghsch studenten Corps (The journalistic and lit. activities of P.T. in the G. student movt), in *J.J.K.*: 34–51.

Toellner, R.: Die Bedeutung d. Niederländ. Univ. f. d. Medizin in Deutschland im 17. Jh., in *D.-N.B.*: 13–24.

The *Biographie Nationale*, 42 1981–82 contains biogs of the following univ. profs: Bouny, F. (Mons 1908–50, Brussels 1950–52); Buttgenbach, H. (Liège 1921–45); Fraeijs de Veubeke, B. (Louvain 1948–76, Liège 1951–76); Goldschmidt, R. (Brussels 1906–30); Henri, V. (Zürich 1920–30, Liège 1931–40); Leclercq, R. (Brussels 1945–70); Lefèvre, M. (Louvain 1940–64); Macar, P. (Liège 1948–76); Muelenaere, R. de (Ghent 1925–52); Olbrechts, F. (Ghent, 1931–58); Straelen, V. van (Ghent 1925–34, Brussels 1928–34); Tulippe, O. (Liège 1934–66); Verriest, G. (Louvain 1906–50).

Trio, P.: De statuten van de laat-middeleeuwse clericale Onze Lieve Vrouw-Broederschap van de studenten van Parijs te Ieper (The statutes

of the late medieval clerical brotherhood of Our Lady of the Paris
students of Ypres), *Bull. de la comm. royale d'hist.*, 148: 91–141.

Verschaeren, J.: De flamingant Vuylsteke aan de univ. 1853–59 (The
Flemish nationalist V. at the univ. (of Ghent)), *Wetenschappelijke
tijdingen*, 41: 165–79.

- - - - - Hoe Julius Vuylsteke flamingant werd. De stichting van 't zal wel
gaan (How J.V. became a Flemish nationalist. The foundation of 't zal
wel gaan (a liberal student soc. of 1852)), *Wetenschappelijke tijdingen*,
41: 15–27.

Vos, L.: De Dietse studentenbeweging 1919–40 (The Flemish student movt
1919–40), in *Colloquium over de geschiedenis van de Belgisch-
Nederlandse betrekkingen tussen 1815 en 1945. Acta*, Ghent: 451–93.

- - - - - *Bloei en ondergang van het A.K.V.S. Geschiedenis van de
Katholieke Vlaamse Studentenbeweging 1914–35* (Flowering and decline
of the A.K.V.S. Hist. of the Cath. Flemish Student Movement 1914–
35), 2 vols, Louvain.

Publications 1983

Auwera, M. van der: Het korte bestaan van de 'Vlaamsche Nor-
maalleergangen' 1884–90 (The 'V.N.', their short existence 1884–90),
Onze alma mater, 37: 307–23. (Educ. of schoolmasters at university).

The *Biographie Nationale*, 43/1, contains biogs of the following univ. profs:
E. Allard (Brussels and Liège), P. Burniat (Brussels), F. Carpentier
(Liège), J. van Breda (Ghent) and F. van den Dungen (Brussels).

Bittlestone, M.: De Gentse Univ. gedurende de eerste wereldoorlog (The
univ. of Ghent during the first world war), *Wetenschappelijke tijdingen*,
42: 1–18 and 65–82.

Blaas, P. B. M.: Van Bosscha tot Kernkamp: een diversiteit van geschiedbeoefening te Amsterdam zonder Amsterdam (From B. to K. A diversity in the practice of hist. in A. without A.), *Theoret. gesch.*, 10: 303–23.

Bosquet, J.: *Le cinquantenaire du département d'acoustique de la Faculté
des sciences 1930–80*, Brussels.

Bots, H. and Frijhoff, W.: Academiereis of educatiereis? Noordbrabantse
studenten in het buitenland 1550–1750 (Acad. trip or educ. trip? Northern Brabant students abroad 1550–1750), *Batavia acad.*, 1: 13–30.

Braive, G.: Le premier prof. d'Antiquité et de latin aux facs 1858–74:
François Deruelle, *Facs univ. Saint-Louis (Brussels)*, *Bull. d'inform.*,
16: 7–8.

Brands, M. C.: Romein en Presser: eender maar vooral anders (R. and P.:
similar, but rather different), *Theoret. gesch.*, 10: 325–34.

*Centième anniversaire de l'Institut d'électricité Montefiore. Université de
Liège*, Liège.

Cohen, A. E.: Bij het afscheid van het Rapenburg (On the departure from
the Rapenburg), in *Boeken Verzamelen. Opstellen aangeboden aan*

Mr J.R. de Groot bij zijn afscheid als bibliothecaris der Rijksuniversiteit te Leiden, Leyden: 105–15.

Damme, D. van: *Universiteit en volksontwikkeling. Het 'Hooger Onderwijs voor het Volk' aan de Gentse universiteit 1892–1914* (The univ. and the devel. of the people. The 'H.O.v.h.V.' at the univ. of Ghent), Ghent.

Despy-Meyer, A.: La prov. de Hainaut et l'univ. de Bruxelles. Profs et étudiants hainuyers de 1834 à 1914, in J.M. Cauchies and J.M. Duvosquel eds: *Recueil d' études d'histoire hainuyère offertes à M.H. Arnould*, 2, Mons: 229–50.

De Verlichting in de Oostenrijkse Nederlanden en het Prinsbisdom Luik (The Enlightenment in the Austrian Neths and the Prince-Bishopric of Liège), Cat. of the exhib. in Brussels July 27-August 20 1983, Brussels: 42–50. (On the church and the univ. of Louvain).

Dewitte, A.: B. Vulcanus Brugensis. Hooglerarenambt, Correspondenten, Edita (B.V.B. Professorship, correspondents, editions), *Sacris erudiri*, 26: 311–62. (B.V.B. prof. of Greek at Leyden 1581–1614).

Dorsman, L. J.: F.J.L. Krämer: leraar, hoogleraar, archivaris 1850–1928 (F.J.L.K.: teacher, prof., archivist), *Ned. archievenblad*, 87: 219–25.

Eijl, E. J. M. van: Belangrijke bron voor de gesch. van de Leuvense Univ.: Centrum voor de studie van het Jansenisme opgericht (An important source for the hist. of L. univ.: the fndation of the centre for the study of Jansenism), *Acad. tijdingen K.U. Leuven*, 18(13) 1: 6–7.

Ellis, J. T.: The Influence of the Cath. Univ. of Louvain on the Church in the United States, *Louvain studies*, 9: 265–83.

Engels, M. H. H.: Bibliothecaris Amama aan curator Saeckma over de Franeker Universiteitsbibliotheek (Librarian A. to curator S.; the Franeker univ. library), *De vrije Fries*, 63: 34–43.

Frank van Westrienen, A.: *De Groote Tour. Tekening van de educatiereis van de Nederlanders in de 17de eeuw* (The Grand Tour. The planning of Dutch educ. visits in the 17th cent.), Amsterdam.

Frijhoff, W.: Wetenschap, beroep en status ten tijde van de Republiek: de intellectueel (Learning, profession and status during the Republic: the intellectuals), *Tijdsch. voor de gesch. der geneeskunde, natuurwetenschappen, wiskunde en tech.*, 6: 18–30.

- - - - - Le médecin selon Jacques Cahaignes 1548–1612: autour de deux soutenances en médecine à Caen au début du 17e s., *Lias*, 10: 193–215.

Geurts, P. A. M.: Voorgesch. van het Statencoll. te Leiden 1575–93 (The early hist. of the State Coll. in L. 1575–93), *Lias*, 10: 1–103.

Groen, M.: *Het wetenschappelijk onderwijs in Nederland van 1815 tot 1980. Een onderwijskundig overzicht. I. De wetgeving* (Scientific teaching in the Neths 1815–1980. I. Legislation), Eindhoven.

Hoekstra, P., Postma, F. and Veenhof, J.: *Het nachtelijke ontslag. Waarom de Kamper docent A. Steketee in 1882 moest gaan. Een gedocumenteerd verslag* (The dismissal at night. Why A.S., lect. at Kampen univ., had to leave in 1882. A doc. account), Delft.

Holk, L. E. van and Schöffer, I. eds: *Gedenkschriften van Prof. Mr R.P. Cleveringa betreffende zijn gevangenschap in 1940–1 en 1944* (Prof. R.P.C.'s memoires relating to his imprisonment in 1940–1 and 1944), Leyden.

Lanoo, I. de: Democratiseringstendensen in de samenstelling van de studentenbevolking. Een andere voorstelling (Trends to democratization in the composition of the student population. Another aspect). *Kultuurleven,* 50: 609–615.

- - - - - Het acad. en wetenschappelijk personeelsbestand. Periode 1967–83 (The acad. and scholarly component 1967–83), *Politica,* 33: 235–76.

Maesschalck, E. de: De invloed van de Leuvense universiteitscoll. op het ontstaan en de uitbouw van de seminaries in de Nederlanden (The influence of the univ. colls of Louvain on the fndation and increase of seminaries in the Neths), *Noordgouw,* 19–20: 7–13.

Mathijsen, J. A. C.: *Inventaris van de archieven van Unitas Studiosorum Rheno-Trajectina* (Inventory of the archives of the USR-T), Utrecht. (Considers the yrs 1882–1969).

Méan, E.: Un centenaire à l'univ.: l'Instit. d'électricité Montefiore, *Bull. du grand Liège,* 100: 27–31.

Meerts, K.: De Leuvense hoogleraar Victor Brants. Soc. ideeën tussen kath. romantiek en realisme 1856–91 (The L. prof. V.B. Soc. ideas between cath. romanticism and realism), *Bijd. tot de gesch.,* 66: 101–130.

Meulemans, A.: Astrologie op het leerplan van de Leuvense univ. in 1430 (Astrology in the study programme of the univ. of L. in 1430), *Volkskunde,* 84: 265–68.

The *Nationaal Biografisch Woordenboek,* 10, contains biogs of the following univ. profs: Cauwelaert, F. van (Freiburg i. Ue. 1907–10); Delva, W. (Ghent 1953–80); Elaut, L. (Ghent 1934–44); Heremans, J. (Ghent 1854–84); Kluyskens, A. (Ghent 1923–55); Lauwerys, J. (London 1932–70); Lemaire, J. F. (Ghent 1826–30, Liège 1830–47); Lipsius, Justus (Jena 1572–74, Louvain 1576–78, Leyden 1578–91, Louvain 1592–1606); Magnel, G. (Ghent 1927–55); Meeren (Mera), K. van der (Louvain 1441–83); Moke, H. (Ghent 1835–62); Verriest, G. (Louvain 1906–52).

Nauta, D.: Het benoemingsbeleid met betrekking tot de hoogleraren in de theol. in de Ned., tot ongeveer 1700 (The pol. of appointment relating to profs of theol. in the Neths around 1700), *Ned. arch. voor kerkgesch.,* 63: 36–41.

Neef, G. de: De toelating van meisjesstudenten tot de Leuvense univ. (The admission of women to L. univ. 1920), *Onze alma mater,* 37: 67–79.

Osborne, T. P.: Le 125e anniv. de la fondation du Coll. américain à Louvain, *Rev. théol. de Louvain,* 14: 260–63.

Paquet, J.: L'immatriculation des étudiants dans les univs médiévales, in

R. Lievens, E. van Mingroot and W. Verbeke eds: *Pascua Mediaevalia. Studies voor Prof. Dr J.M. de Smet,* Louvain: 159–71.

Put, E.: De hervorming van het Leuvense H. Drievuldigheidscoll. in 1755 (The reform of the Coll. of the Holy Trinity at L. in 1755), in *Onderwijs en opvoeding in de Nederlanden in de achttiende eeuw—Enseignement et éducation dans les Pays-Bas au dix-huitième siècle,* Amsterdam/ Maarssen: 85–92.

Rademaeker, C. S. M.: Het Athenaeum Illustre en de geschiedbeoefening in onze Gouden Eeuw (The A.I. and hist. research in our Golden Age), *Theoret. gesch.,* 10: 259–79.

Ramaekers, A.: De Kruisheren en de Leuvense univ., 2 (The crusaders and the univ. of L., 2), *Clairlieu,* 41: 13–138.

Ridder-Symoens, H. de: Peregrinatio Acad. doorheen Europa 13de–18de eeuw in vogelvlucht (A bird's-eye view of the Peregrinatio Acad. throughout Europe, 13th–18th cent.), *Batavia acad.,* 1: 3–11.

Robaye, R.: Droit, hist. et philol. au 16e s. Quelques exemples d'utilisation des scs auxiliaires tirés d'un cours de Gabriel Mudée, *Rev. interdisciplinaire d'études juridiques,* 10: 157–69. (G.M. law prof. at Louvain).

- - - - - Droit romain en Belg.: œuvres et bibliog. de Gabriel Mudée 1500–60, *Rev. internat. des droits de l'Antiquité,* 30: 193–209.

Roelevink, J.: *Historia* en *Antiquitates.* Het geschiedenisonderwijs aan het Athenaeum Illustre van Amsterdam in de 18de eeuw tussen Polyhist. en Verlichting (Hist. educ. at the A.I. of A. in the 18th cent. between Polyhist. and Enlightenment), *Theoret. gesch.,* 10: 281–301.

Roorda, D.J. and Looyenga, A.J.: Het prosopografisch onderzoek naar de Leidse hoogleraren 1575–1815 (Prosopographical research on profs from L. 1575–1815), *Bull. werkgroep 'Elites',* 5: 30–32.

Schoenaerts, A.-M.: Le centenaire de l'Instit. de pharmacie, *Liège-Univ.,* 34: 13.

Snelders, H. A. M.: Science in the Low Countries during the 16th cent. A survey, *Janus,* 70: 213–27. (The univs of Louvain and Leyden).

Vanbeveren, L.: Literaire wandeling door Leuven (A lit. stroll through L.), *Brabantse folklore,* 238: 61–82.

Vandermeersch, P.: Een boedelrekening van Jan Adornes 1494–1537 als bron voor universiteitsgesch. (An estate account of J. A. as a source for univ. hist.), *Lias,* 10: 175–92. (The travels of J.A.'s sons for study to Paris, Orléans, Louvain and Dôle 1550–54).

- - - - - Jacob Reyvaert, humanist en rechtsgeleerde. Enkele biog. aanvullingen (J.R. humanist and jurist. Some biograph. additions), *Brugs ommeland,* 23: 483–88. (Reconstruction of his univ. studies and univ. career).

Weijers, O.: Collège, une institution avant la lettre, *Vivarium,* 21: 73–82. (Origins of the use of the word 'college' in the medieval period).

Yakemtchouk, R.: *L'université Lovanium et sa faculté de théologie. L'action éducative de l'Univ. catholique de Louvain en Afrique centrale,* Chastre.

Publications 1984

Abeele, A. van den: Jan van Hese 1757–1803 studeerde te Leuven (J.v.H. student at L.), *Biekorf*, 84: 164–66.

Acker, A. van: *Slavische studenten aan de R.U.G. 1855–1914. Een evocatie* (Slav students at the R.U.G. 1855–1914. An evocation), Ghent.

Ashmann, M. and Feenstra, R.: *Bibliografie van Hoogleraren in de Rechten aan de Leidse Universiteit tot 1811* (Bibliogs of profs of Law at L. univ. to 1811), Amsterdam/Oxford/New York.

Aubert, R.: Les débuts de l'univ. de Louvain, *Scripta theol.*, 16: 347–58.

Betz, E. H.: Centenaire des découvertes d'Edouard van Beneden. E. van Beneden et l'univ. de Liège, *Bull. de la soc. royale des scs de Liège*, 53: 215–216.

The *Biographie Nationale*, 43/2, contains biogs of the following 19th–20th cent. univ. profs: F.-H. Kupfferschlaeger (Liège), E. Mahaim (Liège), E. Noulet (Brussels), F. Peeters (Brussels), O. Plisnier (Brussels), P. Seeldrayers (Brussels), M. Wilmotte (Liège).

Botke, Y.: *Jacobus Albertus Uilkens 1772–1825: Predikant te Lellens en Eenrum, hoogleraar in de landhuishoudkunde te Groningen* (J. A. U. 1772–1825: minister at L. and E., prof. of agronomy at G.), Groningen.

Bots, H.: L'enseignement de la médecine de l'ancienne univ. de Nimègue 1656–79, in A.H.M. Kerkhoff, A.M. Luyendijk-Elshout and M.J.D. Poulissen eds: *De novis inventis. Essays in the History of Medicine in Honour of Daniel De Moulin on the Occasion of his 65th Birthday*, Amsterdam/Maarssen: 13–25.

Coultre, M. F. le and Fraenkel, M. P.: *De platen bij de Leidse studentenalmanak 1838–97* (Pictures in the L. student almanac), Alphen a/d Rijn.

Courtois, L.: les étudiantes et l'univ. de Louvain. Les tractations préliminaires 1873–1920. Etude statistique 1920–40, *Assoc. des hists de Louvain. Résumés des mémoires de licence en hist.*, 6 (1983): 42–43.

Debrock, W.: De strijd om de 'Vlaamsche Hoogeschool' (The struggle for the Flemish univ.), in W. Debrock ed.: *Pamflet over een verborgen verleden. Links en de Vlaamse Beweging 1780–1914*, Ghent: 88–93.

Despy-Meyer, A. etc.: *1834–1984. 150 ans de vie estudiantine à l'Université Libre de Bruxelles*, Brussels.

Doumes, T. M. S. and Lonkes, P. L. J.: *Hoog Bezoek: De regerende Oranjes op bezoek bij de Groninger Universiteit 1738–1984* (Important visits: The reigning house of Orange visits G. univ. 1738–1984), Groningen.

Dronkers, J. and Stockman, F. N. eds: *Nederlandse elites in beeld: recrutering, samenhang en verandering* (Dutch elites portrayed: recruitment, cohesion and changes), Deventer.

Dunk, H. W. van der: *Spes patriae pro patria*. Studenten in het Duitse Keizerrijk (S.p.p.p. Students in the German Empire), *Theoret. gesch.*, 11: 285–90.

Dunk, H. W. van der: Van fil. tot experiment. Episoden uit de Utrechtse wiskunde en natuurwetenschappen van Regius tot Jordan (From phil. to experiment. Periods of U. maths and physics from R. to J.). Special issue of *Tijdsch. voor de gesch. der geneeskunde, natuurwetenschappen, wiskunde en tech.*, 7.

Fontaine, J.: Les laïcs et les études patristiques latines dans l'univ. fr. au 20e s., *Rev. bénédictine*, 94: 444–61.

Fontaine, P. F. M.: De lange adem van het geschiedenisonderwijs (The long inspiration of hist. teaching), *Spiegel hist.*, 19: 485–91. (Considers also univ. teaching).

Frank van Westrienen, A.: 'De Groote Tour' in de 17de eeuw (The Grand Tour in the 17th cent.), *Spiegel hist.*, 19: 404–19.

Frijhoff, W.: Matricule de la nat. germano-néerlandaise de Bourges: le second registre 1642–71 retrouvé et de nouveau transcrit, *Lias*, 11: 83–116.

Geirnaert, N.: *Inventaris van de handschriften in het stadsarchief te Brugge* (Inventory of the MSS in the archives of the City of B.), Bruges. (Some items relate to dissertations and lectures of profs of the univ. of Louvain 18th–early 19th century).

Geurts, P. A. M.: *Voorgeschiedenis van het Statencollege te Leiden 1575–93* (The early hist. of the State Coll. in L.), Leyden. (Also published in *Lias*, 10 (1983): 1–103).

Gonsalves de Mello, J. A.: Johan Bodecher Banning. Um prof. da univ. de Leiden no Brasil Holandes 1638–39, in H. Bots and M. Kerkhof eds: *Forum Litterarum. Miscelânea de Estudios Literários, Lingüisticos e Históricos oferecida a J.J. van den Besselar*, Amsterdam/Maarssen: 81–85.

Groen, M.: *Het wetenschappelijk onderwijs in Nederland van 1815 tot 1980. Een onderwijskundig overzicht. 2. Maatschappelijke Bevoegdheid* (Scientific teaching in the Neths 1815–1980. 2. Soc. Responsibility), Eindhoven.

Heesakkers, C. L. and Kamerbeek, W. G.: *Carmina Scholastica Amstelodamensia. A Selection of 16th century School-songs from Amsterdam*, Leyden.

Heisburg, G.: La dissolution de l'assoc. cath. des étudiants luxembourgeois (A.V.) par l'occupant en 1940, *Hémecht*, 36: 11–49.

Helderman, J.: Jablonski en Te Water. Twee theol. uit de tijd van de Verlichting (J. and T.W. 2 theols of the Enlightenment), *Phoenix*, 30: 54–62.

Hermans, J. M. M.: A Frenchman present at an Acad. Jubilee in Groningen. Notes on a 14th cent. Bible Historiale, now The Hague, Royal Library, MS 78 D 43, in M. Gosman and J. van Os eds: *Non Nova sed Nove. Mélanges de Civilisation médiévale dédiés à Willem Noomen*, Groningen: 95–108.

Indekeu, B.: Johannes Huybrechts (Van Loemel) 1466 ?–1532, hoogleraar, aartsdiaken, raadsheer, pauselijk commissaris en beurzenstichter (J.H. univ. prof., archdeacon, councillor, papal commissary and fnder of bursaries), *Jb. van de gesch.—en oudheidkundige kring voor Leuven en omgeving*, 24: 50–75. (J.H. taught at univ. of Louvain 1501–1515).

La Barre, A.: L'imprimerie et l'éd. à Douai au 16e at au 17e s., *De Franse Ned.-Les Pays-Bas Fr., Jb.: 99–112.* (The printing-house had close connections with the university).

Laporte, W.: *75 jaar lichamelijke opvoeding aan de R.U.G. 1908–83* (75 yrs of physical educ. at the R.U.G.), Ghent.

Leader, D. R.: John Argentein and learning in medieval Cambridge, *Humanistica Lovaniensia*, 33: 71–85.

Leeuw, R. de: Nederlanders op Grand Tour; Herinneringen aan Italië (Dutchmen on the Grand Tour. Memories of Italy), in R. de Leeuw ed.: *Kunst en Tourisme in de 18de Eeuw. Tentoonstellingskataloog*, Zwolle: 11–33.

Maes, H.: Jef van den Eynde 1879–1929, weeldekind en trekpaard van het Leuvense studentenleven (J.v.d.E., rich child and draught-horse of L. student-life), *Bijd. tot de gesch. der stad Deinze en van het land aan Leie en Schelde*, 51: 73–125.

Maesschalck, E. de: Beurzenstichtingen door Johannes van Loemel (ob. 1532) (The foundation of scholarships by J. v. L.), *Jb. van de gesch.-en oudheidkundige kring voor Leuven en omgeving*, 24: 76–88. (J. v. L. or Huybrechts taught at univ. of Louvain 1501–1515).

- - - - - De strijd om de Leuvense pedagogieën 1426–1569. Eigendomsrecht en macht in de fac. van de artes (The struggle for the Halls at L. 1426–1569. Property rights and power in the fac. of Arts), *Brabantse folklore*, 243: 162–202.

Moorman van Kappen, O. and Neve, P. L.: *Het Gerard Noodt Instituut. Studiencentrum voor Rechtsgeschiedenis aan de Faculteit der Rechtsgeleerdheid van de Katholieke Universiteit te Nijmegen* (The G. N. Inst. Centre for the study of legal hist. in the fac. of Law of the cath. univ. of N.), Nijmegen.

Otterspeer, W. ed.: *Een universiteit herleeft. Wetenschapsbeoefening aan de Leidse universiteit vanaf de tweede helft van de negentiende eeuw* (A univ. revives. Scholarly research at L. from the 2nd half of the 19th cent. onwards), Leyden.

- - - - - *Huizinga voor de afgrond. Het incident Von Leers aan de Leidse universiteit in 1933* (H. on the edge of the precipice. The V.L. incident at L. univ. 1933), Utrecht.

Peeters, V. J. D.: Anderhalve eeuw Vrije Univ. te Brussel of van ULB naar VUB (One cent. and a half of the Free Univ. of Brussels or from ULB, Frenchspeaking, to VUB, Dutchspeaking), *Brabantse folklore*, 243: 249–58.

Reinink, A. W.: De Uithof, pionieren buiten de stad om (The U., pioneering round the city), *Wonen TABK*, 14: 23–30.

- - - - - *Van Johannapolder tot Uithof. Ontstaan en ontwikkeling van een universitaire vestiging* (From J. to U. The rise and devel. of a univ. establishment), Utrecht.

Roegiers, J.: De Brabantse omwenteling in haar pol., relig. en cult. context (The Brabantine revol. in its pol., relig. and cult. context), in J. Lorette, P. Lefèvre and P. de Gryse eds: *Actes du Colloque sur la Révolution brabançonne 13–14 octobre 1983,* Brussels: 75–91. (Inform. about univ. of Louvain).

- - - - - Vijf eeuwen bibliotheekgesch. (Five cents of library hist.), *Ex officina,* 1: 7–13.

Stachurski, E.: De Poolse studenten aan de univ. te Gent van 1856 tot de eerste wereldoorlog (Polish students at the univ. of G. from 1856 to World War One), *Vlaams-Poolse tijdingen,* 2: 3–16.

- - - - - De Poolse studenten aan de univ. te Gent van 1856 tot de eerste wereldoorlog. 2. Alfabetische lijst van de studenten (Polish students at the univ. of G. from 1856 to World War One. 2. Alphabetical list of students), *Vlaams-Poolse tijdingen,* 3: 21–38.

Stroobant, J.: Les 'promoti' de la fac. des arts de l'univ. de Louvain 1535–68. Essai d'analyse statistique, *Assoc. des hists de Louvain. Résumés des mémoires de licence en hist.,* 6 (1983): 31–33.

Trio, P.: Financiering van universiteitsstudenten in de late middeleeuwen (Univ. students' finances in the late middle ages), *Onze alma mater,* 38: 141–50.

Troch, L.: *Professor J.F.J. Heremans 1825–84, pionier van het moedertaalonderwijs in Vlaanderen* (Prof. H. pioneer of teaching in the mother-tongue in Flanders), Ghent.

Uyttebrouck, A. and Despy-Meyer, A. eds: *Les cent cinquante ans de l'Université Libre de Bruxelles 1834–1984,* Brussels.

Vey Mestdagh, J.H. de: De zegels van de univ. en hogescholen in Ned. (The seals of the univs and centres of higher educ. in the Neths), in J. Meinema etc. eds: *Verzegeld Verleden. Zegels: bronnen voor de geschiedenis,* Groningen: 149–215.

Vijftig jaar Nederlandstalig Diergeneeskundig Onderwijs aan de R.U.G. (50 yrs of the teaching of Veterinary Med. at the R.U.G.), Ghent.

Weijers, O.: De terminologie van de univ. in de 13de eeuw (Terminology of the univ. in the 13th cent.), *Batavia acad.,* 2: 1–11.

Zonneveld, P. van ed.: *Het dagboek van de student Nicolaas Beets 1833–36* (The diary of the student N.B.), The Hague.

- - - - - Romantiek in de regen: de Leidse maskarade van 1835 (Romanticism in the rain: the L. masquerade of 1835), *Literatuur. Tijdsch. over Ned. letterkunde,* 1: 238–45.

Publications 1985

Academisch onderwijs te Franeker en Groningen 1585–1843: Ijver en Wedijver. Tentoonstellingscatalogus (Acad. educ. at F. and G. 1585–1843. Zeal and rivalry. Exhib. cat.), Groningen.

Bailleul, B. etc.: Een toren voor boeken 1935–85: Henry van de Velde en de bouw van de Universiteitsbiblioth. en het Hoger Inst. voor Kunstgesch. en Oudheidkunde te Gent (A tower for books 1935–85: H. van de V. and the construction of the univ. library and the Higher Inst. for Art Hist. and Archeol. in Ghent), *Monumenten en landschappen*, 4 (4): 35–42.

Bazan, B. C. etc. eds: *Les questions disputées et les questions quodlibétiques dans les facultés de théologie, de droit et de médecine*, Turnhout.

Bedaux, J. C. etc.: *Stads- of Athenaeumbibliotheek Deventer 1560–1985* (City or Athenaeum library D. 1560–1985), Deventer.

- - - - - De Stads- of Atheneumbibliotheek van Deventer 1560–1985 (The City or Athenaeum library of D. 1560–1985), *Open. Vaktijdsch. voor bibliothecarissen*, 17, 7/8: 323–28.

Berg, J. van den: Willem Bentinck 1704–74 en de theol. fac. te Leiden (W. B. and the fac. of theol. at L.), in S. Groenveld, M. Mout and I. Schöffer eds: *Bestuurders en Geleerden. Opstellen aangeboden aan Prof. Dr J.J. Woltjer bij zijn afscheid als hoogleraar van de Rijksuniversiteit te Leiden*, Amsterdam (henceforth noted as *Bestuurders en Geleerden*): 169–77.

Braive, G.: *Histoire des Facultés Universitaires Saint-Louis des Origines à 1918*, Brussels.

Brulard, T. and Wilmet, J.: Louvain-la-Neuve, une ville nouvelle originale, trois s. après Charleroi, *La Cité belge d'aujourd'hui: Quel avenir? Bull. trimestriel du Crédit Communal de Belg.* Special issue, 39 (154): 63–78. (English summary).

Briels, J. etc.: *Zuid-Nederlanders in de Republiek 1572–1630. Een demografische en cultuurhistorische studie* (South Netherlanders in the Repub. 1572–1630. A demog. and cult. study), Sint-Niklaas. (Considers univ. professors).

Bueren, H. G. van: De univ. als dierbare en dienstbare instelling. Functie en betekenis van de univ. in de informatiemaatschappij (The univ. as a beloved and serviceable inst. The univ's function and meaning in the computer soc.), *De gids*, 148, 9/10: 697–712.

Clerck, K. de: *Rector Bouckaert had toch gelijk* (Rect. Bouckaert was right after all), Ghent. (B. rect. univ. of Ghent).

Cohen, A. E.: Acht februari 1775: Gaubius' eeuwfeestrede (Feb. 8 1775. Gaubius's centenary speech), in *Bestuurders en Geleerden*: 178–86. (Considers univ. of Leyden).

Coppens, C.: Une bibl. imaginaire: de Leuvense universiteitsbiblioth. 1914–40, *Ex officina*, 2: 64–69. (Private libraries obtained by univ. between the world wars and destroyed May 1940).

Crahay, R.: Les censeurs louvanistes d'Erasme, in J. Marx ed.: *D'Erasme à Campanella*, Brussels: 14–39.

Depaepe, M.: De toelatingsvoorwaarden tot de univ. in België. Een hist. overzicht (Conditions of admission to the univ. in Belgium. A hist. survey), *Onze alma mater*, 39: 119–50. (Post 1816).

Decavele, J.: Kerk en Onderwijs tijdens de Gentse Calvinistische Repub. (Church and educ. during the Ghent Calvinistic Repub.), in J. Decavele ed.: *Het eind van een rebelse droom. Opstellen over het calvinistisch bewind te Gent 1577–84 en de terugkeer van de stad onder de gehoorzaamheid van de koning van Spanje 17 sept. 1584*, Ghent: 63–88.

Derez, M.: Met soetigheyt en stantvasticheyt. Een Leuvens Juristengeslacht 1680–1840 (With sweetness and firmness. A family of L. jurist profs: the Winix), *Ex officina*, 2: 37–38.

Dolderer, W.: Van aktivisme naar bolsjevisme? Het studentengenootschap 'Flandria' te Göttingen (From activism to bolshevism? The student soc. 'Flandria' in G.), *Wetenschappelijke tijdingen*, 44 (2): 111–22.

300 jaar chemie te Leuven 1685–1985. Tentoonstelling in de Universiteitshal 14 nov.–7 dec. 1985 (300 yrs of Chem. in L. Exhib. in the univ. hall), Louvain.

'Een toren voor boeken' 1935–85. Henry van de Velde en de bouw van de Universiteitsbibliotheek en het Hoger Instituut voor Kunstgeschiedenis en Oudheidkunde te Gent (A tower for books 1935–85. H. van de V. and the construction of the univ. library and the Higher Inst. for Art Hist. and Archaeol. in Ghent), Cat. of an exhib., Ghent.

Evers, M.: De Illustre Schl te Harderwijk 1600–47. De gesch. van een moeizaam bestaan (The I. Schl at H.1600–47. The hist. of a difficult existence), *Batavia acad.*, 3 (2): 25–35.

- - - - - The Illustre Schl at Harderwijk 1600–47, *Lias*, 12: 81–113.

Feenstra, R.: Johann Friedrich Boeckelmann 1632–81. Een markant Leids hoogleraar in de rechten (J.F.B. An outstanding L. prof. of Law), in *Bestuurders en Geleerden*: 137–50.

- - - - - Een terugblik op de dissertatie als element in de juridische opleiding (A rev. of the dissertation as an element in legal educ.), *Ars aequi*, 34: 18–20.

Figures de Professeurs de Pharmacie à l'Université de Louvain. Debiève, Marius: Un pharmacien révolutionnaire Jean-Baptiste Van Mons. Bruylants, Albert: Gustave Bruylants, Fernand Ranwez et leur école de pharmacie, Louvain-la-Neuve.

Franeker Folianten. Frieslands Universiteitsbibliotheek 1585–1713 (F. volumes. Friesland's univ. library 1585–1713), Franeker.

Franeker hogeschool en Athenaeum: Wegwijzer voor documenten in de Provinciale Bibliotheek van Friesland (F. univ. and Atheneum. Guide to docs in the prov. library of Friesland), Leeuwarden.

Frijhoff, W.: Crisis of Modernisering. Hypothesen over de ontwikkeling van het voortgezet en het hoger onderwijs in Holland in de 18e eeuw (Crisis or Modernization. Hypotheses on the devel. of higher educ. in Holland in the 18th cent.), *Holland*, 17 (1): 37–56.

- - - - - *L'intellectuel néerlandais à l'époque moderne: citoyen de deux Républiques, Liège.* (Considers univs and secondary schools).

Geurts, P. A. M.: De eerste Limburgse priesters naar een Ned. univ.: het voorbeeld van A. H. Geurts 1889–93 (The first priests from L. at a Dutch univ.: the example of A.H.G.), *De Maasgouw*, 104: 183–90.

Goeyse, M. de: Drie Leuvense studentikoze historieliederen (3 student-like hist. songs from L.), *Brabantse folklore*, 248: 335–49. (From the 20th century).

- - - - - Een symbool. Het vaandel van het Vlaams Verbond te Leuven (A symbol. The banner of the Flemish soc. at L.), *Onze alma mater*, 39: 231–43.

Groen, M.: *Het wetenschappelijk onderwijs in Nederland van 1815 tot 1980. Een onderwijskundig overzicht. 3 Godsgeleerdheid; 4 Rechts-geleerdheid; 5 Geneeskunde; 6 Maatschappelijke Bevoegdheid de wet-geving* (Scholarly teaching in the Neths 1815–1980. 3 Theol.; 4 Jurisprudence; 5 Med.; 6 Soc. responsibility: legislation), Eindhoven.

Ijsseling, S.: Fil. in de moderne univ. Centraal punt en randverschijnsel (Phil. in the modern univ. Main thrust and fringe devels), *Wijsgerig perspectief*, 26: 111–117.

Janssen, J. and Voestermans, P.: *Politiek, universiteit en student* (Pols, univ. and the student), Baarn.

Jensma, G. T.: De Franeker Hogeschl- een (buiten)gewestelijke univ? (F. highschl. An outer-prov. univ.?), *Batavia acad.*, 3 (2): 36–40.

- - - - - Smit, F. R. H. and Westra, F. eds: *Universiteit te Franeker 1585–1811. Bijdragen tot de Geschiedenis van de Friese Hogeschool* (F. univ. 1585–1811. Contributions to the hist. of the Friesian highschl), Leeuwarden.

Juvens-Geerkens, J.: Studiebeurzen, rijke bron aan informatie voor famil-ievorsers (Scholarships, a rich source of inform. for family research), *Vlaamse stam*, 21: 147–74, 228.

Lambotte, R.: L'enseignement de l'obstétrique à Liège, in *Mille ans d'aide sociale 985–1985. L'art de guérir, la pauvreté, l'enfance. Exposition*, Liège: 12–13.

Langendries, E.: *De 'Vlaamse Hoogeschool' te Gent 1916–18. Deel A* (The 'Flemish Univ.' at Ghent 1916–18, Part A), Ghent.

Luyendijk-Elshout, A. M.: Leidse medische studenten over 'anima pathemata' in de 18de-eeuwse proefschriften (Students from L. on the 'anima pathemata' in 18th cent. dissertations), in *Bestuurders en Geleerden: 161–68.*

Martens, P.: La fac. des scs agronomiques de Gembloux de 1860 à 1895, *Bull. du cercle art et hist. de Gembloux et environs*, 2: 353–67, 369–77, 385–92.

Martin, D.: *De Rijksuniversiteit te Gent tijdens de bezetting 1940–44* (The R.U.G. during the occupation 1940–44), Ghent.

Muijen, A. S. C. A.: Oriëntatie: Salomons huis als fakkel van de vooruitgang (Orientation: S.'s house as a torch of progress), *Wijsgerig perspectief*, 26: 133–6. (Scientif. Revoln of 17th cent. at Dutch universities).

Napjus, J. W. and Lindeboom, G. A.: *De hoogleraren in de geneeskunde aan de hogeschool en het Athenaeum te Franeker. Verzamelde opstellen*

(Profs in Med. at the highschl and athenaeum at F. Collected papers), Amsterdam.

Nave, F. de: Editeurs et imprimeurs dans le Nord de 1580 au 18e s. La signification de l'émigration anversoise, *Bull. vereniging voor de gesch. van het Belg. Protestantisme*, 10: 109–18.

Nienes, A. P. van etc.: *De archieven van de universiteit te Franeker 1585– 1812* (The archives of the univ. of F. 1585–1812), Leeuwarden.

Nissen, P. J. A.: Waar studeerde Johannes de Lovanio? (Where did J. de L. study?), *De Maasgouw*, 104: 172–9. (At Bologna 1412 and 1438).

Orléans en Leiden. De universitaire geschiedenis van Orléans vanuit Leiden belicht (O. and L. O.'s univ. hist. from a L. point of view). Cat. of an exhib., Leyden.

Otterspeer, W.: Vereenvoudiging en bezuiniging. Een 19de-eeuwse discussie over taakverdeling en concentratie (Simplification and economizing. A 19th cent. discussion on the division of tasks and concentration), in F. van der Meer ed.: *Universiteit in Beweging. Een aantal beschouwingen bij gelegenheid van het 410-jarig bestaan van de R.U. Leiden*, Leyden: 239–61.

- - - - - and Aerts-van Bueren, J.E.: *Werkplaatsen van Wijsheid, Geleerdheid en het Ware Geloof of de wisselwerking tussen de Universiteiten van Leiden en Franeker* (Workcentres for wisdom. Learning and the mixture of beliefs between the univs of L. and F.), Franeker.

Postma, F.: Abbe Wybes, drukker van acad. disputaties te Franeker 1597–99 (A. W., printer of acad. disputations in F. 1597–99), *De vrije Fries*, 65: 87–98.

- - - - - *Disputationes exercitii gratia. Een inventarisatie van disputaties verdedigd onder Sibrandus Lubbertus, professor Theologiae te Franeker 1585–1625 (D. e. g.* An inventory of disputations defended under S. L. prof. of Theol. in F. 1585–1625), Amsterdam.

Reinink, A. W.: Univ. onderkomens en hun bestudering (The study of univ. lodgings), *Batavia acad.*, 3 (1): 1–10.

Ridderikhoff, C. M., Ridder-Symoens, H. de and Illmer, D. eds: *Premier livre des procurateurs de la nation germanique de l'ancienne université d'Orléans, 3. Tables, Additions et Corrections, Illustrations*, Leyden.

Schavemaker, C.: Bijna twee eeuwen grondwettelijke staatszorg voor de univ. (Almost 2 cents of govt concern for the univs), *Wijsgerig perspectief*, 26: 128–33.

Schoeffer, I.: Een kortstondig hoogleraarschap. Johan Valckenaer in Leiden 1795–96 (A short professorship. J.V. in L. 1795–96), in *Bestuurders en Geleerden*: 193–208.

- - - - - Een Leids hoogleraar in pol. moeilijkheden. Het ontslag van Johan Luzac in 1796 (A prof. from L. in trouble. J.L.'s dismissal in 1796), in J.F. Heijbroek, A. Lammers and A.P.G.J. van der Linde eds: *Geen schepsel wordt vergeten. Liber amicorum voor Jan Willem Schulte Nordholt*, Amsterdam: 61–80.

Schramme, A.: De Universitasbeweging 1940–60 (The univ. movt 1940–60). Thesis. Louvain.

- - - - - Univ., meer dan een studentenbeweging (Univs, more than a movt of students), *Onze alma mater,* 39: 251–64.

Servotte, H.: Rector De Somer: een visie, een beleid (Rect. De S. An attitude with discretion), *Onze alma mater,* 39: 189–97.

Simon-Vandermeersch, A. M.: *Inventaris Archief RUG 1817–1981* (Inventary of the Archives of the R.U.G. 1817–1981), Ghent.

Simons, E. J. and Felling, A. J. A.: De kath. intellect. elite 1946–75 (The cath. intellect. elite 1946–75), *Mens en maatschappij,* 60 (1): 26–42.

Soetens, C. and Sauvage, P.: *Les années 30 aux Facultés Saint-Louis,* Brussels.

Somer, P. de: *Een visie op de universiteit* (A view of the univ.), Louvain.

Stachurski, E.: Poolse studenten en navorsers aan de univ. te Gent van 1856 tot 1980 (Polish students and researchers at Ghent univ. 1856–1980), in F. Vyncke ed.: *Handelingen van het Internationaal Colloquium, Nederlands-Poolse Kulturele Ontmoetingen,* Ghent: 121–34.

Trio, P.: Een handschrift van de clericale Onze Lieve Vrouw-broederschap van studenten van Parijs in het Rijksarchief te Brugge, 14de eeuw (A MS of the clerical confraternity of Our Lady of students of Paris from Ypres preserved in the State Archives in Bruges, 14th cent.), *Handelingen van het genootschap voor gesch. Soc. d'émulation de Bruges,* 122: 5–25.

Uyttebrouck, A.: 'L'incident Reclus' à travers les archives officielles de l'Univ. Libre de Bruxelles, in *Elisée Reclus. Colloque organisé à Bruxelles les 1 et 2 février 1985 par l'Institut des Hautes Etudes de Belgique et la Société royale belge de géographie,* Brussels: 23–52. (E.R., geographer and anarchist 1830–1905, prof. at univ. of Brussels).

Vandenghoer, C.: Van aqua sublimata tot hexametyleentetramine: 300 jaar chemie te Leuven (From a.s. to h.: 300 yrs of Chem. at L.), *Ex officina,* 2: 115–118.

Vandermeersch, P.: Brugse studenten aan de univ. Studiekosten en studiefinanciering in de tweede helft van de zestiende eeuw (Students from B. at the univ. Cost of and payment for studies in the second half of the 16th cent.), *Handelingen van het genootschap voor gesch. Soc. d'émulation de Bruges,* 122: 27–63. (Inform. about univ. of Louvain).

- - - - - Het onderwijs aan de Leuvense univ. einde 16de-begin 17de eeuw (Teaching at univ. of L. late 16th-early 17th cent.), *Spiegel hist.,* 20 (5): 215–22.

- - - - - The Reconstruction of the Liber Quintus Intitulatorum Universitatis Lovaniensis 1569–1616. An Application: the Theologians 1562–78, *Lias,* 12: 1–80.

Veen, T.: Hardewijkse promoti en Nijmeegse Studenten (H. promotions and students from N.), in P.L. Nève and E.C.C. Coppens eds: *Sine invidia communico. Opstellen aangeboden aan Prof. Dr A.J. de Groot, Nijmegen* (henceforth noted as *Sine invidia communico*): 243–72.

Visser, J.: *Album collegii studiosorum ex gymnasio Leovardiensi 1626–68*, Franeker.

Weijers, O.: L'appellation des profs au 13e s., in *Sine invidia communico:* 303–20.

Zonneveld, P. van and Berkvens-Stevelinck, C.: *De Leidse maskerade van 1835* (The L. pageant of 1835), Leyden.

The British Isles

Additions to Earlier Lists

For 1978
Highfield, J. R. L. ed.: H. W. Garrod: An indenture between William Rede, bish. of Chichester, and John Bloxham and Henry Stapilton, fellows of Merton College, Oxford, London, 22 Oct. 1374, *Bodleian library record*, 10: 9–19.

For 1979
Jessup, F. W.: *Wolfson College, Oxford. The Early Years*, Oxford.

Williams, M. E.: *The Venerable English College Rome: A History 1579–1979*, London.

For 1980
Cobban, A. B.: The medieval Cambridge colls: a quantitative study of higher degrees to *c.*1500, *Hist. of educ.*, 9: 1–12.

- - - - - The King's Hall, Cambridge, and English medieval coll. hist., in B. Tierney and P. Linehan eds: *Authority and Power. Studies on Medieval Law and Government Presented to Walter Ullman on his Seventieth Birthday*, Cambridge: 183–95.

Simpson, A. H.: Opportunities for Higher Education in the USSR, with special reference to the period 1956–72. Thesis. Birmingham.

Szreter, R.: Landmarks in the institutionalisation of sociology of educ. in Britain, *Educ. rev.*, 32: 293–300. (Considers the period 1954–80).

For 1981
Brockliss, L. W. B.: Aristotle, Descartes and the new sciences. Nat. Phil. at the univ. of Paris 1600–1740, *Annals of science*, 38: 33–69.

Davie, G. E.: *The Democratic Intellect: Scotland and her Universities in the Nineteenth Century*, Edinburgh.

Hammerton, E. and Cannadine, D.: Conflict and consensus on a ceremonial occasion: The Diamond Jubilee in Cambridge in 1897, *Hist. jnl*, 24: 111–46.

Le Guillou, M.: Tech. educ. 1850–1914, in G. Roderick and M. Stephens eds: *Where did we go wrong? Industrial Performance Education and the Economy in Victorian England*, Lewes (henceforth noted as *Where did we go wrong?*): 173–84.

Looney, J.: Undergraduate educ. at early Stuart Cambridge, *Hist. of educ.*, 10: 9–19.

Roderick, G. and Stephens, M.: The univs, in *Where did we go wrong?*: 185–201.

Tolley, B.: Tech. educ. and the Univ. Coll. of Nottingham, in *Where did we go wrong?*: 203–217.

Publications 1982

Allan, A. R.: The study and teaching of Theol. at the univ. of Liverpool, *Univ. of Liverpool recorder*, 90: 31–37.

Anning, S. T. and Walls, W. K. J.: *History of the Leeds School of Medicine*, Leeds.

Bettenson, E. M.: The Hutchens affair, *Durham univ. jnl*, 43: 159–98. (A *cause celebre* at the Coll. of Med. in Newcastle).

Bondos-Greene, S. A.: The end of an era: Cambridge Puritanism and the Christ's Coll. election of 1609, *Hist. jnl*, 25: 197–208.

Claeys, G. A.: A utopian Tory revolutionary at Cambridge: the pol. ideas and schemes of James Bernard 1834–39, *Hist. jnl*, 25: 583–603.

Clapp, B. W.: *The University of Exeter: A History*, Exeter.

Cobban, A. B.: Theol. and Law in the medieval colls of Oxford and Cambridge, *Bull. of the John Rylands library*, 65: 57–77.

Cohen, L., Thomas, J. and Manion, L. eds: *Educational Research and Development in Britain 1970–80*, Windsor. (Notes hist. studies on the devel. of higher education).

Courtenay, W. J. and Tachau, K. H.: Ockham, Ockhamists, and the Eng.–German nat. at Paris 1339–41, *Hist. of univs*, 2: 53–96.

Cruickshank, M. ed.: *Thirty Years of education at Keele 1951–81*, Chester/Keele.

Ellis, E. L.: Dr Thomas Jones, C. H., and educ., *Trans of the honourable soc. of Cymmrodorian*: 86–109. (T.J. active in univ. and extension education).

Forster, H.: The rise and fall of the Cambridge muses 1603–1763, *Trans of the Cambridge bibl. soc.*, 8 (2): 141–72. (Celebratory verse produced in the university).

Griffith, W. P.: Welsh Students at Oxford, Cambridge and the Inns of Court in the 16th Century. Thesis. Univ. of Wales.

Harding, A. F.: Durham univ. museum 1833–1982, *Trans of the architect, and archaeol. soc. of Durham and Northumberland*, 6: 37–43.

Heesom, A.: *The founding of the University of Durham*, Durham.

- - - - - Who thought of the idea of the univ. of Durham? *Durham county local hist. soc. bull.*, 29: 10–20.

Hird, M.: *Doves and dons: a history of St Mary's College Durham, an account of the women's Hostel 1899–1920 and some impressions of later college life*, Durham.

Hughes, Q.: Before the Bauhaus. The experiment at the Liverpool schl of Architect. and Applied Arts, *Architect. hist.*, 25: 102–13.

Jarausch, K. H.: Students, sex and politics in Imperial Germany, *Jnl of contemp. hist.*, 17: 285–303.

Jones, G. L.: *The Discovery of Hebrew in Tudor England. A Third Language*, Manchester. (Contains much inform. about univ. study of Hebrew).

Kadish, A.: *The Oxford Economists in the late Nineteenth Century*, Oxford.

Madden, F. and Fieldhouse, D. K. eds: *Oxford and the Idea of Commonwealth*, Beckenham.

McDowell, R. B. and Webb, D. A.: *Trinity College, Dublin 1592–1952: An Academic History*, Cambridge.

Moore, G.: *The University of Bath: the Formative Years 1949–69*, Bath.

Paquet, J.: Coût des études, pauvreté et labeur. Functions et métiers d'étudiants au Moyen Age, *Hist. of univs*, 2: 15–52.

Porter, R.: The nat. sciences tripos and the Cambridge schl of Geology 1850–1914, *Hist. of univs*, 2: 193–216.

Powers, A. A. R.: Architectural Education in Britain 1880–1914. Thesis. Cambridge.

Rosa, S. de: Studi sull'univ. di Pisa, 1, Alcune fonti inedite: Diari, lettere e rapporti dei bidelli 1473–1700, *Hist. of univs*, 2: 97–125.

Rother, W.: Zur Gesch. d. Basler Universitätsphil. im 17 Jh., *Hist. of univs*, 2: 153–91.

Shafe, M.: *University Education in Dundee 1881–1981. A Pictorial History*, Dundee.

Sharpe, K.: The fndation of the chairs of hist. at Oxford and Cambridge: an episode in Jacobean pols, *Hist. of univs*, 2: 127–52.

Southgate, D. G.: *University Education in Dundee: a centenary history*, Edinburgh.

Swanson, R. N.: *A History of Christ's College Boat Club 1830–1980*, Cambridge.

Twiss, G. P.: *Famous Rectors of St Andrews*, St Andrews.

Tyacke, N.: Science and relig. at Oxford before the Civil War, in D. Pennington and K. Thomas eds: *Puritans and Revolutionaries. Essays in 17th Century History Presented to Christopher Hill*, Oxford: 73–93.

Williams, M.: The contribution of University Extension towards Adult Education on Merseyside before 1918. Thesis. Liverpool.

Wright, H. M.: *Lord Leverhulme's Unknown Venture. The Lever Chair and the Beginnings of Town and Regional Planning 1908–48*, London. (Lever Chair of Civic Design and its holders at the univ. of Liverpool).

Yates, T. E.: *A College remembered: St John's College Durham 1909–79*, Durham.

Publications 1983

Anderson, R. D.: *Education and opportunity in Victorian Scotland: Schools and Universities*, Oxford.

Binns, J. W.: Dr John Rainolds. An Elizabethan Scholar, *The pelican*: 51–55.

Blyth, J. A.: *English University Adult Education 1908–1958: The Unique Tradition*, Manchester.

Davies, J. M.: Student libraries in 16th cent. Toulouse, *Hist. of univs*, 3: 61–86.

Dent, C. M.: *Protestant Reformers in Elizabethan Oxford*, Oxford.

Dodd, C.: *The Oxford and Cambridge Boat Race*, London.

Donaldson, G. ed.: *Four centuries: Edinburgh University Life 1583–1983*, Edinburgh.

Fletcher, J. M. and Upton, C. A.: Destruction, repair and removal: An Oxford coll. chapel during the Refn, *Oxoniensia*, 48: 119–30.

Fozzard, J. A. F.: *Professors of Anatomy in the University of Cambridge: the first two hundred and sixty one years of the Cambridge University Department of Anatomy 1707–1968*, Cambridge.

French, R.: Med. teaching in Aberdeen: From the fndation of the univ. to the middle of the 17th cent., *Hist. of univs*, 3: 127–57.

Giles, G. J.: National Socialism and the educ. elite in the Weimar Repub., in P. D. Stachura ed.: *The Nazi Machtergreifung 1933*, London: 49–67.

Grave, W. W.: *FitzWilliam College, Cambridge 1869–1969. Its History as the Non-Collegiate Institution of the University and its beginnings as an Independent College*, Cambridge.

Gregor, I.: Newman's *Idea of a University* a text for today, in T. R. Wright ed., *John Henry Newman: A man for our Time?* Newcastle upon Tyne: 18–27.

Halliday, J. S.: The Dept of Indust. Studies, *Univ. of Liverpool recorder*, 92: 137–47.

Jack, D. B.: The univ. of Tartu (Dorpat) 1632–1982: A rev. of its contrib. to the pharmacol. sciences, *Trends in pharmacol. sciences*, 4 (3): 99–101.

James, R. R.: *Albert, Prince Consort*, London. (Inform. about A's period as chancellor of Cambridge).

Jones, G. and Quinn, M.: *Fountains of Praise: University College, Cardiff 1883–1983*, Cardiff.

Parker, R.: *Town and Gown: the 700 years' war in Cambridge*, Cambridge.

Philip, I.: *The Bodleian Library in the Seventeenth and Eighteenth Centuries*, Oxford.

Phillips, D. ed.: *German Universities after the Surrender. British Occupation Policy and the Control of Higher Education*, Oxford.

Simpson, R.: *How the PhD Came to Britain. A Century of Struggle for Postgraduate Education*, Guildford.

Sondheimer, J.: *Castle Adamant in Hampstead: A History of Westfield College 1882–1982*, London.

Stubbings, F. H.: *The Statutes of Sir Walter Mildmay for Emmanuel College*, Cambridge.

- - - - - *Emmanuel College: An Historical Guide*, Cambridge.

Szreter, R.: Opportunities for women as univ. teachers in England since the Robbins Report of 1963, *Studies in higher educ.*, 8: 139–50.

Publications 1984

Allan, A. R.: The building of Abercromby Square, *Univ. of Liverpool recorder*, 95: 318–25, 97 (1985): 93–102.

Black, M.: *Cambridge University Press 1584–1984*, Cambridge.

Briggs, A.: *Toynbee Hall. The First Hundred Years*, London.

Carey, H: *Mansfield Forbes and his Cambridge*, Cambridge. (Inform. about the fac. of Eng. between the wars).

Catto, J. l. ed.: *The History of the University of Oxford*, 1, *The Early Oxford Schools*, Oxford.

Couve de Murville, M. N. L. and Jenkins, P.: *Catholic Cambridge*, London.

Dooley, B.: Science teaching as a career at Padua in the early 18th cent., *Hist. of univs*, 3: 115–51.

Dransfield, A.: Applied Sciences at the Colleges of the Victoria University. Thesis. Leeds.

Engel, A. J.: *From Clergyman to Don; the Rise of the Academic Profession in 19th Century Oxford*, Oxford.

Feingold, M.: *The mathematicians' apprenticeship. Science, universities and society in England 1560–1640*, Cambridge.

Fisher, J. R.: The Centre for Latin American Studies, *Univ. of Liverpool recorder*, 95: 311–18.

Fowler, L. and H.: *Cambridge Commemorated: An Anthology of University Life*, Cambridge.

Furlong, B.: *Liverpool University Athletic Union: The first one hundred years 1884–1984*, Liverpool.

Gascoigne, J.: Maths and meritocracy: The emergence of the Cambridge math. tripos, *Soc. studies of science*, 14: 547–84.

– – – – – Politics, patronage and Newtonianism: the Cambridge example, *Hist. jnl*, 27: 1–24.

Gwynn Williams, J.: *Centenary Lecture: The Founding of the University College of North Wales, Bangor*, Newtown.

Hendry, J. ed.: *Cambridge Physics in the Thirties*, Bristol.

Henry, H. E. M. and Crook, A. C. ed.: Use of Rooms from Early Times to 1983. Part 1 of *Use and Occupancy of Rooms in St John's College*, Oxford.

Keynes, M.: *A House by the River. Newnham Grange to Darwin College: a history of the site, buildings and former inhabitants*, Cambridge. (Reprint of the limited ed. of 1976).

Kibre, P.: *Studies in Medieval Science: Alchemy, Astrology, Mathematics and Medicine*, London. (Many essays relating to universities).

McKitterick, D.: *Four Hundred Years of University Printing and Publishing in Cambridge 1584–1984. A Catalogue of the Exhibition in the University Library, Cambridge,* Cambridge.

Oldfield, S.: *Spinsters of this Parish: The Life and Times of F.M. Mayor and Mary Sheepshanks,* London. (Life at Newnham Coll. in the late 19th century).

Pauwels, J. R.: *Women, Nazis and Universities: Female University Students in the Third Reich 1933–45,* London.

Roderick, G. W.: *Post-School Education. England and America in the Nineteenth Century,* London.

Schmitt, C. B.: *The Aristotelian Tradition and Renaissance Universities,* London.

Sutherland, L. S. (ed. A. Newman): *Politics and Finance in the Eighteenth Century,* London. (Several essays relating to Oxford university).

Szreter. R.: Some forerunners of sociology of educ. in Britain: an account of the lit. and influences c.1900–50, *Westminster studies in educ.,* 7: 13–43. (Refs especially to the L.S.E.).

Thomas, J.B.: The origins of teacher training at Univ. Coll. Cardiff, *Jnl of educ. admin. and hist.,* 16 (1): 10–16.

Publications 1985

Boylan, M.: *The University of Sheffield: A Pictorial History,* Sheffield.

Brooke, C.: *The History of Gonville and Caius College,* Woodbridge.

Brooke, C. N. L.: The churches of medieval Cambridge, in D. Beales and G. Best eds: *History, Society and the Churches. Essays in Honour of Owen Chadwick,* Cambridge: 49–76. (Inform. about coll. chapels).

Deacon, R.: *The Cambridge Apostles: A History of Cambridge University's Elite Intellectual Secret Society,* London.

Fletcher, J. M. and Upton, C. A.: The cost of undergraduate study at Oxford in the 15th cent.: the evidence of the Merton Coll. 'Founder's Kin', *Hist. of educ.,* 14: 1–20.

– – – – – Expenses at admission and determination in 15th cent. Oxford: new evidence, *Eng. hist. rev.,* 100: 331–38.

Footman, D.: *Antonin Besse of Aden. The Founder of St Antony's College, Oxford,* London.

Gascoigne, J.: The univs and the scientific revoln. The case of Newton and Restoration Cambridge, *Hist. of science,* 23: 391–434.

Hall, J. T. D. ed.: *The Tounis College: An Anthology of Edinburgh University Student Journals 1823–1923,* Edinburgh.

Ker, N. R. (ed. A. G. Watson): *Books, Collectors and Libraries: Studies in the Medieval Heritage,* London.

Godwin, H.: *Cambridge and Clare,* Cambridge. (Life at Clare Coll. 1919–85).

Gwynn Williams, J.: *The University College of North Wales: Foundations 1884–1927*, Cardiff.

Harman, P. M. ed.: *Wranglers and Physicists: Studies on Cambridge Mathematical Physics in the Nineteenth Century*. Manchester.

Mabro, J.: *I Ban Everything. Free Speech and Censorship in Oxford between the Wars: Some Episodes in the History of the University of Oxford and Ruskin College*, Oxford.

Macfarlane, L. J.: *William Elphinstone and the Kingdom of Scotland 1431–1514: The Struggle for Order*, Aberdeen. (Detailed discussion of fndation of univ. of Aberdeen).

Marriott, S.: *University Extension Lecturers: The Organisation of Extramural Employment in England 1873–1914*, Leeds.

Moss, G. P.: *From Palace to College: An Illustrated Account of Queen Mary College*, London.

Phillips, D. E.: *Student Protest 1960–70: An analysis of the Issues and Speeches*, London.

Roderick, G. W.: *Universities: The Pursuit of Bread, Knowledge and Freedom*, Swansea.

Russell, E.: Marian Oxford and the Counter Refn, in C. M. Barron and C. Harper-Bill eds: *The Church in Pre-Reformation Society. Essays in Honour of F.R.H. Du Boulay*, Woodbridge: 212–27.

Smalley, B.: *The Gospels in the Schools c.1100–c.1280*, London.

Publications 1986

Brockliss, L. W. B.: *French Higher Education in the 17th and 18th Centuries. A Cultural History*, Oxford.

Bush, Jr, S. and Rasmussen, C. J. eds: *The Library of Emmanuel College, Cambridge 1584–1637*, Cambridge.

Carswell, J.: *Government and the Universities in Britain: Programme and Performance 1960–80*, Cambridge.

Feingold, M.: The occult tradition in the English univs of the Renaissance: a reassessment, in B. Vickers ed., *Occult and Scientific Mentalities in the Renaissance*, Cambridge: 73–94.

Fletcher, I.: An English tragedy: the acad. lawyer as jurist, in T. M. Charles-Edwards, M. E. Owen and D. B. Walters eds: *Lawyers and Laymen. Studies in the History of Law presented to Professor Dafydd Jenkins on his seventy-fifth birthday*, Cardiff: 316–35.

Gash, N.: Peel and the Oxford Univ. election of 1829, in N. Gash: *Pillars of Government and other Essays on State and Society c.1770–c.1880*, London: 67–76.

- - - - - Oxford pols in the chancellor's election of 1834, in N. Gash: *Pillars of Government and other Essays on State and Society c.1770–c.1880*, London: 93–97.

Griffin, P.: *St Hugh's: One Hundred Years of Women's Education in Oxford*, Basingstoke.

Harte, N.: *The University of London 1836–1986: An Illustrated History*, London.

Jack, D. B.: Dastardly deeds at Dorpat, *Pharmaceut. hist.*, 14 (3): 9–12.

Logan, D.: *The Birth of a Pension Scheme: A History of the Universities Superannuation Scheme*, Liverpool.

Marsh, N.: *The History of Queen Elizabeth College: One Hundred Years of University Education in Kensington*, London.

McKitterick, D.: *Cambridge University Library: A History. The 18th and 19th Centuries*, Cambridge.

McLaren, C. A.: The process of curricular change. The pathol. question at Aberdeen 1875–84, *Aberdeen univ. rev.*, 51: 474–84.

- - - - - P. J. Anderson and the hist. of the univ., *Aberdeen univ. rev.*, 51: 83–101.

Molland, A. G.: Duncan Liddell 1561–1613. An early benefactor of Marischal Coll. Library, *Aberdeen univ. rev.*, 51: 495–99.

Morgan, J.: *Godly Learning. Puritan Attitudes towards Reason, Learning and Education 1560–1640*, Cambridge. (Discusses role of coll. tutors).

Oates, J. C. T.: *Cambridge University Library: A History From the Beginnings to the Copyright Act of Queen Anne*, Cambridge.

Ovenall, R. F.: *The Ashmolean Museum 1683–1894*, Oxford.

Patrick Edwards, G.: Aberdeen and its classical traditions, *Aberdeen univ. rev.*, 51: 410–26.

- - - - - William Elphinstone, his coll. chapel and the second of April, *Aberdeen univ. rev.*, 51: 1–17.

Queen Alexandra's House. 'For Present Comfort and Future Good?' The Story of Queen Alexandra's House 1884–1984, London. (A residence of London University).

Reid, J. S.: Patrick Copland 1748–1822. Connections outside the coll. courtyard, *Aberdeen univ. rev.*, 51: 226–50.

Slee, P. R. H.: *Learning and a Liberal Education: The Study of History in the Universities of Oxford, Cambridge and Manchester*, Manchester.

Symonds, R.: *Oxford and Empire: The Last Lost Cause?* London.

Weber, R. G. S.: *The German Student Corps in the Third Reich*, London.

Williams, M. E.: *St Alban's College, Valladolid. Four Centuries of English Catholic Presence in Spain*, London.

Canada

Additions to Earlier Lists

For 1979

Descoteaux, J. G.: *Faculté de Droit, Université d'Ottawa 1953–78*, Ottawa.

Peel, B.: *The University of Alberta Library*, Edmonton.

For 1980

Hughes, J. L.: *The First Athabaska University*, Edmonton.

Matais, R.: *Le Centre médicale de l'Université de Sherbrooke: un esquisse de son histoire 1961–79*, Sherbrooke.

Publications 1982

Desilets, A. etc.: *Les 25 ans de l'Université de Sherbrooke,* Sherbrooke.
Milne, D. etc. eds: *The Garden Transformed,* Charlottetown. (Concerns univ. of Prince Edward Island).
Osmond Lewry, P.: Four graduation speeches from Oxford MSS *c.*1270–1310, *Mediaeval studies,* 44: 138–80.
Saint-Jean: une institution qui s'adapte . . . 1908–83, Edmonton.

Publications 1983

Boyle, L. E.: 'Alia lectura fratris Thome', *Mediaeval studies,* 45: 418–29.
Gibson, F.W.: *Queen's University, 2, 1917–61,* Kingston.
Hayden, M.: *Seeking a Place. University of Saskatchewan 1907–82,* Vancouver.
McCalla, A. G.: *The Development of Graduate Studies at the University of Alberta 1908–83,* Edmonton.
McPhedan, M. G.: *Reflections. Nursing Education at U.N.B. 1958–83,* Fredericton.
Thomson, D.: The Oxford grammar masters revisited, *Mediaeval studies,* 45: 298–310.

Publications 1984

Archer, J. H.: *The University of Regina: A History,* Regina.
Ferns, H. S.: *Reading from Left to Right: One Man's Political History,* Toronto. (Communist activities at Cambridge in 1930's).
Frost, S. B.: *McGill University: For the Advancement of Learning, 2, 1895–1971,* Montreal.
Millard, P. ed.: Roger North: *General Preface and Life of Dr John North,* Toronto. (Ed. of biog. of Mast. of Trinity coll. Cambridge in 17th cent. by his brother).
Murray, D. R. and R. A.: *The Prairie Builder. Walter Murray of Saskatchewan,* Edmonton.
Reid, J. G.: *Mount Allison University: A History to 1963,* 2 vols, Toronto.

Publications 1985

Farge, J. K., Bujanda, J. M. de and Higman, F. M.: *Index de L'Université de Paris, 1544, 1545, 1547, 1549, 1551, 1556,* Sherbrooke. (Vol. 1 of the collection 'Index des Livres Interdits', ed. J. M. de Bujanda).
Osmund Lewry, P. ed.: *The Rise of British Logic,* Toronto. (Several papers on Oxford logicians of late Middle Ages and their connections with the continent).

Czechoslovakia

Additions to Earlier Lists

For 1979

Danilák, M., Srogoň, T. and Tylešová, M.: *Pedagogická fakulta v Prešove UPJŠ v Košiciach* (The fac. of Pedagogics at Prešov), Prešov.

For 1980

Vysoká škola ekonomická v Bratislave 1940–80 (The univ. for Economics at Bratislava 1940–80), Bratislava.

For 1981

Čech, F. ed.: *Přírodovědecká fakulta Univerzity Karlovy 1920–80. Dějiny—současnost—perspektivy* (The fac. of Nat. Sciences of the Charles Univ. Prague 1920–80), Prague.

Magdolenová, A.: Slovenské školstvo v prvých poprevratových rokoch (The Slovak schl system in the yrs after 1918), *Hist. časopis*, 29: 482–505. (Summaries in French and Russian).

Tříška, J.: Životopisný slovník předhusitské pražské univerzity 1348–1409—Repertorium biographicum Universitatis Pragensis prehussiticae (A biograph. reg. of the univ. of Prague 1348–1409), Prague. (Text in Latin).

Vidmanová, A.: Stoupenci a protivníci mistra Jana Husi (The supporters and opponents of master J.H.), *Husitský Tábor,* 4: 49–56.

Publications 1982

Čedík, M.: Národnostní otázka a rozdělení pražské univ. (The nat. question and the division of the univ. of Prague 1882), *AUC: Hist. Univ. Carol. Prag.,* 22, Fasc. 1: 15–25. (Summary in German).

Hájek, B., Manová, I. and Niklíček, L.: Prof. Vojtěch Šafařík a počátky výuky chemie na české univ. v Praze (Prof. V.Š., the promotor of chem. studies at the Czech univ. Prague), *AUC: Hist. Univ. Carol. Prag.,* 22, Fasc. 1: 71–79. (Summary in German).

Havránek, J.: Česká univ. v jednání rakouských úřadů do roku 1881 (The division of Prague univ. in the Viennese insts before 1881), *AUC: Hist. Univ. Carol. Prag.,* 22, Fasc. 1: 35–69. (Summary in German).

Hlaváčková, L.: Vybudování toretických ústavů české lékařské fak. v letech 1883–84 (The construction of the theoret. insts of the Czech med. fac. in Prague 1883–84), *AUC: Hist. Univ. Carol. Prag.,* 22: Fasc. 1: 123–52. (Summary in German).

Kapišinská, K. and Klička, K.: *Univerzita P. J. Šafárika v Košiciach* (The P.J.Š. univ. at Košice. A bibliog.), Košice.

Kejř, J.: Neznámý aparát ke Klementinám (A previously unknown MS with remarks on the Clementinum), *Studie o rukopisech,* 21: 61–72. (Summary in German).

Kouřil, M.: Moravští šlechtici na olomoucké univ: do konce 17. st. (Moravian noblemen at the univ. of Olomouc to the end of the 17th cent.), in *Pokrokové proudy ve výchově a vzdělání na jižní Moravě v uplynulých 350 letech. 11. mikulovské symposium 1981*, Prague (henceforth noted as *Symposium 1981*): 169–71.

Krejčová, H.: Soupis fondů prof. a docentů pražské univ., uložených v Literárním archivu Památníku národního písemnictví (A list of personal papers of profs of Prague univ. in the Lit. archive in Prague), *Zprávy Archivu Univ. Karlovy*, 4: 100–121.

Lekárska fakulta UK v Bratislave 1919–79 (The fac. of Med. of the univ. at Bratislava 1919–79), Bratislava.

Litsch, K.: F. L. Rieger o univ. otázce v českém sněmu roku 1866 (The question of a Czech univ. in the diet of Bohemia in 1866 and the activities of F.L.R.), *AUC: Hist. Univ. Carol. Prag.*, 22, Fasc. 1: 27–33. (Summary in German).

Lomič, V.: *Vznik, vývoj a současnost Českého vysokého učení technického v Praze* (The origin, devel. and present state of the Czech TU in Prague), Prague. (Summaries in English and Russian).

Magdolenová, A.: Slovenské školstvo v predmníchovskom Československu (The Slovak schl system in interwar Czechoslovakia), *Hist. časopis*, 30: 272–311.

Pešek, J.: Tiskárna a sklad knih mistra Daniela Adama z Veleslavína (The printing office of master D.A. de V.), *Zprávy Archivu Univ. Karlovy*, 4: 64–79.

- - - - - and Svatoš, M.: Mistr Koldín a právní kultura pražských měst (Master K. and the legal culture of Prague towns in the 16th cent.), in K. Maly ed.: *Městské právo v 16.–18. st. v Evropě*, Prague: 289–97. (Summary in German).

Polišenský, O.: Zápisní kniha Akčního výboru SPF a Spolku posluchačů fil. z let 1945–47 (The book of the assoc. of students of the fac. of Phil. 1945–47), *Zprávy Archivu Univ. Karlovy*, 4: 122–30.

Raková, I.: Činnost pražské univ. v době bavorského kralování v Čechách 1741–43 (The activities of Prague univ. in the period of Bavarian rule over Bohemia 1741–43), *AUC: Hist. Univ. Carol. Prag.*, 22, Fasc. 2: 43–64. (Summary in German).

- - - - - and Svatoš, M.: Proměny vztahu pražské univ. a nižšího školství v 16. a 17. st. (The changing relations of Prague univ. with lower schls in the 16th and 17th cents), in *Symposium 1981: 194–99*.

Schmid, L.: Prof. Mikuláš Franchimont z Frankenfeldu a jeho rod (Prof. M.F. de F. and the genealogy of his family), *Zprávy Archivu Univ. Karlovy*, 4: 89–99.

Šmahel, F.: Regionální původ, profesionální uplatnění a soc. mobilita graduovaných studentů Karlovy univ. v letech 1433–1622 (Prague graduate students, their origins and careers 1433–1622), *Zprávy Archivu Univ. Karlovy*, 4: 3–28.

- - - - - Univ. kvestie a polemiky mistra Jeronýma Pražského (Univ. *quaestiones* and the polemics of master Hieronymus of Prague), *AUC: Hist. Univ. Carol. Prag.*, 22, Fasc. 2: 7–41. (Summary in German).

Spurný, F.: Studenti z jižní Moravy na olomoucké univ. v 16.–17.st. (Students from southern Moravia in the univ. of Olomouc in the 16th–17th cents), in *Symposium 1981:* 215–217.

Svatoš, Ma.: Univ. působení filologa Josefa Krále (The univ. activities of the philologist J.K.), *AUC: Hist. Univ. Carol. Prag.*, 22, Fasc. 2: 65–108. (Summary in German).

Svatoš, Mi.: Studenti z českých zemí na univ. v Siené 1573–1738 (Bohemian students at the univ. of Siena 1573–1738), *Zprávy Archivu Univ. Karlovy*, 4: 29–63.

Syllaba, T.: První český vědecký seminář na pražské univ. (Gebauerův slovanský seminář) (The first Czech inst. at Prague univ.—the slavonic dept under J. Gebauer), *AUC: Hist. Univ. Carol. Prag.*, 22, Fasc. 1: 95–112. (Summary in German).

Urfus, V.: Právní romanistika na české univ. v Praze před sto lety (K zakladatelskému dílu Leopolda Heyrovského) (The study of Roman Law in Prague under Prof. L.H. a cent. ago), *AUC: Hist. Univ. Carol. Prag.*, 22, Fasc. 1: 113–121. (Summary in German).

Vaněček, V.: 'V Praze budou . . . dvé univ . . . ' (The law concerning the organ. of the Prague univs from 1882), *AUC: Hist. Univ. Carol. Prag.*, 22, Fasc. 1: 7–14. (Summary in German).

France

Additions to Earlier Lists

For 1978

Favreau, R.: *La ville de Poitiers à la fin du Moyen Age. Une capitale régionale*, 2 vols, Poitiers. (Inform. about univ. of Poitiers 15th century).

Viguerie, J. de: Quelques observations au sujet des univs fr. au 18e s., in *Travaux sur le 18e s.*, Angers: 57–74.

For 1979

Dulieu, L.: *La médecine à Montpellier*, 2: *La Renaissance*, Avignon.

Miaille, M.: Sur l'enseignement des facs de droit en France, *Procès* (Lyon), 3: 78–107. (Considers reforms of 1905, 1922 and 1954).

Poupard, P.: Trente ans d'enseignement sup. cath. 1945–75, *Rev. de droit canonique*, 29: 94–103.

For 1980

Gallego Barnés. A.: Reforma de las clase de Gramática 1561–89 en la Univ. de Valencia, in *Actes du I Colloque sur le Pays Valencien à l'époque moderne, Pau 1978*, Pau: 55–74.

Le Van-Lemesle, L.: La promotion de l'écon. pol. en France au 19e s. jusqu'à son introduction dans les facs 1815–81, *Rev. d'hist. moderne et contemp.*, 27: 270–94.

Merlin, P.: *L'université assassinée. Vincennes 1968–80,* Paris.

For 1981

Barman, G. and Dulioust, N.: *Etudiants-ouvriers chinois en France 1920– 40,* Paris. (Cat. of archives).

Beltran, E. and Dahan, G.: Un hébraïsant à Paris vers 1400: Jacques Legrand, *Arch. juives,* 17: 41–49.

Caudron, A.: Un vivier de militants chrétiens: la fac. libre de droit de Lille entre 1895 et 1914, *Ensemble d'écs sup. et de facs cath.* (Lille), n.s., 1: 3–11.

Chevallier, P.: Jacques Hennequin, doct. de Sorbonne et fond. de la Bibl. de Troyes, *Mém. de la soc. acad. du dépt de l'Aube,* 1979–81, 110: 245– 72.

Clemens, J.: Dossier d'un étudiant de l'univ. Pau (18e s.), *Rev. de Pau et du Béarn,* 9: 77–79.

Compere, M.-M. and Julia, D.: Les colls sous l'Ancien Régime. Présentation d'un instrument de travail, *Hist. de l'éduc.,* 13: 1–27.

Ciurana, A.: *La création de l'Ecole de Pharmacie de Montpellier et ses premiers maîtres 1803–60,* Montpellier.

Deguy, J.: Lanson enseignant progressiste, *L'amitié Charles Péguy,* 4: 39–56. (Considers the position around 1900).

Dehon, G.: La réforme du statut de l'univ. de Douai en 1749, *Rev. du Nord,* 63: 289–90.

Dulieu, L.: *La faculté des sciences de Montpellier depuis ses origines jusqu'à nos jours,* Avignon.

Favre, P.: Les scs d'Etat entre déterminisme et libéralisme. Emile Boutmy 1835–1096 et la création de l'Ec. libre des scs pol., *Rev. fr. de sociologie,* 22: 429–65.

Flahaut, J.: La révolte des étudiants en pharmacie de Paris en avril-mai 1886, *Rev. d'hist. de la pharmacie,* 28: 229–41.

Gerbod, P.: Les univs fr. à l'époque de Péguy 1890–1914, *L'amitié Charles Péguy,* 4: 27–38.

Grimal, P., Carcopino, C. and Ourliac, P.: *Jérôme Carcopino: un historien au service de l'humanisme,* Paris. (J.C. held several important educ. positions, especially ministry for nat. educ. and youth 1940–1941).

Jarousseau, G.: Les officiers de l'univ. de Poitiers portant la masse ou la verge à la fin du 16e s., *Bull. de la soc. des antiquaires de l'ouest,* 4e sér., 16:125–32.

Julia, D.: *Les trois couleurs du tableau noir. La Revolution,* Paris. (Considers projects for reform of education).

Ory, P.: L'univ. fr. face à la persécution antisémite, in *La France et la question juive. Colloque,* Paris: 79–94.

Oulhiou, Y.: *L'Ecole Normale supérieure de Fontenay-aux-Roses à travers le temps: 1880–1980,* Fontenay-aux-Roses.

Ourliac, P.: L'*epistola tholosana* de 1402, in *Mélanges P. Vigreux,* Paris: 563–78. (A work from univ. of Toulouse relating to the Schism).

Plattard, J.: Un étudiant écossais en France en 1665–66, *Bull. de l'assoc. Guillaume Budé,* 2: 215–23. (Concerns John Lauder).

Ribaut, J.-P.: En marge d'un centenaire; l'univ. cath. de Lille et le premier Congrès eucharistique internat., *Ensemble d'écs sup. et de facs cath.* (Lille), 2; 73–81.

Shinn, T.: Des scs indust. aux scs fondamentales: la mutation de l'Ec. sup. de physique et de chimie 1882–1970, *Rev. fr. de sociologie,* 22: 167–82.

Steegmann, R.: Etudiants et profs: la fac. de médecine de Strasbourg au 18e s., *Saisons d'Alsace,* 75: 171–84.

Thuillier, G.: Les projets d'E.N.A. et de nationalisation de l'Ec. libre des scs pol. 1876-81, *Rev. admin.,* 201: 250–57 and 202: 352–60.

Trocchio, F. di: Paul-Joseph Barthez et l'*Encyclopédie, Rev. d'hist. des scs,* 34: 123–36. (P.-J.B. prof. of Med. at Montpellier).

Publications 1982

Beylard, H.: Les Jésuites à Douai aux 17e et 18e s., *Les amis de Douai,* 8: 189–91.

Bindet, J.: L'univ. de Paris et le clergé d'Avranches aux 17e et 18e s., *Rev. de l'Avranchin et du pays de Granville,* 59: 210–211.

Brunot, A. and Coquand, R.: *Le corps des Ponts-et-Chaussées,* Paris. (The training of French engineers in 19th and 20th centuries).

Burney, J.: La fac. des Lettres de Toulouse de 1830 à 1875, *Annales du Midi,* 94: 277–99.

Buttoud, G.: Les elèves de l'Ec. des eaux-et-forêts 1825–1964: contribution à une soc. hist. de l'admin. forestière fr., *Rev. forestière fr.,* 34: 6–14.

Callot, J.-P. and Journau, P.: *Histoire de l'Ecole Polytechnique,* Paris/ Limoges. (Re-ed. of the commemorative work 1958).

Cassagnes-Brouquet, S.: La violence des étudiants à Toulouse à la fin du 15e et au 16e s. 1460–1610, *Annales du Midi,* 94: 245–62.

Coquerel, R.: De quelques lettres d'étudiants du début du 19e s., *Bull. de la soc. Ramond* (Bagnères-de-Bigorre, Htes Pyrénées), 117: 81–96.

Dastugue, P. and Wagner, N.: L'univ. de Strasbourg à Clermont 1939–44, *Rev. d'Auvergne,* 96: 436–49.

Dillemann, G. ed.: *La Faculté de pharmacie de Paris 1882–1982,* Saint-Cloud.

Dumas, A.; De la manière dont était nommé le rect. de l'ancienne univ. d'Angers, *Mém. de l'acad. des scs, belles-lettres et arts d'Angers,* 1981–82, 5/6: 57–63.

- - - - - D'un procès survenu en 1744 au sujet de la nomination du rect. de l'univ. d'Angers, *Mém. de l'acad, des scs, belles-lettres et arts d'Angers,* 1981–82, 5/6: 247–55.

Frijhoff, W. and Sonnet, M.: Bibliog. d'hist. de l'éduc. fr. (année 1979 et suppléments des années antérieures), *Hist. de l'éduc, 15–16: 3–205.*

Guenée, S.: *Les Universités françaises des origines à la Révolution. Notices historiques sur les Universités, Studia et Académies protestantes,* Paris.

Guenoun, A. S.: Gérard de Solo, maître de l'univ. de médecine de Montpellier et practicien du 14e s., *Ec. Nat. des Chartes. Position des thèses*: 75–82.

Hermet, S.: Le coll. de Foix de Toulouse et son rétablissement à la veille de la Rév., *Archistra (Arch.-Hist.-Traditions)* (Toulouse), 54: 23–24.

Histoire de l'Université d'Orléans, Orléans.

Lefrançois, M.: Philippe Le Bas, fils de conventionnel et admin. de la Bibl. de la Sorbonne 1846–60, *Mél. de la Bibl. de la Sorbonne,* 3: 89–109.

Luc, J.-N. and Barbe, A.: *Des Normaliens. Histoire de l'Ecole normale supérieure de Saint-Cloud,* Paris.

Magliulo, B.: *Les Grandes Ecoles,* Paris.

Menache, S.: La naissance d'une nouvelle source d'autorité: l'univ. de Paris, *Rev. hist.,* 544: 305–27. (The univ. of Paris as pol. and theol. authority early 14th century).

Nebbiai Dalla Guarda, D.: Le coll. de Paris de l'abbaye de Saint-Denis en France, in *Sous la Règle de Saint-Benoît,* Paris/Geneva: 461–88.

Noël, J.-C.: Daily life at the Irish Coll. in Nantes 1775–80, *Cahiers du Centre d'Etudes Irlandaises,* 7: 81–88.

Peach, T.: Le droit romain en français au 16e s.: deux oraisons de François de Némond 1555, *Rev. hist. de droit fr. et étranger,* 60: 5–44. (F. de N. prof. univ. of Poitiers).

Revel, J.: Univ. et soc. dans l'Europe moderne: position des problèmes, in J. Le Goff and B. Köpeczi eds: *Objet et méthodes de l'histoire de la culture,* Paris/Budapest: 53–72.

Rivet, R.: Un médecin de Perpignan, prof. à l'univ. de Montpellier: Joseph Anglada 1775–1833, in *Comptes rendus du 106e Congrés national des Sociétés savantes. Section des Sciences,* 4, Paris: 111–117.

Thuillier, G. and Guiral, P.: *La vie quotidienne des professeurs en France de 1870 à 1940,* Paris.

Tuilier, A.: La fond. de la Sorbonne, les querelles univ. et la pol. du temps, *Mél. de la Bibl. de la Sorbonne,* 3: 7–43.

Verger, J.: Des écs à l'univ.: la mutation institutionnelle, in R. H. Bautier ed.: *La France de Philippe Auguste. Le temps des mutations,* Paris: 817–46.

Vulliez, C.: Le monde univ. orléanais au temps de Jeanne d'Arc, in *Jeanne d'Arc. Une époque, un rayonnement. Colloque d'histoire médiévale,* Paris: 123–37.

- - - - - Une étape privilégiée de l'entrée dans la vie: le temps des études univ. à travers l'exemple orléanais des derniers s. du Moyen Age, in *Les entrées dans la vie. Initiations et apprentissages,* Nancy: 149–81.

Publications 1983

Bataillon, L.-J.: Les conditions de travail des maîtres de l'Univ. de Paris au 13e s., *Rev. des scs phil. et théol.*, 67: 417–32.

Bibliog. d'hist. de l'éduc. fr. Titres parus au cours de l'année 1980 et supplément des années antérieures, *Hist. de l'éduc.*, 19–20: 5–218.

Bozzolo, C. and Ornato, E.: La production du livre manuscrit en France du Nord, ch. in *Pour une histoire du livre manuscrit au Moyen Age. Trois essais de codicologie quantitative*, Paris: 13–121. (Considers univ. MSS and libraries).

Bruneau, W. A.: Sc., opportunisme, pol. Deux perspectives sur Louis Liard et la rénovation de l'enseignement sup. fr. 1884–1902, in W. Frijhoff ed.: *L'offre d'Ecole. Colloque de Sèvres*, Paris: 277–84.

Carbonell, C.-O. and Livet, G. eds: *Au berceau des Annales. Le milieu strasbourgeois, l'histoire en France au début de 20e siècle*, Toulouse. (Inform. about univ. of Strasbourg).

Charle, C.: Le champ univ. parisien à la fin du 19e s., *Actes de la recherche en scs soc.*, 47/48: 77–89. (Consequences of the reform of Fr. universities).

Colin, M.: Univ. de Dijon et figures univ. à la fin du 19e s. d'après des souvenirs familiaux 1888–1902, *Mém. de l'acad. des scs, arts et belles-lettres de Dijon*, 125: 103–119.

Debal, J. ed.: *Histoire d'Orléans et de son terroir*, 3 vols, Roanne. (Refs to univ. of Orléans).

Dulieu, L.: *La médecine à Montpellier*, 3/1, *L'Epoque Classique. Histoire*, Lille.

Geffre, J.: Les relations univ.-écon. à Bordeaux de 1925 à 1975. L'action de l'Union de l'univ., de l'agriculture, du commerce et de l'industrie de Bordeaux et de la région, *Actes de l'acad. de Bordeaux*, 8: 79–98.

Gerbod, P.: Le financement de l'enseignement sup. et de la recherche en France au 19e s. 1801–1900, *La rev. admin.*, 36: 544–50.

Giard, L.: Hist. de l'Univ. et hist. du savoir: Padoue 14e–16e s., *Rev. de synthèse*, 110: 139–69.

Godin, A.: Origénisme et antiorigénisme à la fac. de théol. de Paris au 16e s., *Mél. de la Bibl. de la Sorbonne*, 4: 6–29.

Jullien de Pommerol, M.-H.: La Bibl. de l'Univ. de Médecine de Montpellier en 1506, *Bibl. de l'Ec. des Chartes*, 141: 344–51.

Karady, V.: Les profs de la Répub. Le marché scolaire, les réformes univ. et les transformations de la fonction prof. à la fin du 19e s., *Actes de la recherche en scs soc.*, 47/48: 90–112.

Le Van-Lemesle, L.: L'écon. pol. à la conquête d'une légitimité 1896–1937, *Actes de la recherche en scs soc.*, 47/48: 113–117. (Origins of the teaching of pol. econ. in fac. of Law).

Magnaudet-Barthe, A.: Edmond Richer et la réforme de l'Univ. de Paris 1594–1610, *Ec. Nat. des Chartes. Position des thèses*: 143–49.

Martin, M. L. trans. and ed.: *De la liberté intellectuelle et de la dignité de la vocation universitaire. Ecrits de Max Weber*, Toulouse.

Mazon, B.: La naissance de la 6e section de l'Ec. pratique des Hautes Etudes: genèse d'une instit., *Commentaires*, 22: 433–36.

Monchablon, A.: *Histoire de l'UNEF de 1956 à 1968*, Paris.

Mornet, E.: Le voyage d'études des jeunes nobles danois du 14e s. à la Réforme, *Jnl des Savants:* 287–318.

Tanaka, M.: La nation anglo-allemande de l'université de Paris à la fin du Moyen Age, 2 vols. Thesis. Ec. des Hautes Etudes en Scs sociales, Paris.

Thepot, A.: Les instits sc. et tech. au 19e s., *Hist. de l'éduc*, 18: 83–95.

Thuillier, G.: *L'ENA avant l'ENA*, Paris.

- - - - - Les projets d'Ec. des scs pol. sous la Rév. et l'Empire, *Rev. admin.*, 36: 124–32.

Tuilier, A.: La notion romano-byzantine de *studium generale* et les origines des nations dans les univs médiévales, *Bull. philol. et hist. (jusqu'à 1610)*, 1981: 7–27.

- - - - - L'Univ. de Paris, le chancelier Gerson et l'union avec les Grecs, *Bull. philol. et hist. (jusqu'à 1610)*, 1980: 165–83.

Tulard, J.: Aux origines de la recherche sc. en France: l'Ec. pratique des Hautes Etudes, *Commentaires*, 22: 430–32.

- - - - - L'Univ. napoléonienne, in *Histoire de l'Administration de l'Enseignement en France 1789–1981*, Paris/Geneva: 11–17.

Publications 1984

Belhoste, B. and Lutzen, J.: Joseph Liouville et le Coll. de France, *Rev. d'hist. des scs*, 37: 255–304. (Teaching of Physics and Maths in 19th century).

Bibliog. d'hist. de l'éduc. fr. Titres parus au cours de l'année 1981 et supplément des années antérieures, *Hist. de l'éduc.*, 23–24: 3–210.

Bressolette, C.: *Le pouvoir dans la société et dans l'Eglise: l'ecclésiologie politique de Mgr Maret, doyen de la faculté de théologie de la Sorbonne au 19e siècle*, Paris.

Cabanis, A. and Martin, M.-L.: Les étudiants étrangers en France: notes préliminaires sur leur démographie 1880–1980, *Annales de l'Univ. des scs soc. de Toulouse*, 32: 197–227.

Calvignac, J.-P.: 1879–83; quand naissait le corps des bibliothécaires univ., *Mél. de la Bibl. de la Sorbonne*, 5: 57–79.

Caujolle, F.: L'œuvre toulousaine de Paul Sabatier 1854–1940, *Auta,* 497: 164–72. (Prof. and Nobel Prize winner for Chemistry).

Chevalier, J.-C.: Victor Cousin et l'enseignement sup., in *Mélanges en l'honneur de Gérald Antoine*, Paris: 487–95.

Cholvy, G. ed.: *Histoire de Montpellier*, Toulouse. (Inform. about university).

Cohen, P.: Les élèves cath. de l'Ec. Normale Sup. 1906–14, *Cahiers d'hist.*, 29: 33–46.

Compere, M.-M. and Julia, D.: *Les collèges français 16e–18e siècles*, 1, *Répertoire*. *France du Midi*, Paris.

Despierres, G.: *Histoire de l'enseignement médical à Lyon, de l'Antiquité à nos jours*, Lyon.

Forado, S.: Difficiles débuts de l'univ. de Toulouse, *Auta*, 499: 227–35.

Frijhoff, W.: Univs et soc. à propos d'un projet de la Conférence europ. des rects, *Hist. de l'éduc.*, 22: 19–25.

Garrisson-Estebe, J.: L'Acad. d'Orthez au 16e s., in *Arnaud de Salette et son Temps*. *Colloque internationale*, Orthez: 77–86.

Gerbod, P.: Les Facs des Lettres de 1809 à 1815, in *Actes du 109e Congrès national des Sociétés savantes. Section d'histoire moderne et contemporaine*, 2, Paris: 377–88.

Haut, F.: Vers la liberté de l'enseignement sup. 1870–75, *Annales d'hist. des facs de droit*, 1: 37–56.

Imbert, J.: Passé, présent et avenir du doctorat en droit en France, *Annales d'hist. des facs de droit*, 1: 11–35.

Kaluza, Z.: Le chancelier Gerson et Jérôme de Prague, *Arch. d'hist. doctrinale et littéraire du Moyen Age*, 51: 81–126.

- - - - - and Vignaux, P.: *Preuve et raisons à l'Université de Paris. Logique, ontologie et théologie au 14e siècle*, Paris.

Limacher, P.: *Inventaire des livres du 16e siècle à la Bibliothèque de la Sorbonne*, 1, *Sciences, science politique, médecine*, Paris.

Marchasson, Y.: Le renouveau de l'enseignement du droit canonique en France; l'œuvre de Pierre Gasparri à l'Instit. cath. de Paris, *Rev. de l'Instit. cath. de Paris*, 9: 57–74.

- - - - - L'Hist. des religions à l'Instit. cath. de Paris de 1880 à 1900: l'œuvre de Paul de Broglie et la *Rev. des Religions*, *Rev. de l'Instit. cath. de Paris*, 9: 41–54.

Masson-Marechal, A.: L'Univ. de Paris au début du 16e s. Ed. des registres 12, 13 et 14 des 'Conclusions des Nats réunies' 1512–37, *Ec. Nat. des Chartes. Position des thèses*: 115–120.

Mathieu, B.: La Fac. de Droit de Dijon sous le Premier Empire, in *Actes du 109e Congrès national des Sociétés savantes. Section d'histoire moderne et contemporaine*, 2, Paris: 97–112.

Maurier, H.: L'enseignement de Mgr Le Roy et l'hist. des religions à l'Instit. cath de Paris, *Rev. de l'Instit. cath. de Paris*, 11: 61–66.

Mayeur, F.: Une réforme réussie de l'enseignement sup. en France, *Hist. de l'éduc.*, 22: 3–17. (Changes at the close of 19th century).

Noailles, P.: *L'Ecole centrale de Paris*, Paris.

Pacaut, M.: L'encadrement péd. d'hist. et de géog. à la fac. des Lettres de Lyon 1838–1938, *Cahiers d'hist.*, 29: 265–84.

Pecker, A. ed.: *La médecine à Paris du 13e au 20e siècle*, Paris.

Perville, G.: *Les étudiants algériens de l'Université française 1880–1962*.

Populisme et nationalisme chez les étudiants et intellectuels musulmans algériens de formation française, Paris.

Rapp, F.: Les Alsaciens et les univs à la fin du Moyen Age, *Acad. des inscriptions et belles-lettres. Comptes rendus*, 2: 250–63.

Retat, L.: Renan et les problèmes de l'enseignement sup., *Commentaires*, 27: 535–45.

Reverdin, O.: *Les premiers cours de grec au Collège de France ou l'enseignement de Pierre Danès d'après un document inédit*, Paris.

Schaub, J.-F.: Les quatre colegios mayores de Salamanque et la crise de l'Université 1700–1730. Thesis. Paris 1.

Sirinelli, J.-F.: Khâgneux et normaliens des années vingt: contribution à l'hist. des intellectuels fr., *Bull. de la soc. d'hist. moderne*, 21: 6–17.

Tachau, K. H.: French Theol. in the Mid-14th cent., *Arch. d'hist. doctrinale et littéraire du Moyen Age*, 51: 41–80.

Thomann, M.: Strasbourg, capitale hist. des droits de l'homme et du citoyen: théorie et pratique d'une doctrine univ. au 17e et au 18e s., *Saisons d'Alsace*, 86: 45–54.

Thuillier, G.: Un projet d'éc. de pol. vers 1780, *La rev. admin.*, 37: 133–37.

Todericiu, D.: Balthasar-Georges Sage 1740–1824 chimiste et minéralogiste fr., fond. de la première Ec. des mines 1783, *Rev. d'hist. des scs*, 37: 29–46.

Theuriot, J.: L'Univ, de Dôle au 15e s., *Mém. de la soc. d'émulation du Jura. Travaux*, 1981–82: 493–518.

Trenard, L.: Univs, colls et écs en France au s. des Lumières, in *Les Lumières en Hongrie. Colloque*, Paris/Budapest: 263–88.

Université d'Avignon. *Etudes Vauclusiennes*, 33. Special edition.

Verdier-Castagne, F.: La délinquance univ. dans les lettres de rémission, in *Actes du 107e Congrès national des Sociétés savantes—Section de philologie et d'histoire jusqu'à 1610*, 1, Paris: 283–98.

Verger, J.: L.exégèse de l'Univ., in P. Riché and G. Lobrichon eds: *Le Moyen Age et la Bible*, Paris: 199–232.

Vulliez, C.: Pouvoir royal, univ. et pouvoir municipal à Orléans dans les 'années 80' du 14e s., in *Actes du 105e Congrès national des Sociétés savantes—Section de philologie et d'histoire jusqu'à 1610*, Paris: 187–200.

Publications 1985

Actes du 110e Congrès national des Sociétés savantes—Section d'histoire des sciences et des techniques, 2, *Histoire de l'Ecole médicale de Montpellier*, Paris.

Bazan, B. C. etc. eds: *Les questions disputées et les questions quodlibétiques dans les facultés de Théologie, de Droit et de Médecine*, Paris.

Bibliog. d'hist. de l'éduc. fr. Titres parus au cours de l'année 1982 et supplément des années antérieures, *Hist. de l'éduc.*, 27–28: 3–192.

Blanc, A., Lorenz, C. and Vire, M.: Origine des matériaux de l'ancien coll.

des Bernardins à Paris, in O. Chapelot and P. Benoit eds: *Pierre et métal dans le bâtiment au Moyen Age*, Paris: 237–54.

Calvignac, J.-P.: Naissance d'une instit. napoléonienne: Conseil et Conseillers de l'Univ. impériale, *Mél. de la Bibl. de la Sorbonne*, 6: 59–82.

Caron, J.-C.: La jeunesse des écs à Paris 1815–48. Approche statistique d'un groupe soc., *Sources—Travaux hist.*, 1: 31–45. (Students of the Paris facs in 1st half of 19th century).

Charle, C. and Ferre, R. eds: *Le Personnel de l'enseignement supérieur en France aux 19e et 20e siècles*, Paris.

Chiavassa-Gouron, I.: Les lectures des maîtres et étudiants du coll. de Navarre: un aspect de la vie intellect. à l'univ. de Paris 1380–1520, *Ec. Nat. des Chartes. Position des thèses*: 31–37.

Chouillet, J.: Un projet de réforme de l'Univ. au 18e s., le *Plan d'une Université* de Denis Diderot pour l'Impératrice de Russie, *Mél. de la Bibl. de la Sorbonne*, 6: 47–58.

Compere, M.-M.: *Du Collège au lycée 1500–1850. Généalogie de l'enseignement secondaire français*, Paris. (Considers univ. colls of Ancien Régime).

Fabiani, J.-L.: Enjeux et usages de la 'crise' dans la phil. univ. en France au tournant du s., *Annales. E.S.C.*, 40e année, 2: 377–409.

Feenstra, R. and Ridderikhoff, C. M. eds: Etudes néerland. de droit et d'hist. présentées à l'univ. d'Orléans pour le 750e anniv. des enseignements juridiques. Special issue of *Bull. de la soc. archéol. et hist. de l'Orléanais*, 9(68). (13 articles relating to legal studies at Orléans 13th–18th centuries).

Gasparri, F.: *La principauté d'Orange au Moyen Age (fin 13e–15e siècle)*, Paris. (Beginnings of univ. of Orange).

Gautier, J.-M.: La re-création de la fac. des Lettres de Clermont 1854, *Bull. hist. et scientif. de l'Auvergne*, 92: 307–20.

Grau, P.: Le 'Nouveau Languedoc', groupement des étudiants régionalistes et fédéralistes de l'univ. de Montpellier 1928–39, in *Actes du 110e Congrès national des Sociétés savantes—Section d'histoire moderne et contemporaine*, 3, Paris: 447–57.

Le Goff, J.: *Les Intellectuels au Moyen Age*, New ed., Paris.

- - - - - and Köpeczi, B. eds: *Intellectuels français, intellectuels hongrois, 13e–20e siècles*, Paris/Budapest.

Les méthodes de l'enseignement du Droit. Colloque, Paris. Number 2 of *Annales d'hist. des facs de droit*.

Le Van-Lemesle, L.: L'enseignement et la réception des scs écon. en France aux 19e et 20e s., *Sources—Travaux hist.*, 1: 65–67.

Mayeur, F.: Fustel de Coulanges et les questions d'enseignement sup., *Rev. hist.*, 556: 387–408.

Poirion, D.: Jean de Meun et la querelle de l'univ. de Paris: du libelle au livre, *Cahiers V.-L. Saulnier*, 2: 9–19. (13th cent. dispute).

Roux, S.: Intrigues au coll., in *Histoire sociale, sensibilités collectives et mentalités: Mélanges Mandrou,* Paris: 181–190. (A late 14th cent. dispute at the coll. d'Autun, Paris).

Shatzmiller, J.: Une expérience univ. renouvelée: le *studium* de Manosque 1299–1300, *Provence hist.,* 34: 195–203.

Sirinelli, J.-F.: Khâgneux et Normaliens des années vingt: histoire politique d'une génération d'intellectuels 1919–45. Thesis. Paris 10-Nanterre.

Thepot, A. ed.: *L'ingénieur dans la société française,* Paris. (Articles on Les Ecs d'ingénieurs).

Thuillier, G.: Aux origines de l'Ec. libre des scs pol.: L'Acad. de législation en 1801–1803, *La rev. admin.,* 38: 23–31.

Vaysse, J.-M.: L'Univ. allemande, *Le temps de la réflexion,* 6: 281–301. (The German romantics and their ideal of a university).

Ventre-Denis, M.: *Les sciences sociales et la Faculté de Droit de Paris sous la Restauration. Un texte précurseur: l'ordonnance du 24 mars 1819,* Paris.

Vicaire, M.-H.: L'action de l'enseignement et de la prédication des Mendiants vis-à-vis des cathares. *Cahiers de Fanjeaux,* 20: 277–304. (The *studia* of the mendicants in 13th century).

- - - - - and Gilles, H.: Rôle de l'univ. de Toulouse dans l'effacement du catharisme, *Cahiers de Fanjeaux,* 20: 257–76.

Publications 1986

Bataillon, L.-J.: De la *lectio* à la *praedicatio.* Commentaires bibliques et sermons au 13e s., *Rev. des scs phil. et théol.,* 70: 559–74.

Bibliog. d'hist. de l'éduc. fr. Titres parus au cours de l'année 1983 et supplément des années antérieures, *Hist. de l'éduc.,* 31–32: 5–191.

Charle, C.: *Les professeurs de la Faculté des Lettres de Paris. Dictionnaire biographique,* 1(1985), *1809–1908,* 2, *1909–39,* Paris.

Costabel, P. etc. eds: *L'enseignement classique: collèges et universités au 18e siècle,* Paris.

Hulin, N.: La rivalité Ec. Normale—Ec. Polytech. Un antécédent: l'action de Pasteur sous le second Empire, *Hist. de l'éduc.,* 30: 71–81.

Julia, D., Revel, J. and Chartier, R.: *Les Universités européennes du 16e au 18e siècle. Histoire sociale des populations étudiantes,* 1, *Bohême, Espagne, Etats italiens, Pays germaniques, Pologne, Provinces-Unies,* Paris.

Obert-Piketty, C.: Benoît XII et les colls cisterciens du Languedoc, *Cahiers de Fanjeaux,* 21: 139–50.

- - - - - Les maîtres et étudiants du coll. Saint-Bernard de Paris de 1224 à 1494, *Ec. Nat. des Chartes. Position des thèses*: 127–32.

Ory, P. and Sirinelli, J.-F.: *Les intellectuels en France de l'Affaire Dreyfus à nos jours,* Paris.

Verger, J. ed.: *Histoire des Universités en France,* Toulouse.

- - - - - Condition de l'intellectuel aux 13e et 14e s., in R. Imbach and

M.-Y. Meleard eds: *Philosophes médiévaux. Anthologie de textes philosophiques (13e–14e siècles)*, Paris: 11–49.

German Democratic Republic

Additions to Earlier Lists

For 1978

Bergner, D.: *Universitas litterarum heute: Zur Tradition und der philosophischen Grundlagen der sozialistischen Universität*, Halle/S.

Die Technische Hochschule Karl-Marx-Stadt in der Zeit von 1963 bis 1975, Leipzig.

Einhundertfünfzig Jahre Physik an der Bergakademie Freiberg, Freiberg.

Folgner, G.: *25 Jahre Fachlehrerausbildung an der Pädagogischen Hochschule Erfurt/Mühlhausen*, Erfurt.

Thal, P. and Pschibert, R.: *Das Studium der Ökonomie an der Martin-Luther-Universität Halle-Wittenberg, in Vergangenheit und Gegenwart 1727–1977*, Halle/S.

For 1979

Ackermann, G.: *10 Jahre Sektion Kraftwerksanlagen und Energieumwandlung an der Ingenieurhochschule Zittau*, Zittau.

Festveranstaltung der Karl-Marx-Universität Leipzig aus Anlaß des 100. Geburtstages von Albert Einstein am 22. Februar 1979, Leipzig.

Heinicke, P.-H.: *Zur Geschichte des Lehrstuhls für Hygiene an der Universität Berlin von der Gründung bis zur Berufung Max Rubners*. Thesis. Erfurt.

Kaiser, W. and Hübner, H.: *Der Hallenser Professor Johann Juncker und seine Zeit. Tagungsprotokoll*, 3 Teile, Halle/S.

For 1980

Beiträge zur Arbeit der Universitätsbibliothek Berlin in Vergangenheit und Gegenwart, Berlin.

Fünfundzwanzig Jahre Industrie-Institut der Technischen Universität Dresden, Dresden.

Geschichten und Anekdoten. Vom Werden und Wachsen der Pädagogischen Hochschule 'Karl Liebknecht' Potsdam 1948–78, Potsdam.

Guntau, M.: Zur gesellsch. Stellung u. Wirksamkeit deutscher Gelehrter im Zeitalter d. Aufklärung, *Rostocker wissenschaftshist. Manuskripte*, 5: 7–30.

Haubelt, J.: Die Rolle d. Gelehrten in d. mitteleurop. Aufklärung u. in d. nat. Wiedergeburt, *Rostocker wissenschaftshist. Manuskripte*, 5: 31–34.

Kaiser, W.: Die ersten promovierten Ärztinnen. Zum 225. Jahrestag d. halleschen Graduierung von Dorothea Christiane Erxleben 1715–62, *Z. f. d. gesamte Innere Medizin u. ihre Grenzgebiete*, 35 (4): 175–83.

- - - - - and Völker, A.: Medizingesch. u. Populärwiss. bei d. Hallenser

Prof. Johann Heinrich Schulze 1687–1744, *Das Altertum*, 4(26), 243–49. (S. fnder of Arabic studies at univ. of Halle).

Kant, H.: Einige Betrachtungen zum Problematik 'Wissenschaftler u. Öffentlichkeit' am Beispiel populärwiss. Aktivitäten von Berliner Physikern während d. Weimarer Zeit, *Rostocker wissenschaftshist. Manuskripte*, 5: 69–80.

Katsch, G. and Schwendler, G.: Das Karzer-Buch d. Univ. Leipzig, in *Jb. zur Gesch. d. Stadt Leipzig*, 1: 148–61.

Laitko, H.: Das Persönlichkeitsbild d. Wissenschaftlers im 19 Jh. im Spannungsfeld von Universalität u. Fachspezilisierung, *Rostocker wissenschaftshist. Manuskripte*, 5: 35–57.

Pädagogische Hochschule 'Karl Friedrich Wilhelm Wander' Dresden, Dresden.

Studien und Dokumente zur Geschichte der Physik an der Bergakademie Freiberg, Freiberg.

Tutzke, D.: *Tradition und Fortschritt in der medizinhistorischen Arbeit des Berliner Instituts für Geschichte der Medizin*, Berlin.

Von der Staatlichen Tierarzneischule in Dresden zur Fachrichtung Veterinärmedizin der Sektion Tierproduktion/Veterinärmedizin der Karl-Marx-Universität 1780–1980, Leipzig.

Wollgast, S.: Die gesellsch. Stellung d. Gelehrten vom 15. bis zum 18. Jh. in Deutschland, *Rostocker wissenschaftshist. Manuskripte*, 4: 45–75.

Zum Stand u. zu d. Aufgaben d. hochschulgesch. Forschung in d. DDR, *Ber. u. Inform. zur Hoch- u. Fachschulbildung*, 6 (1): 1–82.

For 1981

Arnhold, R. and Hexelschneider, E.: *Beiträge zur Geschichte des Herder-Instituts an der Karl-Marx Universität Leipzig*, Leipzig.

Baum, H.: *Chronologie zum Hochschulwesen der DDR. Literaturzusammenstellung . . . 1976*, Berlin.

Beiträge des Kolloquiums anläßlich der Gründung des Wissenschaftsbereichs 'Wissenschaftstheorie und-geschichte' an der Martin-Luther-Universität Halle-Wittenberg am 18. Sept. 1980, Halle/S.

Blumenthal, E.: *Altes Ägypten und Leipzig. Zur Geschichte des Ägyptischen Museums und des Ägyptologischen Instituts an der Universität Leipzig*, Leipzig.

Das Physiologische Institut der Friedrich-Schiller-Universität Jena, Jena.

Deutsche Hochschule für Körperkultur und Sport Leipzig. Zeittafel 1950–80, Leipzig.

Dreißig Jahre Ausländerstudium in der DDR—Fünfundzwanzig Jahre Herder-Institut an der Karl-Marx-Universität Leipzig, Leipzig.

Dreißig Jahre marxistisch–leninistisches Grundlagenstudium an der Bergakademie Freiberg, Freiberg.

Einsporn, K.: *Tradition-Vorbild-Ziel. Beiträge zur Traditionsforschung und-pflege an der Pädagogischen Hochschule Halle-Kröllwitz*, Halle/S.

Erfahrungen bei der Erforschung der Geschichte der FDJ an der Technischen Hochschule/Technischen Universität Dresden, Dresden.

FDJ-Geschichte der Friedrich-Schiller-Universität Jena. Ein chronologischer Überblick, 1, 1945–49, Jena.

Fläschendräger, W. in *Atlas zur Geschichte*, Gotha/Leipzig. (3 maps relating to univ. hist. to *c.* 1900 and to origins of Wittenberg students 1502–22).

Gluch, R. and Fürmann, A.: Fritz Foerster-Begründer d. Elektrochemie in Dresden, *Wiss. Z. d. TU Dresden*, 30 (4): 37–40.

Ingenieurhochschule Wismar, Wismar.

Ingenieurhochschule Zittau, Zittau.

Irmscher, J., Lemper, E. H. and Mühlpfordt, G.: *Die Oberlausitz in der Epoche der bürgerlichen Emanzipation*, Görlitz. (Inform. about univs of Halle, Leipzig and Jena).

John, M.: Karl Liebknecht—ein bedeutender Student d. Leipziger Univ., *Leipzig aus Vergangenheit u. Gegenwart*, 1: 188–205.

Kaiser, W. and Hübner, H.: *Hallesche Physiologie im Werden. Hallesches Symposium 1981*, Halle/S.

Klaus, W., *Chronik der Technischen Universität Dresden 1971–79*, Dresden.

Kleineidam, E.: *Universitas studii Erffordensis. Überblick über die Geschichte der Universität Erfurt. 4: Die Universität Erfurt von 1633 bis 1816*, Leipzig.

Landel, H.: Schinkels Planungen zum Augusteum in Leipzig, d. Hauptgebäude d. Univ., in *Bauinformationen*, Berlin: 36–43.

Loh, G.: *Chronologie zur Geschichte der Universitätsbibliothek Leipzig*, Leipzig.

Schmidt, E.: Die Entwicklung der Hochbauabteilung an der Technischen Hochschule Dresden 1900–45. Thesis. Dresden.

Schmidt, H.: Trommsdorff-Forschung-Beispiel f. d. Traditionspflege an d. Medizin. Akad. Erfurt, *Pharmazeut. Praxis*, 36 (5): 230–32.

Schönrock, A.: Zur antifaschistisch-demokratischen Umgestaltung der Universität Greifswald (Mai 1945–Ende 1946). Thesis. Greifswald.

Schrammek, W.: *Museum Musicum. Historische Musikinstrumente im Musikinstrumentenmuseum der Universität Leipzig*, Leipzig.

Schulz, H.-J.: *Die Hoch-und Fachschulbildung in der DDR*, Berlin.

Sonnemann, R.: Der Mißbrauch d. wiss.-tech. Fortschritts im imperialistischen Deutschland, dargestellt am Beispiel von Prof. Hugershoff, Dresden, in Wiss, u. Tech.-Humanismus u. Fortschritt, *Kolloquiumsreihe d. Inst. f. Theorie, Gesch. u. Organisation d. Wiss. Berlin*, 22: 185–88.

Stützner, H.: Das Wirken Carl Julius von Bachs 1847–1931 als Technikwissenschaftler u. Hochschullehrer, *Rostocker wissenschaftshist. Manuskripte*, 7: 87–91.

- - - - - *Zur Geschichte der Technischen Hochschule Karl-Marx-Stadt*, Karl-Marx-Stadt.

Thiermann, W.: Zur Geschichte des Leipziger Psychologischen Instituts 1875–1945. Thesis. Leipzig.

Überblick zur Geschichte des marxistisch-leninistischen Grundlagenstudiums an den Universitäten, Hoch-und Fachschulen der DDR, Leipzig.

Winter, E.: Deutsch-slawische Wechselseitigkeit, besonders in d.Gesch.d. Wiss. Deutsch-russische Wissenschaftsbeziehungen im 18.Jh., *Sitzungsber. d. Akad. d. Wiss. d. DDR, Berlin,* 4(G): 1–42.

Publications 1982

Abe, H.-R.: Die Medizin. Akad. Erfurt u. ihre progressiven Traditionen, *Beitr. zur Gesch. d. Univ. Erfurt,* 19: 9–51.

- - - - - Zur Rolle Erfurts im Leben u. Werk Martin Luthers, *Beitr. zur Gesch. d. Univ. Erfurt,* 19: 53–112.

Aus Anlass des 50. Todestages von Wilhelm Ostwald am 6.4.1982, Berlin. (Contribs to hist. of Med. 1870–1930, of Biology and to hist. of scholarly communication 19th and 20th centuries).

Baum, H. ed.: *Chronologie zum Hochschulwesen der DDR. Literaturzusammenstellung . . . 1977,* Berlin.

Bergakademie Freiberg. Hochschulführer, Freiberg. (Short ch. on hist. of academy).

Birnbaum, D.: Erbe u. Verpflichtung (an d. Ernst-Moritz-Arndt-Univ. Greifswald), *Wiss. Z. d. Ernst-Moritz-Arndt-Univ. Greifswald, gesellsch.-u. sprachwiss. Reihe,* 31 (4): 3–6.

Böhmer, W.: Das Wittenberger Medizinalwesen d. Reformationsära, *Wiss. Beitr. d. Martin-Luther-Univ. Halle-Wittenberg,* 82/7 (T 45): 107–26.

Christ, C.: Zur Herausbildung der marxistisch-leninistischen Wirtschaftswissenschaften in der DDR am Beispiel der Humboldt-Universität zu Berlin. Thesis. Berlin.

Die Bestände der Universitätsbibliothek Berlin. Konferenzprotokoll, Berlin.

Die Gründung des Zentralinstituts für Hochschulbildung—Beginn eines neuen Abschnitts des Forschungen über das Hoch—und Fachschulwesen, Berlin.

Die Entwicklung Berlins als Wissenschaftszentrum 1870–1930. Zur Geschichte der Mathematik (an der Universität) Berlin, Berlin.

Döring, D.: Eine bisher unbekannte Bewerbung Albert Einsteins um eine Assistentenstelle an d. Leipziger Univ., *Arbeitsblätter zur Wissenschaftsgesch.,* 12: 85–100.

Elsner, L.: 30 Jahre Wiss. Z. d. Wilhelm-Pieck-Univ. Rostock, *Beitr. zur Gesch. d. Wilhelm-Pieck-Univ. Rostock,* 2: 66–68.

- - - - - Zur Gesch. d. Hist. Inst. d. Landes Mecklenburg 1948–50 in Rostock, *Beitr. zur Gesch. d. Wilhelm-Pieck-Univ. Rostock,* 2: 51–54.

Feudell, P.: Die Anfänge d. Neurologie an d. Leipziger Univ., *Wiss. Z. d. Karl-Marx-Univ. Leipzig, mathem.-naturwiss. Reihe,* 31: 131–37.

Fläschendräger, W.: Akademie, in H. Hörz etc. eds: *Philosophie und Naturwissenschaften*, Berlin: 21–23.

Fliess, G.: *Universität und Zweijahrplan. Ergebnisse konstruktiver Intelligenz- und Jugendpolitik der SED aus den Jahren des antifaschistisch-demokratischen Neuaufbaus*, Jena.

Franke, M.: Zu d. Bemühungen Leipziger Physiker um eine Profilierung d. Physikalischen Inst. d. Univ. Leipzig im 2. Viertel d. 20. Jh., *NTM*, 19 (1): 68–76.

Friedrich, C.: Zur Entwicklung der Pharmazie an der Ernst-Moritz-Arndt-Universität Greifswald von 1903 bis 1968. Thesis. Greifswald.

Fünfundzwanzig Jahre 'Beiträge zur Geschichte der Universität Erfurt 1392–1816' 1956–81, Leipzig.

Geerdts, H.-J.: Der 'Wiecker Bote', d. Univ. Greifswald u. unser Kulturerbe, *Wiss. Z. d. Ernst-Moritz-Arndt-Univ. Greifswald, gesellsch. -u. sprachwiss. Reihe*, 31 (4): 21–28.

Geschichte der Akademie für Staats- und Rechtswissenschaften der DDR Potsdam–Babelsberg, Potsdam.

Grau, C.: Die Petersburger Akad. d. Wissenschaften in d. interakad. Beziehungen 1899 bis 1915, *Jb. f. Gesch. d. soz. Länder Europas*, 25/2: 51–68.

Güthert, H. and Abe, H.-R.: Zur Entstehungsgesch. d. Medizin.-Wiss. Gesellschaft an d. Medizin. Akad. Erfurt, *Beitr. zur Gesch. d. Univ. Erfurt*, 19: 339–60.

Hellfeldt, G.: Auswirkungen d. lutherischen Refn auf d. Schulwesen in norddeutschen Städten, *Wiss. Z. d. Wilhelm-Pieck-Univ. Rostock, gesellsch.-u. sprachwiss. Reihe*, 31 (6): 1–6.

Hergt, R.: Zur Entwicklung d. Lehrstuhls f. Allgemeine u. Kommunalhygiene im Hygiene-Inst. d. Univ. Rostock, *Beitr. zur Gesch. d. Wilhelm-Pieck-Univ. Rostock*, 2: 44–45.

Herrmann, D.-B.: *Karl Friedrich Zöllner—Astrophysiker an der Universität Leipzig*, Leipzig.

Hiersemann, L.: Jacob Leupold—ein Wegbereiter d. tech. Bildung in Leipzig. Ein Beitr. zur Vorgesch. d. TH Leipzig, *Wiss. Ber. d. TH Leipzig*, 17: 1–128.

Hiller, I. and Schmidmaier, D.: *Heinrich David Wilcken—Student an der Bergakademie Freiberg und erster Professor des Forstinstituts in Schemnitz*, Freiberg.

Hochschule für Verkehrswesen 'Friedrich List' Dresden. Hochschul- und Studienführer, Dresden. (Contains a ch. on hist. of the High School).

Hoffmann, L.: 30 Jahre fachsprachliche Lehre u. Forschung an d. Univ. u. Hochschulen d. DDR, *Wiss. Z. d. Karl-Marx-Univ. Leipzig, gesellsch.—u. sprachwiss. Reihe*, 31 (1): 3–4.

Ingenieurhochschule Dresden, Dresden. (Contains a ch. on hist. of the High School).

Jubiläumsansprachen und Festvorträge zum 525. Gründungstag der Universität Greifswald am 17. Oktober 1981, Greifswald.

Kabus, R.: Die Entwicklung d. Universitätsstadt Wittenberg unter kommunalhygienischem Aspekt, *Wiss. Beitr. d. Martin-Luther-Univ. Halle-Wittenberg,* 82/7 (T 45): 83–106.

Kaiser, W.: Martin Luther u. d. Ars medica Vitebergensis, *Wiss. Beitr. d. Martin-Luther-Univ. Halle-Wittenberg,* 82/7 (T 45): 9–31.

- - - - - and Völker, A.: Ungarländische Absolventen d. Leucorea u. d. Acad. Fridericiana als Initiatoren einer landessprachlichen Fachliteratur, *Wiss. Beitr. d. Martin-Luther-Univ. Halle-Wittenberg,* 82/7 (T 45): 323–39.

Katsch, G.: Zur Entwicklung d. Geschichtswiss. an d. Karl-Marx-Univ. Leipzig von d. demokratischen Neueröffnung bis zur Gründung d. Sektion Gesch., *Wiss. Z. d. Karl-Marx-Univ. Leipzig, gesellsch.-u. sprachwiss. Reihe,* 31 (6): 544–58.

- - - - - and Schwendler, G.: Hermann Duncker an d. Univ. Leipzig, *Leipzig aus Vergangenheit u. Gegenwart,* 2: 225–33.

- - - - - Kuriositäten aus d. Leipziger Universitätsarchiv 2, *Leipzig aus Vergangenheit u. Gegenwart,* 2: 234–40.

Kersten, E.: Zur Entwicklung d. Lehrstuhls f. Arbeitshygiene an d. Wilhelm-Pieck-Univ. Rostock, *Beitr. zur Gesch. d. Wilhelm-Pieck-Univ. Rostock,* 2: 39–43.

Koch, H.-T.: Medizin. Promotionen an d. Univ. Wittenberg in d. Vorreformationszeit. *Wiss. Beitr. d. Martin-Luther-Univ. Halle-Wittenberg,* 82/7 (T 45): 69–81.

Köhler, R.: Universität, in H. Hörz etc. eds: *Philosophie und Naturwissenschaften,* Berlin: 949–52.

König, F.: Die Entstehung des Mathematischen Seminars an der Universität Leipzig im Rahmen des Institutionalisierungsprozesses der Mathematik an den deutschen Universitäten des 19. Jh. Thesis. Leipzig.

Künzel, W.: Stomatologie—eine neue Grundstudienrichtung an d. Medizin. Akad. Erfurt 1975–80, *Beitr. zur Gesch. d. Univ. Erfurt,* 19: 305–38.

Linkesch, W.: Ungarländische Absolventen d. Univ. Wittenberg als Initiatoren einer frühen Tatra-Forschung, *Wiss. Beitr. d. Martin-Luther-Univ. Halle-Wittenberg,* 82/7 (T 45): 293–98.

Litschke, E.: Über die Entwicklung der Pädagogischen Hochschule 'Karl Liebknecht' Potsdam 1955–58. Thesis. Potsdam.

Lück, E.: Die Spruchtätigkeit der Wittenberger Juristenfakultät. Thesis. Halle/S.

- - - - - Die Wittenberger Juristenfak. als Spruchkollegium u. ihr Platz in d. kursächsischen Gerichtsverfassung, *Wiss. Z. d. Martin-Luther-Univ. Halle-Wittenberg, gesellsch.-u. sprachwiss. Reihe,* 31 (3): 101–106.

Mau, R. ed.: Rationis Latomianae pro incendariis Lovaniensis scholae sophistis redditae, Lutherianae confutatio, in H.-U. Delius ed.: *Martin Luther. Studienausgabe,* 2, Berlin: 405–519. (Discusses condemnation of M.L. by univ. of Louvain).

Mehlan, K. H.: Rückblick auf Entwicklung, Aufgaben u. Leistungen d.

Lehrstuhls f. Sozialhygiene an d. Univ. Rostock zwischen 1956 u. 1981, *Beitr. zur Gesch. d. Wilhelm-Pieck-Univ. Rostock,* 2: 33–38.

Mohrmann, W.: Die Humboldt-Universität zu Berlin während der Jahre der Herausbildung und Gestaltung der entwickelten sozialistischen Gesellschaft in der DDR 1961–81. Thesis. Berlin.

- - - - - Die Berliner Univ. im 19. Jh., *Beitr. zur Gesch. d. Humboldt-Univ. zu Berlin,* 8: 1–96.

- - - - - etc.: Die Geschichtswiss. an d. Humboldt-Univ.—Traditionen, Leistungen, Wege. Joachim Streisand zum Gedenken, *Beitr. zur Gesch. d. Humboldt-Univ. zu Berlin,* 6: 1–56.

Mühlpfordt, G.: Johann Herbin—ein Dozent d. Leucorea (1657). Der Auftakt d. neueren Frauenrechtsbestrebungen an d. 'sächsischen Univ.' Wittenberg, Halle, Leipzig u. Jena, *Wiss. Beitr. d. Martin-Luther-Univ. Halle-Wittenberg,* 82/5 (A 57): 75–90.

- - - - - Petersburg u. Halle. Begegnungen im Zeichen d. Aufklärung, *Jb. f. Gesch. d. soz. Länder Europas,* 25/2: 155–71.

Mylnikov, A.: Zu einigen kulturhist. Aspekten d. slawisch-deutschen Wissenschaftsbeziehungen Ende d. 18./Anfang d. 19. Jhs, *Jb. f. Gesch. d. soz. Länder Europas,* 25/2; 123–38.

Namhafte Hochschullehrer der Karl-Marx-Universität, Leipzig. (Important biograph. material).

Poeckern, H.-J.: Die Pharmazie in Wittenberg zur Reformationszeit, *Wiss. Beitr. d. Martin-Luther-Univ. Halle-Wittenberg,* 82/7 (T 45): 181–202.

Rackow, G.: Martin Luther u. d. 'Schulehalten', *Wiss. Z. d. Wilhelm-Pieck-Univ. Rostock, gesellsch.-u. sprachwiss. Reihe,* 31 (6): 7–12.

Schmid, I.: Die Oberaufsicht über d. naturwiss. Inst. an d. Univ. Jena unter Goethes Leitung, 'Impulse', *Aufsätze, Quellen, Ber. zur deutschen Klassik u. Romantik,* 4: 148–93.

Schulze, G.: 30 Jahre wirtschaftswiss. Ausbildung u. Forschung f. d. Praxis an d. Wilhelm-Pieck-Univ. Rostock, *Beitr. zur Gesch. d. Wilhelm-Pieck-Univ. Rostock,* 2: 16–24.

Schuster-Šewc, H.: 30 Jahre Inst. f. Sorabistik an d. Karl-Marx-Univ., *Wiss. Z. d. Karl-Marx-Univ. Leipzig, gesellsch.-u. sprachwiss. Reihe,* 31 (6): 559–65.

Schwann, H.: Richard Kochs Beziehungen zum Karl-Sudhoff-Inst. d. Univ. Leipzig, *NTM,* 19 (1): 94–103.

Schweinitz, B. and Steiger, G. eds: *Reichtümer und Raritäten, 2: Kulturhistorische Sammlungen, Museen, Archive, Denkmale und Gärten der Friedrich-Schiller-Universität Jena,* Jena.

Seemann, U.: Die Entstehung d. Hygiene-Inst. an d. Univ. Rostock vor 100 Jahren u. seine Entwicklung bis zum Ende d. Faschismus, *Beitr. zur Gesch. d. Wilhelm-Pieck-Univ. Rostock,* 2: 25–32.

Snelders, H. A. M.: Die Naturwiss. in d. nördlichen Niederlanden in d. zweiten Hälfte d. 16. u. zu Beginn d. 17. Jhs (mit Berücksichtigung ihrer

Ausstrahlung auf deutsche Univ.), *Wiss. Beitr. d. Martin-Luther-Univ. Halle-Wittenberg*, 82/7 (T 45): 273–83.

Sonntag, L.: Der absolute Geist auf d. Katheder—Hegels Berliner Professorenjahre 1818–31, *Das Hochschulwesen*, 30 (1): 12–17.

Steiger, G.: *'Diesem Geschöpfe leidenschaftlich zugetan'. Bryophyllum calycinum—Goethes 'patheistische Pflanze'*, Jena. (Notes G.'s part in creating a new botanical garden for univ. of Jena).

Stengel, H.: 30 Jahre schiffstech. Ausbildung u. Forschung f. d. Praxis an d. Wilhelm-Pieck-Univ. Rostock, *Beitr. zur Gesch. d. Wilhelm-Pieck-Univ. Rostock*, 2: 6–15.

Technische Hochschule 'Carl Schorlemmer' Leuna-Merseburg, Merseburg. (A ch. on hist. of the High School).

Thal, P.: *30 Jahre marxistisch–leninistische Wirtschaftswissenschaften an der Martin-Luther-Universität Halle-Wittenberg*, Halle/S.

Vida, M.: Kosmas u. Damian, d. Schutzheiligen d. Univ. Wittenberg, *Wiss. Beitr. d. Martin-Luther-Univ. Halle-Wittenberg*, 82/7 (T 45): 33–67.

Vogt, A.: Zur Gesch. d. Mathem. Seminars an d. Berliner Univ., *Berliner wissenschaftshist. Kolloquien*, 7: 37–59.

Völker, A.: Die jüngere Entwicklung d. medizinhist. Unterrichts an d. Martin-Luther-Univ. Halle-Wittenberg, *Wiss. Beitr. d. Martin-Luther-Univ. Halle-Wittenberg*, 82/6 (E 43): 275–78.

- - - - - and Kaiser, W.: Zur sprachwiss. Lehre u. Forschung an d. Univ. von Wittenberg u. Halle, *Wiss. Beitr. d. Martin-Luther-Univ. Halle-Wittenberg*, 82/7 (T 45): 299–322.

- - - - - and Thaler, B.: *Die Entwicklung des medizinhistorischen Unterrichts an deutschen Universitäten und Hochschulen*, Halle/S.

Voigt, W. and Sucker, U.: *Johann Wolfgang von Goethe als Naturwissenschaftler*, Leipzig. (A ch. about G.'s relations with univ. of Jena).

Wilhelmus, W. etc.: *Universität Greifswald 525 Jahre*, Berlin.

Wittig, J.: *Sektion Physik. Zur Physikentwicklung nach 1945 an der Friedrich-Schiller-Universität Jena*, Jena.

Zobel, H.-J.: Palästinawiss. in Greifswald, *Wiss. Z. d. Ernst-Moritz-Arndt-Univ. Greifswald, gesellsch.-u. sprachwiss. Reihe*, 31 (H 4): 59–65.

Zur Geschichte der FDJ-Organisation an der Technischen Universität Dresden, Dresden.

Publications 1983

Abe, H.-R.: *Martin Luther und 12 seiner Zeitgenossen in Erfurt*, Erfurt.

Arnhardt, G.: Zur Ausprägung d. humanistischen hochschulvorbereitenden Bildungstradition in Sachsen an d. Wende vom 17. zum 18. Jh., *Sächsische Heimatblätter*, 29 (6): 265–67.

Benthien, B. and Kliewe, H.: Zur physisch-geograph. Forschung 1975–80 an d. Ernst-Moritz-Arndt-Univ. Greifswald-Rückschau u. Ausblick,

Wiss. Z. d. Ernst-Moritz-Arndt-Univ. Greifswald, mathem.-naturwiss. Reihe, 32 (H 1–2): 2–5.

Biermann, K.-R.: *Alexander von Humboldt,* Leipzig. (Inform. about A. v. H. at univ. of Frankfurt (Oder) and other aspects of univ. history).

Billwitz, K.: Zur Weiterführung d. physisch-geograph. Forschung an d. Ernst-Moritz-Arndt-Univ. Greifswald, *Wiss. Z. d. Ernst-Moritz-Arndt-Univ. Greifswald, mathem.-naturwiss. Reihe,* 32, (H. 1–2): 121–24.

Bolck, F.: *Aufsätze und Reden als Rektor der Friedrich-Schiller-Universität Jena,* Jena.

Box, H.-J.: Hermann Roesler—ein Vertreter d. jurist. Weltanschauung in Rostock, *Wiss. Z. d. Wilhelm-Pieck-Univ. Rostock, gesellsch.-u. sprachwiss. Reihe,* 32 (H 1): 105–108.

Bräuer, S.: Das Lutherjubiläum 1933 u. d. deutschen Univ., *Theol. Literaturzeitung,* 108 (9): 641–62.

Breuste, J. and Bernhardt, P.: Schriftftum über Carl Ritter, *Geograph. Jb.,* 66, Gotha/Leipzig. (C.R. 1820 first prof. of Geog. in Germany, Berlin).

Czok, K.: Über Traditionen sächsischer Landesgesch., *Sitzungsber. d. sächsischen Akad. d. Wiss. zu Leipzig, Phil.—Hist. Klasse,* 123 (4): 1–44.

Fabian, E.: Gerhard Harigs wissenschaftshist. Credo, in G. Harig and G. Wendel eds: *Gerhard Harig-Schriften zur Geschichte der Naturwissenschaften,* Berlin: 319–30. (G.H. 1957–65 director of Inst. for Hist. of Med. and Science 'Karl Sudhoff', Leipzig).

Fahrenbach, S.: Zur Entstehung d. Berliner Medizin. Gesellschaft (1860) u. ihrer wiss. Tätigkeit in d. ersten Jahren ihres Bestehens, *Wiss. Z. d. Wilhelm-Pieck-Univ. Rostock, gesellsch.-u. sprachwiss. Reihe,* 32 (H 9): 61–65.

Festerling, H.: Johann August Christian Roeper—ein Naturwissenschaftler an d. Univ. Rostock in d. ausklingenden Blütezeit d. deutschen Naturphil., *Beitr. zur Gesch. d. Wilhelm-Pieck-Univ. Rostock,* 3: 56–63.

Feyl, R.: *Der lautlose Aufbruch. Frauen in der Wissenschaft,* Berlin. (Biogs of early women at university).

Fläschendräger, W.: Die Gesch. d. Univ. u. ihre Erforschung (Tagungsbericht vom 10./11.10.1982), *Z. f. Geschichtswiss.,* 31 (H 9): 831–32.

- - - - - '. . . mocht geschehenn gutte reformation der universitetenn . . .'. Zu Luthers Wirken als Prof. u. als Universitätsreformer, *Jb. f. Regionalgesch.,* 10: 26–36.

- - - - - Universität, in *Wörterbuch der Geschichte,* Berlin: 1083–1085.

Genschorek, W.: *Carl Gustav Carus 1789–1869—Professor in Dresden,* Leipzig, (C.G.C. first rect. Coll. Medico-Chirurgicum, Dresden).

- - - - - *Wegbereiter der Chirurgie: Johann Friedrich Dieffenbach (Begründer der plastischen Chirurgie, Prof. an der Charité der Universität Berlin) und Theodor Billroth (Begründer der modernen Bauchchirurgie, Prof. in Zürich und Wien),* Leipzig.

Gilardon, K.: *Medizinhistorische Instrumente und Geräte aus dem Karl-*

Sudhoff-Institut für Geschichte der Medizin und der Naturwissenschaften der Karl-Marx-Universität Leipzig, Leipzig.

Girnus, W.: 'Der chemischen Gesellschaft Sitzung jetzt eröffnet ist . . .', *Spectrum*, (H 11): 30–32.

Grau, C. and Hartkopf, W.: *Die Akademie der Wissenschaften der DDR. Ein Beitrag zu ihrer Geschichte. Biographischer Index*, Berlin. (Some 3000 short biogs; many refs to univ. history).

Guntau, M.: Die Beziehung von Geologen u. Mineralogen d. Freiberger Schule zu französischen Gelehrten, *Z. f. geolog. Wiss.*, 11 (4): 499–504.

Haase, G. and Winkler, J. eds: *Die Oder-Universität Frankfurt. Beiträge zu ihrer Geschichte*, Weimar.

Hamel, J.: Karl Friedrich Zöllners Tätigkeit als Hochschullehrer an d. Univ. Leipzig, *NTM*, 20 (H 1): 35–44.

Händel, A.: Die Bibliothek d. Herzogs Albrecht zu Mecklenburg (im Bestand d. Universitätsbibliothek Rostock) u. ihre Kostbarkeiten, *Beitr. zur Gesch. d. Wilhelm-Pieck-Univ. Rostock*, 4: 17–33.

Harig, G., Tutzke, D. and Winter, I.: *Geschichte der Medizin*, Berlin. (Refs to univ. history).

Hesse, P.-G.: Das erste zahnärztliche Inst. Deutschlands u. sein Gründer Friedrich Louis Hesse, *Stomatologie d. DDR*, 33 (12): 861–63.

Irmscher, J.: Die Entwicklung d. klassischen Philologie an d. Humboldt-Univ. zu Berlin, *Wiss. Z. d. Humboldt-Univ. zu Berlin, gesellsch.-u. sprachwiss. Reihe*, 32 (H 3): 355–60.

Jäger, R.: *Nummotheca Lipsiensis. Münzen und Medaillen aus der Münzsammlung der Universitätsbibliothek Leipzig*, Leipzig.

Janke, D.: Grundlinien der Entwicklung des politökonomischen Inhalts der akademischen Lehre an der Universität Leipzig vom Beginn des 16. Jh. bis zur bürgerlich-demokratischen Revolution von 1848. Thesis. Leipzig.

John, J.: Die Weimarer Repub., d. Land Thüringen u. d. Univ. Jena 1918–19—1923–24, *Jb. f. Regionalgesch.*, 10: 177–207.

- - - - - Zum Wirken kommunistischer Studenten in Jena 1922–23. Die kommunistische Studentengruppe an d. Univ. Jena u. d. Kartell d. Deutschen Repub. Studentenschaft, *Z. f. Geschichtswiss.* 31 (H 7): 607–25.

Jonscher, R.: Geschichte der Friedrich-Schiller-Universität Jena von der 400-Jahr-Feier 1958 bis zur Mitte der 60er Jahre. Thesis. Jena.

Kaiser, W. and Völker, A.: Zur Entwicklung klinischer Spezialdisziplinen an d. Univ. Halle, *Wiss. Z. d. Wilhelm-Pieck-Univ. Rostock, gesellsch.-u. sprachwiss. Reihe*, 32 (H 9): 66–70.

- - - - - Zur Gesch. d. ärztlichen Fortbildung an d. Medizin. Fak. Halle u. durch wiss. Gesellschaften, *Z. f. d. gesamte Innere Medizin u. ihre Grenzgebiete*, 38 (H 13): 347–58.

Karl, H.-V.: Naturalien-u. Kunstkabinett d. Franckeschen Stiftungen zu Halle/Saale, *Wiss. Beitr. d. Martin-Luther-Univ. Halle-Wittenberg*, 40 (T 53): 1–20.

Katsch, G. and Schwendler, G.: Gewisse Beziehungen zur marxistischen Erkenntnis gefunden. Hermann Duncker an d. Univ. Leipzig, *Leipzig aus Vergangenheit u. Gegenwart*, 2: 225–33.

- - - - - Hermann Dunckers Promotion an d. Univ. Leipzig. Eine Dokumentation, *Wiss. Z. d. Karl-Marx-Univ. Leipzig, gesellsch.-u. sprachwiss. Reihe*, 32 (1): 92–96.

Kind, R. and Ranneberg, M.: 25 Jahre Wiss. Z. d. TH 'Carl Schorlemmer' Leuna-Merseburg, *Wiss. Z. d. TH Leuna Merseburg*, 25 (H 4): 443–46.

Kottas, E.: Gründung d. Deutschen Hochschule f. Körperkultur Leipzig am 22.10.1950—Ausdruck revolutionärer Veränderungen, *Theorie u. Praxis d. Körperkultur*, 32 (10): 733–39.

Lange, E. etc.: *Die Promotion von Karl Marx in Jena 1841, Eine Quellenedition*, Berlin.

Loh, G.: Beiträge zu einer Geschichte der Universitätsbibliothek Leipzig 1543 bis 1832. Thesis. Leipzig.

Mägdefrau, W.: Die Univ. Jena u. d. lutherische Erbe zwischen Refn u. Aufklärung, *Wiss. Z. d. Friedrich-Schiller-Univ. Jena, gesellsch.-u. sprachwiss. Reihe*, 32 (H 1–2): 163–202.

Marwinski, K.: *Bibliographie zur Geschichte der Universität Jena. Literatur der Jahre 1945–80*, Jena.

Mehls, E.: Die internat. Hochschulbeziehungen d. Humboldt-Univ. zu Berlin von 1946 bis 1980. Ein Überblick, *Beitr. zur Gesch. d. Humboldt-Univ. zu Berlin*, 8: 1–77.

Moldenhauer, D.: Forschungsorganisationen und Institutionalisierungen der Biologie zwischen 1870 und 1930 in Deutschland. Thesis. Köthen.

Moschke, G.: Ein Jahr Abteilung f. Gesch. d. Medizin an d. Medizin. Akad. Magdeburg, *Das Hochschulwesen*, 31 (H 1): 23–24.

- - - - - Zur Bedeutung d. SMAD-Befehls Nr 234 f. d. Entwicklung d. Lehre über Sozialhygiene an d. Leipziger Univ. in d. Jahren 1948–52, *Z. f. d. gesamte Hygiene*, 29 (10): 620–23.

Mühlpfordt, G.: Der Wittenberger Magister legens Johann Herbin-d. erste Frauenrechtler d. deutschen Aufklärung, *Z. f. Geschichtswiss.*, 31 (4): 325–38.

Müller, G. and Köhler, H.: 15 Jahre Botanischer Garten an d. Sektion Biowiss. d. Karl-Marx-Univ. Leipzig. Eine Dokumentation, *Wiss. Z. d. Karl-Marx-Univ. Leipzig, mathem.-naturwiss. Reihe*, 32 (H 5): 515–26.

Ortmann, F.: Die Entstehung der Psychiatrie (als Fachdisziplin) an der Universität Jena. Thesis. Jena.

Palme, P.: Das Rostocker Universitätshauptgebäude u. seine Vorgesch. im 19. Jh., *Beitr. zur Gesch. d. Wilhelm-Pieck-Univ. Rostock*, 3: 4–49.

Papendieck, C.: Die Entwicklung der akademischen landwirtschaftlichen Ausbildung in Berlin von der Gründung der Landwirtschaftlichen Hochschule bis zur Bildung der agrarwissenschaftlichen Sektionen an der Humboldt-Universität zu Berlin. Thesis. Berlin.

Pischel, J. etc.: 125 Jahre Germanistik an d. Univ. Rostock 1858–1983, *Beitr. zur Gesch. d. Wilhelm-Pieck-Univ. Rostock*, 5: 1–60.

Preuss, D.: 30 Jahre Hochschule f. Verkehrswesen 'Friedrich List' Dresden, *Das Hochschulwesen*, 31 (H 1): 22–23.

Rek, K.: Die Janaer Gesellschaft d. freien Männer 1794–99. *Wiss. Z. d. Karl-Marx-Univ. Leipzig, gesellsch.-u. sprachwiss. Reihe*, 32 (6): 577–83.

Richter, H.: Zur Ehrenpromotion Willi Bredels am 3. Nov. 1945, *Beitr. zur Gesch. d. Wilhelm-Pieck-Univ. Rostock*, 3: 64–67.

Schilfert, S.: Grundzüge der Bibliotheksentwicklung an den preußischen technischen Hochschulen bis zum 1. Weltkrieg. Thesis. Berlin.

Schlicker, W.: Physiker im faschistischen Deutschland. Zum Geschehen um eine naturwiss.-tech. Grundlagendisziplin (d. Univ.) seit 1933 bis 1945, *Jb. f. Gesch.*, 27: 109–42.

- - - - - Tendenzen u. Konsequenzen faschistischer Wissenschaftspol. nach d. 30.1.1933, *Z. f. Geschichtswiss.*, 31 (10): 881–95.

- - - - - Eugen Fischer. Faschisierung in Hochschule u. Wiss., in H. Bock, W. Ruge and M. Thoms eds: *Sturz ins Dritte Reich. Historische Miniaturen und Porträt*, Leipzig/Jena/Berlin: 259–65.

Schmidt, S., Elm, L. and Steiger, G. eds: *Alma mater Jenensis. Geschichte der Universität Jena*, Weimar.

- - - - - and Arnold, L. eds: *Wissenschaft und Sozialismus. Beiträge zur Geschichte der Friedrich-Schiller-Universität Jena von 1945 bis 1981*, Jena.

Schwab, M., Pfeiffer, H. and Koehn, H.: Johann Jacob Lerche 1703–80. Geologie u. Mineralogie an d. Univ. Halle im 18. Jh., *Wiss. Beitr. d. Martin-Luther-Univ. Halle-Wittenberg*, 1 (T 48): 1–55.

Schwabe, H.: Julius Bernstein als Hochschullehrer, wissenschaftstheoret. u. Bildungspol., *Wiss. Beitr. d. Martin-Luther-Univ. Halle-Wittenberg*, 32 (T 51): 59–72.

Schwann, H.: Carl Ludwig als Förderer einer wiss. Zahnheilkunde—Archivstudie zur Gründungsgesch. d. Leipziger Zahnärztlichen Universitätsinst., *Stomatologie. DDR*, 33 (9): 652–57.

Schwendler, G.: Aus d. Arbeit d. Archivs d. Karl-Marx-Univ. Leipzig, *Archivmitt.*, 32 (4): 140–43.

Stolze, E.: Die Martin-Luther-Universität Halle-Wittenberg während des Faschismus 1933–45. Thesis. Halle/S.

Stützner, H. etc.: Zur Gesch. d. TH Karl-Marx-Stadt, *Wiss. Schriftenreihe d. TH Karl-Marx-Stadt*, 9: 1–95.

Vogt, A.: Ein Seminar f. Auserwählte. Zur Gesch. d. Mathem. Seminars an d. Univ. Berlin, *Spectrum*, 6: 30–31.

Wahl, V.: *Das Foto-Album der Akademischen Senatsmitglieder der Universität Jena von 1858*, Jena.

- - - - - Aus d. Gesch. d. akad. Brau-u. Schank-wesens: die älteste (Jenaer) Universitätsschenke 'Im Faulloch', *Jena-Inform.*, 7: 18–19.

- - - - - Die Dokumente d. Univ. Jena zur Doktorpromotion von Karl Marx 1841—ein Beitr. aus d. Universitätsarchiv zum Karl-Marx-Jahr

1983 u. zum 425jährigen Gründungsjubiläum d. Univ. Jena, *Archivmitt.*, 33: 6–12.

- - - - - Universitätsjubiläen d. Vergangenheit, *Jena-Inform.*, 9: 18–19.

Wandt, B.: Die Ehrensenatoren unserer Univ. ab 1919 u. Dokumentation über d. ab 1946 Geehrten, *Beitr. zur Gesch. d. Wilhelm-Pieck-Univ. Rostock*, 3: 68–74.

- - - - - Die Insignien d. Univ. Rostock, *Beitr. zur Gesch. d. Wilhelm-Pieck-Univ. Rostock*, 4: 6–16.

- - - - - Die Univ. Rostock u. Johannes Kepler, *Beitr. zur Gesch. d. Wilhelm-Pieck-Univ. Rostock*, 3: 50–55.

Wiele, B.: Studienprogramm u. Studienziel d. Klassischen Philologie, Neogräzistik u. Byzantinistik an d. Humboldt-Univ. zu Berlin, *Wiss. Z. d. Humboldt-Univ. zu Berlin, gesellsch.-u. sprachwiss. Reihe*, 32 (H 3): 363–66.

Zwahr, H.: Die Univ. Leipzig am Beginn d. bürgerlichen Umwälzung in Sachsen, *Sächsische Heimatblätter*, 29 (1): 30–34.

Publications 1984

Arndt, H.: Die Gründung d. Inst. f. Leibesübungen an d. Univ. Leipzig u. seine Entwicklung 1925–33. Ein Beitrag zum 575. Jahrestag d. Gründung d. Alma mater Lipsiensis, *Theorie u. Praxis d. Körperkultur*, 11: 831–50.

- - - - - Die Univ. Leipzig im Vorfeld d. Errichtung d. faschistischen Hitlerdiktatur 1929–33, *Leipzig aus Vergangenheit u. Gegenwart*, 3: 95–109.

Bartschat, B.: Ottmar Dittrich—ein Leipziger Sprachwissenschaftler zwischen Psychol. u. Phil. 1865–1951, *Linguistische Arbeitsber. d. Karl-Marx-Univ. Leipzig*, 42: 68–88.

Bastian, M.: Die Gesch. d. Lehrstuhls f. Vorgesch. an d. Leipziger Univ. 1934–45, *Wiss. Z. d. Karl-Marx-Univ. Leipzig, gesellsch.-u. sprachwiss. Reihe*, 33 (4): 393–99.

Bensing, M. and Katsch, G.: 15 Jahre Sektion Gesch. an d. Karl-Marx-Univ. Leipzig, *Wiss. Z. d. Karl-Marx-Univ. Leipzig*, 33 (4): 381–92.

Blumenthal, E.: *Museum Aegypticum*, Leipzig. (The M.A. of univ. of Leipzig).

Böhme, W. and Klaus, W.; Der Kampf zur Durchsetzung d. Arbeiter-u.-Bauern-Studiums, *Wiss. Z. d. TU Dresden*, 33 (6): 47–52.

Bretschneider, J.: Zur Herausbildung u. zum Stand d. theoret. Biologie als wiss. Spezialdisziplin, *Rostocker wissenschaftshist. Manuskripte*, 10: 3–14.

Bues, A.: Die Entwicklung d. internat. Wissenschaftsbeziehungen d. Martin-Luther-Univ. Halle-Wittenberg, *Wiss. Beitr. d. Martin-Luther-Univ. Halle-Wittenberg (Beitr. zur Universitätsgesch.)*, T 50: 105–114.

Christ-Tilo, C. etc.: Die Herausbildung u. Entwicklung d. marxistisch–leninistischen Wirtschaftsgesch. an d. Humboldt-Univ. zu Berlin. Jürgen Kuczynski zum 80. Geburtstag, *Beitr. zur Gesch. d. Humboldt-Univ. zu Berlin*, 10: 1–77.

Czok, K.: Karl Lamprechts Wirken an d. Leipziger Univ., *Sitzungsber. d. sächsischen Akad. d. Wiss. zu Leipzig, Phil.-Hist. Klasse*, 124 (6): 1–30.

- - - - - Leipzig u. seine Univ. im Wandel d. Jh., *Leipzig aus Vergangenheit u. Gegenwart*, 3: 55–76, and also *Schriftenreihe zum Veteranen-Koll. d. Karl-Marx-Univ. Leipzig*, 7: 1–20.

Diecke, G.: Die Klärung d. soz. Perspektive unter d. Studenten d. Martin-Luther-Univ. 1956–58, *Wiss. Beitr. d. Martin-Luther-Univ. Halle-Wittenberg*, T 50: 74–87.

Döring, D.: Das Leben in Leipzig in d. Zeit d. Dreißigjährigen Krieges, *Leipzig aus Vergangenheit u. Gegenwart*, 3: 151–75. (Refs to univ. of Leipzig).

Drewelow, H.: Zur Traditionslinie pädagog. Forschung in Rostock, *Erziehungswiss. Beitr. d. Wilhelm-Pieck-Univ. Rostock*, 9: 3–8.

Elkar, R. S.: Elitebildung oder Massenuniv. Zu Problemen d. Bildungsrekrutierung im 19. Jh., in S. Hoyer and W. Fläschendräger eds: *Die Geschichte der Universitäten und ihre Erforschung. Theorie-Empire-Methode*, Leipzig (henceforth noted as *Gesch. d. Univ.*): 108–31.

Ewe, H. and Herling, M.: Hoher Staatsbesuch in Stadtarchiv Stralsund u. im Universitätsarchiv Greifswald, *Archivmitt.*, 5: 155–57.

Fahrenbach, S.: Zur Herausbildung der Ophthalmologie als eigenständige Wissenschaftsdisziplin in Preußen unter Berücksichtigung zwischen Disziplinbildungsprozeß und der Tätigkeit der wissenschaftlichen Schule Albrecht von Gräfes. Thesis. Rostock.

Feige, H.-U.: Zur Vorgesch. d. Gründung d. Franz-Mehring-Inst. 1945–48, *Wiss. Z. d. Karl-Marx-Univ. Leipzig, gesellsch.-u. sprachwiss. Reihe*, 33 (4): 372–80.

- - - - - Schwendler, G. and Volkmer, R.: Zeittafel zur Gesch. d. Karl-Marx-Univ. Leipzig 1945–84, *Wiss. Z. d. Karl-Marx-Univ. Leipzig, gesellsch.-u. sprachwiss. Reihe*, 33: 628–81.

Feige, R.: *Königliche Gewerbeschule Chemnitz—Technische Hochschule Karl-Marx-Stadt. Ein Überblick in Daten*, Karl-Marx-Stadt.

Feyl, O.: Die Aspirantenseminare f. Staatsstipendiaten aus Rußland an d. Univ. d. kaiserlichen Deutschlands, in *Gesch. d. Univ.*: 132–45.

Fläschendräger, W.: Tagungsbericht 'Die Gesch. d. Univ. u. ihre Erforschung. Theorie-Empire-Methode', *Gesch. d. Univ.*: 182–84.

- - - - - 'Demnach verlautet, daß von den beyden Professoribus Born und Hilscher zu Leipzig aufwieglerische Gesinnungen geäußert worden . . .'. Zwei 'Jakobiner' an d. Univ. Leipzig? *Jb. f. Regionalgesch.*, 11: 187–90.

- - - - - '. . . Welche hohe Gnade niemahls einiger Deutschen Universität widerfahren . . .'. Anmerkungen zur 200-Jahr-Feier d. Viadrina im April 1706, *Frankfurter Beitr. zur Gesch.*, 13: 2–13.

Fletcher, J. M. and Upton, C. A.: A short description of the 16th cent. domestic accounts of Merton Coll., Oxford, in *Gesch. d. Univ.*: 54–67.

Frost, W.: Die Entwicklung d. Sportwiss. an d. Martin-Luther-Univ.—ein Beitr. zur Universitas Litterarum als Widerspiegelung d. humanistischen Charakters d. soz. Gesellschaft, *Wiss. Beitr. d. Martin-Luther-Univ. Halle-Wittenberg*, T 50: 96–104.

Gabka, K.: Slawistische Lehre u. Forschung an d. Univ. Greifswald, *Wiss. Z. d. Ernst-Moritz-Arndt-Univ. Greifswald*, 33 (1): 3–7.

Gabriel, A. L.: Heinrich von Langenstein—Theoretiker u. Reformator d. mittelalterlichen Univ., in *Gesch. d. Univ.*: 25–36.

Gatzer, H.: 13 Jahre internat. Wissenschaftskooperation Wilhelm-Pieck-Univ. Rostock—Schiffbauversuchsanstalt d. VEB Kombinat Schiffbau—Zentrales Wiss. Forschungsinst. Leningrad, *Schiffbauforschung*, 23 (3): 134–39.

Glier, W.: Zu einigen Erfahrungen u. Aufgaben d. Pflege d. Erbes u. d. progressiven Traditionen an d. TH Karl-Marx-Stadt, *Wiss. Schriftenreihe d. TH Karl-Marx-Stadt, Sonderheft*: 74–75.

Grau, C.: Zur Gesch. d. Orientalistik u. d. Botanik an d. Leipziger Univ. im beginnenden 18. Jh., in *Gesch. d. Univ.*: 78–88.

Hamel, J.: *Friedrich Wilhelm Bessel*, Leipzig. (F.W.B. erected the observatory at Königsberg univ. 1811 with English instruments).

Haschke, H.-D.: Die Entwicklung d. Köthener Polytechnikums als Stätte produktionsorientierter Ingenieurausbildung, *Wiss. Schriftenreihe d. TH Karl-Marx-Stadt, Sonderheft*: 30–35.

Heinemann, M.: Gesch. d. Hochschulwesens in Westdeutschland seit 1945. Methodenfragen u. Forschungsstrategie, in *Gesch. d. Univ.*: 156–81.

Hessel, M.: Zur Gesch. d. maritimen Hochschulausbildung, *Wiss. Schriftenreihe d. TH Karl-Marx-Stadt, Sonderheft*: 44–61.

- - - - - Zur Vorbereitung u. Durchführung d. Hochschulbildung f. Schiffsoffiziere u. Kapitäne in d. DDR Ende d. sechziger u. zu Beginn. d. siebziger Jahre, *Beitr. zur Gesch. d. Hochschulwesens d. DDR, T. I (Ber. u. Inform. zur Hochschulentwicklung)*, Berlin (henceforth noted as *Hochschulentwicklung)*: 29–34.

Heyne, W.: Zur Entwicklung d. Ingenieurhochschule Zwickau, *Schriftenreihe d. TH Karl-Marx-Stadt, Sonderheft*: 62–65.

Hoffmann, D.: Die Physik an d. Berliner Univ. in d. ersten Hälfte unseres Jhs. Zur personellen u. institutionellen Entwicklung, *Kolloquienheft*, 35: 5–30.

- - - - - Max Planck als akad. Lehrer, *Kolloquienheft*, 35: 55–72.

Hofmann, F.: Bemerkungen zur wirksamkeit von Ernst Christian Trapp als Prof. f. Pädagog. an d. Univ. Halle, *Wiss. Beitr. d. Martin-Luther-Univ. Halle-Wittenberg*, T 50: 20–35.

Hondt, J. d' and Wilke, J.: *Hegel in seiner Zeit (als Professor in Berlin),* Berlin.

Hoyer, S.: Die Gründung einer Univ. in Leipzig 1409, *Leipzig aus Vergangenheit u. Gegenwart,* 3: 77–93.

- - - - - and Fläschendräger, W. eds: *Die Geschichte der Universitäten und ihre Erforschung. Theorie-Empirie-Methode,* Leipzig. (Individual items noted separately).

Jahnke, K.-H.: 15 Jahre Forschungsgruppe 'Gesch. d. Jugendbewegung' an d. Sektion Gesch. d. Wilhelm-Pieck-Univ. Rostock, *Beitr. zur Gesch. d. Wilhelm-Pieck-Univ. Rostock,* 6: 94–102.

Janke, D.: Grundlinien d. Herausbildung einer bürgerlichen politökonomischen Lehre an d. Univ. Leipzig 1409–1848, *Wiss. Z. d. Karl-Marx-Univ. Leipzig, gesellsch.-u. sprachwiss. Reihe,* 33 (4): 355–63.

Jannermann, G.: Der Beitr. d. Wilhelm-Pieck-Univ. Rostock zum wiss.-tech. Fortschritt im Meliorationswesen, *Melioration u. Landwirtschaftsbau,* 18 (7): 273–76.

John, J.: Jenaer Studenten in d. bayerischen Putschvorbereitungen 1923, *Z. f. Geschichtwiss.,* 32 (4): 313–31.

Jügelt, K.-H.: Die Nordamerika-Sammlung d. Rostocker Hist. Karl Türk u. d. Univ. Rostock, *Wiss. Z. d. Wilhelm-Pieck-Univ. Rostock, gesellsch.-u. sprachwiss. Reihe,* 33 (2): 66–73.

Jugendlexikon 'Jugend in Studium', Leipzig.

Junghans, H.: *Der junge Luther und die Humanisten (an der Univ. Erfurt),* Berlin.

Kaiser, W.: Eichsfelder Mediziner d. 19. Jhs als hallesche Doktoranden, *Eichsfelder Heimathefte,* 24: 327–46.

- - - - - Zur Entwicklung klinischer Spezialdisziplinen an d. Univ. Halle, *Wiss. Z. d. Wilhelm-Pieck-Univ. Rostock, gesellsch.-u. sprachwiss. Reihe,* 32 (9): 66–70.

- - - - - 275 Jahre hallesche Medikamenten-Expedition. Aus d. Frühgesch. d. pharmazeutischen Industrie in Deutschland, *Beitr. zur Gesch. d. Pharmazie,* 36 (31/22): 185–96.

- - - - - and Völker, A.: Kurt Sprengel als Ordinarius d. Medizin. Fak. Halle, *Arbeitsblätter zur Wissenschaftsgesch.,* 13: 8–38.

Kathe, H.: Die Univ. Halle unter d. Einfluß d. Französischen Revol., *Wiss. Beitr. d. Martin-Luther-Univ. Halle-Wittenberg,* T 50: 36–44.

Kiefer, J.: Neue Erkenntnisse zur Mitgliedschaft Alexander von Humboldts in d.'Akad. nützlicher Wissenschaften' zu Erfurt, *NTM,* 21 (2): 65–79.

Kirsten, C.: *Die Altertumswissenschaften an der Berliner Akademie. Wahlvorschläge zur Aufnahme von Mitgliedern (aus Universitäten),* Berlin.

Klaus, W.: Zur Gesch. d. Freien Deutschen Jugend an d. TU Dresden, 1, *Beitr. zur Gesch. d. TU Dresden,* 11 (5): 1–100.

- - - - - Chronik d. TU Dresden 1962–70, *Beitr. zur Gesch. d. TU Dresden,* 15: 1–200.

Kobuch, A.: Der Einfluß d. westeurop. Aufklärung auf Gottsched u. seine Mitarbeiter in Leipzig im vierten Jahrzehnt d. 18. Jhs, *Wiss. Z. d. Humboldt-Univ. zu Berlin, gesellsch.-u. sprachwiss. Reihe*, 33 (3): 261–65.

Köhler, R.: Lenin u. d. soz. Hochschule, in *Gesch. d. Univ.*: 146–55.

- - - - - Zur Gesch. d. Hochschulwesens d. DDR in d. siebziger Jahren, *Hochschulentwicklung*: 5–22.

- - - - - Zur Gesch. d. tech. Bildungswesens in Deutschland u. d. DDR—Gegenstand-Methoden-Erfahrungen, *Wiss. Schriftenreihe d. TH Karl-Marx-Stadt, Sonderheft*: 75–79.

- - - - - Zur weiteren Verwirklichung d. Marxschen Idee vom Bündnis d. Arbeiterklasse mit d. Intelligenz durch d. Wiss.-u. Hochschulpol. d. SED in d. 60er u. 70er Jahren, in R. Köhler ed.: *Die Auffassung von Karl Marx über die gesellschaftliche Rolle von Wissenschaft und Bildung*, Berlin: 59–67.

Kossok, M.: Universitates Indiarum-Aufklärung-Independencia, in *Gesch. d. Univ.*: 89–107.

Kraus, A.: Bemerkungen zur Reform an d. deutschen TH in d. Jahren d. Weimarer Repub., *Wiss. Schriftenreihe d. TH Karl-Marx-Stadt, Sonderheft*: 36–43.

- - - - - Zur Entwicklung d. Forschung an d. Univ. u. Hochschulen (d. DDR) in d. ersten Hälfte d. siebziger Jahre, *Hochschulentwicklung*: 41–49.

Kröplin, M.: Die Tätigkeit von Prof. Dr August Friedrich Hecker (1763–1811) in Erfurt während der Jahre 1790–1805. Thesis. Erfurt.

Lieberwirth, R.: Die Außenwirksamkeit d. Wittenberger Juristenfak., *Wiss. Beitr. d. Martin-Luther-Univ. Halle-Wittenberg*, T 50: 5–19.

Mahnke, R.: Das wiss. Werk Paul Waldens in Rahmen d. Traditionen d. Elektrolytforschung an d. Univ. Rostock, *Wiss. Z. d. Wilhelm-Pieck-Univ. Rostock, mathem.-naturwiss. Reihe*, 33 (3): 65–72.

Pahnke, W.: Zur Errichtung eines Sportinst. an d. Univ. Rostock 1927, *Beitr. zur Gesch. d. Wilhelm-Pieck-Univ. Rostock*, 6: 42–48.

Piazza, H., Fläschendräger, W. and Katsch, G. eds: *Berühmte Leipziger Studenten*, Leipzig/Jena/Berlin. (25 biographies).

Prokoph, W.: Eine Kommunistische Studentenfraktion an d. Univ. Halle zur Zeit d. Weltwirtschaftskrise, *Wiss. Beitr. d. Martin-Luther-Univ. Halle-Wittenberg*, T 50: 45–55.

Rachold, J. ed.: *Die Illuminaten, Quellen und Texte zur Aufklärungsideologie des Illuminatenordens 1776–85*, Berlin. (Study of student group founded Ingolstadt 1776).

Rathmann, L.: *Erinnerungen an Georg Mayer*, Leipzig. (The present rect. of univ. of Leipzig writes on his predecessor).

- - - - - ed.: *Alma Mater Lipsiensis. Geschichte der Karl-Marx-Universität Leipzig*, Leipzig.

Raue, G.: Journalistikwiss. in d. DDR- Vor 30 Jahren Gründung d. Fak. f.

Journalistik an d. Karl-Marx-Univ. Leipzig, *Wiss. Z. d. Karl-Marx-Univ. Leipzig, gesellsch.-u. sprachwiss. Reihe*, 33 (4), 364–71.

Renker, U. and Franzen, E.: Das Hygiene-Inst. d. Martin-Luther-Univ. Halle-Wittenberg, *Wiss. Beitr. d. Martin-Luther-Univ. Halle-Wittenberg (Beitr. zur Universitätsgesch.)*, T 55: 1–60.

Roger, G.: Zur Entwicklung d. Hoch-u. Fachschulpädagog. in Rostock, *Beitr. zur Gesch. d. Wilhelm-Pieck-Univ. Rostock*, 6: 49–54.

Rothe, R.: Zur Gesch. d. Hochschulbauplanung in d. DDR, *Wiss. Schriftenreihe d. TH Karl-Marx-Stadt, Sonderheft*: 66–68.

Rüdiger, B.: Hochschulwesen, Wiss. u. Kunst in Sachsen während d. Weimarer Repub., *Sächsische Heimatblätter*, 30 (4): 149–52.

Schellbach, A.: Das Arbeiter-u. Bauern-Studium als Bestandteil d. antifaschistisch-demokratischen Umgestaltung d. Martin-Luther-Univ. Zur Entstehung u. Wirksamkeit d. Vorsemesters, *Wiss. Beitr. d. Martin-Luther-Univ. Halle-Wittenberg*, T 50: 56–73.

Schiller, K.-H.: Der Beginn d. Vorbereitung von Auslandsstudenten d. DDR an d. Martin-Luther-Univ., *Wiss. Beitr. d. Martin-Luther-Univ. Halle-Wittenberg*, T 50: 88–95.

Schmid, I.: Goethes amtliche Einflußnahme auf d. Univ. Jena über d. naturwiss. Inst., *Wiss. Beitr. d. Friedrich-Schiller-Univ. Jena*: 30–41.

Schubring, G.: Die (Ehren-) Promotion von P. G. Lejenne Dirichlet an d. Univ. Bonn 1827, *NTM*, 21 (1): 45–66.

Schumacher, G.-H.: Die Entwicklung d. Anatomie in Rostock, *Die Heilberufe*, 36 (11): 426–27.

Sinkovics, I.: Die Periodisierung d. Universitätsgesch., in *Gesch. d. Univ.*: 68–77.

Steiger, G.: Goethe, d. Univ. Jena u. d. Naturwiss., *Wiss. Beitr. d. Friedrich-Schiller-Univ. Jena*: 12–29.

Steinmetz, M.: Einleitung, in *Gesch. d. Univ.*: 6–24.

Stützner, H.: Gedanken zur Erforschung u. Darstellung d. Gesch. höherer tech. Bildungsstätten, *Beitr. zur Gesch. d. Hochschulwesens d. DDR*, 1: 56–63.

- - - - - Zur Erforschung u. Darstellung d. Gesch. d. tech. Bildungswesens in Deutschland u. d. DDR von d. Anfängen bis zur Gegenwart, *Wiss. Schriftenreihe d. TH Karl-Marx-Stadt, Sonderheft*: 1–22.

Tobies, R.: Untersuchungen zur Rolle d. Carl-Zeiss-Stiftung f. d. Entwicklung d. Mathem. an d. Univ. Jena, *NTM*, 21 (1): 33–44.

Totzek, W., Möller, K. and Lubsch, H.: 30 Jahre Industrie-Inst. (an Hochschulen d. DDR)—30 Jahre erfolgreiches Wirken im Interesse soz. Bildungspol., *Das Hochschulwesen*, 32 (5): 123–25.

Trillitzsch, W.: Humanismus u. Refn: Erfurter Humanistenkreis u. d. 'Dichterkönig' Helius Eobanus Hessus, *Wiss. Z. d. Friedrich-Schiller-Univ. Jena, gesellsch.—u. sprachwiss. Reihe*, 33 (3): 343–58.

Verger, J.: L'hist. soc. des univs à la fin du Moyen Age. Problèmes, Sources, Méthodes (à propos des univs du Midi de la France), in *Gesch. d. Univ.*: 37–53.

Wahl, V.: '. . . ein Denkmal d. Fortschritts in d. Kunst': 75 Jahre Ferdinand Hodlers Universitätsbild in Jena, *Jena-Inform.*, 11: 24–26.

- - - - - Friedrich Schiller: Dokumente u. Monumente in Jena. Die Dokumente im Archiv d.Univ., *Jena-Inform.*, 11: 18–20.

- - - - - *Schillers Erbe in Jena. Eine Dokumentation zur Wirkungsgeschichte Friedrich Schillers in der Universitätsstadt*, Jena.

Walter, U.: 'Goethe ist wohl fleißig . . .', *Leipzig aus Vergangenheit u. Gegenwart*, 3: 223–33. (Docs of G.'s student days in Leipzig).

Wandt, B.: Das Promotionsrecht u. d. Verleihung d. Würde eines Ehrendoktors an d. Univ. Rostock Beitr. zur Gesch d. Wilhelm-Pieck-Univ. Rostock, 6: 4–17.

- - - - - Ehrenpromotionen auf d. Gebiet d. Gesellschaftswiss. an d. Univ. Rostock, *Beitr. zur Gesch. d. Wilhelm-Pieck-Univ. Rostock*, 6: 55–70.

Wartenberg, G.: 575 Jahre Alma mater Lipsiensis, *Standpunkt*, 12: 325–27. (The L. Theol. faculty).

Wendel, G.: Die Berliner Inst. d. Kaiser-Wilhelm-Gesellschaft u. ihr Platz im system d. Wissenschaftspol. d. imperialistischen Deutschland in d. Zeit bis 1933, *Kolloquiumsreihe*, 39: 27–69.

Wonneberger, G. and Simon, H.: Gesch. d. Körperkultur als Lehrgebiet an d. Deutschen Hochschule f. Körperkultur u. Sport Leipzig, *Wiss. Z. d. Deutschen Hochschule f. Körperkultur u. Sport Leipzig*, 25 (3): 26–35.

German Federal Republic

Additions to Earlier Lists

For 1977

Kukuch, M.: *Student und Klassenkampf. Studentenbewegung in der BRD seit 1967*, Hamburg.

Schmitz, R.: *Die Naturwissenschaften an der Philipps-Universität Marburg 1527–1977*, Marburg.

For 1980

Boehm, L. and Spörl, J. eds: *Die Ludwig-Maximilians-Universität in ihren Fakultäten*, 2, Berlin.

Burchardt, L.: Science pol. in imperial Germany, *Hist. soc. research*, 13: 271–89.

For 1981

Hammerstein, N.: Humanismus u. Univ., in A. Buck and E. Hauswedell eds: *Die Rezeption der Antike. Zum Problem der Kontinuität zwischen Mittelalter und Renaissance*, Hamburg: 23–39.

Publications 1982

Alter, P.: *Wissenschaft, Staat, Mäzene. Anfänge moderner Wissenschaftspolitik in Großbritannien 1850–1920*, Stuttgart.

Baum, R. J. etc.: *1582–1982 Studentenschaft und Korporationswesen an der Universität Würzburg*, Würzburg.

Baumgart, P. ed.: *Vierhundert Jahre Universität Würzburg*, Neustadt a.d. Aisch.

Benedum, J. ed.: *Th. L. W. Bischoff: Das neue Anatomiegebäude zu Gießen, Gießen 1852*, Gießen.

- - - - - and Michler, M.: *Das Siegel der Medizinischen Fakultät Gießen*, Gießen.

- - - - - and Giese, C.: *375 Jahre Medizin in Gießen. Ausstellungskatalog anläßlich der 375-Jahrfeier der Universität Gießen*, Gießen.

Binding, G. ed.: *Aus der Geschichte der Universität zu Köln*, Cologne.

Bruch, R. vom: *Weltpolitik als Kulturmisssion. Auswärtige Kulturpolitik und Bildungsbürgertum in Deutschland am Vorabend des ersten Weltkrieges*, Paderborn etc.

Conrads, N.: *Ritterakademien der frühen Neuzeit. Bildung als Standesprivileg im 16. und 17. Jahrhundert*, Göttingen.

Dickerhof, H.: Gelehrte Gesellschaften, Akad., Ordenstudien u. Univ., *Z. f. bayerische Landesgesch.*, 45: 37–66.

Ehrhardt, W.: *Das akademische Kunstmuseum der Universität Bonn unter der Direktion von Friedrich Gottlob Welcker und Otto Jahn*, Opladen.

Gundel, H. G. ed.: *Statuta Academicae Marpurgensis deinde Gissensis de anno 1629. Die Statuten der Hessen-Darmstädtischen Landesuniversität Marburg 1629–50/Gießen 1650–1879*, Marburg.

- - - - - Moraw, P. and Press, V. eds: *Gießener Gelehrte in der ersten Hälfte des 20. Jahrhunderts*, 2 vols, Marburg.

Hissette, R.: Albert le Grand et Thomas d'Aquin dans la censure parisienne du 7 mars 1277, in A. Zimmermann ed.: *Studien zur mittelalterlichen Geistesgeschichte und ihren Quellen*, Berlin/New York: 226–46.

Hofmann, N.: *Die Artistenfakultät an der Universität Tübingen 1534–1601*, Tübingen.

Huppertz, A.: *Die Vertreter der Anatomie und des anatomischen Unterrichts in Gießen von 1702–48*, Gießen.

Kleinart, A.: Akad. Disputierschriften aus d. 'Bibliothek Schimank', in P. Vodosek etc. eds: *Bibliothekswissenschaft, Musikbibliothek, soziale Bibliotheksarbeit. Festschrift für H. Waßner zum 60. Geburtstag*, Wiesbaden: 77–86.

Köhler, G.: *Gießener juristische Vorlesungen. Praelectiones iuridicae Giessensis 1607–1982*, Gießen.

Konrad, M.: *Die Hochschulschriften zur Geschichte der Zahnheilkunde. Eine Bibliographie*, Tecklenburg.

Kühlmann, W.: *Gelehrtenrepublik und Fürstenstaat*, Tübingen.

Maffei, D.: Quattro lettere del Capei al Savigny e l'insegnamento del diritto romano a Siena nel 1834, in N. Horn ed.: *Europäisches Rechtsdenken in Geschichte und Gegenwart. Festschrift für Helmut Coing zum 70. Geburtstag*, Munich, 1: 203–24.

Marti, H.: *Philosophische Dissertationen deutscher Universitäten 1660–1750*, Munich/New York.

Moraw, P.: *Kleine Geschichte der Universität Gießen 1607–1982*, Gießen.

- - - - - - and Press, V. eds: *Academia Gissensis. Beiträge zur älteren Gießener Universitätsgeschichte. Zum 375jährigen Jubiläum dargebracht vom Historischen Institut der Justus-Liebig-Universität Gießen*, Marburg.

Nissen, W.: Otto von Bismarcks Göttinger Studentenjahre 1823–33, Göttingen.

Nörr, K. W.: Zum instit. Rahmen d. gelehrten Rechte im 12. Jh., in *Aspecte europäischer Rechtsgeschichte. Festgabe H. Coing*, Frankfurt a. M. (henceforth noted as *Festgabe H.C.*): 233–44. (Organ. of study of Law at Bologna and Paris).

Ott, H. and Schadek, H. eds: *Freiburg im Breisgau. Universität und Stadt. Katalog zur Ausstellung vom 21. 10.–21. 11. 1982 im Colombischlößchen*, Freiberg i. Br.

Prange, W.: Die Siegesfeier d. Kieler Univ. 1815. Nachlese zu Dahlmanns Waterloo-Rede, *Z. d. Gesellschaft f. Schleswig-Holsteinische Gesch.*, 107: 327–46.

Reiter, E.: *Die Eichstätter Bischöfe und ihre Hochschule im Dritten Reich. Abwehr der Versuche zur Politisierung der Hochschule und Sorge um deren Bestand*, Regensburg.

Schimpf, W.: *Die Rezensenten der Göttingischen Gelehrten Anzeigen 1760–68*, Göttingen.

Schormann, G.: *Academia Ernestina. Die schaumburgische Universität zu Rinteln an der Weser 1610/21–1810*, Marburg.

Schrey, H.: *Die Universität Duisburg. Geschichte und Gegenwart*, Duisburg.

Schulte, G.: *Institut für Hochschulkunde an der Universität Würzburg. Werden und Wirken 1882–1982. Aus Anlaß des 400jährigen Bestehens der Universität Würzburg 1582–1982*, Würzburg.

Schwaiger, G.: Sailers frühe Lehrtätigkeit in Ingolstadt u. Dillingen, *Beitr. zur Gesch. d. Bistums Regensburg*, 16: 51–96.

Schwinges, R. C.: Student. Kleingruppen im späten Mittelalter, in H. Ludat and R. C. Schwinges eds: *Politik, Gesellschaft, Geschichtsschreibung. Gießener Festgabe für F. Graus*, Cologne: 319–61.

Vezina, B.: *'Die Gleichschaltung' der Universität Heidelberg im Zuge der nationalsozialistischen Machtergreifung*, Heidelberg.

Weimar, P.: Zur Doktorwurde d. Bologneser Legisten, in *Festgabe H. C.*: 421–43.

Wendehorst, A. and C. eds: *Die Matrikel der Universität Würzburg. 2. Personen-und Ortsregister 1582–1830*, Berlin.

Werner, N.: *375 Jahre Universität Gießen. Geschichte und Gegenwart. Katalog der Jubiläumsausstellung*, Gießen.

Winkel, H. ed.: *Geschichte und Naturwissenschaft in Hohenheim. Beiträge*

zur Natur-, Agrar-, Wirtschafts- und Sozialgeschichte Südwestdeutsch-
lands. Festschrift für Günther Franz zum 80. Geburtstag, Sigmaringen.

Publications 1983

Hammerstein, N.: Die deutschen Univ. im Zeitalter d. Aufklärung, *Z. f.*
hist. Forschung, 10: 73–89.

- - - - - Christian Wolf u. d. Univ. Zur Wirkungsgesch. d. Wolfianismus im
18. Jh., in W. Schneiders ed., *Christian Wolf,* Hamburg: 266–77.

- - - - - Jubiläumsschrift u. Alltagsarbeit. Tendenzen Bildungsgesch. Literatur, *Hist. Z.,* 236: 601–33.

Hanschmidt, A.: Doktoren d. Akad. zu Harderwijk aus d. Amt Mappen in
d. Jahren 1690–1805, *Jb. d. Emsländischen Heimatbundes,* 29: 27–33.

Jarausch, K. H. ed.: *The Transformation of Higher Learning 1860–1930.*
Expansion, Diversification, Social Opening and Professionalization in
England, Germany, Russia and the United States, Stuttgart/Chicago.

Moraw, P.: Heidelberg: Univ. Hof u. Stadt im ausgehenden Mittelalter, in
B. Moeller etc. eds: *Studien zum städtischen Bildungswesen des späten*
Mittelalters und der frühen Neuzeit, Göttingen: 524–52.

Publications 1984

Bruch, R. vom: Die deutsche Hochschule in d. hist. Forschung, in D.
Goldschmidt etc. eds: *Forschungsgegenstand Hochschule. überblick*
und Trendbericht, Frankfurt/New York: 1–27.

- - - - - Universitätsreform als soz. Bewegung, *Gesch. u. Gesellschaft,* 10:
72–91.

Epp, G. K.: *The educational policies of Catherine II: the era of enlighten-*
ment in Russia, Frankfurt a. M.

Hammerstein, N.: 'Die Zeiten verlangen ihre Entsprechungen in d. Gesinnungen'. Die Gesch. d. Frankfurter univ. in ihren Festreden, in
Akademischer Festakt anläßlich des 70. Geburtstages der J. W. G.—Uni-
versität Frankfurt am Main, Frankfurt a. M.: 14–24.

Hanschmidt, A.: Doctoren d. Akad. zu Harderwijk aus d. Aemtern Clop-
penburg u. Vecht im 19. Jh., *Jb. f. d. Oldenburger Münsterland,* Vechta:
100–104.

Jarausch, K. H.: *Deutsche Studenten 1800–1970,* Frankfurt a. M.

Moraw, P.: Humboldt in Gießen. Zur Professorenberufung im 19. Jh.,
Gesch. u. Gesellschaft, 10: 47–71.

Müller, R. A.: Aristokratisierung d. Studiums? Bemerkungen zur Ade-
lsfrequenz an süddeutschen Univ. im 17. Jh., *Gesch. u. Gesellschaft,* 10:
31–46.

Peset, M.: Univ. españolas y univ. europ., *Ius commune,* 12: 71–89.

Ridder-Symoens, H. de: Deutsche Studenten an italienischen Rechtsfak.

Ein Bericht über unveröffentlichtes Quellen-u. Archivmaterial, *Ius commune*, 12: 287–315.

Schwinges, R. C.: Universitätsbesuch im Reich vom 14. zum 16. Jh.: Wachstum u. Konjunkturen, *Gesch. u. Gesellschaft*, 10: 5–30.

Titze, H.: Die zyklische Überproduktion von Akad. im 19. u. 20 Jh., *Gesch. u. Gesellschaft*, 10: 92–121.

Publications 1985

Asmuth, M.: *Die Studentenschaft der Handelshochschule Köln 1901 bis 1919*, Cologne/Vienna.

Boehm, L.: Wilhelm von Humboldt 1767–1835 and the Univ. Idea and implementation, *Alexander von Humboldt Stiftung. Mitt.*, 46: 1–8.

Brinkhus, G.: Stadt.-Univ.-Bibliotheken. Zur Tübinger Bibliotheksgesch. im 16. Jh., in H. G. Göpfert etc. eds: *Beiträge zur Geschichte des Buchwesens in konfessionellen Zeitalter*, Wiesbaden: 179–88.

Ellwein, T.: *Die deutsche Universität. Vom Mittelalter bis zur Gegenwart*, Königstein.

Hammerstein, N.: Zur Gesch. u. Bedeutung d. Univ. im heiligen römischen Reich Deutscher Nat., *Hist. Z.*, 241: 287–328.

Hochgerner, J.: Die Univ. in Österreich. Eine hist. Skizze ihrer Entwicklung, *Z. f. Hochschul-didaktik*, 9: 359–74.

Lungreen, P. ed.: *Wissenschaft im Dritten Reich*, Frankfurt a. M.

Miethke, J.: Die Studenten, in J. Kunisch etc. eds: *Unterwegssein im Spätmittelalter*. Beiheft 1 zur *Z. f. hist. Forschung*, Berlin: 49–70.

Ribhegge, W.: *Geschichte der Universität Münster*, Münster.

Publications 1986

Berning, E.: *Unterschiedliche Fachstudiendauer in gleichen Studiengängen an verschiedenen Universitäten in Bayern*, Munich.

Beyme, K. von: *Politikwissenschaft in der Bundesrepublik Deutschland. Entwicklungsprobleme einer Disziplin*, Opladen.

Boockmann, H.: Ikonographie d. Univ. Bemerkungen über bildliche u. gegenständliche Zeugnisse d. spätmittelalterlichen deutschen Univ.-Gesch., in J. Fried ed.: *Schulen und Studium im sozialem Wandel des hohen und späten Mittelalters*, Sigmaringen (henceforth noted as *S. u. S.*): 565–99.

Brim, S.: *Universitäten und Studentenbewegung in Russland im Zeitalter der Grossen Reformen 1855–81*, Frankfurt a. M.

Bruch, R. vom and Roegele, O. B. eds: *Von der Zeitungskunde zur Publizistik. Biographisch-institutionelle Stationen der deutschen Zeitungswissenschaft in der ersten Hälfte des 20. Jahrhunderts*, Frankfurt a. M.

Bruch, R. vom and Müller, R. A.: *Erlebte und Gelebte Universität. Die Universität München im 19. und 20. Jahrhundert,* Pfaffenhofen.

- - - - - Krieg u. Frieden. Zur Frage d. Militarisierung deutscher Hochschullehrer u. Univ. im späten Kaiserreich, in J. Dülffer and K. Holl eds: *Bereit zum Krieg. Kriegsmentalität im wilhelminischen Deutschland 1890–1914,* Göttingen: 74–98.

- - - - - 'Militarismus', 'Realpolitik', Pazifismus'. Außenpol. u. Aufrüstung in d. Sicht deutscher Hochschullehrer (Historiker) im späten Kaiserreich, *Militärgesch. Mitt.,* 39: 37–58.

- - - - - Moderne Wissenschaftsgesch. als Bildungs-Soz.-u. Disziplingesch. Das Beispiel d. frühen deutschen Soziologie, *Hist. Z.,* 242: 361–73.

Bulst, N.: Studium u. Karriere im königlichen Dienst in Frankreich im 15. Jh., in *S. u. S.:* 375–405.

Diener, H.: Die Hohen Schulen, ihre Lehrer u. Schüler in d. Registern d. päpstlichen Verwaltung d. 14. u. 15 Jhs, in *S. u. S.:* 351–74.

Drüll, G.: *Heidelberger Gelehrtenlexikon 1803–1932, Berlin,* Heidelberg.

Ehlers, J.: Deutsche Scholaren in Frankreich während d. 12. Jhs, in *S. u. S.:* 97–120.

Fried, J. ed.: *Schulen und Studium im sozialen Wandel des hohen und späten Mittelalters,* Sigmaringen. (Items noted separately).

Gilch, E. etc.: *Volkskunde an der Universität München 1933–45. Zwei Studien von Eva Gilch und Carmen Schramka mit einem dokumentarischen Beitrag von Hildegunde Prütting,* Munich.

Gladen, P.: *Gaudeamus igitur. Die studentischen Verbindungen einst und jetzt,* Munich.

Hammerstein, N.: Univ.-Territorialstaaten-Gelehrte Räte, in R. Schnur ed.: *Die Rolle der Juristen bei der Entstehung des modernen Staates,* Berlin: 687–735.

Heckel, M.: *Die theologischen Fakultäten im weltlichen Verfassungsstaat,* Tübingen.

Hecker, H.: *Kolonialforschung und Studentenschaft an der 'Hansischen Universität' im 2 Weltkrieg. Die NSDStB-Kameradschaft 'Hermann von Wißmann' und die 'übersee- und Kolonial-Arbeitsgemeinschaft',* Baden-Baden.

Heimpel, H., Kamp, N.´ and Kertz, W.: *Der Neubeginn der Georgia Augusta zum Wintersemester 1945–46. Akademische Feier zur Erinnerung an die Wiedereröffnung der Georgia Augusta vor vierzig Jahren,* Göttingen.

Illmer, D.: Der Rechtsschule von Orléans u. ihre deutschen Studenten im späten Mittelalter, in *S. u. S.:* 407–38.

Jaspers, K.: *Erneuerung der Universität. Reden und Schriften 1945–46. Nachwort: Renato de Rosa: Politische Akzente im Leben eines Philosophen. Karl Jaspers in Heidelberg 1901–46,* Heidelberg.

Laubach, H.-C.: *Die Politik des Philologenverbandes im Deutschen Reich und in Preußen während der Weimarer Republik. Die Lehrer an höheren*

Schulen mit Universitätsausbildung im politischen und gesellschaftlichen Spannungsfeld der Schulpolitik von 1918–33, Frankfurt a. M./Bern/New York.

Maissen, F. and Arnold, K.: Walliser Studenten an d. Univ. Ingolstadt-Landshut-München 1472–1914, *Blätter aus d. Walliser Gesch.*, 19.

Martin, B.: Heidegger u. d. Reform d. deutschen Univ. 1933, *Freiburger Universitätsblätter*, 92: 49–69.

Miethke, J.: Die Kirche u. d. Univ. im 13 Jh., in *S. u. S.*: 285–320.

Moraw, P.: Die Juristenuniv. in Prag 1372–1419, verfassungs-u. sozialgesch. betrachtet, in *S. u. S.*: 439–86.

Müller, R. A.: *Akademische Ausbildung zwischen Staat und Kirche. Das bayerische Lyzealwesen 1773–1849*, Paderborn/Munich/Vienna/Zürich.

Müller, W.: *Universität und Orden. Die bayerische Landes-universität Ingolstadt zwischen der Aufhebung des Jesuitenordens und der Säkularisation 1773–1803*, Berlin.

Neumann, K. ed.: *Vierzig Jahre Pädagogische Hochschule Göttingen. Jubiläumsfeier am 7. und 8. Februar 1986 im Fachbereich Erziehungswissenschaften der Georg-August-Universität Göttingen*, Göttingen.

Ortmann, R.: *Die Jüngere Geschichte des Anatomischen Instituts der Universität zu Köln 1919–84. 65 Jahre in bewegter Zeit*, Cologne/Vienna.

Röhrich, H.: *Die Frau: Rolle, Studium und Beruf. Eine Literaturanalyse*, Munich.

Schmidt, G. and Rüsen, J. eds: *Gelehrtenpolitik und politische Kultur in Deutschland 1830–1930*, Bochum.

Schnuer, G.: *Die Deutsche Bildungskatastrophe. 20 Jahre nach Pflicht— Lehren und Lernen in Deutschland*, Herford.

Schneider, R.: Studium u. Zisterzienorden, in *S. u. S.*: 321–50.

Schwinges, R. C.: Sozialgesch. Aspekte spätmittelalterlicher Studentenbursen in Deutschland, in *S. u. S.*: 527–64.

- - - - - *Deutsche Universitätsbesucher im 14. und 15. Jahrhundert*, Stuttgart.

Stackmann, K. etc.: *Jacob und Wilhelm Grimm. Vorträge und Ansprachen in den Veranstaltungen der Akademie der Wissenschaften und der Georg-August-Universität in Göttingen anläßlich der 200-Wiederkehr ihrer Geburtstage, am 24., 26. und 28. Juni 1985 in der Aula der Georg-August-Universität Göttingen*, Göttingen.

Stölting, E.: *Akademische Soziologie in der Weimarer Republik*, Berlin.

Syre, L.: *Die Universitätsbibliothek Tübingen auf dem Weg ins 20. Jahrhundert. Die Amtszeit Karl Geigers 1895–1920*, Tübingen.

Theis, A., Graumann, W. and Oppermann, T. eds: *Wissenschaftstransfer zwischen Universität und Wirtschaft. Neue Formen der Kooperation in Westeuropa*, Baden-Baden.

Urban, K.: *Das Ausbildungswesen unter dem Nationalsozialismus. Wissenschaftstheoretische Begründung und Erziehungswirkliche Praxis*, Frankfurt a. M./Bern/New York.

Verger, J.: A propos de la naissance de l'univ. de Paris: contexte social, enjeu pol., portée intellect., in *S. u. S.*: 69–96.
Wiggershaus, R.: *Die Frankfurter Schule. Geschichte, Theoretische Entwicklung, Politische Bedeutung*, Munich/Vienna.
Wriedt, K.: Bürgertum u. Studium in Norddeutschland während d. Spätmittelalters, in *S. u. S.*: 487–525.

Hungary

Publications 1982

Kulcsár, E.: *Egyetemünk kérdései az országgyűlésen 1825–1944* (Discussion concerning the univ. of Budapest in Parliament 1825–1944), Budapest.
Papp, J.: *Hagyományok és tárgyi emlékek az Eötvös Loránd Tudományegyetemen* (Traditions and survivals in the Eötvös Loránd univ.), Budapest.
Polinszky, K.: A Műegyetem bicentenáriuma (The bicent. of the TU), *Felsőoktatási Szemle*, 12: 705–710.
Szögi, L.: *A Semmelweis Orvostudományi Egyetem Levéltára 1770–1970* (The archives of the Semmelweis univ. of Med. 1770–1970), Budapest.
- - - - - ed.: *Egyetemünk történetének levéltári és kézirattári forrásai 1635–1970* (Archive and MS refs to the Eötvös Loránd univ. 1635–1970), 1–2, Budapest.
Szabadváry, F. ed.: *A Budapesti Műszaki Egyetem 200 éve 1782–1982* (200 yrs of the TU of Budapest 1782–1982), Budapest.
Tóth, A. and Vértesy, M.: *A Budapesti egyetemi könyvtár története 1561–1944* (The hist. of the Budapest univ. library 1561–1944), Budapest.
Végh, F.: *Műegyetemi rektori beszédek. Bibliográfia* (Orations of the rects of the TU. A bibliog.), Budapest.

Publications 1983

Bodor, F. ed.: *Dokumentumok a magyar Iparművészeti Főiskola életéből 1945–83* (Docs illustrating life at the Hungarian schl for Indust. Art), Budapest.
Hiller, I.: *H. D. Wilckens az erdészettudomány első professzora Magyarországon* (H.D.W. 1st prof. of Forestry Science in Hungary), Sopron.
- - - - - and Igmándy, Z. eds: *Mindnyájan voltunk egyszer az Akadémián . . . Az erdészeti felsőoktatás 175. évfordulója* (All of us were once at the Acad. . . . The 175th anniv. of higher educ. in Forestry), Sopron.
Tok, M.: Az elmélet és a gyakorlat viszonya a selmeci Akad. pedagóg. (The relation between theory and practice in the Pedagogy of the acad. of Selmecbánya), *Felsőoktatási Szemle*, 2: 123–28.

Bibliography 441

5ary** 441

Zsámboki, L. ed.: *A selmecbányai akadémia oktatóinak lexikona* (Encyclop. of profs of the acad. of Selmecbánya 1735–1918), Miskolc.
Bereczki, U.: A tartui egyetem szerepe Oroszország kult., társadalmi és pol. életében a századfordulón (The role of the univ. of Tartu in Russian cult., soc. and pol. life at the turn of the cent.), *Történelmi Szemle*, 3: 421–32.
Kemény, G. G.: Felsőoktatásunk a dualizmus korában (Hungarian higher educ. under the Dual Monarchy), *Századok*, 1: 64–91.
Sinkovics, I.: A magyar egyetemtörténeti kutatások nemzetközi kapcsolatai, szervezeti és kutatási kérdések (The internal position of Hungarian research into the hist. of univs. Questions of organ. and investigation), *Felsőoktatási Szemle*, 4: 247–51.
Szögi, L.: Az ELTE jubileumi előkészületeinek eredményeiről (Preparations for the celebration of the anniv. of the Eötvös Loránd univ.), *Felsőoktatási Szemle*, 3: 179–84.

Publications 1985

Bakó, K. etc.: *Vivat Academia . . . A bányászati, kohászati és erdészeti felsőoktatás 250. évfordulója* (Vivat Academia . . . The 250th anniv. of higher educ. in Mining, Metallurgy and Forestry), Budapest.
Baráz, M.: A győri tanítóképzés 25 éve 1959–84. Kiadvány ismertetése (25 yrs of teachers' training in Győr. Rev. of a publication), *Felsőoktatási Szemle*, 4: 255–56.
Horváth, P. ed.: *Az Állam- és Jogtudományi Kar szerepe a magyar jogtudomány fejlődésében* (The role of the fac. of Law in the devel. of Hungarian jurisprudence), Budapest.
Márkus, G., Mészáros, I. and Gazda, I.: *Magyar neveléstörténeti irodalom 1800–1944* (Bibliog. of Hungarian educ. hist. 1800–1944), Budapest.
Sinkovics, I. ed.: *Az Eötvös Loránd Tudományegyetem története 1635–1985* (The hist. of the Eötvös Loránd univ. 1635–1985), Budapest. (Summaries in Russian, English and German.)
Szögi, L.: *A Budapesti Eötvös Loránd Tudományegyetem rövid története 1635–1985* (A short hist. of the Eötvös Loránd univ. 1635–1985), Budapest. (Also available in Russian, English and German).
- - - - - *Az Állatorvostudományi Egyetem Levéltára (1741) 1787–1972. Repertórium* (The archives of the veterinary univ. (1741) 1787–1972. A repertorium), Budapest.
Tar, S. ed.: *1735–1985. Nehézipari Műszaki Egyetem* (1735–1985. The Polytech. for Heavy Industries), Miskolc.
Zsámboki, L. ed.: *Selmectől Miskolcig 1735–1985* (From Selmec to Miskolc 1735–1985), Miskolc.

Publications 1986

Dóka, K. ed: *Az egyetemi levéltárak* (The archives of univs (in Hungary and Austria)), Budapest.

Győrffy, S. and Hunyadi, Z. eds: *A soproni Líceum 1557–1982* (The Lyceum of Sopron 1557–1982), Budapest.

Hegyi, I.: Az ének és a zene szerepe Európa felsőoktatásában régen és ma (The role of singing and music in European higher educ. in the past and today), *Felsőoktatási Szemle*, 3: 174–80.

Horváth, P.: Történelmi tapasztalatok szerepe a modern egyetemi munka fejlesztésében (The role of hist. experience in the devel. of modern univ. work), *Felsőoktatási Szemle*, 7–8: 393–98.

Ködöböcz, J.: *Tanítóképzés Sárospatakon. A kollégiumi és középfokú képzés négy évszázada* (Teachers' training in Sárospatek. Four cents of coll. and secondary educ.), Budapest.

Kovács, G. and Fehér, G.: *Biographia. Elhunyt tanáraink és előadóink életrajza 1787–1987* (Biographia. Biogs of former profs and lects of the veterinary univ. 1787–1987), Budapest.

Ladányi, A.: *Felsőoktatási politika 1949–58* (Higher educ. pol. in Hungary 1949–58), Budapest.

Némedi, L.: Hatvan éves a Debreceni Nyári Egyetem (60 yrs of the summer univ. of Debrecen), *Felsőoktatási Szemle*, 10: 610–38.

Szabó, T. and Zallár, A.: Szent-Györgyi Albert az egyetemi oktatásról (A.S.-G. on univ. educ.), *Felsőoktatási Szemle*, 7–8: 489–91.

Szögi, L.: A magyarországi egyetemek történetének forrásai (Sources for univ. hist. in Hungary), *Felsőoktatási Szemle*, 6: 380–84.

- - - - - Az egyetemi levéltárak feladatai (Functions of the univ. archives), *Levéltári Szemle*, 3: 3–10.

Italy

Additions to Earlier Lists

For 1978

Franceschini, E.: *Concetto Marchesi. Linee per l'intepretazione di un uomo inquieto*, Padua. (Inform. about univ. of Padua 20th century).

Maschietto, F. L.: *Elena Lucrezia Cornaro Piscopia 1646–84 prima donna laureata nel mondo*, Padua. (Inform. about univ. of Padua 17th century).

For 1980

Bosna, E.: *Storia dell'Università di Bari, I. Le origini (dal Collegio dei Gesuiti al Reale Liceo delle puglie)*, Bari.

Re, N. del: *Il cardinale Belisario Cristaldi e il canonico Antonio Muccioli*, Vatican. (Inform. about univ. of Rome 19th century).

For 1981

Bo, D.: L'Europa medica nella Genova settecentesca. Alle origini dell'Univ. 1750–1800, *Misc. storica ligure*, 13.

Morelli, G.: De Studio scolarium civitatis Bononie manutenendo. Gli statuti del Comune 1335–1454 per la tutela dello Studio e delle Univ. degli scolari, *L'Archiginnasio*, 76: 79–165.

Roggero, M.: Prof. e studenti nelle univ. tra crisi e riforma, in *Storia d'Italia. Annali*, 4: 1038–81.

Trotti, G. B.: Lo stato dell'Univ. di Parma nel periodo di transizione dai Farnese ai Borboni, *Arch. storico per le prov. parmensi*, 33: 291–308.

Publications 1982

Arnaldi, G.: Fondazione e rifondazioni dello Studio di Napoli in età sveva, in E. Gistiani ed.: *Università e società nei secoli 12–16*, Pistoia (henceforth noted as *Univ. e soc.*): 81–106.

- - - - - Studenti e prof. nell'Italia del sec. 13: la prospettiva degli studi in 'terra aliena', *La cultura*, 20: 415–24.

Arrighi, G.: La matematica fra bottega d'abaco e Studio in Toscana nel Medio Evo, in *Univ. e soc.*: 107–20.

Baker, J. H.: The Inns of Court and Chancery as voluntary associations, *Quad. fiorentini per la storia del pensiero giuridico moderno*, 11/12: 9–38. (Inform. about univs of Oxford and Cambridge).

Bellomo, M.: Studenti e 'populus' nelle città univ. italiane del sec. 12 al 14, in *Univ. e soc.*: 61–80.

Belloni, A.: Giovanni Dondi, Albertino da Salso e le origini dello Studio pavese, *Boll. della soc. pavese di storia patria*, 82: 17–47.

Berengo, M.: Il numero chiuso all'Univ. di Padova. Un dibattito della Restaurazione, *Quad. per la storia dell'Univ. di Padova*, 14 (1981) (henceforth noted as *Q.U.P.*): 41–53.

Bernuzzi, M.: *La Facoltà teologica dell'Università di Pavia nel periodo delle riforme 1767–97*, Milan.

Caldani, L. M. A. and Spallanzani, L.: *Carteggio 1768–98*, Milan. (Inform. about univ. of Pavia 18th century).

Caroti, S.: L'inedita quaestio 'Numquid generatio sit verus motus' di Alessandro Sermoneta, *Giornale critico della fil. ital.*, 61: 168–82. (Inform. about univ. of Florence 15th century).

Catoni, G.: Il comune di Siena e l'ammin. della Sapienza nel sec. 15, in *Univ. e soc.*: 121–29.

Cecchi, D.: Un'inchiesta dell'ammin. pontificia sulla pubblica istruzione nella delegazione apostolica di Macerata (aprile-giugno 1817), *Univ. di Macerata. Annali della fac. di giurisprud.*, 34: 1533–68.

Colliva, P.: Pillio da Medicina (. . . 1169–1207 . . .) nei suoi problematici rapporti con lo studio ed il comune di Bologna, *Clio*, 18: 190–99.

Cortese, E.: Legisti, canonisti e feudisti: la formazione di un ceto medievale, in *Univ. e soc.*: 195–284. (Inform. about Italian universities).

- - - - - Esperienza scientif. Storia del diritto ital., in *Cinquanta anni di esperienza giuridica in Italia*, Milan: 785–858. (Contains bibliog. of Italian universities).

- - - - - Scienza di giudici e scienza di prof. tra 12 e 13 sec., in *Legge, giudici, giuristi*. *Atti del convegno tenuto a Cagliari nei giorni 18–21 maggio 1981*, Milan (henceforth noted as *Legge, giudici, giuristi*): 93–148. (Inform. about Italian universities).

Coturri, E.: L'insegnamento dell'anatomia nelle univ. medioevali, in *Univ. e soc.*: 131–43.

Dolezalek, G.: Libros juridicos anteriores a 1800 en la bibl. de la Univ. Nacional Mayor de san Marcos en Lima. Bases para la formación juridíca de los abogados latinoamericanos del s. 19, in *Diritto romano, codificazioni e sistema giuridico latino-americano. Atti del colloquio internazionale. Sassari, 13–15 gennaio 1978*, Milan (henceforth noted as *Diritto romano, codificazioni*): 491–518.

Donnelly, J. P.: The Jesuit Coll. at Padua: Growth, Suppression, Attempts at Restoration 1552–1606, *Arch. hist. Soc. Jesu*, 51: 45–79.

Fasoli, G.: Rapporti tra le città e gli Studia, in *Univ. e soc.*: 1–21.

Ferrari, S.: L'insegnamento del diritto eccles. nell'univ. di Padova dal 1800 al 1866, *Univ. di Macerata. Annali della fac. di giurisprud.*, 34: 227–53.

Fried, J.: Vermögensbildung d. bologneser Juristen im 12. u. 13. Jh., in *Univ. e soc.*: 27–59.

Gambasin, A.: and Padovan, G.: Problemi del metodo teol. e insegnamento univ. della teol. pastorale in Giovanni Prosdocimo Zabeo 1753–1828, in *Contributi alla storia della chiesa padovana nell' età moderna e contemporanea, 1. Fonti e ricerche di storia eccles. padovana*, 13, Padua: 87–188.

Gaudemet, J.: La réception du droit romain dans les pays latins, in *Diritto romano, codificazioni*: 477–90. (Inform. about univs in Latin countries).

Gouron, A.: La crise des univs fr. à la fin du 14e s., in D. Maffei and P. Nardi eds: *Atti del Simposio internazionale cateriniano-bernardiniano*, Siena: 907–15.

Grandi, R.: Le tombe dei dottori bolognesi: ideologia e coltura, in *Univ. e soc.*: 429–45.

Gratta, R. del: Alcuni aspetti dei privilegi dottorali nel tardo diritto comune, in *Légge, giudici, giuristi*: 197–99.

- - - - - Spigolature storiche sull'univ. di Pisa nel 1400 e 1500, in *Univ. e soc.*: 285–326.

Iacovelli, G.: Niccolò Andria, prof. di medicina in Napoli e la crisi del pensiero medico ital. del primo Ottocento, *Arch. storico pugliese*, 35: 459–65.

Infelise, M.: Il progetto di Gasparo Gozzi per una stamperia dell'univ. di Padova 1766, *Q.U.P.*: 81–87.

Kirshner, J.: Cocchi (de Curribus, Canali) Giovanni (Giovanni da Ferrara), *Dizionario biografico degli Italiani* (henceforth noted as *DBI*), 26: 472–73. (Inform. about univ. of Ferrara 15th century).

Leclercq, J.: Lo sviluppo dell'atteggiamento critico degli allievi verso i maestri dal 10 al 13 sec., in *Univ. e soc.*: 401–28.

Marco, M. de: Comandi Comando, in *DBI*, 27: 513–15. (Inform. about univ. of Florence 15th century).

Marrara, D.: Bernardo Tanucci scol. e lettore nello studio di Pisa 1712–33, *Annali della scl. normale sup. di Pisa*, 12: 241–59.

- - - - - Le cattedre ed i programmi d'insegnamento dello studio di Pisa nell'ultima età medicea 1712–37, *Boll. storico pisano*, 51: 105–46.

Martellozzo Forin, E.: *Acta graduum academicorum Gymnasii Patavini ab anno 1501 ad annum 1550. Index nominum cum aliis praemissis*, Padua.

Mastellotto, E.: Ritrovati 29 giornali di cassa dello studio patavino, *Q.U.P.*: 89–92. (Sources for hist. of univ. of Padua 17th century).

Miglio, L.: Cocchi Donati (Cochius, de' Cocchi, de' Donatis, de Florentia) Donato, *DBI*, 26: 498–501. (Inform. about univs of Bologna and Florence 15th century).

- - - - - Cocchi Donati (Choco, Coccus, de' Cocchis) Antonio, *DBI*, 26: 495–98. (Inform. about univ. of Pisa 15th century).

Musselli, L.: L'insegnamento del diritto eccles. nell'univ. di Pavia dall'Unità ai Patti Lateranensi 1861–1929, *Boll. della soc. pavese di storia patria*, 82: 182–97.

Nardella, T.: Celestino Galiani e l'Accad. degli Illuminati, *Arch. storico pugliese*, 35: 453–58.

Nardi, P.: Introduzione ad una ricerca sulle origini dello studio di Siena, *Studi senesi*, 94: 348–61.

Onofri, L.: Clerico (Cherico, Chierico) Ubertino, *DBI*, 26: 404–406. (Inform. about univ. of Pavia and schls of Casale and Chivasso 15th century).

Pesenti, T.: Generi e pubblico della letteratura medica padovana nel Tre e Quattrocento, in *Univ. e soc.*: 523–51.

Piana, C.: Una 'determinatio' inedita di Guglielmo Alnwick o.f.m. (ob. 1333) come saggio di alcune fonti tacitamente usate dall'autore, *Studi francescani*, 79: 191–231. (Inform. about univ. of Bologna 14th century).

Pozzi, R.: Il problema scolastico in epoca napoleonica. Il caso di Napoli, *Critica storica*, 19: 22–41.

Ricuperati, G.: Univ. e scl. in Italia, in *La Letteratura Italiana*, 1. *Il Letterato e le Istituzioni*, Turin: 983–1007.

Rosa, S. de: La pol. libraria del Coll. di Sapienza dell'univ. di Pisa in un 'Registro' inedito del '600, *La bibliofilia*, 84: 249–64.

Sambin, P.: Giuristi padovani del Quattrocento tra attività univ. et attività pubblica. I. Paolo d'Arezzo (ob. 1443) e i suoi libri, in *Univ. e soc.*: 367–400.

Santini, G.: Univ. e soc. a Modena tra il 12 e il 13 sec., in *Univ. e soc.*: 327–66.

Steffen, W.: Il potere studentesco a Bologna nei sec. 13 e 14, in *Univ. e soc.*: 177–93.

Strnad, A. S. and Walsh, K.: Coltellini (de Cultellinis, de Bononia) Giovanni, *DBI*, 27: 485–87. (Inform. about univ. of Bologna 14th–15th centuries).

Tramontana, S.: Scl., allievi e maestri in Sicilia nel sec. 15, *Quad. catanesi di studi classici e medievali*, 4: 369–93.

Turtas, R.: La nascita dell'univ. sarda, in *La Sardegna*, 1. *La geografia, la storia, l'arte e la letteratura*, Sassari: 137–44.

- - - - - *Un contributo per la storia dell'Università di Sassari*, Sassari.

Ulvioni, P.: Astrol, astron. e medicina nella Repub. veneta tra Cinque e Seicento, *Studi trentini di scienze storiche*, 61: 3–69. (Inform. about univ. of Padua and several schls of Venetia).

Vasoli, C.: Cittadini Antonio, *DBI*, 26: 66–71. (Inform. about univs of Ferrara, Pisa and Padua 15th–16th centuries).

Verde, A. F.: Un terzo soggiorno romano del Poliziano, *Rinascimento*, 22: 257–62. (Inform. about univ. of Florence).

- - - - - Vita univ. nello studio della repub. fiorentina alla fine del Quattrocento, in *Univ. e soc.*: 495–522.

Verger, J.: *Le Università del Medioevo*, Bologna.

- - - - - Les rapports entre univs ital. et univs fr. méridionales 12e–15e s., in *Univ. e soc.*: 145–76.

Veronese Ceseracciu, E.: Il soggiorno padovano dello studente tedesco Anton Edelman 1552–55, *Q.U.P.*: 95–103.

Villani, P.: Conforti Gian Francesco, *DBI*, 27: 793–802. (Inform. about univ. of Naples 18th century).

Zanetti, G.: *Profilo storico dell'Università di Sassari*, Milan.

Zorzoli, M. C.: La formazione dei giuristi lombardi nell'età di Maria Teresa, *Materiali per una storia della cult. giuridica*, 12: 3–27. (Inform. about univ. of Pavia 18th century).

- - - - - Interventi dei duchi e del senato di Milano per l'univ. di Pavia sec. 15–16, in *Univ. e soc.*: 553–73.

Publications 1983

Alfonso, R. d': Ancora su Dante e la fil. a Bologna, in *Studi e Memorie per la Storia dell' Università di Bologna*, 3, Bologna (henceforth noted as *S.M.*): 39–82. (Inform. about univ. of Bologna 13th–14th centuries).

Anselmi, G. M.: Mito classico e allegoresi mitologica tra Beroaldo e Codro, in *S.M.*: 157–95. (Inform. about univ. of Bologna 15th century).

Antonaci, A.: La posizione fil. e scientif. di Marcantonio Zimara negli anni del suo primo insegnamento a Padova 1501–09, in A. Poppi, ed.: *Scienza e filosofia all'Università di Padova nel Quattrocento*, Trieste (henceforth noted as *S.F.*): 315–28.

Avellini, L.: Per uno studio del problema dell'eloquenza nell'opera di

Giovanni Garzoni, *S.M.*: 83–104. (Inform. about univ. of Bologna 15th century).

Barile, E. and Suriano, R. eds: *Il 'Catalogo di Libri' di Giambattista Morgagni*, Trieste.

Bellone, E.: I primi decenni della univ. a Torino 1404–36, *Studi piemontesi*, 12: 352–69.

Bernardin, S. de: I riformatori dello Studio: indirizzi di pol. cult. nell'univ. di Padova, in G. Arnaldi and M. Pastore Zocchi eds: *Storia della cultura veneta*, 4.1. *Il Seicento*, Vicenza: 61–91.

Biliński, B.: Il periodo padovano di Niccolò Copernico 1501–03, in *S.F.*: 223–85.

Bottin, F.: Gaetano da Thiene e i 'Calculatores', in *S.F.*: 125–34. (Inform. about univ. of Padua 15th century).

- - - - - Logica e fil. naturale nelle opere di Paolo Veneto, in *S.F.*: 85–124. (Inform. about univ. of Padua 15th century).

Calore, A.: Il 'Palazzo-Collegio' Priuli (sec. 16) in Borgo S. Croce a Padova, *Quad. per la storia dell'Univ. di Padova*, 15 (1982) (henceforth noted as *Q.U.P.*): 121–30. (Inform. about univ. of Padua 16th century).

Cappelluti, G.: Ricerche sulla cult. fil. e teol. pre-post tridentina nel sud Italia. La Prov. domenicana di S. Tommaso d'Aquino in Puglia e il suo Studio generale, *Memorie domenicane*, 14: 239–328.

Chartularium Studii Bononiensis. Documenti per la storia dell'Università di Bologna dalle origini fino al secolo 15, 14, Bologna (1981).

Gambasin, A.: La cattedra di teol. pastorale all'univ. di Padova dal 1815 al 1828, *Atti e memorie dell'Accad. Patavina di scienze lettere ed arti già Accad. dei Recovrati*, 94 (1981–82): 101–106.

- - - - - Il Frintaneum di Vienna e i *Testimonia* sui prof. della fac. teol. dell'univ. di Padova dal 1816 al 1873, *Q.U.P.*: 61–104.

Graziosi, E.: Fra retorica e giurisprud., in *S.M.*: 3–38. (Inform. about univ of Bologna 12th–13th centuries).

Kohl, B. G.: Conversini (Conversano, Conversino) Giovanni (Giovanni da Ravenna), *Dizionario biografico degli Italiani*, 28 (henceforth noted as *DBI*): 574–78. (Inform. about univ. of Padua 14th–15th centuries).

- - - - - Conti Prosdocimo, *DBI*: 463–65. (Inform. about univ. of Padua 14th–15th centuries).

- - - - - Conti (de Comite, de Comitibus) Ildebrandino, *DBI*: 438–40. (Inform. about univ. of Padua 14th century).

Luca, L. de: L'insegnamento del diritto canonico nelle univ. ital., *Studi parmensi*, 32: 5–21.

Mahoney, E. P.: Phil. and Science in Nicoletto Vernia e Agostino Nifo, in *S.F.*: 135–202. (Inform. about univ. of Padua 15th–16th centuries).

Maria, S. de: Sull'antiquaria bolognese del Seicento, in *S.M.*: 497–540.

Marrara, D.: Lo Studio di Pisa e la discussione settecentesca sull'insegnamento del diritto patrio, *Boll. storico pisano*, 52: 17–41.

Mazzacane, A.: Conticini Pietro, *DBI*: 490–94. (Inform about univs of Pisa and Siena 19th century).

Nardi, P.: Comune, Impero e Papato alle origini dell'insegnamento univ. in Siena 1240–75, *Bull. senese di storia patria,* 90: 50–94.

Olivieri, L.: La scientificità della teoria dell'anima nell'insegnamento padovano di Pietro Pomponazzi, in *S.F.*: 203–222. (Inform. about univ. of Padua 16th century).

Palmer, R.: *The 'studio' of Venice and its Graduates in the 16th Century,* Trieste.

Passicos, J.: L'enseignement du droit canonique en France, *Studi parmesi,* 32: 23–32.

Pezzarossa, F.: Un profilo quattrocentesco dello studio Bolognese, in *S.M.*: 105–56.

Piana, C.: Il traduttore e commentatore della Divina Commedia fra Giovanni Bertoldi da Serravalle o.f.m. baccalario a Ferrara nel 1379 ed altri documenti per la storia degli Studi francescani, *Analecta Pomposiana,* 7 (1982): 131–83.

- - - - - Il mag. Ottaviano Strambiati da Ravenna o.f.m. conv. lettore di metafisica 'in via Scoti' nell'univ. di Padova 1607–28, *Studi francescani,* 80: 471–75.

- - - - - Lancellotto de Mercuriis da Reggio lettore di retorica e poesia nell'univ. di Bologna e una sua lettera spirituale (a. 1475), *Italia medioevale e umanistica,* 24 (1981): 360–83.

Poppi, A.: Scienza e fil. nelle scl. tomista e scotista all'univ. di Padova nel sec. 15, in *S.F.*: 329–43.

Premuda, L.: Le conquiste metodologiche e tecnico-operative della medicina nella scl. padovana del sec. 15, in *S.F.*: 395–428.

Reina, V.: La enseñanza del derecho canónico en España, *Studi parmesi,* 32: 33–42.

Ricciardi, R.: Conti (Comes, Maioragius) Antonio Maria (Marcus Antonius), *DBI*: 359–64. (Inform. about univs of Ferrara and Milan 16th century).

- - - - - Conti (Quintianus Stoa) Giovanni Francesco, *DBI*: 429–31. (Inform. about univ. of Pavia 16th century).

Rosa, S. de: *Una biblioteca universitaria del secondo '600: la libraria di Sapienza dello Studio pisano 1666–1700,* Florence.

Rossetti, L.: Lo Studio di Padova nel Quattrocento. Nota informativa, in *S.F.*: 11–15.

Santinello, G.: Prosdocimo de'Beldomandi, in *S.F.*: 71–84. (Inform. about univ. of Padua 15th century).

Todescan, F.: Logica e 'scientia iuris' a Padova nel Quattrocento. Il'De interpretatione legis extensiva' di Bartolomeo Cepolla, in *S.F.*: 463–89. (Inform. about univ. of Padua 15th century).

Tognoni Campitelli, A.: Coppoli (de Coppolis, de Copulis) Ivo (Ivo da Perugia), *DBI*: 678–80. (Inform. about univs of Perugia and Rome 15th century).

Tomasi Stussi, G.: Per la storia dell'Accad. Imperiale di Pisa 1810–14, *Critica storica,* 20: 60–120.

Veronese Ceseracciu, E.: Documenti per la biog. di Pietro Catena, *Q.U.P.*: 113–20. (Inform. about univ. of Padua 16th century).

Vivo, F. de: *L'insegnamento della pedagogia nell'Università di Padova durante il 19 secolo*, Trieste.

Japan

Publication 1982

Hayashima, A.: *Der Kölner Weg zum Promotionsrecht. Zur Geschichte einer deutschen Handels hochschule*, Nishinomiya.

Poland

Addition to Earlier Lists

For 1981

Karolewicz, G.: 'Lowańczycy' wśród prof. Katol. Uniw. Lubelskiego w okresie międzywojennym (Louvain students among profs of the Cath. univ. of Lublin 1918–39), *Archiwa, Biblioteki i Muzea Kóscielne*, 43: 217–29.

Publications 1982

Catoni, G.: Stampa e univ. nella Siena dei Lumi, in A. Gieysztor and M. Koczerska eds: *Universitates Studiorum saec. 18 et 19*, Warsaw (henceforth noted as *U.S.*): 133–56.

Domonkos, L.: The Enlightenment and higher educ. in early America, in *U.S.*: 185–206.

Fläschendräger, W.: Rezensenten u. Autoren d. 'Acta Eruditorum' 1682–1731, in *U.S.*: 61–80.

Fletcher, J. M.: British univs in the age of the Enlightenment, in *U.S.*: 157–84.

Garlicki, A. ed.: *Dzieje Uniwersytetu Warszawskiego 1915–39* (The hist. of Warsaw univ. 1915–39), Warsaw. (Summaries in French and English).

Gieysztor, A. and Koczerska, M. eds: *Universitates Studiorum saec. 18 et 19*, Warsaw. (Items noted separately).

Kielanowski, T.: Wspomnienia z pierwszych lat budowy Uniw. Marii Curie-Skłodowskiej (Beginnings and early yrs of work at the M. C.-S. univ. at Lublin), *KHNiT*, 27: 599–619. (Summary in French).

Kieniewicz, S.: La première univ. de Varsovie et les Lumières, in *U.S.*: 21–34.

Michalewska, K.: Uniw. Jagielloński a wychodźstwo w latach 1889–1939

(The Jagellonian univ. and Polish emigré circles 1889–1939), *Studia Hist.*, 25: 215–41. (Summary in English).

Molik, W.: Polacy na Uniw. w Heidelbergu 1803–70 (Poles at the univ. of Heidelberg 1803–70), *KHNiT*, 27: 313–35. (Summary in German).

Mrozowska, K.: Les univs polonaises à l'époque de la Comm. de l'Educ. Nat. 1773–94, in *U.S.*: 7–19.

Ostromęcka, H.: Z badań nad dziejami polskiego Wydziału Lekarskiego przy Uniw. w. Edynburgu (The hist. of the Polish fac. of Med. at Edinburgh univ.), *KHNiT*, 27: 291–311.

Ruta, Z. ed.: *Źródła do dziejów Wyższej Szkoły Pedagogicznej im. Komisji Edukacji Narodowej w Krakowie 1946–81* (Sources for the hist. of the Ec. Normale Sup. of Cracow 1946–81), 1, Cracow.

Średniawa, B.: Fizyka teoretyczna na Uniw. Jagiellońskim w latach 1815–90 (Theoret. Physics at the Jagellonian univ. during the yrs 1815–90), *KHNiT*, 27: 621–55.

Stasiewicz-Jasiukowa, I. ed.: *Dzieje nauczania historii nauki i historii techniki w Polsce* (The teaching of the hist. of science and tech. in Poland), Wrocław. (Summary in English).

Steinmetz, M.: Glanz u. Elend deutscher Univ. im Zeitalter d. Aufklärung, in *U.S.*: 35–60.

Zorzoli, M.C.: Alcuni aspetti dell'insegnamento del diritto nella Lombardia austriaca: piano di riforma teresiano e tesi legali nell'Univ. di Pavia 1772–96, in *U.S.*: 81–131.

Publications 1983

Beauvois, D.: L'univ. de Vilna et les écs des Congrégations 1803–32, in M. Kulczykowski ed.: *L'Université et l'Enseignement Extra-universitaire 16e–19e siècles*, Warsaw/Cracow (henceforth noted as *Univ. et Enseignement*): 133–43.

Brańska, E.: Andrzej Stanisław Załuski a reforma Uniw. Krakowskiego i innych wyższych uczelni w Polsce Wettinów. Przyczynki źródłowe (A.S.Z. and the reform of Cracow univ. and other higher schls in Poland in the reign of Wettin. Some sources), *KHNiT*, 28: 177–99.

Dutkowa, R.: L'univ. Jagellon et les écs secondaires au 19e s., in *Univ. et Enseignement*: 69–83.

Dybiec, J.: L'univ. de Vilna et l'enseignement dans les écs secondaires, in *Univ. et Enseignement*: 145–57.

Frijhoff, W.: L'univ. et l'enseignement extra-univ. dans un état naissant: position des problèmes dans la Répub. des Provinces—Unies 17e—18e s., in *Univ et Enseignement*: 47–68.

Hajdukiewicz, L.: Les colonies acad. de l'univ. de Cracovie aux 16e–18e s., in *Univ. et Enseignement*: 13–25.

Havránek, J.: L'univ. de Prague et l'enseignement non-univ. aux 16e–19e s., in *Univ. et Enseignement*: 159–70.

Kulczykowski, M. ed.: *L'Université et l'Enseignement Extra-universitaire 16e–19e siècles. 2e Session Scientifique Internationale, Cracovie, 11–12 mai 1979,* Warsaw/Cracow. (Items noted separately).

Lipkowski, O.: *Wyższa Szkoła Pedagogiki Specjalnej im. Marii Grzegorzewskiej w Warszawie 1922–82* (The higher schl for special educ. at Warsaw 1922–82), Warsaw. (Summary in French, English and German).

Michalewicz, J.: L'ancien système de bourse et sa fonction dans les rapports de l'univ. Jagellon avec l'enseignement non-univ. en Pologne, in *Univ. et Enseignement*: 27–38.

Michalewiczowa, M.: Les aspects soc. du système boursier de l'acad. de Cracovie, in *Univ. et Enseignement*: 39–45.

Miśkiewicz, B.: *Uniwersytet Poznański. Fakty, refleksje, wspomnienia* (The univ. of Poznań. Details, reflections, memories), Poznań.

Mrozowska, K.: L'Ec. Centrale de la Couronne et l'enseignement secondaire à l'époque de la Comm. de l'Educ. Nat., in *Univ. et Enseignement*: 85–96.

Rakova, I.: L'univ. de Prague de 1654 à 1773 et son rôle dans l'enseignement non-univ., in *Univ. et Enseignement*: 171–75.

Ruta, Z. ed.: *Źródła do dziejów Wyższej Szkoły Pedagogicznej im. Komisji Edukacji Narodowej w Krakowie 1946–81* (Sources for the hist. of the Ec. Normale Sup. of Cracow 1946–81), 2, Cracow.

Sapia-Drewniak, E.: La participation des profs de l'univ. Jagellonne aux travaux de l'instruction publique à la fin du 19e et au debut du 20e s., in *Univ. et Enseignement*: 177–82.

Skowronek, J.: L'enseignement non-univ. par nécessité; les problèmes de l'enseignement sup. dans le royaume de Pologne de 1832 à 1857, in *Univ. et Enseignement*: 97–117.

Romania

Publication 1983

Carbonell, C.-O.: Les profs d'hist. de l'enseignement sup. en France au début du 20e s., *Anal. Univ. Bucuresti. Seria sñinte soc., ist.*, 22: 19–33.

Scandinavia

Addition to Earlier Lists

For 1979

Pinborg, J. ed.: *Universitas Studii Haffnensis. Stiftelsesdokumenter og Statutter 1479,* Copenhagen. (Facsimile with Danish and English trans. by J. P. and B. P. McGuire).

Publication 1986

Hammerstein, N.: Zum Fortwirken von Pufendorfs Naturrechts-Lehre an d. Univ. d. Heligen Römischen Reiches Deutscher Nat. während d. 18. Jhs, in *Samuel von Pufendorf 1632–1982. Ett rättshistoriskt symposium i Lund 15–16 jan. 1982,* Lund: 31–51.

South America

Publication 1983

Carabias Torres, A. M.: Los col. mayores salmantinos en el gobierno de las Indias s. 16, *Res gesta* (Rosario, Argentina), 13: 23–30.

Publication 1986

Phillips, W. D.: Univ. graduates in Castellian royal service in the 15th cent., in *Estudios en homenaje a Don Claudio Sánchez Albornoz en sus 90 años,* Buenos Aires, 4: 475–90.

Spain and Portugal

Additions to Earlier Lists

For 1977
Dios, A. M. de: Inventario de los bracarenses en la Univ. de Salamanca durante la monarquía dual, *O distrito de B raga 2,* 2 serie, 6.
Echeverría, L. de: *De oratoria universitaria salmantina,* Salamanca.
Puig, F.: *La enseñanza de la cirugía en el Colegio de Mallorca. Plan para perfeccionar los estudios de cirugía 1790,* Valladolid.
For 1978
García Lasoasa, J.: *Planes de reforma de estudios de la Universidad de Zaragoza en la segunda mitad del s. 18,* Saragossa.
For 1980
Ayala, F.: La Univ. y la Repúb., *ARBOR,* 115 (426–27): 67–74.
Closa Farrés, J.: *Latín clásico, latín medieval y latín humanístico en los documentos de estudiantes irlandeses e ingleses de la Universidad de Salamanca en el s. 16,* Salamanca.
Echeverría, L. de: La celebración de la Semana Santa en la capilla de la Univ., in *Triduo sacro en rito hispano antiguo o mozárabe*: 17–24.
García Oro, J.: Cisneros y la Univ. de Salamanca, in *5 Simposio. Toledo Renacentista,* 1, Madrid; 73–167.
Gómez-Sánchez, F.: *Biografía de la Universidad de Toledo,* Toledo.

Solsona Climent, F. and Boleda Isarre, P.: *El Archivo de la Universidad de Cervera. El fondo bibliográfico grecolatino de la Universidad de Cervera*, Cervera.

Vico Monteoliva, M.: *Los colegios de estudios valencianos post-tridentinos: vertiente pedagógica a través de sus constituciones*, Valencia.

For 1981

Carrizzo San Millán, M. G.: *Obras de interés médico y científico en las Bibliotecas Universitarias y de Santa Cruz de Valladolid hasta 1877*, Valladolid.

Cortina Iceta, J. L.: *El siglo 18 en la preilustración salmantina. Vida y pensamiento de Luis de Losada 1681–1748*, Madrid.

Esteban Mateo, L.: La enseñanza de la teol. en las Univ. españolas. La ilustración valenciana, *Cuadernos de hist. de la teol.*, 24.

Falcón, M.: *Cristóbal Colón y la Universidad de Salamanca*, Salamanca.

Gallego, J. and Felipo, A.: Grados concedidos por la Univ. de Valencia durante la primera mitad del s. 16, *Analecta sacra Tarraconensia*, 51–52: 323–80.

Madurell i Marimón, J. M.: Antoni Jolís, catedratic de Gramática de l'Univ. de Barcelona 1588–1600, *Analecta sacra Tarraconensia*, 53–54: 187–215.

Malagón, J.: Los profs españoles exiliados enla Univ. de Santo Domingo 1939–49, *ARBOR*, 108 (423): 49–64.

Martín Abad, J.: *La oratoria sagrad contribución a la bibliografía salmantina de s. 18*, Salamanca.

Mestre, A.: Jerarquía católica y oligarquía municipal ante el control de la univ. de Valencia (el obispo Esteve y la cuestión contra el patriarca Ribera), *Anal. de la univ. de Alicante. Hist. moderna*, 1: 9–35.

San Vicente, A.: *Monumentos diplomáticos sobre los edificios fundacionales de la Universidad de Zaragoza y sus construcciones*, Saragossa.

Publications 1982

Albiñana, S.: Francisco Ballester y la enseñanza de las matemáticas en la univ. de Valencia 1745–52, in *Estudios . . . Peset Aleixandre*, Valencia (henceforth noted as *Estudios P.A.*), 3: 65–77.

Balaguer Perigüell, E.: Continuidad y ruptura en La Renovación científica valenciana, *Anal. de la univ. de Alicante. Hist. moderna*, 2: 251–58.

Baldo Lacomba, M.: *La Universidad de Valencia en la crisis del antiguo régimen*. Thesis. Valencia.

- - - - - La hisenda de la univ. de Valencia durante la crisi del régim feudal 1807–36, in *Estudios P.A.*, 1: 241–60.

Bartolomé Martínez, B.: Las cátedras de Gramática de los jesuitas en las univ. de Aragón, *Hispania sacra*, 34: 389–448.

Blasco Carrascosa, J. A.: *El krausisme valencià*, Valencia.

Cervera Vera, L.: *Arquitectura del Colegio Mayor de Santa Cruz de Valladolid*, Valladolid.

Delgado, B.: *El cartulario del colegio universitario de santa María de Lérida 1376–1564*, Barcelona.

Díaz-Trechuelo López-Spínola, L.: *La vida universitaria en Indias. Siglos 16 y 17*, Cordova.

Fernández-Villamil Ingunza, M. del C.: *Catálogo de impresos del s. 17 de la Biblioteca Universitaria de Murcia*, Murcia.

Garín y Ortiz de Taranco, F. M.: *La Universidad literaria de Valencia y sus obras de arte*, Valencia.

Gutiérrez Cuadrado, J.: La ciencia lingüística en la univ. de Barcelona en el s. 19, in *Estudios P.A.*, 2: 327–51.

Hernández, B.: El Libro Becerro de la Univ. Salamanca, *Rev. Española de derecho canónico*, 38: 237–52.

Isasmendi, F. and J. and Tamayo, J.: *Catálogo de incunables de la Biblioteca Universitaria y Suplemento*, Seville.

Jesus Marques, A. de: *Um escolar de direito em Coimbra y Salamanca, o lic. Fernando Alvares 1548–66*, Mafra.

Kagan, R.: Universities in Castile 1500–1700, *Past and present*, 49 (1970): 44–71. Trans. into Spanish in J.H. Elliot ed., *Poder y sociedad en la España de los Austrias*, Barcelona.

Lluch Adelantado, A. and Sevilla Merino, C.: Biblioteca univ. y provincial, in *Estudios P.A.*, 2: 599–615.

Mancebo, F.: La univ. de Valencia en el tránsito de la dictadura a la repúb. La F.U.E., *Estudis d'hist. contemp. del país valencià*, 3: 175–235.

Martín González, J. J.: Alonso Berruguete y la fachada de la Univ. de Salamanca, *Bol. del seminario de arte y arqueol.*, 48: 398–405.

Mayordomo Pérez, A. and Ruiz Rodrigo, C.: *La universidad como problema en los intelectuales regeneracionistas*, Valencia.

Mesa, R. ed.: *Jaraneros y alborotadores. Documentos sobre los sucesos estudiantiles de febrero de 1956 en la universidad complutense de Madrid*, Madrid.

Miralles Vives, F.: La fac. de artes entre 1600–1611: provisión de cátedras y graduados en la univ. de Valencia, *Saitabi*, 32: 43–60.

Pendas García, M.: Los colegiales mayores de Santa Cruz de Valladolid 1660–1785. Estudio soc, *Pedralbes. Rev. d'hist. moderna*, 2.

Pérez García, J.: Los orígenes de la escuela de Veterinaria de Zaragoza, *Asclepio*, 34: 101–80.

Peset, J. L.: De la Univ. de ayer a la de hoy, in A. Dou ed.: *Sobre la Universidad*, Bilbao: 21–53.

Peset, M.: Estudiantes hispanos en las univ. francesas s. 14, in *Estudios P.A.*, 3: 273–94.

Riera Palmero, J.: Nota sobre Antonio Cibac y la cátedra de Física experimental, *Dynamis*, 2: 357–62.

Robles, L.: Francisco de Castro, 'conjunt' de la univ. y hermano de Guillem de Castro, in *Estudios P.A.*, 3: 429–45.

Seisdedos Sánchez, C.: El Brocenze y la univ. de Salamanca, *Studia Zamorensia,* 3: 481–88.
Vico Monteoliva, M.: El prof. univ. valenciano del s. 16: Formación y promoción, *Ciencias da la educ.,* 3, 293–300.
- - - - - La obra pedagóg. de Melchor de Villena, catedrático de medicina, director del jardín botánico y médico de Felipe IV. Análisis constitucional, in *Estudios P.A.,* 3: 723–41.
- - - - - *La universidad de Valencia en el s. 16,* Valencia.

Publications 1983

Alomar Esteve, C.: Los estudios de derecho en Mallorca 1721–1829, *Estudis Baleàrics,* 11 (3): 21–33.
Alvarez Villar, J.: *Heráldica universitaria salmantina,* Salamanca.
Barrientos García, J.: *El maestro Pedro de Herrera y la Universidad de Salamanca,* Salamanca.
Bartolomé Martínez, B.: Las cátedras de Gramática de los jesuitas en las univs de su prov. de Castilla, *Hispania sacra,* 35: 449–97.
Beltrán de Heredia, V.: *Los orígenes de la Universidad de Salamanca,* Salamanca.
Bustos Rodríguez, M.: *Los cirujanos del Real Colegio de Cádiz en la encrucijada de la Ilustración 1749–96,* Cadiz.
Carabias Torres, A. M.: *El Colegio Mayor de Cuenca en el s. 16: Estudio institucional,* Salamanca.
- - - - - Evolución hist. del Col. Trilingüe de Salamanca 1550–1812, *Studia hist. Hist. moderna,* 1: 143–68.
Carrete Parrondo, C.: *Hebraistas judeoconversos en la Universidad de Salamanca s. 15–16,* Salamanca.
Cuart Moner, B.: Colegiales y burócratas. El caso del Col. de San Clemente de los Españoles de Bolonia en la primera mitad del s. 16, *Studia hist. Hist. moderna,* 1 (3): 65–93.
Felipo, A.: Las Constituciones de la Univ. de Valencia de 1563, *Escritos del Vedat,* 13: 233–54.
Felipo Orts, A.: Provisión de cátedras entre 1620–30. Datos para la hist. de la Univ. de Valencia, *Estudis. Rev. de hist. moderna,* 9: 81–100.
Fernández Alvarez, M.: El diario de un estudiante: la Salamanca del barroco, in *La sociedad española en el Siglo de Oro,* Madrid: 955–87.
Ferrer, D.: *Historia del Real Colegio de Cirugía de la Armada de Cádiz,* Cadiz.
Gallego Salvadores, J. and Felipo Orts, A.: Grados concedidos en Valencia entre 1526–61, *Analecta sacra Tarraconensia,* 55–56: 7–107.
García Cué, J. R.: *El hegelianismo en la Universidad de Sevilla,* Seville.
García Domínguez, L. M.: Vida religiosa y estudios en el Colegio Real de la Compañ'ia de Jesús en Salamanca 1665–1700. Thesis. Salamanca.
Hernández, R.: Algunos aspectos de la crisis univ. de Salamanca a finales

del s. 16 y principios del s. 17: falta de inteligencia de los Colegios, *Estudios*, 34: 65–98.

Jiménez, F.: El libro de los nombres, una costumbre de la Univ. Salamanca? *Salamanca. Rev. prov. de estudios*, 7: 115–18.

Moll Blanes, I.: La crisis de la Univ. en Mallorca, *Estudis Baleàrics*, 11 (3): 53–61.

Moralejo Alvarez, M. R. and Delgado Casado, J.: *4 Centenario de la Universidad de Zaragoza. Exposición del tesoro documental y bibliográfico de la Universidad de Zaragoza. Catálogo*, Saragossa.

Pedraza, P.: Los jeroglíficos del patio de la Univ. de Salamanca y la Hypnerotomachia Poliphili, *Traza y Baza*, 8: 36–58.

Peset, J. L. and Peset, M.: *Carlos IV y la Universidad de Salamanca*, Madrid.

- - - - - and Hernández Sandoica, E.: *Estudiantes de Alcalá*, Alcalá de Henares.

Robles, L.: Profs de la Fac. de Teol. de la Univ. de Valencia 1550–1600, in *Corrientes espirituales en la Valencia del s. 16 1550–1600*, Valencia: 80–133.

Rodríguez Sampedro Bezares, L. E.: Estudiantes en Salamanca 1590–1621: el hospedaje, bachilleres y pupilos, in *El pasado histórico de Castilla y León. Actas del 1 Congreso de Historia de Castilla y León, 2: Edad Moderna*, Burgos: 187–200.

- - - - - Pupilajes, gobernaciones y casas de estudiantes en Salamanca 1590–1630, *Studia hist. Hist. moderna*, 1: 185–210.

- - - - - Vascos en Salamanca s. 16: D. Juan López de Arizmendi, in *Homenaje a J. Ignacio Tellechea Idígoras (Bol. de Estudios Hist. sobre S. Sebastián)*, 1: 423–51.

Sánchez Reyes, E.: *Miscelánea de Estudios sobre las sabias piedras de la Universidad de Salamanca*, Salamanca.

Santander Rodríguez, M. T.: La iglesia de San Nicolás y el antiguo teatro anatómico de la Univ. de Salamanca, *Rev. Española de teol.*, 43: 253–73.

Varela, J.: *Modos de educación en la España de la contrarreforma*, Madrid.

Various authors: *Historia de la Universidad de Zaragoza*, Madrid.

- - - - - *La enseñanza superior en Castilla y León 1940–80*, Salamanca.

Publications 1984

Arribas Jimeno, S.: *La facultad de ciencias de la Universidad de Oviedo, Estudio histórico*, Oviedo.

Arroyo Ilera, R.: *Numerario de la Universidad de Valencia*, Valencia.

Baldó i Lacomba, M.: *Profesores y estudiantes en la época romántica. La Universidad de Valencia en la crisis del antiguo régimen 1786–1843*, Valencia.

Barrientos García, J.: El maestro Pedro de Ledesma y la Univ. de Salamanca, *Archivo Dominicano*, 5: 201–69.

Campo del Pozo, F.: Método y prof. de la Univ. de S. Nicolás en Bogotá, *Archivo Agustiniano*, 68: 183–223.

Carbonell Boria, M. J.: Noticia de tres títulos univ. de la Corona de Aragón s. 18, *Estudis. Rev. de hist. moderna*, 11: 95–101.

Espinel Marcos, J. L.: Cristóbal Colón en Salamanca, *Salamanca. Rev. prov. de estudios*, 14: 63–84.

Figueres i Pàmies, M.: Alguns trets sobre el procés ideològic de la Univ. a Catalunya s. 18 i 19, *Miscellània Cerverina*, 2: 75–116.

Fuertes Herreros, J. L. ed.: *Estatutos de la Universidad de Salamanca 1529. Mandato de Pérez de Oliva, Rector*, Salamanca.

García Sánchez, J.: Consideraciones histórico-jurídicas referentes a la fundación de la Univ. de Oviedo, *Studium Ovetense*, 12: 59–108.

González Navarro, R. and Larios y Bernaldo de Quirós, A.: *Universidad Complutense. Constituciones originales cisnerianas. Edición bilingüe y comentario. Estudio de los textos legislativos, su evolución y las reformas posteriores durante el s. 16*, Alcalá de Henares.

Hernández Montes, B.: Col. y Hospital de Nuestra Señora de la Paz de Salamanca, *Salamanca. Rev. prov. de estudios*, 12: 97–130.

Menéndez Peláez, J.: El 4 Concilio de Letrán, La Univ. de Palencia y el Mester de Clerecía, *Studium Ovetense*, 12: 27–39.

Otero Túñez, C.: *Más libros y folletos de la Universidad Compostelana*, 1–2. Catálogos de la Biblioteca Univ., Santiago, 1982–84.

Perarnau i Espelt, J.: Les primeres gestions per a l'erecció d'Estudi Univ. a Barcelona (1310) i a Girona (1446), *Arxiu de textos Catalans antics*, 3: 243–50.

Rodríguez, I.: Maestros y lectores del col. de Valladolid, *Archivo Agustiniano*, 68: 225–324.

Rodriguez Cruz, A. M.: Dominicos en la Univ. de Salamanca, *Archivo Dominicano*, 5: 91–118.

- - - - - Discípulos de la Univ. de Salamanca en América, in *La ética en la conquista de América*, Madrid: 499–550.

Sánchez Herrero, J.: Centros de enseñanza y estudiantes de Sevilla durante los s. 13 al 15, in *La España Medieval: Estudios dedicados al Prof. D. Angel Ferrari Núñez*, 2, Madrid: 875–98.

Santamaría, A.: Quinto Centenario del privilegio fac. del Estudio General de Mallorca 1483–1983. Contexto hist. del privilegio fac. del Estudio General de Mallorca, *Boll. de la soc. arqueol. Luliana*, 40: 187–202.

Santander Rodríguez, T.: *Escolares médicos en Salamanca s. 16*, Salamanca.

Tort i Mitjans, F.: La Univ. de Cervera: una institució conflictiva, *Miscellània Cerverina*, 2: 67–74.

Various authors: *Educación e Ilustración en España. 3 Coloquio de Historia de la Educación*, Barcelona.

Publications 1985

Alcaraz Quiñonero, J. J.: La formación del prof. univ.: hist. y posibilidades, in *Higher Education and Society. Historical Perspectives/ Educación superior y sociedad. Perspectivas históricas*, 1 and 2, 7 Congreso internacional de Hist. de la Educ., Salamanca (henceforth noted as *H.E.S.*), 2: 25–32.

Ávila de Azevedo, R.: L'Univ. dans la formation des élites portugaises 1834–70, in *H.E.S.*, 1: 36–45.

Barcala Muñoz, A.: Las univ. españolas durante la Edad Media, *Anu. de estudios medievales*, 15: 83–126.

Barrientos García, J.: El estatuto y juramento (1627) de enseñar y leer a San Agustín y Santo Tomás en la Univ. de Salamanca: un simple proyecto? *Cuadernos Salmantinos de filos.*, 12: 103–24.

Bartolomé Martínez, B.: Estudiantes y profs españoles en univ. extranjeras, *Hist. de la educ. Rev. interuniv.*, 4: 7–33.

- - - - - Aranceles de depósitos y propinas para la colación de grados en las univ. españolas, in *H.E.S.*, 1: 62–75.

Calatayud Soler, R.: Facs y estudiantes en la Univ. de Valencia (primera mitad del s. 19), in *H.E.S.*, 2: 62–74.

Canella Secades, F.: *Historia de la Universidad de Oviedo y noticia de los establecimientos de enseñanza de su distrito*, Oviedo.

Canes Garrido, F. and Gutiérrez Zuluaga, I.: La primera Asamblea Univ. Española 1902, in *H.E.S.*, 2: 75–89.

Carabias Torres, A. M.: Catálogo de col. del Col. Mayor de Oviedo s. 16, *Studia hist. Hist. moderna*, 3: 63–105.

- - - - - Catálogo de col. del Col. Mayor de S. Bartolomé, *Prov. de Salamanca. Rev. de estudios*, 18: 223–82.

- - - - - Estudiantes burgaleses y col. mayores s. 16, in *La ciudad de Burgos. Actas del Congreso de Historia de Burgos*, Madrid: 343–60.

- - - - - Evolución del concepto de Fac. de Artes en España s. 13 al 18, in *Actas del 4 Seminario de Historia de la Filosofía*, Salamanca: 303–33.

- - - - - Reformas de la fac. de artes salmantina. Período renacentista, *Azafea*, 1: 89–128.

Cid Fernández, M.: La condición univ. del magisterio. Planteamientos teóricos y realizaciones en el contexto repub. español, in *H.E.S.*, 2: 160–73.

Cieza García, J. A.: Intelectuales y Univ. Las Letras Españolas ante el problema univ. durante el primer tercio del s.20, in *H.E.S.*, 2: 141–49.

Colmenar Orzaes, C. and Carreño Rivero, M.: El acceso de la mujer a la enseñanza oficial en la Univ. Central durante el s. 19 español, in *H.E.S.*, 1: 100–114.

Corchón, C. L.: La formación de profs para la enseñanza superior en el Inst. Nacional Superior del Prof. 'Joaquín V. González' de Buenos Aires, Repúb. Argentina, in *H.E.S.*, 2: 191–200.

Cortés Vázquez, L.: *La vida estudiantil en la Salamanca clásica*, Salamanca.

Corts Giner, M. I.: La Univ. española de principios de siglo a través de los discursos de apertura de la Univ. de Sevilla 1900–25, in *H.E.S.*, 2: 201–214.

Echeverría, L. de: *Presentación de la Univ. de Salamanca*, Salamanca.

Escarbajal de Haro, A.: Autonomía univ.: Análisis hist. de la relación Univ.-Estado, in *H.E.S.*, 2: 240–48.

Esteban Mateo, L.: Las cátedras lulistas en Valencia. Materiales para su estudio, in *H.E.S.*, 1: 123–32.

Fernández Soria, J. M. and Mayordomo Pérez, A.: En torno a la idea de Univ. en la España de la postguerra 1939–43, in *H.E.S.*, 2: 249–62.

Ferreira Gomes, J.: L'Univ. et la formation psychopéd. des profs de l'enseignement secondaire au Portugal pendant la première Repub. 1910–26, in *H.E.S.*, 2: 263–71.

Ferrero Blanco, J. J.: Educ. superior y conciencia de identidad en el pueblo vasco, in *H.E.S.*, 2: 272–83.

Flecha García, C.: La mujer en la Univ. de Sevilla de 1900 a 1930, in *H.E.S.*, 1: 133–42.

Gómez García, M. N.: El preámbulo de la LRU: contraste con el pensamiento de Giner de los Ríos sobre la reforma de la Univ., in *H.E.S.*, 1: 171–82.

Gómez R. de Castro, F.: La libertad acad. del estudiante de la preclara Fac. de Artes y Filos. de la Univ. Complutense en el s. 16, in *H.E.S.*, 2: 284–94.

González Gallego, I.: Autonomía jurisdiccional univ. a mediados del s. 18, in *H.E.S.*, 2: 295–310.

González González, E.: La definición de las normas legales en la Real Univ. de México 1553–63, in *H.E.S.*, 1: 195–207.

Gonzallo Aizpuru, P.: El discurso de las armas y las letras en la Nueva España, in *H.E.S.*, 1: 183–94.

Guereña, J. L.: La projection soc. de l'univ. à la fin du 19e s.: l'extension univ. en Espagne, in *H.E.S.*, 1: 208–218.

Hernández Díaz, J. M.: La condición de los estudiantes en Salamanca en el umbral del s. 20, in *H.E.S.*, 2: 336–49.

Higher Education and Society. Historical Perspectives. Educación superior y sociedad. Perspectivas históricas, 1 and 2. 7 Congreso Internacional de Hist. de la Educ., Salamanca. (Relevant items noted separately).

Hurtado Rodríguez, F.: *Salamanca en el s. 18. La Salamanca que conoció Jovellanos*, Salamanca.

Lamouroux, F.: La revelación contable en la Salamanca histórica. La Universidad de Salamanca en la encrucijada contable de los s. 15 y 16 a través de sus cuentas. Thesis. Madrid.

Lázaro Lorente, L. M.: La inquisición y la renovación de la filos. en la Univ. española del s. 18, in *H.E.S.*, 2: 393–404.

Lechner, J.: Estudiantes de origen hispánico y portugués en la Univ. de

Leiden 1575–1875, in *Estudios Románicos dedicados al Prof. Andrés Soria Ortega*, 2, Granada: 587–603.

López Martín, R.: Análisis legislativo de la pol. univ. primorriverista, in *H.E.S.*, 2: 416–26.

López Torrijo, M.: La Univ. de Valencia: un proceso autonómico a principios del s. 20, in *H.E.S.*, 1: 382–412.

Luna Díaz, L. M.: El desarrollo de la conciencia corporativa univ. y la pol. ecles. univ. en Nueva España, in *H.E.S.*, 1: 423–36.

Marques i Sureda, S.: La univ. en Cataluña: de la 2 Repúb. al actual estado de las autonomías, in *H.E.S.*, 2: 444–55.

Marsiske, M.: La autonomía de la Univ. Nacional de México 1910–29, in *H.E.S.*, 1: 452–63.

Martín Zúñiga, F.: Relación del Col.-Seminario San Dionisio de Areopagita del Sacro-Monte de Granada con la Univ. y. demás col. contemporáneos s. 17–18, in *H.E.S.*, 2: 456–67.

Martínez Tuya, M.: El Mayo francés y las Univ.: hechos y mitos, in *H.E.S.*, 2: 468–80.

Menegus Bonemann, M.: Dos proyectos de educ. superior en la Nueva España en el s. 16. La exclusión de los índigenas de la Univ., in *H.E.S.*, 1: 464–78.

Mones i Pujol-Busquets, J.: Univ.-soc. en el marco del segundo Congreso univ. catalán 1917–19, in *H.E.S.*, 2: 481–94.

Moreno-A. Viñao, P. L.: El cuerpo de catedráticos de Univ. como grupo profesional. Análisis sociológico 1907–58, in *H.E.S.*, 1: 492–502.

Navarro Hinojosa, R.: La reforma de los estudios jurídicos de 1842 y su aplicación en la Univ. Canaria, in *H.E.S.*, 2: 497–508.

Negrín Fajardo, O.: Rivalidad religiosa y conflictos interinsulares en las primeras etapas de la Univ. Canaria, in *H.E.S.*, 2: 509–523.

Núñez Gil, M. and Collado Broncano, M.: La univ. popular de Sevilla 1933–36: una labor de extensión univ., in *H.E.S.*, 1: 505–517.

Ossenbach Sauter, G.: La idea de la Univ. en el pensamiento del positivismo hispanoamericano s. 19. El problema de la utilidad de la enseñanza superior, in *H.E.S.*, 2: 556–69.

Palacio Lis, I.: La Univ. de Oviedo y su programa americanista 1900–10, in *H.E.S.*, 1: 535–36.

Pérez Varas, F.: *Salamanca y su Universidad en la cultura española*, Salamanca.

Pérez White, T.: *La Escuela Universitaria de Béjar y los estudios de ingeniería técnica industrial*, Salamanca.

Pozo Andrés, M. del M. del: El movimiento romántico liberal y la Univ. española en el s. 19 1824–45, in *H.E.S.*, 1: 537–53.

Rodríguez Cruz, A. M.: La pedagog. de la Univ. de Salamanca y su proyección en las Univs Hispanoamericanas del período hispano, in *H.E.S.*, 1: 554–66.

Rodríguez Fernández, J. R.: Newman y la univ. católica de irlanda, *Studium Ovetense*, 13: 99–127.

Rodríguez-Sampedro Bezares, L. E.: Cuantificación y problemática de la matrícula univ. salmantina en el Siglo de Oro: 1590–1630, in *H.E.S.*, 2: 583–92.

- - - - - Libros de Artes-Filos. en la Librería de la Univ. de Salamanca en el s. 16. Inventario de 1600, *Studia hist.*, 3: 107–17.

Ruiz Rodrigo, C.: Acción sociocultural de la FUE (Valencia 1932–36), in *H.E.S.*, 1: 578–89.

Sanz, F.: La fundación de la Univ. de Santo Tomás de Avila, in *H.E.S.*, 2: 593–602.

Sauras Herrera, C.: Autonomía univ. en la España contemp. El decreto Silió (1919) y la LRU (1983), in *H.E.S.*, 2: 604–615.

Soetermeer, F.: Un prof. de l'Univ. de Salamanque au 13e s., Guillaume d'Accurse, *Anu. de hist. del derecho Español*, 55: 754–65.

Sola, P.: Entre el mérito y la ciencia: Apuntes para un retrato del prof. de acad. de Matemáticas s. 18, in *H.E.S.*, 1: 615–22.

Sosa Also, P.: Reforma y cambio soc. de la Univ. española de principios de s., in *H.E.S.*, 2: 642–54.

Soto Arango, D.: Los inicios de la univ. pública en Nueva Granada, in *H.E.S.*, 1: 633–48.

Various authors: Declive y regionalización de la matrícula salmantina de los s. 17 y 18. Aproximación descriptiva, *Studia hist.*, 3: 143–150.

Vega Gil, L.: A pedagog. and soc. perspective of the Spanish student of the 19th cent. Realistic literature and educ., in *H.E.S.*, 1: 670–91.

Publications 1986

Barrientos García, J.: Pleito de la Compañía de Jesús con la Univ. de Salamanca, *Studia Zamorensia*, 7: 465–505.

Carabias, A. M.: *Colegios Mayores: Centros de poder*, 1–3, Salamanca.

Delgado, B.: *El Colegio de S. Bartolomé de Salamanca*, Salamanca.

Echeverría, L. de: La Univ. en que estudió Cortés, in *Actas del 1 Congreso Internacional sobre Hernán Cortés*, Salamanca (henceforth noted as *Hernán Cortés*).

Felipo Orts, A.: Nuevas noticias sobre la problemática de la concesión de grados en la Univ. de Valencia 1621–34, *Escritos del Vedat*, 16: 313–69.

Fernández Álvarez, M.: *Universidad y Sociedad (Entre la Historia y el recuerdo). Discurso pronunciado en la solemne apertura del Curso Académico 1986–87*, Salamanca.

García Cortés, C.: Ecles mindonienses graduados en el Seminario Central y Univ. Pontificia de Santiago, *Estudios Mindonienses*, 2: 259–307.

Guitarte Izquierdo, V.: *El pensamiento jurídico valenciano del s. 13 al 19. Aportaciones a su historia*, Castellón.

Jesus Marques, A. de: *Da estirpe portuguesa de um candidato a São Bartolomeu de Salamanca, o licenciado D. Pedro Portocarrero 1564*, Porto.

Julia, D.: Frontières étatiques, clivages confessionnels et cloisonnements intellect. dans l'Europe des 16e–17e s., in J.-P. Genet and B. Vincent eds: *État et Église dans la Genèse de l'État moderne*, Madrid (henceforth noted as *État et Église*): 73–84.

Muñoz Delgado, V.: Los mercedarios en el Perú durante el período español. Colaboración hispano-peruana en estudios prof., col., univ. y escritos, in *Actas del 4 Seminario de Historia de la Filosofía Española*, Salamanca: 77–173.

Peset, M.: Clérigos y univ. en la Baja Edad Media castellanoleonesa, in *État et Église*: 63–71.

Rodríguez Cruz, A. M.: Proyección de la Univ. de Salamanca en México, in *Hernán Cortés*: 167–85.

Rodríguez-Sampedro Bezares, L. E.: *La Universidad Salmantina del Barroco, período 1598–1625*, 1–3, Salamanca.

Switzerland

Publications 1986

Calder, W. M., and Hoffmann, C.: Ulrich von Wilamowitz-Moellendorff on the Basel Greek chair, *Museum Helveticum*, 43: 258–63.

Centre Universitaire Patiño, Genève ed.: *25 ans de formation universitaire pour le développement: Le Centre universitaire Patiño*, Geneva.

Donzé, M.: La théol. pastorale dans l'enseignement univ., *Freiburger Z. f. Phil. u. Theol.*, 33: 431–43.

Döring, D.: Eine bisher unbekannte Handschrift mit d. Text von Heinrich Bullingers 'Ratio Studiorum' in d. Leipziger Universitätsbibliothek, *Zwingliana*, 17: 27–32.

Driesche, R. van den and Gäbler, U.: Schweizer Theologiestudenten in Franeker 1585–1650, *Zwingliana*, 17: 48–61.

Im Hof, U.: Deutsche Studenten u. Dozenten an d. Hohen Schulen d. reformierten Schweiz, in U. Im Hof and S. Stehelin eds: *Das Reich und die Eidgenossenschaft 1580–1650. Kulturelle Wechselwirkungen im konfessionellen Zeitalter*, Freiburg i. Ue. (henceforth noted as *Das Reich u. d. Eidgenossenschaft*): 33–54.

Koelbing, H. M. and Mörgeli, C. eds: *Johann Friedrich Horner, 1831–86, der Begründer der Schweizer Augenheilkunde in seiner Autobiographie*, Zürich. (Inform. about univ. of Zürich).

Kreis, G.: *Die Universität Basel 1960–85*, Basel.

Maissen, F.: Westschweizer Prof. u. Studenten an d. Univ. Ingolstadt-Landshut-München 1472–1914, *Z. f. Schweiz. Kirchengesch.*, 80: 117–80.

Martin-Achard, R.: Aperçus sur l'enseignement de l'Ancien Testament à l'Acad. et à l'Univ. de Genève, *Rev. de Théol. et de Phil.*, 118: 373–88.

Meylan, H.: *La Haute Ecole de Lausanne 1537–1937. Esquisse historique publiée à l'occasion de son quatrième centenaire. 2e edition. Préface d'Eric Junod*, Lausanne.

Rother, W.: Deutsche Autoren in Basler phil. Disputationen 1600–1700, in *Das Reich u. d. Eidgenossenschaft*: 77–99.

Screech, M. A.: Greek in the 'Coll. Trilingue' of Paris and the 'Coll. Trilingue' at Louvain. 'A propos' of prof. O. Reverdin's lect. at the 'Coll. de France', *Bibl. d'Humanisme et Renaissance*, 48: 85–90.

Schmid, H.-P.: Entwicklung der medizinischen Radiologie an der Universität Zürich 1918–85, unter besonderer Berücksichtigung der Radiotherapie und der Nuklearmedizin, Thesis. Zürich.

Schmid, H.: Kurt von Neergaard 1887–1947, Professor für physikalische Therapie, Thesis. Zürich.

Staehelin, A.: Die Univ. Basel u. ihre deutschen Besucher 1580–1620, in *Das Reich u. d. Eidgenossenschaft*: 11–32.

Studhalter, J.: Deutschland u. d. Bildungswesen d. kath. Schweiz 1580–1650, in *Das Reich u. d. Eidgenossenschaft*: 55–75.

The United States

Additions to Earlier Lists

For 1977

Lichteig, F.-B.: The German Carmelites at the Medieval Universities. Thesis. Cath. Univ. of America. (See also *Hist. of Europ. Univs: Work in Progress and Publications*, 5 (1981): 47).

Rose, P.: Erasmians and mathematicians at Cambridge in the early 16th cent., *16th cent. jnl*, 8: 47–59.

For 1979

Bender, J. L.: Nicholas Aston: A Study in Oxford Thought after the Black Death. Thesis. Wisconsin, Madison.

Bruneau, W.: Logic and pragmatism; the fndations of hist. research and training in France 1880–1914, *Proceedings of the Western soc. for Fr. hist.*, 6: 306–316.

Halley, A. M.: Arts, Law and other Studies in Orléans in the 12th, 13th and 14th Centuries. Thesis. City Univ. of New York.

Horn, M.: *The Intercollegiate Socialist Society 1905–21: Origins of the Modern American student Movement*, Boulder, Colo.

Jungnickel, C.: Teaching and research in the physical sciences and Maths in Saxony 1820–50, *Hist. studies in the physical sciences*, 10: 3–47.

Leonard, E. P.: *A Cornell Heritage: Veterinary Medicine 1868–1908*, Ithaca, N.Y.

Wolkowski, L. A.: The Polish Commission for National Education 1773–94. Its Significance and Influence on Russian and American Education. Thesis. Loyola Univ. of Chicago.

For 1980

Becher, H. W.: William Whewell and Cambridge Maths, *Hist. studies in the physical sciences*, 11: 1–48.

Cobb, J. D.: The Forgotten Reforms. Non-Prussian Universities 1797–1817. Thesis. Wisconsin, Madison.

Evans, J. W.: *The Newman Movement: Roman Catholics in American Higher Education 1883–1971*, Notre Dame, Ind.

Melikokis, G. C.: The Origins and Development of the Pedagogic Academies in Greece 1933–72. Thesis. New York University.

Roberts, G. K.: The liberally educ. chemist: Chem. in the Cambridge Nat. Sciences tripos 1851–1914, *Hist studies in the physical sciences*, 11: 157–83.

Westfall, R. S.: Isaac Newton in Cambridge: the Restoration univ. and scientific creativity, in P. Zagorin ed., *Culture and Politics from Puritanism to the Enlightenment*, Berkeley, Calif.: 135–64.

For 1981

Bruneau, W.: An apologia for biog. in Fr. hist., *Proceedings of the Western soc. for Fr. hist.*, 8: 568–76. (Uses the case of Louis Liard Director of Higher Educ. for Fr. 1884–1902).

Edmonson, J. M.: *From mecanicien to ingenieur: Technical Education and the Machine Building Industry in 19th Century France*, New York.

Frank, R. G.: *Harvey and the Oxford Physiologists. A Study of Scientific Ideas and Social Interaction*, Berkeley, Calif.

Gorelick, S.: *City college and the Jewish Poor: Education in New York 1880–1924*, New Brunswick, N.J.

Schubring, G.: Maths and teacher training. Plans for a Polytech. in Berlin, *Hist. studies in the physical sciences*, 12: 161–94.

Siraisi, N. G.: *Taddeo Alderotti and his pupils: two generations of Italian medical learning*, Princeton, N.J. (A summary of the early hist. of med. teaching at Bologna).

Publications 1982

Berman, J. W.: A Sense of Achievement. The Significance of Higher Education for British Women 1890–1930. Thesis. State Univ. of New York at Buffalo.

Engel, A. J.: Oxford Dons and Professional Men in Victorian England, *Hist. of higher educ. annual*, 2: 3–34.

Giles, G. J.: Nazi pol. towards student fraternities, in M.B. Barrett ed.: *Proceedings of the Citadel Symposium on Hitler and the National Socialist Era*, Charleston: 46–53.

Jarausch, K. H.: *Students, Society and Politics in Imperial Germany. The rise of academic illiberalism*, Princeton, N.J.

Jones, D. R.: The Origins of Civic Universities: Manchester, Leeds and Liverpool. Thesis. Yale.

Meiners, F.: *A History of Rice University: The Institute Years 1907–63*, Houston, Tex.

Peck, E. S.: *Berea's First 125 Years 1855–1980*, Lexington.

Smith, R. J.: *The Ecole Normale Supérieure and the Third Republic*, Albany.

Sullivan, J. E.: Studia Monastica: Benedictine and Cluniac Monks at the University of Paris 1228–1500. Thesis. Wisconsin, Madison.

Turner, R. S.: Justus Liebig versus Prussian Chem. Reflections on early inst.-building in Germany, *Hist. studies in the physical sciences*, 13: 129–62.

Weiss, J. H.: *The Making of Technological Man: the social Origins of French Engineering education*, Cambridge, Mass. (Discusses the Ec. Centrale in the first half of the 19th century).

Weisz, G.; *The Emergence of Modern Universities in France, 1863–1914*, Princeton, N.J.

Publications 1983

Cline, P.: *Mountain Campus: The Story of Northern Arizona University*, Flagstaff, Ariz.

Dippel, S. A.: A Study of Religious Thought at Oxford and Cambridge from 1560 to 1640. Thesis. Ohio State University.

Engel, A. J.: The English univs and professional educ., in K.H. Jarausch ed.: *The Transformation of Higher Learning 1860–1930*, Chicago/Cologne: 293–305.

Lytle, G. F.: The Church Fathers and Oxford profs in the Late Middle Ages, Renaissance and Refn, in R.J. Schoeck ed.: *Acta Conventus Neo-Latina Bononiensis*, Binghamton: 101–115.

Osborne, T. R.: *A Grande Ecole for the Grands Corps: the recruitment and training of the French administrative elite in the 19th and 20th centuries*, Columbia.

Skelton, J. T.: The Effect of National Socialism on the German Educational system 1933–45. Thesis. Southern Illinois Univ. at Carbondale.

Publications 1984

Boney, F. N.: *A Pictorial History of the University of Georgia*, Athens, Ga.

Bridgforth, L. R.: *Medical Education in Mississippi: A History of the School of Medicine*, Jackson, Miss.

Courtenay, W. J.: The role of English thought in the transformation of univ. educ. in the Late Middle Ages, in J. M. Kittelson and P. J. Transue eds: *Rebirth, Reform and Resilience: Universities in Transition 1300–1700*, Columbus, Ohio (henceforth noted as *R.R.R.*): 103–162.

Craig, J. E.: *Scholarship and Nation Building: The Universities of Strasbourg and Alsatian Society 1870–1939*, Chicago.

Fletcher, J. M.: Univ. migrations in the Late Middle Ages with particular ref. to the Stamford secession, in *R.R.R.*: 163–89.

- - - - - and Deahl, J.: European univs 1300–1700: The development of research 1969–81 and a summary bibliog., in *R.R.R.*: 324–57.

Gallagher, C. T.: A Scottish Contribution to American Higher Education: The Saint Andrew's Society of New York 1756–1806 and the Founding of King's College. Thesis. Kentucky.

Grant, E.: Science and the medieval univ., in *R.R.R.*: 68–102.

Holland, A. F.: Nathan B. Young and the development of black higher education. Thesis. Univ. of Missouri, Columbia.

Kilman, G. A.: Southern Collegiate Women Higher Education at Wesleyan Female College and Randolph-Macon Woman's College 1893–1907. Thesis. Delaware.

Kittelson, J. M.: Introduction: The durability of the univs of old Europe, in *R.R.R.*: 1–18.

- - - - - and Transue, P. J. eds: *Rebirth, Reform and Resilience: Universities in Transition 1300–1700,* Columbus, Ohio (Items noted separately).

Knoll, P. W.: The Univ. of Cracow in the Conciliar Movt, in *R.R.R.*: 190–212.

Lytle, G. F.: The careers of Oxford students in the Later Middle Ages, in *R.R.R.*: 213–53.

Mey, M. de: Sarton's earliest ambitions at the univ. of Ghent, *Isis*, 57: 39–45. (S. and the univ. 1902).

Oberman, H. O.: Univ. and soc. on the threshold of modern times: The German connection, in *R.R.R.*: 19–41.

Overfield, J. H.: *Humanism and scholasticism in late medieval Germany,* Princeton, N.J.

- - - - - Univ. studies and the clergy in pre-refn Germany, in *R.R.R.*: 254–92.

Reinhart, T. E.: The Parliamentary Visitation of Oxford University 1646–52. Thesis. Brown University.

Spitz, L. W.: The importance of the Refn for univs: Culture and confession in the critical years, in *R.R.R.*: 42–67.

Stoops, M.: *The Heritage: The Education of Women at St Mary's College, Raleigh, North Carolina 1842–1982,* Raleigh, N.C.

Publications 1985

Conkin, P. K.: *Gone with the Ivy: A Biography of Vanderbilt University,* Knoxville, Tenn.

Corley, F. M.: Higher Education For Southern women. Four church-related Women's Colleges in Georgia, Agnes Scott. Shorter, Spelman and Wesleyan 1900–20. Thesis. Georgia State University.

Deering, T. E.: Academic Freedom: Issues and controversies 1963–85. Thesis. Univ. of Missouri, Columbia.

Dyer, T. G.: *The University of Georgia: A Bicentennial History 1785–1985*, Athens, Ga.

Gavin, D. P.: *John Carroll University. A Century of Service*, Kent, Ohio.

Giles, G. J.: *Students and National Socialism in Germany*, Princeton, N.J.

Heintze, M. R.: *Private Black Colleges in Texas 1865–1954*, College Station, Tex.

Hylander, G. L.: The Educational Features of the G.I. Bill and its Impact on Selected Boston Area Universities. Thesis. Boston College.

Ibish, J. S.: Emmanuel College: The Founding Generation with a Biographical Register of Members of the college 1584–1604. Thesis. Harvard.

Killian, J. R.: *The Education of a College President: A Memoir*, Cambridge, Mass.

Knoll, P. W.: The Univ. context of Kochanowski's era: Humanism and the acad. culture of the Renaissance in Poland, in S. Fiszman ed.: *The Polish Renaissance in its European Context*, Bloomington, Ind.

McMath, R.: *Engineering the New South: Georgia Tech 1885–1985*, Athens, Ga.

Middlebrooks, D. J.: A History of the Associate Degree Nursing Program in Nevada 1963–1983. Thesis. Univ. of Nevada, Las Vegas.

Peck, D. C. ed.: *'Leicester's Commonwealth': the copy of a letter written by a Master of Art of Cambridge (1584) and related documents*, Ohio.

Phillips, D. E.: *Student Protest 1960–1970. Analysis of the Issues and Speeches*, Lanham, MD.

Reeves, M. G.: Economic Depression in Higher Education: Emory University, the University of Georgia and Georgia Tech 1930–40. Thesis. Georgia State University.

Robson, D. W.: *Educating Republicans, The college in the Era of the American Revolution 1750–1800*, Wesport, Conn.

Roche, J. F.: *The Colonial Colleges in the War for American Independence*, Millwood, N.Y.

Senseney, J. E.: The Influences of the Western Allies on German Adult Education 1945–53. Thesis. Texas Tech. University.

Sher, R. B.: *Church and University in the Scottish Enlightenment. The Moderate Literati of Edinburgh*, Princeton, N.J.

Stameshkin, D.: *The Town's College: Middlebury College 1800–1915*, Middlebury, Ut.

Swann, J. P.: The Emergence of Cooperative Research between American Universities and the Pharmaceutical Industry 1920–40. Thesis. Wisconsin, Madison.

Tuchman, A. M.: Science, Medicine and the State: The Institutionalization of Scientific Medicine at the University of Heidelberg. Thesis. Wisconsin, Madison.

Vincent, A. W.: A Fair Chance for the Girls: A Case Study in the Function of Prestige in the Controversy over Admission of Women to Tufts College 1852–1912. Thesis. Schl of Theol. at Claremont.

Publications 1986

Avi-Yonah, R. S.: The Aristotelian Revolution: A Study of the Transformation of Medieval Cosmology, 1150–1250. Thesis, Harvard.

Gabriel, A. L.: *The University of Paris and its Hungarian Students and Masters during the Reign of Louis XII and Francois Ier*, Notre Dame/Frankfurt a. M.

Graffam, A. E.: On the Persistence of Denominational Evangelical Higher Education: Case Studies in the History of Geneva College, Roberts Wesleyan College, Nyack College and Houghton College. Thesis. State Univ. of New York at Buffalo.

Horowitz, H. and Kramer, W. M.: A Stamp of Approval: Oklahoma Oilman and Rosh Ha-Yeshiva Bernard Revel, *Western states Jewish hist.*, 18 (3): 256–61. (B.R. pres. of Yeshiva University).

Kolozsvari, I. B.: The Organizational Development of the Keszthely Agricultural University 1797–1962. Thesis. San Francisco.

McMillan, J. T.: The Development of Higher Education for Blacks During the Late Nineteenth Century: A Study of the African Methodist Episcopal Church, Wilberforce University, The American Missionary Association, Hampton Institute and Fisk University. Thesis. Columbia Univ. Teachers' College.

Miller, K. K.: Black Studies in California Higher Education 1965. Thesis. Univ. of California.

Nyhart, L. K.: Morphology and the German University 1860–1900. Thesis. Univ. of Pennsylvania.

Rosner, L.: Students and Apprentices. Medical Education at Edinburgh University 1760–1810. Thesis. John Hopkins University.

Trusty, L.: All Talk and No 'Kash': Valparaiso Univ. and the Ku Klux Klan, *Indiana mag. of hist.*, 82 (1): 1–36.

Walker, W. H.: Foundations of Higher Education: Adult Education prior to 1860. Thesis. Univ. of Oklahoma.

Wechsler, H. S.: Community and acad.: Jewish Learning at the Univ. of California 1870–1920, *Western states Jewish hist.*, 18 (2): 131–42.

Index of Continents, Towns and Institutions

Volume VIII 1989

Volume VIII of *History of Universities* will follow the same format as the present volume. The articles section will contain papers devoted to all periods of university history. Among papers already accepted for the 1989 volume are the following:

The Medical Faculty at Early Fourteenth Century Lerida *Michael McVaugh and Luis Garcia Ballester*

University, Administration, Taxation and Society in Italy in the Sixteenth Century: The Case of Fiscal Exemptions for the University of Pavia *Mario Rizzo*

Dutch Professors (1576–1876): Learned Individuals or a Professional Group? *Willem Frijhoff*

Experimental Science in Early-Nineteenth Century Oxford *G. L. E. Turner*

The Teaching of Cameralism, *Staatswissenchaften*, and Economics in Early Nineteenth Century Germany *Norbert Waszek*